The Royal Houses of Israel and Judah: An Interwoven History With A Harmony Of Parallel Passages

George Obadiah Little

Nabu Public Domain Reprints:

You are holding a reproduction of an original work published before 1923 that is in the public domain in the United States of America, and possibly other countries. You may freely copy and distribute this work as no entity (individual or corporate) has a copyright on the body of the work. This book may contain prior copyright references, and library stamps (as most of these works were scanned from library copies). These have been scanned and retained as part of the historical artifact.

This book may have occasional imperfections such as missing or blurred pages, poor pictures, errant marks, etc. that were either part of the original artifact, or were introduced by the scanning process. We believe this work is culturally important, and despite the imperfections, have elected to bring it back into print as part of our continuing commitment to the preservation of printed works worldwide. We appreciate your understanding of the imperfections in the preservation process, and hope you enjoy this valuable book.

344.5
Little

Harvard University
Library of the Divinity School

———

THE BEQUEST OF

JOSEPH HENRY THAYER
LATE PROFESSOR IN THE SCHOOL.

———

20 March 1902

THE ROYAL HOUSES
OF
ISRAEL AND JUDAH

THE ROYAL HOUSES

OF

ISRAEL AND JUDAH

An Interwoven History with a Harmony of
Parallel Passages

BY
REV. GEORGE O. *Obadiah* LITTLE, D.D.

PROFESSOR OF PASTORAL THEOLOGY AND OLD TESTAMENT LITERATURE
HOWARD UNIVERSITY, WASHINGTON, D. C.

FUNK & WAGNALLS COMPANY
NEW YORK AND LONDON
MDCCCCI

Bequest of
Prof. J. H. Thayer
March 20, 1902.
(977)

Copyright 1900
by
FUNK & WAGNALLS COMPANY
[Registered at Stationers' Hall, London, England]
Printed in the United States of America

Dedicated
TO MY FATHER,
Rev. HENRY LITTLE, D.D.,
WHO, IN A MINISTRY OF OVER A HALF OF A CEN-
TURY, IMPARTED TO HIS FOUR MINISTER SONS
A LOVE FOR, AND THE PRACTICAL USE OF,
THE OLD TESTAMENT SCRIPTURES.

CONTENTS

	PAGE
Preface	ix
Synopsis of Sections	xi
TABLES { I For Finding any Passage in the History or Harmony	xvii
II For Finding any Parallel Passages in the Harmony	xx
III Chronological Chart	xxii

		PAGES
PART I	THE FOUNDING OF THE MONARCHY	1–42
PART II	THE UNITED KINGDOM	43–151
PART III	THE DIVIDED KINGDOM	152–243
PART IV	THE SURVIVING SOUTHERN KINGDOM	244–304

Appendices:
- A. Chronology 307–309
- B. The Duplications of Incidents in I Samuel 310–316
- C. The Peculiarities of Chronicles 317–329

PREFACE

In my pastorate of a quarter of a century at the Capital of the Nation, I have taught the Old Testament in two of the educational institutions of the city. While thus teaching the historical books in 1894, I was impressed with the need of a harmony for the profitable study of the period of the kings of Israel and Judah. I made inquiries at the Congressional Library, and wrote to several theological professors for information concerning an Old Testament harmony, and could find none.

I read a paper before the Presbyterian Association on the Peculiarities of Chronicles, the substance of which will be found in Appendix C, and was requested to prepare such a harmony for publication. I first prepared a harmony of the historical books, Samuel, Kings, and Chronicles. Later I enlarged the plan so as to include all parallel passages in the poetical and prophetical books narrating the history of the Monarchy from the first king to the return from exile.

My double labor of preaching and teaching prevented me from typewriting it for publication. While thus delayed, two works appeared almost simultaneously, one in America, and one in England,* that were similar in plan to the two I had prepared, but in neither of the two was the harmony arranged in parallel columns so as to correspond line for line, the parallel parts being often on different parts of the page, and sometimes on different pages.

Having resigned my pastorate in 1898, I for the third time enlarged the plan of the book, and prepared, as I think, the first interwoven history of the period of the Monarchy, and combined with it the first harmony of parallel passages, which correspond to each other, and to the history on the opposite page, line for line.

This Interwoven History, which comprises all of six consecutive books and parts of four others, does for the Old Testament what the several Interwoven Gospels do for the New Testament. It is presented in modern literary form, doing away with the arbitrary divisions of Chapter and verse, save for reference. The Scripture language is not changed, but there is a rearrangement of the

---

* A Harmony of Samuel, Kings and Chronicles.
  By William Day Crockett, A.M., New York, 1897.
The Hebrew Monarchy: A Commentary with a Harmony of Parallel Texts.
  By Andrew Wood, A.M., London, 1896.

PREFACE

narrative of the teachings, incidents, and events of each book, and combining and interweaving the narrative of different books so as to make a complete, comprehensive and connected *e pluribus unum* story of the Royal Houses of Israel and Judah that attracts and interests and helps to a clear view of the period, as the separated narratives can not do.

Whenever and wherever there is more than one record of the same incident or event, there is an accurately arranged harmony of the parallel passages showing to the eye the likenesses or unlikenesses, the agreements or disagreements of the two records, and also the omissions or additions of either record. This correspondence of the parallel columns is made apparent 1, By blank spaces, which indicate the omission of either record. 2 By a parenthesis ( ), enclosing parts of passages in both columns which are similar in subject matter, but dissimilar in other respects. 3 By parentheses (( )) which indicate a difference, disagreement or discrepancy in the subject matter of the enclosed corresponding parts.

The harmony thus arranged is put on the page opposite the history, and corresponds to it line for line, so that the history is explained and verified by the harmony, and the harmony is unified and made available to the reader by the history interwoven from it.

It is my hope that this first interwoven history of six consecutive books and parts of nearly as many other books of the Old Testament will furnish a ready reference for the busy clergyman, Sabbath School teacher and Bible reader, to obtain a complete knowledge of every incident, event or teaching recorded in one or more of the Scriptures of this period, and at the same time give a clearer understanding of the unified history as a comprehensive whole.   G. O. L.

SYNOPSIS OF SECTIONS

I—The Israelites Demand a King

Elders Ask for a King—God's Consent—Protest and Warning of Samuel—Saul the Benjamite Designated and Anointed by Samuel—Elected King at National Assembly—Jabesh-Gilead Delivered—Saul Inaugurated at Gilgal—Samuel's Address............ 1

II—Saul's Double Disobedience

Saul Offers the Burnt Offering—The First Sentence for First Disobedience—Jonathan's Daring Exploit—Philistines' Discomfiture—Hasty Oath of Saul—Pursuit Stopped—Saul's Wars—Second Disobedience and Sentence—The Kingdom Rent from Saul.... 7

III—David's Victory Over Goliath

David Privately Chosen and Anointed by Samuel—Introduced to the Court of Saul as a Harper—Goliath's Challenge—David Sent to His Brethren—David's Fight with Goliath—Jealousy of Saul Aroused by Women's Song............................ 13

IV—Saul's Injustice and Violence to David

Saul's Two Artful Proposals for David's Marriage with His Two Daughters—Attempts on David's Life—Escape to Samuel—Flight to Jonathan—The Mutual Covenant—The Final Parting 18

V—David a Fugitive and Outlaw

David's Final Flight—Goes to Achish King of Gath—An Outlaw at Adullam—Psalms LXVI, XXXIV—Saul's Massacre of Priests of Nob by Doeg—Psalm LII—Keilah Saved—Philistines Smitten—David Betrayed by the Ziphites—Coming of New Warriors—Psalm LIV—David Spares Saul's Life at Engedi—His Interview and Covenant With Saul—Psalms LVII, CXLII—Death and Burial of Samuel—Nabal and Abigail—Second Betrayal by the Ziphites—Second Sparing of Saul's Life—Psalm LXIII 22

VI—An Exile in the Land of the Philistines

Second Flight to Achish King of Gath—Ziklag Assigned to Him—New Accessions—Confidence of Achish—Suspicion of Rulers—David Sent Back—Ziklag Smitten and Burned—David's Pursuit, Rescue of Captives and Recovery of Spoil—Divison and Distribution of the Spoil... 32

VII—THE FALL OF THE HOUSE OF SAUL

Saul's Visit to the Witch of Endor—Death of Saul and His Sons on Mount Gilboa—Report of Brought to David by an Amalekite—David's Dirge in Lamentation for Saul and Jonathan 35

VIII—THE RISE OF THE HOUSE OF DAVID

David Anointed King of Judah at Hebron—Ishbosheth Made King of Israel at Mahanaim—Death of Asahel—The Civil War—Abner Offers to Bring Over Benjamin and Israel to David—Assassination of Abner and Ishbosheth—David's Lamentation for Abner... 39

PART II—THE UNITED KINGDOM

IX—DAVID MADE KING OVER ALL ISRAEL

The Armed Men of the Tribes of Israel That Came to David at Hebron—David Elected and Anointed King Over All Israel at Hebron—Jerusalem Captured and Called the City of David—David's Wives and Sons—David's Heroes—The Thirty............. 43

X—DAVID'S WARS WITH THE PHILISTINES

Two Philistine Invasions Repelled—Exploits against Philistine Giants—Hiram King of Tyre Sends Messengers, Masons and Carpenters to David—David's Song of Thanksgiving—Chief Officials—David's Kindness to Jonathan's Son Mephibosheth.......... 48

XI—THE ARK REMOVED FROM KIRJATH-JEARIM

David Assembles the Chosen Men of Israel to Bring up the Ark into the New Capital—Uzzah's Error and Death—Ark Carried into the House of Obed-edom—David's Instructions to the Levites—Appointment of Singers—Ark Brought Up from the House of Obed-edom with Sacrifices—Set in the Tent David Had Pitched for It—Levites Appointed to Minister before It—David's Service of Song and Thanksgiving........ 56

XII—DAVID'S VICTORIES

First Victory Over the Ammonites—Victory Over the Syrians—Second Victory Over the Ammonites—David's Double Sin—Death of Uriah—Marriage with Bath-sheba—Nathan's Parable and Rebuke—David's Penitence—Penitential Psalm—Death of Child Born to Them—Capture of Rabbah—Victory Over Moab—Syrians Defeated—Victory in the Valley of Salt—David's Proposal to Build an House for the Ark—God's Promises to David—David's Response.. 64

XIII—FAMILY TROUBLES

Amnon's Incest—Absalom's Revenge in Death of Amnon—Flight to Geshur—Joab and the Wise Woman of Tekoa—Absalom Recalled to Jerusalem—Absalom's Conspiracy and Rebellion—Flight of David and His Household—Hushai Sent Back—Ziba's Slander of Mephibosheth—The Rival Counsellors in Jerusalem—David at Mahanaim—Defeat and Death of Absalom—David's Grief for Absalom.................... 76

SYNOPSIS OF SECTIONS

XIV—The Restoration

David Recalled by Judah—David's Return—Sparing of Shimei—Mephibosheth Righted—Barzillai's Welcome—Israel Aggrieved with Judah—Rebellion of Sheba—Amasa Slain—Gibeonites Avenged—Numbering the People—Repentance and Punishment—Sacrifice at the Threshing Floor of Araunah—Chosen Place for Sacrifice and Site for Temple 85

XV—Final Arrangements for the Temple

Charge to Solomon—Command to Princes of Israel—Number and Service of the Levites—Twenty-four Courses of the Priests—Twenty-four Classes of Singers—Courses of Doorkeepers—Levites Over the Treasuries—Twelve Courses of the Army—Chiefs of Tribes—Officers of State... 94

XVI—David's Last Words and Acts

Address to National Assembly—Address to Solomon—David Gives Pattern of the Temple—Address to the Congregation—Blesses, Thanks and Praises the Lord—Congregation Sacrifices and Offers Burnt Offerings—The Ideal Ruler—The Last Words of David—The Virgin Abishag Found for the Aged David—Adonijah's Rebellion—Solomon Twice Made King—Dying Charge to Solomon—David's Death............. 102

XVII—Solomon's Accession to the Throne

Solomon Rights Past Wrongs—Joab's Death—Restriction of Shimei—Shimei's Death—Princes of Solomon—Marriage with Pharaoh's Daughter—Solomon's Prayer at Gibeon, God's Answer—Exhibition of Wisdom—Plans for Building of the House for the Lord—Arrangements with Hiram.. 110

XVIII—Building the Temple

Site Chosen on Mount Moriah in the Threshing Floor of Araunah—The Fabric—The Fittings and Contents—The Courts—Hiram and His Works—Two Pillars of Brass—The Molten Sea—Ten Bases and Lavers—Summary of Hiram's Works............... 120

XIX—Dedication of the Temple

Ark Brought Out of Zion—Psalm CXXXVI—Solomon's Address—Prayer for David's House—Prayer for Israel in Time of Defeat, Drought, Famine, Battle, Captivity—Solomon's Blessing—Fire from Heaven—Three Houses of Solomon—The Lord's Second Appearance to Solomon at Gibeon—Blessing and Warning.................. 128

XX—Solomon's Fame, Greatness, and Works

Dominion and Peace—Glory and Revenue—Splendor and Wisdom—The Coming of the Queen of Sheba—Hiram and Solomon—Levy Raised................................. 140

SYNOPSIS OF SECTIONS

XXI—Downfall and Division

Polygamy and Idolatry—The Lord's Anger and Sentence—Adversaries Raised Up—Hadad—Rezon the Son of Eliada—Jereboam the Son of Nebat—Ahijah the Shilonite Promises Him Ten Tribes—Solomon's Death and Burial—Rehoboam Made King—Jereboam's Proposition—Rehoboam's Answer—Rebellion of Israel.................. 146

PART III—THE DIVIDED KINGDOM

XXII—Rival Houses of David and Jereboam

Civil War Forbidden—Initiatory Enterprises—Two Calves and Feast—Prophecy of Man of God—Deception and Disobedience—Rehoboam's Household—Forsaking God in Prosperity—Summary of Rehoboam's Reign—Accession and Character of Abijah—Victory Over Israel—Summary of the Reign of Abijah—Accession and Character of Asa—Jereboam's Retributive Punishment—Fulfillment of Prophecy in Nadab........ 152

XXIII—Rival Houses of David and Baasha

Accession and Character of Baasha—Asa's Victory Over Zerah at Mareshah—Azariah's Approval and Encouragement—Reformation, Sacrifice, and Covenant—Alliance with Ben-hadad—Hanani's Reproof—Condemnation of Baasha by Jehu—Accession and Assassination of Elah.. 163

XXIV—Rival Houses of David and Omri

Zimri's One Week's Reign—Accession and Character of Omri—Accession and Character of Ahab—Asa's Disease and Death—Accession and Character of Jehoshaphat—The Kingdom Established—Judah Taught—Increasing Power and Greatness—Prophecy and Hiding of Elijah—Reviving the Widow's Child—Meeting of Elijah and Ahab—Challenge to Sacrifice With Test of Fire—Prophecy of and Prayer for Rain—Flight and Despondency of Elijah—Manifestation and Message of the Lord—Call of Elisha—Ben-haded Besieges Samaria—Ahab's Victory—Ben-hadad's Second Victory—Ahab's Second Victory—Life Spared and Life Forfeited—Ahab's Sin Against Naboth—Retributive Punishment Foretold... 167

XXV—Allied Houses of David and Omri (Elijah).

Alliance of Jehoshaphat and Ahab—Micaiah's Adverse Prediction—Ahab Puts Micaiah in Prison—Defiance, Disguise, and Death—Rebuke of Jehoshaphat by Jehu—Accession and Character of Ahaziah—Reforms of Jehoshaphat—Alliance of Jehoshaphat and Ahaziah—Sentence of Elijah Upon Ahaziah—Wondrous Deliverance by Prayer—Praise, Song, Thanksgiving, and Blessing—Mantle of Elijah Falls upon Elisha—Beginning of Elisha's Miracles... 178

SYNOPSIS OF SECTIONS

XXVI—Allied Houses of David and Omri (Elisha).

Accession and Character of Jehoram—Alliance of Jehoshaphat and Jehoram—Prediction and Prophecy of Elisha—Prophet's Chamber at Shunem—Elisha's Appreciation and Reward—Shunamite's Son Restored to Life—Saved from Famine and Loss of Land—Healing of Naaman's Leprosy—Leprosy of Naaman Put on Gehazi—Syrian Bands Smitten with Blindness—Ben-hadad Besieges Samaria—Predicts Plenty and Deliverance—Elisha's Word to Ben-hadad and Hazael—Co-regency of Jehoram—Wicked and Disastrous Reign—Posthumous Message from Elijah—Accession and Character of Azariah—Alliance with Joram of Israel—Anointing of Jehu—Conspiracy and Ride to Jezreel—Jehoram Slain and Cast in Naboth's Plat—Jehu Slays Ahaziah and His Brethren—Death of Jezebel as Predicted—Jehu Slays all of Ahab in Jezreel—Jehu Smites all of Ahab in Samaria.. 188

XXVII—Rival Houses of David and Jehu

Jehu Subtilly Slays all of Baal—Athaliah's Usurpation—Joash Made King—Death of Athaliah—Jehoiada's Covenant—Accession and Character of Joash—Transjordanic Raid of Hazael—Death of Jehu—Accession and Character of Jehoahaz—Renewal and Repairs by Joash—New Device of a Chest for Gifts—Oppression by Hazael and Ben-haded—Jehoiada's Death—Judah's Apostasy—Joash's Triple Retributive Punishment—Oppression by Hazael—Death of Jehoiada—Accession and Character of Jehoash—Accession and Character of Amaziah—Military Preparations—Amaziah's Idolatry Rebuked—Elisha and Joash King of Israel—Death and Burial of Elisha—Amaziah's Boastful Challenge—Amaziah's Disastrous Defeat—Death of Joash and Amaziah—Accession and Character of Jereboam II—Accession and Character of Uzziah—Subjection of Philistines, Arabians and Ammonites—Uzziah's Presumption and Leprosy—Jereboam's Death and Burial.. 205

XXVIII—The House of David and Last Four Houses of Israel

Shallum's One Month's Reign—Accession and Character of Menahen—Accession and Character of Pekahiah—Accession and Character of Pekah—Death and Burial of Uzziah—Jotham Reigns Alone—Character, Works, and Wars of Jotham—Accession and Character of Ahaz—Rezin and Pekah Besiege Jerusalem—Isaiah's First Message to Ahaz—Isaiah's Second Message—Ahaz Punished for Idolatry and Unbelief—Ahaz Sends to Tiglath-pileser for Help—Material Gain but Spiritual Loss—Israel's First Captivity—Conspiracy Against Pekah—Accession and Character of Hoshea—Death and Burial of Ahaz—Accession and Character of Hezekiah—Sixteen Days Cleansing of the Temple—Congregation Bring Thank Offerings—Proclamation for Passover Second Month—Israel Divided but Judah United—Keeping Passover—Oblations Given, Stored and Distributed—Hezekiah Commended—Hoshea's Conspiracy and Imprisonment—Shalmoneser Besieges and Takes Samaria—The Lord's Bitter Indictment Against Israel—Other Nations Brought into Samaria—A Priest Sent Back from the Captives—Self-made Priests—Their Own Gods Served........................ 224

SYNOPSIS OF SECTIONS

XXIX—The Reign of Hezekiah After Captivity of Israel

Hezekiah's Sickness and Recovery—Return of the Shadow Ten Steps—Ambassadors from Babylon—Babylonian Captivity Foretold—Prosperous End of Life and Reign—Sennacherib Invades Judah—Brave Words to the People—Humble Words to the King of Assyria—Sennacherib's Messengers—Rabshakeh's Insulting Message—Insolent Repetition of Insult—Hezekiah's Message to Isaiah—Isaiah's Prediction—Prayer of Hezekiah—God's Answer by Isaiah—Prophecy and Fulfillment.......... 244

XXX—The Wicked Reigns of Manasseh and Amon

Accession and Character of Manasseh—The Lord's Indictment and Sentence—Repentance, Remission and Reformation—Accession and Character of Amon—Violent Death and Burial 258

XXXI—Josiah's Piety and Reformations

Accession and Character of Josiah—Repairs of the House of the Lord—Finding Book of the Law of the Lord—King Inquires of Huldah the Prophetess—Huldah's Answer—National Renewal of the Covenant—Suppression of Idolatry in Jerusalem—Fulfillment of Prophecy on the Altar—Josiah's Great Passover—Summary of Josiah's Reforms—Disastrous Attack on Pharaoh-Necoh.................................... 264

XXXII—Josiah's Successors the Vassals of Babylon

Jehoahaz Made King by the People—Jehoiakim Made King by Neco—Jeremiah Foretells Captivity—Words Put in the Roll of a Book—Roll Read in the House of the Lord—The First Captivity—Daniel, Hananiah, Mishael, and Azariah—Accession and Character of Jehoiachin—The Second Captivity—Vision of Good and Bad Figs—Accession and Character of Zedekiah—Hananiah's False Predictions—Jeremiah's True Prophecies—The Prophet Consulted the First Time—The Prophet Consulted the Second Time—Jeremiah Put in Prison—Jeremiah Released—The Prophet Consulted the Third Time—Zedekiah's Rebellion—Jerusalem Besieged—Death and Burial of Zedekiah Foretold—Jerusalem Captured—Zedekiah's Punishment—Jerusalem's Houses Burnt—The Final Captivity—The Temple Despoiled—Treatment and Number of Captives—The Final Indictment and Sentence—Gedaliah the Governor and Jeremiah—Gedaliah Murdered—Johanan Rescues Captives—Inquiry and Answer—Disobedience and Destruction—Idolatry Denounced—Retributive Punishment—Captivity and Promised Return—Proclamation for the Return—The Return......................... 276

TABLE I
For Finding Any Passage in the History and Harmony

CHAP.	VERSE	PART	SECTION	PAGE	CHAP.	VERSE	PART	SECTION	PAGE
I SAMUEL					**I KINGS**				
8	1-22	I	I	1, 2	1	1-53	II	XVI	105, 106, 108
9	1-23	I	I	2, 3	2	1-11	II	XVI	108, 109
10	1-27	I	I	3, 4	2	12	II	XVII	111
11	1-15	I	I	4, 5	2	13-46	II	XVII	110, 112
12	1-25	I	I	5, 6	3	1-3	II	XVII	113
13	1-23	I	II	7, 8	3	4-15	II	XVII	115
14	1-52	I	II	8, 10	3	16-28	II	XVII	114, 116
15	1-35	I	II	10, 12	4	1-20	II	XVII	113
16	1-23	I	III	13, 14	4	21	II	XVII	141
17	1-58	I	III	14, 16	4	22, 23	II	XVII	113
18	1-16	I	III	16, 17	4	24-26	II	XX	141
18	17-30	I	IV	18	4	27, 28	II	XVII	113
19	1-24	I	IV	18, 20	4	29-34	II	XX	141
20	1-42	I	IV	20, 21	5	1-18	II	XVII	117, 119
21	1-15	I	V	22, 23	6	1-3	II	XVIII	121
22	1-23	I	V	23, 24	6	4-16	II	XVIII	120, 122
23	1-29	I	V	25, 26	6	17-27	II	XVIII	123
24	1-22	I	V	27	6	28-38	II	XVIII	122
25	1-44	I	V	27-30	7	1-12	II	XIX	136
26	1-25	I	V	30, 31	7	13-26	II	XVIII	125
27	1-12	I	VI	32	7	27-37	II	XVIII	125, 127
28	1, 2	I	VI	32	8	1-32	II	XIX	129, 131
28	3-25	I	VII	35, 36	8	33-66	II	XIX	133, 135, 137
29	1-22	I	VI	32, 33	9	1-9	II	XIX	149
30	1-30	I	VI	33, 34	9	10-23	II	XX	145
31	1-11	I	VII	37	9	24, 25	II	XIX	137
					9	26-28	II	XX	143
					10	1-10, 13	II	XX	143
					10	11, 12, 22	II	XX	145
					10	14-25	II	XX	141, 143
					10	26-29	II	XX	141
II SAMUEL					11	1-40	II	XXI	146-148
1	1-27	I	VII	36, 38	11	41-43	II	XXI	149
2	1-32	I	VIII	38, 40	12	1-19	II	XXI	140, 151
3	1-39	I	VIII	40, 41	12	20-25	III	XXII	152, 153
4	1-12	I	VIII	41, 42	12	26-33	III	XXII	154
5	1-10	II	IX	45	13	1-34	III	XXII	154-156
5	11, 12	II	X	51	14	1-20	III	XXII	160, 162
5	13-16	II	IX	45	14	21-31	III	XXII	157, 159
5	17-25	II	X	49	15	1-7b	III	XXII	150
6	1-12a	II	XI	57	15	7a-15	III	XXII	161
6	12b-14	II	XI	59	15	16-22, 32	III	XXIII	165
6	15-23	II	XI	61	15	23, 24	III	XXIV	169
7	1-29	II	XII	73, 75	15	25-31	III	XXII	162
8	1	II	X	49	15	33, 34	III	XXIII	163
8	2-14	II	XII	71	16	1-14	III	XXIII	160
8	15-18	II	X	51	16	15-23	III	XXIV	167, 168
9	1-13	II	X	54	17	1-24	III	XXIV	170, 171
10	1-19	II	XII	65, 67	18	1-46	III	XXIV	171-173
11	1	II	XII	67	19	1-21	III	XXIV	173, 174
11	2-27	II	XII	66, 68	20	1-43	III	XXIV	174-176
12	1-25	II	XII	68, 69	21	1-29	III	XXIV	176, 177
12	26-31	II	XII	71	22	1-38	III	XXV	179, 181
13	1-39	II	XIII	76, 77	22	39, 40	III	XXV	182
14	1-33	II	XIII	77-79	22	51-53	III	XXV	182
15	1-37	II	XIII	79, 80	22	41-43, 46	III	XXIV	169
16	1-23	II	XIII	80, 81	22	44, 47-49	III	XXV	183
17	1-29	II	XIII	81-83	22	43, 50	III	XXVI	197
18	1-33	II	XIII	83, 84					
19	1-43	II	XIII	84-86	**II KINGS**				
20	1-22	II	XIII	88					
20	23-26	II	X	51	1	1, 17b	III	XXVI	189
21	1-14	II	XIV	88	1	2-18	III	XXV	184
21	15-22	II	X	48-50	2	1-25	III	XXV	186, 187
22	1-51	II	X	50, 52, 54	3	1-5	III	XXVI	189
23	1-7	II	XVI	104, 105	3	6-27	III	XXVI	190
23	8-12	II	IX	47	4	1-7	III	XXV	187
23	13-17	II	X	51					
23	18-39	II	IX	47					
24	1-25	II	XIV	89, 91, 93					

Table I (Continued)—For Finding Any Passage in the History and Harmony

II KINGS—Continued

CHAP.	VERSE	PART	SECTION	PAGE	CHAP.	VERSE	PART	SECTION	PAGE
4	8–37	III	XXVI	191, 192	15	1–4	III	XXVII	221
4	38–44	III	XXV	187	15	5	III	XXVII	223
5	1–27	III	XXVI	192, 193	15	6, 7	III	XXVIII	225, 227
6	1–7	III	XXV	187, 188	15	8–12	III	XXVIII	222
6	8–33	III	XXVI	193, 194	15	13–28	III	XXVIII	224
7	1–20	III	XXVI	194, 195	15	29–31	III	XXVIII	232
8	1–6	III	XXVI	192	15	32–38	III	XXVIII	227, 229
8	7–15	III	XXVI	195, 196	16	1–9	III	XXVIII	229, 231
8	16–29	III	XXVI	197, 199	16	10–18	III	XXVIII	232
9	1–26	III	XXVI	198, 200, 201	16	19, 20	III	XXVIII	233
9	27, 28	III	XXVI	203	17	1–3	III	XXVIII	232
9	29	III	XXVI	199	17	4–8	III	XXVIII	241
9	30–37	III	XXVI	202	17	9–41	III	XXVIII	240, 242, 243
10	1–12a	III	XXVI	204	18	1–3	III	XXVIII	235
10	12b–14	III	XXVI	203	18	4–8	III	XXVIII	239, 241
10	15–17	III	XXVI	204	18	9–12	III	XXVIII	241
10	18–29	III	XXVII	205	18	13–27	IV	XXIX	249, 251
10	30, 31	III	XXVI	204	18	28–37	IV	XXIX	251
10	32–36	III	XXVII	206	19	1–37	IV	XXIX	255, 257
11	1–21	III	XXVII	207, 209	20	1–19	IV	XXIX	245, 247, 249
12	1–16	III	XXVII	209, 211	20	20, 21	IV	XXIX	257
12	17–21	III	XXVII	213	21	1–26	IV	XXX	259, 261, 263
13	1, 2	III	XXVII	208	22	1–20	IV	XXXI	265, 267
13	3–7	III	XXVII	210, 212	23	1–3	IV	XXXI	267, 269
13	8–11	III	XXVII	214	23	4–21	IV	XXXI	268, 270, 271
13	12, 13	III	XXVII	219	23	22, 23	IV	XXXI	273
13	14–21	III	XXVII	216	23	24–30a	IV	XXXI	274, 275
13	22, 23	III	XXVII	214	23	30b–37	IV	XXXI	277
13	24, 25	III	XXVII	216	24	1–4	IV	XXXII	281, 280
14	1–7	III	XXVII	215	24	5–19	IV	XXXII	283, 285
14	8–20	III	XXVII	217, 219	24	20	IV	XXXII	289
14	21, 22	III	XXVII	221	25	1–21	IV	XXXII	289, 291, 293
14	23, 27	III	XXVII	219	25	22–24	IV	XXXII	295
14	28, 29	III	XXVII	222	25	25, 26	IV	XXXII	297

I CHRONICLES

CHAP.	VERSE	PART	SECTION	PAGE	CHAP.	VERSE	PART	SECTION	PAGE
3	1–9	I	IX	45	20	1b–3	II	XII	71
10	1–14	I	VII	37	20	4–8	II	X	49
11	1–9	II	IX	45	21	1–30	II	XIV	89, 91, 93
11	10–14	II	IX	47	22	1, 2–19	II	XIV	93–95
11	15–19	II	X	49	23	1–15	II	XV	95
11	20–47	II	IX	47	23	16–24	II	XV	97
12	1–7	I	VI	32, 33	23	25–32	II	XV	96
12	8–18	I	V	26	24	1–19	II	XV	96, 98
12	19–22	I	VI	33	24	20–31	II	XV	97
12	23–40	II	IX	43, 44	25	1–31	II	XV	98, 99
13	1–14	II	XI	57	26	1–32	II	XV	99, 100
14	1, 2	II	X	51	27	1–22	II	XV	100
14	3–7	II	IX	45	27	23, 24	II	XIV	91
14	8–17	II	X	49	27	25–34	II	XV	101
15	1–29	II	XI	56, 58, 59	28	1–21	II	XVI	102, 103
16	1–43	II	XI	61, 63	29	1–22a	II	XVI	103, 104
17	1–27	II	XII	74, 76	29	22b	II	XVI	107
18	1, 14–17	II	X	49, 51	29	23–25	II	XVII	111
18	2–13	II	XII	71	29	26, 27	I	IX	45
19	1–19	II	XI	65, 67	29	28–30	II	XVI	109
20	1a	II	XII	67					

II CHRONICLES

CHAP.	VERSE	PART	SECTION	PAGE	CHAP	VERSE	PART	SECTION	PAGE
1	1	II	XVII	111	2	1–12	II	XVII	117, 119
1	2, 3–13	II	XVII	113, 115	2	13, 14	II	XVIII	125
1	14–17	II	XX	141	2	15–18	II	XVII	119

Table I (Continued)—For Finding Any Passage in the History and Harmony

II CHRONICLES—Continued

CHAP.	VERSE	PART	SECTION	PAGE	CHAP.	VERSE	PART	SECTION	PAGE
3	1-14	II	XVIII	121, 123	22	10-12	III	XXVII	207
3	15-17	II	XVIII	125	23	1-21	III	XXVII	207, 209
4	1-5	II	XVIII	125	24	1-14	III	XXVII	209, 211
4	6-22	II	XVIII	127	24	15-22	III	XXVII	212
5	1-14	II	XVIII	127, 129	24	23-27	III	XXVII	213
6	1-23	II	XIX	131	25	1-4	III	XXVII	215
6	24-42	II	XIX	133, 135	25	5-16	III	XXVII	214, 216
7	1-10	II	XIX	135, 137	25	17-28	III	XXVII	217, 219
7	11-22	II	XIX	139	26	1-5	III	XXVII	221
8	1-10	II	XX	145	26	6-20a	III	XXVII	220, 222
8	11-16	II	XIX	137, 139	26	20b, 21	III	XXVII	223
8	17, 18	II	XX	143	26	22, 23	III	XXVIII	225, 227
9	1-9, 12	II	XX	143	27	1-9	III	XXVIII	227
9	10, 11, 21	II	XX	145	28	1-4	III	XXVIII	229
9	13, 22, 24	II	XX	141, 143	28	5-15	III	XXVIII	228, 230
9	25-28	II	XX	141	28	16-27	III	XXVIII	231-233
9	29-31	II	XXI	149	29	1, 2	III	XXVIII	235
10	1-19	II	XXI	149, 151	29	3-36	III	XXVIII	234, 236
11	1-4	III	XXII	153	30	1-27	III	XXVIII	236, 237
11	5-17	III	XXII	152	31	1-19	III	XXVIII	238, 240
11	18-23	III	XXII	156	31	20, 21	III	XXVIII	241
12	1-16	III	XXII	157, 159	32	1-13a	IV	XXIX	249, 251
13	1, 2, 22	III	XXII	159, 161	32	13b-19	IV	XXIX	253
13	3-21	III	XXII	158, 160	32	20-23	IV	XXIX	255, 257
14	1-7	III	XXII	161	32	24, 25	IV	XXIX	245, 246
14	8-15	III	XXIII	163	32	26-31	IV	XXIX	246
15	1-15	III	XXIII	163, 164	32	32, 33	IV	XXIX	257
15	16-18	III	XXIII	161	33	1-25	IV	XXX	259, 261, 263
16	1-6	III	XXIII	165	34	1-33	IV	XXXI	265, 267, 269
16	11-14	III	XXIV	169	35	1, 18, 19	IV	XXXI	271, 273
17	1-19	III	XXIV	169, 168, 170	35	2-17	IV	XXXI	270, 272
18	1-34	III	XXV	179, 181	35	18, 19	IV	XXXI	271, 273
19	1-11	III	XXV	182	35	20-27	IV	XXXI	275
20	1-30	III	XXV	184, 186	36	1-5	IV	XXXII	277
20	31-33	III	XXIV	169	36	6, 7	IV	XXXII	281
20	34	III	XXVI	197	36	8-12	IV	XXXII	283, 285
20	35-37	III	XXV	183	36	13	IV	XXXII	289
21	1-20	III	XXVI	197, 199	36	14-21	IV	XXXII	292, 294
22	1-6	III	XXVI	199	36	22, 23	IV	XXXII	303
22	7-9	III	XXVI	203					

REMAINING O. T. BOOKS

CHAP.	VERSE	PART	SECTION	PAGE	CHAP.	VERSE	PART	SECTION	PAGE
Dan. 1	1-7	IV	XXXII	281, 280	Jer. 37	2-10	IV	XXXII	285, 287
Dan. 1	17-21	IV	XXXII	280, 282	Jer. 38	1-18	IV	XXXII	287, 288
Deut. 17	14-20	I	I	4	Jer. 39	1-10	IV	XXXII	289, 291, 293
Ez. 17	11-21	IV	XXXII	268	Jer. 40	2-16	IV	XXXII	294-296
Ezra 1	1-4	IV	XXXII	303	Jer. 41	1-18	IV	XXXII	296-298
Ezra 1	5-11	IV	XXXII	304	Jer. 42	1-22	IV	XXXII	298, 300
Is. 6	1-13	III	XXVIII	226	Jer. 43	1-13	IV	XXXII	300
Is. 7	1-9	III	XXVIII	229	Jer. 44	1-30	IV	XXXII	300-302
Is. 7	10-17	III	XXVIII	228	Jer. 52	1, 2	IV	XXXII	285
Is. 8	5-8	III	XXVIII	229	Jer. 52	3-16	IV	XXXII	289, 291, 293
Is. 36	1-22	IV	XXIX	249, 251, 253	Jer. 52	17-30	IV	XXXII	293
Is. 37	1-38	IV	XXIX	255, 257	Jer. 52	31-34	IV	XXXII	283, 285
Is. 38	1-8	IV	XXIX	245	Ps. 18	1-50	II	X	51-55
Is. 38	9-20	IV	XXIX	246	Ps. 32	1-7	II	XII	69
Is. 38	21, 22	IV	XXIX	245	Ps. 34	1-22	II	V	23, 24
Is. 39	1-8	IV	XXIX	247, 249	Pss. 46-48		III	XXV	186
Jer. 3	6-11	IV	XXXI	272	Ps. 51	1-19	II	XII	69
Jer. 15	1-6	IV	XXX	260	Ps. 52	1-9	I	V	24
Jer. 19	1-15	IV	XXXI	268, 269	Ps. 54	1-7	I	V	26
Jer. 21	1-10	IV	XXXII	286, 287	Ps. 56	1-13	I	V	28
Jer. 22	6a, 10-12	IV	XXXII	277	Ps. 57	1-11	I	IV	27, 28
Jer. 22	24-30	IV	XXXII	285	Ps. 59	1-17	I	IV	19
Jer. 24	1-10	IV	XXXII	284	Ps. 83	1-18	III	XXV	185
Jer. 25	1-14	IV	XXXII	276, 278	Ps. 96	1-13	II	XI	63
Jer. 28	1-17	IV	XXXII	284, 286	Ps. 105	1-15	II	XI	61-63
Jer. 29	1-14	IV	XXXII	302	Ps. 106	1, 47, 48	II	XI	63
Jer. 32	1-5	IV	XXXII	288	Ps. 136	1-26	II	XIX	134, 135
Jer. 34	1-7	IV	XXXII	288, 290	Ps. 147	1-7	I	V	27, 28
Jer. 36	1-32	IV	XXXII	278-280					

TABLE II
For Finding Parallel Passages in the Harmony

I SAM.	II SAM.	I KINGS	II KINGS	I CHRON.	II CHRON.	REMAINING O. T. BOOKS	PAGE
xxxi: 1-13				x: 1-14			37
	iii: 2-5			iii: 1-4			43
	v: 1-3			xi: 1-3			45
	v: 4, 5			{xxxix: 26, 27 / xi: 4b}			45
	v: 6-10			xi: 4-9			45
	v: 11, 12			xiv: 1, 2			51
	v: 13-16			{xiv: 3-7 / iii: 5-9}			45
	v: 17-25			xiv: 8-17			49
	vi: 1-12a			xiii: 1-14			57
	{vi: 12b-16 / 20-23}			xv: 25-29			58, 59, 61
	vi: 17-19			xvi: 1-7			61
	vii: 1-29			xvii: 1-27			73, 75
	viii: 1			xviii: 1			49
	viii: 2-14			xviii: 2-13			71
	viii: 15-18			xviii: 14-17			51
	x: 1-19			xix: 1-19			65, 67
	xi: 1a			xx: 1a			67
	xii: 26-31			xx: 1b-3			71
	xxi: 18-22			xx: 4-8			49
	xxii: 2-51					Ps. xviii: 1-50	61, 63
	xxiii: 8-12			xi: 10-14			47
	xxiii: 13-17			xi: 15-19			49
	xxiii: 20-39			xi: 22-47			47
	xxiv: 1-25			{xxi: 1-30 / xxii: 1}			89, 93
				xvi: 8-22			61, 63
				xvi: 23-33		Ps. cv: 1-15	65
				xvi: 34-36		Ps. xcvi: 1-11	65
						Ps. cvi: 1, 47, 48	63
							97
		i: 39, 40					107
		ii: 10, 11					109
		ii: 12		xxix: 22			111
				xxix: 26-30			
				xxix: 23-25	l: 1		
		iii: 4-15			i: 3-13		115
		v: 1-18			ii: 1-12, 15-18		117, 119
		vi: 1-3			iii: 1-4		121
		vi: 37-27			iii: 5-14		123
		vii: 13-26			{ii: 11, 13, 14 / iii: 15-17 / iv: 1-5 / iv: 6-21 / v: 1}		125
		viii: 22-51					127
		viii: 2-11			v: 2-14		129
		viii: 12-53			vi: 1-42		131, 133, 135
		viii: 54-61			vii: 1-3		135
		viii: 62-66			vii: 4-10		137
		ix: 24, 25			viii: 12-16		127, 129
		ix: 1-8			vii: 11-22		139
		iv: 21-25			ix: 25, 26		141
		x: 26-29			ix: 27, 28		141, 143
		x: 14-25			ix: 13-24		143
		x: 1-10, 13	i: 14-17		ix: 1-9, 12		145
		x: 11, 12, 22			ix: 10, 11, 21		143
		ix: 26-28			viii: 17, 18		145
		ix: 10-23			viii: 1-10		149
		xi: 41, 43			ix: 29-31		149, 151
		xii: 1-19			x: 1-19		153
		xiii: 22-24			xi: 1-4		155
		xv: 2b			xiii: 2b		157
		xiv: 25			xii: 2		157, 159
		xiv: 21-31			xii: 9-16		159
		xv: 1-7b			xiii: 1, 2		
					{xiii: 22 / xiv: 1-7 / xv: 16-18}		161
		xv: 7c-15			xvi: 1-6		163
		xv: 16-22, 32			{xvi: 7-10 / xvii: 1a}		169
		xv: 23, 24			xvi: 11-14		169
		xxii: 41-43, 46			xx: 31-33		

Table II (Continued)—For Finding Parallel Passages in the Harmony

I SAM.	II SAM.	I KINGS	II KINGS	I CHRON.	II CHRON.	REMAINING O. T. BOOKS	PAGE
		xxii: 1-15			xviii: 1-14		179
		xxii: 16-38			xviii: 15-34		181
		xxii: 41, 42-49			xx: 35-37		183
		xxii: 45, 50			xx: 34		197
			i: 1, 17b				189
			iii: 1-3				
			viii: 16-22			xxi: 1-11	197
			viii: 23, 24		xxi: 20b		199
					xxii: 1a		
			viii: 25		xxii: 1b		199
			ix: 29				
			viii: 26-29		xxii: 2-6		199
			ix: 27, 28		xxii: 7, 9		203
			x: 12b, 14		xxii: 8		203
			xi: 1-21		xxii: 10-21		207, 209
			xii: 1-16		xxiv: 1-14		209, 211
			xii: 17-21		xxiv: 23-27		213
			xiv: 1-7		xxv: 1-4, 11		215
			xiv: 8-14, 18, 19		xxv: 17-24, 26, 28		217, 219
			xiv: 15-17		xxv: 5		219
			xiii: 12, 13				
			xiv: 21, 22		xxvi: 1, 2		221
			xv: 1-4		xxvi: 3-5		221
			xv: 5, 6		xxvi: 20b-22		223, 225
			xv: 7		xxvi: 23		227
			xv: 32-36, 38		xxvii: 1-9		227
			xv: 37				
			xvi: 5			Is. vii: 1-9	229
			xvi: 1-4		xxviii: 1-4		229
			xvi: 6-9		xxviii: 16-21		231
			xvi: 19, 20		xxviii: 26, 27		233
			xviii: 1-3		xxix: 1, 2		235
			xviii: 4a		xxxi: 1		239
			xviii: 4b-8		xxxi: 20, 21		241
			xviii: 9-12				
			xvii: 1-8				241
			xx: 1-11	xxxii: 24		Is. xxxviii: 1-8	245
			xx: 12-18			Is. xxxix: 1-7	247, 249
			xx: 19			Is. xxxix: 8	249
			xviii: 13-17	xxxii: 1-13		Is. xxxvi: 1-12	249, 251
			xviii: 18-37	xxxii: 14-19		Is. xxxvi: 13-22	253
			xix: 1			Is. xxxvii: 1	255
			xix: 2-34			Is. xxxvii: 2-35	255, 257
			xix: 35-37		xxxii: 20	Is. xxxvii: 36-38	255, 257
			xx: 20, 21		xxxii: 21-23		257
			xxi: 1-18		xxxiii: 1-20		259, 261
			xxi: 19-26		xxxiii: 21-25		263
			xxii: 1-20		xxxiv: 1-28		265, 267
			xxiii: 1-3		xxxiv: 29-33		267, 269
			xxiii: 21		xxxv: 1		271
			xxiii: 22, 23		xxxv: 18, 19		273
			xxiii: 28-30a		xxxv: 20-26		275
			xxiii: 30b-37		xxxvi: 1-5		277
			xxiv: 1		xxxvi: 6, 7		281
			xxiv: 5-17		xxxvi: 8-10	Jer. xxii: 24-30	285
			xxiv: 18, 19		xxxvi: 11, 12	Jer. lii: 1, 2	285
						Jer. xxxvii: 2	
			xxiv: 20		xxxvi: 13	Jer. lii: 3	289
						Jer. xxxix: 1	289
			xxv: 1			Jer. lii: 4	
			xxv: 2-12			Jer. xxxix: 2-10	291, 293
						Jer. lii: 5-16	
			xxv: 13-21			Jer. lii: 17-30	293
			xxv: 22-24			Jer. xl: 1-9	295
			xxv: 25			Jer. xli: 1-3	297
			xxv: 26			Jer. xlii: 17, 18	297
			xxv: 27-30			Jer. lii: 31-34	283, 285
					xxxvi: 22, 23	Ezra i: 1-4	303

CHRONOLOGICAL CHART

ISRAEL			B.C. COMMON USHER	B.C. REVISED KENT*	ISRAEL		
		THE HOUSE			OF SAUL		
I Saul	(Samuel)		1096	1037	I Saul		(Samuel)
		THE HOUSE	1056	1017	OF DAVID		
I David made king of Judah		UNITED			KINGDOM		
		(Nathan)	1049	1010	I David made king of Israel		
II Solomon		(Nathan)	1016	977	II Solomon		(Nathan)
	JUDAH	DIVIDED			KINGDOM	ISRAEL	
	THE HOUSE OF DAVID				THE HOUSE OF JEREBOAM		(First)
III Rehoboam	(Shemaiah)	(1)	976	957	I Jereboam		(1)
IV Abijam		(2)	959	920			
V Asa	(Azariah) (Hanani)	(3)	956	917			
			955	915	II Nadab		(2)
					THE HOUSE OF BAASHA		(Second)
			953	914	I Baasha	(Jehu)	(3)
			931	890	II Elah		(4)
					THE HOUSE OF ZIMRI		(Third)
			930	889	I Zimri		(5)
					THE HOUSE OF OMRI		(Fourth)
			930	889	I Omri		(6)
		A	917	887	II A Ahab	(Micaiah) (Elijah)	(7)
VI Jehoshaphat	(Jehu) (Eliezer)	L L (4)	915	876	L L		
		I	898	855	III I Ahaziah	(Elijah)	(8)
		A	897	854	IV A Jehoram	(Elijah)	(9)
VII Jehoram		N C (5)	889	851	MAR C RIAGE		
VIII Ahaziah	INTER	E (6)	885	843	E		
					THE HOUSE OF JEHU		(Fifth)
Athaliah usurps the throne			883	842	I Jehu		(10)
IX Joash		(7)	877	856			
			855	814	II Jehoahaz		(11)
			838	797	III Jehoash	(Elisha)	(12)
X Amaziah	(Joel)	(8)	838	796			
			823	781	IV Jereboam II	(Amos) (Hosea)	(13)
XI Uzziah	(Isaiah) (Micah)	(9)	808	782		(Jonah)	
				763	The Great Eclipse		
			771	740	V Zechariah		(14)
					THE HOUSE OF SHALLUM		(Sixth)
			770	740	I Shallum	(Amos)	(15)
					THE HOUSE OF MENAHEM		(Seventh)
	Jotham Co-Regent		770	740	I Menahem	(Hosea)	(16)
			761	737	II Pekahiah		(17)
					THE HOUSE OF PEKAH		(Eighth)
			759	735	I Pekah		(18)
XII Jotham		(10)	756	737			
XIII Ahaz	(Isaiah) (Micah)	(11)	742	735			
					THE HOUSE OF HOSHEA		(Ninth)
					I Hoshea		(19)
XIV Hezekiah	(Isaiah) (Micah)	(12)	726	725 715	or		
			721	722	Captivity of Israel		
XV Manasseh		(13)	697	686			
XVI Amon	(Nahum)	(14)	642	641			
XVII Josiah	(Zephaniah) (Habakkuk)	(15)	640	639			
XVIII Jehoahaz		(16)	609	609			
XIX Jehoiakim	(Jeremiah)	(17)	609	609			
First Captivity			606	599			
XX Jehoiachin		(18)	599	597			
XXI Zedekiah	(Jeremiah)	(19)	599	597			
Final Captivity			588	586			

* Students' Chart of Biblical History
History of the Hebrew People
Charles F. Kent, Ph.D.

PART I

The Founding of the Monarchy

THE HOUSE OF SAUL
B. C. 1096 (Usher)*

I Saul
B. C. 1037 (Rev.)*

SECTION I

The Israelites Demand a King

I Sam. 8:1. And it came to pass, when Samuel was old, that he made his sons judges over Israel. 2. Now the name of his firstborn was Joel; and the name of his second, Abijah: they were judges in Beer-sheba. 3. And his sons walked not in his ways, but turned aside after lucre, and took bribes, and perverted judgment.

Elders Ask for a King
4. Then all the elders of Israel gathered themselves together, and came to Samuel unto Ramah: 5. and they said unto him, Behold thou art old, and thy sons walk not in thy ways: now make us a king to judge us like all the nations. 6. But the thing displeased Samuel, when they said, Give us a king to judge us. And Samuel prayed unto the Lord. 7. And the Lord said unto Samuel, Hearken unto the voice of the people in all that they say unto thee: for they have not rejected thee, but they have rejected me, that I should not be king over them. 8. According to all the works which they have done since the day that I brought them out of Egypt even unto this day, in that they have forsaken me, and served other gods, so do they also unto thee. 9. Now therefore hearken unto their voice: howbeit thou shalt protest solemnly unto them, and shalt show them the manner of the king that shall reign over them.

Protest and Warning of Samuel
10. And Samuel told all the words of the Lord unto the people that asked of him a king. 11. And he said, This will be the manner of the king that shall reign over you: he will take your sons, and appoint them unto him, for his chariots, and to be his horsemen; and they shall run before his chariots: 12. and he will appoint them unto him for captains of thousands and captains of fifties; and he will set some to plow his ground, and to reap his harvest, and to make his instruments of war, and the instruments of his chariots. 13. And he will take your daughters to be confectionaries, and to be cooks, and to be bakers. 14. And he will take your fields and your vineyards, and your oliveyards, even the best of them, and give them to his servants. 15. And he will take the tenth of your seed, and of your vineyards, and give to his officers, and to his servants. 16. And he will take your menservants, and your maidservants, and your goodliest young men, and your asses, and put them to his work. 17. He will take the tenth of your flocks: and ye shall be his servants. 18. And ye shall cry out in that day because of your king which ye shall have chosen you; and the Lord will not answer you in that day. 19. But the people refused to hearken unto the voice of Samuel; and they said, Nay; but we will have a king over us: 20. that we also may be like all the nations; and that our king

---
*See Chronology. Appendix A. Both the Usher and the Revised Chronology is given.

may judge us, and go out before us, and fight our battles. 21. And Samuel heard all the words of the people, and he rehearsed them in the ears of the Lord. 22. And the Lord said to Samuel, Hearken unto their voice, and make them a king. And Samuel said unto the men of Israel, Go ye every man unto his city.

Saul the Benjamite

I Sam. 9:1. Now there was a man of Benjamin, whose name was Kish, the son of Abiel, the son of Zeror, the son of Becorath, the son of Aphiah, the son of a Benjamite, a mighty man of valour. 2. And he had a son, whose name was Saul, a young man and a goodly: and there was not among the children of Israel a goodlier person than he: from his shoulders and upward he was higher than any of the people. 3. And the asses of Kish Saul's father were lost. And Kish said to Saul, his son, Take now one of the servants with thee, and arise, go seek the asses. 4. And he passed through the hill country of Ephraim, and passed through the land of Shalishah, but they found them not: then they passed through the land of Shaalim, and there they were not: and he passed through the land of the Benjamites, but they found them not. 5. When they were come to the land of Zuph, Saul said to his servant that was with him, Come and let us return; lest my father leave caring for the asses, and take thought for us. 6. And he said unto him, Behold now, there is in this city a man of God, and he is a man that is held in honour; all that he saith cometh surely to pass: now let us go thither; peradventure he can tell us concerning our journey whereon we go. 7. Then said Saul to his servant, But, behold, if we go, what shall we bring the man? for the bread is spent in our vessels, and there is not a present to bring to the man of God: what have we? 8. And the servant answered Saul again, and said, Behold, I have in my hand the fourth part of a shekel of silver: that will I give to the man of God, to tell us our way. 9. (Beforetime in Israel, when a man went to inquire of God, thus he said, Come, and let us go to the seer: for he that is now called a Prophet was beforetime called a Seer.) 10. Then said Saul to his servant, Well said; come, let us go. So they went unto the city where the man of God was. 11. As they went up the ascent to the city, they found young maidens going out to draw water, and said unto them, Is the seer here? 12. And they answered them, and said, He is; behold, he is before thee: make haste now, for he is come to-day into the city; for the people have a sacrifice to-day in the high place: 13. as soon as ye be come into the city, ye shall straightway find him, before he go up to the high place to eat: for the people will not eat until he come, because he doth bless the sacrifice; and afterwards they eat that be bidden. Now therefore get you up; for at this time ye shall find him. 14. And they went up to the city; and as they came within the city, behold, Samuel came out against them, for to go up to the high place.

Anointed to Be Prince

15. Now the Lord had revealed unto Samuel a day before Saul came, saying, 16. To-morrow about this time I will send thee a man out of the land of Benjamin, and thou shalt anoint him to be prince over my people Israel, and he shall save my people out of the hand of the Philistines: for I have looked upon my people, because their cry is come unto me. 17. And when Samuel saw Saul, the Lord said unto him, Behold, the man of whom I spake to thee! this same shall have authority over my people. 18. Then Saul drew near to Samuel in the gate, and said, Tell me, I pray thee, where the seer's house is. 19. And Samuel answered Saul, and said, I am the seer; go up before me unto the high place, for ye shall eat with me to-day: and in the morning I will let thee go, and will tell thee all that is within thine heart. 20. And as for thine asses that were lost three days ago, set not thy mind on them; for they are found. And for whom is all that is desirable in Israel? Is it not for thee, and for all thy father's house?

21. And Saul answered and said, Am not I a Benjamite, of the smallest of the tribes of Israel? and my family the least of all the families of the tribe of Benjamin? wherefore then speakest thou to me after this manner? 22. And Samuel took Saul and his servant, and brought them into the guest chamber, and made them sit in the chiefest place among them that were bidden, which were about thirty persons. 23. And Samuel said unto the cook, Bring me the portion which I gave thee, of which I said unto thee, Set it by thee. 24. And the cook took up the thigh, and that which was upon it, and set it before Saul. And Samuel said, Behold that which has been reserved! set it before thee and eat; because unto the appointed time hath it been kept for thee, for I said, I have invited the people. So Saul did eat with Samuel that day. 25. And when they were come down from the high place into the city, he communed with Saul upon the housetop. 26. And they arose early: and it came to pass about the spring of the day, that Samuel called to Saul on the housetop, saying, Up, that I may send thee away. And Saul arose, and they went out both of them, he and Samuel, abroad. 27. As they were going down at the end of the city, Samuel said to Saul, Bid the servant pass on before us, (and he passed on) but stand thou still at this time, that I may cause thee to hear the word of God.

I Sam. 10:1 * Then Samuel took the vial of oil, and poured it upon his head, and kissed him, and said, Is it not that the Lord hath anointed thee to be prince over his inheritance? 2. When thou art departed from me to-day, then thou shalt find two men by Rachel's sepulchre, in the border of Benjamin at Zelzah; and they will say unto thee, The asses which thou wentest to seek are found: and, lo, thy father hath left the care of the asses, and taketh thought for you, saying, what shall I do for my son? 3. Then shalt thou go on forward from thence, and thou shalt come to the oak of Tabor, and there shall meet thee there three men going up to God to Bethel, one carrying three kids, and another carrying three loaves of bread, and another carrying a bottle of wine. 4. And they will salute thee, and give thee two loaves of bread; which thou shalt receive of their hand. 5. After that thou shalt come to the hill of God, where is the garrison of the Philistines: and it shall come to pass, when thou art come thither to the city, that thou shalt meet a band of prophets coming down from the high place with a psaltery, and a timbrel, and a pipe, and a harp, before them; and they shall be prophesying. 6. And the spirit of the Lord will come mightily upon thee, and thou shalt prophesy with them, and shalt be turned into another man. 7. And let it be, when these signs are come unto thee, that thou do as occasion serve thee; for God is with thee. 8. And thou shalt go down before me to Gilgal; and, behold, I will come down unto thee, to offer burnt offerings, and to sacrifice sacrifices of peace offerings: seven days shalt thou tarry, till I come unto thee, and shew thee what thou shalt do. 9. And it was so, that when he had turned his back to go from Samuel, God gave him another heart: and all those signs came to pass that day. 10. And when they came thither to the hill, behold, a band of prophets met him; and the spirit of God came mightily upon him, and he prophesied among them. 11. And it came to pass, when all that knew him beforetime saw that, behold he prophesied with the prophets, then the people said one to another, What is this that is come unto the son of Kish? Is Saul also among the prophets? 12. And one of the same place answered, and said, And who is their father? Therefore it became a proverb, Is Saul among the prophets? 13. And when he had made an end of prophesying, he came to the high place.

14. And Saul's uncle said unto him and to his servant, Whither went ye? And he said, To

*See Samuel, Appendix B. Duplication of incidents, 2, 3.

seek the asses: and when we saw that they were not found, we came to Samuel. 15. And Saul's uncle said, Tell me, I pray thee, what Samuel said unto you. 16. And Saul said unto his uncle, He told us plainly that the asses were found. But concerning the matter of the kingdom, whereof Samuel spake, he told him not.

Elected King at National Assembly

17.* And Samuel called the people together unto the Lord to Mizpah; 18. and he said unto the children of Israel, Thus saith the Lord, the God of Israel, I brought up Israel out of Egypt, and I delivered you out of the hand of the Egyptians, and out of the hand of all the kingdoms that oppressed you: 19. but ye have this day rejected your God, who himself saveth you out of all your calamities and your distresses; and ye have said unto him, Nay, but set a king over us. Now therefore present yourselves before the Lord by your tribes, and by your thousands. 20. So Samuel brought all the tribes of Israel near, and the tribe of Benjamin was taken. 21. And he brought the tribe of Benjamin near by their families, and the family of Matrites was taken: and Saul the son of Kish was taken; but when they sought him, he could not be found. 22. Therefore they asked of the Lord further, Is there yet a man to come hither? And the Lord answered, Behold, he hath hid himself among the stuff. 23. And they ran and fetched him thence; and when he stood among the people he was higher than any of the people from his shoulders and upward. 24. And Samuel said to all the people,† See ye him whom the Lord hath chosen, that there is none like him among all the people? And all the people shouted, and said, God save the King. 25. Then Samuel told the people the manner of the kingdom, and wrote it in a book, and laid it up before the Lord. And Samuel sent all the people away, every man to his house. 26. And Saul also went to his house to Gibeah; and there went with him the host, whose heart God had touched. 27. But certain sons of Belial said, How shall this man save us? And they despised him, and brought him no present. But he held his peace.

Saul Delivers Jabesh-gilead

I Sam. 11:1. Then Nahash the Ammonite came up, and encamped against Jabesh-gilead: and all the men of Jabesh said unto Nahash, Make a covenant with us, and we will serve thee. 2. And Nahash the Ammonite said unto them, On this condition will I make it with you, that all your right eyes be put out; and I will lay it for a reproach upon all Israel. 3. And the elders of Jabesh said unto him, Give us seven days respite, that we may send messengers unto all the borders of Israel: and then, if there be none to save us, we will come out to thee. 4. Then came the messengers to Gibeah of Saul, and spake these words in the ears of the people: and all the people lifted up their voice and wept. 5. And, behold, Saul came following the oxen out of the field; and Saul said, What aileth the people that they weep? And they told him the words of the men of Jabesh. 6. And the spirit of God came mightily upon Saul when he heard those words, and his anger was kindled greatly. 7. And he took a yoke of oxen, and cut them in pieces, and sent them throughout all the borders of

---

* See God's commandment concerning the choice of a king. Deut. 17:14-20. When thou art come unto the land which the Lord thy God giveth thee, and shalt possess it, and shall dwell therein; and shalt say, I will set a king over me, like as all the nations that are round about me; thou shalt in any wise set him king over thee, whom the Lord thy God shall choose: one from among thy brethren shalt thou set king over thee, thou mayest not put a foreigner over thee, which is not thy brother. Only he shall not multiply horses to himself, nor cause the people to return to Egypt, to the end that he should multiply horses: forasmuch as the Lord hath said unto you, Ye shall henceforth return no more that way. Neither shall he multiply wives to himself, that his heart turn not away; neither shall he greatly multiply to himself silver and gold. And it shall be, when he sitteth upon the throne of his kingdom, that he shall write him a copy of this law in a book, out of that which is before the priests the Levites: and it shall be with him, and he shall read therein all the days of his life: that he may learn to fear the Lord his God, to keep all the words of this law and these statutes to do them; that his heart be not lifted up above his brethren, and that he turn not aside from the commandment, to the right hand, or to the left: to the end that he may prolong his days in his kingdom, he and his children, in the midst of Israel.

† See Samuel, Appendix B. Duplication of Incidents, 2.

Israel by the hand of messengers, saying, Whosoever cometh not forth after Saul and after Samuel, so shall it be done unto his oxen. And the dread of the Lord fell on the people, and they came out as one man. 8. And he numbered them in Bezek; and the children of Israel were three hundred thousand, and the men of Judah thirty thousand. 9. And they said unto the messengers that came, Thus shall ye say unto the men of Jabesh-gilead, To-morrow, by the time the sun is hot, ye shall have deliverance. And the messengers came and told the men of Jabesh; and they were glad. 10. Therefore the men of Jabesh said, To-morrow we will come out unto you, and ye shall do with us all that seemeth good unto you. 11. And it was so on the morrow, that Saul put the people in three companies; and they came into the midst of the camp in the morning watch, and smote the Ammonites until the heat of the day: and it came to pass, that they which remained were scattered, so that two of them were not left together. 12. And the people said unto Samuel, Who is he that said, Shall Saul reign over us? bring the men that we may put them to death. 13. And Saul said, There shall not a man be put to death this day: for to-day the Lord hath wrought deliverance in Israel.

Inauguration at Gilgal

14. Then said Samuel to the people, Come and let us go to Gilgal, and renew the kingdom there. 15. And all the people went to Gilgal;* and there they made Saul king before the Lord in Gilgal; and there they sacrificed sacrifices of peace offerings before the Lord; and there Saul and all the men of Israel rejoiced greatly.

Samuel's Address

I Sam. 12:1. And Samuel said unto all Israel, Behold, I have hearkened unto your voice in all that ye said unto me, and have made a king over you. 2. And now, behold, the king walketh before you: and I am old and greyheaded; and, behold, my sons are with you: and I have walked before you from my youth unto this day. 3. Here I am; witness against me before the Lord, and before † his anointed: whose ox have I taken? or whose ass have I taken? or whom have I defrauded? whom have I oppressed? or of whose hand have I taken a ransom to blind mine eyes therewith? and I will restore it you. 4. And they said, Thou hast not defrauded us, nor oppressed us, neither hast thou taken aught of any man's hand. 5. And he said unto them, The Lord is witness against you, and * his anointed is witness this day, that ye have not found aught in my hand. 6. And they said, He is witness. And Samuel said unto the people, It is the Lord that appointed Moses and Aaron, and that brought your fathers up out of the land of Egypt. 7. Now therefore stand still, that I may plead with you before the Lord concerning all the righteous acts of the Lord, which he did to you and to your fathers. 8. When Jacob was come into Egypt, and your fathers cried unto the Lord, then the Lord sent Moses and Aaron, who brought

---

*See Samuel, A. Duplication of incidents, 2.

†Note. His Anointed. This title Heb. Maschiah (whence Messiah through the Greek, Messias) Sept. the Christ, had been already applied to Aaron and his sons, (Lev. 4:3, 5. 6:20) and Hannah, in her thanksgiving song, had in prophetic anticipation coupled it with the title king. (I Sam. 1:10).

> The Lord shall judge the ends of the earth,
> And he shall give strength unto his king;
> And exalt the horn of his anointed.

It is now applied by Samuel to Saul the first king, and although both the priests and the prophets were anointed, the title The Lord's anointed was henceforward limited to the Theocratic King. It proclaimed that the king, chosen of Jehovah, represented the power and the authority of the Covenant God. This idea was sanctioned and confirmed by God's promise to David of an house, and a kingdom, and a throne that should be established forever. (2 Sam. 7:12-16.) Thenceforth the hope of Israel centered in an ideal Davidic king, whose person, work, and sure coming, is foretold and minutely described in the Messianic psalms and prophecies of the Old Testament. Andrew announces to Simon the fulfillment of these prophecies, saying, We have found the Messiah (which is, being interpreted, Christ). Jn. 1:41. The woman of Samaria asks in wonder, Can this be the Christ? The Samaritans said later, Now we believe, not because of thy speaking: for we have heard him for ourselves, and know that this is indeed the Saviour of the world. Jn. 4:29, 42.

forth your fathers out of Egypt, and made them to dwell in this place. 9. But they forgat the Lord their God, and he sold them into the hand of Sisera, captain of the host of Hazor, and into the hand of the Philistines, and into the hand of the king of Moab, and they fought against them. 10. And they cried unto the Lord, and said, We have sinned, because we have forsaken the Lord, and have served the Baalim and the Ashtaroth: but now deliver us out of the hand of our enemies, and we will serve thee. 11. And the Lord sent Jerubbaal, and Bedan, and Jephthah, and Samuel, and delivered you out of the hand of your enemies on every side, and ye dwelled in safety. 12. And when ye saw that Nahash the king of the children of Ammon came against you, ye said unto me, Nay, but a king shall reign over us: when the Lord your God was your king. 13. Now therefore behold the king whom ye have chosen, and whom ye have asked for: and, behold, the Lord hath set a king over you. 14. If ye will fear the Lord, and serve him, and hearken unto his voice, and not rebel against the commandment of the Lord, and both ye and also the king that reigneth over you be followers of the Lord your God, well: 15. but if ye will not hearken unto the voice of the Lord, but rebel against the commandment of the Lord, then shall the hand of the Lord be against you, as it was against your fathers. 16. Now therefore stand still and see this great thing, which the Lord will do before your eyes. 17. Is it not wheat harvest to-day? I will call unto the Lord, that he may send thunder and rain; and ye shall know and see that your wickedness is great, which ye have done in the sight of the Lord, in asking you a king. 18. So Samuel called unto the Lord; and the Lord sent thunder and rain that day: and all the people greatly feared the Lord and Samuel. 19. And all the people said unto Samuel, Pray for thy servants unto the Lord thy God, that we die not: for we have added unto all our sins this evil, to ask us a king. 20. And Samuel said unto the people, Fear not: ye have indeed done all this evil: yet turn not aside, from following the Lord, but serve the Lord with all your heart; 21. and turn ye not aside for then should ye go after vain things which can not profit nor deliver, for they are vain. 22. For the Lord will not forsake his people for his great name's sake: because it hath pleased the Lord to make you a people unto himself. 23. Moreover as for me, God forbid that I should sin against the Lord in ceasing to pray for you; but I will instruct you in good and the right way. 24. Only fear the Lord, and serve him in truth with all your heart: for consider how great things he hath done for you. 25. But if ye shall still do wickedly, ye shall be consumed, both ye and your king.

THE HOUSE OF SAUL
  B. C. 1096 (Usher)
I Saul
  B. C. 1037 (Rev.)

SAMUEL

SECTION II

Saul's Double Disobedience

I Sam. 13:1. Saul was (thirty) * years old when he began to reign; and he reigned two years over Israel. 2. And Saul chose him three thousand men of Israel; whereof two thousand were with Saul in Michmash and in the mount of Bethel, and a thousand were with Jonathan in Gibeah of Benjamin: and the rest of the people he sent every man to his tent. 3. And Jonathan smote the garrison of the Philistines that was in Geba, and the Philistines heard of it. And Saul blew the trumpet throughout all the land, saying, Let the Hebrews hear. 4. And all Israel heard say that Saul had smitten the garrison of the Philistines, and that Israel also was had in abomination with the Philistines. And the people were gathered together after Saul to Gilgal. 5. And the Philistines assembled themselves together to fight with Israel, thirty thousand chariots, and six thousand horsemen, and people as the sand which is on the seashore in multitude: and they came up, and pitched in Michmash, eastward of Beth-aven. 6. When the men of Israel saw that they were in a strait, (for the people were distressed,) then the people did hide themselves in caves, and in thickets, and in rocks, and in holds, and in pits. 7. Now some of the Hebrews had gone over Jordan to the land of Gad and Gilead; but as for Saul, he was yet in Gilgal, and all the people followed him trembling.

Saul Offers the Burnt Offering

†8. And he tarried seven days, according to the set time that Samuel had appointed: but Samuel came not to Gilgal; and the people were scattered from him. 9. And Saul said, Bring hither the burnt offering to me, and the peace offerings. And he offered the burnt offering. 10. And it came to pass that, as soon as he had made an end of offering the burnt offering, behold, Samuel came; and Saul went out to meet him, that he might salute him. 11. And Samuel said, What hast thou done? And Saul said, Because I saw that the people were scattered from me, and that thou camest not within the days appointed, and that the Philistines assembled themselves together at Michmash; 12. therefore said I, Now will the Philistines come down upon me to Gilgal, and I have not intreated the favour of the Lord: I forced myself, therefore, and offered the burnt offering. 13. And Samuel said to Saul, Thou hast done foolishly: thou hast not kept the commandment of the Lord thy God, which he commanded thee: for now would the Lord have established thy kingdom upon

---

*Note R. V. Margin. The Hebrew text has, Saul was a year old. The whole verse is omitted in the unrevised Sept. but in a later recension the number thirty is inserted. A. V. Saul reigned one year; and when he had reigned two years over Israel, Saul chose him three thousand men of Israel: This rendering connects the two verses, and gives the reason for specifying two years, as the interval between Samuel's address and Saul's organizing a national force. Andrew Wood says, "Apparently, two numbers are wanting in the Hebrew text (which is the customary heading to future reigns). Render, Saul was (? thirty) years old when he began to reign, and he reigned (? thirty) and two years over Israel. In the Hebrew, v. 2 has no grammatical connection with v. 1." This rendering would allow a much longer interval than two years, and so better account for his having a grown son able to command one third of the army, and take independent action as in v. 3; and also for the manifest development in Saul's character from the mistrustful and retiring king-elect, to the self reliant and even presumptuous king.

†See Samuel, Appendix B. Duplication of incidents. 4.

Sentence for First Disobedience

Israel for ever. 14. But now thy kingdom shall not continue: the Lord hath sought him a man after his own heart, and the Lord hath appointed him to be prince over his people, because thou hast not kept that which the Lord commanded thee. 15. And Samuel arose, and gat him up from Gilgal unto Gibeah of Benjamin. And Saul numbered the people that were present with him, about six hundred men. 16. And Saul, and Jonathan his son, and the people that were present with them, abode in Geba of Benjamin: but the Philistines encamped in Michmash. 17. And the spoilers came out of the camp of the Philistines in three companies: one company turned unto the way that leadeth to Ophrah, unto the land of Shual: 18. and another company turned the way to Beth-horon: and another company turned the way of the border that looketh down upon the valley of Zeboim toward the wilderness. 19. Now there was no smith found throughout all the land of Israel: for the Philistines said, Lest the Hebrews make them swords or spears: 20. but all the Israelites went down to the Philistines, to sharpen every man his share, and his coulter, and his axe, and his mattock; 21. yet they had a file for the mattocks, and for the coulters, and for the forks, and for the axes; and to set the goads. 22. So it came to pass in the day of battle, that there was neither sword nor spear found in the hand of any of the people that were with Saul and Jonathan; but with Saul and with Jonathan his son was there found. 23. And the garrison of the Philistines went out unto the pass of Michmash.

Jonathan's Daring Exploit

I Sam. 14:1. Now it fell upon a day, that Jonathan the son of Saul said unto the young man that bare his armour, Come and let us go over to the Philistines' garrison, that is on yonder side. But he told not his father. 2. And Saul abode in the uttermost part of Gibeah under the pomegranate tree which is in Migron: and the people that were with him were about six hundred men: 3. and Ahijah, the son of Ahitub, Ichabod's brother, the son of Phinehas, the son of Eli, the priest of the Lord in Shiloh, wearing an ephod. And the people knew not that Jonathan was gone. 4. And between the passes, by which Jonathan sought to go over unto the Philistines' garrison, there was a rocky crag on the one side, and a rocky crag on the other side: and the name of the one was Bozez, and the name of the other Seneh. 5. The one crag rose up on the north in front of Michmash, and the other on the south in front of Geba. 6. And Jonathan said to the young man that bare his armour, Come and let us go over unto the garrison of these uncircumcised: it may be that the Lord will work for us: for there is no restraint to the Lord to save by many or by few. 7. And his armourbearer said unto him, Do all that is in thine heart: turn thee, behold I am with thee according to thy heart. 8. Then said Jonathan, Behold, we will pass over unto the men, and we will discover ourselves unto them. 9. If they say thus unto us, Tarry until we come to you; then we will stand still in our place, and will not go up unto them. 10. But if they say thus, Come up unto us; then we will go up: for the Lord hath delivered them into our hand: and this shall be a sign unto us. 11. And both of them discovered themselves unto the garrison of the Philistines: and the Philistines said, behold, the Hebrews come forth out of the holes where they had hid themselves. And the men of the garrison answered Jonathan and his armourbearer, and said, Come up to us, and we will shew you a thing. And Jonathan said unto his armourbearer, Come up after me: for the Lord hath delivered them into the hand of Israel. 13. And Jonathan climbed up upon his hands and upon his feet, and his armourbearer after him: and they fell before Jonathan; and his armourbearer slew them after him. 14. And that first slaughter, which

Jonathan and his armourbearer made, was about twenty men, within as it were half a furrows length in an acre of land. 15. And there was a trembling in the camp, in the field, and among all the people; the garrison, and the spoilers, they also trembled: and the earth quaked; so there was an exceeding great trembling. 16. And the watchmen of Saul in Gibeah of Benjamin looked; and, behold, the multitude melted away, and they went hither and thither. 17. Then said Saul unto the people that were with him, Number now, and see who is gone from us. And when they had numbered, behold, Jonathan and his armourbearer were not there. 18. And Saul said unto Ahijah, Bring hither the ark of God. For the ark of God was there at that time with the children of Israel.

Philistine's Discomfiture
19. And it came to pass, while Saul talked unto the priest, that the tumult that was in the camp of the Philistines went on and increased: and Saul said unto the priest, Withdraw thine hand. 20. And Saul and all the people that were with him were gathered together, and came to the battle: and, behold, every man's sword was against his fellow, and there was a very great discomfiture. 21. Now the Hebrews that were with the Philistines as before time, which went up with them into the camp from the country round about: even they also turned to be with the Israelites that were with Saul and Jonathan. 22. Likewise all the men of Israel which had hid themselves in the hill country of Ephraim, when they heard that the Philistines fled, even they also followed hard after them in the battle. 23. So the Lord saved Israel that day: and the battle passed over by Beth-aven.

Hasty Oath of Saul
24. And the men of Israel were distressed that day: but Saul adjured the people, saying, Cursed be the man that eateth any food until it be evening, and I be avenged on mine enemies. So none of the people tasted food. 25. And all the people came into the forest; and there was honey upon the ground. 26. And when the people were come unto the forest, behold, the honey dropped: but no man put his hand to his mouth, for the people feared the oath. 27. But Jonathan heard not when his father charged the people with the oath: wherefore he put forth the end of the rod that was in his hand, and dipped it in the honeycomb, and put his hand to his mouth; and his eyes were enlightened. 28. Then answered one of the people, and said, Thy father straitly charged the people with an oath, saying, Cursed be the man that eateth food this day. 29. And the people were faint. Then said Jonathan, My father hath troubled the land: see, I pray you, how mine eyes have been enlightened, because I tasted a little of this honey. 30. How much more, if haply the people had eaten freely to-day of the spoil of their enemies which they found? for now hath there been no great slaughter among the Philistines. 31. And they smote of the Philistines that day from Michmash to Aijalon: and the people were very faint. 32. And the people flew upon the spoil, and took sheep, and oxen, and calves, and slew them on the ground: and the people did eat them with the blood. 33. Then they told Saul, saying, Behold, the people sin against the Lord, in that they eat with the blood. And he said, Ye have dealt treacherously: roll a great stone unto me this day. 34. And Saul said, Disperse yourselves among the people, and say unto them, Bring me hither every man his ox, and every man his sheep, and slay them here, and eat; and sin not against the Lord in eating with the blood. And all the people brought every man his ox with him that night, and slew them there. 35. And Saul built an altar unto the Lord: the same was the first altar that he built unto the Lord.

36. And Saul said, Let us go down after the Philistines by night, and spoil them until the

morning light, and let us not leave a man of them. And they said, Do whatsoever seemeth good unto thee. Then said the priest, Let us draw near hither unto God. 37. And Saul asked counsel of God. Shall I go down after the Philistines? wilt thou deliver them into the hand of Israel? But he answered him not that day. 38. And Saul said, Draw nigh hither, all ye chiefs of the people; and know and see wherein this sin hath been this day. 39. For as the Lord liveth, which saveth Israel, though it be in Jonathan my son, he shall surely die. But there was not a man among all the people that answered him. 40. Then said he unto all Israel, Be ye on one side, and I and Jonathan my son will be on the other side. And the people said unto Saul, Do what seemeth good unto thee. 41. Therefore Saul said unto the Lord, the God of Israel, Shew the right. And Jonathan and Saul were taken by lot: but the people escaped. 42. And Saul said, Cast lots between me and Jonathan my son. And Jonathan was taken. 43. Then Saul said to Jonathan, Tell me what thou hast done. And Jonathan told him, and said, I did certainly taste a little honey with the end of the rod that was in mine hand; and, lo, I must die. 44. And Saul said, God do so and more also: for thou shalt surely die, Jonathan. 45. And the people said unto Saul, Shall Jonathan die, who hath wrought this great salvation in Israel? God forbid: as the Lord liveth, there shall not one hair of his head fall to the ground; for he hath wrought with God this day. So the people rescued Jonathan, that he died not. 46. Then Saul went up from following the Philistines: and the Philistines went to their own place.

Pursuit Stopped

Saul's Wars and Family

47. Now when Saul had taken the kingdom over Israel, he fought against all his enemies on every side, against Moab, and against the children of Ammon, and against Edom, and against the kings of Zobah, and against the Philistines: and whithersoever he turned himself, he vexed them. 48. And he did valiantly, and smote the Amalekites, and delivered Israel out of the hands of them that spoiled them.

49. Now the sons of Saul were Jonathan, and Ishvi, and Malchishua: and the names of his two daughters were these; the name of the firstborn Merab, and the name of the younger Michal; 50. and the name of Saul's wife was Ahinoam the daughter of Ahimaaz: and the name of the captain of his host was Abner the son of Ner, Saul's uncle. 51. And Kish was the father of Saul; and Ner the father of Abner was the son of Abiel. 52. And there was sore war against the Philistines all the days of Saul: and when Saul saw any mighty man, or any valiant man, he took him unto him. I Sam. 15:1. And Samuel said unto Saul, The Lord sent me to anoint thee to be king over his people, over Israel: now therefore hearken thou unto the voice of the words of the Lord. 2. Thus saith the Lord of hosts, I have marked that which Amalek did to Israel, how he set himself against him in the way, when he came up out of Egypt. 3. Now go and smite Amalek, and utterly destroy all that they have, and spare them not; but slay both man and woman, infant and suckling, ox and sheep, camel and ass. 4. And Saul summoned the people, and numbered them in Telaim, two hundred thousand footmen, and ten thousand men of Judah. 5. And Saul came to the city of Amalek, and laid wait in the valley. 6. And Saul said unto the Kenites, Go, depart, get you down from among the Amalekites, lest I destroy you with them: for ye shewed kindness to all the children of Israel, when they came up out of Egypt. So the Kenites departed from among the Amalekites. 7. And Saul smote the Amalekites, from Havilah as thou goest to Shur, that is before Egypt. 8. And he

Saul's Second Disobedience

took Agag the king of the Amalekites alive, and utterly destroyed all the people with the edge of the sword. 9. But Saul and the people spared Agag, and the best of the sheep, and of the oxen, and of the fatlings, and the lambs, and all that was good, and would not utterly destroy them: but everything that was vile and refuse, that they destroyed utterly.

Sentence for Second Disobedience 10. Then came the word of the Lord unto Samuel, saying, 11. It repenteth me that I have set up Saul to be king; for he is turned back from following me, and hath not performed my commandments. And Samuel was wroth; and he cried unto the Lord all night. 12. And Samuel rose early to meet Saul in the morning; and it was told Samuel, saying, Saul came to Carmel, and, behold, he set him up a monument, and is gone about, and passed on, and gone down to Gilgal. 13. And Samuel came to Saul: and Saul said unto him, Blessed be thou of the Lord: I have performed the commandment of the Lord. 14. And Samuel said, What meaneth then this bleating of the sheep in mine ears, and the lowing of the oxen which I hear? 15. And Saul said, They have brought them from the Amalekites: for the people spared the best of the sheep and of the oxen, to sacrifice unto the Lord thy God; and the rest we have utterly destroyed. 16. *Then Samuel said unto Saul, Stay, and I will tell thee what the Lord hath said to me this night. And he said unto him, Say on. 17. And Samuel said, Though thou wast little in thine own sight, wast thou not made the head of the tribes of Israel? And the Lord anointed thee king over Israel; 18 and the Lord sent thee on a journey, and said, Go and utterly destroy the sinners the Amalekites, and fight against them until they be consumed. 19. Wherefore then didst thou not obey the voice of the Lord, but didst fly upon the spoil, and didst that which was evil in the sight of the Lord? 20. And Saul said unto Samuel, Yea, I have obeyed the voice of the Lord, and have gone the way which the Lord sent me, and have brought Agag the king of Amalek, and have utterly destroyed the Amalekites. 21. But the people took of the spoil, sheep, and oxen, the chief of the devoted things, to sacrifice unto the Lord thy God in Gilgal. 22. And Samuel said,

> Hath the Lord as great delight in burnt offerings and sacrifices,
>   As in obeying the voice of the Lord?
> Behold, to obey is better than sacrifice,
>   And to hearken than the fat of rams.
> 23 For rebellion is as the sin of witchcraft,
>   And stubbornness is as idolatry and teraphim.
> Because thou hast rejected the word of the Lord,
>   He hath also rejected thee from being king.

24. And Saul said unto Samuel,
I have sinned: for I have transgressed the commandment of the Lord, and thy words: because I feared the people, and obeyed their voice. 25. Now therefore, I pray thee, pardon my sin, and turn again with me, that I may worship the Lord. 26. And Samuel said unto Saul, I will not return with thee: for thou hast rejected the word of the Lord, and the Lord hath rejected thee from being king over Israel. 27. And as Samuel turned about to go away, he laid hold upon the skirt of his robe, and it rent. 28. And Samuel said unto him, The Lord hath rent the kingdom of Israel from thee this day, and hath given it to a neighbour of thine, that is better than thou. 29. And also the Strength of Israel will not lie nor repent: for he is not a man that he should repent. 30. Then he said, I have sinned: yet honour me now, I pray

---
* See Samuel, Appendix B. Duplication of incidents, 4.

thee, before the elders of my people, and before Israel, and turn again with me, that I may worship the Lord thy God. 31. So Samuel turned again after Saul: and Saul worshipped the Lord. 32. Then said Samuel, Bring ye hither to me Agag the king of the Amalekites. And Agag came unto him delicately. And Agag said, Surely the bitterness of death is past. 33. And Samuel said, As thy sword hath made women childless, so shall thy mother be childless among women. And Samuel hewed Agag in pieces before the Lord in Gilgal. 34. Then Samuel went to Ramah, and Saul went up to his house to Gibeah of Saul. 35. And Samuel came no more to see Saul until the day of his death: for Samuel mourned for Saul: and the Lord repented that he had made Saul king over Israel.

THE HOUSE OF SAUL
  B. C. 1096 (Usher
I Saul
  B. C. 1037 (Rev.)

SAMUEL

SECTION III

David's Victory over Goliath

David Chosen and Anointed

I Sam. 16:1. And the Lord said unto Samuel, How long wilt thou mourn for Saul, seeing I have rejected him from being king over Israel? fill thine horn with oil, and go, I will send thee to Jesse the Beth-lehemite: for I have provided me a king among his sons. 2. And Samuel said, How can I go? if Saul hear it, he will kill me. And the Lord said, Take an heifer with thee, and say, I am come to sacrifice to the Lord. 3. And call Jesse to the sacrifice, and I will shew thee what thou shalt do: and thou shalt anoint unto me him whom I name unto thee. 4. And Samuel did that which the Lord spake, and came to Bethlehem. And the elders of the city came to meet him trembling, and said, Comest thou peaceably? 5. And he said, Peaceably: I am come to sacrifice unto the Lord: sanctify yourselves, and come with me to the sacrifice. And he sanctified Jesse and his sons, and called them to the sacrifice. 6. And it came to pass, when they were come, that he looked on Eliab, and said, Surely the Lord's anointed is before him. 7. But the Lord said unto Samuel, Look not on his countenance, or on the height of his stature; because I have rejected him: for the Lord seeth not as man seeth; for man looketh on the outward appearance, but the Lord looketh on the heart. 8. Then Jesse called Abinadab, and made him pass before Samuel. And he said, Neither hath the Lord chosen this. 9. Then Jesse made Shammah to pass by. And he said, Neither hath the Lord chosen this. 10. And Jesse made seven of his sons to pass before Samuel. And Samuel said unto Jesse, The Lord hath not chosen these. 11. And Samuel said unto Jesse, Are here all thy children? And he said, There remaineth yet the youngest, and, behold, he keepeth the sheep. And Samuel said unto Jesse, Send and fetch him: for we will not sit down till he come hither. 12. And he sent, and brought him in. Now he was ruddy, and withal of a beautiful countenance, and goodly to look upon. And the Lord said, Arise, anoint him: for this is he. 13. Then Samuel took the horn of oil, and anointed him in the midst of his brethren: and the spirit of the Lord came mightily upon David from that day forward. So Samuel rose up, and went to Ramah.

David Comes to Saul

14. *Now the spirit of the Lord had departed from Saul, and an evil spirit from the Lord troubled him. 15. And Saul's servants said unto him, Behold now, an evil spirit from God troubleth thee. 16. Let our Lord now command thy servants, which are before thee, to seek out a man who is a cunning player on the harp: and it shall come to pass, when the evil spirit of God is upon thee, that he shall play with his hand, and thou shalt be well. 17. And Saul said unto his servants, Provide me now a man that can play well, and bring him to me. 18. Then answered one of the young men, and said, Behold, I have seen

* See Samuel, Appendix B. Duplication of incidents, 5.

a son of Jesse the Beth-lehemite, that is cunning in playing, and a mighty man of valour, and a man of war, and prudent in speech, and a comely person, and the Lord is with him. 19. Wherefore Saul sent messengers unto Jesse, and said, Send me David thy son, which is with the sheep. 20. And Jesse took an ass laden with bread, and a bottle of wine, and a kid, and sent them by David his son unto Saul. 21. And David came to Saul, and stood before him: and he loved him greatly; and he became his armourbearer. 22. And Saul sent to Jesse, saying, Let David, I pray thee, stand before me; for he hath found favour in my sight. 23. And it came to pass, when the evil spirit from God was upon Saul, that David took the harp, and played with his hand: so Saul was refreshed, and was well, and the evil spirit departed from him.

Goliath's Challenge I Sam. 17:1. Now the Philistines gathered together their armies to battle, and they were gathered together at Socoh, which belongeth to Judah, and pitched between Socoh and Azekah, in Ephes-dammim. 2. And Saul and the men of Israel were gathered together, and pitched in the vale of Elah, and set the battle in array against the Philistines. 3. And the Philistines stood on the mountain on the one side, and Israel stood on the mountain on the other side: and there was a valley between them. 4. And there went out a champion out of the camp of the Philistines, named Goliath, of Gath, whose height was six cubits and a span. 5. And he had a helmet of brass upon his head, and he was clad with a coat of mail; and the weight of the coat was five thousand shekels of brass. 6. And he had greaves of brass upon his legs, and a javelin of brass between his shoulders. 7. And the staff of his spear was like a weaver's beam; and his spear's head weighed six hundred shekels of iron: and his shieldbearer went before him. 8. And he stood and cried unto the armies of Israel, and said unto them, Why are ye come out to set your battle in array? am not I a Philistine, and ye servants to Saul? choose you a man for you, and let him come down to me. 9. If he be able to fight with me, and kill me, then will we be your servants: but if I prevail against him, and kill him, then shall ye be our servants, and serve us. 10. And the Philistine said, I defy the armies of Israel this day; give me a man, that we may fight together. 11. And when Saul and all Israel heard those words of the Philistine, they were dismayed, and greatly afraid.

* 12. (Now David was the son of that Ephrathite of Beth-lehem-judah, whose name was Jesse; and he had eight sons: and the man was an old man in the days of Saul, stricken in years among men. 13. And the three eldest sons of Jesse had gone after Saul to the battle: and the names of his three sons that went to the battle were Eliab the firstborn, and next unto him Abinadab, and the third Shammah. 14. And David was the youngest: and the three eldest followed Saul. 15. Now David went to and fro from Saul to feed his father's sheep at Beth-lehem. 16. And the Philistine drew near morning and evening and presented himself forty days.

† 17. And Jesse said unto David his son, Take now for thy brethren an ephah of this

---

* Note. At this point of the narrative of David's coming to Saul, there is inserted in the Hebrew text what is omitted in the Sept. (which being some 600 years older than the earliest extant Hebrew MS. carries great weight), viz. 17: 12-31, 55-58. 18: 1-5, 8-11, 17-19, 21, 26, 30. These inserted passages are supposed to be parts of another written tradition, interwoven with this shorter consistent story, without a thorough alteration to harmonize the differences. A partial effort seems to be made in 17:15, in the statement, "Now David went to and fro from Saul to feed his father's sheep at Beth-lehem." The greatest of these differences, and the only irreconcilable one, is found in 55-58, which contain Saul's inquiry of Abner, Whose son is this youth? when he saw David go forth against the Philistine; and on Abner's inability to answer, his inquiry of David himself on his return, Whose son art thou? and his answer. This ignorance of the King and of the captain of his host, is unexplainable with David's prior coming to Saul, whether he remained constantly with him, or went to and fro between sheep and court, as often as he was needed by Saul to banish the evil spirit with his music. The above omissions are marked with a ( ).

† See Samuel, Appendix B. Duplication of incidents, 5.

parched corn, and these ten loaves, and carry them quickly to the camp to thy brethren; 18. and bring these ten cheeses to the captain of their thousand, and look how thy brethren fare, and take their pledge. 19. Now Saul, and they, and all the men of Israel, were in the vale of Elah, fighting with the Philistines. 20. And David rose up early in the morning, and left the sheep with a keeper, and took, and went, as Jesse had commanded him; and he came to the place of the wagons, as the host which was going forth to the fight shouted for the battle. 21. And Israel and the Philistines put the battle in array, army against army. 22. And David left his baggage in the hand of the keeper of the baggage, and ran to the army, and came and saluted his brethren. 23. And as he talked with them, behold, there came up the champion, the Philistine of Gath, Goliath by name, out of the ranks of the Philistines, and spake according to the same words: and David heard them. 24. And all the men of Israel, when they saw the man, fled from him, and were sore afraid. 25. And the men of Israel said, Have ye seen this man that is come up? surely to defy Israel is he come up: and it shall be, that the man who killeth him, the king will enrich him with great riches, and will give him his daughter, and make his father's house free in Israel. 26. And David spake to the men that stood by him, saying, What shall be done to the man that killeth this Philistine, and taketh away the reproach from Israel? for who is this uncircumcised Philistine, that he should defy the armies of the living God? 27. And the people answered him after this manner, saying, so shall it be done to the man that killeth him. 28. And Eliab his eldest brother heard when he spake unto the men; and Eliab's anger was kindled against David, and he said, Why art thou come down? and with whom hast thou left those few sheep in the wilderness? I know thy pride, and the naughtiness of thine heart; for thou art come down that thou mightest see the battle. 29. And David said, What have I now done? Is there not a cause? 30. And he turned away from him toward another, and spake after the same manner: and the people answered him again after the former manner. 31. And when the words were heard which David spake, they rehearsed them before Saul: and he sent for him.) 32. And David said to Saul, Let no man's heart fail because of him; thy servant will go and fight with this Philistine. 33. And Saul said to David, Thou art not able to go against this Philistine to fight with him: for thou art but a youth, and he a man of war from his youth. 34. And David said unto Saul, Thy servant kept his father's sheep; and when there came a lion, and a bear, and took a lamb out of the flock, 35. I went out after him, and smote him, and delivered it out of his mouth: and when he arose against me, I caught him by his beard, and smote him, and slew him. 36. Thy servant smote both the lion and the bear: and this uncircumcised Philistine shall be as one of them, seeing he hath defied the armies of the living God. 37. And David said, The Lord that delivered me out of the paw of the lion, and out of the paw of the bear, he will deliver me out of the hand of this Philistine. And Saul said unto David, Go, and the Lord shall be with thee. 38. And Saul clad David with his apparel, and he put an helmet of brass upon his head, and he clad him with a coat of mail. 39. And David girded his sword upon his apparel, and he assayed to go; for he had not proved it. And David said unto Saul, I cannot go with these; for I have not proved them. And David put them off him.

40. And he took his staff in his hand, and chose him five smooth stones out of the brook, and put them in the shepard's bag which he had, even in his scrip; and his sling was in his hand: and he drew near to the Philistine. 41. And the Philistine came on and drew near unto David; and the man that bare the shield went before him. 42. And when the Philistine

looked about, and saw David, he disdained him: for he was but a youth, and ruddy, and withal of a fair countenance. 43. And the Philistine said unto David, Am I a dog, that thou comest to me with staves? And the Philistine cursed David by his gods. 44. And the Philistine said to David, Come to me, and I will give thy flesh unto the fowls of the air, and unto the beasts of the field. 45. Then said David to the Philistine, Thou comest to me with a sword, and with a spear, and with a javelin: but I come to thee in the name of the Lord of hosts, the God of the armies of Israel, which thou hast defied. 46. This day will the Lord deliver thee into mine hand; and I will smite thee, and take thine head from off thee; and I will give the carcases of the host of the Philistines this day unto the fowls of the air, and to the wild beasts of the earth; that all the earth may know that there is a God in Israel: 47. and that all this assembly may know that the Lord saveth not with sword and spear: for the battle is the Lord's, and he will give you into our hand. 48. And it came to pass, when the Philistine arose, and came and drew nigh to meet David, that David hastened, and ran toward the army to meet the Philistine. 49. And David put his hand in his bag, and took thence a stone, and slang it, and smote the Philistine in his forehead; and the stone sank into his forehead, and he fell upon his face to the earth. 50. So David prevailed over the Philistine with a sling and with a stone, and smote the Philistine, and slew him; but there was no sword in the hand of David. 51. Then David ran, and stood over the Philistine, and took his sword, and drew it out of the sheath thereof, and slew him, and cut off his head therewith. And when the Philistines saw that their champion was dead, they fled. 52. And the men of Israel and Judah arose, and shouted, and pursued the Philistines, until thou comest to Gai, and to the gates of Ekron. And the wounded of the Philistines fell down by the way to Shaarim, even unto Gath, and unto Ekron. 53. And the children of Israel returned from chasing after the Philistines, and they spoiled their camp. 54. And David took the head of the Philistine, and brought it to Jerusalem; but he put his armour in his tent.

David's Fight with Goliath

* (55. And when Saul saw David go forth against the Philistine, he said unto Abner, the captain of the host, Abner, whose son is this youth? And Abner said, As thy soul liveth, O king, I cannot tell. 56. And the king said, Inquire thou whose son the stripling is. 57. And as David returned from the slaughter of the Philistine, Abner took him, and brought him before Saul with the head of the Philistine in his hand. 58. And Saul said to him, Whose son art thou, thou young man? And David answered, I am the son of thy servant Jesse the Beth-lehemite.)

I Sam. 18:1. (And it came to pass, when he had made an end of speaking unto Saul, that the soul of Jonathan was knit with the soul of David, and Jonathan loved him as his own soul. 2. And Saul took him that day, and would let him go no more home to his father's house. 3. Then Jonathan and David made a covenant, because he loved him as his own soul. 4. And Jonathan stripped himself of the robe that was upon him, and gave it to David, and his apparel, even to his sword, and to his bow, and to his girdle. 5. And David went out whithersoever Saul sent him, and behaved himself wisely: and Saul set him over the men of war, and it was good in the sight of all the people, and also in the sight of Saul's servants.)

---

* If verses 55-58 be considered as an interpolation, and so omitted in the reading, the greatest difficulty in harmonizing Chapters 16-18 is removed. Smith on Samuel, Introduction XXIV-XXV. divides these two Chapters into two narratives as follows: First, the Sections 16:14-23. 18:6-13. 20-29. Second, the Sections 16:1-13. 17:1-58. 18:1-5, 14-19, 30.

SECT. III THE FOUNDING OF THE MONARCHY

Jealousy of Saul Aroused

6. And it came to pass as they came, when David returned from the slaughter of the Philistine, that the women came out of all the cities of Israel, singing and dancing, to meet king Saul, with timbrels, with joy, and with instruments of music. 7. And the women sang one to another in their play, and said,

> Saul hath slain his thousands,
> And David his ten thousands.

8. And Saul was very wroth, and this saying displeased him; and he said, They have ascribed unto David ten thousands, and to me they have ascribed but thousands: and what can he have more but the kingdom? 9. And Saul eyed David from that day and forward. * 10. And it came to pass on the morrow, that an evil spirit from God came mightily upon Saul, and he prophesied in the midst of the house: and David played with his hand, as he did day by day: and Saul had his spear in his hand. 11. And Saul cast the spear; for he said, I will smite David even to the wall. And David avoided out of his presence twice.) 12. And Saul was afraid of David, because the Lord was with him, and was departed from Saul. 13. Therefore Saul removed him from him, and made him his captain over a thousand; and he went out and came in before the people. 14. And David behaved himself wisely in all his ways; and the Lord was with him. 15. And when Saul saw that he behaved himself very wisely, he stood in awe of him. 16. But all Israel and Judah loved David; for he went out and came in before them.

---

* See Samuel, Appendix B. Duplication of incidents, 6.

THE HOUSE OF SAUL
  B. C. 1096 (Usher)
I Saul
  B. C. 1037 (Rev.)

SAMUEL

SECTION IV

Saul's Injustice and Violence to David

Two Artful Proposals for Marriage
I Sam. 18:17. (*And Saul said to David, Behold, my eldest daughter Merab, her will I give thee to wife: only be thou valiant for me, and fight the Lord's battles. For Saul said, Let not mine hand be upon him, but let the hand of the Philistines be upon him. 18. And David said unto Saul, Who am I, and what is my life, or my father's family in Israel, that I should be son in law to the king? 19. But it came to pass at the time when Merab Saul's daughter should have been given to David, that she was given unto Adriel the Meholathite to wife.) 20. And Michal Saul's daughter loved David: and they told Saul, and the thing pleased him. 21. (And Saul said, I will give him her, that she may be a snare to him, and that the hand of the Philistine may be against him. Wherefore Saul said to David, Thou shalt this day be my son in law a second time.) 22. And Saul commanded his servants, saying, Commune with David secretly, and say, Behold the king hath delight in thee, and all his servants love thee: now therefore be the king's son in law. 23. And Saul's servants spake these words in the ears of David. And David said, Seemeth it to you a light thing to be the king's son in law, seeing that I am a poor man, and lightly esteemed? 24. And the servants of Saul told him, saying, On this manner spake David. 25. And Saul said, Thus shall ye say to David, The king desireth not any dowry, but an hundred foreskins of the Philistines, to be avenged of the king's enemies. Now Saul thought to make David fall by the hand of the Philistines. 26. (And when his servants told David these words, it pleased David well to be the king's son in law. And the days were not expired;) 27. and David arose and went, he and his men, and slew of the Philistines two hundred men; and David brought their foreskins, and they gave them in full tale to the king, that he might be the king's son in law. And Saul gave him Michal his daughter to wife. 28. And Saul saw and knew that the Lord was with David; and Michal Saul's daughter loved him. 29. And Saul was yet the more afraid of David; and Saul was David's enemy continually. 30. (Then the princes of the Philistines went forth: and it came to pass, as often as they went forth, that David behaved himself more wisely than all the servants of Saul; so that his name was much set by.)

Attempts on David's Life
I Sam. 19:1. And Saul spake to Jonathan his son, and to all his servants, that they should slay David. 2. But Jonathan Saul's son delighted much in David. And Jonathan told David, saying, Saul my father seeketh to slay thee: now therefore, I pray thee, take heed to thyself in the morning, and abide in a secret place, and hide thyself: 3. and I will go out and stand beside my father in the field where thou art, and I will commune with my

---
* See Samuel, Appendix B. Duplication of incidents, 7.

father of thee; and if I see aught I will tell thee. 4. And Jonathan spake good of David unto Saul his father, and said unto him, Let not the king sin against his servant, against David; because he has not sinned against thee, and because his works have been to thee-ward very good: 5. for he put his life in his hand, and smote the Philistine, and the Lord wrought a great victory for all Israel: thou sawest it and didst rejoice: wherefore then wilt thou sin against innocent blood, to slay David without a cause? 6. And Saul hearkened unto the voice of Jonathan: and Saul sware, As the Lord liveth, he shall not be put to death. 7. And Jonathan called David, and Jonathan shewed him all those things. And Jonathan brought David to Saul, and he was in his presence, as beforetime. 8. And there was war again: and David went out and fought with the Philistines, and slew them with a great slaughter; and they fled before him. 9. And an evil spirit from the Lord was upon Saul, as he sat in his house with his spear in his hand; and David played with his hand. 10. * And Saul sought to smite David even to the wall with the spear; but he slipped away out of Saul's presence, and he smote the spear into the wall: and David fled, and escaped that night. 11. And Saul sent messengers unto David's house, to watch him, and to slay him in the morning: and Michal David's wife told him, saying, If thou save not thy life to-night, to-morrow thou shalt be slain. 12. So Michal let David down through the window: and he went, and fled, and escaped. 13. And Michal took the teraphim, and laid it in the bed, and put a pillow of goat's hair at the head thereof, and covered it with the clothes. 14. And when Saul sent messengers to take David, she said, He is sick. 15. And Saul sent the messengers to see David, saying, Bring him up to me in the bed, that I may slay him. 16. And when the messengers came in, behold, the teraphim was in the bed, with the pillow of goat's hair at the head thereof. 17. And Saul said unto Michal, Why hast thou deceived me thus, and let mine enemy go, that he is escaped? And Michal answered Saul, He said unto me, Let me go; why should I kill thee? †

David's Escape to Samuel

18. Now David fled, and escaped, and came to Samuel to Ramah, and told him all that Saul had done to him. And he and Samuel went and dwelt in Naioth. 19. And it was told Saul, saying, Behold, David is at Naioth in Ramah. 20. And Saul sent messengers to take David: and when they saw the company of the prophets prophesying, and Samuel standing as head over them, the spirit of God came upon the messengers of Saul, and they

---

* See Samuel, Appendix B. Duplication of incidents, 6.
† PS. 59. A Psalm of David: when Saul sent, and they watched the house to kill him.

1. Deliver me from mine enemies, O my God:
   Set me on high from them that rise up against me.
2. Deliver me from the workers of iniquity,
   And save me from the bloodthirsty men.
3. For, lo, they lie in wait for my soul,
   The mighty gather themselves together against me
   Not for my transgression, nor for my sin, O Lord.
4. They run and prepare themselves without my fault:
   Awake thou to help me, and behold.
5. Even thou, O Lord God of hosts, the God of Israel,
   Arise to visit all the heathen:
   Be not merciful to any wicked transgressors. Selah
6. They return at evening, they make a noise like a dog,
   And go round about the city.
7. Behold, they belch out with their mouth;
   Swords are in their lips:
   For who, say they, doth hear?
8. But thou, O Lord, shalt laugh at them;
   Thou shalt have all the heathen in derision.
9. O my strength, I will wait upon thee:
   For God is my high tower.
10. The God of my mercy shall prevent me:
    God shall let me see my desire upon mine enemies.
11. Slay them not, lest my people forget:
    Scatter them by thy power, and bring them down, O Lord our shield.
12. For the sin of their mouth, and the words of their lips,
    Let them even be taken in their pride,
    And for cursing and lying which they speak.
13. Consume them in wrath, consume them, that they be no more:
    And let them know that God ruleth in Jacob
    Unto the ends of the earth.
14. And at evening let them return, let them make a noise like a dog,
    And go round about the city.
15. They shall wander up and down for meat,
    And tarry all night if they be not satisfied.
16. But I will sing of thy strength;
    Yea, I will sing aloud of thy mercy in the morning:
    For thou hast been my high tower,
    And a refuge in the day of my distress.
17. Unto thee, O my strength, will I sing praises:
    For God is my high tower, the God of my mercy.

also prophesied. 21. And when it was told Saul, he sent other messengers, and they also prophesied. And Saul sent messengers again the third time, and they also prophesied. 22. Then went he also to Ramah, and came to the great well that is in Secu: and he asked and said, Where are Samuel and David? And one said, Behold, they be at Naioth in Ramah. 23. And he went thither to Naioth in Ramah: and the spirit of God came upon him also, and he went on, and prophesied, until he came to Naioth in Ramah. 24. And he also stripped off his clothes, and he also prophesied before Samuel, and lay down naked all that day and all that night. Wherefore they say, Is Saul also among the prophets? *

David's Flight to Jonathan

I Sam. 20:1. And David fled from Naioth in Ramah, and came and said before Jonathan, What have I done? what is mine iniquity? and what is my sin before thy father, that he seeketh my life? 2. And he said unto him, God forbid; thou shalt not die: behold, my father doeth nothing either great or small, but that he discloseth it unto me: and why should my father hide this thing from me? it is not so. 3. And David sware moreover, and said, Thy father knoweth well that I have found grace in thine eyes; and he saith, Let not Jonathan know this, lest he be grieved: but truly as the Lord liveth, and as thy soul liveth, there is but a step between me and death. 4. Then said Jonathan unto David, Whatsoever thy soul desireth, I will even do it for thee. 5. And David said unto Jonathan, Behold, tomorrow is the new moon, and I should not fail to sit with the king at meat: but let me go, that I may hide myself in the field unto the third day at even. 6. If thy father miss me at all, then say, David earnestly asked leave of me that he might run to Beth-lehem his city: for it is the yearly sacrifice there for all the family. 7. If he say thus, it is well; thy servant shall have peace; but if he be wroth, then know that evil is determined by him. 8. Therefore deal kindly with thy servant; for thou hast brought thy servant into a covenant of the Lord with thee: but if there be in me iniquity, slay me thyself; for why shouldest thou bring me to thy father? 9. And Jonathan said, Far be it from thee: for if I should at all know that evil were determined by my father to come upon thee, then would not I tell it thee? 10. Then said David to Jonathan, Who shall tell me if perchance thy father answer thee roughly? 11. And Jonathan said unto David, Come and let us go out into the field. And they went out both of them into the field.

The Mutual Covenant

12. And Jonathan said unto David, The Lord, the God of Israel, be witness; when I have sounded my father about this time tomorrow, or the third day, behold, if there be good toward David, shall I not then send unto thee, and disclose it unto thee? 13. The Lord do so to Jonathan, and more also, should it please my father to do thee evil, if I disclose it not unto thee, and send thee away, that thou mayest go in peace: and the Lord be with thee, as he hath been with my father. 14. And thou shalt not only while yet I live shew me the kindness of the Lord, that I die not: 15. but also thou shalt not cut off thy kindness from my house for ever: no, not when the Lord hath cut off the enemies of David every one from the face of the earth. 16. So Jonathan made a covenant with the house of David, saying, And the Lord shall require it at the hand of David's enemies. 17. And Jonathan caused David to swear again, for the love that he had to him: for he loved him as he loved his own soul. 18. Then Jonathan said unto him, To-morrow is the new moon: and thou shalt be missed, because thy seat will be empty. 19. And when thou hast stayed three

---

* See Samuel, Appendix B. Duplication of incidents, 3.

days, thou shalt go down quickly, and come to the place where thou didst hide thyself when the business was in hand, and shalt remain by the stone Ezel. 20. And I will shoot three arrows on the side thereof, as though I shot at a mark. 21. And, behold, I will send the lad, saying, Go, find the arrows. If I say unto the lad, Behold, the arrows are on this side of thee: take them and come; for there is peace to thee and no hurt, as the Lord liveth. 22. But if I say thus unto the boy, Behold, the arrows are beyond thee: go thy way; for the Lord hath sent thee away. 23. And as touching the matter which thou and I have spoken of, behold, the Lord is between thee and me for ever.

The Final Parting

24. So David hid himself in the field: and when the new moon was come, the king sat him down to eat meat. 25. And the king sat upon his seat, as at other times, even upon the seat by the wall; and Jonathan stood up, and Abner sat by Saul's side: but David's place was empty. 26. Nevertheless Saul spake not anything that day: for he thought, Something hath befallen him, he is not clean; surely he is not clean. 27. And it came to pass on the morrow after the new moon, which was the second day, that David's place was empty: and Saul said unto Jonathan his son, Wherefore cometh not the son of Jesse to meat, neither yesterday nor to-day? 28. And Jonathan answered Saul, David earnestly asked leave of me to go to Beth-lehem: 29. and he said, Let me go, I pray thee, for our family hath a sacrifice in the city; and my brother he hath commanded me to be there: and now, if I have found favour in thine eyes, let me get away, I pray thee, and see my brethren. Therefore he is not come unto the king's table. 30. Then Saul's anger was kindled against Jonathan, and he said unto him, Thou son of a perverse rebellious woman, do not I know that thou hast chosen the son of Jesse to thine own shame, and unto the shame of thy mother's nakedness? 31. For as long as the son of Jesse liveth upon the ground, thou shalt not be stablished, nor thy kingdom. Wherefore now send and fetch him unto me, for he shall surely die. 32. And Jonathan answered Saul his father, and said unto him, Wherefore should he be put to death? what hath he done? 33. And Saul cast his spear at him to smite him: whereby Jonathan knew that it was determined of his father to put David to death. 34. So Jonathan arose from the table in fierce anger, and did eat no meat the second day of the month: for he was grieved for David, because his father had done him shame. 35. And it came to pass in the morning, that Jonathan went out into the field at the time appointed with David, and a little lad with him. 36. And he said unto his lad, Run, find now the arrows which I shoot. And as the lad ran, he shot an arrow beyond him. 37. And when the lad was come to the place of the arrow which Jonathan had shot, Jonathan cried after the lad, and said, Is not the arrow beyond thee? 38. And Jonathan cried after the lad, Make speed, haste, stay not. And Jonathan's lad gathered up the arrows, and came to his master. 39. But the lad knew not anything: only Jonathan and David knew the matter. 40. And Jonathan gave his weapons unto his lad, and said unto him, Go, carry them to the city. 41. And as soon as the lad was gone, David arose out of the place toward the South, and fell on his face to the ground, and bowed himself three times: and they kissed one another, and wept one with another, until David exceeded. 42. And Jonathan said to David, Go in peace, forasmuch as we have sworn both of us in the name of the Lord, saying, the Lord shall be between me and thee, and between my seed and thy seed, for ever. And he arose and departed: and Jonathan went in to the city.

THE HOUSE OF SAUL
    B. C. 1096 (Usher)
I Saul
    B. C. 1037 (Rev.)

SAMUEL
GAD

SECTION V

David a Fugitive and Outlaw

The Final Flight

I Sam. 21:1. Then came David to Nob to Ahimelech the priest: and Ahimelech came to meet David trembling, and said unto him, Why art thou alone, and no man with thee? 2. And David said unto Ahimelech the priest, The king hath commanded me a business, and hath said unto me, Let no man know any thing of the business whereabout I send thee, and what I have commanded thee: and I have appointed the young men to such and such a place. 3. Now therefore what is under thine hand? give me five loaves of bread in mine hand, or whatsoever there is present. 4. And the priest answered David, and said, There is no common bread under mine hand, but there is * holy bread; if only the young men have kept themselves from women. 5. And David answered the priest, and said unto him, Of a truth women have been kept from us about these three days; when I came out, the vessels of the young men were holy, though it was but a common journey; how much more then to-day shall their vessels be holy? 6. So the priest gave him holy bread: for there was no bread there but the shewbread, that was taken from before the Lord, to put hot bread in the day when it was taken away. 7. Now a certain man of the servants of Saul was there that day, detained before the Lord; and his name was Doeg the Edomite, the chiefest of the herdmen that belonged to Saul. 8. And David said unto Ahimelech, And is there not here under thine hand spear or sword? for I have neither brought my sword nor my weapons with me, because the king's business required haste. 9. And the priest said, The sword of Goliath the Philistine, whom thou slewest in the vale of Elah, behold, it is here wrapped in a cloth behind the ephod: if thou wilt take that, take it: for there is no other save that here. And David said, There is none like that; give it me.

Goes to Achish King of Gath

10. And David arose, and fled that day for fear of Saul, and went to † Achish the king of Gath. 11. And the servants of Achish said unto him, Is not this David the king of the land? did they not sing one to another of him in dances, saying

> Saul hath slain his thousands,
> And David his ten thousands?

12. And David laid up these words in his heart, and was sore afraid of Achish the king

---

* See Matt. 12:1-8. To the Pharisees who, when they saw the hungered disciples pluck the ears of corn and eat them on the Sabbath, said to Jesus, Behold thy disciples do that which is not lawful to do upon the Sabbath. He said unto them, Have ye not read what David did, when he was an hungered, and they that were with him, how he entered into the house of God, and did eat the shewbread, which it was not lawful for him to eat, neither for them that were with him, but only for the priests?
† See Samuel. Duplication of incidents, 8.

of *Gath. 13. And he †changed his behaviour before them, and feigned himself mad in their hands, and scrabbled on the doors of the gate, and let his spittle fall down upon his beard. 14. Then said Achish unto his servants, Lo, ye see that the man is mad: wherefore then have ye brought him to me? 15. Do I lack mad men, that ye have brought this fellow to play the mad man in my presence? shall this fellow come into my house?

An Outlaw at Adullam

I Sam. 22:1. David therefore departed thence, and escaped to the cave of Adullam: and when his brethren and all his father's house heard it, they went down thither to him. 2. And every one that was in distress, and every one that was in debt, and every one that was discontented, gathered themselves unto him; and he became captain over them: and there were with him about four hundred men. 3. And David went thence to Mizpeh of Moab: and he said unto the king of Moab, Let my father and my mother, I pray thee, come forth, and be with you, till I know what God will do for me. 4. And he brought them before the king of Moab: and they dwelt with him all the while that David was in the hold. 5. And the prophet Gad said unto David, Abide not in the hold; depart, and get thee into the land of Judah. Then David departed, and came into the forest of Hereth. 6. And Saul heard that David was discovered, and the men that were with him: now Saul was sitting in Gibeah, under the tamarisk tree in Ramah, with his spear in his hand, and all his servants were standing about him. 7. And Saul said unto his servants that stood about him, Hear now, ye Benjamites; will the son of Jesse give every one of you fields and vineyards, will he make you all captains of thousands and captains of hundreds; 8. that all of you have conspired against me, and there is none that discloseth to me when my son maketh a league with the son of Jesse, and there is none of you that is sorry for me, or discloseth unto me that my son hath stirred up my servant against me, to lie in wait, as at this day?

---

*PSALM 56.

A Psalm of David: Michtam: when the Philistines took him in Gath.

1. Be merciful unto me, O God; for man would swallow me up:
   All the day long he fighting oppresseth me.
2. Mine enemies would swallow me up all the day long:
   For they be many that fight proudly against me.
3. What time I am afraid,
   I will put my trust in thee.
4. In God I will praise his word:
   In God have I put my trust, I will not be afraid;
   What can flesh do unto me?
5. All the day long they wrest my words:
   All their thoughts are against me for evil.
6. They gather themselves together, they hide themselves,
   They mark my steps,
   Even as they have waited for my soul.
7. Shall they escape by iniquity?
   In anger cast down the peoples, O God.
8. Thou tellest my wanderings:
   Put thou my tears into thy bottle;
   Are they not in thy book?
9. Then shall mine enemies turn back in the day that I call:
   This I know, that God is for me.
10. In God will I praise his word,
    In the Lord will I praise his word.
11. In God have I put my trust, I will not be afraid,
    What can man do unto me?
12. Thy vows are upon me, O God:
    I will render thank offerings unto thee.
13. For thou hast delivered my soul from death:
    Hast thou not delivered my feet from falling?
    That I may walk before God in the light of the living.

†PSALM 34.

A Psalm of David: when he changed his behaviour before (Achish the) Abimelech, who drove him away, and he departed.

1. I will bless the Lord at all times:
   His praise shall be continually in my mouth.
2. My soul shall make her boast in the Lord:
   The meek shall hear thereof and be glad.
3. O magnify the Lord with me,
   And let us exalt his name together.
4. I sought the Lord, and he answered me,
   And delivered me from all my fears.
5. They looked unto him, and were lightened:
   And their faces shall never be confounded.
6. This poor man cried, and the Lord heard him,
   And saved him out of all his troubles.
7. The angel of the Lord encampeth round about them that fear him,
   And delivereth them.
8. O taste and see that the Lord is good:
   Blessed is the man that trusteth in him.
9. O fear the Lord, ye his saints:
   For there is no want to them that fear him.
10. The young lions do lack, and suffer hunger:
    But they that seek the Lord shall not want any good thing.
11. Come, ye children, hearken unto me:
    I will teach you the fear of the Lord.
12. What man is he that desireth life,
    And loveth many days, that he may see good?
13. Keep thy tongue from evil,
    And thy lips from speaking guile.

Saul's Massacre of Priests of Nob by Doeg

9. Then answered * Doeg the Edomite, which stood by the servants of Saul, and said, I saw the son of Jesse coming to Nob, to Ahimelech the son of Ahitub. 10. And he inquired of the Lord for him, and gave him victuals, and gave him the sword of Goliath the Philistine. 11. Then the king sent to call Ahimelech the priest, the son of Ahitub, and all his father's house, the priests that were in Nob: and they came all of them to the king. 12. And Saul said, Hear now, thou son of Ahitub. And he answered, Here I am, my lord. 13. And Saul said unto him, Why have ye conspired against me, thou and the son of Jesse, in that thou hast given him bread, and a sword, and hast inquired of God for him, that he should rise against me, to lie in wait, as at this day? 14. Then Ahimelech answered the king, and said, And who among all thy servants is so faithful as David, which is the king's son in law, and is taken into thy council, and is honourable in thy house? 15. Have I to-day begun to inquire of God for him? be it far from me: let not the king impute any thing unto his servant, nor to all the house of my father: for thy servant knoweth nothing of all this, less or more. 16. And the king said, Thou shalt surely die, Ahimelech, thou, and all thy father's house. 17. And the king said unto the guard that stood about him, Turn, and slay the priests of the Lord; because their hand also is with David, and because they knew that he fled, and did not disclose it to me. But the servants of the king would not put forth their hand to fall upon the priests of the Lord. 18. And the king said to Doeg, Turn thou, and fall upon the priests. And Doeg the Edomite turned, and he † fell upon the priests, and he slew on that day fourscore and five persons that did wear a linen ephod. 19. And Nob, the city of the priests, smote he with the edge of the sword, both men and women, children and sucklings, and oxen and asses and sheep, with the edge of the sword. 20. And one of the sons of Ahimelech the son of Ahitub, named Abiathar, escaped, and fled after David. 21. And Abiathar told David that Saul had slain the Lord's priests. 22. And David said unto Abiathar, I knew on that day, when Doeg the Edomite was there, that he would surely tell Saul: I have occasioned the death of all the persons of thy father's house. 23. Abide thou with me, fear not: for he that seeketh my life seeketh thy life: for with me thou shalt be in safeguard.

---

* PSALM 52.

Maschil of David: when Doeg the Edomite came and told Saul, and said unto him, David is come to the house of Ahimelech.

1. Why boasteth thou thyself in mischief, O mighty man?
   The mercy of God endureth continually.
2. Thy tongue deviseth very wickedness:
   Like a sharp razor, working deceitfully.
3. Thou lovest evil more than good;
   And lying rather than to speak righteousness.
4. Thou lovest all devouring words,
   O thou deceitful tongue.
5. God shall likewise destroy thee for ever,
   He shall take thee up, and pluck thee out of thy tent,
   And root thee out of the land of the living.
6. The righteous also shall see it, and fear,
   And shall laugh at him, saying,
7. Lo, this is the man that made not God his strength;
   But trusted in the abundance of his riches,
   And strengthened himself in his wickedness. [God:
8. But as for me I am like a green olive tree in the house of
   I trust in the mercy of God for ever and ever. [it
9. I will give thee thanks for ever, because thou hast done
   And I will wait on thy name, for it is good, in the presence of thy saints.

PSALM 34.

14. Depart from evil, and do good;
    Seek peace and pursue it
15. The eyes of the Lord are toward the righteous,
    And his ears are open unto their cry.
16. The face of the Lord is against them that do evil,
    To cut off the remembrance of them from the earth.
17. The righteous cried, and the Lord heard
    And delivered them out of all their troubles.
18. The Lord is nigh unto them that are of a broken heart,
    And saveth such as be of a contrite spirit.
19. Many are the afflictions of the righteous:
    But the Lord delivereth him out of them all
20. He keepeth all his bones:
    Not one of them is broken.
21. Evil shall slay the wicked:
    And they that hate the righteous shall be condemned.
22. The Lord redeemeth the soul of his servants:
    And none of them that trust in him shall be condemned.

† See 2:31-36. Prophecy against Eli and his house, as fulfilled (1) 4:11 in the death of Hophni and Phinehas. (2) In this massacre of the priests of Nob by Saul. (3) In the removal of Abiathar by Solomon for his defection to Adonijah. I Kings 2:26, 27. (4) In the appointment of Zadock in his room. I Kings 2:35.

SECT. V — THE FOUNDING OF THE MONARCHY

**Keilah Saved
Philistines Smitten**

I Sam. 23:1. And they told David, saying, Behold, the Philistines are fighting against Keilah, and they rob the threshing floors. 2. Therefore David inquired of the Lord, saying, Shall I go and smite these Philistines? And the Lord said unto David, Go, and smite the Philistines, and save Keilah. 3. And David's men said unto him, Behold we be afraid here in Judah: how much more then if we go to Keilah against the armies of the Philistines? 4. Then David inquired of the Lord yet again. And the Lord answered him and said, Arise, go down to Keilah; for I will deliver the Philistines into thine hand. 5. And David and his men went to Keilah, and fought with the Philistines, and brought away their cattle, and slew them with a great slaughter. So David saved the inhabitants of Keilah.
6. And it came to pass, when Abiathar the son of Ahimelech fled to David to Keilah, that he came down with an ephod in his hand. 7. And it was told Saul that David was come to Keilah. And Saul said, God hath delivered him into mine hand: for he is shut in, by entering into a town that hath gates and bars. 8. And Saul summoned all the people to war, to go down to Keilah, to besiege David and his men. 9. And David knew that Saul devised mischief against him: and he said to Abiathar the priest, Bring hither the ephod. 10. Then said David, O Lord, the God of Israel, thy servant hath surely heard that Soul seeketh to come to Keilah, to destroy the city for my sake. 11. Will the men of Keilah deliver me up into his hand? will Saul come down, as thy servant hath heard? O Lord, the God of Israel, I beseech thee, tell thy servant. And the Lord said, He will come down. 12. Then said David, Will the men of Keilah deliver up me and my men into the hand of Saul? And the Lord said, They will deliver thee up. 13. Then David and his men, which were about six hundred, arose and departed out of Keilah, and went whithersoever they could go. And it was told Saul that David was escaped from Keilah: and he forbare to go forth.

**Betrayed by the
Ziphites**

14. And David abode in the wilderness in the strong holds, and remained in the hill country in the wilderness of Ziph. And Saul sought him every day, but God delivered him not into his hand.
15. And David saw that Saul was come out to seek his life: and David was in the wilderness of Ziph in the wood. 16. And Jonathan Saul's son arose, and went to David in the wood, and strengthened his hand in God. 17. And he said unto him, Fear not: for the hand of Saul my father shall not find thee; and thou shalt be king over Israel, and I shall be next unto thee; and that also Saul my father knoweth. 18. And they two made a covenant before the Lord: and David abode in the wood, and Jonathan went to his house. 19. Then came up the * Ziphites to Saul to Gibeah, saying, Doth not David hide himself with us in the strong holds in the wood, in the hill of Hachilah, which is on the south of the desert? 20. Now therefore, O king, come down, according to all the desire of thy soul to come down; and our part shall be to deliver him up into the king's hand. 21. And Saul said, Blessed be ye of the Lord; for ye have had compassion on me. 22. Go, I pray you, make yet more sure, and know and see his place where his haunt is, and who hath seen him there: for it is told me that he dealeth very subtilly. 23. See therefore, and take knowledge of all the lurking places where he hideth himself, and come ye again to me of a certainty, and I will go with you: and it shall come to pass, if he be in the land, that I will search him out among all the thousands of

---

* See Samuel, Appendix B. Duplication of incidents, 9...

Judah.* 24. And they arose, and went to Ziph before Saul: but David and his men were in the wilderness of Maon, in the Arabah on the south of the desert. 25. And Saul and his men went to seek him. And they told David: wherefore he came down to the rock, and abode in the wilderness of Maon. And when Saul heard that, he pursued after David in the wilderness of Maon. 26. And Saul went on this side of the mountain, and David and his men on that side of the mountain: and David made haste to get away for fear of Saul; for Saul and his men compassed David and his men round about to take them. 27. But there came a messenger unto Saul, saying, Haste thee, and come; for the Philistines have made a raid upon the land. 28. So Saul returned from pursuing after David, and went against the Philistines: therefore they called that place Sela-hammahlekoth. 29. And David went up from thence, and dwelt in the strong holds of En-gedi.

Coming of New Warriors

I Chron. 12:8. And of the Gadites there separated themselves unto David to the hold in the wilderness, mighty men of valour, men trained for war, that could handle shield and spear; whose faces were like the faces of lions, and they were as swift as the roes upon the mountains; 9. Ezer the chief, Obadiah the second, Eliab the third; 10. Mismannah the fourth, Jeremiah the fifth; 11. Attai the sixth, Eliel the seventh; 12. Johanan the eighth, Elzabad the ninth; 13. Jeremiah the tenth, Machbanni the eleventh. 14. These of the sons of Gad were captains of the host: he that was least was equal to an hundred, and the greatest to a thousand. 15. These are they that went over Jordan in the first month, when it had overflown all its banks; and they put to flight all them of the valleys, both toward the east and toward the west. 16. And there came of the children of Benjamin and Judah to the hold unto David. 17. And David went out to meet them, and answered and said unto them, If ye be come peaceably unto me to help me, mine heart shall be knit unto you: but if ye be come to betray me to mine adversaries, seeing there is no wrong in mine hands, the God of our fathers look thereon and rebuke it. 18. Then the spirit came upon Amasai, who was chief of the thirty, and he said, thine are we, David, and on thy side, thou son of Jesse: peace, peace be unto thee, and peace be to thine helpers; for thy God helpeth thee. Then David received them, and made them captains of the band.

David Spares Saul's Life

I Sam. 24:1. And it came to pass, when Saul was returned from following the Philistines, that it was told him, saying, Behold, David is in the wilderness of En-gedi. 2. Then Saul took three thousand chosen men out of all Israel, and went to seek David and his men upon the rocks of the wild goats. 3. And he came to the sheepcotes by the way, where was a cave; and Saul went in to cover his feet. Now David and his men were abiding

---

* PSALM 54.

Maschil of David: when the Ziphites came and said to Saul, Doth not David hide himself with us?

1. Save me, O God, by thy name,
   And judge me in thy might.
2. Hear my prayer, O God;
   Give ear to the words of my mouth.
3. For strangers are risen up against me,
   And violent men have sought after my soul
   They have not set God before them.
4. Behold, God is mine helper;
   The Lord is of them that uphold my soul.
5. He shall requite the evil unto mine enemies:
   Destroy thou them in thy truth.
6. With a free will offering will I sacrifice unto thee:
   I will give thanks unto thy name, O Lord, for it is good.
7. For he hath delivered me out of all trouble;
   And mine eye hath seen my desire upon mine enemies.

in the innermost parts of the *cave. 4. †And the men of David said unto him, Behold, the day of which the Lord said unto thee, Behold, I will deliver thine enemy into thine hand, and thou shalt do to him as it shall seem good unto thee. Then David arose, and cut off the skirt of Saul's robe privily. 5. And it came to pass afterward, that David's heart smote him, because he had cut off Saul's skirt. 6. And he said unto his men, The Lord forbid that I should do this thing unto my lord, the Lord's anointed, to put forth my hand against him, seeing he is the Lord's anointed. 7. So David checked his men with these words, and suffered them not to rise against Saul. And Saul rose up out of the cave, and went on his way. 8. David also arose afterward, and went out of the cave, and cried after Saul, saying, My lord the king. And when Saul looked behind him, David bowed with his face to the earth, and did obeisance. 9. And David said to Saul, Wherefore harkenest thou to men's words, saying, Behold, David seeketh thy hurt? 10. Behold, this day thine eyes have seen how that the Lord had delivered thee to-day into mine hand in the cave: and some bade me kill thee: but mine eye spared thee; and I said, I will not put forth mine hand against my lord; for he is the Lord's anointed. 11. Moreover, my father, see, yea, see the skirt of thy robe in my hand: for in that I cut off the skirt of thy robe, and killed thee not, know thou and see that there is neither evil nor transgression in mine hand, and I have not sinned against thee, though thou huntest after my soul to take it. 12. The Lord judge between me and thee, and the Lord avenge me of thee: but mine hand shall not be upon thee. 13. As saith the proverb of the ancients, Out of the wicked cometh forth wickedness: but mine hand shall not be upon thee. 14. After whom is the king of Israel come out? after whom dost thou pursue? after a dead dog, after a flea. 15. The Lord therefore be judge, and give sentence between me and thee, and see, and plead my cause, and deliver me out of thine hand. 16. And it came to pass, when David had made an end of speaking these words unto Saul, that Saul said, Is this thy voice, my son David? And Saul lifted up his voice and wept. 17. And he said to David, Thou art more righteous than I: for thou hast rendered unto me good, whereas I have rendered unto thee evil. 18. And thou hast declared this day how that thou hast dealt well with me: forasmuch as when the Lord had delivered me up into thine hand, thou killest me not. 19. For if a man find his enemy, will he let him go well away? wherefore the Lord reward thee good for that thou hast done unto me this day. 20. And now, behold, I know that thou shalt surely be king, and that the kingdom of Israel shall be established in thine hand. 21. Swear now therefore unto me by the Lord, that thou wilt not cut off my seed after me, and that thou wilt not destroy my name out of my father's house. 22. And David sware unto Saul. And Saul went home; but David and his men gat them up into the hold.

Death and Burial of Samuel — I Sam. 25:1. And Samuel died, and all Israel gathered themselves together, and lamented him, and buried him in his house at Ramah. And David arose, and went down to the wilderness of Paran. 2. And there was a man in Maon, whose possessions were in Carmel; and the man was very great, and he had three thousand sheep, and a thousand goats: and he was shearing his sheep in Carmel.

---

*PS. 57. A Psalm of David when he fled from Saul, in the cave.
1. Be merciful unto me, O God, be merciful unto me;
   For my soul taketh refuge in thee;

†See Samuel, Appendix B. Duplication of incidents, 10.

*PS. 142. Maschil of David, when he was in the cave; a Prayer.
1. I cry with my voice unto the Lord;
   With my voice unto the Lord do I make supplication.

Nabal and Abigail

3. Now the name of the man was Nabal; and the name of his wife Abigail: and the woman was of good understanding, and of a beautiful countenance: but the man was churlish and evil in his doings; and he was of the house of Caleb. 4. And David heard in the wilderness that Nabal did shear his sheep. 5. And David sent ten young men, and David said unto the young men, Get you up to Carmel, and go to Nabal, and greet him in my name: 6. and thus shall ye say to him that liveth in prosperity, Peace be both unto thee, and peace be to thine house, and peace be unto all that thou hast. 7. And now I have heard that thou hast shearers: thy shepherds have now been with us, and we did them no hurt, neither was there aught missing unto them, all the while they were in Carmel. 8. Ask thy young men, and they will tell thee: wherefore let the young men find favour in thine eyes: for we come in a good day: give, I pray thee, whatsoever cometh to thine hand, unto thy servants, and to thy son David. 9. And when David's young men came, they spake to Nabal according to all those words in the name of David, and ceased. 10. And Nabal answered David's servants, and said, Who is David? and who is the son of Jesse? there be many servants now a days that break away every man from his master. 11. Shall I then take my bread, and my water, and my flesh that I have killed for my shearers, and give it unto men of whom I know not whence they be? 12. So David's young men turned on their way, and went back, and came and told him according to all these words. 13. And David said unto his men, Gird ye every man his sword. And they girded on every man his sword; and David also girded on his sword: and there went up after David about four hundred men; and two hundred abode by the stuff. 14. But one of the young men told Abigail, Nabal's wife, saying, Behold, David sent messengers out of the wilderness to salute our master; and he flew upon them. 15. But the men were very good unto us, and we were not hurt, neither missed we any thing, as long as we were conversant with them, when we were in the fields; 16. they were a wall unto us both by night and by day, all the while we were with them keeping the sheep. 17. Now therefore know and consider what thou wilt do; for evil is determined against our master, and against all his house: for he is such a son of Belial, that one cannot speak to him. 18. Then Abigail made haste, and took two hundred loaves, and two bottles of wine, and five sheep ready

Yea, in the shadow of thy wings will I take refuge,
Until these calamities be overpast.
2. I will cry unto God most high;
Unto God that performeth all things for me.
3. He shall send from heaven, and save me,
When he that would swallow me up reproacheth;
God shall send forth his mercy and his truth.
4 My soul is among lions;
I lie among them that are set on fire,
Even the sons of men, whose teeth are spears and arrows,
And their tongue a sharp sword.
5. Be thou exalted, O God, above the heavens:
Let thy glory be above all the earth.
6. They have prepared a net for my steps.
My soul is bowed down:
They have digged a pit before me;
They have fallen into the midst thereof themselves.
7. My heart is fixed, O God, my heart is fixed.
I will sing, yea, I will sing praises.
8. Awake up, my glory; awake psaltery and harp.
I myself will awake right early.
9. I will give thanks unto thee, O Lord, among the peoples:
I will sing praises unto thee among the nations.
10. For thy mercy is great unto the heavens,
And thy truth unto the skies.
11. Be thou exalted, O God, above the heavens;
Let thy glory be above all the earth.

2. I pour out my complaint before him;
I shew before him my trouble.
3. When my spirit was overwhelmed within me, thou knewest my path.
In the way wherein I walk have they hidden a snare for me.
4. Look on my right hand, and see; for there is no man that knoweth me:
Refuge hath failed me: no man careth for my soul.
5. I cried unto thee, O Lord;
I said, thou art my refuge,
My portion in the land of the living
6. Attend unto my cry; for I am brought very low:
Deliver me from my persecutors; for they are stronger than I.
7. Bring my soul out of prison, that I may give thanks unto thy name:
The righteous shall compass me about;
For thou shalt deal bountifully with me

dressed, and five measures of parched corn, and an hundred clusters of raisins, and two hundred cakes of figs, and laid them on asses. 19. And she said unto her young men, Go on before me; behold, I come after you. But she told not her husband Nabal. 20. And it was so, as she rode on her ass, and came down by the covert of the mountain, that, behold, David and his men came down against her; and she met them. 21. Now David had said, Surely in vain have I kept all that this fellow hath in the wilderness, so that nothing was missed of all that pertained unto him: and he hath returned me evil for good. 22. God do so unto the enemies of David, and more also, if I leave of all that pertain to him by the morning light so much as one man child. 23. And when Abigail saw David, she hasted, and lighted off her ass, and fell before David on her face, and bowed herself to the ground. 24. And she fell at his feet, and said, Upon me, my lord, upon me be the iniquity: and let thine handmaid, I pray thee, speak in thine ears, and hear thou the words of thine handmaid. 25. Let not my lord, I pray thee, regard this man of Belial, even Nabal: for as his name is, so is he: Nabal is his name, and folly is with him: but I thine handmaid saw not the young men of my lord, whom thou didst send. 26. Now therefore, my lord, as the Lord liveth, and as thy soul liveth, seeing the Lord hath withholden thee from blood-guiltiness, and from avenging thyself with thine own hand, now therefore, let thine enemies, and them that seek evil to my lord, be as Nabal. 27. And now this present which thy servant hath brought unto my lord, let it be given unto the young men that follow my lord. 28. Forgive, I pray thee, the trespass of thine handmaid: for the Lord will certainly make my lord a sure house, because my lord fighteth the battles of the Lord; and evil shall not be found in thee all thy days. 29. And though man be risen up to pursue thee, and to seek thy soul, yet the soul of my lord shall be bound in the bundle of life with the Lord thy God; and the souls of thine enemies, them shall he sling out, as from the hollow of a sling. 30. And it shall come to pass, when the Lord shall have done to my lord according to all the good that he hath spoken concerning thee, and shall have appointed thee prince over Israel; 31. that this shall be no grief unto thee, nor offence of heart unto my lord, either that thou hast shed blood causeless, or that my lord hath avenged himself: and when the Lord shall have dealt well with my lord, then remember thine handmaid. 32. And David said to Abigail, Blessed be the Lord, the God of Israel, which sent thee this day to meet me: 33. and blessed be thy wisdom, and blessed be thou, which hast kept me this day from bloodguiltiness, and from avenging myself with mine own hand. 34. For in very deed, as the Lord, the God of Israel, liveth, which hath withholden me from hurting thee, except that thou hadst hasted and come to meet me, surely there had not been left unto Nabal by the morning light so much as one man child. 35. So David received of her hand that which she had brought him: and he said unto her, Go up in peace to thine house; see, I have hearkened to thy voice, and have accepted thy person. 36. And Abigail came to Nabal; and, behold, he held a feast in his house, like the feast of a king; and Nabal's heart was merry within him, for he was very drunken: wherefore she told him nothing, less or more, until the morning light. 37. And it came to pass in the morning, when the wine was gone out of Nabal, that his wife told him these things, and his heart died within him, and he became as a stone. 38. And it came to pass about ten days after, that the Lord smote Nabal, that he died. 39. And when David heard that Nabal was dead, he said, Blessed be the Lord, that hath pleaded the cause of my reproach from the hand of Nabal, and hath kept back his servant from evil: and the evil-doing of Nabal hath the Lord returned upon his own head. And David sent and spake concerning Abigail, to take her to him to wife. 40. And when the servants of David were come to Abigail to Carmel, they spake unto her, saying, David hath sent us unto thee, to take thee to him to wife. 41. And she arose, and bowed herself with her face to the earth, and said, Behold, thine handmaid is a servant to wash the feet of the servants of my lord. 42. And Abigail hasted, and arose, and rode upon an ass, with five damsels of hers that followed her: and she went after the messengers of David, and became his wife. 43. David also took Ahinoam of Jezreel, and they became both of them his wives. 44. Now Saul had given Michal his daughter, David's wife, to Palti the son of Laish, which was of Gallim.

Second Betrayal by the Ziphites

I Sam. 26:1.* And the Ziphites came unto Saul to Gibeah, saying, Doth not David hide himself in the hill of Hachilah, which is before the desert? 2. Then Saul arose, and went down to the wilderness of Ziph, having three thousand chosen men of Israel with him, to seek David in the wilderness of Ziph. 3. And Saul pitched in the hill of Hachilah, which is before the desert, by the way. But David abode in the wilderness, and he saw that Saul came after him into the wilderness. 4. David therefore sent out spies, and understood that Saul was come of a certainty. 5. And David arose, and came to the place where Saul had pitched: and David beheld the place where Saul lay, and Abner the son of Ner, the captain of the host: and Saul lay within the place of the wagons, and the people pitched round about him. 6. Then answered David and said to Ahimelech the Hittite and to Abishai the son of Zeruiah, brother to Joab, saying, Who will go down with me to Saul to the camp? And Abishai said, I will go down with thee. 7. So David and Abishai came to the people by night: and, behold, Saul lay sleeping within the place of the wagons, with his spear stuck in the ground at his head: and Abner and the people lay round about him. 8. Then said Abishai to David, God hath delivered up thine enemy into thine hand this day: now therefore let me smite him, I pray thee, with the spear to the earth at one stroke, and I will not smite him the second time.

Second Sparing of Saul's Life

*9. And David said to Abishai, Destroy him not: for who can put forth his hand against the Lord's anointed, and be guiltless? 10. And David said, As the Lord liveth, the Lord shall smite him; or his day shall come to die; or he shall go down into battle, and perish. 11. The Lord forbid that I should put forth mine against the Lord's anointed: but now take, I pray thee, the spear that is at his head, and the cruse of water, and let us go. 12. So David took the spear and the cruse of water from Saul's head; and they gat them away, and no man saw it, nor knew it, neither did any awake: for they were all asleep; because a deep sleep from the Lord was fallen upon them. 13. Then David went over to the other side, and stood on the top of the mountain afar off; a great space being between them: 14. and David cried to the people, and to Abner the son of Ner, saying, Answerest thou not Abner? Then Abner answered and said, Who art thou that criest to the king? 15. And David said to Abner, Art not thou a valiant man? and who is like to thee in Israel? wherefore then hast thou not kept watch over thy lord the king? for there came one of the people in to destroy the king thy lord. 16. This thing is not good that thou hast done. As the Lord liveth, ye are worthy to die, because ye have not kept watch over your lord, the Lord's anointed. And now, see, where the king's spear is, and the cruse of water that was at his head. 17. And Saul knew David's voice, and said, Is this thy voice, my son David? And David said, It is my voice, my lord, O king. 18. And he said, Wherefore doth my lord pursue after his servant? for what have I done? or what evil is in mine hand? 19. Now therefore, I pray thee, let my lord the king hear the

---

* See Samuel, Appendix B. Duplication of incidents, 9, 10.

words of his servant. If it be the Lord that hath stirred thee up against me, let him accept an offering: but if it be the children of men, cursed be they before the Lord; for they have driven me out this day that I should not cleave unto the inheritance of the Lord, saying, Go serve other gods. 20. Now therefore, let not my blood fall to the earth away from the presence of the Lord: for the king of Israel is come out to seek a flea, as when one doth hunt a partridge in the mountains. 21. Then said Saul, I have sinned: return, my son David: for I will no more do thee harm, because my life was precious in thine eyes this day: behold, I have played the fool, and have erred exceedingly. 22. And David answered and said, Behold the spear, O king! let then one of the young men come over and fetch it. 23. And the Lord shall render to every man his righteousness and his faithfulness: forasmuch as the Lord delivered thee into my hand to-day, and I would not put forth mine hand against the Lord's anointed. 24. And, behold, as thy life was much set by this day in mine eyes, so let my life be much set by in the eyes of the Lord, and let him deliver me out of all tribulation. 25. Then Saul said to David, Blessed be thou, my son David: thou shalt both do mightily, and shalt surely prevail. So David went his way, and Saul returned to his place.

THE HOUSE OF SAUL
B. C. 1096 (Usher)
I Saul
B. C. 1037 (Rev.)

SAMUEL

SECTION VI

An Exile in the Land of the Philistines

Second Flight Unto Achish at Gath

I Sam. 27:1. And David said in his heart, I shall now perish one day by the hand of Saul: there is nothing better for me than that I should* escape into the land of the Philistines; and Saul shall despair of me, to seek me any more in all the borders of Israel: so shall I escape out of his hand. 2. And David arose, and passed over, he and the six hundred men that were with him, unto Achish the son of Maoch, king of Gath. 3. And David dwelt with Achish at Gath, he and his men, every man with his household, even David with his two wives, Ahinoam the Jezreelitess, and Abigail the Carmelitess, Nabal's wife. 4. And it was told Saul that David was fled to Gath: and he sought no more again for him. 5. And David said unto Achish, If now I have found grace in thine eyes, let them give me a place in one of the cities in the country, that I may dwell there: for why should thy servant dwell in the royal city with thee? 6. Then Achish gave him Ziklag that day: wherefore Ziklag pertaineth unto the kings of Judah unto this day. 7. And the number of the days that David dwelt in the country of the Philistines was a full year and four months. 8. And David and his men went up, and made a raid upon the Geshurites, and the Girzites, and the Amalekites: for those nations were the inhabitants of the land, which were of old, as thou goest to Shur, even unto the land of Egypt. 9. And David smote the land, and saved neither man nor woman alive, and took away the sheep, and the oxen, and the asses, and the camels, and the apparel; and he returned and came to Achish. 10. And Achish said, Whither have ye made a raid to-day? And David said, Against the South of Judah, and against the South of the Jerahmeelites, and against the South of the Kenites. 11. And David saved neither man nor woman alive, to bring them to Gath, saying, Lest they should tell on us, saying, So did David, and so hath been his manner all the while he hath dwelt in the country of the Philistines. 12. And Achish believed David, saying, He hath made his people Israel utterly to abhor him; therefore he shall be my servant forever. I Chron. 12:1. Now these are they that came to David to Ziklag, while he yet kept himself close because of Saul the son of Kish: and they were among the mighty men, his helpers in war. 2. They were armed with bows, and they could use both the right hand and the left in slinging stones and in shooting arrows from the bow; they were of Saul's brethren of Benjamin. 3. The chief was Ahiezer, then Joash, the sons of Shemaah the Gibeathite; and Jeziel, and Pelet, the sons of Azmaveth; and Beracah, and Jehu the Anathothite; 4. and Ishmaiah the Gibeonite, a mighty man among the thirty, and over the thirty; and Jeremiah, and Jehaziel, and Johanan, and Jozabad the Gederathite; 5. Eluzai and Jerimoth, and Bealiah, and Shemariah, and Shephatiah the Haruphite; 6. Elkanah, and Isshiah, and Azarel, and Joezer, and Jashobeam, the Korahites; 7. and Joelah, and Zebediah, the sons of Jeroham of Gedor.

Confidence In and Suspicion Of David

I Sam. 28:1. And it came to pass in those days, that the Philistines gathered their hosts together for warfare, to fight with Israel. And Achish said unto David, Know thou assuredly, that thou shalt go out with me in the host, thou and thy men. 2. And David said to Achish, Therefore shalt thou know what thy servant will do. And Achish said to David, Therefore will I make thee keeper of mine head forever. I Sam. 29:1. Now the Philistines gathered together all their hosts to Aphek: and the Israelites pitched by the fountain which is in Jezreel.

---
* See Samuel, Appendix B. Duplication of Incidents, 8.

2. And the lords of the Philistines passed on by hundreds, and by thousands: and David and his men passed on in the rearward with Achish. 3. Then said the princes of the Philistines, What do these Hebrews here? And Achish said unto the princes of the Philistines, Is not this David, the servant of Saul the king of Israel, which hath been with me these days or these years, and I have found no fault in him since he fell away unto me unto this day? 4. But the princes of the Philistines were wroth with him; and the princes of the Philistines said unto him, Make the man return, that he may go back to his place where thou hast appointed him, and let him not go down with us to battle, lest in the battle he become an adversary to us: for wherewith should this fellow reconcile himself unto his lord? should it not be with the heads of these men? 5. Is not this David, of whom they sang one to another in dances, saying,

> Saul hath slain his thousands,
> And David his ten thousands?

6. Then Achish called David, and said unto him, As the Lord liveth, thou hast been upright, and thy going out and thy coming in with me in the host is good in my sight: for I have not found evil in thee since the day of thy coming unto me unto this day: nevertheless the lords favour thee not. 7. Wherefore now return, and go in peace, that thou displease not the lords of the Philistines. 8. And David said unto Achish, But what have I done? and what hast thou found in thy servant so long as I have been before thee unto this day, that I may not go and fight against the enemies of my lord the king? 9. And Achish answered and said to David I know that thou art good in my sight, as an angel of God: notwithstanding the princes of the Philistines have said, He shall not go up with us to the battle. 10. Wherefore now rise up early in the morning with the servants of thy lord that are come with thee: and as soon as ye be up early in the morning, and have light, depart. 11. So David rose up early, he and his men, to depart in the morning, to return into the land of the Philistines. And the Philistines went up to Jezreel. I Chron. 12:19. Of Manasseh also there fell away some to David, when he came with the Philistines against Saul to battle, but they helped them not: for the lords of the Philistines upon advisement sent him away, saying, He will fall away to his master Saul to the jeopardy of our heads. 20. As he went to Ziklag, there fell to him of Manasseh, Adnah, and Jozabad, and Jediael, and Michael, and Jozabad, and Elihu and Zillethai, captains of thousands that were of Manasseh. 21. And they helped David against the band of rovers: for they were all mighty men of valour, and were captains in the host. 22. For from day to day there came to David to help him, until it was a great host, like the host of God.

Ziklag Smitten and Burned

I Sam. 30:1. And it came to pass, when David and his men were come to Ziklag on the third day, that the Amalekites had made a raid upon the South, and upon Ziklag, and had smitten Ziklag, and burned it with fire; 2. and had taken captive the women and all that were therein, both small and great: they slew not any, but carried them off, and went their way. 3. And when David and his men came to the city, behold, it was burned with fire; and their wives, and their sons, and their daughters, were taken captives. 4. Then David and the people that were with him lifted up their voice and wept, until they had no more power to weep. 5. And David's two wives were taken captive, Ahinoam the Jezreelitess, and Abigail the wife of Nabal the Carmelite. 6. And David was greatly distressed; for the people spake of stoning him, because the soul of all the people was grieved, every man for his sons and for his daughters: but David strengthened himself in the Lord his God. 7. And David said to Abiathar the priest, the son of Ahimelech, I pray thee, bring me hither the ephod. And Abiathar brought thither the ephod to David. 8. And David inquired of the Lord, saying, If I pursue after this troop, shall I overtake them? And he answered him, Pursue: for thou shalt surely overtake them, and shalt without fail recover all. 9. So David went, he and the six hundred men that were with him, and came to the brook Besor, where those that were left behind stayed. 10. But David pursued, he and four hundred men: for two hundred stayed behind, which were so faint that they could not go over the brook Besor: 11. and they found an Egyptian in the field, and brought him to David, and gave him bread, and he did eat; and they gave him water to drink: 12. and they gave him a piece of a cake of figs, and two clusters of raisins; and when he had eaten, his spirit came again to him: for he had eaten no bread, nor drunk any water, three days and three nights. 13. And David said unto him, To whom belongest thou? and whence art thou? And he said, I am a young man of Egypt, servant to an Amalekite; and my master left me, because three days agone I fell sick. 14. We made a raid upon the South of the Cherethites, and upon that which belongeth to Judah, and upon the South of Caleb, and we burned Ziklag with fire. 15. And David said, Wilt thou bring me down to this troop? And he said, Swear unto me by God, that thou wilt neither kill me, nor deliver me up into the hands of my master, and I will bring thee down to this troop. 16. And when he had brought him down, behold, they were spread abroad over all the ground, eating and drinking, and feasting, because of all the great spoil that they had taken out of the land of the Philistines, and out of the land of Judah.

David's Rescue and Recovery
17. And David smote them from the twilight even unto the evening of the next day: and there escaped not a man of them save four hundred young men, which rode upon camels and fled. 18. And David recovered all that the Amalekites had taken: and David rescued his two wives. 19. And there was nothing lacking to them, neither small nor great, neither sons nor daughters, neither spoil, nor anything that they had taken to them: David brought back all. 20. And David took all the flocks and the herds, which they drave before those other cattle, and said, This is David's spoil. 21. And David came to the two hundred men, which were so faint that they could not follow David, whom also they had made to abide at the brook Besor: and they went forth to meet David, and to meet the people that were with him: and when David came near to the people, he saluted them. 22. Then answered all the wicked men and men of Belial, of those that went with David, and said, Because they went not with us, we will not give them aught of the spoil that we have recovered, save to every man his wife and his children, that they may lead them away and depart.

Division and Distribution of the Spoil
23. Then said David, Ye shall not do so, my brethren, with that which the Lord hath given unto us, who hath preserved us, and delivered the troop that came against us into our hand. 24. And who will hearken unto you in this matter? for as his share is which goeth down to the battle, so shall his share be that tarrieth by the stuff: they shall share alike. 25. And it was so from that day forward, that he made it a statute and an ordinance for Israel, unto this day. 26. And when David came to Ziklag, he sent of the spoil unto the elders of Judah, even to his friends, saying, Behold a present for you of the spoil of the enemies of the Lord; 27. to them which were in Bethel, and to them which were in Ramoth of the South, and to them which were in Jattir, 28. and to them which were in Aroer, and to them which were in Siphmoth, and to them which were in Eshtemoa; 29. and to them which were in Racal, and to them which were in the cities of the Jerahmeelites, and to them which were in the cities of the Kenites; 30. and to them which were in Hormah, and to them which were in Cor-ashan, and to them which were in Athach; 31. and to them which were in Hebron, and to all the places where David himself and his men were wont to haunt.

THE HOUSE OF SAUL
B. C. 1056 (Usher)
I Saul
B. C. 1017 (Rev.)

SECTION VII

The Fall of the House of Saul

I Sam. 28:3. Now Samuel was dead, and all Israel had lamented him, and buried him in Ramah, even in his own city. And Saul had put away those that had familiar spirits, and the wizards, out of the land. 4. And the Philistines gathered themselves together, and came and pitched in Shunem: and Saul gathered all Israel together, and they pitched in Gilboa. 5. And when Saul saw the host of the Philistines, he was afraid, and his heart trembled greatly. 6. And when Saul inquired of the Lord, the Lord answered him not, neither by dreams, nor by Urim, nor by prophets.

Saul Visits the Witch of Endor

7. Then said Saul unto his servants, Seek me a woman that hath a familiar spirit, that I may go to her, and inquire of her. And his servants said to him, Behold, there is a woman that hath a familiar spirit at Endor. 8. And Saul disguised himself, and put on other raiment, and went, he and two men with him, and they came to the woman by night: and he said, Divine unto me, I pray thee, by the familiar spirit, and bring me up whomsoever I shall name unto thee. 9. And the woman said unto him, Behold, thou knowest what Saul hath done, how he hath cut off those that have familiar spirits, and the wizards, out of the land: wherefore then layest a snare for my life to cause me to die? 10. and Saul sware to her by the Lord, saying, As the Lord liveth, there shall no punishment happen to thee for this thing. 11. Then said the woman, whom shall I bring up unto thee? And he said, bring me up Samuel. 12. And when the woman saw Samuel, she cried with a loud voice: and the woman spake to Saul, saying, Why hast thou deceived me? for thou art Saul. 13. And the king said unto her, Be not afraid: for what seest thou? And the woman said unto Saul, I see a god coming up out of the earth. 14. And he said unto her, What form is he of? And she said, An old man cometh up: and he is covered with a robe. And Saul perceived that it was Samuel, and he bowed with his face to the ground, and did obeisance. 15. And Samuel said to Saul, Why hast thou disquieted me, to bring me up? And Saul answered, I am sore distressed; for the Philistines make war against me, and God is departed from me, and answereth me no more, neither by prophets, nor by dreams; therefore I have called thee, that thou mayest make known unto me what I shall do. 16. And Samuel said, Wherefore then dost thou ask of me, seeing the Lord is departed from thee, and is become thy adversary? 17. And the Lord hath wrought for himself, as he spake by me: and the Lord hath rent the kingdom out of thine hand, and given it to thy neighbour, even to David. 18. Because thou obeyedst not the voice of the Lord and didst not execute his fierce wrath upon Amelek, therefore hath the Lord done this thing unto thee this day. 19. Moreover the Lord will deliver Israel also with thee into the hands of the Philistines, and to-morrow shalt thou and thy sons be with me: the Lord shall deliver the host of Israel also into the hand of the Philistines. 20. Then Saul fell straightway his full length upon the earth, and was sore afraid, because of the words of Samuel: and there was no strength in him; for he had eaten no bread all the day, nor all the night. 21. And the woman came unto Saul, and saw that he was sore troubled, and said unto him, Behold, thine handmaid hath hearkened unto thy voice, and I have put my life in my hand and have hearkened unto thy words which thou spakest unto me. 22. Now therefore, I pray thee, hearken thou also unto the voice of thine handmaid, and let me set a morsel of bread before thee; and eat, that thou mayest have strength, when thou goest on thy way. 23. But he refused, and said, I will not eat. But his servants, together with the woman, constrained him: and he hearkened unto their voice. So he arose from the earth, and sat upon the bed. 24. And the woman had a fatted

calf in the house: and she hasted, and killed it; and she took flour, and kneaded it, and did bake unleavened bread thereof, 25. and she brought it before Saul, and before his servants, and they did eat. Then they rose up, and went away that night.

Saul's Death on Mount Gilboa Now the Philistines fought against Israel, and the men of Israel fled from before the Philistines, and fell down slain in mount Gilboa. And the Philistines followed hard upon Saul and upon his sons; and the Philistines slew Jonathan, and Abinadab, and Melchi-shua, Saul's sons. And the battle went sore against Saul, and the archers overtook him; and he was greatly distressed by reason of the archers. Then said Saul unto his armourbearer, Draw thy sword and thrust me through therewith; lest these uncircumcised come and thrust me through and abuse me. But his armourbearer would not, for he was sore afraid. Therefore Saul took a sword and fell upon it.

And when his armourbearer saw that Saul was dead, he fell likewise upon his sword, and died with him. So Saul died, and his three sons, and his armourbearer, and all his men, that same day together. And when the men of Israel that were upon the other side of the valley, and they that were beyond Jordan, saw that the men of Israel fled, and that Saul and his sons were dead, they forsook the cities, and fled; and the Philistines came and dwelt in them. And it came to pass on the morrow, when the Philistines came to strip the slain, that they found Saul and his three sons fallen in mount Gilboa. And they stripped him, and took his head, and his armour, and sent into the land of the Philistines round about, to carry tidings unto the house of their idols, and to the people. And they put his armour in the house of the Ashtaroth, and they fastened his head in the house of Dagon, and his body to the wall of Bethshan. And when all Jabesh-gilead heard all that the Philistines had done to Saul, all the valiant men arose, and went all night, and took the body of Saul, and the bodies of his sons, and they came to Jabesh, and burnt them there and buried their bones under the tamerisk tree in Jabesh, and fasted seven days. So Saul died for his trespass which he committed against the Lord, because of the word of the Lord which he kept not; and also for that he asked counsel of one that had a familiar spirit, to inquire thereby, and inquired not of the Lord: therefore he slew him, and turned the kingdom unto David the son of Jesse. II Sam. 1:1. And it came to pass after the death of Saul, when David was returned from the slaughter of the Amalekites, and David had abode two days in Ziklag; 2. it came even to pass on the third day, that, behold, a man came out of the camp from Saul with his clothes rent, and earth upon his head; and so it was, when he came to David that he fell to the earth, and did obeisance, 3. and David said unto him, From whence cometh thou?

Saul's Death Reported to David And he said unto him, Out of the camp of Israel am I escaped. 4. And David said unto him, How went the matter! I pray thee, tell me. And he answered, The people are fled from the battle, and many of the people also are fallen and dead; and Saul and Jonathan, his son, are dead also. 5. And David said unto the young man that told him, How knowest thou that Saul and Jonathan, his son, be dead? 6. And the young man that told him said, As I happened by chance on mount Gilboa, behold, Saul leaned upon his spear; and, lo, the chariots and the horsemen followed hard after him. 7. And when he looked behind him, he saw me, and called unto me. And I answered, Here am I. 8. And he said unto me, Who are thou? And I answered him, I am an Amalekite. 9. And he said unto me, Stand, I pray thee, beside me, and slay me, for anguish hath taken hold of me; because my life is yet whole in me. 10. So I stood beside him and slew him because I was sure that he could not live after that he was

Death of Saul on Mount Gilboa

I. Sam., xxxi., 1-13.

1. Now the Philistines fought against Israel, and the men of Israel fled from before the Philistines, and fell down slain in mount Gilboa.
2. And the Philistines followed hard upon Saul and upon his sons; and the Philistines slew Jonathan, and Abindab, and Melchi-shua, the sons of Saul. 3. And the battle went sore against Saul, and the archers overtook him; and he was greatly distressed by reason of the archers. 4. Then said Saul unto his armourbearer, Draw thy sword, and thrust me through therewith; lest these uncircumcised come and thrust me through and abuse me. But his armourbearer would not; for he was sore afraid. Therefore Saul took his sword, and fell upon it.
5. And when his armourbearer saw that Saul was dead, he likewise fell upon his sword, and died with him. 6. So Saul died, and his three sons and his armourbearer, and all his men, that same day together. 7. And when the men of Israel that were upon the other side of the valley, and they that were beyond Jordan saw that they fled and that Saul and his sons were dead, they forsook the cities, and fled: and the Philistines came and dwelt in them. 8. And it came to pass on the morrow, when the Philistines came to strip the slain, that they found Saul and his three sons fallen in mount Gilboa. 9. And they cut off his head, and stripped off his armour, and sent into the land of the Philistines round about, to carry the tidings unto the house of their idols, and to the people. 10. And they put his armour in the house of the Ashtaroth; and they fastened* ((his body to the wall of Bethshan)). 11. And when the inhabitants of Jabesh-gilead heard concerning him that which the Philistines had done to Saul, 12 all the valiant men arose, and went all night, and took the body of Saul, and the bodies of his sons from the wall of Bethshan, and they came to Jabesh, and burnt them there. 13. And they took their bones, and buried them under the tamerisk tree in Jabesh, and fasted seven days.

---

*See Appendix C. Chronicles II. 1.

*I. Chron., x., 1-14.

1. Now the Philistines fought against Israel, and the men of Israel fled from before the Philistines, and fell down slain in mount Gilboa.
2. And the Philistines followed hard after Saul and after his sons; and the Philistines slew Jonathan, and Abindab, and Melchi-shua, the sons of Saul. 3. And the battle went sore against Saul, and the archers overtook him; and he was distressed by reason of the archers. 4. Then said Saul unto his armourbearer, Draw thy sword and thrust me through therewith; lest these uncircumcised come and abuse me. But his armourbearer would not; for he was sore afraid. Therefore Saul took his sword, and fell upon it.
5. And when his armourbearer saw that Saul was dead, he likewise fell upon his sword, and died 6. So Saul died, and his three sons; and all his house died together. 7. And when all the men of Israel that were in the valley, saw that they fled and that Saul and his sons were dead, they forsook the cities, and fled; and the Philistines came and dwelt in them. 8. And it came to pass on the morrow, when the Philistines came to strip the slain, that they found Saul and his sons fallen in mount Gilboa. 9. And they stripped him, and took his head, and his armour, and sent into the land of the Philistines round about, to carry the tidings unto their idols, and to the people. 10. And they put his armour in the house of their gods, and they fastened ((his head in the house of Dagon)).
11. And when all Jabesh-gilead heard all that the Philistines had done to Saul, 12 all the valiant men arose and took away the body of Saul, and the bodies of his sons, and brought them to Jabesh, and buried their bones under the oak in Jabesh, and fasted seven days.
13. So Saul died for his trespass which he committed against the Lord, because of the word of the Lord which he kept not; and also for that he asked counsel of one that had a familiar spirit, to inquire thereby, 14 and inquired not of the Lord: therefore he slew him, and turned the kingdom unto David the son of Jesse.

fallen: and I took the crown that was upon his head, and the bracelet that was upon his arm, and have brought them hither unto my lord. 11. Then David took hold on his clothes, and rent them; and likewise all the men that were with him: 12. and they mourned and wept, and fasted until even for Saul, and for Jonathan his son, and for the people of the Lord, and for the house of Israel; because they were fallen by the sword. 13. And David said unto the young man that told him, Whence art thou? And he answered I am the son of a stranger, an Amalekite. 14. And David said unto him, How was thou not afraid to put forth thine hand to destroy the Lord's anointed? 15. And David called one of the young men, and said, go near, and fall upon him. And he smote him that he died. 16. And David said unto him, Thy blood be upon thy head; for thy mouth hath testified against thee, saying, I have slain the Lord's anointed.

David's Dirge for Saul and Jonathan 17. And David lamented with this lamentation over Saul and over Jonathan his son: 18. and he bade them teach the children of Judah the song of the bow: behold it is written in the book of Jashar.

19. Thy glory, O Israel, is slain upon thy high places!
    How are the mighty fallen!
20. Tell it not in Gath,
    Publish it not in the streets of Askelon;
    Lest the daughters of the Philistines rejoice,
    Lest the daughters of the uncircumcised triumph.
21. Ye mountains of Gilboa,
    Let there be no dew nor rain upon you, neither fields of offerings:
    For there the shield of the mighty was vilely cast away,
    The shield of Saul, not anointed with oil.
22. From the blood of the slain, from the fat of the mighty,
    The bow of Jonathan turned not back,
    And the sword of Saul returned not back empty.
23. Saul and Jonathan were lovely and pleasant in their lives,
    And in their death they were not divided;
    They were swifter than eagles,
    They were stronger than lions.
24. Ye daughters of Israel weep over Saul,
    Who clothed you in scarlet delicately,
    Who put ornaments of gold upon your apparel.
25. How are the mighty fallen in the midst of the battle!
    Jonathan is slain upon thy high places.
26. I am distressed for thee, my brother Jonathan:
    Very pleasant hast thou been unto me:
    Thy love to me was wonderful,
    Passing the love of women.
27. How are the mighty fallen,
    And the weapons of war perished!

II Sam. 2:1. And it came to pass after this, that David inquired of the Lord, saying, Shall I go up into any of the cities of Judah? And the Lord said unto him, Go up. And David said, Whither shall I go up? And he said, Unto Hebron. 2. So David went up thither, and his two wives also, Ahinoam the Jezreelitess, and Abigail the wife of Nabal the Carmelite. 3. And his men that were with him did David bring up, every man with his household; and they dwelt in the cities of Hebron.

THE HOUSE OF DAVID
  B. C. 1056 (Usher)
I David
  B. C. 1017 (Rev.)

SECTION VIII

The Rise of the House of David

David Anointed King of Judah

II Sam. 2:4. And the men of Judah came, and there they anointed David king over the house of Judah. And they told David, saying, The men of Jabesh-gilead were they that buried Saul. 5. And David sent messengers unto the men of Jabesh-gilead, and said unto them, Blessed be ye of the Lord, that ye have showed this kindness unto your Lord, even unto Saul, and have buried him. 6. And now the Lord show kindness and truth unto you: and I also will requite you this kindness, because ye have done this thing. 7. Now therefore let your hands be strong, and be ye valiant: for Saul your lord is dead, and also the house of Judah have anointed me king over them.

Ish-bosheth Made King of Israel

8. Now Abner the son of Ner captain of Saul's host had taken Ish-bosheth the son of Saul, and brought him over to Mahanaim; 9. and he made him king over Gilead, and over the Ashurites, and over Jezreel, and over Ephraim, and over Benjamin, and over all Israel. 10. (Ish-bosheth Saul's son was forty years old when he began to reign over Israel, and he reigned two years.) But the house of Judah followed David. 11. And the time that David was king in Hebron over the house of Judah was seven years and six months. 12. And Abner the son of Ner, and the servants of Ish-bosheth the son of Saul, went out from Mahanaim to Gibeon. 13. And Joab the son of Zeruiah, and the servants of David, went out, and met them by the pool of Gibeon, and they sat down, one on the one side of the pool, and the other on the other side of the pool. 14. And Abner said to Joab, Let the young men, I pray thee, arise and play before us. And Joab said, Let them arise. 15. Then they arose and went over by number; twelve for Benjamin, and for Ish-bosheth the son of Saul, and twelve of the servants of David. 16. And they caught every one his fellow by the head, and thrust his sword in his fellow's side; so they fell down together: wherefore that place was called Helkath-hazzurim, which is in Gibeon. 17. And the battle was very sore that day, and Abner was beaten, and the men of Israel, before the servants of David. 18. And the three sons of Zeruiah were there, Joab, and Abishai, and Asahel: and Asahel was as light of foot as a wild roe. 19. And Asahel pursued after Abner; and in going he turned not to the right hand nor to the left from following Abner. 20. Then Abner looked behind him, and said, Is it thou, Asahel? And he answered, It is I. 21. And Abner said to him, Turn thee aside to thy right hand or to thy left, and lay thee hold of one of the young men, and take thee his armour. But Asahel would not turn aside from following of him. 22. And Abner said again to Asahel, Turn thee aside from following me; wherefore should I smite thee to the ground? how then should I hold up my face to Joab thy brother? 23. Howbeit he refused to turn aside; wherefore Abner with the hinder end of the spear smote him in the belly, that the spear came out behind him; and he fell down

there, and died in the same place: and it came to pass, that as many as came to the place where Asahel fell down and died stood still. 24. But Joab and Abishai pursued after Abner: and the sun went down when they were come to the hill of Ammah, that lieth before Giah by the way of the wilderness of Gibeon. 25. And the children of Benjamin gathered themselves together after Abner, and became one band, and stood on the top of an hill. 26. Then Abner called to Joab, and said, Shall the sword devour forever? knowest thou not that it will be bitterness in the latter end? how long shall it be then, ere thou bid the people return from following their brethren? 27. And Joab said, As God liveth, if thou hadst not spoken, surely then in the morning the people had gone away, nor followed every one his brother. 28. So Joab blew the trumpet, and all the people stood still, and pursued after Israel no more, neither fought they any more. 29. And Abner and his men went all that night through the Arabah; and they passed over Jordan, and went through all Bithron, and came to Mahanaim. 30. And Joab returned from following Abner: and when he had gathered all the people together, there lacked of David's servants nineteen men and Asahel. 31. But the servants of David had smitten of Benjamin, and of Abner's men, so that three hundred and threescore men died. 32. And they took up Asahel, and buried him in the sepulchre of his father, which was in Beth-lehem. And Joab and his men went all night, and the day brake upon them at Hebron.

The Civil War

II Sam. 3:1. Now there was long war between the house of Saul and the house of David: and David waxed stronger and stronger, but the house of Saul waxed weaker and weaker. 2. And unto David were sons born in Hebron: and his firstborn was Amnon, of Ahinoam the Jezreelitess; 3. and his second, Chileab, of Abigail the wife of Nabal the Carmelite, and the third, Absalom the son of Maacah the daughter of Talmai king of Geshur; 4. and the fourth, Adonijah the son of Haggith; and the fifth, Shepthatiah the son of Abital; 5. and the sixth, Ithream, of Eglah David's wife. These were born to David in Hebron. 6. And it came to pass, while there was war between the house of Saul and the house of David, that Abner made himself strong in the house of Saul. 7. Now Saul had a concubine, whose name was Rizpah, the daughter of Aiah: and Ish-bosheth said to Abner, wherefore hast thou gone into my father's concubine? 8. Then was Abner very wroth for the words of Ish-bosheth, and said, Am I a dog's head that belongeth to Judah? This day do I shew kindness unto the house of Saul thy father, to his brethren, and to his friends, and have not delivered thee into the hand of David, and yet thou chargeth me this day with a fault concerning this woman. 9. God do so to Abner, and more also, if, as the Lord has sworn to David, I do not even so to him; 10. to translate the kingdom from the house of Saul, and to set up the throne of David over Israel and over Judah, and from Dan even to Beer-sheba. 11. And he could not answer Abner another word, because he feared him. 12. And Abner sent messengers to David on his behalf, saying, Whose is the land? saying also, Make thy league with me, and, behold, my hand shall be with thee, to bring about all Israel unto thee. 13. And he said, Well; I will make a league with thee: but one thing will require of thee, that is, thou shalt not see my face, except thou first bring Michal Saul's daughter, when thou comest to see my face. 14. And David sent messengers to Ish-bosheth Saul's son, saying, Deliver me my wife Michal, whom I betrothed to for an hundred foreskins of the Philistines. 15. And Ish-bosheth sent, and took her from her husband, even from Paltiel the son of Laish. 16. And her husband went with her, weeping as he went, and followed her to Bahurin. Then said Abner unto him, Go, return; and he returned. 17. And Abner had communication with the elders of Israel, saying, In times past

SECT. VIII   *THE FOUNDING OF THE MONARCHY*

ye sought for David to be king over you: now then do it: 18. for the Lord hath spoken of David, saying, By the hand of my servant David I will save my people Israel out of the hand of the Philistines, and out of the hand of all their enemies. 19. And Abner also spake in the ears of Benjamin: and Abner went also to speak in the ears of David in Hebron all that seemed good to Israel, and to the whole house of Benjamin. 20. So Abner came to David to Hebron, and twenty men with him. And David made Abner and the men that were with him a feast. 21. And Abner said unto David, I will arise and go, and will gather all Israel unto my lord the king, that they may make a covenant with thee, and that thou mayest reign over all that thy soul desireth. And David sent Abner away; and he went in peace. 22. And, behold, the servants of David and Joab came from a foray, and brought in a great spoil with them: but Abner was not with David in Hebron; for he had sent him away, and he was gone in peace. 23. When Joab and all the host that was with him were come, they told Joab, saying, Abner the son of Ner came to the king, and he hath sent him away, and he is gone in peace. 24. Then Joab came to the king, and said, What hast thou done? behold, Abner came unto thee; why is it that thou hast sent him away, and he is quite gone? 25. Thou knowest Abner the son of Ner, that he came to deceive thee, and to know thy going out and thy coming in, and to know all that thou doest. 26. And when Joab was come out from David, he sent messengers after Abner, and they brought him back from the well of Sirah:

Assassination of Abner and Ish-bosheth but David knew it not. 27. And when Abner was returned to Hebron, Joab took him aside into the midst of the gate to speak with him quietly, and smote him there in the belly, that he died, for the blood of Asahel his brother. 28. And after when David heard it, he said, I and my kingdom are guiltless before the Lord forever from the blood of Abner the son of Ner: 29. let it fall upon the head of Joab, and upon all his father's house, and let there not fail from the house of Joab one that hath an issue, or that is a leper, or that leaneth on a staff, or that falleth by the sword, or that lacketh bread. 30. So Joab and Abishai his brother slew Abner, because he had killed their brother Asahel at Gibeon in the battle. 31. And David said to Joab, and to all the people that were with him, Rend your clothes, and gird you with sackcloth, and mourn before Abner. And king David followed the bier. 32. And they buried Abner in Hebron: and the king lifted up his voice, and wept at the grave of Abner; and all the people wept. 33. And the king lamented for Abner, and said,

Should Abner die as the fool dieth?

34. Thy hands were not bound, nor thy feet put into fetters:
As a man falleth before the children of iniquity, so didst thou fall.

And all the people wept again over him. 35. And all the people came to cause David to eat bread while it was yet day; but David sware, saying, God do so to me, and more also, if I taste bread, or aught else, till the sun be down. 36. And all the people took notice of it, and it pleased them: as whatsoever the king did pleased all the people. 37. So all the people and all Israel understood that day that it was not of the king to slay Abner the son of Ner. 38. And the king said unto his servants, Know ye not that there is a prince and a great man fallen this day in Israel? 39. And I am this day weak, though anointed king; and these men the sons of Zeruiah be too hard for me: the Lord reward the wicked doer according to his wickedness. II Sam. 4:1. And when Ishbosheth, Saul's son, heard that Abner was dead in Hebron, his hands became feeble, and all the Israelites were troubled. 2. And Ishbosheth, Saul's son, had two men that were captains of bands: the name of one was

Baanah, and the name of the other Rechab the sons of Rimmon the Beerothite, of the children of Benjamin: (for Beeroth also is reckoned to Benjamin: 3. and the Beerothites fled to Gittaim, and have been sojourners there until this day.) 4. Now Jonathan, Saul's son, had a son that was lame of his feet. He was five years old when the tidings came of Saul and Jonathan out of Jezreel, and his nurse took him up, and fled: and it came to pass, as she made haste to flee, that he fell, and became lame. And his name was Mephibosheth. 5. And the sons of Rimmon the Beerothite, Rechab and Baanah, went, and came about the heat of the day to the house of Ish-bosheth, as he took his rest at noon. 6. And they came thither into the midst of the house, as though they would have fetched wheat; and they smote him in the belly: and Rechab and Baanah his brother escaped. 7. Now when they came into the house, as he lay on his bed in his bedchamber, they smote him, and slew him, and beheaded him, and took his head, and went by the way of the Arabah all night. 8. And they brought the head of Ish-bosheth unto David to Hebron, and said to the king, Behold the head of Ish-bosheth the son of Saul thine enemy, which sought thy life; and the Lord hath avenged my lord the king this day of Saul, and of his seed. 9. And David answered Rechab and Baanah his brother, the sons of Rimmon the Beerothite, and said unto them, as the Lord liveth, who hath redeemed my soul out of all adversity, 10. when one told me, saying, Behold, Saul is dead, thinking to have brought good tidings, I took hold of him, and slew him in Ziklag, which was the reward I gave him for his tidings. 11. How much more, when wicked men have slain a righteous person in his own house upon his bed, shall I not require his blood of your hand, and take you away from the earth? 12. And David commanded his young men, and they slew them, and cut off their hands and their feet, and hanged them up beside the pool in Hebron. But they took the head of Ish-bosheth, and buried it in the grave of Abner in Hebron.

PART II

The United Kingdom

THE HOUSE OF DAVID
B. C. 1049 (Usher)
I David
B. C. 1010 (Rev.)

SECTION IX

David Made King Over All Israel

The Armed Men of the Twelve Tribes

I Chron. 12:23. And these are the numbers of the heads of them that were armed for war, which came to David to Hebron, to turn the kingdom of Saul to him, according to the word of the Lord.

24. The CHILDREN OF JUDAH that bare shield and spear were six thousand and eight hundred, armed for war.
25. Of the CHILDREN OF SIMEON, mighty men of valour for the war, seven thousand and one hundred.
26. Of the CHILDREN OF LEVI four thousand and six hundred. 27. And Jehoiada was the leader of the house of Aaron, and with him were three thousand and seven hundred; 28. and Zadok, a young man mighty of valour, and of his father's house twenty and two captains.
29. And of the CHILDREN OF BENJAMIN, the brethren of Saul, three thousand: for hitherto the greatest part of them had kept their allegiance to the house of Saul.
30. And of the CHILDREN OF EPHRAIM twenty thousand and eight hundred, mighty men of valour, famous men in their fathers' houses.
31. And of the HALF TRIBE OF MANASSEH eighteen thousand, which were expressed by name, to come and make David king.
32. And of the CHILDREN OF ISSACHAR, men that had understanding of the times, to know what Israel ought to do; the heads of them were two hundred; and all their brethren were at their commandment.
33. OF ZEBULON, such as were able to go out in the host, that could set the battle in array, with all manner of instruments of war, fifty thousand; and that could order the battle array, and were not of double heart.
34. And OF NAPHTALI, a thousand captains, and with them with shield and spear thirty and seven thousand.
35. And OF THE DANITES, that could set the battle in array, twenty and eight thousand and six hundred.
36. And OF ASHER, such as were able to go out in the host, that could set the battle in array, forty thousand.
37. And on the other side of Jordan, OF THE REUBENITES, AND THE GADITES, and OF THE HALF TRIBE OF MANASSEH, with all manner of instruments of war for the battle, an hundred and twenty thousand.

38. All these, being men of war, that could order the battle array, came with a perfect heart to Hebron, to make David king over all Israel: and all the rest also of Israel were of one heart to make David king.
39. And they were there with David three days, eating and drinking; for their brethren had made preparation for them.
40. Moreover they that were nigh unto them, even as far as Issachar and Zebulon and Naphtali, brought bread on asses, and on camels, and on mules, and on oxen, victual of meal, cakes of figs, and clusters of raisins, and wine, and oil, and oxen, and sheep in abundance: for there was joy in Israel.

The Tribes Come to David Unto Hebron

Then all the tribes of Israel gathered themselves to David unto Hebron, and spake, saying, Behold, we are thy bone and thy flesh. In times past, when Saul was king over us, it was thou that leddest out and broughtest in Israel, and the Lord thy God said unto thee, Thou shalt feed my people Israel, and thou shalt be prince over my people Israel. So all the elders of Israel came to the king to Hebron; and king David made a covenant with them in Hebron before the Lord: and they anointed David king over Israel, according to the word of the Lord by the hand of Samuel. Now David the son of Jesse reigned over all Israel. David was thirty years old when he began to reign, and the time that he reigned over Israel was forty years. In Hebron he reigned over Judah seven years and six months: and in Jerusalem he reigned thirty and three years over all Israel and Judah. And David and all Israel went to

Jerusalem Captured and Called The City of David

Jerusalem (the same is Jebus), against the Jebusites, the inhabitants of the land. And the inhabitants of Jebus spake to David, saying, Except thou take away the blind and the lame, thou shalt not come in hither: thinking, David cannot come in hither. Nevertheless David took the strong hold of Zion; the same is the city of David. And David said on that day, Whosoever smiteth the Jebusites, let him go up to the watercourse, and smite the lame and the blind, that are hated of David's soul. Wherefore they say, There are the blind and the lame; he cannot come into the house; and, Whosoever smiteth the Jebusites first shall be chief and captain. And Joab the son of Zeruiah went up first, and was made chief. And David dwelt in the strong hold; therefore they called it the city of David. And David built the city round about from Millo and inward: and Joab repaired the rest of the city. And David waxed greater and greater; for the Lord, the God of hosts, was with him. And unto David were sons born in Hebron: and his firstborn was Amnon of Ahinoam the

David's Wives and Sons

Jezreelitess; the second, Chileab, of Abigail the wife of Nabal the Carmelite; the third, Absalom the son of Maachah the daughter of Talmai, king of Geshur; the fourth, Adonijah the son of Haggith; the fifth, Shephatiah the son of Abital; the sixth, Ithrea, by Eglah his wife. These six were born to David in Hebron. And David took him more concubines and wives out of Jerusalem, after he was come from Hebron; and David begat more sons and daughters. And these are the names of the children that were born unto him in Jerusalem; Shimea, and Shobab, and Nathan, and Solomon, four, of Bath-shua the daughter of Ammiel: and Ibhar, and Elishama, and Eliphelet; and Nogah, and Nepheg, and Japhia; and Elishama, and Eliada, and Eliphelet, nine. All these were the sons of David, beside the sons of the concubines; and Tamar was their sister.

Tribes of Israel come to David unto Jerusalem

(II Sam. 5:) 1. Then came all the tribes of Israel to David to Hebron, and spake, saying, Behold we are thy bone and thy flesh. 2. In times past, when Saul was king over us, it was thou that leddest out and broughtest in Israel: and the Lord said to thee, Thou shalt feed my people Israel, and thou shalt be prince over Israel. 3. So all the elders of Israel came to the king to Hebron; and king David made a covenant with them in Hebron before the Lord: and they anointed David king over Israel.

(I Chron. 11:) 1. Then all Israel gathered themselves to David unto Hebron, saying, Behold, we are thy bone and thy flesh 2. In times past even when Saul was king, it was thou that leddest out and broughtest in Israel: and the Lord thy God said to thee, Thou shalt feed my people Israel, and thou shalt be prince over my people Israel. 3. So all the elders of Israel came to the king to Hebron; and David made a covenant with them in Hebron before the Lord: and they anointed David king over Israel, according to the word of the Lord by the hand of Samuel.

(I Chron. 29:) 26. Now David the son of Jesse reigned over all Israel.

4. David was thirty years old when he began to reign, and he reigned forty years.

27. And the time that he reigned over Israel was forty years;

5. In Hebron he reigned over Judah seven years and six months: and in Jerusalem he reigned thirty and three years over all Israel and Judah.

seven years reigned he in Hebron, thirty and three years reigned he in Jerusalem.

(I Chron. 3:) 4b. and there he reigned seven years and six months: and in Jerusalem he reigned thirty and three years.

6. And the king and his men went to Jerusalem against the Jebusites, the inhabitants of the land;

(I Chron. 11:) 4. And David and all Israel went to Jerusalem (the same is Jebus); and the Jebusites, the inhabitants of the land were there. 5. And the inhabitants of Jebus said to David,

which spake unto David, saying Except thou take away the blind and the lame thou shalt not come in hither: thinking, David cannot come in hither. Nevertheless David took the strong hold of Zion; the same is the city of David. 8. And David said on that day, Whosoever smiteth the Jebusites, let him get up to the watercourse, and smite the lame and the blind, that are hated of David's soul. Wherefore they say, There are the blind and the lame; he cannot come into the house.

Thou shalt not come in hither. Nevertheless David took the strong hold of Zion; the same is the city of David. 6. And David said, Whosoever smiteth the Jebusites first shall be chief and captain. And Joab the son of Zeruiah went up first, and was made chief. 7. And David dwelt in the strong hold; therefore they called it the city of David. 8. And he built the city round about, from Millo even round about: and Joab repaired the rest of the city.

9. And David dwelt in the strong hold, and called it the city of David and David built round about from Millo and inward.

10. And David waxed greater and greater: for the Lord the God of hosts, was with him.

9. And David waxed greater and greater; for the Lord of hosts was with him.

(II Sam. 3:) 2. And unto David were sons born in Hebron: and his first-born was Amnon, of Ahinoam the Jezreelitess; 3. And his second, Chileab, of Abigail the wife of Nabal the Carmelite; and the third Absalom, the son of Maachah the daughter of Talmai, king of Geshur; 4. And the fourth, Adonijah the son of Haggith; and the fifth, Shephatiah the son of Abital; 5. And the sixth, Ithream, by Eglah, David's wife. These were born to David in Hebron.

(I Chron. 3:) 1. Now these were the sons of David, which were born unto him in Hebron: the first-born Amnon, of Ahinoam the Jezreelitess; the second, Daniel of Abigail the Carmelitess. 2. The third Absalom the son of Maachah the daughter of Talmai, king of Geshur; the fourth, Adonijah the son of Haggith; 3. The fifth, Shephatiah the son of Abital; the sixth Ithream, by Eglah his wife. 4a. Six were born unto him in Hebron.

(II Sam. 5:) 13. And David took him more concubines and wives out of Jerusalem, after he was come from Hebron: and there were yet sons and daughters born to David.

(I Chron. 14:) 3. And David took more wives at Jerusalem: and David begat more sons and daughters.

14. And these be the names of those that were born unto him in Jerusalem; Shammua, and Shobab, and Nathan, and Solomon,

4. And these are the names of the children which he had in Jerusalem, Shammua, and Shobab, Nathan, and Solomon,

(I Chron. 3:) 5. And these were born unto him in Jerusalem; Shimea, and Shobab, and Nathan, and Solomon, four, of Bath-shua the daughter of Ammiel: 6. and Ibhar, and Elishama, and Eliphelet; 7. and Nogah, and Nepheg, and Japhia; 8. and Elishama, and Eliada, and Eliphelet, nine. 9. All these were the sons of David, beside the sons of the concubines; and Tamar was their sister.

15. and Ibhar, and Elishua, and Nepheg, and Japhia; 16. and Elishama, and Eliada, and Eliphelet.

5. and Ibhar, and Elishua, and Elpalet; 6. and Nogah and Nepheg, and Japhia; 7. and Elishama, and Beeliada, and Eliphelet.

Now these are the chief of the mighty men whom David had, who shewed themselves strong with him in his kingdom, together with all Israel to make him king, according to the word of the Lord concerning Israel. These be the names and number of the mighty men whom David had: Jashobeam, an Hachmonite, chief of the captains;

David's Heroes

the same was Adino the Eznite, he lifted up his spear against eight hundred* whom he slew at one time. And after him was Eleazer the son of Dodo the Ahoite who was one of the three mighty men with David, when they defied the Philistines that were gathered together to battle, and the men of Israel were gone away: he arose, and smote the Philistines until his hand was weary, and his hand clave unto the sword: and the Lord wrought a great victory that day; and the people returned after him that day only to spoil. And after him was Shammah the son of Agee a Haraite, who was with David at Pasdammin. And the Philistines were gathered together into a troop, where was a plot of ground full of lentiles; and the people fled before the Philistines. But he stood in the midst of the plot, and defended it, and the Lord saved them by a great victory which he wrought.

The Second Three Mighty Men

And Abishai, the brother of Joab, the son of Zeruiah, was chief of the three. And he lifted up his spear against three hundred and slew them, and had a name among the three. Of the three, he was more honourable than the two, and was made their captain: howbeit he attained not to the first three. And Benaiah the son of Jehoiada, the son of a valiant man of Kabzeel, who had done mighty deeds, he slew the two sons of Ariel of Moab; he went down also and slew a lion in the time of snow: And he slew an Egyptian, a goodly man of great stature, five cubits high; and in the Egyptian's hand was a spear like a weaver's beam; and he went down to him with a staff, and plucked the spear out of the Egyptian's hand, and slew him with his own spear. These things did Benaiah the son of Jehoiada, and had a name among the three mighty men. Behold he was more honourable than the thirty, but he attained not to the first three: and David set him over his guard. Also the mighty men of the armies; Asahel the brother of Joab was one of the thirty;

The Thirty

Elhanan the son of Dodo of Beth-lehem; Shammah the Harodite, Elika the Harodite, Helez the Pelonite; Ira the son of Ikkesh the Tekoite, Abiezer the Anathothite; Sibbecai the Hushathite; Zalmon the Ahoite, Maharai the Netophathite; Heled the son of Baanah the Netophathite; Ittai the son of Ribai of Gibeah of the children of Benjamin; Benaiah the Pirathonite; Hiddai of the brooks of Gaash, Abiel the Arbathite; Azmaveth the Barhumite; Eliahba the Shaalbonite, the sons of Hashem the Gizonite; Jonathan; Shammah the Harorite; Ahiam the son of Sacar the Harorite; Eliphelet the son of Ahasbai, the son of Maacathite; Eliam the son of Ahithophel the Gilonite, Hezro the Carmelite, Naarai the son of Ezbai; Igal the son of Nathan of Zobah; Mibhar the son of Hagri; Zelek the Ammonite, Naharai the Beerothite, armourbearer to Joab the son of Zeruiah; Ira the Ithrite, Gareb the Ithrite; Uriah the Hittite: thirty and seven in all. Zabad the son of Ahli; Adina the son of Shiza the Reubenite, a chief of the Reubenites, and thirty with him; Hanan the son of Maachah, and Joshaphat the Mithnite; Uzzia the Ashtrathite, Shama and Jeiel the sons of Hotham the Aroerite; Jediael the son of Shimri, and Joha his brother, the Tizite; Eliel the Mahavite, and Jeribai, and Joshaviah, the sons of Elnaam, and Ithmah the Moabite; Eliel, and Obed, and Jaasiel the Mezobaite.

---
*Chronicles, three hundred. See Appendix G, Chronicles III 1 (2).

DAVID'S HEROES.

(II Sam. 23:) 8. These be the names of the mighty men whom David had: Josheb-basshebeth a Tahchmonite, chief of the captains; the same was Adino the Eznite, against ((eight hundred)) slain at one time.   9. And after him was Eleazer the son of Dodai the son of an Ahoite, one of the three mighty men with David when they defied the Philistines that were there gathered together to battle, and the men of Israel were gone away: 10. he arose, and smote the Philistines until his hand was weary, and his hand clave unto the sword: and the Lord wrought a great victory that day; and the people returned after him only to spoil.   11. And after him was Shammah the son of Agee a Hararite. And the Philistines were gathered together into a troop, where was a plot of ground full of lentils; and the people fled from the Philistines. 12. But he stood in the midst of the plot, and defended it, and slew the Philistines: and the Lord wrought a great victory.

(I Chron. 11:) 10. Now these are the chief of the mighty men whom David had, who shewed themselves strong with him in his kingdom, together with all Israel, to make him king, according to the word of the Lord concerning Israel   11. And this is the number of the mighty men whom David had: Jashobeam, the son of a Hachmonite, the chief of the thirty, he lifted up his spear against ((three hundred)) and slew them at one time.   12. And after him was Eleazer the son of Dodo, the Ahoite, who was one of the three mighty men.   13. He was with David at Pas-dammin, and there the Philistines were gathered together to battle, where was a plot of ground full of barley, and the people fled from before the Philistines.   14. And they stood in the midst of the plot, and defended it, and slew the Philistines: and the Lord saved them by a great victory.

18. And Abishai, the brother of Joab, the son of Zeruiah, was chief of the three. And he lifted up his spear against three hundred and slew them, and had a name among the three. 19. Was he not most honourable of the three? therefore he was made their captain: howbeit he attained not unto the first three.

20. And Abishai, the brother of Joab, he was chief of the three: for he lifted up his spear against three hundred and slew them, and had a name among the three. 21. Of the three he was more honourable than the two, and was made their captain: howbeit he attained not to the first three.

20. And Benaiah the son of Jehoiada, the son of a valiant man of Kabzeel, who had done mighty deeds, he slew the two sons of Ariel of Moab: he went down also and slew a lion in the midst of a pit in time of snow:
21. and he slew an Egyptian, a goodly man: and the Egyptian had a spear in his hand; but he went down to him with a staff, and plucked the spear out of the Egyptian's hand, and slew him with his own spear. 22. These things did Benaiah the son of Jehoiada, and had a name among the three mighty men.   23. He was more honourable than the thirty, but he attained not to the first three. And David set him over his guard.

22. Benaiah the son of Jehoiada, the son of a valiant man of Kabzeel, who had done mighty deeds, he slew the two sons of Ariel of Moab: he went down also and slew a lion in the midst of a pit in time of snow:
23. And he slew an Egyptian, a man of great stature, five cubits high; and in the Egyptian's hand was a spear like a weaver's beam; and he went down to him with a staff, and plucked the spear out of the Egyptian's hand, and slew him with his own spear. 24. These things did Benaiah the son of Jehoiada, and had a name among the three mighty men.   25. Behold he was more honourable than the thirty, but he attained not to the first three: and David set him over his guard. 26. Also the mighty men of the armies;

24. Asahel the brother of Joab was one of the thirty; Elhanan the son of Dodo of Beth-lehem; 25. Shammah the Harodite, Elika the Harodite; 26. Helez the Paltite, Ira the son of Ikkesh the Tekoite; 27. Abiezer the Anothothite, ((Mebunnai the Hushathite;)) 28. Zalmon the Ahohite, Maharai the Netophathite; 29. Heleb the son of Baanah the Netophathite, Ittai the son of Ribai of Gibeah of the children of Benjamin; 30. Benaiah a Pirathonite, Hiddai of the brooks of Gaash; 31. Abialbon the Arbathite, Azmaveth the Barhumite; 32. Eliahba the Shaalbonite, the sons of Jashen, Jonathan;   33. Shammah the Harorite, Ahiam the son of Sharar the Ararite; 34. Eliphelet the son of Ahasbai, the son of Maacathite, Eliam the son of Ahithophel the Gilonite; 35. Hezro the Carmelite, Paarai the Arbite; 36. Igal the son of Nathan of Zobah, Bani the Gadite;

Asahel the brother of Joab, Elhanan the son of Dodo of Beth-lehem. 27. Shommoth the Harorite, Helez the Pelonite; 28. Ira the son of Ikkesh the Tekoite, Abiezer the Anothothite; ((Sibbecai the Hushathite,)) Ilai the Ahohite; 30. Maharai the Netophathite, Heled the son of Baanah the Netophathite; 31. Ithai the son of Ribai of Gibeah of the children of Benjamin, Benaiah the Pirathonite; 32. Hurai of the brooks of Gaash, Abiel the Arbathite; 33. Azmaveth the Barhumite, Eliahba the Shaalbonite; 34. the sons of Hashem the Gizonite, Jonathan the son of Shage the Harorite; 35. Ahiam the son of Sacar the Harorite, Eliphal the son of Ur;   36. Hepher the Mecherathite, Ahijah the Pelonite; 37. Hezro the Carmelite, Naarai the son of Ezbai; 38. Joel the brother of Nathan, Mibhar the son of Hagri; 39. Zelek the Ammonite, Naharai the Berothite, the armour-bearer to Joab the son of Zeruiah; 40. Ira the Ithrite, Gareb the Ithrite; 41. Uriah the Hittite, Zabod the son of Ahli; 42. Adina the son of Shiza the Reubenite, a chief of the Reubenites, and thirty with him. 43. Hanan the son of Maachah, and Joshaphat the Mithnite; 44. Uzzia the Ashtrathite, Shama and Jeiel the sons of Hotham the Aroerite; 45. Jediel the son of Shimri, and Joha his brother, the Tizite; 46. Eliel the Mahavite, and Jeribai, and Joshaviah, the sons of Elnaam, and Ithmah the Moabite; 47. Eliel, and Obed, and Jaasiel the Mezobaite.

37. Zelek the Ammonite, Naharai the Beerothite, armour-bearers to Joab the son of Zeruiah;   38. Ira the Ithrite, Gareb the Ithrite; 39. Uriah the Hittite: thirty and seven in all.

THE HOUSE OF DAVID
B. C. 1049 (Usher)
I David
B. C. 1010 (Rev.)

SECTION X

David's War with the Philistines

Two Invasions Repelled

And when the Philistines heard that David was anointed king over all Israel, all the Philistines went up to seek David: and David heard of it, and went out against them down to the hold. Now the Philistines had come and made a raid and spread themselves in the valley of Rephaim. And three of the thirty chief went down to the rock, and came to David in the harvest time unto the cave of Adullam; and the troop of the Philistines were encamped in the valley of Rephaim. And David was then in the hold, and the garrison of the Philistines was then in Beth-lehem. And David longed, and said, Oh that one would give me water to drink of the well of Beth-lehem, which is by the gate! And the three mighty men brake through the host of the Philistines, and drew water out of the well of Beth-lehem, that was by the gate, and took it, and brought it to David: but David would not drink thereof, but poured it out unto the Lord, and said My God forbid it me, that I should do this: shall I drink the blood of these men that have put their lives in jeopardy? for with the jeopardy of their lives they brought it. Therefore he would not drink it. These things did the three mighty men. And David inquired of the Lord, saying, Shall I go up against the Philistines? wilt thou deliver them into mine hand? And the Lord said unto David, Go up; for I will certainly deliver the Philistines into thine hand. So they came up to Baal-perazim, and David smote them there; and David said, God hath broken mine enemies by my hand, like the breach of waters. Therefore they called the name of that place Baal-perazim. And they left their images there; and David gave commandment, and his men took them away and they were burned with fire. And the Philistines came up yet again, and made a raid and spread themselves in the valley of Rephaim. And when David inquired of the Lord, God said unto him, Thou shalt not go up after them: turn away from them, make a circuit behind them, and come upon them over against the mulberry trees. And it shall be, when thou hearest the sound of marching in the tops of the mulberry trees that thou shalt bestir thyself and go out to battle for God is gone out before thee to smite the host of the Philistines. And David did as the Lord commanded him: and they smote the host of the Philistines from Gibeon even to Gezer. And the fame of David went out into all lands, and the Lord brought the fear of him upon all nations.

Exploits Against Philistine Giants

And after this it came to pass, that David smote the Philistines, and subdued them: and took Gath, the bridle of the mother city, and her towns out of the hands of the Philistines. And it came to pass after this, that there arose war at Gezer with the Philistines: then Sibbecai the Hushathite slew Sippai, of the sons of the giant, and they were subdued. And there was war again with the Philistines at Gob; and Elhanan the son of Jaareoregim the Beth-lehemite slew Lahmi the brother of Goliath the Gittite, the staff of whose spear was like a weaver's beam. And there was war again at Gath, where was a man of great stature, that had on every hand six fingers, and on every foot six toes, four and twenty in number; and he also was born of the giant. And when he defied Israel, Jonathan the son of Shimei David's brother slew him. These four were born to the giant in Gath; and they fell by the hand of David, and by the hand of his servants. II Sam. 21:15. And the Philistines had war again with Israel: and David went down, and his servants with him, and fought against the Philistines: and David waxed faint. 16. And Ishbi-benob, which was of the sons of the giant, the weight of whose spear was three hundred shekels of brass in weight, he being

David's Wars with the Philistines

(II Sam. 5:) 17. And when the Philistines heard that they had anointed David king over Israel, all the Philistines went up to seek David; and David heard of it, and went down to the hold. 18. Now the Philistines had come and spread themselves in the valley of Rephaim.
(II Sam. 23:)
13. And three of the thirty chief went down, and came to David in the harvest time unto the cave of Adullam; and the troop of the Philistines were encamped in the valley of Rephaim. 14. And David was then in the hold, and the garrison of the Philistines was then in Beth-lehem.

15. And David longed, and said, Oh that one would give me water to drink of the well of Beth-lehem, which is by the gate! 16. And the three mighty men break through the host of the Philistines, and drew water out of the well of Beth-lehem, that was by the gate, and took it, and brought it to David but he would not drink thereof, but poured it out unto the Lord.
17. And he said, Be it far from me, O Lord, that I should do this: shall I drink the blood of the men that went in jeopardy of their lives?
therefore he would not drink it. These things did the three mighty men.
(II Sam. 5:)
19. And David inquired of the Lord, saying, Shall I go up against the Philistines? wilt thou deliver them into mine hand? and the Lord said unto David, Go up: for I will certainly deliver the Philistines into thine hand. 20. And David came to Baal-perazim, and David smote them there; and he said, the Lord hath broken mine enemies before me, like the breach of waters. Therefore he called the name of that place Baal-perazim.

21. And they left their images there, ((and David and his men took them away.))
22. And the Philistines came up yet again, and spread themselves in the valley of Rephaim.

23. And when David inquired of the Lord, he said, Thou shalt not go up: make a circuit behind them, and come upon them over against the mulberry trees. 24. And it shall be, when thou hearest the sound of the marching in the tops of the mulberry trees that then thou bestir thyself: for then is the Lord gone out before thee to smite the host of the Philistines. 25. And David did so, as the Lord commanded him; and smote the Philistines from Geba until thou come to Gezer.

(II Sam. 8:)
1. And after this it came to pass, that David smote the Philistines, and subdued them: and David took the bridle of the mother city out of the hand of the Philistines.
(II Sam. 21:)
18. And it came to pass after this, that there was again war with the Philistines at Gob: then Sibbecai the Hushathite slew Saph, which was of the sons of the giant.
19. And there was again war with the Philistines at Gob: and Elhanan the son of Jaareoregim the Beth-lehemite slew ((Goliath the Gittite,)) the staff of whose spear was like a weaver's beam. 20. And there was war at Gath, where was a man of great stature, that had on every hand six fingers, and on every foot six toes, four and twenty in number; and he also was born to the giant. 21. and when he defied Israel, Jonathan the son of Shimei David's brother slew him.
22. These four were born to the giant on Gath; and they fell by the hand of David, and by the hand of his servants.

(I Chron. 14:) 8. And when the Philistines heard that David was anointed king over all Israel, all the Philistines went up to seek David: and David heard of it, and went out against them. 9. Now the Philistines had come and made a raid in the valley of Rephaim.
(I Chron. 11:)
15. And three of the thirty chief went down to the rock to David, into the cave of Adullam; and the host of the Philistines were encamped in the valley of the Rephaim. 16. And David was then in the hold, and the garrison of the Philistines was then in Beth-lehem.

17. And David longed, and said, Oh that one would give me water to drink of the well of Beth-lehem, which is by the gate! 18. And the three break through the host of the Philistines, and drew water out of the well of Beth-lehem, that was by the gate, and took it, and brought it to David: but David would not drink thereof but poured it out unto the Lord,
and said, 19. My God forbid it me, that I should do this: shall I drink the blood of these men that have put their lives in jeopardy? for with the jeopardy of their lives they brought it. Therefore he would not drink it. These things did the three mighty men.
(I Chron. 14:)
10. And David inquired of God, saying, Shall I go up against the Philistines? and wilt thou deliver them into mine hand? And the Lord said unto him, Go up; for I will deliver them into thine hand. 11. So they came up to Baal-perazim, and David smote them there; and David said, God hath broken mine enemies by mine hand, like the breach of waters. Therefore they called the name of that place Baal-perazim.

12. And they left their gods there; ((and David gave commandment, and they were burned with fire.))
13. And the Philistines yet again and made a raid in the valley.

14. And David inquired again of God; and God said unto him, Thou shalt not go up after them: turn away from them and come upon them over against the mulberry trees. 15. And it shall be, when thou hearest the sound of marching in the tops of the mulberry trees that then thou shalt go out to battle; for God is gone out before thee to smite the host of the Philistines. 16. And David did as God commanded him: and they smote the host of the Philistines from Gibeon even to Gezer.

17. And the fame of David went out into all lands; and the Lord brought the fear of him upon all nations.

(I Chron. 18:)
1. And after this it came to pass, that David smote the Philistines, and subdued them, and took Gath and her towns out of the hand of the Philistines.
(I Chron. 20:)
4. And it came to pass after this, that there arose war at Gezer with the Philistines: then Sibbecai the Hushathite slew Sippai, of the sons of the giant: and they were subdued.
5. And there was again war with the Philistines; and Elhanan the son of Jair slew ((Lahmi the brother of Goliath the Gittite,)) the staff of whose spear was like a weaver's beam. 6. And there was again war at Gath, where was a man of great stature, whose fingers and toes were four and twenty, six on each hand, and six on each foot; and he also was born unto the giant. 7. and when he defied Israel, Jonathan the son of Shimea David's brother slew him.
8. These were born unto the giant in Gath; and they fell by the hand of David, and by the hand of his servants.

girded with a new sword, thought to have slain David. 17. But Abishai the son of Zeruiah succored him, and smote the Philistine, and killed him. Then the men of David sware unto him, saying, Thou shall go no more out with us to battle, that thou quench not the light of Israel.

And Hiram king of Tyre sent messengers to David, and cedar trees, and carpenters and masons; and they built David an house. And David perceived that the Lord had established him king over Israel, and that he had exalted his kingdom on high, for his people Israel's sake. And David reigned over all Israel; and David executed judgment and justice unto all his people. And Joab the son of Zeruiah was over the host; and Jehoshaphat the son of Ahilud was recorder; and Zadok the son of Ahitub, and Abimelech the son of Abiathar, were priests; and Zeraiah was scribe; And Benaiah the son of Jehoiada was over the Cherethites and Pelethites; and Adoram was over the tribute: and the sons of David were chief about the king. II Sam. 22:1. And David spake unto the Lord the words of this song in the day that the Lord delivered him out of the hand of all his enemies, and out of the hand of Saul: 2. and he said,

 The Lord is my rock and my fortress, and my deliverer, even mine.
3. The God of my rock, in him will I trust;
 My shield, and the horn of my salvation, my high tower, and my refuge;
 My saviour, thou savest me from violence.
4. I will call upon the Lord, who is worthy to be praised:
 So shall I be saved from mine enemies.
5. For the waves of death compassed me,
 The floods of ungodliness made me afraid.
6. The cords of Sheol were round about me:
 The snares of death came upon me.
7. In my distress I called upon the Lord,
 Yea, I called unto my God:
 And he heard my voice out of his temple,
 And my cry came into his ears.
8. Then the earth shook and trembled,
 The foundations of heaven moved
 And were shaken, because he was wroth.
9. There went up a smoke out of his nostrils,
 And fire out of his mouth devoured:
 Coals were kindled by it.
10. He bowed the heavens also and came down;
 And thick darkness was under his feet.
11. And he rode upon a cherub, and did fly:
 Yea, he was seen upon the wings of the wind.
12. And he made darkness pavilions round about him,
 Gathering of waters, thick clouds of the skies.
13. At the brightness before him
 Coals of fire were kindled.
14. The Lord thundered from heaven,
 And the most high uttered his voice.
15. And he sent out arrows, and scattered them;
 Lightning, and discomfited them;
16. Then the channels of the sea appeared,
 The foundations of the world were laid bare,
 By the rebuke of the Lord,
 At the blast of the breath of his nostrils.
17. He sent from on high, he took me;
 He drew me out of many waters;
18. He delivered me from my strong enemy,
 From them that hated me; for they were too mighty for me.

SECT. X — THE UNITED KINGDOM — 51

(II Sam. 5:) 11. And Hiram king of Tyre sent messengers to David, and cedar trees, and carpenters, and masons: and they built David an house. 12. And David perceived that the Lord had established him king over Israel, and that he had exalted his kingdom for his people Israel's sake.

(II Sam. 8:) 15. And David reigned over all Israel; and David executed judgment and justice unto all his people. 16. And Joab the son of Zeruiah was over the host; and Jehoshaphat the son of Ahilud was recorder; 17. and Zadok the son of Ahitub, and Ahimelech the son of Abiathar, were priests; and Seraiah was scribe; 18. and Benaiah the son of Jehoiada was over the Cherethites and the Pelethites; and David's sons were priests.

(II Sam. 20:) 23-26. Now Joab was over all the host of Israel; and Jehoshaphat the son of Ahilud was recorder; and Zadok and Abiathar were priests; and Sheva was scribe; and Benaiah the son of Jehoiada was over the Cherethites and over the Pelethites; and Adoram was over the tribute: and Ira also the Jairite was a chief minister unto David.

(I Chron. 14:) 1. And Hiram king of Tyre sent messengers to David, and cedar trees, and masons, and carpenters, to build him an house. 2. And David perceived that the Lord had established him king over Israel, for his kingdom was exalted on high, for his people Israel's sake.

(I Chron. 18:) 14. And David reigned over all Israel; and he executed judgment and justice unto all his people. 15. And Joab the son of Zeruiah was over the host; and Jehoshaphat the son of Ahilud was recorder; 16. and Zadok the son of Ahitub, and Abimelech the son of Abiathar were priests; and Shavsha was scribe; 17. and Benaiah the son of Jehoiada was over the Cherethites and the Pelethites; and the sons of David were chief about the king.

II. Sam. 22: 2-51.

2. The Lord is my rock, and my fortress, and my deliverer, even mine;
3. The God of my rock, in him will I trust;
 My shield, and the horn of my salvation, my high tower and my refuge,
 My saviour, thou savest me from violence.
4. I will call upon the Lord, who is worthy to be praised:
 So shall I be saved from mine enemies.
5. For the waves of death compassed me,
 The floods of ungodliness made me afraid.
6. The cords of Sheol were round about me:
 The snares of death came upon me.
7. In my distress I called upon the Lord,
 Yea, I called unto my God:
 And he heard my voice out of his temple,
 And my cry came into his ears.
8. Then the earth shook and trembled,
 The foundations of heaven moved
 And were shaken, because he was wroth.
9. There went up a smoke out of his nostrils,
 And fire out of his mouth devoured:
 Coals were kindled by it.
10. He bowed the heavens also, and came down;
 And thick darkness was under his feet.
11. And he rode upon a cherub, and did fly:
 Yea, he was seen upon the wings of the wind.
12. And he made darkness pavilions round about him,
 Gathering of waters, thick clouds of the skies.
13. At the brightness before him
 Coals of fire were kindled.
14. The Lord thundered from heaven,
 And the most high uttered his voice.
15. And he sent out arrows, and scattered them;
 Lightning, and discomfited them.
16. Then the channels of the sea appeared,
 The foundations of the world were laid bare,
 By the rebuke of the Lord,
 At the blast of the breath of his nostrils.
17. He sent from on high, he took me;
 He drew me out of many waters;
18. He delivered me from my strong enemy,
 From them that hated me; for they were too mighty for me.

Psalm 18: 1-50.

1. I love thee, O Lord, my strength.
2. The Lord is my rock, and my fortress, and my deliverer;
 My God, my strong rock, in him will I trust;
 My shield, and the horn of my salvation, my high tower;
3. I will call upon the Lord, who is worthy to be praised:
 So shall I be saved from mine enemies.
4. The cords of death compassed me,
 And the floods of ungodliness made me afraid.
5. The cords of Sheol were round about me:
 The snares of death came upon me.
6. In my distress I called upon the Lord,
 And cried unto my God:
 He heard my voice out of his temple,
 And my cry before him came into his ears.
7. Then the earth shook and trembled,
 The foundations also of the mountains moved
 And were shaken, because he was wroth.
8. There went up a smoke out of his nostrils,
 And fire out of his mouth devoured:
 Coals were kindled by it.
9. He bowed the heavens also, and came down;
 And thick darkness was under his feet.
10. And he rode upon a cherub, and did fly:
 Yea, he flew swiftly upon the wings of the wind.
11. And he made darkness his hiding-place, his pavilion round about him;
 Darkness of waters, thick clouds of the skies.
12. At the brightness before him his thick clouds passed,
 Hailstones and coals of fire.
13. The Lord also thundered in the heavens,—
 And the most high uttered his voice;
 Hailstones and coals of fire.
14. And he sent out his arrows, and scattered them;
 Yea, lightnings manifold, and discomfited them.
15. Then the channels of waters appeared,
 The foundations of the world were laid bare,
 At thy rebuke, O Lord,
 At the blast of the breath of thy nostrils.
16. He sent from on high, he took me;
 He drew me out of many waters;
17. He delivered me from my strong enemy,
 And from them that hated me, for they were too mighty for me.

19. They came upon me in the day of my calamity:
    But the Lord was my stay.
20. He brought me forth also into a large place:
    He delivered me, because he delighted in me.
21. The Lord rewarded me according to my righteousness:
    According to the cleanness of my hands hath he recompensed me.
22. For I have kept the ways of the Lord,
    And have not wickedly departed from my God.
23. For all his judgments were before me:
    And as for his statutes, I did not depart from them.
24. I was also perfect toward him,
    And I kept myself from mine iniquity.
25. Therefore hath the Lord recompensed me according to my righteousness;
    According to my cleanness in his eyesight.
26. With the merciful thou wilt shew thyself merciful,
    With the perfect man thou wilt shew thyself perfect;
27. With the pure thou wilt shew thyself pure;
    And with the perverse thou wilt shew thyself froward.
28. And the afflicted people thou wilt save:
    But thine eyes are upon the haughty, that thou mayest bring them down.
29. For thou art my lamp, O Lord:
    And the Lord will lighten my darkness.
30. For by thee I run upon a troop:
    By my God do I leap over a wall.
31. As for God, his way is perfect;
    The word of the Lord is tried;
    He is a shield unto all them that trust in him.
32. For who is God, save the Lord?
    And who is a rock, save our God?
33. God is my strong fortress:
    And he guideth the perfect in his way.
34. He maketh his feet like hind's feet:
    And setteth me upon my high places.
35. He teacheth my hands to war;
    So that mine arms do bend a bow of brass.
36. Thou hast also given me the shield of thy salvation:
    And thy gentleness hath made me great.
37. Thou hast enlarged my steps under me,
    And my feet have not slipped.
38. I have pursued mine enemies, and destroyed them;
    Neither did I turn again till they were consumed.
39. And I have consumed them, and smitten them through, that they cannot arise:
    Yea, they are fallen under my feet.
40. For thou hast girded me with strength unto the battle:
    Thou hast subdued under me those that rose up against me.
41. Thou hast also made mine enemies turn their backs unto me,
    That I might cut off them that hate me.
42. They looked, but there was none to save;
    Even unto the Lord, but he answered them not.
43. Then did I beat them small as the dust of the earth,
    I did stamp them as the mire of the streets, and did spread them abroad.
44. Thou also hast delivered me from the strivings of my people;
    Thou hast kept me to be the head of the nations:
    A people whom I have not known shall serve me.

19. They came upon me in the day of my calamity: But the Lord was my stay.	18. They came upon me in the day of my calamity: But the Lord was my stay.
20. He brought me forth also into a large place: He delivered me because he delighted in me.	19. He brought me forth also into a large place: He delivered me because he delighted in me.
21. The Lord rewarded me according to my righteousness. According to the cleanness of my hands hath he recompensed me.	20. The Lord rewarded me according to my righteousness: According to the cleanness of my hands hath he recompensed me.
22. For I have kept the ways of the Lord, And have not wickedly departed from my God.	21. For I have kept the ways of the Lord, And have not wickedly departed from my God.
23. For all his judgments were before me: And as for his statutes, I did not depart from them.	22. For all his judgments were before me, And put not away his statutes from me.
24. I was also perfect toward him, And I kept myself from mine iniquity.	23. I was also perfect with him, And I kept myself from mine iniquity.
25. Therefore hath the Lord recompensed me according to my righteousness, According to my cleanness in his eyesight.	24. Therefore hath the Lord recompensed me according to my righteousness, According to the cleanness of my hands in his eyesight.
26. With the merciful thou wilt shew thyself merciful, With the perfect man thou wilt shew thyself perfect;	25. With the merciful thou wilt shew thyself merciful; With the perfect man thou wilt shew thyself perfect;
27. With the pure thou wilt shew thyself pure; And with the perverse thou wilt shew thyself froward.	26. With the pure thou wilt shew thyself pure; And with the perverse thou wilt shew thyself froward.
28. And the afflicted people thou wilt save: But thine eyes are upon the haughty, that thou mayest bring them down.	27. For thou wilt save the afflicted people; But the haughty eyes thou wilt bring down.
29. For thou art my lamp, O Lord; And the Lord will lighten my darkness.	28. For thou wilt light my lamp: The Lord my God will lighten my darkness.
30. For by thee I run upon a troop: By my God do I leap over a wall.	29. For by thee I run upon a troop; And by my God do I leap over a wall.
31. As for God, his way is perfect: The word of the Lord is tried: He is a shield unto all them that trust in him.	30. As for God, his way is perfect: The word of the Lord is tried; He is a shield unto all them that trust in him.
32. For who is God, save the Lord? And who is a rock, save our God?	31. For who is God save the Lord? And who is a rock, beside our God?
33. God is my strong fortress: And he guideth the perfect in his way.	32. The God that girdeth me with strength, And maketh my way perfect.
34. He maketh his feet like hinds' feet: And setteth me upon my high places.	33. He maketh my feet like hinds' feet: And setteth me upon my high places.
35. He teacheth my hands to war; So that mine arms do bend a bow of brass.	34. He teacheth my hands to war; So that mine arms do bend a bow of brass.
36. Thou hast also given me the shield of thy salvation: And thy gentleness hath made me great.	35. Thou hast also given me the shield of thy salvation: And thy right hand hath holden me up, And thy gentleness hath made me great.
37. Thou hast enlarged my steps under me, And my feet have not slipped.	36. Thou hast enlarged my steps under me, And my feet have not slipped.
38. I have pursued mine enemies, and destroyed them; Neither did I turn again till they were consumed.	37. I will pursue mine enemies, and overtake them; Neither will I turn again till they are consumed.
39. And I have consumed them, and smitten them through, that they cannot arise: Yea they are fallen under my feet.	38. I will smite them through that they shall not be able to rise: They shall fall under my feet.
40. For thou hast girded me with strength unto the battle: Thou hast subdued under me those that rose up against me.	39. For thou hast girded me with strength unto the battle: Thou hast subdued under me those that rose up against me.
41. Thou hast also made mine enemies turn their backs unto me, That I might cut off them that hate me.	40. Thou hast also made mine enemies turn their backs unto me, That I might cut off them that hate me.
42. They looked, but there was none to save; Even unto the Lord, but he answered them not.	41. They cried, but there was none to save: Even unto the Lord, but he answered them not.
43. Then did I beat them small as the dust of the earth, I did stamp them as the mire of the streets, and did spread them abroad.	42. Then did I beat them small as the dust before the wind: I did cast them out as the mire of the streets.
44. Thou also hast delivered me from the strivings of my people: Thou hast kept me to be the head of the nations: A people whom I have not known shall serve me.	43. Thou hast delivered me from the strivings of the people Thou hast made me the head of the nations: A people whom I have not known shall serve me.

45. The strangers shall submit themselves unto me:
    As soon as they hear of me, they shall obey me.
46. The strangers shall fade away,
    And shall come trembling out of their close places.
47. The Lord liveth; and blessed be my rock;
    And exalted be the God of the rock of my salvation:
48. Even the God that executeth vengeance for me,
    And bringeth down peoples under me,
49. And that bringeth me forth from mine enemies:
    Yea, thou liftest me up above them that rise up against me:
    Thou deliverest me from the violent man.
50. Therefore I will give thanks unto thee, O Lord, among the nations,
    And will sing praises unto thy name.
51. Great deliverance giveth he to his king:
    And sheweth loving kindness to his anointed,
    To David and to his seed, for evermore.

David's Kindness to Jonathan's Son

II Sam. 9: 1. And David said, Is there yet any that is left of the house of Saul, that I may shew him kindness for Jonathan's sake? 2. And there was of the house of Saul a servant whose name was Ziba, and they called him unto David; and the king said unto him, Art thou Ziba? And he said, Thy servant is he. 3. And the king said, Is there not yet any of the house of Saul, that I may shew the kindness of God unto him? And Ziba said unto the king, Jonathan hath yet a son, which is lame on his feet. II Sam. 4: 4. He was five years old when the tidings came of Saul and Jonathan out of Jezreel, and his nurse took him up, and fled: and it came to pass, as she made haste to flee, that he fell, and became lame. And his name was Mephibosheth. II Sam. 9: 4. And the king said unto him, Where is he? And Ziba said unto the king, Behold, he is in the house of Machir the son of Ammiel, in Lo-debar. 5. Then king David sent, and fetched him out of the house of Machir the son of Ammiel, from Lo-debar. 6. And Mephibosheth, the son of Jonathan, the son of Saul, came unto David, and fell on his face, and did obeisance. And David said, Mephibosheth. And he answered, Behold thy servant! 7. And David said unto him, Fear not: for I will surely shew thee kindness for Jonathan's thy father's sake, and will restore thee all the land of Saul thy father; and thou shalt eat bread at my table continually. 8. And he did obeisance, and said, What is thy servant; that thou should look upon such a dead dog as I am? 9. Then the king called to Ziba, Saul's servant, and said unto him, All that pertained to Saul and to all his house have I given unto thy master's son. 10. And thou shalt till the land for him, thou, and thy sons, and thy servants; and thou shalt bring in the fruits, that thy master's son may have bread to eat: but Mephibosheth thy master's son shall eat bread alway at my table. Now Ziba had fifteen sons and twenty servants. 11. Then said Ziba unto the king, According to all that my lord the king commandeth his servant, so shall thy servant do. As for Mephibosheth, said the king, he shall eat at my table, as one of the king's sons. 12. And Mephibosheth had a young son, whose name was Mica. And all that dwelt in the house of Ziba were servants to Mephibosheth. 13. So Mephibosheth dwelt in Jerusalem; for he did eat continually at the king's table; and he was lame on both his feet.

45. The strangers shall submit themselves unto me: As soon as they hear of me they shall obey me.	44. As soon as they hear of me they shall obey me: The strangers shall submit themselves unto me.
46. The strangers shall fade away, And shall come trembling out of their close places.	45. The strangers shall fade away, And shall come trembling out of their close places.
47. The Lord liveth; and blessed be my rock; And exalted be the God of the rock of my salvation:	46. The Lord liveth; and blessed be my rock; And exalted be the God of my salvation:
48. Even the God that executeth vengeance for me, And bringeth down peoples under me,	47. Even the God that executeth vengeance for me, And subdueth peoples under me.
49. And that bringeth me forth from mine enemies: Yea, thou liftest me up above them that rise up against me: Thou deliverest me from the violent man.	48. He rescueth me from mine enemies; Yea, thou liftest me up above them that rise up against me: Thou deliverest me from the violent man.
50. Therefore I will give thanks unto thee, O Lord, among the nations And will sing praises unto thy name.	49. Therefore I will give thanks unto thee, O Lord, among the nations. And will sing praises unto thy name.
51. Great deliverance giveth he to his king: And sheweth loving kindness to his anointed, To David and to his seed for evermore.	50. Great deliverance giveth he to his king: And sheweth loving kindness to his anointed, To David and to his seed for evermore.

THE HOUSE OF DAVID
  B. C. 1049 (Usher)
I David
  B. C. 1010 (Rev.)

SECTION XI

The Ark Removed from Kiriath-jearim

And David consulted with the captains of thousands and of hundreds, even with every leader. And David said unto all the assembly of Israel, If it seem good unto you, and if it be of the Lord our God, let us send abroad every where unto our brethren that are left in all the land of Israel, with whom the priests and Levites are in their cities that have suburbs, that they may gather themselves unto us: and let us bring again the ark of our God to us: for we sought not unto it in the days of Saul. And all the assembly said that they would do so: for the thing was right in the eyes of all the people. And David assembled all the chosen men of Israel together, from Sihor the brook of Egypt even unto the entering of Hamath, thirty thousand, to bring the ark of God from Kiriath-jearim. And David arose, and went up, with all the people that were with him, to Baalah, that is, to Kiriath-jearim, which belonged to Judah, to bring up from thence the ark of God, which is called by the Name, even the name of the Lord of hosts that sitteth upon the Cherubim. And they carried the ark of God upon a new cart, and brought it out of the house of Abinadab that was in the hill: and Uzzah and Ahio drave the new cart. And they brought it out of the house of Abinadab, which was in the hill, with the ark of God: and Ahio went before the ark.

And David and all the house of Israel played before the Lord God with all their might even with songs, and with harps, and with psalteries, and with timbrels, and with cymbals, and with trumpets. And when they came unto the threshing-floor of Nacon, Uzzah put forth his hand to take hold of the ark of God: for the oxen stumbled. And the anger of the Lord was kindled against Uzzah; and God smote him there for his error, because he put forth his hand to the ark: and there he died by the ark of God. And David was displeased, because the Lord had broken forth upon Uzzah: and he called that place Perez-uzzah, unto this day. And David was afraid of the Lord that day: and he said, How shall I bring the ark of God home to me? So David would not remove the ark of the Lord unto him into the city of David; but carried it aside into the house of Obed-edom the Gittite. And the ark of God remained with the family of Obed-edom in his house three months: and the Lord blessed the house of Obed-edom, and all that he had. And it was told king David, saying: The Lord hath blessed the house of Obed-edom, and all that pertaineth unto him, because of the ark of God. I Chron. 15: 1. And David made him houses in the city of

Ark Carried Into House of Obed-edom

SECT. XI   THE UNITED KINGDOM

The Ark Removed From Kiriath-jearim

II SAM. 6:1-12.	I CHRON. 13:1-14.
	1. And David consulted with the captains of thousands and of hundreds, even with every leader. 2. And David said unto all the assembly of Israel, If it seem good unto you, and if it be of the Lord, our God, let us send abroad everywhere unto our brethren that are left in all the land of Israel, with whom the priests and Levites are in their cities that have suburbs, that they may gather themselves unto us: 3. and let us bring again the ark of our God to us: for we sought not unto it in the days of Saul. 4. And all the assembly said that they would do so: for the thing was right in the eyes of all the people.
	5. So David assembled all Israel together, (from Sihor the brook of Egypt even unto the entering of Hamath,) to bring the ark of God from Kiriath-jearim.
1. And David again gathered together all the chosen men of Israel, (thirty thousand) 2. And David arose and went with all the people that were with him, (from Baale Judah,) to bring up from thence the ark of God, which is called by the Name, even the name of the Lord of hosts that sitteth upon the cherubim.	6. And David went up, and all Israel, (to Baalah, that is, to Kiriath-jearim, which belonged to Judah,) to bring up from thence the ark of God, the Lord that sitteth upon the cherubim, which is called by the Name.
3. And they set the ark of God upon a new cart, and brought it out of the house of Abinadab that was in the hill: and Uzzah and Ahio, the sons of Abinadab drave the new cart. 4. And they brought it out of the house of Abinadab, which was in the hill, with the ark of God: and Ahio went before the ark.	7. And they carried the ark of God upon a new cart, and brought it out of the house of Abinadab: and Uzza and Ahio drave the cart.
5. And David and all the house of Israel played before the Lord (with all manner of instruments made of fir wood, and with harps, and with psalteries, and with timbrels, and with castanets, and with cymbals.)	8. And David and all Israel played before God (with all their might even with songs, and with harps, and with psalteries, and with timbrels, and with cymbals and with trumpets.)
6. And when they came to the threshing-floor of Nacon, Uzzah put forth his hand to the ark of God and took hold of it; for the oxen stumbled. 7. And the anger of the Lord was kindled against Uzzah; and God smote him there for his error; and there he died by the ark of God.	9. And when they came unto the threshing-floor of Chidon, Uzza put forth his hand to hold the ark; for the oxen stumbled. 10. And the anger of the Lord was kindled against Uzza; and he smote him, because he put forth his hand to the ark: and there he died before God.
8. And David was displeased, because the Lord had broken forth upon Uzzah: and he called that place Perez-uzzah, unto this day. 9. And David was afraid of the Lord that day; and he said, How shall the ark of the Lord come unto me?	11. And David was displeased, because the Lord had broken forth upon Uzza; and he called that place Perez-uzza, unto this day. 12. And David was afraid of God that day, saying, How shall I bring the ark of God home to me?
10. So David would not remove the ark of the Lord unto him into the city of David; but David carried it aside into the house of Obed-edom the Gittite.	13. So David removed not the ark unto him into the city of David, but carried it aside into the house of Obed-edom the Gittite.
11. And the ark of the Lord remained in the house of Obed-edom the Gittite three months: and the Lord blessed Obed-edom, and all his house.	14. And the ark of God remained with the family of Obed-edom in his house three months: and the Lord blessed the house of Obed-edom, and all that he had.
12a. And it was told king David, saying, The Lord hath blessed the house of Obed-edom, and all that pertaineth unto him, because of the ark of God.	

*Critical Notes. Chronicles, II, 2 (1). Appendix C.

David; and he prepared a place for the ark of God, and pitched for it a tent. 2. Then David said, None ought to carry the ark of God but the Levites: for them hath the Lord chosen to carry the ark of God, and to minister unto him forever. 3. And David assembled all Israel at Jerusalem, to bring up the ark of the Lord unto its place, which he had prepared for it. 4. And David gathered together the sons of Aaron, and the Levites: 5. of the sons of Kohath; Uriel the chief, and his brethren an hundred and twenty: 6. of the sons of Merari; Asaiah the chief, and his brethren two hundred and twenty: 7. of the sons of Gershom; Joel the chief, and his brethren an hundred and thirty: 8. of the sons of Elizaphan; Shemaiah the chief, and his brethren two hundred: 9. of the sons of Hebron; Eliel the chief, and his brethren fourscore: 10. of the sons of Uzziel; Amminadab the chief, and his brethren an hundred and twelve. 11. And David called for Zadok and Abiathar the priests, and for the Levites, for Uriel, Asaiah, and Joel, Shemaiah, and Eliel, and Amminadab and said unto them, Ye are the heads of the fathers' houses of the Levites: sanctify yourselves, both ye and your brethren, that ye may bring up the ark of the Lord, the God of Israel, unto the place that I have prepared for it. 13. For because ye bare it not at the first, the Lord our God made a breach upon us, for that we sought him not according to the ordinance. 14. So the priests and the Levites sanctified themselves to bring up the ark of the Lord, the God of Israel. 15. * And the children of the Levites bare the ark of God upon their shoulders with the staves thereon, as Moses commanded according to the word of the Lord. 16. And David spake to the chief of the Levites to appoint their brethren the singers, with instruments of music, psalteries and harps and cymbals, sounding aloud and lifting up the voice with joy. 17. So the Levites appointed Heman the son of Joel; and of his brethren, Asaph the son of Berechiah; and of the sons of Merari their brethren, Ethan the son of Kushaiah; 18. and with them their brethren of the second degree, Zechariah, Ben, and Jaaziel, and Shemiramoth, and Jehiel, and Unni, Eliab, and Benaiah, and Maaseiah, and Mattithiah, and Eliphelehu, and Mikneiah, and Obed-edom, and Jeiel, the doorkeepers. 19. So the singers, Heman, Asaph, and Ethan, were appointed, with cymbals of brass to sound aloud; 20. and Zechariah, and Aziel, and Shemiramoth, and Jehiel, and Unni, and Eliab, and Maaseiah, and Benaiah with psalteries set to Alamoth; 21. and Mattithiah, and Eliphelehu, and Mikneiah, and Obed-edom, and Jeiel, and Azaziah, with harps set to the Sheminith, to lead. 22. And Chenaniah, chief of the Levites, was over the song: he instructed about the song, because he was skilful. 23. And Berechiah and Elkanah were doorkeepers for the ark. 24. And Shebaniah, and Joshaphat, and Nethanel, and Amasai, and Zechariah, and Benaiah, and Eliezer, the priests, did blow with the trumpets before the ark of God: and Obed-edom and Jehiah were doorkeepers for the ark.

Ark Brought From the House of Obed-edom

So David, and the elders of Israel, and the captains over thousands, went to bring up the ark of the covenant of the Lord out of the house of Obed-edom into the city of David with joy: and it came to pass, when God helped the Levites that bare the ark of the covenant of the Lord, that they sacrificed seven bullocks and seven rams. And it was so, that when they that bare the ark of the Lord had gone six paces, he sacrificed an ox and a fatling. And David was clothed with a robe of fine linen, and all the Levites that bare the ark, and the singers, and Chenaniah the master of the song with the singers: And David danced before the Lord with all his might: and David was girded with a linen ephod. So David

---

* Critical Notes. Chronicles II, 2 (1). Appendix C.

Ark Brought From the House of Obed-edom

(II Sam. 6:) 12b. And David God went and brought up the ark of God from the house of Obed-edom, into the city of David, with joy.
13. And it was so, that when they that bare the ark of the Lord had gone six paces, he sacrificed an ox and a fatling.

14. And David danced before the Lord with all his might: and David was girded with a linen ephod.

(I Chron. 15:) 25. So David, and the elders of Israel, and the captains over thousands, went to bring up the ark of the covenant of the Lord out of the house of Obed-edom with joy: 26. and it came to pass, when God helped the Levites that bare the ark of the covenant of the Lord, that they sacrificed seven bullocks and seven rams.

27. And David was clothed with a robe of fine linen, and all the Levites that bare the ark, and the singers, and Chenaniah the master of the song with the singers:

and David had upon him an ephod of linen.

and all the house of Israel brought up the ark of the covenant of the Lord with shouting, and with the sound of the cornet, and with trumpets, and with cymbals, sounding aloud with psalteries and harps. And it came to pass, as the ark of the covenant of the Lord came into the city of David that Michal the daughter of Saul looked out of the window, and saw king David leaping and dancing before the Lord; and she despised him in her heart. Then David returned to bless his household. And Michal came out to meet David, and said, How glorious was the king of Israel to-day, who uncovered himself to-day in the eyes of the handmaids of his servants, as one of the vain fellows shamelessly uncovereth himself! And David said unto Michal, It was before the Lord, which chose me above thy father, and above all his house, to appoint me prince over the people of the Lord, over Israel: therefore will I play before the Lord. And I will be yet more vile than thus, and will be base in mine own sight: but of the handmaids which thou hast spoken of, of them shall I be had in honour. And Michal the daughter had no child unto the day of her death.

Ark Set in the Tent David Pitched for It And they brought in the ark of the Lord, and set it in the midst of the tent that David had pitched for it: and David offered burnt offerings and peace offerings before the Lord. And when David had made an end of offering the burnt offering and the peace offerings, he blessed the people in the name of the Lord of hosts. And he dealt among all the people, even among the whole multitude of Israel, both to men and women, to every one a cake of bread, and a portion of flesh, and a cake of raisins. So all the people departed every one to his house. And he appointed certain of the Levites to minister before the ark of the Lord, and to celebrate and to thank and to praise the Lord, the God of Israel: Asaph the chief, and second to him Zechariah, Jeiel, and Shemiramoth, and Jehiel, and Mattithiah, and Eliab, and Benaiah and Obed-edom, and Jeiel, with psalteries and with harps; and Asaph with cymbals, sounding aloud; and Benaiah and Jahaziel the priests with trumpets continually, before the ark of the covenant of God. I Chron. 16:7. Then on that day did David first ordain to give thanks unto the Lord by the hand of Asaph and his brethren.

8. O give thanks unto the Lord, call upon his name;
   Make known his doings among the peoples.
9. Sing unto him, sing praises unto him;
   Talk ye of all his marvellous works.
10. Glory ye in his holy name:
    Let the heart of them rejoice that seek the Lord.
11. Seek ye the Lord and his strength,
    Seek ye his face evermore.
12. Remember his marvellous works that he hath done;
    His wonders, and the judgments of his mouth;
13. O ye seed of Israel his servant,
    Ye children of Jacob, his chosen ones.
14. He is the Lord our God:
    His judgments are in all the earth.
15. Remember his covenant forever,
    The word which he commanded to a thousand generations;
16. The covenant which he made with Abraham,
    And his oath unto Isaac;
17. And confirmed the same unto Jacob for a statute,
    To Israel for an everlasting covenant:

15. So David and all the house of Israel brought up the ark of the Lord with shouting, and with the sound of the trumpet. 16. And it was so, as the ark of the Lord came into the city of David, that Michal the daughter of Saul looked out at the window, and saw king David leaping and dancing before the Lord; and she despised him in her heart.
20. Then David returned to bless his household. And Michal the daughter of Saul came out to meet David, and said, How glorious was the king of Israel to-day, who uncovered himself to-day in the eyes of the handmaids of his servants, as one of the vain fellows shamelessly uncovereth himself! 21. And David said unto Michal, It was before the Lord, which chose me above thy father, and above all his house, to appoint me prince over the people of the Lord, over Israel: therefore will I play before the Lord. 22. And I will be yet more vile than thus, and will be base in mine own sight: but of the handmaids which thou hast spoken of, of them shall I be had in honour. 23. And Michal the daughter of Saul had no child unto the day of her death.

17. And they brought in the ark of the Lord, and set it in its place in the midst of the tent that David had pitched for it: and David offered burnt offerings and peace offerings before the Lord. 18. And when David had made an end of offering the burnt offering and the peace offerings, he blessed the people in the name of the Lord of hosts. 19. And he dealt among all the people, even among the whole multitude of Israel, both to men and women, to every one a cake of bread, and a portion of flesh, and a cake of raisins. So all the people departed every one to his house.

28. Thus all Israel brought up the ark of the covenant of the Lord with shouting, and with the sound of the cornet, and with trumpets, and with cymbals, sounding aloud with psalteries and harps. 29. And it came to pass, as the ark of the covenant of the Lord came to the city of David, that Michal the daughter of Saul looked out at the window, and saw king David dancing and playing; and she despised him in her heart.

(I Chron. 16:) 1. And they brought in the ark of God, and set it in the midst of the tent that David had pitched for it: and they offered burnt offerings and peace offerings before God. 2. And when David had made an end of offering the burnt offering and the peace offerings, he blessed the people in the name of the Lord. 3. And he dealt to every one of Israel, both to man and woman, to every one a loaf of bread, and a portion of flesh, and a cake of raisins.

4. And he appointed certain of the Levites to minister before the ark of the Lord, and to celebrate and to thank and praise the Lord, the God of Israel: 5. Asaph the chief, and second to him Zechariah, Jeiel, and Shemiramoth, and Jehiel, and Mattithiah, and Eliab, and Benaiah, and Obed-edom, and Jeiel, with psalteries and with harps; and Asaph with cymbals, sounding aloud; 6. and Benaiah and Jahaziel the priests with trumpets continually, before the ark of the covenant of God.
7. Then on that day did David first ordain to give thanks unto the Lord, by the hand of Asaph and his brethren.

PSALM 105:

1. O give thanks unto the Lord, call upon his name;
Make known his doings among the peoples.

2. Sing unto him, sing praises unto him;
Talk ye of all his marvellous works.

3. Glory ye in his holy name:
Let the heart of them rejoice that seek the Lord.

4. Seek ye the Lord and his strength,
Seek ye his face evermore.

5. Remember his marvellous works which he hath done;
His wonders, and the judgements of his mouth;

6. O ye seed of Abraham his servant,
Ye children of Jacob, his chosen ones.

7. He is the Lord our God:
His judgements are in all the earth.

8. He hath remembered his covenant forever,
The word which he commanded to a thousand generations.

9. The covenant which he made with Abraham,
And his oath unto Isaac;

10. And confirmed the same unto Jacob for a statute,
To Israel for an everlasting covenant.

I CHRON. 16:

8. O give thanks unto the Lord, call upon his name;
Make known his doings among the peoples.

9. Sing unto him, sing praises unto him;
Talk ye of all his marvellous works.

10. Glory ye in his holy name:
Let the heart of them rejoice that seek the Lord.

11. Seek ye the Lord and his strength,
Seek ye his face evermore.

12. Remember his marvellous works which he hath done;
His wonders, and the judgements of his mouth;

13. O ye seed of Israel his servant,
Ye children of Jacob, his chosen ones.

14. He is the Lord our God:
His judgements are in all the earth.

15. Remember his covenant forever,
The word which he commanded to a thousand generations;

16. The covenant which he made with Abraham,
And his oath unto Isaac;

17. And he confirmed the same unto Jacob for a statute,
To Israel for an everlasting covenant.

18. Saying, Unto thee will I give the land of Canaan,
    The lot of your inheritance:
19. When ye were but a few men in number;
    Yea, very few, and sojourners in it;
20. And they went about from nation to nation,
    And from one kingdom to another people.
21. He suffered no man to do them wrong;
    Yea, he reproved kings for their sakes;
22. Saying, Touch not mine anointed ones,
    And do my prophets no harm.
23. Sing unto the Lord, all the earth;
    Shew forth his salvation from day to day.
24. Declare his glory among the nations,
    His marvellous works among all the peoples.
25. For great is the Lord, and highly to be praised:
    He also is to be feared above all gods.
26. For all the gods of the peoples are idols:
    But the Lord made the heavens.
27. Honour and majesty are before him:
    Strength and gladness are in his place.
28. Give unto the Lord, ye kindreds of the peoples,
    Give unto the Lord glory and strength.
29. Give unto the Lord the glory due unto his name:
    Bring an offering, and come before him:
    Worship the Lord in the beauty of holiness.
30. Tremble before him all the earth:
    The world also is stablished that it cannot be moved.
31. Let the heavens be glad, and let the earth rejoice;
    And let them say among the nations, The Lord reigneth.
32. Let the sea roar, and the fulness thereof;
    Let the field exult, and all that is therein;
33. Then shall the trees of the wood sing for joy before the Lord,
    For he cometh to judge the earth.
34. O give thanks unto the Lord; for he is good:
    For his mercy endureth forever.
35. And say ye, Save us, O God of our salvation,
    And gather us together and deliver us from the nations,
    To give thanks unto thy holy name,
    And to triumph in thy praise.
36. Blessed be the Lord, the God of Israel,
    From everlasting ever to everlasting.
    And all the people said, Amen, and praised the Lord.

37. So he left there, before the ark of the covenant of the Lord, Asaph and his brethren, to minister before the ark continually, as every day's work required: 38. and Obed-edom with their brethren, threescore and eight; Obed-edom also the son of Jeduthun and Hosah to be doorkeepers: 39. and Zadok the priest, and his brethren the priests, before the tabernacle of the Lord in the high place that was at Gibeon, to offer burnt offerings unto the Lord upon the altar of burnt offering continually morning and evening, even according to all that is written in the law of the Lord, which he commanded unto Israel; 41. and with them Heman and Jeduthun, and the rest that were chosen, who were expressed by name, to give thanks to the Lord, because his mercy endureth forever; 42. and with them Heman and Jeduthun with trumpets and cymbals for those that should sound aloud, and with instruments for the songs of God: and the sons of Jeduthun to be at the gate. 43. And all the people departed every man to his house: and David returned to bless his house.

11. Saying, Unto thee will I give the land of Canaan,
    The lot of your inheritance:
12. When they were but a few men in number;
    Yea, very few, and sojourners in it;
13. And they went about from nation to nation,
    From one kingdom to another people.
14. He suffered no man to do them wrong;
    Yea, he reproved kings for their sakes;
15. Saying, Touch not mine anointed ones,
    And do my prophets no harm.

PSALM 96.

^b_a1. Sing unto the Lord, all the earth.
2. Shew forth his salvation from day to day.
3. Declare his glory among the nations,
   His marvellous works among all the peoples.
4. For great is the Lord, and highly to be praised.
   He is to be feared above all gods.
5. For all the gods of the peoples are idols:
   But the Lord made the heavens.
6. Honour and majesty are before him:
   Strength and beauty are in his sanctuary.
7. Give unto the Lord, ye kindreds of the peoples,
   Give unto the Lord glory and strength.
8. Give unto the Lord the glory due unto his name:
   Bring an offering, and come into his courts.
9. O worship the Lord in the beauty of holiness:
   Tremble before him, all the earth.
10. (Say among the nations, the Lord reigneth:
    The world also is stablished that it cannot be moved:
    He shall judge the people with equity.
11. Let the heavens be glad, and let the earth rejoice;)
    Let the sea roar, and the fulness thereof;
12. Let the field exult, and all that is therein;
    Then shall all the trees of the wood sing for joy;
13. Before the Lord, for he cometh;
    For he cometh to judge the earth:

PSALM 106:1.

O give thanks unto the Lord; for he is good:
For his mercy endureth forever.
47. Save us, O Lord our God,
    And gather us from among the nations,
    To give thanks unto thy holy name,
    And to triumph in thy praise.
48. Blessed be the Lord, the God of Israel,
    From everlasting even to everlasting.
    And let all the people say, Amen.
    Praise ye the Lord.

18. Saying, Unto thee will I give the land of Canaan,
    The lot of your inheritance:
19. When they were but a few men in number;
    Yea, very few, and sojourners in it;
20. And they went about from nation to nation,
    And from one kingdom to another people.
21. He suffered no man to do them wrong;
    Yea, he reproved kings for their sakes;
22. Saying, Touch not mine anointed ones,
    And do my prophets no harm.
23. Sing unto the Lord, all the earth;
    Shew forth his salvation from day to day.
24. Declare his glory among the nations,
    His marvellous works among all the peoples.
25. For great is the Lord, and highly to be praised:
    He also is to be feared above all gods.
26. For all the gods of the peoples are idols:
    But the Lord made the heavens.
27. Honour and majesty are before him:
    Strength and gladness are in his place.
28. Give unto the Lord, ye kindreds of the peoples,
    Give unto the Lord glory and strength.
29. Give unto the Lord the glory due unto his name:
    Bring an offering, and come before him:

    Worship the Lord in the beauty of holiness.
30. Tremble before him all the earth:

    (The world is stablished that it cannot be moved.
31. Let the heavens be glad, and let the earth rejoice;
    And let them say among the nations, The Lord reigneth.)
32. Let the sea roar, and the fulness thereof;
    Let the field exult, and all that is therein;
33. Then shall all the trees of the wood sing for joy before
    the Lord,

    For he cometh to judge the earth.

34. O give thanks unto the Lord; for he is good:
    For his mercy endureth forever.
35. And say ye, Save us, O God of our salvation,
    And gather us together and deliver us from the nations,
    To give thanks unto thy holy name,
    And to triumph in thy praise.
36. Blessed be the Lord, the God of Israel,
    From everlasting even to everlasting.
    And all the people said, Amen, and praised the Lord.

THE HOUSE OF DAVID
    B. C. 1040 (Usher)
I David
    B. C. 1010 (Rev.)

SECTION XII

David's Victories

First Victory over the Ammonites

And it came to pass after this, that Nahash, the king of the children of Ammon, died and his son reigned in his stead. And David said, I will shew kindness unto Hanun the son of Nahash, because his father shewed kindness to me. So David sent messengers to comfort him concerning his father. And David's servants came into the land of the children of Ammon to Hanun, to comfort him. But the princes of the children of Ammon said unto Hanun their lord, Thinkest thou that David dost honour thy father, that he hath sent comforters unto thee? hath not David sent his servants unto thee to search the city, and to spy it out, and to overthrow it? So Hanun took David's servants, and shaved off the one half of their beards, and cut off their garments in the middle, even to their buttocks, and sent them away. Then there went certain, and told David how the men were served. And he sent to meet them; for they were greatly ashamed. And the king said, Tarry at Jericho until your beards be grown, and then return. And when the children of Ammon saw that they had made themselves odious to David, Hanun and the children of Ammon sent a thousand talents of silver and hired the Syrians of Beth-rehob, and the Syrians of Zobah, twenty thousand footmen, and the men of Tob twelve thousand men. So they hired them thirty and two thousand chariots, and the king of Maacah with a thousand men; who came and pitched before Medeba. And the children of Ammon gathered themselves together from their cities, and came to battle. And when David heard of it, he sent Joab, and all the host of the mighty men. And the children of Ammon came out, and put the battle in array at the entering of the gate: and the Syrians of Zobah and of Rehob, and the men of Tob and Maacah, were by themselves in the field. Now when Joab saw that the battle was set against him before and behind, he chose of all the choice men of Israel, and put them in array against the Syrians: And the rest of the people he committed into the hand of Abishai his brother, and they put themselves in array against the children of Ammon. And he said, If the Syrians be too strong for me, then thou shalt help me: but if the children of Ammon be too strong for thee, then I will come and help thee. Be of good courage, and let us play the men for our people, and for the cities of our God: and the Lord do that which seemeth him good. So Joab and the people that were with him drew nigh before the Syrians unto the battle: and they fled before him. And when the children of Ammon saw that the Syrians were fled, they likewise fled before Abishai his brother, and entered into the city. Then Joab returned from the children of Ammon, and came to Jerusalem.

SECT. XII   THE UNITED KINGDOM

David's Victories

(II Sam. 10:) 1. And it came to pass after this, that the king of the children of Ammon died, and Hanun his son reigned in his stead. 2. And David said, I will shew kindness unto Hanun the son of Nahash, as his father shewed kindness unto me. So David sent by the hand of his servants to comfort him concerning his father. And David's servants came into the land of the children of Ammon.

3. But the princes of the children of Ammon said unto Hanun their lord, Thinkest thou that David doth honour thy father, that he hath sent comforters unto thee? hath not David sent his servants unto thee to search the city, and to spy it out, and to overthrow it? 4. So Hanun took David's servants, and shaved off the one half of their beards, and cut off their garments in the middle, even to their buttocks, and sent them away.

5. When they told it unto David, he sent to meet them: for the men were greatly ashamed. And the king said, Tarry at Jericho until your beards be grown, and then return. 6. And when the children of Ammon saw that they were become odious to David, the children of Ammon sent ((and hired the Syrians of Beth-rehob, and the Syrians of Zobah, twenty thousand footmen, and the king of Maacah with a thousand men, and the men of Tob twelve thousand men.))

7. And when David heard of it, he sent Joab, and all the host of the mighty men. 8. And the children of Ammon came out, and put the battle in array at the entering in of the gate: (and the Syrians of Zobah, and of Rehob, and the men of Tob and Maacah), were by themselves in the field. 9. Now when Joab saw that the battle was set against him before and behind, he chose of all the choice men of Israel, and put them in array against the Syrians: 10. and the rest of the people he committed into the hand of Abishai his brother, and he put them in array against the children of Ammon. 11. And he said, If the Syrians be too strong for me, then thou shalt help me; but if the children of Ammon be too strong for thee, then I will come and help thee. 12. Be of good courage, and let us play the men for our people, and for the cities of our God: and the Lord do that which seemeth him good. 13. So Joab and the people that were with him drew nigh unto the battle against the Syrians: and they fled before him. 14. And when the children of Ammon saw that the Syrians were fled, they likewise fled before Abishai, and entered into the city. Then Joab returned from the children of Ammon, and came to Jerusalem.

(I Chron. 19:) 1. And it came to pass after this, that Nahash the king of the children of Ammon died, and his son reigned in his stead. 2. And David said, I will shew kindness unto Hanun the son of Nahash, because his father shewed kindness unto me. So David sent messengers to comfort him concerning his father. And David's servants came into the land of the children of Ammon to Hanun, to comfort him.

3. But the princes of the children of Ammon said to Hanun, Thinkest thou that David dost honour thy father, that he hath sent comforters unto thee? are not his servants come unto thee for to search, and to overthrow, and to spy out the land? 4. So Hanun took David's servants, and shaved them, and cut off their garments in the middle, even to their buttocks, and sent them away.

5. Then there were certain that told David how the men were served. And he sent to meet them: for the men were greatly ashamed. And the king said, Tarry at Jericho until your beards be grown, and then return. 6. And when the children of Ammon saw that they had made themselves odious to David, Hanun and the children of Ammon sent ((a thousand talents of silver to hire them chariots and horsemen out of Mesopotamia, and out of Aram-maacah, and out of Zobah. 7. So they hired them thirty and two thousand chariots, and the king of Maacah and his people:)) who came and pitched before Medeba. And the children of Ammon gathered themselves together from their cities, and came to battle.

8. And when David heard of it, he sent Joab and all the host of the mighty men. 9. And the children of Ammon came out, and put the battle in array at the gate of the city: (and the kings that were come) were by themselves in the field. 10. Now when Joab saw that the battle was set against him before and behind, he chose of all the choice men of Israel, and put them in array against the Syrians: 11. And the rest of the people he committed into the hand of Abishai his brother, and they put themselves in array against the children of Ammon. 12. And he said, If the Syrians be too strong for me, then thou shalt help me; but if the children of Ammon be too strong for thee, then I will come and help thee. 13. Be of good courage, and let us play the men for our people, and for the cities of our God; and the Lord do that which seemeth him good. 14. So Joab and the people that were with him drew nigh before the Syrians unto the battle; and they fled before him. 15. And when the children of Ammon saw that the Syrians were fled, they likewise fled before Abishai, and entered into the city. Then Joab came to Jerusalem.

Victory over the Syrians

And when the Syrians saw that they were put to the worse before Israel, they gathered themselves together. And Hadarezer sent, and drew out the Syrians that were beyond the River: and they came to Helam, with Shobach the captain of the host of Hadarezer at their head. And it was told David: and he gathered all Israel together, and passed over Jordan, and came upon them at Helam, and set the battle in array against them. And the Syrians set themselves in array against David, and fought with him. And the Syrians fled before Israel; and David slew of the Syrians the men of seven hundred * chariots, and forty thousand footmen, and killed Shobach the captain of their hosts, that he died there.

And when all the kings that were servants to Hadarezer saw that they were put to the worse before Israel, they made peace with David, and served him. So the Syrians feared to help the children of Ammon any more.

Second Victory over the Ammonites

And it came to pass, at the time of the return of the year, at the time when kings go out to battle, that David sent Joab, and his servants with him, and all Israel: and they wasted the country of the children of Ammon, and came and besieged Rabbah. But David tarried at Jerusalem.

David's Double Sin

II Sam. 11:2. And it came to pass at eventide, that David arose from off his bed, and walked upon the roof of the king's house: and from the roof he saw a woman bathing: and the woman was very beautiful to look upon. 3. And David sent and inquired after the woman. And one said, Is not this Bath-sheba, the daughter of Eliam, the wife of Uriah the Hittite? 4. And David sent messengers, and took her; and she came in unto him, and he lay with her, (for she was purified from her uncleanness;) and she returned unto her house. 5. And the woman conceived, and she sent and told David, and said, I am with child. 6. And David sent to Joab, saying, Send me Uriah the Hittite. And Joab sent Uriah to David. 7. And when Uriah was come unto him, David asked of him how Joab did, and how the people fared, and how the war prospered. 8. And David said to Uriah, Go down to thy house and wash thy feet. And Uriah departed out of the king's house, and there followed him a mess of meat from the king. But Uriah slept at the door of the king's house with all the servants of his lord, and went not down to his house. 10. And when they had told David, saying, Uriah went not down unto his house, David said unto Uriah, Art thou not come from a journey? wherefore didst thou not go down unto thine house? 11. And Uriah said unto David, The ark, and Israel, and Judah, abide in booths, and my lord Joab, and the servants of my lord are encamped in the open field; shall I then go into mine house, to eat and to drink, and to lie with my wife? as thou livest, and as thy soul liveth, I will not do this thing. 12. And David said to Uriah, Tarry here to-day also, and to-morrow I will let thee depart. So Uriah abode in Jerusalem that day, and the morrow. 13. And when David did call him, he did eat and drink before him; and he made him drunk: and at even he went out to lie on his bed with the servants of his lord, but went not down to his house. 14. And it came to pass in the morning, that David wrote a letter to Joab, and sent it by the hand of Uriah. 15. And he wrote in the letter, saying, Set ye Uriah in the forefront of the hottest battle, and retire ye from him, that he may be smitten, and die. 16. And it came to pass, when Joab kept watch upon the city, that he assigned Uriah unto the place where he knew that valiant men were. 17. And the men of the city went out, and fought with Joab: and there fell some of the people, even of the servants of David; and Uriah the Hittite died also. 18. Then Joab sent and told David all the things concerning the war;

---
* Chronicles, seven thousand. Appendix C. Chronicles III. i (1).

SECT. XII　　　　THE UNITED KINGDOM　　　　67

15. And when the Syrians saw that they were put to the worse before Israel, they gathered themselves together. 16. And Hadarezer sent, and brought out the Syrians that were beyond the River: and they came to Helam, with Shobach the captain of the host of Hadarezer at their head. 17. And it was told David: and he gathered all Israel together, and passed over Jordan, and came to Helam.

(And the Syrians set themselves in array against David,) and fought with him. 18. And the Syrians fled before Israel; and David slew of the Syrians the men of ((seven hundred)) chariots, and forty thousand horsemen, and smote Shobach the captain of their hosts, that he died there. 19. And when all the kings that were servants to Hadarezer saw that they were put to worse before Israel, they made peace with Israel, and served them. So the Syrians feared to help the children of Ammon any more.

II Sam. 11:

1. And it came to pass, at the return of the year, at the time when kings go out to battle, (that David sent Joab, and his servants with him, and all Israel: and they destroyed the children of Ammon,) and besieged Rabbah. But David tarried at Jerusalem.

16. And when the Syrians saw that they were put to the worse before Israel, they sent messengers, and drew forth the Syrians that were beyond the River, with Shophach the captain of the host of Hadarezer at their head. 17. And it was told David: and he gathered all Israel together, and passed over Jordan, and came upon them, and set the battle in array against them.

(So when David had put the battle in array against the Syrians,) they fought with him. 18. And the Syrians fled before Israel; and David slew of the Syrians the men of ((seven thousand)) chariots, and forty thousand footmen, and killed Shophach the captain of the host. 19. And when the servants of Hadarezer saw that they were put to worse before Israel, they made peace with David, and served him: neither would the Syrians help the children of Ammon any more.

I Chron. 20:

1ª. And it came to pass, at the time of the return of the year, at the time when kings go out to battle, (that Joab led forth the power of the army, and wasted the country of the children of Ammon,) and came and besieged Rabbah. But David tarried at Jerusalem.

19. and he charged the messenger, saying, When thou hast made an end of telling all the things concerning the war unto the king, 20. it shall be that, if the king's wrath arise, and he say unto thee, Wherefore went ye so nigh unto the city to fight? knew ye not that they would shoot from the wall? 21. who smote Abimelech the son of Jerubbesheth? did not a woman cast an upper millstone upon him from the wall, that he died at Thebez? why went ye so nigh the wall? then shalt thou say, Thy servant Uriah the Hittite is dead also. 22. So the messenger went, and came and shewed David all that Joab had sent him for. 23. And the messenger said unto David, The men prevailed against us, and came out unto us into the field, and we were upon them even unto the entering of the gate. 24. And the shooters shot at thy servants from off the wall: and some of the king's servants be dead, and thy servant Uriah the Hittite is dead also. 25. Then David said unto the messenger, Thus shalt thou say unto Joab, Let not this thing displease thee, for the sword devoureth one as well as another: make thy battle more strong against the city, and overthrow it: and encourage thou him. 26. And when the wife of Uriah heard that Uriah her husband was dead, she made lamentation for her husband. 27. And when the mourning was past, David sent and took her home to his house, and she became his wife, and bare him a son. But the thing that David had done displeased the Lord.

Nathan's Rebuke and David's Penitence

II Sam. 12:1. And the Lord sent Nathan unto David. And he came unto him, and said unto him. There were two men in one city: the one rich, and the other poor. 2. The rich man had exceeding many flocks and herds: 3. but the poor man had nothing save one little ewe lamb, which he had bought and nourished up: and it grew up together with him, and with his children; it did eat of his own morsel, and drank of his own cup, and lay in his bosom, and was unto him as a daughter. 4. And there came a traveler unto the rich man, and he spared to take of his own flock and of his own herd, to dress for the wayfaring man that was come unto him, but took the poor man's lamb, and dressed it for the man that was come to him. 5. And David's anger was greatly kindled against the man; and he said to Nathan, As the Lord liveth, the man that hath done this is worthy to die: 6. and he shall restore the lamb fourfold—because he did this thing, and because he had no pity. 7. And Nathan said to David, Thou art the man. Thus saith the Lord, the God of Israel, I anointed thee king over Israel, and I delivered thee out of the hand of Saul, 8. and I gave thee thy master's house, and thy master's wives into thy bosom, and gave thee the house of Israel and of Judah and if that had been too little, I would have added unto thee such and such things. 9. Wherefore hast thou despised the word of the Lord, to do that which is evil in his sight? thou hast smitten Uriah the Hittite with the sword, and hast taken his wife to be thy wife, and hast slain him with the sword of the children of Ammon. 10. Now therefore, the sword shall never depart from thine house; because thou hast despised me, and hast taken the wife of Uriah the Hittite to be thy wife. 11. Thus saith the Lord, Behold, I will raise up evil against thee out of thine own house, and I will take thy wives before thine eyes, and give them unto thy neighbour, and he shall lie with thy wives in the sight of this sun. 12. For thou didst it secretly: but I will do this thing before all Israel, and before the sun. 13. And David said unto Nathan, I have sinned against the Lord. And Nathan said unto David, The Lord hath put away thy sin; thou shalt not die. 14. Howbeit, because by this deed thou hast given great occasion to the enemies of the Lord to blaspheme, the child also that is born unto thee shall surely die. 15. And Nathan departed unto his house.* And the Lord struck the child that Uriah's wife bare unto David, and it was very sick. 16. David therefore besought God for the child, and David fasted, and went in, and lay all night upon the earth. 17. And the elders of his house arose, and stood beside him, to raise him up from the earth: but he would not, neither did he eat bread with them. 18. And it came to pass on the seventh day, that the child died. And the servants of David feared to tell him that the child was dead: for they said, Behold, while the child was yet alive, we spake unto him, and he hearkened not unto our voice: how will he then vex himself, if we tell him that the child is dead? 19. But when David saw that his servants whispered together, David perceived that the child was dead: and David said unto his servants, Is the child dead? And they said, He is dead. 20. Then David arose from the earth, and washed, and anointed himself, and changed his apparel; and he came into the house of the Lord, and worshipped: then he came to his own house; and when he required they set bread before him, and he did eat. 21. Then said his servants unto him, What thing is this that thou hast done? thou didst fast and weep for the child, while it was alive; but when the child was dead, thou didst rise and eat bread. 22. And he said, While the child was yet alive, I fasted and wept: for I said, Who knoweth whether the Lord will not be gracious to me, that the child may live? 23. But now he is dead, Wherefore should I fast? can I bring him back again? I shall go to him, but he shall not return to me. 24. And David comforted Bath-sheba his wife, and went in unto her, and lay with her: and she bare a son, and he called his name Solomon. 25. And the Lord loved him; and he sent by the hand of Nathan the prophet, and he called his name Jedidiah, for the Lord's sake,

*A Psalm of David: when Nathan the prophet came unto him, after he had gone in to Bath-sheba.

PSALM 51.

1. Have mercy upon me, O God, according to thy loving kindness:
   According to the multitude of thy tender mercies blot out my transgressions.
2. Wash me throughly from mine iniquity,
   And cleanse me from my sin.
3. For I acknowledge my transgressions:
   And my sin is ever before me.
4. Against thee, thee only, have I sinned,
   And done that which is evil in thy sight:
   That thou mayest be justified when thou speakest,
   And be clear when thou judgest.
5. Behold, I was shapen in iniquity:
   And in sin did my mother conceive me.
6. Behold thou desirest truth in the inward parts:
   And in the hidden part thou shalt make me to know wisdom.
7. Purge me with hyssop, and I shall be clean:
   Wash me, and I shall be whiter than snow.
8. Make me to hear joy and gladness;
   That the bones which thou hast broken may rejoice.
9. Hide thy face from my sins,
   And blot out all mine iniquities.
10. Create in me a clean heart, O God;
    And renew a right spirit within me.
11. Cast me not away from thy presence;
    And take not thy holy spirit from me.
12. Restore unto me the joy of thy salvation:
    And uphold me with a free spirit.
13. Then will I teach transgressors thy ways;
    And sinners shall be converted unto thee.
14. Deliver me from bloodguiltiness, O God, thou God of my salvation;
    And my tongue shall sing aloud of thy righteousness.
15. O Lord, open thou my lips;
    And my mouth shall shew forth thy praise.
16. For thou delightest not in sacrifice; else would I give it:
    Thou hast no pleasure in burnt offering.
17. The sacrifices of God are a broken spirit:
    A broken and a contrite heart, O God, thou wilt not despise.
18. Do good in thy good pleasure unto Zion:
    Build thou the walls of Jerusalem.
19. Then shalt thou delight in the sacrifices of righteousness, in burnt offering and whole burnt offering:
    Then shall they offer bullocks upon thine altar.

PSALM 32.

1. Blessed is the man whose transgression is forgiven, whose sin is covered.
2. Blessed is the man unto whom the Lord imputeth not iniquity,
   And in whose spirit there is no guile.
3. When I kept silence, my bones waxed old
   Through my roaring all the day long.
4. For day and night thy hand was heavy upon me:
   My moisture was changed as with the drought of summer.
   Selah
5. I acknowledge my sin unto thee, and mine iniquity have I not hid:
   I said I will confess my transgressions unto the Lord;
   And thou forgavest the iniquity of my sin. Selah
6. For this let every one that is godly pray unto thee in a time when thou mayest be found:
   Surely when the great waters overflow they shall not reach unto him.
7. Thou art my hiding place; thou wilt preserve me from trouble;
   Thou wilt compass me about with songs of deliverance.
   Selah

Capture of Rabbah

Now Joab fought against Rabbah of the children of Ammon, and smote, overthrew, and took the royal city. And Joab sent messengers to David, and said, I have fought against Rabbah, yea, I have taken the city of waters. Now therefore gather the rest of the people together, and encamp against the city and take it: lest I take the city, and it be called after my name. And David gathered all the people together, and went to Rabbah, and fought against it, and took it. And David took the crown of their king from off his head; and the weight thereof was a talent of gold, and in it were precious stones; and it was set on David's head: and he brought forth the spoil of the city exceeding much. And he brought forth the people that were therein, and put them under saws, and under harrows of iron, and under axes of iron, and made them pass through the brickkiln: and thus did he unto all the cities of Ammon. And David and all the people returned unto Jerusalem.

Victory over Moab

And he smote Moab, and measured them with a line, making them to lie down on the ground: and he measured two lines to put to death and one full line to keep alive. And the Moabites became servants to David, and brought presents.

Victory over Hadadezer

David smote also Hadadezer the son of Rehob, king of Zobah unto Hamath, as he went to stablish his dominion by the river Euphrates. And David took from him a thousand chariots and seven* thousand horsemen, and twenty thousand footmen: and David houghed all the chariot horses, but reserved of them for an hundred chariots.

Victory over the Syrians

And when the Syrians of Damascus came to succour Hadadezer king of Zobah, David smote of the Syrians two and twenty thousand men. Then David put garrisons in Syria of Damascus: and the Syrians became servants to David, and brought presents. And the Lord gave victory to David whithersoever he went. And David took the shields of gold that were on the servants of Hadadezer, and brought them to Jerusalem. And from Betah and from Berothai, cities of Hadadezer, king David took exceeding much brass, wherewith Solomon made the brazen sea, and the pillars and the vessels of brass. And when Toi king of Hamath heard that David had smitten all the host of Hadadezer king of Zobah, then Toi sent Joram his son unto king David, to salute him, and to bless him, because he had fought against Hadadezer and smitten him: for Hadadezer had wars with Toi. And Joram brought with him vessels of silver, and vessels of gold, and vessels of brass. These also did king David dedicate unto the Lord, with the silver and the gold that he carried away from all the nations which he subdued: of Syria, and of Moab, and of the children of Ammon, and of Amelek, and of the spoil of Hadadezer, son of Rehob king of Zobah.

Victory in the Valley of Salt

† And David gat him a name when he returned with Abishai the son of Zeruiah from smiting of the ‡ Syrians in the Valley of Salt, even eighteen thousand men. And he put garrisons in Edom: throughout all Edom put he garrisons, and all the Edomites became servants to David. And the Lord gave victory to David whithersoever he went.

---

* In Samuel 1700. See Chronicles Appendix C. III. 1 (3).
† Psalm LX.
‡ In Chronicles, *Edomites*.

SECT. XII   THE UNITED KINGDOM   71

The Capture of Rabbah

(II Sam. 12:) 26. Now Joab fought against Rabbah of the children of Ammon, and took the royal city. 27. And Joab sent messengers to David, and said, I have fought against Rabbah, yea, I have taken the city of waters. 28. Now therefore gather the rest of the people together, and encamp against the city and take it: lest I take the city, and it be called after my name. 29. And David gathered all the people together, and went to Rabbah, and fought against it, and took it. 30. And he took the crown of their king from off his head; and the weight thereof was a talent of gold, and in it were precious stones; and it was set on David's head. And he brought forth the spoil of the city exceeding much. 31. And he brought forth the people that were therein, and put them under saws, and under harrows of iron, and under axes of iron, and made them pass through the brickkiln: and thus did he unto all the cities of Ammon. And David and all the people returned unto Jerusalem.

(II Sam. 8:) 2. And he smote Moab, and measured them with a line, making them to lie down on the ground; and he measured two lines to put to death, and one full line to keep alive. And the Moabites became servants to David, and brought presents.

3. David smote also Hadadezer the son of Rehob king of Zobah, as he went to recover his dominion at the River. 4. And David took from him ((a thousand and seven hundred horsemen)) and twenty thousand footmen: and David houghed all the chariot horses, but reserved of them for an hundred chariots.

5. And when the Syrians of Damascus came to succour Hadadezer king of Zobah, David smote of the Syrians two and twenty thousand men. 6. Then David put garrisons in Syria of Damascus: and the Syrians became servants to David, and brought presents. And the Lord gave victory to David whithersoever he went.

7. And David took the shields of gold that were on the servants of Hadadezer, and brought them to Jerusalem. 8. And from Betah and from Berothai, cities of Hadadezer, king David took exceeding much brass.

9. And when Toi king of Hamath heard that David had smitten all the host of Hadadezer, 10. then Toi sent Joram his son unto king David, to salute him, and to bless him, because he had fought against Hadadezer and smitten him: for Hadadezer had wars with Toi. And Joram brought with him vessels of silver, and vessels of gold, and vessels of brass: 11. these also did king David dedicate unto the Lord, with the silver and gold that he dedicated of all the nations which he subdued; 12. of Syria, and of Moab, and of the children of Ammon, and of the Philistines, and of Amalek, and of the spoil of Hadadezer, son of Rehob king of Zobah.

13. (And David gat him a name when he returned from smiting of the Syrians in the Valley of Salt, even eighteen thousand men.) 14. And he put garrisons in Edom: throughout all Edom put he garrisons, and all the Edomites became servants to David. And the Lord gave victory to David whithersoever he went.

(I Chron. 20:) 1b. And Joab smote Rabbah, and overthrew it.

2. And David took the crown of their king from off his head, and found it to weigh a talent of gold, and there were precious stones in it; and it was set upon David's head: and he brought forth the spoil of the city, exceeding much. 3. And he brought forth the people that were therein, and cut them with saws, and with harrows of iron, and with axes. and thus did David unto all the cities of Ammon. And David and all the people returned to Jerusalem.

(I Chron. 18:) 2. And he smote Moab;

and the Moabites became servants to David and brought presents.

3. And David smote Hadarezer king of Zobah unto Hamath, as he went to stablish his dominion by the river Euphrates. 4. And David took from him ((a thousand chariots and seven thousand horsemen)) and twenty thousand footmen: and David houghed all the chariot horses, but reserved of them for an hundred chariots.

5. And when the Syrians of Damascus came to succour Hadarezer king of Zobah, David smote of the Syrians two and twenty thousand men. 6. Then David put garrisons in Syria of Damascus: and the Syrians became servants to David, and brought presents. And the Lord gave victory to David whithersoever he went.

7. And David took the shields of gold that were on the servants of Hadarezer, and brought them to Jerusalem. 8. And from Tibhath and from Cun, cities of Hadarezer, David took very much brass, wherewith Solomon made the brasen sea, and the pillars, and the vessels of brass.

9. And when Tou king of Hamath heard that David had smitten all the host of Hadarezer king of Zobah, 10. he sent Hadoram his son to king David, to salute him, and to bless him, because he had fought against Hadarezer and smitten him: for Hadarezer had wars with Tou, and he had with him all manner of vessels of gold and silver and brass. 11. These also did king David dedicate unto the Lord, with the silver and the gold that he carried away from all the nations; from Edom, and from Moab, and from the children of Ammon, and from the Philistines, and from Amalek.

12. (Moreover Abishai the son of Zeruiah smote of the Edomites in the valley of Salt eighteen thousand.) 13. And he put garrisons in Edom; and all the Edomites became servants to David. And the Lord gave victory to David whithersoever he went.

A House for the Ark

And it came to pass, when David dwelt in his house and the Lord had given him rest from all his enemies round about, that David said unto Nathan the prophet, Lo, I dwell in an house of cedar, but the ark of the covenant of the Lord dwelleth within curtains. And Nathan said unto David, Do all that is in thine heart, for God is with thee. And it came to pass the same night that the word of God came to Nathan, saying, Go and tell David my servant, Thus saith the Lord, Thou shalt not build me an house to dwell in: for I have not dwelt in an house since the day that I brought up the children of Israel out of Egypt even to this day, but have gone from tent to tent, and from one tabernacle to another. In all places wherein I have walked with all the children of Israel, spake I a word to any of the tribes of Israel, whom I commanded to feed my people Israel, saying, Why have ye not built me an house of cedar?

Promises Made to David

Now therefore thus shalt thou say unto my servant David, Thus saith the Lord of hosts, I took thee from the sheepcote, from following the sheep, that thou shouldest be prince over my people Israel: and I have been with thee whithersoever thou wentest, and have cut off all thine enemies from before thee, and I will make thee a great name, like unto the name of the great ones that are in the earth. And I will appoint a place for my people Israel, and will plant them, that they may dwell in their own place, and be moved no more, neither shall the children of wickedness afflict them any more, as at the first, and as from the day that I commanded judges to be over my people Israel; and I will subdue all thine enemies. Moreover I tell thee that the Lord will build thee an house. And it shall come to pass, when thy days be fulfilled, and thou shalt sleep with thy fathers, I will set up thy seed after thee, which shall proceed out of thy bowels, and I will establish his kingdom. He shall build me an house for my name, and I will establish the throne of his kingdom for ever. I will be his father, and he shall be my son: if he commit iniquity, I will chasten him with the rod of men, and with the stripes of the children of men: and I will not take my mercy away from him, as I took it away from Saul, whom I put away from before thee. And thine house and thy kingdom shall be made sure for ever before thee: thy throne shall be established for ever. According to all these words, and according to all this vision, so did Nathan speak unto David.

David's Response

Then David the king went in, and sat before the Lord; and he said, Who am I, O Lord God, and what is my house, that thou hast brought me thus far? And this was yet a small thing in thine eyes, O Lord God: but thou hast spoken also of thy servant's house for a great while to come, and hast regarded me according to the estate of a man of high degree, O Lord God. And what can David say yet more unto thee concerning the honour which is done unto thy servant? for thou knowest thy servant, O Lord God. For thy word's sake, and according to thine own heart, hast thou wrought all this greatness, to make thy servant know it. Wherefore thou art great, O Lord God: for there is none like thee, neither is there any God beside thee, according to all that we have heard with our ears. And what one nation in the earth is like thy people Israel, whom God went to redeem unto himself for a people, and to make him a name by great and terrible things, in driving out nations from before thy people, which thou redeemest out of Egypt, from the nations and

David's Desire to Build an House for the Ark

(II Sam. 7:) 1. And it came to pass, when the king dwelt in his house, and the Lord had given him rest from all his enemies round about, 2. that the king said unto Nathan the prophet, See now I dwell in an house of cedar, but the ark of God dwelleth within curtains. 3. And Nathan said to the king, Go, do all that is in thine heart, for the Lord is with thee. 4. And it came to pass the same night that the word of the Lord came unto Nathan, saying, 5. Go and tell my servant David, Thus saith the Lord, Shalt thou build me an house for me to dwell in? 6. for I have not dwelt in an house since the day that I brought up the children of Israel out of Egypt even to this day, but have walked in a tent and in a tabernacle.

7. In all places wherein I have walked with all the children of Israel, spake I a word with any of the tribes of Israel, whom I commanded to feed my people Israel, saying, Why have ye not built me an house of cedar?

8. Now therefore thus shalt thou say unto my servant David, Thus saith the Lord of hosts, I took thee from the sheepcote, from following the sheep, that thou shouldest be prince over my people, over Israel: 9. and I have been with thee whithersoever thou wentest, and have cut off all thine enemies from before thee; and I will make thee a great name, like unto the name of the great ones that are in the earth.

10. And I will appoint a place for my people Israel, and will plant them, that they may dwell in their own place, and be moved no more, neither shall the children of wickedness afflict them any more, as at the first, 11. and as from the day that I commanded judges to be over my people Israel; and I will cause thee to rest from all thine enemies. Moreover the Lord telleth thee that the Lord will make thee an house. 12. When thy days be fulfilled, and thou shalt sleep with thy fathers, I will set up thy seed after thee, which shall proceed out of thy bowels, and I will establish his kingdom. 13. He shall build an house for my name, and I will establish the throne of his kingdom for ever.

14. I will be his father, and he shall be my son: if he commit iniquity, I will chasten him with the rod of men, and with the stripes of the children of men; 15. but my mercy shall not depart from him, as I took it from Saul, whom I put away before thee. 16. And thine house and thy kingdom shall be made sure for ever before thee: thy throne shall be established for ever. 17. According to all these words, and according to all this vision, so did Nathan speak unto David.

18. Then David the king went in, and sat before the Lord; and he said, Who am I, O Lord God, and what is my house, that thou hast brought me thus far? 19. And this was yet a small thing in thine eyes, O Lord God; but thou hast spoken also of thy servant's house for a great while to come, (and this too after the manner of men, O Lord God!) 20. And what can David say more unto thee? for thou knowest thy servant, O Lord God. 21. For thy word's sake, and according to thine own heart, hast thou wrought all this greatness, to make thy servant know it.

22. Wherefore thou art great, O Lord God: for there is none like thee, neither is there any God beside thee, according to all that we have heard with our ears. 23. And what one nation in the earth is like thy people, even like Israel, whom God went to redeem unto himself for a people, (and to make him a name, and to do great things for you, and terrible things for thy land, before thy people,) which thou redeemest to thee out of Egypt, from the nations and their gods?

(I Chron. 17:) 1. And it came to pass, when David dwelt in his house, that David said to Nathan the prophet, Lo, I dwell in an house of cedar, but the ark of the covenant of the Lord dwelleth under curtains. 2. And Nathan said unto David, Do all that is in thine heart, for God is with thee. 3. And it came to pass the same night, that the word of God came to Nathan, saying, 4. Go, and tell David my servant, Thus saith the Lord, Thou shalt not build me an house to dwell in: 5. for I have not dwelt in an house since the day that I brought up Israel unto this day, but have gone from tent to tent, and from one tabernacle to another.

6. In all places wherein I have walked with all Israel, spake I a word with any of the judges of Israel, whom I commanded to feed my people saying, Why have ye not built me an house of cedar?

7. Now therefore thus shalt thou say unto my servant David, Thus saith the Lord of hosts, I took thee from the sheepcote, from following the sheep, that thou shouldest be prince over my people Israel: 8. and I have been with thee whithersoever thou wentest, and have cut off all thine enemies from before thee; and I will make thee a name, like unto the name of the great ones that are in the earth.

9. And I will appoint a place for my people Israel, and will plant them, that they may dwell in their own place, and be moved no more; neither shall the children of wickedness waste them any more, as at the first, 10. and as from the day that I commanded judges to be over my people Israel; and I will subdue all thine enemies. Moreover I tell thee that the Lord will build thee an house. 11. And it shall come to pass, when thy days be fulfilled that thou must go to be with thy fathers, I will set up thy seed after thee, which shall be of thy sons; and I will establish his kingdom. 12. He shall build me an house, and I will establish his throne for ever.

13. I will be his father, and he shall be my son; and I will not take my mercy away from him, as I took it from him that was before thee: 14. but I will settle him in mine house and in my kingdom for ever: and his throne shall be established for ever. 15. According to all these words, and according to all this vision, so did Nathan speak unto David.

16 Then David the king went in, and sat before the Lord; and he said, Who am I, O Lord God, and what is my house, that thou hast brought me thus far? 17. And this was a small thing in thine eyes, O God; but thou hast spoken of thy servant's house for a great while to come, (and hast regarded me according to the estate of a man of high degree, O Lord God.) 18. What can David say yet more unto thee concerning the honour which is done to thy servant? for thou knowest thy servant, 19. O Lord. For thy servant's sake, and according to thine own heart, hast thou wrought all this greatness, to make known all these great things.

20. O Lord, there is none like thee, neither is there any God beside thee, according to all that we have heard with our ears. 21. And what one nation in the earth is like thy people, Israel, whom God went to redeem unto himself for a people, (and to make thee a name by great and terrible things, in driving out nations from before thy people,) which thou redeemest out of Egypt?

their gods? And thou didst establish to thyself thy people Israel to be a people unto thee for ever; and thou Lord, becamest their God. And now, O Lord God, let the word that thou hast spoken concerning thy servant, and concerning his house, be established for ever, and do as thou hast spoken. And let thy name be established and magnified for ever, saying, The Lord of hosts is the God of Israel, even a God to Israel: and the house of thy servant David shall be established before thee. For thou, O Lord of hosts, the God of Israel, hast revealed to thy servant, saying, I will build thee a house: therefore hast thy servant found in his heart to pray this prayer unto thee. And now, O Lord God, thou art God, and thy words are truth, and thou hast promised this good thing unto thy servant: now therefore let it please thee to bless the house of thy servant, that it may continue for ever before thee: for thou, O Lord God, hast spoken it: and with thy blessing let the house of thy servant be blessed for ever.

24. (And thou didst establish to thyself thy people Israel to be a people unto thee for ever;) and thou, Lord, becamest their God.
25. And now, O Lord God, the word that thou hast spoken concerning thy servant, and concerning his house, confirm thou it for ever, and do as thou hast spoken.
26. And let thy name be   magnified for ever, saying, The Lord of hosts is God over Israel:
        and the house of thy servant David shall be established before thee. 27. For thou, O Lord of hosts, the God of Israel, hast revealed to thy servant, saying, I will build thee a house: therefore hath thy servant found in his heart to pray this prayer unto thee.
28. And now, O Lord God, thou art God, and thy words are truth, and thou hast promised this good thing unto thy servant: 30. now therefore let it please thee to bless the house of thy servant, that it may continue for ever before thee: for thou, O Lord God, hast spoken it: and with thy blessing let the house of thy servant be blessed for ever.

22. (For thy people Israel didst thou make thine own people for ever:)   and thou, Lord, becamest their God.
23. And now, O Lord, let the word that thou hast spoken concerning thy servant, and concerning his house, be established for ever, and do as thou hast spoken.
24. And let thy name be established and magnified for ever, saying, The Lord of hosts is the God of Israel, even a God to Israel: and the house of David thy servant is established before thee. 25. For thou, O my God,
        hast revealed to thy servant that thou wilt build him an house: therefore hath thy servant found in his heart to pray   before thee.
26. And now, O Lord,   thou art God,
        and   hast promised this good thing unto thy servant: 27. and now it hath pleased thee to bless the house of thy servant, that it may continue for ever before thee: for thou, O Lord, hast blessed,
        and it is blessed for ever.

THE HOUSE OF DAVID
    B. C. 1049 (Usher)
I David
    B. C. 1010 (Rev.)

NATHAN

SECTION XIII

Family Troubles

Amnon's Incest

II Sam. 13:1. And it came to pass after this, that Absalom the son of David had a fair sister, whose name was Tamar; and Amnon the son of David loved her. 2. And Amnon was so vexed that he fell sick because of his sister Tamar; for she was a virgin; and it seemed hard to Amnon to do anything unto her. 3. But Amnon had a friend, whose name was Jonadab, the son of Shimeah David's brother: and Jonadab was a very subtil man. 4. And he said unto him, Why, O son of the king, art thou thus lean from day to day? wilt thou not tell me? And Amnon said unto him, I love Tamar, my brother Absalom's sister. 5. And Jonadab said unto him, Lay thee down on thy bed, and feign thyself sick: and when thy father cometh to see thee say unto him, Let my sister Tamar come, I pray thee, and give me bread to eat, and dress the food in my sight, that I may see it, and eat at her hand. 6. So Amnon lay down, and feigned himself sick: and when the king was come to see him, Amnon said unto the king, Let my sister Tamar come, I pray thee, and make a couple of cakes in my sight, that I may eat at her hand. 7. Then David sent home to Tamar, saying, Go now to thy brother Amnon's house, and dress him food. 8. So Tamar went to her brother Amnon's house; and he was laid down. And she took dough, and kneaded it, and made cakes in his sight, and did bake the cakes. 9. And she took the pan, and poured them out before him; but he refused to eat. And Amnon said, Have out all men from me. And they went out every man from him. 10. And Amnon said unto Tamar, Bring the food into the chamber, that I may eat of thine hand. And Tamar took the cakes which she had made, and brought them into the chamber to Amnon her brother. 11. And when she had brought them near unto him to eat, he took hold of her, and said unto her, Come lie with me my sister. 12. And she answered him, Nay, my brother, do not force me; for no such thing ought to be done in Israel: do not thou this folly. 13. And I, whither shall I carry my shame? and as for thee, thou shalt be as one of the fools in Israel. Now therefore, I pray thee, speak unto the king; for he will not withhold me from thee. 14. Howbeit he would not hearken unto her voice: but being stronger than she, he forced her, and lay with her. 15. Then Amnon hated her with exceeding great hatred, for the hatred wherewith he hated her was greater than the love wherewith he had loved her. And Amnon said unto her, Arise, be gone. 16. And she said unto him, Not so, because this great wrong in putting me forth is worse than the other that thou didst unto me. But he would not hearken unto her. 17. Then he called his servant that ministered unto him, and said, Put now this woman out from me, and bolt the door after her. 18. And she had a garment of divers colours upon her; for with such robes were the king's daughters that were virgins apparelled. Then his servant brought her out, and bolted the door after her. 19. And Tamar put ashes on her head, and rent her garment of divers colours that was on her; and she laid her hand on her head, and went her way, crying aloud as she went. 20. And Absalom her brother said unto her, Hath Amnon thy brother been with thee? but now hold thy peace, my sister: he is thy brother; take not this thing to heart. So Tamar remained desolate in her brother Absalom's house. 21. But when king David heard of all these things, he was very wroth. 22. And Absalom spake unto Amnon neither good nor bad: for Absalom hated Amnon, because he had forced his sister Tamar. 23.

Amnon Killed by Absalom
And it came to pass after two full years, that Absalom had sheepshearers in Baal-hazor, which is beside Ephraim: and Absalom invited all the king's sons. 24. And Absalom came to the king, and said, Behold now, thy servant hath sheepshearers: let the king, I pray thee, and his servants go with thy servant. 25. And the king said to Absalom, Nay, my son, let us not all go, lest we be burdensome unto thee. And he pressed him: howbeit he would not go, but blessed him. 26. Then said Absalom, If not, I pray thee, let my brother Amnon go with us. And the king said unto him, Why should he go with thee? 27. But Absalom pressed him, that he let Amnon and all the king's sons go with him. 28. And Absalom commanded his servants, saying, Mark ye now when Amnon's heart is merry with wine; and when I say unto you, Smite Amnon, then kill him, fear not: have not I commanded you? be courageous, and be valiant. 29. And the servants of Absalom did unto Amnon as Absalom had commanded. Then all the king's sons arose, and every man got him upon his mule, and fled. 30. And it came to pass, while they were in the way, that the tidings came to David, saying, Absalom hath slain all the King's sons, and there is not one of them left. 31. Then the king arose, and rent his garments, and lay on the earth; and all his servants stood by with their clothes rent. 32. And Jonadab, the son of Shimeah David's brother, answered and said, Let not my lord suppose that they have killed all the young men the king's sons; for Amnon only is dead: for by the appointment of Absalom this has been determined from the day that he forced his sister Tamar. 33. Now therefore let not my lord the king take the thing to his heart, to think that all the king's sons are dead: for Amnon only is dead. But Absalom fled. 34. And the young man that kept the watch lifted up his eyes, and looked, and, behold, there came much people by the way of the hill side behind him. 35. And Jonadab said unto the king, Behold, the king's sons are come: as thy servant said, so it is. 36. And it came to pass, as soon as he had made an end of speaking, that, behold, the king's sons came, and lifted up their voice, and wept: and the king also and all his servants wept very sore. 37. But Absalom

Absalom's Flight
fled, and went to Talmai the son of Ammihur, king of Geshur. And David mourned for his son every day. 38. So Absalom fled, and went to Geshur, and was there three years. 39. And the soul of king David longed to go forth unto Absalom: for he was comforted concerning Amnon, seeing he was dead.

14:1. Now Joab the son of Zeruiah perceived that the king's heart was toward Absalom. 2. And Joab sent to Tekoa, and fetched thence a wise woman, and said unto her, I pray thee feign thyself to be a mourner, and put on mourning apparel, I pray thee, and

Joab and the Wise Woman of Tekoa
anoint not thyself with oil, but be as a woman that had a long time mourned for the dead: 3. and go into the king, and speak on this manner unto him. So Joab put the words in her mouth. 4. And when the woman of Tekoa spake to the king, she fell on her face to the ground, and did obeisance, and said, Help, O king. 5. And the king said unto her,

What aileth thee? And she answered, Of a truth I am a widow woman, and mine husband is dead. 6. And thy handmaid had two sons, and they two strove together in the field, and there was none to part them, but the one smote the other, and killed him. 7. And, behold, the whole family is risen against thine handmaid, and they said, Deliver him that smote his brother, that we may kill him for the life of his brother whom he slew, and so destroy the heir also: thus shall they quench my coal which is left, and shall leave to my husband neither name nor remainder upon the face of the earth. 8. And the king said unto the woman, Go to thine house, and I will give charge concerning thee. 9. And the woman of Tekoa said unto the king, My lord, O king, the iniquity be on me, and on my father's house: and the king and his throne be guiltless. 10. And the king said, Whosoever saith aught unto thee, bring him to me, and he shall not touch thee any more. 11. Then said she, I pray thee, let the king remember the Lord thy God, that the avenger of blood destroy not any more, lest they destroy my son. And he said, As the Lord liveth, there shall not one hair of thy son fall to the earth. 12. Then the woman said, let thine handmaid, I pray thee, speak a word unto my lord the king. And he said, Say on. 13. And the woman said, Wherefore then hast thou devised such a thing against the people of God? for in speaking this word the king is as one which is guilty, in that the king doth not fetch home again his banished one. 14. For we must needs die, and are as water spilt on the ground, which cannot be gathered up again; neither doth God take away life, but deviseth means, that he that is banished be not an outcast from him. 15. Now therefore seeing that I am come to speak this word unto my lord the king, it is because the people have made me afraid: and thy handmaid said, I will now speak unto the king; it may be that the king will perform the request of his servant. 16. For the king will hear, to deliver his servant out of the hand of the man that would destroy me and my son together out of the inheritance of God. 17. Then thine handmaid said, Let, I pray thee, the word of my lord the king be comfortable: for as an angel of God, so is my lord the king to discern good and bad: and the Lord thy God be with thee. 18. Then the king answered and said unto the woman, Hide not from me, I pray thee, aught that I shall ask thee. And the woman said, Let my lord the king now speak. 19. And the king said, Is the hand of Joab with thee in all this? And the woman answered and said, As thy soul liveth, my lord the king, none can turn to the right hand or to the left from aught that my lord the king hath spoken: for thy servant Joab, he bade me, and he put all these words in the mouth of thine handmaid: 20. to change the face of the matter hath thy servant Joab done this thing: and my lord is wise, according to the wisdom of an angel of God, to know all things that are in the earth. 21. And the king said unto Joab, Behold now, I have done this thing: go therefore, bring the young man Absalom again. 22. And Joab fell to the ground on his face, and did obeisance, and blessed the king: and Joab said, To-day thy servant knoweth that I have found grace in thy sight, my lord, O king, in that the king hath performed the request of his servant. 23. So Joab arose and went to Geshur, and brought Absalom to Jerusalem. 24. And the king said, Let him turn to his own house but let him not see my face. So Absalom turned to his own house and saw not the king's face. 25. Now in all Israel there was none to be so much praised as Absalom for his beauty: from the sole of his foot even to the crown of his head there was no blemish in him. 26. And when he polled his head, (now it was at every year's end that he polled it: because the hair was heavy on him, therefore he polled it:) he weighed the hair of his head at two hundred shekels, after the king's weight. 27. And unto Absalom there were born three sons, and one daughter whose name was Tamar: she

Absalom Recalled

was a woman of a fair countenance. 28. And Absalom dwelt two full years in Jerusalem; and he saw not the king's face. 29. Then Absalom sent for Joab, to send him to the king; but he would not come to him: and he sent again the second time, but he would not come. 30. Therefore he said unto his servants, See, Joab's field is near mine and he hath barley there; go and set it on fire. And Absalom's servants set the field on fire. 31. Then Joab arose, and came to Absalom unto his house, and said unto him, Wherefore have thy servants set my field on fire? 32. And Absalom answered Joab, Behold, I sent unto thee, saying, Come hither, that I may send thee to the king, to say, Wherefore am I come from Geshur? it were better for me to be there still: now therefore let me see the king's face; and if there be iniquity in me, let him kill me. 33. So Joab came to the king, and told him: and when he had called for Absalom, he came to the king, and bowed himself on his face to the ground before the king: and the king kissed Absalom.

II Sam. 15:1. And it came to pass after this, that Absalom prepared him a chariot and horses, and fifty men to run before him. 2. And Absalom rose up early, and stood beside the way of the gate: and it was so, that when any man had a suit which should come to the king for judgment, then Absalom called unto him, and said, Of what city art thou? And he said thy servant is of one of the tribes of Israel. 3. And Absalom said unto him, See, thy matters are good and right; but there is no man deputed of the king to hear thee. 4. Absalom said moreover, Oh that I were made judge in the land, that every man which hath any suit or cause might come unto me, and I would do him justice! 5. And it was so, that when any man came nigh to do him obeisance, he put forth his hand, and took hold of him, and kissed him. 6. And on this manner did Absalom to all Israel that came to the king for judgment: so Absalom stole the hearts of the men of Israel. 7. And it came to pass at the

Absalom's Rebellion

end of forty * years, that Absalom said unto the king, I pray thee, let me go and pay my vow, which I have vowed unto the Lord, in Hebron. 8. For thy servant vowed a vow while I abode at Geshur in Syria, saying, If the Lord shall indeed bring me again to Jerusalem, then I will serve the Lord. 9. And the king said unto him, Go in peace, So he arose, and went to Hebron. 10. But Absalom sent spies throughout all the tribes of Israel, saying, as soon as ye hear the sound of the trumpet, then ye shall say, Absalom is king in Hebron. 11. And with Absalom went two hundred men out of Jerusalem that were invited, and went in their simplicity; and they knew not any thing. 12. And Absalom sent for Ahithophel the Gilonite, David's counsellor, from his city, even from Giloh, while he offered the sacrifices. And the conspiracy was strong; for the people increased continually with Absalom. 13. And there came a messenger to David, saying, The hearts of the men of Israel are after Absalom. 14. And David said unto all his servants that

David's Flight

were with him at Jerusalem, Arise, and let us flee; for else none of us shall escape from Absalom: make speed to depart, lest he overtake us quickly, and bring down evil upon us, and smite the city with the edge of the sword. 15. And the king's servants said unto the king, Behold, thy servants are ready to do whatsoever my lord the king shall choose. 16. And the king went forth, and all his household after him. And the king left ten women, which were concubines, to keep the house. 17. And the king went forth, and all the people after him; and they tarried in Beth-merhak. 18. And all his servants passed on beside him; and all the Cherethites, and all the Pelethites,

---

* Four according to some ancient authorities

and all the Gittites, six hundred men which came after him from Gath, passed on before the king. 19. Then saith the king to Ittai the Gittite, Wherefore goest thou also with us? return, and abide with the king: for thou art a stranger, and also an exile; return to thine own place. 20. Whereas thou camest but yesterday, should I this day make thee go up and down with us, seeing I go whither I may? return thou, and take back thy brethren; mercy and truth be with thee. 21. And Ittai answered the king, and said, As the Lord liveth, and as my lord the king liveth, surely in what place my lord the king shall be, whether for death or for life, even there also will thy servant be. 22. And David said to Ittai, Go and pass over. And Ittai the Gittite passed over, and all his men, and all the little ones that were with him. 23. And all the country wept with a loud voice, and all the people passed over: the king also himself passed over the brook Kidron, and all the people passed over, toward the way of the wilderness. 24. And, lo, Zadok also came, and all the Levites with him, bearing the ark of the covenant of God; and they set down the ark of God, and Abiathar went up, until all the people had done passing out of the city. 25. And the king said unto Zadok, Carry back the ark of God into the city: if I shall find favour in the eyes of the Lord, he will bring me again, and shew me both it, and his habitation: but if he say thus, I have no delight in thee; behold, here am I, let him do to me as seemeth good unto him. 27. The king said also unto Zadok the priest, Art thou not a seer? return into the city in peace, and your two sons with thee, Ahimaaz thy son, and Jonathan the son of Abiathar. 28. See, I will tarry at the fords of the wilderness, until there come word from you to certify me. 29. Zadok therefore and Abiathar carried the ark of God again to Jerusalem: and they abode there. 30. And David went up by the ascent of the mount of Olives and wept as he went up; and he had his head covered, and went barefoot: and all the people that were with him covered every man his head, and they went up, weeping as they went up. 31. And one told David, saying, Ahithophel is among the conspirators with Absalom. And David said, O Lord, I pray thee, turn the counsel of Ahithophel into foolishness. 32. And it came to pass, that when David was come to the top of the ascent, where God was worshipped, behold, Hushai the Archite came to meet him with his coat rent, and earth upon his head: 33. and David said unto him, If thou passest on with me, then thou shalt be a burden unto me: but if thou return to the city, and say unto Absalom, I will be thy servant, O king; as I have been thy father's servant in time past, so will I now be thy servant: then shalt thou defeat for me the counsel of Ahithophel. 35. And hast thou not there with thee Zadok and Abiathar the priests? therefore it shall be, that what thing soever thou shalt hear out of the king's house, thou shalt tell it to Zadok and Abiathar the priests. 36. Behold, they have there with them their two sons, Ahimaaz Zadok's son, and Jonathan Abiathar's son; and by them ye shall send unto me everything that ye shall hear. 37. So Hushai David's friend came into the city; and Absalom came into Jerusalem.

David's Ascent of the Mount of Olives

II Sam. 16:1. And when David was a little past the top of the ascent, behold Ziba the servant of Mephibosheth met him, with a couple of asses saddled, and upon them two hundred loaves of bread, and an hundred clusters of raisins, and an hundred of summer fruits, and a bottle of wine. 2. And the king said unto Ziba, What meanest thou by these? And Ziba said, the asses be for the king's household to ride on, and the bread and summer fruit for the young men to eat; and the wine, that as such as be faint in the wilderness may drink. 3. And the king said, And where is thy master's son? And Ziba said unto the king, Behold, he abideth at Jerusalem: for he said, To-day shall the house of Israel restore me the kingdom of my father. 4. Then said the king to Ziba, Behold, thine is all that pertaineth unto Mephibosheth. And Ziba said, I do obeisance; let me find favour in thy sight, my lord, O king. 5. And when king David came to Bahurim, behold, there came out thence a man of the family of the house of Saul, whose name was Shimei, the son of Gera; he came out, and cursed still as he came. 6. And he cast stones at David, and at all the servants of king David: and all the people and all the mighty men were on his right hand and on his left. 7. And thus said Shimei when he cursed, Begone, begone, thou man of blood, and man of Belial: the Lord hath returned upon thee all the blood of the house of Saul, in whose stead thou hast reigned; and the Lord hath delivered the kingdom into the hand of Absalom thy son: and, behold, thou art taken in thine own mischief, because thou art a man of blood. 9. Then said Abishai the son of Zeruiah unto the king, Why should this dead dog curse my lord the king? let me go over, I pray thee, and take off his head. 10. And the king said, What have I to do with you, ye sons of Zeruiah? Because he curseth, and because the Lord hath said unto him, Curse David; who then shall say, Wherefore hast thou done so? 11. And David said to Abishai, and to all his servants, Behold, my son, which came forth of my bowels, seeketh my life; how much more may this Benjamite now do it? let him alone, and let him curse; for the Lord hath bidden him. 12. It may be that the Lord will look on the wrong done unto me, and that the Lord will requite me good for his cursing of me this day. 13. So David and his men went by the way: and Shimei went along on the hillside over against him, and cursed as he went, and threw stones at him, and cast dust. 14. And the king, and all the people that were with him, came weary; and he refreshed himself there. 15. And Absalom, and all the people the men of Israel, came to Jerusalem, and Ahithophel with him. 16. And it came to pass when Hushai the Archite, David's friend, was come unto Absalom, that Hushai said unto Absalom, God save the king, God save the king. 17. And Absalom said to Hushai, Is this thy kindness to thy friends, why wentest thou not with thy friend? 18. And Hushai said unto Absalom, Nay; but whom the Lord, and this people, and all the men of Israel have chosen, his will I be, and with him will I abide. 19. And again, whom should I serve? should I not serve in the presence of his son? as I have served in thy father's presence, so will I be in thy presence. 20. Then said Absalom to Ahithophel, Give your counsel what we shall do. 21. And Ahithophel said unto Absalom, Go in unto thy father's concubines, which he hath left to keep the house; and all Israel shall hear that thou art abhorred of thy father; then shall the hands of all that are with thee be strong. 22. So they spread Absalom a tent upon the top of the house; and Absalom went in unto his father's concubines in the sight of all Israel. 23. And the counsel of Ahithophel, which he counselled in those days, was as if a man inquired at the oracle of God: so was all the counsel of Ahithophel both with David and with Absalom.

The Rival Counsellors in Jerusalem

II Sam. 17:1. Moreover Ahithophel said unto Absalom, Let me now choose out twelve thousand men, and I will arise and pursue after David this night: and I will come upon him while he is weary and weak handed, and will make him afraid: and all the people that are with him shall flee; and I will smite the king only: 3. and I will bring back all the people unto thee: the man whom thou seekest is as if all returned: so all the people shall be in peace. 4. And the saying pleased Absalom well, and all the elders of Israel. 5. Then said Absalom, Call now Hushai the Archite also, and let us hear likewise what he saith. 6. And when Hushai was come to Absalom, Absalom spake unto him, saying, Ahithophel hath spoken after this manner: shall we do after his saying? if not, speak thou. 7. And Hushai said unto Absalom, the counsel that Ahithophel hath given this time is not good. 8. Hushai said moreover, Thou knowest thy father and his men, that they be mighty men, and they be chafed in their minds, as a bear robbed of her whelps in the field: and thy father is a man of war, and will not lodge with the people. 9. Behold, he is hid now in some pit, or in some other place: and it will come to pass, when some of them be fallen at the first, that whosoever heareth it will say, There is a slaughter among the people that follow Absalom. 10. And even he that is valiant, whose heart is as the heart of a lion, shall utterly melt: for all Israel knoweth that thy father is a mighty man, and they which be with him are valiant men. 11. But I counsel that all Israel be gathered together unto thee, from Dan even to Beer-sheba, as the sand that is by the sea for multitude; and that thou go to battle in thine own person. 12. So shall we come upon him in some place where he shall be found, and we will light upon him as the dew falleth on the ground: and of him and of all the men that are with him we will not leave so much as one. 13. Moreover, if he be gotten into a city, then shall all Israel bring ropes to that city, and we will draw it into the river, until there be not one small stone found there. 14. And Absalom and all the men of Israel said, The counsel of Hushai is better than the counsel of Ahithophel. For the Lord had ordained to defeat the good counsel of Ahithophel, to the intent that the Lord might bring evil upon Absalom. 15. Then said Hushai unto Zadok and to Abiathar the priests, Thus and thus did Ahithophel counsel Absalom and the elders of Israel; and thus and thus have I counselled. 16. Now therefore send quickly and tell David, saying, Lodge not this night at the fords of the wilderness, but in any wise pass over; lest the king be swallowed up, and all the people that are with him. 17. Now Jonathan and Ahimaaz stayed by Enrogel; and a maidservant used to go and tell them; and they went and told king David: for they might not be seen to come into the city. 18. But a lad saw them, and told Absalom: and they went both of them away quickly, and came to the house of a man in Bahurim, who had a well in his court; and they went down thither. 19. And the woman took and spread the covering over the well's mouth, and strewed bruised corn thereon; and nothing was known. 20. And Absalom's servants came to the woman to the house; and they said, Where are Ahimaaz and Jonathan? And the woman said unto them, They be gone over the brook of water. And when they had sought and could not find them, they returned to Jerusalem. 21. And it came to pass, after they were departed, that they came up out of the well, and went and told king David; and they said unto David, Arise ye, and pass quickly over the water: for thus hath Ahithopel counselled against you. 22. Then David arose, and all the people that were with him, and they passed over Jordan: by the morning light there lacked not one of them that was not gone over Jordan. 23. And when Ahithophel saw that his counsel was not followed, he saddled his ass, and arose and gat him home, unto his city, and set his house in order, and hanged himself; and he died, and was buried in the sepulchre of his father.

David at Mahanaim
24. Then David came to Mahanaim. And Absalom passed over Jordan, he and all the men of Israel with him. 25. And Absalom set Amasa over the host instead of Joab. Now Amasa was the son of a man, whose name was Ithra the Israelite, that went into Abigal the daughter of Nahash sister to Zeruiah Joab's mother. 26. And Israel and Absalom pitched in the land of Gilead. 27. And it came to pass, when David was come to Mahanaim, that Shobi the son of Nahash of Rabbah of the children of Ammon, and Machir the son of Ammiel of Lo-debar, and Barzillai the Gileadite of Rogelim, 28. brought beds, and basons, and earthen vessels, and wheat, and barley, and meal, and parched corn, and beans, and

lentils, and parched pulse, 29. and honey, and butter, and sheep, and cheese of kine, for David, and the people that were with him to eat: for they said, the people are hungry, and weary, and thirsty, in the wilderness.

II Sam. 18:1. And David numbered the people that were with him, and set captains of thousands, and captains of hundreds over them. 2. And David sent forth the people, a third part under the hand of Joab, and a third part under the hand of Abishai the son of Zeruiah, Joab's brother, and a third part under the hand of Ittai the Gittite. And the king said unto the people, I will surely go forth with you myself also. 3. But the people said, Thou shalt not go forth: for if we flee away, they will not care for us; neither if half of us die, will they care for us: but thou art worth ten thousand of us: therefore now it is better that thou be ready to succour us out of the city. 4. And the king said unto them, what seemeth you best I will do. And the king stood by the gate side, and all the people went out by hundreds and by thousands. 5. And the king commanded Joab and Abishai and Ittai, saying, Deal gently for my sake with the young man, even with Absalom. And all the people heard when the king gave all the captains charge concerning

Defeat and Death of Absalom

Absalom. 6. So the people went out into the field against Israel: and the battle was in the forest of Ephraim. 7. And the people of Israel were smitten there before the servants of David, and there was a great slaughter there that day of twenty thousand men. For the battle was there spread over the face of all the country: and the forest devoured more people that day than the sword devoured. 9. And Absalom chanced to meet the servants of David. And Absalom rode upon his mule, and the mule went under the thick boughs of a great oak, and his head caught hold of the oak, and he was taken up between the heaven and the earth; and the mule that was under him went on. 10. And a certain man saw it, and told Joab, and said, Behold, I saw Absalom hanging in an oak. 11. And Joab said unto the man that told him, And behold, thou sawest it, and why didst thou not smite him there to the ground? and I would have given thee ten pieces of silver and a girdle. 12. And the man said unto Joab, Though I should receive a thousand pieces of silver in mine hand, yet would I not put forth mine hand against the king's son; for in our hearing the king charged thee and Abishai and Ittai, saying, Beware that none touch the young man Absalom. 13. Otherwise if I had dealt falsely against his life, (and there is no matter hid from the king) then thou thyself would have stood aloof. 14. Then said Joab, I may not tarry thus with thee. And he took three darts in his hand, and thrust them through the heart of Absalom, while he was yet alive in the midst of the oak. 15. And ten young men that bare Joab's armour compassed about and smote Absalom, and slew him. 16. And Joab blew the trumpet, and the people returned from pursuing after Israel: for Joab held back the people. 17. And they took Absalom, and cast him into the great pit in the forest, and raised over him a very great heap of stones: and all Israel fled every one to his tent. 18. Now Absalom in his lifetime had taken and reared up for himself the pillar, which is in the king's dale: for he said, I have no son to keep my name in remembrance: and he called the pillar after his own name: and it is called Absalom's monument unto this day. Then said Ahimaaz the son of Zadok Let me now run, and bear the king tidings, how that the Lord hath avenged him of his enemies. 20. And Joab said unto him, Thou shalt not be the bearer of tidings this day, but thou shalt bear tidings another day: but this day thou shalt bear no tidings, because the king's son is dead. 21. Then said Joab to the Cushite, Go tell the king what thou hast seen. And the Cushite bowed himself unto Joab, and ran. 22.

Then said Ahimaaz the son of Zadok yet again to Joab, But come what may, let me, I pray thee, also run after the Cushite. And Joab said, Wherefore wilt thou run, my son, seeing that thou wilt have no reward for the tidings? 23. But come what may, said he, I will run. And he said unto him, Run. Then Ahimaaz ran by the way of the Plain, and overran the Cushite. 24. Now David sat between the two gates: and the watchman went up to the roof of the gate unto the wall, and lifted up his eyes, and looked, and, behold, a man running alone. 25. And the watchman cried, and told the king. And the king said, If he be alone, there is tidings in his mouth. And he came apace, and drew near. 26. And the watchman saw another man running: and the watchman called unto the porter, and said, Behold another man running alone. And the king said, He also bringeth tidings. 27. And the watchman said, Me thinketh the running of the foremost is like the running of Ahimaaz the son of Zadok. And the king said, He is a good man, and cometh with good tidings. 28. And Ahimaaz called, and said unto the king All is well. And he bowed himself before the king with his face to the earth, and said, Blessed be the Lord thy God, which hath delivered up the men that lifted up their hand against my lord the king. 29. And the king said, Is it well with the young man Absalom? And Ahimaaz answered, When Joab sent the king's servant, even me thy servant, I saw a great tumult, but I knew not what it was. 30. And the king said, Turn aside, and stand here. And he turned aside, and stood still. 31. And behold, the Cushite came; and the Cushite said, Tidings for my lord the king: for the Lord hath avenged thee this day of all them that rose up against thee. 32. And the king said Is it well with the young man Absalom? And the Cushite answered, The enemies of my lord the king, and all that rise up against thee to do thee hurt, be as that young man is. 33. And the king was much moved, and went up to the chamber over the gate, and wept: and as he went, thus he said, O my son Absalom, my son, my son, Absalom! would God I had died for thee, O Absalom, my son, my son.

David's Grief

II Sam. 19:1. And it was told Joab, Behold the king weepeth and mourneth for Absalom. 2. And the victory that day was turned into mourning unto all the people: for the people heard say that day, The king grieveth for his son. 3. And the people gat them by stealth that day into the city, as people that are ashamed steal away when they flee in battle. 4. And the king covered his face, and the king cried with a loud voice, O my son Absalom, O Absalom, my son, my son! 5. And Joab came into the house to the king, and said, Thou hast shamed this day the faces of all thy servants, which this day have saved thy life, and the lives of thy sons and of thy daughters, and the lives of thy wives, and the lives of thy concubines; 6. in that thou lovest them that hate thee, and hatest them that love thee. For thou hast declared this day that princes and servants are nought unto thee: for this day I perceive, that if Absalom had lived, and all we had died this day, then it had pleased thee well. 7. Now therefore arise, go forth, and speak comfortably unto thy servants: for I swear by the Lord, if thou go not forth, there will not tarry a man with thee this night: and that will be worse unto thee than all the evil that hath befallen thee from thy youth until now. 8. Then the king arose, and sat in the gate. And they told unto all the people, saying, Behold, the king doth sit in the gate: and all the people came before the king.

SECT. XIV THE UNITED KINGDOM 85

THE HOUSE OF DAVID
    B. C. 1049 (Usher)
I David
    B. C. 1010 (Rev.)

NATHAN

SECTION XIV

The Restoration

David's Recall

Now Israel had fled every man to his tent. 9. And all the people were at strife throughout all the tribes of Israel, saying, The king delivered us out of the hand of our enemies, and he saved us out of the hand of the Philistines; and now he is fled out of the land from Absalom. 10. And Absalom, whom we anointed over us, is dead in battle. Now therefore why speak ye not a word of bringing the king back? 11. And king David sent to Zadok and to Abiathar the priests, saying, Speak unto the elders of Judah, saying, Why are ye the last to bring the king back to his house? seeing the speech of all Israel is come to the king, to bring him to his house. 12. Ye are my brethren, ye are my bone and my flesh: wherefore then are ye the last to bring back the king? 13. And say ye to Amasa, Art thou not my bone and my flesh? God do so to me, and more also, if thou be not captain of the host before me continually in the room of Joab. 14. And he bowed the heart of all the men of Judah, even as the heart of one man; so that they sent unto the king, saying, return thou, and all thy servants.

David's Return

15. So the king returned, and came to Jordan. And Judah came to Gilgal, to go to meet the king, to bring the king over Jordan. 16. And Shimei the son of Gera, the Benjamite, which was of Bahurim, hasted and came down with the men of Judah to meet king David. 17. And there were a thousand men of Benjamin with him, and Ziba the servant of the house of Saul, and his fifteen sons and his twenty servants with him; and they went through Jordan in the presence of the king. 18. And there went over a ferry boat to bring over the king's household, and to do what he thought good. And Shimei the son of Gera fell down before the king when he was come over Jordan. 19. And he said unto the king, Let not my lord impute iniquity unto me, neither do thou remember that which thy servant did perversely the day that my lord the king went out of Jerusalem, that the king should take it to his heart. 20. For thy servant doth know that I have sinned: therefore, behold, I am come this day the first of all the house of Joseph to go down to meet my lord the king. 21. But Abishai the son of Zeruiah answered and said, Shall not Shimei be put to death for this, because he cursed the Lord's anointed? 22. And David said, What have I to do with you, ye sons of Zeruiah, that ye should this day be adversaries unto me? shall there any man be put to death this day in Israel? for do not I know that I am this day king over Israel? 23. And the king said unto Shimei, Thou shalt not die. And the king sware unto him.

Mephibosheth meets David

24. And Mephibosheth the son of Saul came down to meet the king; and he had neither dressed his feet, nor trimmed his beard, nor washed his clothes, from the day the king departed until the day he came home in peace. 25. And it came to pass, when he was come to Jerusalem to meet the king that the king said unto him, Wherefore wentest thou not with me, Mephibosheth? 26. And he answered, My Lord, O king, my servant deceived me:

for thy servant said, I will saddle me an ass, that I may ride thereon, and go with the king; because thy servant is lame. 27. And he hath slandered thy servant unto my lord the king; but my lord the king is as an angel of God: do therefore what is good in thine eyes. 28. For all my father's house were but dead men before my lord the king: yet didst thou set thy servant among them that did eat at thine own table. What right therefore have I yet that I should cry any more unto the king? 29. And the king said unto him, Why speakest thou any more of thy matters? I say, Thou and Ziba divide the land. 30. And Mephibosheth said unto the king, Yea let him take all, forasmuch as my lord the king is come in peace unto his own house.

Barzillai's Welcome 31. And Barzillai the Gileadite came down from Rogelim; and he went over Jordan with the king, to conduct him over Jordan. 32. Now Barzillai was a very aged man, even fourscore years old: and he had provided the king with sustenance while he lay at Mahanaim; for he was a very great man. 33. And the king said unto Barzillai, Come thou over with me, and I will sustain thee with me in Jerusalem. 34. And Barzillai said unto the king, How many are the days of the years of my life, that I should go up with the king unto Jerusalem? 35. I am this day fourscore years old: can I discern between good and bad? can thy servant taste what I eat or what I drink? can I hear any more the voice of singing men and singing women? wherefore then should thy servant be yet a burden unto my lord the king? 36. Thy servant would but just go over Jordan with the king: and why should the king recompense it me with such a reward? 37. Let thy servant, I pray thee, turn back again, that I may die in mine own city, by the grave of my father and my mother. But behold, thy servant Chimham; let him go over with my lord the king; and do to him what shall seem good unto thee. 38. And the king answered, Chimham shall go over with me, and I will do unto him that which shall seem good unto thee: and whatsoever thou shalt require of me, that will I do for thee. 39. And all the people went over Jordan, and the king went over: and the king kissed Barzillai, and blessed him and he returned unto his own place. 40. So the king went over to Gilgal, and Chimham went over with him: and all the people of Judah brought the king over, and also half the people of Israel.

Israel Aggrieved 41. And, behold, all the men of Israel came to the king, and said unto the king, Why have our brethren the men of Judah stolen thee away, and brought the king, and his household over Jordan, and all David's men with him? And all the men of Judah answered the men of Israel, Because the king is near of kin to us: wherefore then be ye angry for this matter? have we eaten at all of the king's cost? or hath he given us any gift? 43. And the men of Israel answered the men of Judah, and said, We have ten parts in the king, and we have also more right in David than ye: why then did ye despise us, that our advice should not be first had in bringing back our king? And the words of the men of Judah were fiercer than the words of the men of Israel.

Rebellion of Sheba II Sam. 20:1. And there happened to be there a man of Belial, whose name was Sheba, the son of Bichri, a Benjamite: and he blew the trumpet, and said, We have no portion in David, neither have we inheritance in the son of Jesse: every man to his tents, O Israel. So all the men of Israel went up from following David, and followed Sheba the son of Bichri: but the men of Judah clave unto their king, from Jordan even to Jerusalem. 3.

And David came to his house at Jerusalem; and the king took the ten women his concubines, whom he had left to keep the house, and put them in ward, and provided them with sustenance, but went not in unto them. So they were shut up unto the day of their death, living in widowhood. 4. Then said the king to Amasa, Call me the men of Judah together within three days, and be thou here present. 5. So Amasa went to call the men of Judah together: but he tarried longer than the set time which he had appointed him. 6. And David said to Abishai, Now shall Sheba the son of Bichri do us more harm than did Absalom: take thou thy lord's servants, and pursue after him, lest he get him fenced cities, and escape out of our sight. 7. And there went out after him Joab's men, and the Cherethites and the Pelethites, and all the mighty men: and they went out of Jerusalem, to pursue after Sheba the son of Bichri. 8. When they were at the great stone which is in Gibeon, Amasa came to meet them.

Amasa Slain

And Joab was girded with his apparel of war that he had put on, and thereon was a girdle with a sword fastened upon his loins in the sheath thereof; and as he went forth it fell out. 9. And Joab said to Amasa, Is it well with thee, my brother? And Joab took Amasa by the beard with his right hand to kiss him. 10. But Amasa took no heed to the sword that was in Joab's hand: so he smote him therewith in the belly, and shed out his bowels to the ground, and struck him not again; and he died. And Joab and Abishai his brother pursued after Sheba the son of Bichri. 11. And there stood by him one of Joab's young men, and said, He that favoureth Joab, and he that is for David, let him follow Joab. 12. And Amasa lay wallowing in his blood in the midst of the high way. And when the man saw that all the people stood still, he carried Amasa out of the high way into the field, and cast a garment over him, when he saw that every one that came by him stood still. 13. When he was removed out of the high way, all the people went on after Joab, to pursue after Sheba the son of Bichri. 14. And he went through all the tribes of Israel unto Abel, and to Beth-maacah, and all the Berites: and they were gathered together, and went also after him. 15. And they came and besieged him in Abel of Beth-maacah, and they cast up a mount against the city, and it stood against the rampart: and all the people that were with Joab battered the wall, to throw it down. 16. Then cried a wise woman out of the city, Hear, hear; say, I pray you, unto Joab, Come near hither, that I may speak with thee. 17. And he came near unto her; and the woman said, Art thou Joab? And he answered, I am. Then she said unto him, Hear the words of thine handmaid. And he answered, I do hear. 18. Then she spake, saying, They were wont to speak in old time, saying, They shall surely ask counsel at Abel: and so they ended the matter. 19. I am of them that are peaceable and faithful in Israel: thou seekest to destroy a city and a mother in Israel: why wilt thou swallow up the inheritance of the Lord? 20. And Joab answered and said Far be it, far be it from me, that I should swallow up or destroy. 21. The matter is not so: but a man of the hill country of Ephraim, Sheba the son of Bichri by name, hath lifted up his hand against the king, even against David: deliver him only, and I will depart from the city. And the woman said unto Joab, Behold, his head shall be thrown to thee over the wall. 22. Then the woman went unto all the people in her wisdom. And they cut off the head of Sheba the son of Bichri, and threw it out to Joab. And he blew the trumpet, and they were dispersed from the city, every man to his tent. And Joab returned to Jerusalem unto the king.

Gibeonites Avenged

II Sam. 21:1. And there was a famine in the days of David three years, year after year; and David sought the face of the Lord. And the Lord said, It is for Saul, and for his bloody house, because he put to death the Gibeonites. 2. And the king called the Gibeonites, and said unto them; (now the Gibeonites were not of the children of Israel, but of the remnant of the Amorites; and the children of Israel had sworn unto them: and Saul sought to slay them in his zeal for the children of Israel and Judah:) 3. and David said unto the Gibeonites, What shall I do for you? and wherewith shall I make atonement, that ye may bless the inheritance of the Lord? 4. And the Gibeonites said unto him, It is no matter of silver or gold between us and Saul, or his house; neither is it for us to put any man to death in Israel. And he said, What ye shall say, that will I do for you. 5. And they said unto the king, The man that consumed us, and that devised against us, that we should be destroyed from remaining in any of the borders of Israel, 6. let seven men of his sons be delivered unto us, and we will hang them up unto the Lord in Gibeah of Saul, the chosen of the Lord. And the king said, I will give them. 7. But the king spared Mephibosheth, the son of Jonathan the son of Saul, because of the Lord's oath that was between them, between David and Jonathan the son of Saul. 8. But the king took the two sons of Rizpah the daughter of Aiah, whom she bare unto Saul, Armoni and Mephibosheth; and the five sons of Michal the daughter of Saul, whom she bare to Adriel the son of Barzillai the Meholathite: 9. and he delivered them into the hands of the Gibeonites, and they hanged them in the mountain before the Lord, and they fell all seven together: and they were put to death in the days of harvest, in the first days, at the beginning of barley harvest. 10. And Rizpah the daughter of Aiah took sackcloth, and spread it for her upon the rock, from the beginning of harvest until water was poured upon them from heaven; and she suffered neither the birds of the air to rest on them by day, nor the beasts of the field by night. 11. And it was told David what Rizpah the daughter of Aiah, the concubine of Saul, had done. 12. And David went and took the bones of Saul and the bones of Jonathan his son from the men of Jabesh-gilead, which had stolen them from the street of Beth-shan, where the Philistines had hanged them, in the day that the Philistines slew Saul in Gilboa: 13. and he brought up from thence the bones of Saul and the bones of Jonathan his son; and they gathered the bones of them that were hanged. 14. And they buried the bones of Saul and Jonathan his son in the country of Benjamin in Zela, in the sepulchre of Kish his father: and they performed all that the king commanded. And after that God was intreated for the land.

Numbering the People

And Satan* stood up against Israel and moved David to number Israel and Judah. And the king said to Joab the captain of the host, which was with him, and to the princes of the people, Go now to and fro through all the tribes of Israel, from Dan even to Beersheba, and number ye the people, and bring me word, that I may know the sum of the people. And Joab said unto the king, Now the Lord thy God add unto the people, how many soever they be, an hundred fold, and may the eyes of my lord the king see it: but my lord the king, are they not all my lord's servants? why doth my lord require this thing? why will he be a cause of guilt unto Israel? Notwithstanding the king's word prevailed against Joab, and against the captains of the host. And Joab and the captains of the host went out from the presence of the king, to number the people of Israel. And they passed

---

* In Samuel, he *i.e.* the Lord. See Chronicles, Appendix C, III, 2 (2).

(II Sam. 24:) 1. And again the anger of the Lord was kindled against Israel, and ((he moved David against them, saying, Go number Israel and Judah.))

2. And the king said to Joab the captain of the host, which was with him, Go now to and fro through all the tribes of Israel, from Dan even to Beersheba, and number ye the people, that I may know the sum of the people.

3. And Joab said unto the king, Now the Lord thy God add unto the people how many soever they be, an hundred fold, and may the eyes of my lord the king see it: but why doth my lord the king delight in this thing?

4. Notwithstanding the king's word prevailed against Joab, and against the captains of the host. And Joab and the captains of the host went out from the presence of the king, to number the people of Israel. 5. And they passed over Jordan, and pitched in Aroer, on the right side of the

(I Chron. 21:) 1. And ((Satan stood up against Israel and moved David to number Israel.))

2. And David said to Joab and to the princes of the people, Go, number Israel from Beersheba even to Dan; and bring me word, that I may know the sum of them.

3. And Joab said, the Lord make his people an hundred times so many more as they be: but, my lord the king, are they not all my lord's servants why doth my lord require this thing? why will he be a cause of guilt unto Israel?

4. Nevertheless the king's word prevailed against Joab. Wherefore Joab departed, and went throughout all Israel.

over Jordan, and pitched in Aroer, on the right side of the city that is in the middle of the valley of Gad, and unto Jazer: Then they came to Gilead, and to the land of Tahtim-hodshi; and they came to Danjaan, and round about to Zidon, and came to the strong hold of Tyre and to all the cities of the Hivites and of the Canaanites: and they went out to the south of Judah, at Beer-sheba. So when they had gone to and fro through all the land, they came to Jerusalem at the end of nine months and twenty days. And Joab gave up the sum of the numbering of the people unto the king: and there were in Israel *[1]eight hundred thousand valiant men that drew sword: and the men of Judah were *[2]five hundred thousand men. But David took not the number of them from twenty years old and under: because the Lord had said he would increase Israel like to the stars of heaven. Joab the son of Zeruiah began to number, but finished not; and there came wrath for this upon Israel; neither was the number put into the account in the chronicles of king David.

But Levi and Benjamin counted he not among them: for the king's word was abominable to Joab. And God was displeased with this thing; therefore he smote Israel.

Repentance and Punishment

And David's heart smote him after that he had numbered the people. And David said unto the Lord, I have sinned greatly in that I have done this thing: but now, O Lord, put away, I beseech thee, the iniquity of thy servant; for I have done very foolishly. And when David rose up in the morning, the word of the Lord came unto Gad, David's seer, Go and speak unto David, saying, Thus saith the Lord, I offer thee three things; choose thee one of them that I may do it unto thee. So Gad came to David, and said unto him, Thus saith the Lord, Take which thou wilt; either †three years of famine in thy land; or three months to be consumed before thy foes, while that the sword of thine enemies overtaketh thee; or else three days, even pestilence in the land, and the angel of the Lord destroying throughout all the coasts of Israel. Now therefore advise thee, and consider what answer I shall return to him that sent me. And David said unto Gad, I am in a great strait: let me fall now into the hand of the Lord; for very great are his mercies: and let me not fall into the hand of man. So the Lord sent a pestilence upon Israel, from the morning even to the time appointed: and there died of the people from Dan even to Beer-sheba seventy thousand men. And God sent an angel unto Jerusalem to destroy it: and when the angel stretched out his hand toward Jerusalem to destroy it, the Lord beheld and he repented him of the evil, and said to the destroying angel, It is enough: now stay thine hand. And the angel of the Lord stood by the threshing-floor of ‡Araunah the Jebusite. And David lifted up his eyes, and saw the angel of the Lord stand between the earth and the heaven, having a drawn sword in his hand stretched out over Jerusalem. Then David and the elders, clothed in sackcloth, fell upon their faces. And David spake unto the Lord when he saw the angel that smote the people, and said, Is it not I that have commanded the people to be numbered? even I it is that have sinned and done very wickedly: but these sheep, what have they done? let thine hand, I pray thee, O Lord my God, be against me, and against my father's house; but not against thy people, that they should be plagued. Then the angel of the Lord commanded Gad to say to David, Go up, rear an altar unto the Lord in the threshing-floor of Araunah the Jebusite. And David went up according to the saying of Gad, as the Lord commanded. And Araunah turned back, and saw the angel; and

---

*[1] In Chronicles, 1,000,000.
*[2] In Chronicles, 470,000. Appendix C, Chronicles III 1. (4). " " (5).
† In Samuel, seven years.
‡ In Chronicles, Ornan.

SECT. XIV THE UNITED KINGDOM

city that is in the middle of the valley of Gad, and unto Jazer: 6. Then they came to Gilead, and to the land of Tahtim-hodshi; and they came to Danjaan, and round about to Zidon, 7. and came to the strong hold of Tyre and to all the cities of the Hivites and of the Canaanites: and they went out to the south of Judah, at Beer-sheba. 8. So when they had gone to and fro through all the land, they came to Jerusalem at the end of nine months and twenty days. 9. And Joab gave up the sum of the numbering of the people unto the king: and there were in Israel ((eight hundred thousand valiant men that drew sword:))

and the men of Judah were ((five hundred thousand men.))

I Chron. 27:23. But David took not the number of them from twenty years old and under: because the Lord had said he would increase Israel like to the stars of heaven. 24. Joab the son of Zeruiah began to number, but finished not; and there came wrath for this upon Israel; neither was the number put into the account in the chronicles of king David.

and came to Jerusalem.
5. And Joab gave up the sum of the numbering of the people unto David; and all they of Israel were ((a *thousand thousand and an hundred thousand men that drew sword.))

and Judah was ((four hundred threescore and ten thousand men that drew sword.))

6. But Levi and Benjamin counted he not among them: for the king's word was abominable to Joab. 7. And God was displeased with this thing; therefore he smote Israel.

10. And David's heart smote him after that he had numbered the people.
And David said unto the Lord, I have sinned greatly in that I have done: but now, O Lord, put away, I beseech thee, the iniquity of thy servant; for I have done very foolishly.

11. And when David rose up in the morning, the word of the Lord came unto the prophet Gad, David's seer, saying, Go and speak unto David, Thus saith the Lord, I offer thee three things; choose thee one of them, that I may do it unto thee. 12. So Gad came to David, and told him and said unto him, Shall ((seven)) years of famine come unto thee in thy land? or wilt thou flee three months before thy foes while they pursue thee? or shall there be three days of pestilence in thy land?
now advise thee, and consider what answer I shall return to him that sent me. 14. And David said unto Gad, I am in a great strait: let us fall now into the hand of the Lord; for his mercies are great: and let me not fall into the hand of man.

15. So the Lord sent a pestilence upon Israel, from the morning even to the time appointed: and there died of the people from Dan even to Beer-sheba seventy thousand men.

16. And when the angel stretched out his hand toward Jerusalem to destroy it, the Lord repented him of the evil, and said to the angel that destroyed the people, It is enough; now stay thine hand. And the angel of the Lord was by the threshing-floor of Araunah the Jebusite.

8. And David said unto God, I have sinned greatly in that I have done this thing: but now, put away, I beseech thee, the iniquity of thy servant; for I have done very foolishly.

9. And the Lord spake unto Gad, David's seer, saying, Go and speak unto David, saying, Thus saith the Lord I offer thee three things; choose thee one of them, that I may do it unto thee. 11. So Gad came to David, and said unto him, Thus saith the Lord, Take which thou wilt; either ((three)) years of famine; or three months to be consumed before thy foes, while that the sword of thine enemies overtaketh thee; or else three days the sword of the Lord, even pestilence in the land, and the angel of the Lord destroying throughout all the coasts of Israel. Now therefore consider what answer I shall return to him that sent me. 13. And David said unto Gad, I am in a great strait: let me fall now into the hand of the Lord; for very great are his mercies: and let me not fall into the hand of man.

14. So the Lord sent a pestilence upon Israel:
and there fell of Israel seventy thousand men.

15. And God sent an angel unto Jerusalem to destroy it: and as he was about to destroy, the Lord beheld and he repented him of the evil, and said to the destroying angel, It is enough; now stay thine hand. And the angel of the Lord stood by the threshing-floor of Ornan the Jebusite. 16. And David lifted up his eyes, and saw the angel of the Lord stand between the earth and the heaven, having a drawn sword in his hand, stretched out over Jerusalem. Then David and the elders, clothed in sackcloth, fell upon their faces.

17. And David spake unto the Lord when he saw the angel that smote the people, and said, Lo,

I have sinned, and I have done perversely: but these sheep, what have they done? let thine hand, I pray thee, be against me, and against my father's house.

17. And David said unto God,

Is it not I that commanded the people to be numbered? even I it is that have sinned and done very wickedly: but these sheep, what have they done? let thine hand, I pray thee, O Lord my God, be against me, and against my father's house; but not against thy people, that they should be plagued.

18. And Gad came that day to David, and said unto him, Go up, rear an altar unto the Lord in the threshing-floor of Araunah the Jebusite.
19. And David went up according to the saying of Gad, as the Lord commanded.

18. Then the angel of the Lord commanded Gad to say to David, that David should go up, and rear an altar unto the Lord in the threshing-floor of Ornan the Jebusite.
19. And David went up at the saying of Gad, which he spake in the name of the Lord. 20. And Ornan turned back, and saw the angel;

his four sons that were with him hid themselves. Now Araunah was threshing wheat. And as David came to Araunah, Araunah looked forth and saw the king and his servants coming toward him: and Araunah went out of the threshing-floor, and bowed himself before the king with his face to the ground. And Araunah said, Wherefore is my lord the king come to his servant? And David said, To buy the threshing-floor of thee, to build thereon an altar unto the Lord: for the full price shalt thou give it me: that the plague may be stayed from the people. And Araunah said unto David, Take it thee, and let my lord the king do that which is good in his eyes: lo, I give thee the oxen for burnt offerings, and the threshing instruments and the furniture of the oxen for the wood, and the wheat for the meal offering: all this, O king, doth Araunah give unto the king. And Araunah said unto the king, The Lord thy God accept thee. And the king said unto Araunah, Nay; but I will verily buy it of thee for the full price: for I will not take what is thine for the Lord, neither will I offer burnt offerings unto the Lord my God which cost me nothing. So David bought the threshing-floor and the oxen for fifty* shekels of silver. And David built there an altar unto the Lord, and offered burnt offerings and peace offerings, and called upon the Lord. So the Lord was intreated for the land, and he answered him from heaven by fire upon the altar of burnt offering. And the Lord commanded the angel: and he put up his sword again into the sheath thereof, and the plague was stayed from Israel.

Made Place for Sacrifice At that time, when David saw that the Lord had answered him in the threshing-floor of Araunah the Jebusite, then he sacrificed there. For the tabernacle of the Lord, which Moses made in the wilderness, and the altar of burnt offering, were at that time in the high place at Gibeon. But David could not go before it to inquire of God: for he was afraid because of the angel of the Lord. I Chron. 22:1. Then David said, This is the house of the Lord God, and this is the altar of burnt offering for Israel.

Site for Temple

---

* In Chronicles, six hundred shekels of gold. Appendix C. Chronicles III., 1 (6).

SECT. XIV   THE UNITED KINGDOM   93

20. And Araunah looked forth and saw the king and his servants coming on toward him: and Araunah went out, and bowed himself before the king with his face to the ground. 21. And Araunah said, Wherefore is my lord the king come to his servant? And David said, To buy the threshing-floor of thee, to build an altar unto the Lord, that the plague may be stayed from the people. 22. And Araunah said unto David, Let my lord the king take and offer up what seemeth good unto him: behold, the oxen for the burnt offering, and the threshing instruments and the furniture of the oxen for the wood: 23. all this, O king, doth Araunah give unto the king. And Araunah said unto the king, The Lord thy God accept thee.	and his four sons that were with him hid themselves. Now Ornan was threshing wheat. 21. And as David came to Ornan, Ornan looked and saw David, and went out of the threshing-floor, and bowed himself to David with his face to the ground. 22. Then David said to Ornan, Give me the place of this threshing-floor, that I may build thereon an altar unto the Lord: for the full price shalt thou give it me: that the plague may be stayed from the people. 23. And Ornan said unto David, Take it to thee, and let my lord the king do that which is good in his eyes: lo, I give thee the oxen for burnt offerings and the threshing instruments for wood, and the wheat for the meal offering: I give it all.
24. And the king said unto Araunah, Nay; but I will verily buy it of thee at a price: neither will I offer burnt offerings unto the Lord my God which cost me nothing. So David bought the threshing-floor and the oxen for ((fifty shekels of silver.)) 25. And David built there an altar unto the Lord, and offered burnt offerings and peace offerings, (So the Lord was intreated for the land, and the plague was stayed from Israel.)	24. And king David said to Ornan, Nay; but I will verily buy it for the full price: for I will not take that which is thine for the Lord, nor offer a burnt offering without cost. 25. So David gave to Ornan for the place ((six hundred shekels of gold by weight.)) 26. And David built there an altar unto the Lord, and offered burnt offerings and peace offerings, and called upon the Lord, (and he answered him from heaven by fire upon the altar of burnt offering. 27. And the Lord commanded the angel; and he put up his sword again into the sheath thereof.)* 28. At that time, when David saw that the Lord had answered him in the threshing-floor of Ornan the Jebusite, then he sacrificed there. 29. For the tabernacle of the Lord, which Moses made in the wilderness, and the altar of burnt offering, were at that time in the high place at Gibeon. 30. But David could not go before it to inquire of God: for he was afraid because of the sword of the angel of the Lord. 22:1. Then David said, This is the house of the Lord God, and this is the altar of burnt offering for Israel.

THE HOUSE OF DAVID
   B. C. 1049 (Usher)
I David
   B. C. 1010 (Rev.)   NATHAN

SECTION XV

Final Arrangements for the Temple

I Chron. 22:2. And David commanded to gather together the strangers that were in the land of Israel; and he set masons to hew wrought stones to build the house of God. 3. And David prepared iron in abundance for the nails for the doors of the gates, and for the couplings; and brass in abundance without weight; 4. and cedar trees without number; for the Zidonians and they of Tyre brought cedar trees in abundance to David. 5. And David said, Solomon my son is young and tender, and the house that is to be builded for the Lord must be exceeding magnifical, of fame and glory throughout all countries: I will therefore make preparation for it. So David prepared abundantly before his death.

Charge to Solomon
6. Then he called for Solomon his son, and charged him to build an house for the Lord, the God of Israel. 7. And David said to Solomon his son, As for me, it was in my heart to build an house unto the name of the Lord my God. 8. But the word of the Lord * came to me, saying, Thou hast shed blood abundantly, and hast made great wars: thou shalt not build an house unto my name, because thou hast shed much blood upon the earth in my sight: 9. behold, a son shall be born to thee, who shall be a man of rest; and I will

---

* Notice the additional reason given in I Chron. 17:4-15. And it came to pass the same night, that the word of God came to Nathan, saying, Go and tell David my servant, Thus saith the Lord, Thou shalt not build me an house to dwell in: for I have not dwelt in an house since the day that I brought up Israel, unto this day; but have gone from tent to tent, and from one tabernacle to another. In all places wherein I have walked with all Israel, spake I a word with any of the judges of Israel, whom I commanded to feed my people, saying, Why have ye not built me an house of cedar? Now therefore thus shalt thou say unto my servant David, Thus saith the Lord of hosts, I took thee from the sheepcote, from following the sheep, that thou shouldest be prince over my people Israel; and I have been with thee whithersoever thou wentest, and have cut off all thine enemies from before thee; and I will make thee a name, like unto the name of the great ones that are in the earth. Moreover I tell thee, that the Lord will build thee an house. And it shall come to pass, when thy days be fulfilled that thou must go to be with thy fathers, that I will set up thy seed after thee, which shall be of thy sons and I will establish his kingdom. He shall build me an house, and I will establish his throne forever. I will be his father, and he shall be my son and I will not take my mercy away from him, as I took it from him that was before thee: but I will settle him in mine house and in my kingdom forever: and his throne shall be established forever.

give him rest from all his enemies round about; for his name shall be Solomon, and I will give peace and quietness unto Israel in his days: 10. he shall build an house for my name; and he shall be my son, and I will be his father; and I will establish the throne of his kingdom over Israel forever. 11. Now, my son, the Lord be with thee: prosper thou, and build the house of the Lord thy God, as he hath spoken concerning thee. 12. Only the Lord give thee discretion and understanding, and give thee charge concerning Israel; that so thou mayest keep the law of the Lord thy God. 13. Then shalt thou prosper, if thou observe to do the statutes and the judgments which the Lord charged Moses with concerning Israel; be strong and of good courage; fear not, neither be dismayed. 14. Now, behold, in my affliction I have prepared for the house of the Lord an hundred thousand talents of gold, and a thousand thousand talents of silver; and of brass and iron without weight; for it is in abundance; timber also and stone have I prepared; and thou mayest add thereto. 15. Moreover there are workmen with thee in abundance, hewers and workers of stone and timber, and all men that are cunning in any manner of work; 16. of the gold, the silver, and the brass, and the iron, there is no number; arise and be doing, and the Lord be with thee.

Command to Princes of Israel

17. David also commanded all the princes of Israel to help Solomon his son, saying, 18. Is not the Lord your God with you? and hath he not given you rest on every side? for he hath delivered the inhabitants of the land into mine hand; and the land is subdued before the Lord, and before his people. 19. Now set your heart and your soul to seek after the Lord your God; arise therefore, and build ye the sanctuary of the Lord God, to bring the ark of the covenant of the Lord, and the holy vessels of God, into the house that is to be built to the name of the Lord.

I Chron. 23:1. Now David was old and full of days; and he made Solomon his son king over Israel. 2. And he gathered together all the princes of Israel, with the priests and the Levites.

Number and Service of the Levites

3. And the Levites were numbered from thirty years old and upward: and their number by their polls, man by man, was thirty and eight thousand. 4. Of these, twenty and four thousand were to oversee the work of the house of the Lord; and six thousand were officers and judges: 5. and four thousand were doorkeepers; and four thousand praised the Lord with the instruments which I made, said David, to praise therewith. 6. And David divided them into courses according to the sons of Levi; GERSHON, KOHATH, and MERARI. 7. Of the GERSHONITES; Ladan and Shimei. 8. The sons of Ladan; Jehiel the chief, and Zetham, and Joel, three. 9. The sons of Shimei; Shelometh, and Haziel, and Haran, three. These were the heads of the fathers' houses of Ladan. 10. And the sons of Shimei; Jahath, Zina, and Jeush, and Beraiah. These four were the sons of Shimei. 11. And Jahath was the chief, and Zizah the second: but Jeush and Beraiah had not many sons; therefore they became a fathers' house in one reckoning. 12. The sons of KOHATH; Amram, Izhar, Hebron, and Uzziel, four. 13. The sons of Amram; Aaron and Moses: and Aaron was separated, that he should sanctify the most holy things, he and his sons, for ever, to burn incense before the Lord, to minister unto him, and to bless in his name for ever. 14. But as for Moses the man of God, his sons were named among the tribe of Levi. 15. The sons of Moses; Gershom and Eliezer.

And of the rest of the sons of Levi: of the sons of Gershom; Shebuel the chief: of the sons of Shebuel, Jehdeiah. And the sons of Eliezer were, Rehabiah the chief. And Eliezer had none other sons: but the sons of Rehabiah were many, Isshiah the chief. The sons of Izhar; Shelomith the chief; of the sons of Shelomith, Jahath. The sons of Hebron; Jeriah the chief, Amariah the second, Jahaziel the third, and Jekameam the fourth. The sons of Uzziel; Micah the chief; of the sons of Micah, Shamir. The brother of Micah, Isshiah; of the sons of Isshiah, Zechariah. The sons of MERARI: Mahli and Mushi; the sons of Jaaziah; Beno, and Shoham, and Zaccur, and Ibri. The sons of Mahli; Eleazar and Kish. And Eleazar died, and had no sons, but daughters only: and their brethren the sons of Kish, Jerameel, took them to wife. The sons of Mushi; Mahli, and Eder, and Jeremoth, three. These were the sons of Levi after their fathers' houses, even the heads of the fathers' houses of those that were counted, in the number of names by their polls, who did the work for the service of the house of the Lord from twenty years old and upward. These likewise cast lots even as their brethren the sons of Aaron in the presence of David the king, and Zadok, and Abimelech, and the heads of the fathers' houses of the priests and of the Levites; the fathers' houses of the chief even as those of his younger brother. I Chron. 23:25. For David said, The Lord, the God of Israel, hath given rest unto his people; and he dwelleth in Jerusalem for ever: 26. and also the Levites shall no more have need to carry the tabernacle and all the vessels of it for the service thereof. 27. For by the last words of David the sons of Levi were numbered, from twenty years old and upward. 28. For their office was to wait on the sons of Aaron for the service of the house of the Lord, in the courts, and in the chambers, and in the purifying of all holy things, even the work of the service of the house of God; 29. for the shewbread also, and for the fine flour for a meal offering, whether of unleavened wafers, or of that which is baked in the pan, or of that which is soaked, and for all manner of measure and size; 30. and to stand every morning to thank and praise the Lord, and likewise at even; 31. and to offer all burnt offerings unto the Lord, in the sabbaths, in the new moons, and on the set feasts, in number according to the ordinance concerning them, continually before the Lord: 32. and that they should keep the charge of the tent of meeting, and the charge of the holy place, and the charge of the sons of Aaron their brethren, for the service of the house of the Lord.

Twenty-four Courses of the Priests

I Chron. 24:1. And the courses of the sons of Aaron were these. The sons of Aaron; Nadab and Abihu, Eleazar and Ithamar. 2. But Nadab and Abihu died before their father, and had no children: therefore Eleazar and Ithamar executed the priest's office. 3. And David with Zadok of the sons of Eleazar, and Ahimelech of the sons of Ithamar, divided them according to their ordering in their service. 4. And there were more chief men found of the sons of Eleazar than of the sons of Ithamar; and thus were they divided: of the sons of Eleazar there were sixteen, heads of fathers' houses; and of the sons of Ithamar, according to their fathers' houses, eight. 5. Thus were they divided by lot, one sort with another; for there were princes of the sanctuary, and princes of God, both of the sons of Eleazar, and of the sons of Ithamar. 6. And Shemaiah the son of Nethanel the scribe, who was of the Levites, wrote them in the presence of the king, and the princes, and Zadok the priest, and Ahimelech the son of Abiathar, and the heads of

I Chron. 23:16. The sons of Gershom; Shebuel the chief. 17. And the sons of Eliezer were, Rehabiah the chief. And Eliezer had none other sons; but the sons of Rehabiah were very many. 18. The sons of Izhar; Shelomith the chief. 19. The sons of Hebron; Jeriah the chief, Amariah the second, Jahaziel the third, and Jekameam the fourth. 20. The sons of Uzziel; Micah the chief, and Isshiah the second.

21. The sons of MERARI; Mahli and Mushi. The sons of Mahli; Eleazar and Kish. 22. And Eleazar died, and had no sons, but daughters only: and their brethren the sons of Kish took them to wife. 23. The sons of Mushi; Mahli, and Eder, and Jeremoth, three. 24. These were the sons of Levi after their fathers' houses, even the heads of the fathers' houses of those of them that were counted, in the number of names by their polls, who did the work for the service of the house of the Lord from twenty years old and upward.

I Chron. 24:20. And of the rest of the sons of Levi: of the sons of Amram, Shubael; of the sons of Shubael, Jehdeiah. 21. Of Rehabiah: of the sons of Rehabiah, Isshiah the chief. 22. Of the Izharites, Shelomoth; of the sons of Shelomoth, Jahath. 23. And the sons of Hebron; Jeriah the chief, Amariah the second, Jahaziel the third, Jakameam the fourth. 24. The sons of Uzziel, Micah; of the sons of Micah, Shamir. 25. The brother of Micah, Isshiah; of the sons of Isshiah, Zechariah. 26. The sons of MERARI; Mahli and Mushi: the sons of Jaaziah; Beno. 27. The sons of MERARI; of Jaaziah, Beno, and Shoham, and Zaccur, and Ibri. 28. Of Mahli; Eleazar, who had no sons. 29. Of Kish; the sons of Kish, Jerahmeel. 30. And the sons of Mushi; Mahli, and Eder, and Jerimoth.

These were the sons of the Levites after their fathers' houses.

31. These likewise cast lots even as their brethren the sons of Aaron in the presence of David the king, and Zadok, and Ahimelech, and the heads of the fathers' houses of the priests and of the Levites; the fathers' houses of the chief even as those of his younger brother.

the fathers' houses of the priests and of the Levites: one fathers' house being taken for Eleazar, and one taken for Ithamar. 7. Now the first lot came forth to Jehoiarib, the second to Jedaiah; 8. the third to Harim, the fourth to Seorim; 9. the fifth to Malchijah, the sixth to Mijamin; 10. the seventh to Hakkoz, the eight to Abijah; 11. the ninth to Jeshua, the tenth to Shecaniah; 12. the eleventh to Eliashib, the twelfth to Jakim, 13. the thirteenth to Huppah, the fourteenth to Jeshebeab; 14. the fifteenth to Bilgah, the sixteenth to Immer; 15. the seventeenth to Hezir, the eighteenth to Happizez; 16. the nineteenth to Pethahiah, the twentieth to Jehezkel; 17. the one and twentieth to Jachin, the two and twentieth to Gamul; 18. the three and twentieth to Delaiah, the four and twentieth to Maaziah. 19. This was the ordering of them in their service, to come into the house of the Lord according to the ordinance given unto them by the hand of Aaron their father, as the Lord, the God of Israel had commanded him.

Twenty-four Classes of Singers

I Chron. 25:1. Moreover David and the captains of the host separated for the service certain of the sons of Asaph, and of Heman, and of Jeduthun, who should prophesy with harps, with psalteries, and with cymbals: and the number of them that did the work according to their service was: 2. of the sons of Asaph; Zaccur, and Joseph, and Nethaniah, and Asharelah, the sons of Asaph; under the hand of Asaph, who prophesied after the order of the king. 3. Of Jeduthun: the sons of Jeduthun; Gedaliah, and Zeri, and Jeshaiah, Hashabiah, and Mattithiah, six; under the hand of their father Jeduthun with the harp, who prophesied in giving thanks and praising the Lord. 4. Of Heman: the sons of Heman; Bukkiah, Mattiniah, Uzziel, Shebuel, and Jerimoth, Hananiah, Hanani, Eliathah, Giddalti, and Romanti-ezer, Joshbekashah, Mallothi, Hothir, Mahazioth: 5. all these were the sons of Heman the king's seer in the words of God, to lift up the horn. And God gave to Heman fourteen sons and three daughters. 6. All these were under the hand of their father for song in the house of the Lord, with cymbals, psalteries, and harps, for the service of the house of God; Asaph, Jeduthun, and Heman being under the order of the king. 7. And the number of them, with their brethren that were instructed in singing unto the Lord, even all that were skilful, was two hundred four-score and eight. 8. And they cast lots for their charges, all alike, as well the small as the great, the teacher as the scholar. 9. Now the first lot came forth for Asaph to Joseph: the second to Gedaliah; he and his brethren and sons were twelve: 10. the third to Zaccur, his sons and his brethren twelve: 11. the fourth to Izri, his sons and his brethren, twelve: 12. the fifth to Nethaniah, his sons and his brethren, twelve: 13. the sixth to Bukkiah, his sons and his brethren, twelve: 14. the seventh to Jesharelah, his sons and his brethren, twelve: 15. the eighth to Jeshiah, his sons and his brethren, twelve: 16. the ninth to Mattinaiah, his sons and his brethren, twelve: 17. the tenth to Shimei, his sons and his brethren, twelve: 18. the eleventh to Azarel, his sons and his brethren, twelve: 19. the twelfth to Hasabiah, his sons and his brethren, twelve: 20. for the thirteenth, Shubael, his sons and his brethren, twelve: 21. for the fourteenth, Mattithiah, his sons and his brethren, twelve: 22. for the fifteenth to Jeremoth, his sons and his brethren, twelve: 23. for the sixteenth to Hananiah, his sons and his brethren, twelve: 24. for the seventeenth to Joshbekashah, his sons and his brethren, twelve: 25. for the eighteenth to Hanani, his sons and his brethren, twelve: 26. for the nineteenth to Mallothi, his sons and his brethren, twelve: 27. for the twentieth to Eliathah, his sons and his brethren, twelve: 28. for the one and twentieth to Hothir, his sons and his brethren, twelve: 29. for the two and twentieth to Giddalti, his sons and his brethren, twelve: 30. for the three and twentieth to Mahazioth, his sons and his brethren, twelve: 31. for the four and twentieth to Romanti-ezer, his sons and his brethren, twelve.

Courses of Doorkeepers

I Chron. 26:1. For the courses of the doorkeepers: of the Korahites; Meshelemiah the son of Kore, of the sons of Asaph. 2. And Meshelemiah had sons; Zechariah the firstborn, Jediael the second, Zebadiah the third, Jathniel the fourth; 3. Elam the fifth, Jehohanan the sixth, Eliehoenai the seventh. 4. And Obed-edom had sons; Shemaiah the firstborn, Jehozabad the second, Joah the third, and Sacar the fourth, and Nethanel the fifth; 5. Ammiel the sixth, Issachar the seventh, Peullethai the eighth: for God blessed him. 6. Also unto Shemaiah his son were sons born, that ruled over the house of their father: for they were mighty men of valour. 7. The sons of Shemaiah; Othni, and Rephael, and Obed, Elzabad, whose brethren were valiant men, Elihu, and Semachiah. 8. All these were of the sons of Obed-edom: they and their sons and their brethren, able men in strength for the service; threescore and two of Obed-edom. 9. And Meshelemiah had sons and brethren, valiant men, eighteen. 10. Also Hosah, of the children of Merari, had sons; Shimri the chief, (for though he was not the firstborn, yet his father made him chief:) 11. Hilkiah the second, Tebeliah the third, Zechariah the fourth: all the sons and brethren of Hosah were thirteen. 12. Of these were the courses of the doorkeepers, even of the chief men, having charges like as their brethren, to minister in the house of the Lord. 13. And they cast lots, as well the small as the great, according to their fathers' houses, for every gate. 14. And the lot eastward fell to Shelemiah. Then for Zechariah his son, a discreet counsellor, they cast lots; and his lot came out northward. 15. To Obed-edom southward; and to his sons the storehouse. 16. To Shuppim and Hosah westward, by the gate of Shallecheth, at the causeway that goeth up, ward against ward. 17. Eastward were six Levites, northward four a day, southward four a day, and for the storehouse two and two. 18. For Parbar westward, four at the causeway, and two at Parbar. 19. These were the courses of the doorkeepers; of the sons of the Korahites, and of the sons of Merari.

Levites over the Treasuries

20. And of the Levites, Ahijah was over the treasuries of the house of God, and over the treasuries of the dedicated things. 21. The sons of Ladan; the sons of the Gershonites belonging to Ladan, the heads of the fathers' houses belonging to Ladan the Gershonite; Jehieli. 22. The sons of Jehieli; Zetham and Joel his brother, over the treasuries of the house of the Lord. 23. Of the Amramites, of the Izharites, of the Hebronites, of the Uzzielites: 24. and Shebuel the son of Gershom, the son of Moses was ruler over the treasuries. 25. And his brethren; of Eliezer came Rehibiah his son, and Jeshaiah his son, and Joram his son, and Zichri his son, and Shelomoth his son. 26. This Shelomoth and his brethren were over all the treasuries of the dedicated things, which David the king, and the heads of the fathers' houses, the captains over thousands and hundreds, and the captains of the host had dedicated. 27. Out of the spoil won in battles did they dedicate to repair the house of the Lord. 28. And all that Samuel the seer, and Saul the son of Kish, and Abner the son of Ner, and Joab the son of Zeruiah, had dedicated; whosoever had dedicated anything, it was under the hand of Shelomoth, and of his brethren. 29. Of the Izharites, Chenaniah and his sons were for the outward business over Israel, for officers and judges.

30. Of the Hebronites, Hashabiah and his brethren, men of valour, a thousand and seven hundred, had the oversight of Israel beyond Jordan westward; for all the business of the Lord, and for the service of the king. 31. Of the Hebronites was Jerijah the chief, even of the Hebronites, according to their generations by fathers' houses. In the fortieth year of the reign of David they were sought for, and there were found among them mighty men of valour at Jazer of Gilead. 32. And his brethren, men of valour, were two thousand and seven hundred, heads of fathers' houses, whom king David made overseers over the Reubenites, and the Gadites, and the half tribe of the Manassites, for every matter pertaining to God, and for the affairs of the king.

Twelve Courses of the Army

I Chron. 27:1. Now the children of Israel after their number, to wit, the heads of the fathers' houses and the captains of thousands and of hundreds, and their officers that served the king, in any matter of the courses which came in and went out month by month throughout all the months of the year, of every course were twenty and four thousand. 2. Over the first course for the first month was Jashobeam the son of Zabdiel: and in his course were twenty and four thousand. 3. He was of the children of Perez, the chief of all the captains of the host for the first month. 4. And over the course of the second month was Dodai the Ahohite, and his course; and Mikloth the ruler: and in his course were twenty and four thousand. 5. The third captain of the host for the third month was Benaiah, the son of Jehoiada the priest, chief: and in his course were twenty and four thousand. 6. This is that Benaiah, who was the mighty man of the thirty, and over the thirty: and of his course was Ammizabad his son. 7. The fourth captain for the fourth month was Asahel the brother of Joab, and Zebadiah his son after him: and in his course were twenty and four thousand. 8. The fifth captain for the fifth month was Shamhuth the Izrahite: and in his course were twenty and four thousand. 9. The sixth captain for the sixth month was Ira the son of Ikkesh the Tekohite: and in his course were twenty and four thousand. 10. The seventh captain for the seventh month was Helez the Pelonite, of the children of Ephraim: and in his course were twenty and four thousand. 11. The eighth captain for the eighth month was Sibbecai the Hushathite, of the Zerahites: and in his course were twenty and four thousand. 12. The ninth captain for the ninth month was Abiezer the Anothothite, of the Benjamites: and in his course were twenty and four thousand. 13. The tenth captain for the tenth month was Maharai the Netophathite, of the Zerahites: and in his course were twenty and four thousand. 14. The eleventh captain for the eleventh month was Benaiah the Pirathonite, of the children of Ephraim: and in his course were twenty and four thousand. 15. The twelfth captain for the twelfth month was Heldai the Netophathite, of Othniel: and in his course were twenty and four thousand.

Chiefs of the Tribes

16. Furthermore over the tribes of Israel: of the Reubenites was Eliezer the son of Zichri the ruler: of the Simeonites, Shephatiah the son of Maacah: 17. of Levi, Hashabiah the son of Kemuel: of Aaron, Zadok: 18. of Judah, Elihu, one of the brethren of David: of Issachar, Omri the son of Michael: 19. of Zebulon, Ishmaiah the son of Obadiah: of Naphtali, Jeremoth the son of Azriel: 20. of the children of Ephraim, Hoshea the son of Azaziah: of the half tribe of Manasseh, Joel the son of Pedaiah: 21. of the half tribe of Manasseh in Gilead; Iddo the son of Zechariah: of Benjamin, Jaasiel the son of Abner: 22. of Dan, Azarel the son of Jeraham. These were the captains of the tribes of Israel.

Rulers over the King's Possessions

25. And over the king's treasuries was Azmaveth the son of Adiel: and over the treasuries in the fields, in the cities, and in the villages, and in the castles, was Jonathan the son of Uzziah: 26. and over them that did the work of the field for tillage of the ground was Ezri the son of Chelub: 27. and over the vineyards was Shimei the Ramathite: and over the increase of the vineyards for the wine cellars was Zabdi the Shipmite: 28. and over the olive trees and the sycamore trees that were in the low plain and was Baal-hanan the Gederite: and over the cellars of oil was Joash: 29. and over the herds that fed in Sharon was Shitrai the Sharonite: and over the herds that were in the valleys was Shaphat the son of Adlai: 30. and over the camels was Obil the Ishmaelite: and over the asses was Jehdeiah the Merothonite: 31. and over the flocks was Jaziz the Hagrite. All these were the rulers of the substance which was king David's.

Officers of State

32. Also Jonathan, David's uncle, was a counsellor, a man of understanding, and a scribe: and Jehiel the son of Hachmoni was with the king's sons: 33. And Ahithophel was the king's counsellor: and Hushai the Archite was the king's friend: 34. and after Ahithophel was Jehoiada the son of Benaiah, and Abiathar: and the captain of the king's host was Joab.

THE HOUSE OF DAVID
B. C. 1049 (Usher)
I David
B. C. 1010 (Rev.)

NATHAN

SECTION XVI

David's Last Words and Acts

Address to National Assembly

I Chron. 28:1. And David assembled all the princes of Israel, the princes of the tribes, and the captains of the companies that served the king by course, and the captains of thousands, and the captains of hundreds, and the rulers over all the substance and possessions of the king and his sons, with the officers, and the mighty men, even all the mighty men of valour, unto Jerusalem. 2. Then David the king stood up upon his feet, and said, Hear me, my brethren, and my people: as for me, it was in mine heart to build an house of rest for the ark of the covenant of the Lord, and for the footstool of our God; and I had made ready for the building. 3. But God said unto me, Thou shalt not build an house for my name, because thou art a man of war, and hast shed blood. 4. Howbeit the Lord, the God of Israel, chose me out of all the house of my father to be king over Israel for ever: for he hath chosen Judah to be prince; and in the house of Judah, the house of my father; and among the sons of my father he took pleasure in me to make me king over all Israel: 5. and of all my sons, (for the Lord hath given me many sons,) he hath chosen Solomon my son to sit upon the throne of the kingdom of the Lord over Israel. 6. And he said unto me, Solomon thy son, he shall build my house and my courts: for I have chosen him to be my son, and I will be his father. 7. And I will establish his kingdom for ever, if he be constant to do my commandments and my judgements, as at this day. 8. Now therefore, in the sight of all Israel, the congregation of the Lord, and in the audience of our God, observe and seek out all the commandments of the Lord your God; that ye may possess this good land, and leave it for an inheritance to your children after you for ever.

Address to Solomon

9. And thou, Solomon my son, know thou the God of thy father, and serve him with a perfect heart and with a willing mind: for the Lord searcheth all hearts, and understandeth all the imaginations of the thoughts: if thou seek him, he will be found of thee; but if thou forsake him, he will cast thee off forever. 10. Take heed now; for the Lord hath chosen thee to build an house for the sanctuary: be strong and do it.

Gives Pattern of the Temple

11. Then David gave to Solomon his son the pattern of the porch of the temple, and of the houses thereof, and of the treasuries thereof, and of the upper rooms thereof, and of the inner chambers thereof, and of the place of the mercy seat: 12. and the pattern of all that he had by the spirit, for the courts of the house of the Lord, and for all the chambers round about, for the treasuries of the house of God, and for the treasuries of the dedicated

things: 13. also for the courses of the priests and the Levites, and for all the work of the service of the house of the Lord, and for all the vessels of service in the house of the Lord: 14. of gold by weight for the vessels of gold, for all vessels of every kind of service; of silver for all the vessels of silver by weight, for all vessels of every kind of service: 15. by weight also for the candlesticks of gold, and for the lamps thereof, of gold, by weight for every candlestick and for the lamps thereof: according to the use of every candlestick: 16. and the gold by weight for the tables of shewbread, for every table; and silver for the tables of silver: 17. and the fleshhooks, and the basons, and the cups, of pure gold: and for the golden bowls by weight for every bowl; and for the silver bowls by weight for every bowl: 18. and for the altar of incense refined gold by weight: and gold for the pattern of the chariot, even the cherubim, that spread out their wings, and covered the ark of the covenant of the Lord. 19. All this, said David, have I been made to understand in writing from the hand of the Lord, even all the works of this pattern. 20. And David said to Solomon his son, Be strong and of good courage, and do it: fear not, nor be dismayed: for the Lord God, even my God, is with thee; he will not fail thee, nor forsake thee, until all the work for the service of the house of the Lord be finished. 21. And, behold, there are the courses of the priests and the Levites for all the service of the house of God: and there shall be with thee in all manner of work every willing man that hath skill, for any manner of service: also the captains and all the people will be wholly at thy commandment.

Address to Congregation

I Chron. 29:1. And David the king said unto all the congregation, Solomon my son, whom alone God hath chosen, is yet young and tender, and the work is great: for the palace is not for man, but for the Lord God. 2. Now I have prepared with all my might for the house of my God the gold for the things of gold, and the silver for the things of silver, and the brass for the things of brass, the iron for the things of iron, and wood for the things of wood; onyx stones, and stones to be set, stones for inlaid work, and of divers colours, and all manner of precious stones, and marble stones in abundance. 3. Moreover also, because I have set my affection to the house of my God, seeing that I have a treasure of mine own of gold and silver, I give it unto the house of my God, over and above all that I have prepared for the holy house: 4. even three thousand talents of gold, of the gold of Ophir, and seven thousand talents of refined silver, to overlay the walls of the houses withal: 5. of gold for the things of gold, and of silver for the things of silver, and for all manner of work to be made by the hand of artificers. Who then offereth willingly to consecrate himself this day unto the Lord? 6. Then the princes of the fathers' houses, and the princes of the tribes of Israel, and the captains of thousands and of hundreds, with the rulers over the king's work, offered willingly: 7. and they gave for the service of the house of God of gold five thousand talents and ten thousand darics, and of silver ten thousand talents, and of brass eighteen thousand talents, and of iron a hundred thousand talents. 8. And they with whom precious stones were found gave them to the treasure of the house of the Lord, under the hand of Jehiel the Gershonite. 9. Then the people rejoiced, for that they offered willingly, because with a perfect heart they offered willingly to the Lord: and David the king also rejoiced with great joy.

Blesses, Thanks, and Praises the Lord

10. Wherefore David blessed the Lord before all the congregation: and David said, Blessed be thou, O Lord, the God of Israel our father, for ever and ever. 11. Thine, O Lord, is the greatness, and the power, and the glory, and the victory, and the majesty: for

all that is in the heaven and in the earth is thine; thine is the kingdom, O Lord, and thou art exalted as head above all. 12. Both riches and honour come of thee, and thou rulest over all; and in thine hand is power and might; and in thine hand it is to make great, and to give strength unto all. 13. Now therefore, our God, we thank thee, and praise thy glorious name. 14. But who am I, and what is my people, that we should be able to offer so willingly after this sort? for all things come of thee, and of thine own have we given thee. 15. For we are strangers before thee, and sojourners, as all our fathers were: our days on the earth are as a shadow, and there is no abiding. 16. O Lord our God, all this store that we have prepared to build thee an house for thine holy name cometh of thine hand, and is all thine own. 17. I know also, my God, that thou triest the heart, and hast pleasure in uprightness. As for me, in the uprightness of mine heart I have willingly offered all these things: and now have I seen with joy thy people, which are present here, to offer willingly unto thee. 18. O Lord, the God of Abraham, of Isaac, and of Israel, our fathers, keep this for ever in the imagination of the thoughts of the heart of thy people, and prepare their heart unto thee: 19. and give unto Solomon my son a perfect heart, to keep thy commandments, thy testimonies, and thy statutes, and to do all these things, and to build the palace, for the which I have made provision.

Congregation Blesses God and Sacrifices

20. And David said to all the congregation, Now bless the Lord your God. And all the congregation blessed the Lord the God of their fathers, and bowed down their heads, and worshipped the Lord, and the king. 21. And they sacrificed sacrifices unto the Lord, and offered burnt offerings unto the Lord, on the morrow after that day, even a thousand bullocks, a thousand rams, and a thousand lambs, with their drink offerings, and sacrifices in abundance for all Israel; 22ª. and did eat and drink before the Lord on that day with great gladness.

The Ideal Ruler

II Sam. 23:1. Now these be the Last words of David.
David the son of Jesse saith,
And the man who was raised on high saith,
The anointed of the God of Jacob,
And the sweet psalmist of Israel:
2. The spirit of the Lord spake by me,
And his word was upon my tongue.
3. The God of Israel said,
The Rock of Israel spake to me:
One that ruleth over men righteously,
That ruleth in the fear of God,
4. He shall be as the light of the morning, when the sun riseth,
A morning without clouds;
When the tender grass springeth out of the earth,
Through clear shining after rain.
5. Verily my house is not so with God;
Yet he hath made with me an everlasting covenant,
Ordered in all things and sure;
For it is all my salvation, and all my desire,
Although he maketh it not to grow.

6. But the ungodly shall be all of them as thorns to be thrust away,
   For they cannot be taken with the hand:
7. But the man that toucheth them
   Must be armed with iron and the staff of a spear;
   And they shall be utterly burned with fire in their place.

I Kings 1:1. Now king David was old and stricken in years; and they covered him with clothes, but he gat no heat. 2. Wherefore his servants said unto him, let there be sought for my lord the king a young virgin: and let her stand before the king, and cherish him; and let her lie in thy bosom that my lord the king may get heat. 3. So they sought for a fair damsel throughout all the coasts of Israel, and found Abishag the Shunamite, and brought her to the king. 4. And the damsel was very fair; and she cherished the king, and ministered to him; but the king knew her not. 5. Then Adonijah the son of Haggith exalted himself, saying, I will be king: and he prepared him chariots and horsemen, and fifty men to run before him. 6. And his father had not displeased him at any time in saying, Why hast thou done so? and he was also a very goodly man; and he was born after Absalom. 7. And he conferred with Joab the son of Zeruiah, and with Abiathar the priest: and they following Adonijah helped him. 8. But Zadok the priest, and Benaiah the son of Jehoiada, and Nathan the prophet, and Shimei, and Rei, and the mighty men which belonged to David, were not with Adonijah. 9. And Adonijah slew sheep and oxen and fatlings by the stone of Zoheleth, which is beside En-rogel; and he called all his brethren the king's sons, and all the men of Judah the king's servants: 10. but Nathan the prophet, and Benaiah, and the mighty men, and Solomon his brother, he called not. 11. Then Nathan spake unto Bath-sheba the mother of Solomon, saying, Hast thou not heard that Adonijah the son of Haggith doth reign, and David our lord knoweth it not? 12. Now therefore come, let me, I pray thee, give thee counsel, that thou mayest save thine own life, and the life of thy son Solomon. 13. Go and get thee in unto king David, and say unto him, Didst not thou, my lord, O king, swear unto thine handmaid, saying, Assuredly Solomon thy son shall reign after me, and he shall sit upon my throne? why then doth Adonijah reign? 14. Behold, while thou yet talkest there with the king, I also will come in after thee, and confirm thy words. 15. And Bath-sheba went in unto the king into the chamber: and the king was very old; and Abishag the Shunamite ministered unto the king. 16. And Bath-sheba bowed, and did obeisance unto the king. And the king said, What wouldest thou? 17. And she said unto him, My lord, thou swarest by the Lord thy God unto thy handmaid, saying, Assuredly Solomon thy son shall reign after me, and he shall sit upon my throne. 18. And now, behold, Adonijah reigneth; and thou, my lord the king, knowest it not: 19. and he hath slain oxen and fatlings and sheep in abundance, and hath called all the sons of the king, and Abiathar the priest, and Joab the captain of the host: but Solomon thy servant hath he not called. 20. And thou, my lord the king, the eyes of all Israel are upon thee, that thou shouldest tell them who shall sit on the throne of my lord the king after him. 21. Otherwise it shall come to pass, when my lord the king shall sleep with his fathers, that I and my son Solomon shall be counted offenders. 22. And, lo, while she yet talked with the king, Nathan the prophet came in. 23. And they told the king, saying, Behold, Nathan the prophet. And when he was come in before the king, he bowed himself before the king with his face to the ground. 24. And Nathan said, My lord,

Abishag Found for David

Adonijah's Rebellion

O king, hast thou said, Adonijah shall reign after me, and he shall sit upon my throne? 25. For he is gone down this day, and hath slain oxen and fatlings and sheep in abundance, and hath called all the king's sons, and the captains of the host, and Abiathar the priest; and, behold, they eat and drink before him, and say, God save king Adonijah. 26. But me, even me thy servant, and Zadok the priest, and Benaiah the son of Jehoiada, and thy servant Solomon, hath he not called. 27. Is this thing done by my lord the king, and thou hast not shewed unto thy servants who should sit on the throne of my lord the king after him? 28. Then king David answered and said, Call me Bath-sheba. And she came into the king's presence, and stood before the king. 29. And the king sware, and said, As the Lord liveth, who hath redeemed my soul out of all adversity, 30. verily as I sware unto thee by the Lord, the God of Israel, saying, Assuredly Solomon thy son shall reign after me, and he shall sit upon my throne in my stead; verily so will I do this day. 31. Then Bath-sheba bowed with her face to the earth, and did obeisance to the king, and said, Let my lord king David live for ever. 32. And king David said, Call me Zadok the priest, and Nathan the prophet, and Benaiah the son of Jehoiada. And they came before the king. 33. And the king said unto them, Take with you the servants of your lord, and cause Solomon my son to ride upon mine own mule, and bring him down to Gihon: 34. And let Zadok the priest and Nathan the prophet anoint him there king over Israel: and blow ye with the trumpet, and say, God save king Solomon. 35. Then ye shall come up after him and he shall come and sit upon my throne; for he shall be king in my stead: and I have appointed him to be prince over Israel and over Judah. 36. And Benaiah the son of Jehoiada answered the king, and said, Amen: the Lord, the God of my lord the king, say so too. 37. As the Lord hath been with my lord the king, even so be he with Solomon, and make his throne greater than the throne of my lord king David. 38. So Zadok the priest, and Nathan the prophet, and Benaiah the son of Jehoiada, and the Cherethites and the Pelethites, went down, and caused Solomon to ride up on king David's mule, and brought him to Gihon. 39. And Zadok the priest took the horn of oil out of the Tent, and anointed Solomon. And they made Solomon the son of David king the second time, and anointed him unto the Lord to be prince, and Zadok to be priest. And they blew the trumpet; and all the people said, God save king Solomon. 40. And all the people came up after him, and the people piped with pipes, and rejoiced with great joy, so that the earth rent with the sound of them. 41. And Adonijah and all the guests that were with him heard it as they had made an end of eating. And when Joab heard the sound of the trumpet, he said, Wherefore is this noise of the city being in an uproar? 42. While he yet spake, behold, Jonathan the son of Abiathar the priest came: And Adonijah said, Come in; for thou art a worthy man and bringest good tidings. 43. And Jonathan answered and said to Adonijah, Verily our lord king David hath made Solomon king: 44. and the king hath sent with him Zadok the priest, and Nathan the prophet, and Benaiah the son of Jehoiada, and the Cherethites and the Pelethites, and they have caused him to ride upon the king's mule: 45. and Zadok the priest and Nathan the prophet have anointed him king in Gihon: and they are come up from thence rejoicing, so that the city rang again. This is the noise that ye have heard. 46. And also Solomon sitteth on the throne of the kingdom. 47. And moreover the king's servants came to bless our lord king David, saying, Thy God make the Name of Solomon better than thy name, and make his throne greater than thy throne: and the king bowed himself upon the bed. 48. And also thus said the king, Blessed be the Lord, the God of Israel, which hath given one to sit on my throne this day,

Solomon Made King the Second Time

I Kings 1:39. (And Zadok the priest took the horn of oil out of the Tent and anointed Solomon.)

And they blew the trumpet; and all the people said, God save king Solomon. 40. And all the people came up after him, and the people piped with pipes, and rejoiced with great joy, so that the earth rent with the sound of them.

I Chron. 29:22^b. (And they made Solomon the son of David king the second time and anointed him unto the Lord to be prince, and Zadok to be priest.)

mine eyes even seeing it. 49. And all the guests of Adonijah were afraid, and rose up, and went every man his way. 50. And Adonijah feared because of Solomon; and he arose, and went and caught hold on the horns of the altar. 51. And it was told Solomon, saying, Behold, Adonijah feareth king Solomon: for lo, he hath laid hold on the horns of the altar, saying, Let king Solomon swear unto me this day that he will not slay his servant with the sword. 52. And Solomon said, If he shall shew himself a worthy man, there shall not a hair of him fall to the earth; but if wickedness be found in him, he shall die. 53. So king Solomon sent, and they brought him down from the altar. And he came and did obeisance to king Solomon: and Solomon said unto him, Go to thine house.

Dying Charge to Solomon I Kings 2:1. Now the days of David drew nigh that he should die; and he charged Solomon his son, saying, 2. I go the way of all the earth: be thou strong therefore, and shew thyself a man; 3. and keep the charge of the Lord thy God, to walk in his ways to keep his statutes, and his commandments, and his judgements, and his testimonies, according to that which is written in the law of Moses, that thou mayest prosper in all that thou doest, and whithersoever thou turnest thyself: 4. that the Lord may establish his word which he spake concerning me, saying, If thy children take heed to their way, to walk before me in truth with all their heart and with all their soul, there shall not fail thee (said he) a man on the throne of Israel. 5. Moreover thou knowest also what Joab the son of Zeruiah did unto me, even what he did to the two captains of the host of Israel, unto Abner the son of Ner, and unto Amasa the son of Jether, whom he slew, and shed the blood of war in peace, and put the blood of war upon his girdle that was about his loins, and in his shoes that were on his feet. 6. Do therefore according to thy wisdom, and let not his hoar head go down to the grave in peace. 7. But shew kindness unto the sons of Barzillai the Gileadite, and let them be of those that eat at thy table: for so they came to me when I fled from Absalom thy brother. 8. And, behold, there is with thee Shimei the son of Gera the Benjamite, of Bahurim, who cursed me with a grievous curse in the day when I went to Mahanaim: but he came down to meet me at Jordan, and I sware to him by the Lord, saying, I will not put thee to death with the sword. 9. Now therefore hold him not guiltless, for thou art a wise man; and thou wilt know what thou oughtest to do unto him, and thou shalt bring his hoar head down to the grave with blood. Now David the son of Jesse reigned over all Israel. And the time that he reigned over Israel was forty years: seven years reigned he in Hebron, and thirty and three years reigned he in Jerusalem. And he died in a good old age, full of days, riches, and honour: and was buried in the city of David. And Solomon his son reigned in his stead. Now the acts of David the king first and last, behold, they are written in the history of Samuel the seer and in the history of Nathan the prophet, and in the history of Gad the seer; with all his reign and his might, and the times that went over him, and over Israel, and over all the kingdoms of the countries.

| I Kings 2:11. And the days that David reigned over Israel were forty years; seven years reigned he in Hebron, and thirty and three years reigned he in Jerusalem. 10. And David slept with his fathers and was buried in the city of David. | I Chron. 29:26. Now David the son of Jesse reigned over all Israel. 27. And the time that he reigned over Israel was forty years: seven years reigned he in Hebron, and thirty and three years reigned he in Jerusalem. 28. And he died in a good old age, full of days, riches, and honour: and Solomon his son reigned in his stead. 29. Now the acts of David the king, first and last, behold, they are written in the history of Samuel the seer, and in the history of Nathan the prophet, and in the history of Gad the seer; 30. with all his reign and his might, and the times that went over him, and over Israel, and over all the kingdoms of the countries. |

THE HOUSE OF DAVID
B. C. 1016 (Usher)
II Solomon
B. C. 977 (Rev.)

NATHAN THE PROPHET

SECTION XVII

Solomon's Accession to the Throne

Then Solomon sat on the throne of the Lord as king instead of David his father, and prospered; and all Israel obeyed him. And all the princes, and the mighty men, and all the sons likewise of king David, submitted themselves unto Solomon the king.

And Solomon the son of David was strengthened in his kingdom, and the Lord his God was with him, and magnified him exceedingly in the sight of all Israel, and bestowed upon him such royal majesty as had not been on any king before him in Israel.

Past Wrongs Righted

I Kings 2:13. Then Adonijah the son of Haggith came to Bath-sheba the mother of Solomon. And she said, Comest thou peaceably? And he said, Peaceably. 14. He said moreover, I have somewhat to say unto thee. And she said, Say on. 15. And he said, Thou knowest that the kingdom was mine, and that all Israel set their faces on me, that I should reign: howbeit the kingdom is turned about, and is become my brother's: for it was his from the Lord. 16. And now I ask one petition of thee, deny me not. And she said unto him, Say on. 17. And he said, Speak, I pray thee unto Solomon the king, (for he will not say thee nay,) that he give me Abishag the Shunamite to wife. 18. And Bath-sheba said, Well; I will speak for thee unto the king. 19. Bath-sheba therefore went unto king Solomon, to speak unto him for Adonijah. And the king rose up to meet her, and bowed himself unto her, and sat down on his throne, and caused a throne to be set for the king's mother; and she sat on his right hand. 20. Then she said, I ask one small petition of thee; deny me not. And the king said unto her, Ask on, my mother: for I will not deny thee. 21. And she said, Let Abishag the Shunamite be given to Adonijah thy brother to wife. 22. And king Solomon answered and said unto his mother, And why dost thou ask Abishag the Shunamite for Adonijah? ask for him the kingdom also; for he is mine elder brother; even for him, and for Abiathar the priest, and for Joab the son of Zeruiah. 23. Then king Solomon sware by the Lord, saying, God do so to me, and more also, if Adonijah have not spoken this word against his own life. 24. Now therefore, as the Lord liveth, who hath established me, and set me on the throne of David my father, and who hath made me an house, as he promised, surely Adonijah shall be put to death this day. 25. And king Solomon sent by the hand of Benaiah the son of Jehoiada; and he fell upon him that he died.

Adonijah and Abiathar

26. And unto Abiathar the priest said the king, Get thee to Anathoth, unto thine own fields; for thou art worthy of death: but I will not at this time put thee to death, because thou barest the ark of the Lord God before David my father and because thou wast

(I Kings 2:) 12. And Solomon sat upon the throne of David his father;	(I Chron. 29:) 23. Then Solomon sat on the throne of the Lord as king instead of David his father, and prospered; and all Israel obeyed him. 24. And all the princes and the mighty men, and all the sons likewise of king David, submitted themselves unto Solomon the king.	
and his kingdom was established greatly.	25. And the Lord magnified Solomon exceedingly in the sight of all Israel, and bestowed upon him such royal majesty as had not been on any king before him in Israel.	(II Chron. 1:) 1. And Solomon the son of David was strengthened in his kingdom, and the Lord his God was with him, and magnified him exceedingly.

afflicted in all wherein my father was afflicted. 27. So Solomon thrust out Abiathar from being priest unto the Lord; that he might fulfill the word of the Lord which he spake concerning the house of *a Eli in Shiloh. 28. And the tidings came to Joab: for Joab had turned after Adonijah, though he turned not after Absalom. And Joab fled unto the Tent of the Lord, and caught hold on the horns of the altar. 29. And it was told king Solomon, Joab is fled unto the Tent of the Lord, and behold, he is by the altar. Then Solomon sent Benaiah the son of Jehoiada, saying, Go, fall upon him. 30. And Benaiah came to the Tent of the Lord, and said unto him, Thus saith the king, Come forth. And he said, Nay; but I will die here. And Benaiah brought the king word again, saying, Thus said Joab, and thus he answered me. 31. And the king said unto him, Do as he hath said, and fall upon him, and bury him; that thou mayest eat take away the blood, which Joab shed without cause, from me and from my father's house. 32. And the Lord shall return his blood upon his own head, because he fell upon two men more righteous and better than he, and slew them with the sword, and my father David knew it not, to wit, *b Abner the son of Ner, captain of the host of Israel, and *c Amasa the son of Jether, captain of the host of Judah. 33. So shall their blood return upon the head of Joab, and upon the head of his seed for ever: but unto David, and unto his seed, and unto his house, and unto his throne, shall there be peace for ever from the Lord. 34. Then Benaiah the son of Jehoiada went up, and fell upon him, and slew him; and he was buried in his own house in the wilderness. 35. And the king put Benaiah the son of Jehoiada in his room over the host: and Zadok the priest did the king put in the room of Abiathar. 36. And the king sent and called for *d Shimei, and said unto him, Build thee an house in Jerusalem, and dwell there, and go not forth thence any whither. 37. For on the day thou goest out, and passest over the brook Kidron, know thou for certain that thou shalt surely die: thy blood shall be upon thine own head. 38. And Shimei said unto the king, The saying is good: as my lord the king hath said, so will thy servant do. And Shimei dwelt in Jerusalem many days. 39. And it came to pass at the end of three years, that two of the servants of Shimei ran away unto Achish, son of Maacah, king of Gath. And they told Shimei, saying, Behold, thy servants be in Gath. 40. And Shimei arose, and saddled his ass, and went to Gath to Achish, to seek his servants: and Shimei went, and brought his servants from Gath. 41. And it was told Solomon that Shimei had gone from Jerusalem to Gath, and was come again. 42. And the king sent and called for Shimei, and said unto him, Did I not make thee to swear by the Lord, and protested unto thee, saying, Know for certain, that on the day thou goest out, and walkest abroad any whither, thou shalt surely die? and thou saidst unto me, The saying that I have heard is good. 43. Why then hast thou not kept the oath of the Lord, and the commandment that I have charged thee with? 44. The king said moreover to Shimei, Thou knowest all the wickedness which thine heart is privy to, that thou didst to David my father: therefore the Lord shall return thy wickedness upon thine own head. 45. But king Solomon shall be blessed and the throne of David shall be established before the Lord for ever. 46. So the king commanded Benaiah the son of Jehoiada; and he went out and fell upon him, that he died. And the kingdom was established in the hand of Solomon.

*a I Sam. 2:30-36. 3:11-14.
*c II Sam. 20:10, 20
*b II Sam. 3:26-30
*d II Sam 16:5-13. 19:16-23.

SECT. XVII   *THE UNITED KINGDOM*

Princes of Solomon
I Kings 4:1. And king Solomon was king over all Israel. 2. And these were the princes which he had; Azariah the son of Zadok the priest; 3. Elihoreph and Ahijah, the sons of Shisha, scribes; Jehoshaphat the son of Ahilud, the recorder; 4. and Benaiah the son of Jehoiada was over the host; and Zadok and Abiathar were priests; 5. and Azariah the son of Nathan was over the officers; and Zabud the son of Nathan was priest, and the king's friend; 6. and Ahishar was over the household; and Adoniram the son of Abda was over the levy.

Officers for Twelve Months
7. And Solomon had twelve officers over all Israel, which provided victuals for the king and his household: each man had to make provision for a month in the year. 8. And these are their names: Ben-hur, in the hill country of Ephraim: 9. Ben-deker, in Makaz, and in Shaalbim, and Beth-shemesh, and Elon-beth-hanan: 10. Ben-hesed, in Aruboth; to him pertained Socoh, and all the land of Hepher: 11. Ben-abibadab, in all the height of Dor; he had Taphath the daughter of Solomon to wife: 12. Baana the son of Ahilud, in Taanach and Megiddo, and all Beth-shean which is beside Zarethan, beneath Jezreel, from Beth-shean to Abel-meholah, as far as beyond Jokmeam: 13. Ben-geber in Ramoth-gilead; to him pertained the towns of Jair the son of Manasseh, which are in Gilead; even to him pertained the region of Argob, which is in Bashan, threescore great cities with walls and brasen bars; 14. Ahinadab the son of Iddo, in Mahanaim: 15. Ahimaaz, in Naphtali; he also took Basemath the daughter of Solomon to wife: 16. Baana the son of Hushai, in Asher and Bealoth: 17. Jehoshaphat the son of Paruah, in Issachar: 18. Shimei the son of Ela, in Benjamin: 19. Geber the son of Uri, in the land of Gilead, the country of Sihon king of the Amorites and of Og king of Bashan; and he was the only officer which was in the land. 20. Judah and Israel were many, as the sand which is by the sea in multitude, eating and drinking and making merry. 22. And Solomon's provision for one day was thirty measures of fine flour and threescore measures of meal; 23. ten fat oxen, and twenty oxen out of the pastures, and an hundred sheep, beside harts, and gazelles, and roebucks and fatted fowl. 27. And those officers provided victual for king Solomon, and for all that came unto king Solomon's table, every man in his month: they let nothing be lacking. 28. Barley also and straw for the horses and swift steeds brought they unto the place where the officers were, every man according to his charge.

Marries Pharaoh's Daughter
I Kings 3:1. And Solomon made affinity with Pharaoh king of Egypt, and took Pharaoh's daughter, and brought her into the city of David, until he had made an end of building his own house, and the house of the Lord, and the wall of Jerusalem round about. 2. Only the people sacrificed in the high places, because there was no house built for the name of the Lord until those days. 3. And Solomon loved the Lord, walking in the statutes of David his father: only he sacrificed and burnt incense in the high places.

II Chron. 1:2. And Solomon spake unto all Israel, to the captains of thousands and of hundreds, and to the judges, and to every prince in all Israel the heads of the fathers' houses.

So Solomon, and all the congregation with him, went to the high place that was at Gibeon to sacrifice there; for there was the tent of meeting with God, which Moses the servant of the Lord had made in the wilderness. But the ark of God had David brought up from Kiriath-jearim to the place that David had prepared for it: for he had pitched a tent for it at Jerusalem. Moreover the brasen altar that Bezalel the son of Uri, the son of Hur, had made, was there before the tabernacle of the Lord: and Solomon and the congregation sought unto it. And Solomon went up thither to the brasen altar before the Lord, which was at the tent of meeting, and offered a thousand burnt offerings. In Gibeon the Lord appeared to Solomon in a dream by night, and God said, Ask what I shall give thee. And Solomon said unto God, Thou hast shewed unto thy servant David my father great kindness, according as he walked before thee in truth, and in righteousness, and in uprightness of heart with thee: and thou hast kept for him this great kindness, that thou hast given him a son to sit on his throne, as it is this day. And now, O Lord my God, thou hast made thy servant king instead of David my father: and I am but a little child; I know not how to go out or come in. Now, O Lord God, let thy promise unto David my father be established: for thou hast made me a king over a people, which thou hast chosen, a great people, that cannot be numbered nor counted for multitude. Give me now wisdom and knowledge, that I may go out and come in before this people, and an understanding heart to judge thy people, that I may discern between good and evil; for who is able to judge this thy people that is so great? And the speech pleased the Lord, that Solomon had asked this thing. And God said unto him, Because thou hast asked this thing, and hast not asked for thyself riches, wealth, or honour, nor hast asked the life of thine enemies, neither yet hast asked for thyself long life; but hast asked wisdom and knowledge for thyself, and understanding to discern judgement, that thou mayest judge my people, over whom I have made thee king: behold, I have done according to thy word: lo, I have given thee a wise and understanding heart; wisdom and knowledge is granted unto thee; so that there hath been none like thee before thee, neither after thee shall any arise like unto thee. And I have also given thee that which thou hast not asked, both riches, and wealth, and honour, such as none of the kings have had that have been before thee, neither shall there any after thee have the like. And if thou wilt walk in my ways, to keep my statutes and my commandments, as thy father David did walk, then I will lengthen thy days. And Solomon awoke, and behold, it was a dream. So Solomon came from his journey to the high place that was at Gibeon, from before the tent of meeting, unto Jerusalem, and stood before the ark of the covenant of the Lord, and offered burnt offerings, and offered peace offerings, and made a feast unto all his servants; and he reigned over Jerusalem.

Prayer and Its Answer

I Kings 3:16. Then came there two women, that were harlots, unto the king, and stood before him. 17. And the one woman said Oh my lord, I and this woman dwell in one house; and I was delivered of a child with her in the house. 18. And it came to pass the third day after I was delivered, that this woman was delivered also; and we were together; there was no stranger with us in the house, save we two in the house. 19. And this woman's child died in the night; because she overlaid it. 20. And she arose at midnight, and took my son from beside me, while thine handmaid slept, and laid it in her bosom, and laid her dead child in my bosom. 21. And when I rose in the morning to give my child suck, behold, it was dead: but when I had considered it in the morning, behold, it was not my son, which I did bear. 22. And the other woman said, Nay;

SECT. XVII — THE UNITED KINGDOM

(I Kings 3:)	(II Chron. 1:)
4. And the king went to Gibeon to sacrifice there; for that was the great high place:	3. So Solomon, and all the congregation with him went to the high place that was at Gibeon; for there was the tent of meeting with God, which Moses the servant of the Lord had made in the wilderness. 4. But the ark of God had David brought up from Kiriath-jearim to the place that David had prepared for it: for he had pitched a tent for it at Jerusalem. 5. Moreover the brasen altar that Bezalel the son of Uri, the son of Hur, had made, was there before the tabernacle of the Lord: and Solomon and the congregation sought unto it. 6. And Solomon went up thither to the brasen altar before the Lord, which was at the tent of meeting, and offered
a thousand burnt offerings did Solomon offer upon that altar. 5. In Gibeon the Lord appeared to Solomon in a dream by night: and God said, Ask what I shall give thee. 6. And Solomon said, Thou hast shewed unto thy servant David my father great kindness, according as he walked before thee in truth, and in righteousness, and in uprightness of heart with thee; and thou hast kept for him this great kindness, that thou hast given him a son to sit on his throne, as it is this day. 7. And	a thousand burnt offerings. 7. In that night did God appear unto Solomon, and said unto him, Ask what I shall give thee. 8. And Solomon said unto God, Thou hast shewed great kindness unto David my father,
now, O Lord my God, thou hast made thy servant king instead of David my father: and I am but a little child; I know not how to go out or come in.	and hast made me king in his stead.
8. (And thy servant is in the midst of thy people, which thou hast chosen, a great people, that cannot be numbered nor counted for multitude. 9. Give thy servant therefore an understanding heart to judge thy people, that I may discern between good and evil; for who is able to judge this thy great people?)	9. (Now, O Lord God, let thy promise unto David my father be established: for thou hast made me king over a people like the dust of the earth in multitude. 10. Give me now wisdom and knowledge, that I may go out and come in before this people: for who can judge this thy people that is so great?)
10. And the speech pleased the Lord, that Solomon had asked this thing. 11. (And God said unto him, Because thou hast asked this thing, and hast not asked for thyself long life; neither hast asked riches for thyself, nor hast asked the life of thine enemies; but hast asked for thyself understanding to discern judgement;	11. (And God said to Solomon, Because this was in thine heart, and thou hast not asked riches, wealth, or honour, nor the life of them that hate thee, neither yet hast asked long life, but hast asked wisdom and knowledge for thyself, that thou mayest judge my people, over whom I have made thee king:
12. behold, I have done according to thy word: lo, I have given thee a wise and an understanding heart; so that there hath been none like thee before thee, neither after thee shall any arise like unto thee. 13. And I have also given thee that which thou hast not asked, both riches and honour, so that there shall not be any among the kings like unto thee, all thy days.)	12. wisdom and knowledge is granted unto thee; and I will give thee riches, and wealth and honour, such as none of the kings have had that have been before thee, neither shall there any after thee have the like.)
14. And if thou wilt walk in my ways, to keep my statutes and my commandments, as thy father David did walk, then I will lengthen thy days. 15. And Solomon awoke, and behold, it was a dream:	13. So Solomon came from his journey to the high place that was at Gibeon, from before the tent of meeting, unto Jerusalem;
and he came to Jerusalem, and stood before the ark of the covenant of the Lord, and offered up burnt offerings, and offered peace offerings, and made a feast to all his servants.	and he reigned over Jerusalem.

but the living is my son, and the dead is thy son. And this said, No; but the dead is thy son, and the living is my son. Thus they spake before the king.

Exhibition of Wisdom

23. Then said the king, The one saith, This is my son that liveth, and thy son is the dead: and the other saith, Nay; but thy son is the dead, and my son is the living. 24. And the king said, Fetch me a sword. And they brought a sword before the king. 25. And the king said, Divide the living child in two, and give half to the one and half to the other. 26. Then spake the woman whose the living child was unto the king, for her bowels yearned upon her son, and she said, Oh my lord give her the living child, and in no wise slay it. But the other said, It shall be neither mine nor thine; divide it. 27. Then the king answered and said, Give her the living child, and in no wise slay it: she is the mother thereof. 28. And all Israel heard of the judgement which the King had judged; and they feared the king: for they saw that the wisdom of God was in him to do judgement.

Plans for Building

Now Solomon proposed to build an house for the name of the Lord, and an house for his kingdom. And Solomon told out threescore and ten thousand men to bear burdens, and fourscore thousand men that were hewers in the mountains, and three thousand and six hundred to oversee them. And Hiram king of Tyre sent his servants unto Solomon; for he had heard that they had anointed him king in the room of his father: for Hiram was ever a lover of David. And Solomon sent to Hiram the king of Tyre, saying, Thou knowest how that David my father could not build an house for the name of the Lord his God for the wars which were about him on every side, until the Lord put them under the soles of his feet. But now the Lord my God hath given me rest on every side; there is neither adversary, nor evil occurent. As thou didst deal with David my father and didst send him cedars to build him an house to dwell therein, even so deal with me. And, behold, I purpose to build an house for the name of the Lord my God (as the Lord spake unto David my father, saying, Thy son, whom I will set upon thy throne in thy room, he shall build the house in my name,) to dedicate it to him, and to burn before him incense of sweet spices, and for the continual shewbread, and for the burnt offerings morning and evening, on the sabbathe, and on the new moons, and on the set feasts of the Lord our God. This is an ordinance for ever to Israel.

Arrangements with Hiram

And the house which I build is great: for great is our God above all gods. But who is able to build him an house, seeing the heaven and the heaven of heavens cannot contain him? who am I then, that I should build him an house, save only to burn incense before him? Now therefore send me a man cunning to work in gold, and in silver, and in brass, and in iron, and in purple, and crimson, and blue, and that can skill to grave all manner of gravings, to be with the cunning men that are with me in Judah and in Jerusalem, whom David my father did provide. Now therefore command thou that they hew me cedar trees, fir trees and algum trees, out of Lebanon: for I know that thy servants can skill to cut timber in Lebanon; and, behold, my servants shall be with thy servants, even to prepare me timber in abundance: for the house which I am about to build shall be wonderful great: and I will give thee hire for thy servants according to all that thou shalt say: for thou knowest that there is not among us any that can skill to hew timber like the Zidonians. And, behold, I will give to thy servants, the hewers that cut timber, twenty thousand measures of beaten wheat for food for his household,* and twenty thousand measures of barley, and twenty thousand baths of wine, and twenty thousand baths of oil: thus gave Solomon to Hiram year by year.

---
* See Chronicles III, 1, (8).

SECT. XVII — THE UNITED KINGDOM — 117

(II Chron. 2:) 1. Now Solomon purposed to build an house for the name of the Lord, and an house for his kingdom. 2. And Solomon told out threescore and ten thousand men to bear burdens and fourscore thousand men that were hewers in the mountains, and three thousand and six hundred to oversee them.

(I Kings 5:) 1. And Hiram king of Tyre sent his servants unto Solomon; for he had heard that they had anointed him king in the room of his father: for Hiram was ever a lover of David. 2. And Solomon sent to Hiram, saying, 3. Thou knowest how that David my father could not build an house for the name of the Lord his God for the wars which were about him on every side, until the Lord put them under the soles of his feet. 4. But now the Lord my God hath given me rest on every side; there is neither adversary, nor evil occurrent.

3. And Solomon sent to Huram the king of Tyre, saying,

As thou didst deal with David my father and didst send him cedars to build him an house to dwell therein, even so deal with me. 4. Behold, I build an house for the name of the Lord my God,

5. And, behold, I purpose to build an house for the name of the Lord my God, as the Lord spake unto David my father, saying, Thy son, whom I will set upon thy throne in thy room, he shall build the house for my name.

to dedicate it to him, and to burn before him incense of sweet spices, and for the continual shewbread, and for the burnt offerings morning and evening, on the sabbaths, and on the new moons, and on the set feasts of the Lord our God. This is an ordinance for ever to Israel.

5. And the house which I build is great: for great is our God above all gods. 6. But who is able to build him an house, seeing the heaven and the heaven of heavens cannot contain him? who am I then, that I should build him an house, save only to burn incense before him? 7. Now therefore send me a man cunning to work in gold, and in silver, and in brass, and in iron, and in purple, and crimson, and blue, and that can skill to grave all manner of gravings, to be with the cunning men that are with me in Judah and in Jerusalem, whom David my father did provide.

6. Now therefore command thou that they hew me cedar trees out of Lebanon; and my servants shall be with thy servants;

and I will give thee hire for thy servants according to all that thou shalt say: for thou knowest that there is not among us any that can skill to hew timber like unto the Zidonians.

8. Send me also cedar trees, fir trees, and algum trees, out of Lebanon: for I know that thy servants can skill to cut timber in Lebanon; and, behold, my servants shall be with thy servants, 9. even to prepare me timber in abundance: for the house which I am about to build shall be wonderful great.

11. And Solomon gave Hiram ((twenty thousand measures of wheat for food to his household, and twenty measures of pure oil)): thus gave Solomon to Hiram year by year.

10. And, behold, I will give to thy servants, the hewers that cut timber, (((twenty thousand measures of beaten wheat, and twenty thousand measures of barley, and twenty thousand baths of wine, and twenty thousand baths of oil.))

Then Hiram king of Tyre answered in writing, which he sent to Solomon, Because the Lord loveth his people, he hath made thee king over them. And it came to pass when Hiram heard the words of Solomon, that he rejoiced greatly, and said, Blessed be the Lord, the God of Israel, that made heaven and earth, who hath given unto David the king a wise son over this great people, endued with discretion and understanding, that should build an house for the Lord and an house for his kingdom. And Hiram sent to Solomon, saying, I have heard the message which thou hast sent unto me: I will do all thy desire concerning timber of cedar, and concerning timber of fir. Now therefore the wheat and the barley, the oil and the wine, which my lord hath spoken of, let him send unto his servants: and we will cut wood out of Lebanon, as much as thou shalt need. My servants shall bring them down from Lebanon unto the sea: and I will make them into rafts to go by sea unto the * place where thou shalt appoint me, and will cause them to be broken up there, and thou shalt receive and carry them up to Jerusalem; and thou shalt accomplish my desire in giving food for my household. So Hiram gave Solomon timber of cedar and timber of fir according to all his desire. And Solomon numbered all the strangers that were in the land of Israel, after the numbering wherewith David his father had numbered them; and they were found an hundred and fifty thousand and three thousand and six hundred. And king Solomon raised a levy out of all Israel; and the levy was thirty thousand men. And he sent them to Lebanon, ten thousand a month by courses: a month they were in Lebanon, and two months at home: and Adoniram was over the levy. And Solomon had threescore and ten thousand that bare burdens, and fourscore thousand that were hewers in the mountains; besides Solomon's chief officers that were over the work, three thousand and † three hundred, which bare rule over the people that wrought in the work.

And the king commanded, and they hewed out great stones, costly stones to lay the foundation of the house with wrought stones. And Solomon's builders and Hiram's builders and the Gebalites did fashion them, and prepared the timber and the stones to build the house. And the Lord gave Solomon wisdom, as he promised him; and there was peace between Hiram and Solomon; and they two made a league together.

---

* Chronicles, to Joppa.   † Chronicles, 36 hundred.   Appendix C, Chronicles III, 1, (10).

SECT. XVII   THE UNITED KINGDOM   119

7. And it came to pass, when Hiram heard the words of Solomon, that he rejoiced greatly, and said Blessed be the Lord this day, given unto David a wise son over this great people. 8. And Hiram sent to Solomon, saying, I have heard the message which thou hast sent unto me: I will do all thy desire concerning timber of cedar, and concerning timber of fir. 9. My servants shall bring them down from Lebanon unto the sea: and I will make them into rafts to go by sea unto the place that thou shalt appoint me, and will cause them to be broken up there, and thou shalt receive them; and thou shalt accomplish my desire in giving food for my household. 10. So Hiram gave Solomon timber of cedar and timber of fir according to all his desire. 13. And king Solomon raised a levy out of all Israel; and the levy was thirty thousand men. 14. And he sent them to Lebanon, ten thousand a month by courses: a month they were in Lebanon, and two months at home: and Adoniram was over the levy. 15. And Solomon had threescore and ten thousand that bare burdens, and fourscore thousand that were hewers in the mountains; 16. besides Solomon's chief officers that were over the work,((three thousand and *three* hundred)), which bare rule over the people that wrought in the work. 17. And the king commanded, and they hewed out great stones, costly stones to lay the foundation of the house with wrought stones. 18. And Solomon's builders and Hiram's builders and the Gebalites did fashion them, and prepared the timber and the stones to build the house. 12. And the Lord gave Solomon wisdom, as he promised him; and there was peace between Hiram and Solomon; and they two made a league together.	11. Then Huram the king of Tyre answered in writing, which he sent to Solomon, Because the Lord loveth his people, he hath made thee king over them. 12. Huram said moreover, Blessed be the Lord, the God of Israel, that made heaven and earth, who hath given to David the king a wise son, endued with discretion and understanding, that should build an house for the Lord, and an house for his kingdom. 15. Now therefore the wheat and the barley, the oil and the wine, which my lord hath spoken of, let him send unto his servants: 16. and we will cut wood out of Lebanon, as much as thou shalt need: and we will bring it to thee in floats by sea to Joppa; and thou shalt carry it up to Jerusalem. 17. And Solomon numbered all the strangers that were in the land of Israel, after the numbering wherewith David his father had numbered them; and they were found an hundred and fifty thousand and three thousand six hundred. 18. And he set threescore and ten thousand to bear burdens, and fourscore thousand that were hewers in the mountains, and ((three thousand and *six* hundred)) overseers to set the people awork.

THE HOUSE OF DAVID
B. C. 1016 (Usher)
II Solomon
B. C. 977 (Rev.)

NATHAN

SECTION XVIII

Building the Temple

And it came to pass in the four hundred and eightieth year after the children of Israel were come out of Egypt, then Solomon began to build the house of the Lord at Jerusalem in mount Moriah, where the Lord appeared unto David his father, which he made ready in the place that David had appointed, in the threshing floor of Ornan the Jebusite. And he began to build in the second day of the month Ziv, which is the second month, in the fourth year of his reign. Now these are the foundations which Solomon laid for the building of the house of God. The length by cubits after the first measure was threescore cubits, and the breadth thereof twenty cubits, and the height thereof thirty cubits. And the porch before the temple of the house, twenty cubits was the length thereof, according to the breadth of the house, and ten cubits was the breadth thereof before the house, and the height an hundred and twenty: and he overlaid it with pure gold. I Kings 6:4. And for the house he made windows of fixed lattice work. 5. And against the wall of the house he built stories round about, against the walls of the house round about, both of the temple and of the oracle: and he made side chambers round about: 6. the nethermost story was five cubits broad, and the middle was six cubits broad, and the third was seven cubits broad: for on the outside he made rebatements in the wall of the house round about, that the beams should not have hold in the walls of the house. 7. And the house when it was in building, was built of stone made ready at the quarry: and there was neither hammer nor axe nor any tool of iron heard in the house, while it was in building. 8. The door for the middle side-chambers was in the right side of the house: and they went up by winding stairs into the middle chambers, and out of the middle into the third. 9. So he built the house and finished it; and he covered the house with beams and planks of cedar. 10. And he built the stories against all the house, each five cubits high: and they rested on the house with timber of cedar. 11. And the word of the Lord came to Solomon, saying, 12. Concerning this house which thou art in building, if thou wilt walk in my statutes, and execute my judgements, and keep all my commandments to walk in them; then will I establish my word with thee, which I spake unto David thy father. 13. And I will dwell among the children of Israel, and will not forsake my people Israel. 14. So Solomon built the house, and finished it. 15. And he built the walls of the house within with boards of cedar; from the floor of the house unto the walls of the ceiling, he covered them on the

SECT. XVIII THE UNITED KINGDOM

(I Kings 6:) 1. And it came to pass in the four hundred and eightieth year after the children of Israel were come out of the land of Egypt

(in the fourth year of Solomon's reign over Israel, in the month Ziv, which is the second month, that he began to build the house of the Lord). 2. And the house which king Solomon built for the Lord, the length thereof

was threescore cubits, and the breadth thereof twenty cubits, and the height thereof thirty cubits. 3. And the porch before the temple of the house, twenty cubits was the length thereof, according to the breadth of the house, and ten cubits was the breadth thereof before the house.

(II Chron. 3:) 1. Then Solomon began to build the house of the Lord at Jerusalem in mount Moriah, where the Lord appeared unto David his father, which he made ready in the place that David had appointed, in the threshing floor of Ornan the Jebusite. 2. (And he began to build in the second day of the second month, in fourth year of his reign.)

3. Now these are the foundations which Solomon laid for the building of the house of God. The length by cubits after the first measure was threescore cubits, and the breadth twenty cubits. 4. And the porch that was before the house, the length of it, according to the breadth of the house was twenty cubits, and the height an hundred and twenty: and he overlaid it within with pure gold.

inside with wood: and he covered the floor of the house with boards of fir. 16. And he built twenty cubits on the hinder part of the house with boards of cedar from the floor unto the walls: he even built them for it within, for an oracle even for the most holy place. And the greater house, that is, the temple before the oracle, was forty cubits long. And there was cedar on the house within, carved with knops and open flowers: all was cedar; there was no stone seen, and he ceiled it with fir tree, which he overlaid with fine gold, and wrought thereon palm trees and chains. And he garnished the house with precious stones for beauty: and the gold was the gold of Parvaim. And he prepared an oracle in the midst of the house within, to set there the ark of the covenant of the Lord. And within the oracle was a space of twenty cubits in length, and twenty cubits in breadth, and twenty cubits in the height thereof; and he overlaid it with fine gold, amounting to six hundred talents. And the weight of the nails was fifteen shekels of gold. And he covered the *altar which was of cedar with gold, and overlaid the upper chambers with gold. So Solomon overlaid the house within with pure gold: and he drew chains of gold across before the oracle; and he overlaid it with gold. He overlaid the whole house, the beams, the thresholds, and the walls thereof, with gold, until all the house was finished: also the whole altar that belonged to the oracle he overlaid with gold. And in the oracle he made two cherubim in image work of olive wood, each ten cubits high and overlaid them with gold. The wing of the one cherub was five cubits, reaching to the wall of the house, and the other wing was likewise five cubits, reaching to the wing of the other cherub. And the wing of the other cherub was five cubits, reaching to the wall of the house: and the other wing was five cubits also, joining to the wing of the other cherub. And the wings of the cherubim were twenty cubits long: from the uttermost part of the one wing unto the uttermost part of the other were ten cubits: both the cherubim were of one measure and of one form. The height of the one cherub was ten cubits, and so was it of the other cherub. And he set the cherubim within the inner house: and the wings of the cherubim spread themselves forth twenty cubits, so that the wing of the one touched the one wall, and the wing of the other cherub touched the other wall; and their wings touched one another in the midst of the house, and they stood on their feet, and their faces were *inward. And he made the veil of blue, and purple, and crimson, and fine linen, and wrought cherubim thereon. I Kings 6:28. And he overlaid the cherubim with gold. 29. And he carved all the walls of the house round about with carved figures of cherubim and palm trees and open flowers, within and without. 30. And the floor of the house he overlaid with gold, within and without. 31. And for the entering of the oracle he made doors of olive wood: the lintel and the door posts were a fifth part of the wall. 32. So he made two doors of olive wood; and he carved upon them carving of cherubim and palm trees and open flowers, and overlaid them with gold; and he spread the gold upon the cherubim, and upon the palm trees. 33. So also made he for the entering of the temple door posts of olive wood, out of a fourth part of the wall; and two doors of fir wood; the two leaves of the one door were folding, and the two leaves of the other door were folding. 35. And he carved thereon cherubim and palm trees and open flowers: and he overlaid them with gold fitted upon the graven work. 36. And he built the inner court with three rows of hewn stone, and a row of cedar beams. 37. In the fourth year was the foundation of the house of the Lord laid, in the month Ziv. 38. And in the eleventh year, in the month Bul, which is the eighth month, was the house finished throughout all the parts thereof, and according to all the fashion of it. So was he seven years in building it.

---
* Marginal reading.

Sect. XVIII THE UNITED KINGDOM

(I Kings 6:)17. And the house, that is, the temple before the oracle, was forty cubits long. 18. And there was cedar on the house within, carved with knops and open flowers: all was cedar; there was no stone seen.

19. And he prepared an oracle in the midst of the house within, to set there the ark of the covenant of the Lord. 20. And within the oracle was a space of twenty cubits in length,
and twenty cubits in breadth, and twenty cubits in the height thereof; and he overlaid it with pure gold: and he covered the altar with cedar.

21. So Solomon overlaid the house within with pure gold: and he drew chains of gold across before the oracle; and he overlaid it with gold. 22. And the whole house he overlaid with gold, until all the house was finished: also the whole altar that belonged to the oracle he overlaid with gold. 23. And in the oracle he made two cherubim of olive wood, each ten cubits high.

24. And five cubits was the one wing of the cherub, and five cubits the other wing of the cherub;

from the uttermost part of the one wing unto the uttermost part of the other were ten cubits. 25. And the other cherub was ten cubits: both the cherubim were of one measure and one form. 26. The height of the one cherub was ten cubits, and so was it of the other cherub. 27. And he set the cherubim within the inner house: and the wings of the cherubim were stretched forth, so that the wing of the one touched the one wall, and the wing of the other cherub touched the other wall; and their wings touched one another in the midst of the house.

(II Chron. 3:)5. And the greater house he cieled with fir tree,
which he overlaid with fine gold, and wrought thereon palm trees and chains. 6. And he garnished the house with precious stones for beauty: and the gold was the gold of Parvaim. 8. And he made the most holy house;
the length thereof, according to the breadth of the house, was twenty cubits, and the breadth thereof twenty cubits:
and he overlaid it with fine gold, amounting to six hundred talents. 9. And the weight of the nails was fifty shekels of gold.

And he overlaid the upper chambers with gold.

7. He overlaid also the house, the beams, the thresholds, and the walls thereof, and the doors thereof with gold;
10. And in the most holy house he made two cherubim of image work; and they overlaid them with gold; 11^b. the wing of the one cherub was five cubits, reaching to the wall of the house; and the other wing was likewise five cubits, reaching to the wing of the other cherub. 12. And the wing of the other cherub was five cubits, reaching to the wall of the house: and the other wing was five cubits also, joining to the wing of the other cherub.

11^a. And the wings of the cherubim were twenty cubits long:

13. The wings of the cherubim spread themselves forth twenty cubits:

and they stood on their feet, and their faces were toward the house. 14. And he made the veil of blue, and purple, and crimson, and fine linen, and wrought cherubim thereon.

Hiram and His Works

Then Hiram the king of Tyre answered in writing, which he sent to Solomon, Because the Lord loveth his people, he hath made thee king over them.* And now I have sent a cunning man endued with understanding, *¹ of Hiram, my father's, the son of a widow woman of the tribe of *² Naphtali, and his father was a man of Tyre, skilful to work in gold, and in silver, in brass, in iron, in stone, and in timber, in purple, in blue, and in fine linen, and in crimson; also to grave in any manner of graving, and to devise any device: that there may be a place appointed unto him with thy cunning men, and with the cunning men of my lord David thy father. And he came to king Solomon, and wrought all his work.

Two Pillars of Brass

For he fashioned two pillars of brass of *³ eighteen cubits high apiece: and a line of twelve cubits compassed either of them about. And he made two chapiters of molten brass, to set upon the tops of the pillars: the height of one chapiter was five cubits, and the height of the other chapiter was five cubits. There were nets of checker work, and wreaths of chain work, as in the oracle, for the chapiters that were upon the top of the pillars; seven for the one chapiter, and seven for the other chapiter. So he made the pillars; and there were two rows round about upon the one network, to cover the chapiters that were upon the top of the pillars: and so did he for the other chapiter. And the chapiters that were upon the top of the pillars in the porch were in lily work, four cubits. And there were chapiters above also upon the two pillars, close by the belly which was beside the network: and the pomegranates were two hundred, in rows round about upon the other chapiter. And he set up the pillars at the porch of the temple: and he set up the right pillar, and called the name thereof Jachin: and he set up the left pillar, and called the name Boaz. And upon the top of the pillars was lily work: so was the work of the pillars finished. Moreover he made an altar of brass, twenty cubits the length thereof, and twenty cubits the breadth thereof, and ten cubits the height thereof. Also he made the

The Molten Sea

molten sea of ten cubits from brim to brim, round in compass, and the height thereof was five cubits: and a line of thirty cubits compassed it round about. And under the brim of it round about there were *⁴ knops which did compass it round about for ten cubits, compassing the sea round about. The *⁴ knops were in two rows, cast when it was cast. It stood upon twelve oxen, three looking toward the north, and three looking toward the west, and three looking toward the south, and three looking toward the east: and the sea was set upon them above, and all their hinder parts were inward. And it was an handbreadth thick; and the brim thereof was wrought like the brim of a cup, like the flower of a lily: it received and held *⁵ *two thousand* baths. 27. And he made the ten

Ten Bases and Lavers

bases of brass; four cubits was the length of one base, and four cubits the breadth thereof, and three cubits the height of it. 28. And the work of the bases was on this manner: they had borders; and there were borders between the ledges: 29. and on the borders that were between the ledges were lions, oxen, and cherubim; and upon the ledges there was a pedestal above: and beneath the lions and oxen were wreaths of hanging work. 30. And every base had four brasen wheels, and axles of brass: and the four feet thereof had undersetters: beneath the laver were the undersetters molten, with wreaths at the side of each. 31. And the mouth of it within the chapiter and above

---

*See Chronicles, Appendix C, III, 2, (3).
*1 cf. II Chronicles 4: 16.   *2 Chronicles, Dan.   *3 Chronicles, Thirty-five, III, 1 (11).   *4 Chronicles Oxen.   *5 Chronicles, three thousand, III, 1, (12).

SECT. XVIII THE UNITED KINGDOM

(I Kings 7:) 13. And king Solomon sent and fetched Hiram out of Tyre. 14. He was the son of a widow woman of the tribe of ((*Naphtali,*)) and his father was a man of Tyre, a worker in brass;

and he was filled with wisdom and understanding and cunning, to work all works of brass.

And he came to king Solomon, and wrought all his work. 15. For he fashioned the two pillars of brass, of ((*eighteen*)) *cubits high apiece*: and a line of twelve cubits compassed either of them about. 16. And he made two chapiters of molten brass, to set upon the tops of the pillars: the height of the one chapiter was five cubits, and the height of the other chapiter was five cubits. 17. There were nets of checker work, and wreaths of chain work, for the chapiters that were upon the top of the pillars; seven for the one chapiter, and seven for the other chapiter. 18. So he made the pillars; and there were two rows round about upon the one network, to cover the chapiters that were upon the top of the pillars: and so did he for the other chapiter. 19. And the chapiters that were upon the top of the pillars in the porch were of lily work, four cubits. 20. And there were chapiters above also upon the two pillars, close by the belly which was beside the network: and the pomegranates were two hundred, in rows round about upon the other chapiter. 21. And he set up the pillars at the porch of the temple:
and he set up the right pillar, and called the name thereof Jachin: and he set up the left pillar, and called the name Boaz. 22. And upon the top of the pillars was lily work: so was the work of the pillars finished.

(II Chron. 2:) 11. Then Huram the king of Tyre answered in writing, which he sent to Solomon, Because the Lord loveth his people, he hath made thee king over them. 13. And now I have sent a cunning man, endued with understanding, of Huram my father's, 14. the son of a woman of the daughters of ((*Dan,*)) and his father was a man of Tyre, skilful to work in gold, and in silver, in brass, in iron, in stone, and in timber, in purple, in blue, and in fine linen, and in crimson; also to grave any manner of graving, and to devise any device:
that there may be a place appointed unto him with thy cunning men, and with the cunning men of my lord David thy father.

3:15. Also he made before the house two pillars of ((*thirty and five*)) *cubits high*,
and the chapiter that was on the top of each of them was five cubits.

16. And he made chains in the oracle, and put them on the tops of the pillars.

and he made an hundred pomegranates, and put them on the chains. 17. And he set up the pillars before the temple, one on the right hand, and the other on the left;
and called the name of that on the right hand Jachin, and the name of that on the left Boaz.

II Chron. 4:1. Moreover he made an altar of brass, twenty cubits the length thereof, and twenty cubits the breadth thereof, and ten cubits the height thereof.
2. Also he made the molten sea of ten cubits, from brim to brim, round in compass, and the height thereof was five cubits; and a line of thirty cubits compassed it round about.

23. And he made the molten sea of ten cubits from brim to brim, round in compass, and the height thereof was five cubits: and a line of thirty cubits compassed it round about. 24. And under the brim of it round about there were ((*knops*)) which did compass it for ten cubits, compassing the sea round about; the *knops* were in two rows, cast when it was cast. 25. It stood upon twelve oxen, three looking toward the north, and three looking toward the west, and three looking toward the south, and three looking toward the east; and the sea was set upon them above, and all their hinder parts were inward. 26. And it was an handbreadth thick; and the brim thereof was wrought like the brim of a cup, like the flower of a lily: it held ((*two thousand baths.*))

3. And under it was the similitude of ((*oxen*)) which did compass it round about, for ten cubits, compassing the sea round about. The *oxen* were in two rows, cast when it was cast. 4. It stood upon twelve oxen, three looking toward the north, and three looking toward the west, and three looking toward the south, and three looking toward the east; and the sea was set upon them above, and all their hinder parts were inward. 5. And it was an handbreadth thick; and the brim thereof was wrought like the brim of a cup, like the flower of a lily: it received and held ((*three thousand baths.*))

was a cubit: and the mouth thereof was round after the work of a pedestal, a cubit and an half: and also upon the mouth of it were gravings, and their borders were foursquare, not round. 32. And the four wheels were underneath the borders; and the axletrees of the wheels were in the base: and the height of a wheel was a cubit and half a cubit. 33. And the work of the wheels was like the work of a chariot wheel: their axletrees, and their felloes, and their spokes, and their naves, were all molten. 34. And there were four undersetters at the four corners of each base: the undersetters thereof were of the base itself. 35. And in the top of the base was there a round compass of half a cubit high: and on the top of the base the stays thereof and the borders thereof were of the same. 36. And on the plates of the stays thereof, and on the borders thereof, he graved cherubim, lions, and palm trees, according to the space of each, with wreaths round about. 37. After this manner he made the ten bases: all of them had one casting, one measure, and one form. He made also ten lavers of brass, and put five on the right hand, and five on the left, to wash in them, such things as belonged to the burnt offering they washed in them: one laver contained forty baths; and every laver was four cubits: and upon every one of the ten bases one laver. And he set the bases, five on the right side of the house, and five on the left side of the house: but the sea was for the priests to wash in. And he set the sea on the right side of the house eastward, toward the south. And he made ten candlesticks of gold according to the ordinance concerning them; and he set them in the temple, five on the right hand, and five on the left. He made also ten tables, and placed them in the temple, five on the right side, and five on the left. And he made an hundred basons of gold. Furthermore he made the court of the priests, and the great court, and the doors for the court, and overlaid the doors of them with brass. And Hiram made the pots, and the shovels, and the basons.

Summary of Hiram's Works

So Hiram made an end of doing all the work that he wrought for king Solomon in the house of God: the two pillars, and the two bowls, and the two chapiters that were on the top of the pillars; and the two networks to cover the two bowls of the chapiters that were on the top of the pillars: and the four hundred pomegranates for the two networks; two rows of pomegranates for each network, to cover the two bowls of the chapiters that were upon the pillars. He made also the ten bases, and the ten lavers on the bases; and the one sea, and the twelve oxen under it. The pots also, and the shovels, and the basons, and the fleshhooks, and all the vessels thereof, did Hiram his father make for king Solomon for the house of the Lord of bright brass. In the plain of Jordan did the king cast them, in the clay ground between Succoth and Zaredah. And Solomon left all the vessels unweighed, because they were exceeding many: the weight of the brass could not be found out. And Solomon made all the vessels that were in the house of God: the golden altar, and the tables whereon was the shewbread, of gold; and the candlesticks with their lamps, that they should burn according to the ordinance before the oracle, of pure gold; and the flowers, and the lamps, and the tongs, of gold, and that perfect gold; and the cups, and the snuffers, and the basons, and the spoons, and the firepans, of pure gold; and the hinges both for the doors of the inner house, the most holy place, and for the doors of the house, to wit, of the temple were of gold. Thus all the work that king Solomon wrought for the house of the Lord was finished. And Solomon brought in the things that David his father had dedicated; even the silver, and the gold, and all the vessels, and put them in the treasuries of the house of the Lord.

(I Kings 7:) 38. And he made ten lavers of brass: one laver contained forty baths; and every laver was four cubits: and upon every one of the ten bases one laver. 39. And he set the bases, five on the right side of the house, and five on the left side of the house: and he set the sea on the right side of the house eastward, toward the south.

40. And Hiram made the lavers, and the shovels, and the basons. So Hiram made an end of doing all the work that he wrought for king Solomon in the house of the Lord: 41. the two pillars, and the two bowls of the chapiters that were on the top of the pillars; and the two network to cover the two bowls of the chapiters that were on the top of the pillars: 42. and the four hundred pomegranates for the two networks; two rows of pomegranates for each network, to cover the two bowls of the chapiters that were upon the pillars: 43. and the ten bases, and the ten lavers on the bases; 44. and the one sea, and the twelve oxen under the sea, 45. and the pots, and the shovels, and the basons: even all these vessels, which Hiram made for king Solomon, in the house of the Lord, were of burnished brass.
46. In the plain of Jordan did the king cast them, in the clay ground between Succoth and Zarethan.
47. And Solomon left all the vessels unweighed, because they were exceeding many: the weight of the brass could not be found out. 48. And Solomon made all the vessels that were in the house of the Lord: the golden altar, and the table whereupon the shewbread was, of gold; 49. and the candlesticks, five on the right side, and five on the left, before the oracle, of pure gold; and the flowers, and the lamps, and the tongs of gold; 50. and the cups, and the snuffers, and the basons, and the spoons, and the firepans, of pure gold; and the hinges both for the doors of the inner house, the most holy place, and for the doors of the house, to wit, of the temple, of gold. 51. Thus all the work that king Solomon wrought in the house of the Lord was finished. And Solomon brought in the things which David his father had dedicated, even the silver, and the gold, and the vessels, and put them in the treasuries of the house of the Lord.

(II Chron. 4:) 6. He made also ten lavers, and put five on the right hand, and five on the left, to wash in them; such things as belonged to the burnt offering they washed in them; but the sea was for the priests to wash in. 10. And he set the sea on the right side of the house eastward, toward the south. 7. And he made the ten candlesticks of gold according to the ordinance concerning them; and he set them in the temple, five on the right hand and five on the left 8. He made also ten tables, and placed them in the temple, five on the right side, and five on the left. And he made an hundred basons of gold. 9. Furthermore he made the court of the priests, and the great court, and doors for the court, and overlaid the doors of them with brass. 11. And Huram made the pots, and the shovels, and the basons. So Huram made an end of doing the work that he wrought for king Solomon in the house of God: 12. the two pillars and the bowls, and the two chapiters which were on the top of the pillars; and the two networks to cover the two bowls of the chapiters that were on the top of the pillars; 13. and the four hundred pomegranates for the two networks; two rows of pomegranates for each network, to cover the two bowls of the chapiters that were upon the pillars. 14. He made also the bases, and the lavers made he upon the bases; 15. one sea, and the twelve oxen under it.
16. The pots also, and the shovels, and the fleshhooks, and all the vessels thereof, did Huram his father make for king Solomon for the house of the Lord of bright brass.
17. In the plain of Jordan did the king cast them, in the clay ground between Succoth and Zaredah.
18. Thus Solomon made all these vessels in great abundance: for the weight of the brass could not be found out. 19. And Solomon made all the vessels that were in the house of God, the golden altar also, and the tables whereon was the shewbread; 20. and the candlesticks with their lamps, that they should burn according to the ordinance before the oracle, of pure gold; 21. and the flowers, and the lamps, and the tongs, of gold, and that perfect gold; 22. and the snuffers, and the basons, and the spoons, and the firepans, of pure gold: and as for the entry of the house, the inner doors thereof for the most holy place, and the doors of the house, to wit, of the temple were of gold. 5:1. Thus all the work that Solomon wrought for the house of the Lord was finished. And Solomon brought in the things that David his father had dedicated; even the silver, and the gold, and all the vessels, and put them in the treasuries of the house of God.

THE HOUSE OF DAVID
  B. C. 1016 (Usher)
II Solomon
  B. C. 977 (Rev.)

NATHAN

SECTION XIX

Dedication of the Temple

Ark Brought Out of Zion

Then Solomon assembled all the elders of Israel, and all the heads of the tribes, the princes of the fathers' houses of the children of Israel, unto king Solomon in Jerusalem, to bring up the ark of the covenant of the Lord out of the city of David, which is Zion. And all the men of Israel assembled themselves unto king Solomon at the feast, in the month Ethanim, which is the seventh month. And all the elders of Israel came, and the priests took up the ark. And they brought up the ark of the Lord, and the Tent of meeting, and all the holy vessels that were in the Tent; even these did the priests and the Levites bring up. And king Solomon and all the congregation of Israel, that were assembled unto him, were with him before the ark, sacrificing sheep and oxen, that could not be told nor numbered for multitude. And the priests brought in the ark of the covenant of the Lord unto its place, into the oracle of the house, to the most holy place, even under the wings of the cherubim. For the cherubim spread forth their wings over the place of the ark, and the cherubim covered the ark and the staves thereof above. And the staves were so long that the ends of the staves were seen from the holy place before the oracle; but they were not seen without; and there they are, unto this day. There was nothing in the ark save the two tables of stone which Moses put there at Horeb, when the Lord made a covenant with the children of Israel, when they came out of the land of Egypt. And it came to pass when the priests were come out of the holy place,*¹ (for all the priests that were present had sanctified themselves, and did not keep their courses; also the Levites which were the singers, all of them, even Asaph, Heman, Jeduthun, and their sons and their brethren, arrayed in fine linen, with cymbals, and psalteries and harps, stood at the east end of the altar, and with them an hundred and twenty priests sounding with trumpets:) it came to pass when the trumpeters and singers were as one, to make one sound to be heard in praising and thanking the Lord; and when they lifted up their voice with the trumpets and cymbals and instruments of music, and praised the Lord, saying, *² For he is good; for his mercy endureth for ever: that then the house was filled with a cloud, even the house of the Lord, so that the priests could not stand to minister by reason of the cloud; for the glory of the Lord filled the house of the Lord.

* 1. See Chronicles II. Appendix C.
* 2. PSALM 136:1-26. O give thanks unto the Lord: for he is good:
    For his mercy endureth for ever.
    O give thanks unto the God of gods:
    For his mercy endureth for ever.
    O give thanks unto the Lord of lords:
    For his mercy endureth for ever.

SECT. XIX THE UNITED KINGDOM

(I Kings 8:)	(II Chron. 5:)
1. Then Solomon assembled the elders of Israel, and all the heads of the tribes, the princes of the fathers' houses of the children of Israel, unto king Solomon in Jerusalem, to bring up the ark of the covenant of the Lord out of the city of David, which is Zion. 2. And all the men of Israel assembled themselves unto king Solomon at the feast, in the month Ethanim, which is the seventh month. 3. And all the elders of Israel came, and the priests took up the ark. 4. And they brought up the ark of the Lord, and the tent of meeting, and all the holy vessels that were in the Tent; even these did the priests and the Levites bring up. 5. And king Solomon and all the congregation of Israel, that were assembled unto him, were with him before the ark, sacrificing sheep and oxen, that could not be told nor numbered for multitude. 6. And the priests brought in the ark of the covenant of the Lord unto its place, into the oracle of the house, to the most holy place, even under the wings of the cherubim. 7. For the cherubim spread forth their wings over the place of the ark, and the cherubim covered the ark and the staves thereof above. 8. And the staves were so long that the ends of the staves were seen from the holy place before the oracle; but they were not seen without: and there they are, unto this day. 9. There was nothing in the ark save the two tables of stone which Moses put there at Horeb, when the Lord made a covenant with the children of Israel, when they came out of the land of Egypt. 10. And it came to pass when the priests were come out of the holy place, that the cloud filled the house of the Lord, 11. so that the priests could not stand to minister by reason of the cloud: for the glory of the Lord filled the house of the Lord..	2. Then Solomon assembled the elders of Israel, and all the heads of the tribes, the princes of the fathers' houses of the children of Israel, unto Jerusalem, to bring up the ark of the covenant of the Lord out of the city of David, which is Zion. 3. And all the men of Israel assembled themselves unto the king at the feast, which was in the seventh month. 4. And all the elders of Israel came, and the Levites took up the ark. 5. And they brought up the ark and the tent of meeting, and all the holy vessels that were in the Tent; these did the priests and the Levites bring up. 6. And king Solomon and all the congregation of Israel, that were assembled unto him, were before the ark, sacrificing sheep and oxen, that could not be told nor numbered, for multitude. 7. And the priests brought in the ark of the covenant of the Lord unto its place, into the oracle of the house, to the most holy place, even under the wings of the cherubim. 8. For the cherubim spread forth their wings over the place of the ark, and the cherubim covered the ark and the staves thereof above. 9. And the staves were so long that the ends of the staves were seen from the ark before the oracle; but they were not seen without: and there it is, unto this day. 10. There was nothing in the ark save the two tables which Moses put there at Horeb, when the Lord made a covenant with the children of Israel, when they came out of Egypt. 11. And it came to pass when the priests were come out of the holy place, (for all the priests that were present had sanctified themselves, and did not keep their courses; 12. also the Levites which were the singers, all of them, even Asaph, Heman, Jeduthun, and their sons and their brethren, arrayed in fine linen, with cymbals, and psalteries and harps, stood at the east end of the altar, and with them an hundred and twenty priests sounding with trumpets:) 13. it came even to pass when the trumpeters and singers were as one, to make one sound to be heard in praising and thanking the Lord; and when they lifted up their voice with the trumpets and cymbals and instruments of music, and praised the Lord, saying, For he is good; For his mercy endureth for ever: that then the house was filled with a cloud, even the house of the Lord, 14. so that the priests could not stand to minister by reason of the cloud; for the glory of the Lord filled the house of God.

Solomon's Address

Then spake Solomon, The Lord hath said that he would dwell in the thick darkness. I have surely built thee an house of habitation, and a place for thee to dwell in for ever. And the king turned his face about, and blessed all the congregation of Israel: and all the congregation of Israel stood. And he said, Blessed be the Lord, the God of Israel, which spake with his mouth unto David my father, and hath with his hand fulfilled it, saying, Since the day that I brought forth my people Israel out of the land of Egypt, I chose no city out of all the tribes of Israel to build an house in, that my name might be there; neither chose I any man to be prince over my people Israel; but I have chosen Jerusalem, that my name might be there, and have chosen David to be over my people Israel. Now it was in the heart of David my father to build an house for the name of the Lord, the God of Israel. But the Lord said unto David my father, Whereas it was in thine heart to build an house for my name, thou didst well that it was in thine heart; nevertheless thou shalt not build the house; but thy son that shall come forth out of thy loins, he shall build the house for my name. And the Lord hath established his word that he spake; for I am risen up in the room of David my father, and sit on the throne of Israel, as the Lord promised, and have built the house for the name of the Lord, the God of Israel. And there have I set a place for the ark, wherein is the covenant of the Lord, which he made with our fathers, when he brought them out of the land of Egypt.

Prayer for David's House

And Solomon stood before the altar of the Lord in the presence of all the congregation of Israel, and spread forth his hands toward heaven: (for Solomon had made a brasen scaffold, of five cubits long, and five cubits broad, and three cubits high and had set it in the midst of the court; and upon it he stood, and kneeled down on his knees before all the congregation of Israel, and spread forth his hands toward heaven:) and he said, O Lord, the God of Israel, there is no God like thee, in heaven above, or on earth beneath; who keepest covenant and mercy with thy servants, that walk before thee with all their heart; who hast kept with thy servant David my father that which thou didst promise him: yea, thou spakest with thy mouth, and hast fulfilled it with thine hand, as it is this day. Now therefore, O Lord, the God of Israel, keep with thy servant David my father that which thou hast promised him, saying, There shall not fail thee a man in my sight to sit on the throne of Israel; if only thy children take heed to their way to walk before me as thou hast walked before me. Now therefore O Lord, the God of Israel, let thy word, I pray thee, be verified, which thou spakest unto thy servant David my father. But will God in very deed dwell with men on the earth? behold, heaven, and the heaven of heavens cannot contain thee; how much less this house that I have builded! Yet have thou respect unto the prayer of thy servant, and to his supplication, O Lord my God, to hearken unto the cry and to the prayer which thy servant prayeth before thee this day: that thine eyes may be open toward this house day and night, even toward the place whereof thou hast said, My name shall be there: to hearken unto the prayer which thy servant shall pray toward this place.

Prayer for Israel

And hearken thou to the supplication of thy servant, and of thy people Israel, when they shall pray toward this place: yea, hear thou in heaven thy dwelling place; and when thou hearest forgive. If a man sin against his neighbour, and an oath be laid upon him to cause him to swear, and he come and swear before thine altar in this house: then hear thou in heaven, and do, and judge thy servants, requiting the wicked, to bring his way upon

SECT. XIX   THE UNITED KINGDOM   131

(I Kings 8:) 12. Then spake Solomon, The Lord hath said that he would dwell in the thick darkness. 13. I have surely built thee an house of habitation,   a place for thee to dwell in for ever. 14. And the king turned his face about, and blessed all the congregation of Israel: and all the congregation of Israel stood. 15. And he said, Blessed be the Lord, the God of Israel, which spake with his mouth unto David my father, and hath with his hand fulfilled it, saying, 16. Since the day that I brought forth my people Israel out of   of Egypt, I chose no city out of all the tribes of Israel to build an house, that my name might be there;

but I chose David to be over my people Israel.

17. Now it was in the heart of David my father to build an house for the name of the Lord, the God of Israel. 18. But the Lord said unto David my father, Whereas it was in thine heart to build an house for my name, thou didst well that it was in thine heart; 19. nevertheless thou shalt not build the house; but thy son that shall come forth out of thy loins, he shall build the house for my name. 20. And the Lord hath established his word that he spake; for I am risen up in the room of David my father, and sit on the throne of Israel, as the Lord promised, and have built the house for the name of the Lord, the God of Israel. 21. And there have I set a place for the ark, wherein is the covenant of the Lord, which he made with our fathers, when he brought them out of the land of Egypt.

22. And Solomon stood before the altar of the Lord in the presence of all the congregation of Israel, and spread forth his hands toward heaven:

23. and he said, O Lord, the God of Israel, there is no God like thee, in heaven above, or on earth beneath; who keepest covenant and mercy with thy servants, that walk before thee with all their heart; 24. who hast kept with thy servant David my father that which thou didst promise him: yea, thou spakest with thy mouth, and hast fulfilled it with thine hand, as it is this day. 25. Now therefore, O Lord, the God of Israel, keep with thy servant David my father that which thou hast promised him, saying, There shall not fail thee a man in my sight to sit on the throne of Israel; if only thy children take heed to their way to walk before me as thou hast walked before me. 26. Now therefore, O   God of Israel, let thy word, I pray thee, be verified, which thou spakest unto thy servant David my father. 27. But will God in very deed dwell   on the earth? behold, heaven, and the heaven of heavens can not contain thee; how much less this house that I have builded! 28. Yet have thou respect unto the prayer of thy servant, and to his supplication, O Lord my God, to hearken unto the cry and to the prayer which thy servant prayeth before thee this day: 29. that thine eyes may be open toward this house night and day, even toward the place whereof thou hast said, My name shall be there: to hearken unto the prayer which thy servant shall pray toward this place.

30. And hearken thou to the supplication of thy servant, and of thy people Israel, when they shall pray toward this place: yea, hear thou in heaven thy dwelling place; and when thou hearest, forgive. 31. If a man sin against his neighbour, and an oath be laid up on him to cause him to swear, and he come and swear before thine altar in this house: 32. then hear thou in heaven, and do, and judge thy servants, condemning the wicked, to bring his way upon

(II Chron. 6:) 1. Then spake Solomon, The Lord hath said that he would dwell in the thick darkness. 2. But I have   built thee an house of habitation, and a place for thee to dwell in for ever. 3. And the king turned his face   and blessed all the congregation of Israel: and all the congregation of Israel stood. 4. And he said, Blessed be the Lord, the God of Israel, which spake with his mouth unto David my father, and hath with his hands fulfilled it, saying, 5. Since the day that I brought forth my people Israel, out of the land of Egypt, I chose no city out of all the tribes of Israel to build an house in, that my name might be there; neither chose I any man to be prince over my people Israel: 6. but I have chosen Jerusalem, that my name might be there, and have chosen David to be over my people Israel.

7. Now it was in the heart of David my father to build an house for the name of the Lord, the God of Israel. 8. But the Lord said unto David my father, Whereas it was in thine heart to build an house for my name, thou didst well that it was in thine heart; 9. nevertheless thou shalt not build the house; but thy son that shall come forth out of thy loins, he shall build the house for my name. 10. And the Lord hath performed his word that he spake; for I am risen up in the room of David my father, and sit on the throne of Israel, as the Lord promised, and have built the house for the name of the Lord, the God of Israel. 11. And there have I set the ark, wherein is the covenant of the Lord, which he made with the children of Israel.

12. And he   stood before the altar of the Lord in the presence of all the congregation of Israel, and spread forth his hands: 13. (for Solomon had made a brasen scaffold, of five cubits long, and five cubits broad, and three cubits high, and had set it in the midst of the court; and upon it he stood, and kneeled down upon his knees before all the congregation of Israel, and spread forth his hands toward heaven:) 14. and he said, O Lord, the God of Israel, there is no God like thee, in the heaven, or in the earth; who keepest covenant and mercy with thy servants, that walk before thee with all their heart; 15. who hast kept with thy servant David my father that which thou didst promise him: yea, thou spakest with thy mouth, and hast fulfilled it with thine hand, as it is this day. 16. Now therefore, O Lord, the God of Israel, keep with thy servant David my father that which thou hast promised him, saying, There shall not fail thee a man in my sight to sit on the throne of Israel; if only thy children take heed to their way, to walk in my law as thou hast walked before me. 17. Now therefore, O Lord the God of Israel, let thy word   be verified, which thou spakest unto thy servant David.   18. But will God in very deed dwell with men on the earth? behold, heaven, and the heaven of heavens can not contain thee; how much less this house which I have builded! 19. Yet have thou respect unto the prayer of thy servant, and to his supplication, O Lord my God, to hearken unto the cry and to the prayer which thy servant prayeth before thee: 20. that thine eyes may be open toward this house day and night, even toward the place whereof thou hast said that thou wouldest put thy name there; to hearken unto the prayer which thy servant shall pray toward this place.

21. And hearken thou to the supplication of thy servant, and of thy people Israel, when they shall pray toward this place: yea, hear thou from thy dwelling place even from heaven; and when thou hearest, forgive. 22. If a man sin against his neighbour, and an oath be laid up on him to cause him to swear, and he come and swear before thine altar in this house: 23. then hear thou from heaven, and do, and judge thy servants, requiting the wicked, to bring his way upon

his own head; and justifying the righteous, to give him according to his righteousness.

When thy people Israel be smitten down before the enemy, because they have sinned against thee; if they turn again to thee, and confess thy name, and pray and make supplication unto thee in this house: then hear thou in heaven, and forgive the sin of thy people Israel, and bring them again unto the land which thou gavest unto their fathers.

When the heaven is shut up, and there is no rain, because they have sinned against thee; if they pray toward this place, and confess thy name, and turn from their sin, when thou dost afflict them: then hear thou in heaven, and forgive the sin of thy servants, and of thy people Israel, when thou teachest them the good way wherein they should walk; and send rain upon thy land, which thou hast given to thy people for an inheritance.

If there be in the land famine, if there be pestilence, if there be blasting or mildew, locust or caterpiller; if their enemy besiege them in the land of their cities; whatsoever plague, whatsoever sickness there be; what prayer and what supplication soever be made by any man, or by all thy people Israel, which shall know every man his own plague and his own sorrow, and shall spread forth his hands toward this house: then hear thou in heaven thy dwelling place, and forgive, and do, and render unto every man according to all his ways, whose heart thou knowest; (for thou even thou only knowest the hearts of all the children of men;) that they may fear thee, to walk in thy ways, so long as they live in the land which thou gavest unto our fathers.

Moreover concerning the stranger, that is not of thy people Israel, when he shall come out of a far country for thy great name's sake (for they shall hear of thy great name, and of thy mighty hand, and of thy stretched out arm;) when he shall come and pray toward this house; then hear thou in heaven thy dwelling place, and do according to all the stranger calleth to thee for; that all the peoples of the earth may know thy name, to fear thee as doth thy people Israel, and that they may know that this house which I have built is called by thy name.

If thy people go out to battle against their enemy, by whatsoever way thou shalt send them, and they pray unto thee toward this city which thou hast chosen, and toward the house which I have built for thy name; then hear thou in heaven their prayer and their supplication, and maintain their cause.

If they sin against thee, (for there is no man that sinneth not,) and thou be angry with them, and deliver them to the enemy, so that they carry them away captive unto the land of the enemy, far off or near; yet if they shall bethink themselves in the land whither they are carried captive, and turn again, and make supplication unto thee in the land of them that carried them captive, saying, We have sinned, we have done perversely, and have dealt wickedly; if they return unto thee with all their heart and with all their soul in the land of their captivity, whither they have carried them captive, and pray unto thee toward their land which thou gavest unto their fathers, and the city which thou hast chosen, and toward the house which I have built for thy name: then hear thou from heaven, even from thy dwelling place, their prayer and their supplications, and maintain their cause; and forgive thy people which have sinned against thee, and all their transgressions wherein they have transgressed against thee; and **give them compassion before those who carried them**

his own head; and justifying the righteous, to give him according to his righteousness.

33. When thy people Israel be smitten down before the enemy, because they have sinned against thee; if they turn again to thee, and confess thy name, and pray and make supplication unto thee in this house: 34. then hear thou in heaven, and forgive the sin of thy people Israel, and bring them again unto the land which thou gavest unto their fathers.

35. When heaven is shut up, and there is no rain, because they have sinned against thee; if they pray toward this place, and confess thy name, and turn from their sin, when thou dost afflict them: 36. then hear thou in heaven, and forgive the sin of thy servants, and of thy people Israel, when thou teachest them the good way wherein they should walk; and send rain upon thy land which thou hast given to thy people for an inheritance.

37. If there be in the land famine, if there be pestilence, if there be blasting or mildew, locust or caterpiller; if their enemy besiege them in the land of their cities; whatsoever plague, whatsoever sickness there be; 38. what prayer and supplication soever be made by any man, or by all thy people Israel, which shall know every man the plague of his own heart, and spread forth his hands toward this house: 39. then hear thou in heaven thy dwelling place, and forgive, and do, and render unto every man according to all his ways, whose heart thou knowest; (for thou, even thou only knowest the hearts of all the children of men;) 40. that they may fear thee all the days that they live in the land which thou gavest unto our fathers.

41. Moreover concerning the stranger, that is not of thy people Israel, when he shall come out of a far country for thy name's sake; 42. (for they shall hear of thy great name, and of thy mighty hand, and of thy stretched out arm;) when he shall come and pray toward this house; 43. hear thou in heaven thy dwelling place, and do according to all that the stranger calleth to thee for; that all the peoples of the earth may know thy name, to fear thee as doth thy people Israel, and that they may know that this house which I have built is called by thy name.

44. If thy people go out to battle against their enemy, by whatsoever way thou shalt send them, and they pray unto the Lord toward the city which thou hast chosen, and toward the house which I have built for thy name; 45. then hear thou in heaven their prayer and their supplication, and maintain their cause.

46. If they sin against thee, (for there is no man that sinneth not,) and thou be angry with them, and deliver them to the enemy, so that they carry them away captive unto the land of the enemy, far off or near; 47. yet if they shall bethink themselves in the land whither they were carried captive, and turn again, and make supplication unto thee in the land of them that carried them captive, saying, We have sinned, and have done perversely, we have dealt wickedly; 48. if they return unto thee with all their heart and with all their soul in the land of their enemies, which carried them captive, and pray unto thee toward their land which thou gavest unto their fathers, the city which thou hast chosen, and the house which I have built for thy name: 49. then hear thou their prayer and their supplication in heaven thy dwelling place, and maintain their cause; 50. and forgive thy people which have sinned against thee, and all their transgressions wherein they have transgressed against thee; and give them compassion before those who carried them captive, that they may have

his own head; and justifying the righteous, to give him according to his righteousness.

24. And if thy people Israel be smitten down before the enemy, because they have sinned against thee; and shall turn again and confess thy name, and pray and make supplication before thee in this house: 25. then hear thou from heaven, and forgive the sin of thy people Israel, and bring them again unto the land which thou gavest to them and to their fathers.

26. When the heaven is shut up, and there is no rain, because they have sinned against thee; if they pray toward this place, and confess thy name, and turn from their sin, when thou dost afflict them: 27. then hear thou in heaven, and forgive the sin of thy servants, and of thy people Israel, when thou teachest them the good way wherein they should walk; and send rain upon thy land, which thou hast given to thy people for an inheritance.

28. If there be in the land famine, if there be pestilence, if there be blasting or mildew, locust or caterpiller; if their enemies besiege them in the land of their cities; whatsoever plague, whatsoever sickness there be; 29. what prayer and supplication soever be made by any man, or by all thy people Israel, which shall know every man his own plague and his own sorrow, and shall spread forth his hands toward this house: 30. then hear thou from heaven thy dwelling place, and forgive, and render unto every man according to all his ways, whose heart thou knowest; (for thou, even thou only, knowest the hearts of the children of men;) 31. that they may fear thee, to walk in thy ways, so long as they live in the land which thou gavest unto our fathers.

32. Moreover concerning the stranger, that is not of thy people Israel, when he shall come out of a far country for thy great name's sake and thy mighty hand, and thy stretched out arm; when they shall come and pray toward this house: 33. then hear thou from heaven, even from thy dwelling place, and do according to all that the stranger calleth to thee for; that all the peoples of the earth may know thy name, and fear thee as doth thy people Israel, and that they may know that this house which I have built is called by thy name.

34. If thy people go out to battle against their enemies, by whatsoever way thou shalt send them, and they pray unto thee toward this city which thou hast chosen, and the house which I have built for thy name; 35. then hear thou from heaven their prayer and their supplication, and maintain their cause.

36. If they sin against thee, (for there is no man that sinneth not,) and thou be angry with them, and deliver them to the enemy, so that they carry them away captive unto a land far off or near; 37. yet if they shall bethink themselves in the land whither they are carried captive and turn again, and make supplication unto thee in the land of their captivity, saying, We have sinned, we have done perversely, and have dealt wickedly; 38. if they return unto thee with all their heart and with all their soul in the land of their captivity, whither they have carried them captive, and pray toward their land which thou gavest unto their fathers, and the city which thou hast chosen, and toward the house which I have built for thy name; 39. then hear thou from heaven, even from thy dwelling place, their prayer and their supplications, and maintain their cause; and forgive thy people which have sinned against thee.

captive, that they may have compassion on them; for they be thy people: and thine inheritance which thou broughtest forth out of Egypt, from the midst of the furnace of iron. Now, O my God, let, I beseech thee, thine eyes be open unto the supplication of thy servant, and unto the supplication of thy people Israel, and let thine ears be attent unto the prayer that is made in this place, to hearken unto them whensoever they cry unto thee. For thou didst separate them from among all the peoples of the earth, to be thine inheritance, as thou spakest by the hand of Moses thy servant, when thou broughtest our fathers out of Egypt, O Lord God. Now therefore arise, O Lord God, into thy resting place, thou, and the ark of thy strength; let thy priests, O Lord God, be clothed with salvation, and let thy saints rejoice in goodness. O Lord God, turn not away the face of thine anointed: remember the mercies of David thy servant.

And it was so, that when Solomon had made an end of praying all this prayer and supplication unto the Lord, he arose from before the altar of the Lord, from kneeling on his knees with his hands spread forth toward heaven. And he stood, and blessed all the congregation of Israel with a loud voice, saying, Blessed be the Lord that hath given rest unto his people Israel, according unto all that he hath promised: there hath not failed one word of all his good promise, which he promised by the hand of Moses his servant. The Lord our God be with us, as he was with our fathers: let him not leave, nor forsake us: that he may incline our hearts unto him, to walk in all his ways, and to keep his commandments, and his statutes, and his judgements, which he commanded our fathers. And let these my words, wherewith I have made supplication before the Lord, be nigh unto the Lord our God day and night, that he maintain the cause of his servant, and the cause of his people Israel, as every day shall require: that all the peoples of the earth may know that the Lord, he is God; there is none else. Let your heart therefore be perfect with the Lord our God, to walk in his statutes, and to keep his commandments, as at this day. Now when Solomon had made an end of praying, the fire came down from heaven, and consumed the burnt offering and the sacrifices; and the glory of the Lord filled the house. And the priests could not enter into the house of the Lord, because the glory of the Lord filled the Lord's house. And all the children of Israel looked on when the fire came down, and the glory of the Lord was upon the house; and they bowed themselves with their faces to the ground upon the pavement, and worshipped, and gave thanks unto the Lord, saying, * For he is good; for his mercy endureth for ever.

---

* PSALM 136:
1. O give thanks unto the Lord; for he is good;
   For his mercy endureth for ever.
2. O give thanks unto the God of gods:
   For his mercy endureth for ever.
3. O give thanks unto the Lord of lords;
   For his mercy endureth for ever.
4. To him alone who doeth great wonders:
   For his mercy endureth for ever.
5. To him that by understanding made the heavens:
   For his mercy endureth for ever
6. To him that spread forth the earth above the waters:
   For his mercy endureth for ever.
7. To him that made great lights:
   For his mercy endureth for ever.
8. The sun to rule by day:
   For his mercy endureth for ever
9. The moon and the stars to rule by night:
   For his mercy endureth for ever
10. To him that smote Egypt in their firstborn:
    For his mercy endureth for ever.
11. And brought out Israel from among them:
    For his mercy endureth for ever.
12. With a strong hand, and with a stretched out arm:
    For his mercy endureth for ever.
13. To him which divided the Red Sea in sunder:
    For his mercy endureth for ever.

compassion on them; 51. for they be thy people; and thine inheritance, which thou broughtest forth out of Egypt, from the midst of the furnace of iron:
52. that thine eyes may be open unto the supplication of thy servant, and unto the supplication of thy people Israel,
to hearken unto them whensoever they cry unto thee.
53. For thou didst separate them from among all the peoples of the earth, to be thine inheritance, as thou spakest by the hand of Moses thy servant, when thou broughtest our fathers out of Egypt, O Lord God.

54. And it was so, that when Solomon had made an end of praying all this prayer and supplication unto the Lord, he arose from before the altar of the Lord, from kneeling on his knees with his hands spread forth toward heaven. 55. And he stood, and blessed all the congregation of Israel with a loud voice, saying, 56. Blessed be the Lord that hath given rest unto his people Israel, according unto all that he promised: there hath not failed one word of all his good promise, which he promised by the hand of Moses his servant. 57. The Lord our God be with us, as he was with our fathers: let him not leave us, nor forsake us: 58. that he may incline our hearts unto him, to walk in all his ways, and to keep his commandments, and his statutes, and his judgements, which he commanded our fathers. 59. And let these my words, wherewith I have made supplication before the Lord, be nigh unto the Lord our God day and night, that he maintain the cause of his servant, and the cause of his people Israel, as every day shall require: 60. that all the peoples of the earth may know that the Lord, he is God; there is none else. 61. Let your heart therefore be perfect with the Lord our God, to walk in his statutes, and to keep his commandments, as at this day.

40. Now, O my God, let, I beseech thee, thine eyes be open,

and let thine ears be attent unto the prayer that is made in this place.

41. Now therefore arise, O Lord God, into thy resting place, thou, and the ark of thy strength: let thy priests, O Lord God, be clothed with salvation, and let thy saints rejoice in goodness. 42. O Lord God, turn not away the face of thine anointed: remember the mercies of David thy servant.

(II Chron. 7:) 1. Now when Solomon had made an end of praying,
the fire came down from heaven, and consumed the burnt offering and the sacrifices; and the glory of the Lord filled the house. 2. And the priests could not enter into the house of the Lord, because the glory of the Lord filled the Lord's house. 3. And all the children of Israel looked on, when the fire came down, and the glory of the Lord was upon the house; and they bowed themselves with their faces to the ground upon the pavement, and worshipped, and gave thanks unto the Lord, saying,
For he is good; For his mercy endureth for ever.

14. And made Israel to pass through the midst of it:
   For his mercy endureth for ever.
15. But overthrew Pharaoh and his host in the Red Sea:
   For his mercy endureth for ever.
16. To him which led his people through the wilderness:
   For his mercy endureth for ever.
17. To him which smote great kings:
   For his mercy endureth for ever.
18. And slew famous kings:
   For his mercy endureth for ever.
19. Sihon king of the Amorites:
   For his mercy endureth for ever.
20. And Og king of Bashan:
   For his mercy endureth for ever.
21. And gave their land for an heritage:
   For his mercy endureth for ever.
22. Even an heritage unto Israel his servant:
   For his mercy endureth for ever.
23. Who remembered us in our low estate:
   For his mercy endureth for ever.
24. And hath delivered us from our adversaries:
   For his mercy endureth for ever.
25. He giveth food to all flesh:
   For his mercy endureth for ever.
26. O give thanks unto the God of heaven:
   For his mercy endureth for ever.

Then the king, and all Israel with him, offered sacrifice before the Lord. And king Solomon offered for the sacrifice of peace offerings, which he offered unto the Lord, two and twenty thousand oxen, and an hundred and twenty thousand sheep. So the king and all the people dedicated the house of God. And the priests stood, according to their offices; the Levites also with instruments of music of the Lord, which David the king had made to give thanks unto the Lord, for his mercy endureth for ever, when David praised by their ministry: and the priests sounded trumpets before them; and all Israel stood.

Moreover Solomon the same day hallowed the middle of the court that was before the house of the Lord; for there he offered the burnt offering, and the meal offering, and the fat of the peace offerings: because the brasen altar which Solomon had made, was not able to receive the burnt offering, and the meal offering, and the fat of the peace offering. So Solomon held the feast at that time seven days, and all Israel with him, a very great congregation, from the entering in of Hamath unto the brook of Egypt, before the Lord our God. And on the eighth day they held a solemn assembly: for they kept the dedication of the altar seven days, and the feast seven days, even fourteen days. On the eighth day, which was the three and twentieth day of the seventh month, he sent the people away, and they blessed the king, and went unto their tents joyful and glad of heart for all the goodness that the Lord had shewed unto David his servant, and to Solomon, and to Israel his people.

Three Houses of Solomon

I Kings 7:1. And Solomon was building his own house thirteen years, and he finished all his house. 2. For he built the house of the forest of Lebanon; the length thereof was an hundred cubits, and the breadth thereof fifty cubits, and the height thereof thirty cubits, upon four rows of cedar pillars, with cedar beams upon the pillars. 3. And it was covered with cedar above over the forty and five beams, that were upon the pillars; fifteen in a row. 4. And there were prospects in three rows, and light was over against light in three ranks. 5. And all the doors and posts were square in prospect: and light was over against light in three ranks. 6. And he made the porch of pillars; the length thereof was fifty cubits, and the breadth thereof thirty cubits; and a porch before them; and pillars and thick beams before them. 7. And he made the porch of the throne where he might judge, even the porch of judgement: and it was covered with cedar from floor to floor. 8. And his house where he might dwell, the other court within the porch, was of like work. (He made also an house for Pharaoh's daughter, whom Solomon had taken to wife,) like unto this porch. 9. All these were of costly stones, even of hewn stone, according to measure, sawed with saws, within and without, even from the foundation unto the coping, and so on the outside unto the great court. 10. And the foundation was of costly stones, even great stones, stones of ten cubits, and stones of eight cubits. 11. And above were costly stones, even hewn stones, according to measure, and cedar wood. 12. And the great court round about had three rows of hewn stone, and a row of cedar beams; like as the inner court of the house of the Lord, and the porch of the house. And Solomon brought up the daughter of Pharaoh out of the city of David unto her house which he had built for her: for he said, My wife shall not dwell in the house of David king of Israel, because the places are holy, whereunto the ark of the Lord hath come: then did he build Millo. And three times in a year Solomon offered burnt and peace offerings unto the Lord on the altar of the Lord, which he had built before the porch, even as the duty of every day required, offering according to the commandments of Moses, on the Sabbaths, and on the new moons, and on the set feasts, three times in the year, even in the feast of unleavened bread, and in the feast of weeks,

SECT. XIX THE UNITED KINGDOM 137

(I Kings 8:) 62. And the king, and all Israel with him, offered sacrifice before the Lord. 63. And Solomon offered for the sacrifice of peace offerings, which he offered unto the Lord, two and twenty thousand oxen, and an hundred and twenty thousand sheep. So the king and all the children of Israel dedicated the house of the Lord.

64. The same day did the king hallow the middle of the court that was before the house of the Lord; for there he offered the burnt offering, and the meal offering, and the fat of the peace offerings; because the brasen altar that was before the Lord was too little to receive the burnt offering, and the meal offering, and the fat of the peace offerings.
65. So Solomon held the feast at that time, and all Israel with him, a great congregation, from the entering in of Hamath unto the brook of Egypt, before the Lord our God,

and seven days, even fourteen days.
66. On the eighth day
he sent the people away, and they blessed the king, and went unto their tents joyful and glad of heart for all the goodness that the Lord had shewed unto David his servant, and to Israel his people.

(II Chron. 7:) 4. Then the king and all the people offered sacrifice before the Lord. 5. And king Solomon offered a sacrifice
 twenty and two thousand oxen, and an hundred and twenty thousand sheep. So the king and all the people dedicated the house of God. 6. And the priests stood, according to their offices; the Levites also with instruments of music of the Lord, which David the king had made to give thanks unto the Lord, for his mercy endureth for ever, when David praised by their ministry: and the priests sounded trumpets before them; and all Israel stood.

7. Moreover Solomon hallowed the middle of the court that was before the house of the Lord; for there he offered the burnt offerings, and the fat of the peace offerings; because the brasen altar which Solomon had made was not able to receive the burnt offering, and the meal offering, and the fat.
8. So Solomon held the feast at that time seven days, and all Israel with him, a very great congregation, from the entering in of Hamath unto the brook of Egypt.

9. And on the eighth day they held a solemn assembly; for they kept the dedication of the altar seven days, and the feast seven days.
10. And on the three and twentieth day of the seventh month he sent the people away
unto their tents, joyful and glad of heart for the goodness that the Lord had shewed unto David, and to Solomon, and to Israel his people.

(I Kings 9:) 24. But Pharaoh's daughter came up out of the city of David unto her house which Solomon had built for her:

then did he build Millo.
25. (And three times in a year did Solomon offer burnt offerings and peace offerings upon the altar which he built unto the Lord, burning incense therewith, upon the altar that was before the Lord.)

(I Chron. 8:) 11. And Solomon brought up the daughter of Pharaoh out of the city of David unto the house that he had built for her: for he said, My wife shall not dwell in the house of David king of Israel, because the places are holy, whereunto the ark of the Lord hath come.

12. (Then Solomon offered burnt offerings unto the Lord on the altar of the Lord, which he had built before the porch,
13. even as the duty of every day required offering according to the commandment of Moses, on the sabbaths, and on the new moons, and on the set feasts, three times in the year, even in the feast of unleavened bread, and in the feast of weeks,

and in the feast of tabernacles. And he appointed, according to the ordinance of David his father, the courses of the priests to their service, and the Levites to their charges, to praise, and to minister before the priests, as the duty of every day required; the doorkeepers also by their courses at every gate: for so had David the man of God commanded. And they departed not from the commandment of the king unto the priests and Levites concerning any matter, or concerning the treasures. Now all the work of Solomon was prepared unto the day of the foundation of the house of the Lord, and until it was finished. So the house of the Lord was perfected. And it came to pass, when Solomon had finished the building of the house of the Lord, and the king's house, and

**Lord Appears
Second Time**

all that came into Solomon's heart to make in the house of the Lord, and in his own house, that the Lord appeared to Solomon by night the second time, as he had appeared unto him at Gibeon. And the Lord said unto him, I have heard thy prayer and thy supplication, that thou hast made before me: I have hallowed this house, which thou hast built, to put my name there for ever; and have chosen this place to myself for an house of sacrifice, and mine eyes and mine heart shall be there perpetually.

If I shut up heaven that there be no rain, or if I command the locust to devour the land, or if I send pestilence among my people; if my people, which are called by my name, shall humble themselves, and pray, and seek my face, and turn from their wicked ways; then I will hear from heaven, and will forgive their sin, and will heal their land. Now mine eyes shall be open, and mine ears attent, unto the prayer that is made in this place. For now have I chosen and hallowed this house, that my name may be there for ever: and mine eyes and mine heart shall be there perpetually.

And as for thee, if thou wilt walk before me, as David thy father walked, in integrity of heart, and in uprightness, and do according to all that I have commanded thee, and wilt keep my statutes and my judgments; then I will establish the throne of thy kingdom over Israel for ever; according as I covenanted with David thy father, saying, There shall not fail thee a man upon the throne of Israel.

But if ye shall turn away from following me, ye or your children, and not keep my commandments and my statutes which I have set before you, but shall go and serve other gods, and worship them: then will I cut off Israel and pluck them up by the roots out of my land which I have given them; and this house, which I have hallowed for my name, will I cast out of my sight; and I will make it a proverb, and a byword among all peoples: and though this house be so high, yet shall every one that passeth by it be astonished, and shall hiss; and they shall say, Why hath the Lord done thus unto this land, and to this house? And they shall answer, Because they forsook the Lord their God, which brought forth their fathers out of the land of Egypt, and laid hold on other gods, and worshipped them, and served them: therefore hath the Lord brought all this evil upon them.

SECT. XIX   THE UNITED KINGDOM   139

So he finished the house.
(I Kings 9:) 1. And it came to pass when Solomon had finished the building of the house of the Lord, and the king's house, and (all Solomon's desire which he was pleased to do,)
2. that the Lord appeared to Solomon the second time, as he had appeared unto him at Gibeon. 3. And the Lord said unto him, I have heard thy prayer and thy supplication, that thou hast made before me; (I have hallowed this house, which thou hast built, to put my name there for ever; and mine eyes and mine heart shall be there perpetually.)

4. And as for thee, if thou wilt walk before me, as David thy father walked, in integrity of heart, and in uprightness, to do according to all that I have commanded thee, and wilt keep my statutes and my judgements; 5. then I will establish the throne of thy kingdom over Israel for ever: according as I promised to David thy father, saying, There shall not fail thee a man upon the throne of Israel.
6. But if ye shall turn away from following me, ye or your children, and not keep my commandments and my statutes which I have set before you, but shall go and serve other gods, and worship them: 7. then will I cut off Israel out of the land which I have given them; and this house, which I have hallowed for my name, will I cast out of my sight; and Israel shall be a proverb and a byword among all peoples: 8. and though this house be so high, yet shall every one that passeth by it be astonished, and shall hiss; and they shall say, Why hath the Lord done thus unto this land, and to this house? 9. And they shall answer, Because they forsook the Lord their God, which brought forth their fathers out of the land of Egypt, and laid hold on other gods, and worshipped them, and served them; therefore hath the Lord brought all this evil upon them.

and in the feast of tabernacles. 14. And he appointed, according to the ordinance of David his father, the courses of the priests to their service, and the Levites to their charges, to praise, and to minister before the priests, as the duty of every day required: the doorkeepers also by their courses at every gate: for so had David the man of God commanded. 15. And they departed not from the commandment of the king unto the priests and Levites concerning any matter, or concerning the treasures. 16. Now all the work of Solomon was prepared unto the day of the foundation of the house of the Lord, and until it was finished. So the house of the Lord was perfected.
(II Chron. 7:) 11. Thus Solomon finished the house of the Lord, and the king's house, and (all that came into Solomon's heart to make in the house of the Lord, and in his own house, he prosperously effected.) 12. And the Lord appeared to Solomon by night,
and said unto him, I have heard thy prayer,
(and have chosen this place to myself for an house of sacrifice.)

13. If I shut up heaven that there be no rain, or if I command the locust to devour the land, or if I send pestilence among my people; 14. if my people, which are called by my name, shall humble themselves, and pray, and seek my face, and turn from their wicked ways; then will I hear from heaven, and will forgive their sin, and will heal their land. 15. Now mine eyes shall be open, and mine ears attent, unto the prayer that is made in this place. 16. For now have I chosen and hallowed this house, that my name may be there for ever: and mine eyes and mine heart shall be there perpetually. 17. And as for thee, if thou wilt walk before me, as David thy father walked, and do according to all that I have commanded thee, and wilt keep my statutes and my judgements; 18. then I will establish the throne of thy kingdom, according as I covenanted with David thy father, saying, There shall not fail thee a man to be ruler in Israel.
19. But if ye turn away,
and forsake my statutes and my commandments, which I have set before you, and shall go and serve other gods, and worship them: 20. then will I pluck them up by the roots out of my land which I have given them; and this house which I have hallowed for my name, will I cast out of my sight; and I will make it a proverb and a byword among all peoples. 21. And this house, which is so high, every one that passeth by it shall be astonished, and shall say, Why hath the Lord done thus unto this land, and to this house? 22. And they shall answer, Because they forsook the Lord, the God of their fathers, which brought them forth out of the land of Egypt, and laid hold on other gods, and worshipped them, and served them: therefore hath he brought all this evil upon them.

THE HOUSE OF DAVID
  B. C. 1016 (Usher)
II Solomon
  B. C. 977 (Rev.)   NATHAN

SECTION XX

Solomon's Fame, Greatness, and Works

Dominion and Peace — And Solomon ruled over all the kingdoms from the River even unto the land of the Philistines and unto the border of Egypt: they brought presents, and served Solomon all the days of his life. For he had dominion over all the region on this side the River, from Tiphsah even to Gaza, over all the kings on this side the River: and he had peace on all sides round about him. And Judah and Israel dwelt safely, every man under his vine and under his fig tree, from Dan even to Beer-sheba all the days of Solomon.

Glory and Revenue — And Solomon had * four thousand stalls for horses and chariots, and twelve thousand horsemen. And Solomon gathered together chariots and horsemen: and he had a thousand and four hundred chariots, and twelve thousand horsemen, which he bestowed in the chariot cities and with the king at Jerusalem. And the horses which Solomon had were brought out of Egypt, and out of all lands; and the king's merchants received them in droves, each drove at a price. And they fetched up and brought out of Egypt a chariot for six hundred shekels of silver, and an horse for an hundred and fifty: and so for all the kings of the Hittites, and for the kings of Syria, did they bring them out by their means. And the king made silver to be in Jerusalem as stones, and cedars made he to be as the sycamore trees that are in the lowland, for abundance. Now the weight of gold that came to Solomon in one year was six hundred threescore and six talents of gold, beside that which the chapmen brought, and the traffic of the merchants, and of all the kings of the mingled people, and of the governors of the country.

Splendor and Wisdom — And king Solomon made two hundred targets of beaten gold: six hundred shekels of beaten gold went to one target. And he made three hundred shields of beaten gold; three † hundred shekels of gold went to one shield: and the king put them in the house of the forest of Lebanon. Moreover the king made a great throne of ivory, and overlaid it with the finest gold. There were six steps to the throne, with a footstool of gold, which were fastened to the throne, and the top of the throne was round behind; and there were stays on either side by the place of the seat, and two lions standing beside the stays. And twelve lions stood there on the one side and on the other upon the six steps:

---
* In Kings forty thousand.   † In Kings three pound. See Appendix C, Chronicles III, 1, (7).

SECT. XX   THE UNITED KINGDOM   141

(I Kings 4:) 21. And Solomon ruled over all the kingdoms from the River unto the land of the Philistines and unto the border of Egypt: they brought presents, and served Solomon all the days of his life. 24. For he had dominion over all the region on this side the River, from Tiphsah even to Gaza, over all the kings on this side the River: and he had peace on all sides round about him. 25. And Judah and Israel dwelt safely, every man under his vine and under his fig tree, from Dan even to Beer-sheba all the days of Solomon. 26. ((And Solomon had *forty* thousand stalls of horses for his chariots, and twelve thousand horsemen.))	(II Chron. 9:) 26. And he ruled over all the kings from the River even unto the land of the Philistines and to the border of Egypt. (II Chron. 9:) 25. ((And Solomon had *four* thousand stalls for horses and chariots, and twelve thousand horsemen.))

(I Kings 10:) 26. And Solomon gathered together chariots and horsemen: and he had a thousand and four hundred chariots, and twelve thousand horsemen, which he bestowed in the chariot cities and with the king at Jerusalem. 28. And the horses which Solomon had were brought out of Egypt; and the king's merchants received them in droves, each drove at a price. 29. And a chariot came up and went out of Egypt for six hundred shekels of silver, and an horse for an hundred and fifty: and so for all the kings of the Hittites, and for the kings of Syria, did they bring them out by their means. 27. And the king made silver to be in Jerusalem as stones, and cedars made he to be as the sycomore trees that are in the lowland, for abundance.	(II Chron. 1:) 14. And Solomon gathered together chariots and horsemen: and he had a thousand and four hundred chariots, and twelve thousand horsemen, which he placed in the chariot cities and with the king at Jerusalem. 16. And the horses which Solomon had were brought out of Egypt; and the king's merchants received them in droves, each drove at a price. 17 And they fetched up, and brought out of Egypt a chariot for six hundred shekels of silver, and an horse for an hundred and fifty, and so for all the kings of the Hittites, and for the kings of Syria, did they bring them out by their means. 15. And the king made silver to be in Jerusalem as stones, and cedars made he to be as the sycomore trees that are in the lowland, for abundance.	which he bestowed in the chariot cities and with the king at Jerusalem. 28. And they brought horses for Solomon out of Egypt, and out of all lands. 27. And the king made silver to be in Jerusalem as stones, and cedars made he to be as the sycomore trees that are in the lowland, for abundance.

(I Kings 10:) 14. Now the weight of gold that came to Solomon in one year was six hundred threescore and six talents of gold, 15. beside that which the chapmen brought, and the traffic of the merchants, and of all the kings of the mingled people, and of the governors of the country. 16. And king Solomon made two hundred targets of beaten gold: six hundred shekels of gold went to one target. 17. And he made three hundred shields of beaten gold ((*three pound* of gold went to one shield)) and the king put them in the house of the forest of Lebanon. 18. Moreover the king made a great throne of ivory, and overlaid it with the finest gold. 19. There were six steps to the throne, and the top of the throne was round behind: and there were stays on either side by the place of the seat, and two lions standing beside the stays. 20. And twelve lions stood there on the one side and on the other upon the six steps:	(II Chron. 9:) 13. Now the weight of gold that came to Solomon in one year was six hundred threescore and six talents of gold; 14. beside that which the chapmen and merchants brought, and all the kings of Arabia, and the governors of the country brought gold and silver to Solomon. 15. And king Solomon made two hundred targets of beaten gold: six hundred shekels of beaten gold went to one target. 16. And he made three hundred shields of beaten gold ((*three hundred shekels* of gold went to one shield)) and the king put them in the house of the forest of Lebanon. 17. Moreover the king made a great throne of ivory, and overlaid it with pure gold. 18. And there were six steps to the throne, with a footstool of gold, which were fastened to the throne, and stays on either side by the place of the seat, and two lions standing beside the stays. 19. And twelve lions stood there on the one side and on the other upon the six steps:

there was not the like made in any kingdom. And all king Solomon's drinking vessels were of gold, and all the vessels of the forest of Lebanon were of pure gold: none were of silver; it was nothing accounted of in the days of Solomon. So king Solomon exceeded all the kings of the earth in riches and in wisdom.

Wisdom of Solomon

And all the kings of the earth sought the presence of Solomon, to hear his wisdom, which God had put in his heart. And they brought every man his present, vessels of silver, and vessels of gold, and raiment, and armour, and spices, horses, and mules a rate year by year. I Kings 4:29. And God gave Solomon wisdom and understanding exceeding much, and largeness of heart, even as the sand that is on the sea shore. 30. And Solomon's wisdom excelled the wisdom of all the children of the east, and all the wisdom of Egypt. 31. For he was wiser than all men; than Ethan the Ezrahite, and Heman, and Calcol, and Darda, the sons of Mahol: and his fame was in all the nations round about. 32. And he spake three thousand proverbs: and his songs were a thousand and five. 33. And he spake of trees, from the cedar that is in Lebanon even unto the hyssop that springeth out of the wall: he spake also of beasts, and of fowl, and of creeping things, and of fishes. 34. And there came of all peoples to hear the wisdom of Solomon, from all the kings of the earth, which had heard of his wisdom.

Queen of Sheba

And when the queen of Sheba heard of the fame of Solomon concerning the name of the Lord, she came to prove him with hard questions. And she came to Jerusalem with a very great train, with camels that bare spices, and gold in abundance, and precious stones: and when she was come to Solomon, she communed with him of all that was in her heart. And Solomon told her all her questions: and there was not anything hid from the king which he told her not. And when the queen of Sheba had seen all the wisdom of Solomon, and the house that he had built, and the meat of his table, and the sitting of his servants, and the attendance of his ministers, and his cupbearers, and their apparel, and his ascent by which he went up into the house of the Lord; there was no more spirit in her. And she said to the king, It was a true report that I heard in mine own land of thine acts, and of thy wisdom. Howbeit I believed not their words, until I came, and mine eyes had seen it: and, behold, the half of the greatness of thy wisdom was not told me: thy wisdom and prosperity exceedeth the fame which I heard. Happy are thy men, happy are these thy servants, which stand continually before thee, and that hear thy wisdom. Blessed be the Lord thy God, which delighted in thee, to set thee on the throne of Israel, to be king for the Lord thy God; because thy God loved Israel, to establish them for ever, therefore made he thee king over them, to do judgment and justice. And she gave the king an hundred and twenty talents of gold, and spices in great abundance, and precious stones: there came no more such abundance of spices, as these which the queen of Sheba gave to king Solomon. And king Solomon gave to the queen of Sheba all her desire, whatsoever she asked, *beside that which Solomon gave her of his royal bounty. So she turned and went to her own land, she and her servants.

Hiram and Solomon

And king Solomon made a navy of ships in Ezion-geber, which is beside Eloth, on the shore of the Red Sea, in the land of Edom. And Hiram sent him, by the hand of his servants, ships, and servants that had knowledge of the sea; and they came with the servants of Solomon to Ophir, and fetched from thence † *four hundred and twenty* talents of gold and brought them to king Solomon.

* See Chronicles III, 2, (4). Appendix C.   † Chronicles, *Four hundred and fifty*. III, 1, (9).

SECT. XX THE UNITED KINGDOM

there was not the like made in any kingdom. 21. And all king Solomon's drinking vessels were of gold, and all the vessels of the forest of Lebanon were of pure gold: none were of silver; it was nothing accounted of in the days of Solomon. 23. So king Solomon exceeded all the kings of the earth in riches and in wisdom. 24. And all the earth sought the presence of Solomon, to hear his wisdom, which God had put in his heart. 25. And they brought every man his present, vessels of silver, and vessels of gold, and raiment, and armour, and spices, horses, and mules, a rate year by year.	there was not the like made in any kingdom. 20. And all king Solomon's drinking vessels were of gold, and all the vessels of the forest of Lebanon were of pure gold: silver was nothing accounted of in the days of Solomon. 22. So king Solomon exceeded all the kings of the earth in riches and in wisdom. 23. And all the kings of the earth sought the presence of Solomon, to hear his wisdom, which God had put in his heart. 24. And they brought every man his present, vessels of silver, and vessels of gold, and raiment, armour, and spices, horses, and mules, a rate year by year.
(1 Kings 10:) 1-13. And when the queen of Sheba heard of the fame of Solomon concerning the name of the Lord, she came to prove him with hard questions. 2. And she came to Jerusalem with a very great train, with camels that bare spices, and very much gold, and precious stones: and when she was come to Solomon, she communed with him of all that was in her heart. 3. And Solomon told her all her questions: there was not anything hid from the king which he told her not. 4. And when the queen of Sheba had seen all the wisdom of Solomon, and the house that he had built, 5. and the meat of his table, and the sitting of his servants, and the attendance of his ministers, and their apparel, and his cupbearers, and his ascent by which he went up into the house of the Lord; there was no more spirit in her. 6. And she said to the king, It was a true report that I heard in mine own land of thine acts and of thy wisdom. 7. Howbeit I believed not the words, until I came, and mine eyes had seen it: and, behold, the half was not told me: thy wisdom and prosperity exceedeth the fame which I heard. 8. Happy are thy men, happy are these thy servants, which stand continually before thee, and that hear thy wisdom. 9. Blessed be the Lord thy God, which delighted in thee, to set thee on the throne of Israel: because the Lord loved Israel for ever, therefore made he thee king, to do judgement and justice. 10. And she gave the king an hundred and twenty talents of gold, and of spices very great store, and precious stones: there came no more such abundance of spices as these which the queen of Sheba gave to king Solomon. 13. And king Solomon gave to the queen of Sheba all her desire, whatsoever she asked, beside ((that which Solomon gave her of his royal bounty.)) So she turned and went to her own land, she and her servants. (I Kings 9:) 26. ((And king Solomon made a navy of ships in Ezion-geber which is beside Eloth, on the shore of the Red Sea, in the land of Edom. 27. And Hiram sent in the navy his *servants*, shipmen that had knowledge of the sea, with the servants of Solomon. 28. And they came to Ophir, and fetched from thence gold, ((four hundred and *twenty* talents)) and brought it to king Solomon.	(II Chron. 9:) 1-12. And when the queen of Sheba heard of the fame of Solomon, she came to prove Solomon with hard questions at Jerusalem, with a very great train, and camels that bare spices, and gold in abundance, and precious stones: and when she was come to Solomon, she communed with him of all that was in her heart. 2. And Solomon told her all her questions: and there was not anything hid from Solomon which he told her not. 3. And when the queen of Sheba had seen the wisdom of Solomon, and the house that he had built, 4. and the meat of his table, and the sitting of his servants, and the attendance of his ministers, and their apparel: his cupbearers also, and their apparel, and his ascent by which he went up unto the house of the Lord, there was no more spirit in her. 5. And she said to the king, It was a true report that I heard in mine own land of thine acts and of thy wisdom. 6 Howbeit I believed not their words, until I came, and mine eyes had seen it · and, behold, the half of the greatness of thy wisdom was not told me: thou exceedeth the fame that I heard. 7. Happy are thy men, happy are these thy servants, which stand continually before thee, and hear thy wisdom. 8. Blessed be the Lord thy God, which delighted in thee, to set thee on his throne, to be king for the Lord thy God: because thy God loved Israel, to establish them forever, therefore made he thee king over them, to do judgement and justice. 9. And she gave the king an hundred and twenty talents of gold, and spices in great abundance, and precious stones: neither was there any such spice as the queen of Sheba gave to king Solomon. 12. And king Solomon gave to the queen of Sheba all her desire, whatsoever she asked, beside ((that which she brought unto the king.)) So she turned and went to her own land, she and her servants (II Chron 8.) 17. ((Then went Solomon to Ezion-geber, and to Eloth, on the sea shore in the land of Edom. 18. And Huram sent him by the hands of his servants *ships*, and servants that had knowledge of the sea; and they came with the servants of Solomon to Ophir, and fetched from thence ((four hundred and *fifty* talents of gold)) and brought them to king Solomon.

For the king had at sea a navy at Tarshish with the navy of Hiram: once every three years came the ships of Tarshish, bringing gold, and silver, ivory, and apes, and peacocks. And the servants also of Hiram, and the servants of Solomon, which brought gold from Ophir, brought great plenty of almug trees and precious stones. And the king made of the almug trees pillars for the house of the Lord, and for the king's house, and harps and psalteries for the singers: there came no such almug trees, and there were none such seen before in the land of Judah, unto this day.

And it came to pass at the end of twenty years, wherein Solomon had built the two houses, the house of the Lord and his own house, (now Hiram the king of Tyre had furnished Solomon with cedar trees and fir trees, and with gold according to all his desire,) that then *King Solomon gave Hiram twenty cities in the land of Galilee. And Hiram came out from Tyre to see the cities which Solomon had given him; and they pleased him not. And he said, what cities are these which thou hast given me, my brother? And he called them the land of Cabul, unto this day. And Hiram sent to the king sixscore talents of gold.

Levy for Building — And this is the reason of the levy which king Solomon raised; for to build the house of the Lord, and his own house, and Millo, and the wall of Jerusalem, and Hazor, and Megiddo, and Gezer. Pharaoh king of Egypt had gone up, and taken Gezer, and burnt it with fire, and slain the Canaanites that dwelt in the city, and given it for a portion unto his daughter, Solomon's wife.

And Solomon went to Hamath-zobah, and prevailed against it. Also he built Gezer, and Beth-horon the upper, and Beth-horon the nether, fenced cities, with walls, gates, and bars, and Baalath. And he built Tadmor in the wilderness in the land, and all the store cities, which he built in Hamath, and all the store cities that Solomon had, and all the cities for his chariots, and the cities for his horsemen, and all that Solomon desired to build for his pleasure in Jerusalem, and in Lebanon, and in all the land of his dominion.

As for all the people that were left of the Hittites, and the Amorites, and the Perezzites, and the Hivites, and the Jebusites, which were not of the children of Israel; of their children that were left after them in the land, whom the children of Israel were not able utterly to destroy, of them did Solomon raise a levy of bondservants, unto this day. But of the children of Israel did Solomon make no bondservants for his work, but they were the men of war, and his servants, and his princes, and chief of his captains, and rulers of his chariots, and of his horsemen. And these were the chief officers that were over king Solomon's work, even †five hundred and fifty, which bare rule over the people that wrought in the work.

---

* In Chronicles, the cities which Huram had given to Solomon, Solomon built them, and caused the children of Israel to dwell there. See Appendix C, Chronicles III, 2, (6).

† In Chronicles, two hundred and fifty. See Chronicles III, 1, (13). Appendix C.

Sect. XX THE UNITED KINGDOM

(I Kings 10:) 22. For the king had at sea a navy of Tarshish with the navy of Hiram: once every three years came the navy of Tarshish, bringing gold, and silver, ivory, and apes, and peacocks. 11. And the navy also of Hiram, that brought gold from Ophir brought in from Ophir great plenty of almug trees and precious stones. 12. And the king made of the almug trees *pillars* for the house of the Lord, and for the king's house, harps also and psalteries for the singers; there came no such almug trees, nor were seen, unto this day.

(I Kings 9:) 10. And it came to pass at the end of twenty years, wherein Solomon had built the two houses, the house of the Lord and the king's house, 11. now Hiram the king of Tyre had furnished Solomon with cedar trees and fir trees, and with gold, according to all his desire, that ((then king Solomon gave Hiram twenty cities in the land of Galilee. 12. And Hiram came out from Tyre to see the cities which Solomon had given him; and they pleased him not. 13. And he said, what cities are these which thou hast given me, my brother? And he called them the land of Cabul, unto this day. 14. And Hiram sent to the king sixscore talents of gold.))

15. And this is the reason of the levy which king Solomon raised; for to build the house of the Lord, and his own house, and Millo, and the wall of Jerusalem, and Hazor, and Megiddo, and Gezer. 16. Pharaoh king of Egypt had gone up, and taken Gezer, and burnt it with fire, and slain the Canaanites that dwelt in the city, and given it for a portion unto his daughter, Solomon's wife.

17. And Solomon built Gezer, and Beth-horon the nether, 18. and Baalath, and Tamar in the wilderness, in the land, 19. and all the store cities that Solomon had, and the cities for his chariots, and the cities for his horsemen, and that which Solomon desired to build for his pleasure in Jerusalem, and in Lebanon, and in all the land of his dominion.

20. As for all the people that were left of the Amorites, the Hittites, the Perizzites, the Hivites, and the Jebusites, which were not of the children of Israel; 21. their children that were left after them in the land, whom the children of Israel were not able utterly to destroy, of them did Solomon raise a levy of bondservants unto this day. 22. But of the children of Israel did Solomon make no bondservants: but they were the men of war, and his servants, and his princes, and his captains, and rulers of his chariots, and of his horsemen. 23. These were the chief officers that were over Solomon's work, ((*five hundred and fifty*, which bare rule over the people that wrought in the work.))

(II Chron. 9:) 21. For the king had ships that went to Tarshish with the servants of Huram: once every three years came the ships of Tarshish, bringing gold, and silver, ivory, and apes, and peacocks. 10. And the servants also of Huram, and the servants of Solomon, which brought gold from Ophir, brought almug trees and precious stones. 11. And the king made of the almug trees *terraces* for the house of the Lord, and for the king's house, and harps and psalteries for the singers; and there were none such seen before in the land of Judah.

(II Chron. 8:) 1. And it came to pass at the end of twenty years, wherein Solomon had built the house of the Lord, and his own house,

2. that ((the cities which Huram had given to Solomon, Solomon built them, and caused the children of Israel to dwell there.))

3. And Solomon went to Hamath-zobah, and prevailed against it. 5. Also he built Beth-horon the upper, and Beth-horon the nether, fenced cities, with walls, gates, and bars; and Baalath. 4. And he built Tadmor in the wilderness, and all the store cities which he built in Hamath. 6. and all the store cities that Solomon had, and all the cities for his chariots, and the cities for his horsemen, and all that Solomon desired to build for his pleasure in Jerusalem, and in Lebanon, and in all the land of his dominion.

7. As for all the people that were left of the Hittites, and the Amorites, and the Perizzites, and the Hivites, and the Jebusites, which were not of Israel; 8. of their children that were left after them in the land, whom the children of Israel consumed not, of them did Solomon raise a levy of bondservants, unto this day. 9. But of the children of Israel did Solomon make no servants, for his work; but they were men of war, and chief of his captains, and rulers of his chariots, and of his horsemen. 10. And these were the chief officers of king Solomon, even ((*two hundred and fifty* that bare rule over the people.))

THE HOUSE OF DAVID
B. C. 1016 (Usher)
II Solomon
B. C. 977 (Rev.)

PROPHET, AHIJAH
THE SHILONITE

SECTION XXI

Downfall and Division

I Kings 11:1. Now king Solomon loved many strange women, together with the daughter of Pharaoh, women of the Moabites, Ammonites, Edomites, Zidonians, and Hittites; 2. of the nations concerning which the Lord said unto the children of Israel,* Ye shall not go among them, neither shall they come among you: for surely they will turn away your heart after their gods: Solomon clave unto these in love.

Polygamy and Idolatry

3. And he had seven hundred wives, princesses, and three hundred concubines: and his wives turned away his heart. 4. For it came to pass, when Solomon was old, that his wives turned away his heart after other gods: and his heart was not perfect with the Lord his God, as was the heart of David his father. 5. For Solomon went after Ashtoreth the goddess of the Zidonians, and after Milcom the abomination of the Ammonites. 6. And Solomon did that which was evil in the sight of the Lord, and went not fully after the Lord, as did David his father. 7. Then did Solomon build an high place for Chemosh the abomination of Moab, in the mount that is before Jerusalem, and for Molech the abomination of the children of Ammon. 8. And so did he for all his strange wives, which burnt incense and sacrificed unto their gods.

---

* Ex. 34:12-17. Take heed to thyself, lest thou make a covenant with the inhabitants of the land whither thou goest, lest it be for a snare in the midst of thee: but ye shall break down their altars, and dash in pieces their pillars, and ye shall cut down their Asherim: for thou shalt worship no other God: for the Lord, whose name is Jealous, is a jealous God: lest thou make a covenant with the inhabitants of the land, and they go a whoring after their gods, and do sacrifice unto their gods, and one call thee and thou eat of his sacrifice; and thou take of their daughters unto thy sons, and their daughters go a whoring after their gods, and make thy sons go a whoring after their gods. Thou shalt make thee no molten gods.

Deut. 7:1-6. When the Lord thy God shall bring thee into the land whither thou goest to possess it, and shall cast out many nations before thee, the Hittite, and the Girgashite, and the Amorite, and the Canaanite, and the Perezzite, and the Hivite, and the Jebusite, seven nations greater and mightier than thou; and when the Lord thy God shall deliver them up before thee, and thou shalt smite them; then thou shalt utterly destroy them; thou shalt make no covenant with them, nor shew mercy unto them: neither shalt thou make marriages with them; thy daughter thou shalt not give unto his son, nor his daughter shalt thou take unto thy son. For he will turn away thy son from following me, that they may serve other gods: so will the anger of the Lord be kindled against you, and he will destroy thee quickly. But thus shall ye deal with them; ye shall break down their altars, and dash in pieces their pillars, and hew down their Asherim, and burn their graven images with fire. For thou art an holy people unto the Lord thy God: the Lord thy God hath chosen thee to be a peculiar people unto himself, above all peoples that are upon the face of the earth.

Josh. 23:11-13. Take good heed therefore unto yourselves, that ye love the Lord your God. Else if ye do in any wise go back, and cleave unto the remnant of these nations, even these that remain among you, and make marriages with them, and go in unto them, and they to you: know for a certainty that the Lord your God will no more drive these nations from out of your sight; but they shall be a snare and a trap unto you, and a scourge in your sides, and thorns in your eyes, until ye perish from off this good land which the Lord your God hath given you.

THE UNITED KINGDOM

Lord's Anger and Sentence

9. And the Lord was angry with Solomon, because his heart was turned away from the Lord, the God of Israel, which had appeared unto him twice, 10. and had commanded him concerning this thing, that he should not go after other gods: but he kept not that which the Lord commanded. 11. Wherefore the Lord said unto Solomon, Forasmuch as this is done of thee, and thou hast not kept my covenant and my statutes, which I have commanded thee, I will surely rend the kingdom from thee, and will give it to thy servant. 12. Notwithstanding in thy days I will not do it, for David thy father's sake: but I will rend it out of the hand of thy son. 13. Howbeit I will not rend away all the kingdom; but I will give one tribe to thy son, for David my servant's sake, and for Jerusalem's sake which I have chosen.

Adversaries Raised Up

14. And the Lord raised up an adversary unto Solomon, Hadad the Edomite: he was of the king's seed in Edom. 15. For it came to pass, when David was in Edom, and Joab the captain of the host was gone up to bury the slain, and had smitten ever male in Edom; 16. (for Joab and all Israel remained there six months, until he had cut off every male in Edom;) 17. that Hadad fled, he and certain Edomites of his father's servants with him, to go into Egypt; Hadad being yet a little child. 18. And they arose out of Midian, and came to Paran: and they took men with them out of Paran, and they came to Egypt, unto Pharaoh king of Egypt; which gave him an house, and appointed him victuals, and gave him land. 19. And Hadad found great favour in the sight of Pharaoh, so that he gave him to wife the sister of his own wife, the sister of Tahpenes the queen. 20. And the sister of Tahpenes bare him Genubath his son, whom Tahpenes weaned in Pharaoh's house: and Genubath was in Pharaoh's house among the sons of Pharaoh. 21. And when Hadad heard in Egypt that David slept with his fathers, and that Joab the captain of the host was dead, Hadad said unto Pharaoh Let me depart, that I may go to mine own country. 22. Then Pharaoh said unto him, But what hast thou lacked with me, that, behold, thou seekest to go to thine own country? And he answered, Nothing: howbeit let me depart in any wise.

23. And God raised up another adversary unto him, Rezon the son of Eliada, which had fled from his lord Hadadezer king of Zobah: 24. and he gathered men unto him, and became captain over a troop, when David slew them of Zobah: and they went to Damascus, and dwelt therein, and reigned in Damascus. 25. And he was an adversary to Israel all the days of Solomon, beside the mischief that Hadad did: and he abhorred Israel, and reigned over Syria.

26. And Jereboam the son of Nebat, an Ephraimite of Zeredah, a servant of Solomon, whose mother's name was Zeruah, a widow woman, he also lifted up his hand against the king. 27. And this was the cause that he lifted up his hand against the king: Solomon built Millo, and repaired the breach of the city of David his father. 28. And the man Jereboam was a mighty man of valour: and Solomon saw the young man that he was industrious, and he gave him charge over all the labour of the house of Joseph. 29. And it came to pass at that time, when Jereboam went out of Jerusalem, that the prophet Ahijah the Shilonite found him in the way; now Ahijah had clad himself with a new garment; and they two alone were in the field. 30. And Ahijah laid hold of the new garment that was on him, and rent it in twelve pieces. 31. And he said to Jereboam, Take thee ten pieces: for thus saith the Lord, the God of Israel, Behold, I will rend the kingdom out of the hand of Solomon, and will give ten tribes to thee: 32. (but he shall have one tribe, for my servant

David's sake, and for Jerusalem's sake, the city which I have chosen out of all the tribes of Israel:) 33. because that they have forsaken me, and have worshipped Ashtoreth the goddess of the Zidonians, Chemosh the god of Moab, and Milcom the god of the children of Ammon; and they have not walked in my ways, to do that which is right in mine eyes, and to keep my statutes and my judgements, as did David his father. 34. Howbeit I will not take the whole kingdom out of his hand: but I will make him prince all the days of his life, for David my servant's sake, whom I chose, because he kept my commandments and my statutes: 35. but I will take the kingdom out of his son's hand, and will give it unto thee, even ten tribes. 36. And unto his son will I give one tribe, that David my servant may have a lamp alway before me in Jerusalem, the city which I have chosen me to put my name there. 37. And I will take thee, and thou shalt reign according to all that thy soul desireth, and shalt be king over Israel. 38. And it shall be, if thou wilt hearken unto all that I command thee, and wilt walk in my ways, and do that which is right in mine eyes, to keep my statutes and my commandments, as David my servant did; that I will be with thee, and will build thee a sure house, as I built for David, and will give Israel unto thee. 39. And I will for this afflict the seed of David, but not for ever. 40. Solomon sought therefore to kill Jereboam: but Jereboam arose, and fled into Egypt, unto Shishak king of Egypt, and was in Egypt until the death of Solomon.

Now the rest of the acts of Solomon, first and last, and all that he did, and his wisdom, are they not written in the book of the acts of Solomon, and in the history of Nathan the prophet, and in the prophecy of Ahijah the Shilonite, and in the visions of Iddo the seer concerning Jereboam the son of Nebat? And the time that Solomon reigned in Jerusalem over all Israel was forty years. And Solomon slept with his fathers, and he was buried in the city of David his father: and Rehoboam his son reigned in his stead.

Answer of Rehoboam to Israel's Question And Rehoboam went to Shechem: for all Israel were come to Shechem to make him king. And it came to pass, when Jereboam the son of Nebat heard of it, (for he was yet in Egypt, whither he had fled from the presence of king Solomon, that Jereboam returned out of Egypt.) And they sent and called him; and Jereboam and all the congregation of Israel came, and spake unto Rehoboam, saying, Thy father made our yoke grievous: now therefore make thou the grievous service of thy father, and his heavy yoke which he put upon us, lighter, and we will serve thee. And he said unto them, Depart yet for three days, then come again to me. And the people departed. And king Rehoboam took counsel with the old men, that had stood before Solomon his father while he yet lived, saying, What counsel give ye me to return answer to this people? And they spake unto him, saying, If thou be kind to this people, and serve them, and please them, and answer them, and speak good words to them, then they will be thy servants for ever.

But he forsook the counsel of the old men which they had given him, and took counsel with the young men that were grown up with him, that stood before him. And he said unto them, What counsel give ye, that we may return answer to this people, who have spoken to me, saying, Make the yoke that thy father did put upon us lighter? And the young men that were grown up with him spake unto him, saying, Thus shalt thou say unto this people that spake unto thee, saying, Thy father made our yoke heavy, but make thou it lighter unto us; thus shalt thou speak unto them, My little finger is thicker than my father's loins. And now whereas my father did lade you with a heavy yoke, I will add to your yoke: my father chastised you with whips, but I will chastise you with scorpions. So

(I Kings 11:) 41. Now the rest of the acts of Solomon, and all that he did, and his wisdom, are they not written in the book of the acts of Solomon?

42. And the time that Solomon reigned in Jerusalem over all Israel was forty years. 43. And Solomon slept with his fathers, and was buried in the city of David his father: and Rehoboam his son reigned in his stead.
(I Kings 12:) 1. And Rehoboam went to Shechem: for all Israel were come to Shechem to make him king. 2. And it came to pass, when Jereboam the son of Nebat heard of it, for he was yet in Egypt, whither he had fled from the presence of king Solomon, and Jereboam dwelt in Egypt. 3. and they sent and called him; that Jereboam and all the congregation of Israel came and spake unto Rehoboam, saying, 4. Thy father made our yoke grievous: now therefore make thou the grievous service of thy father, and his heavy yoke which he put upon us, lighter, and we will serve thee. 5. And he said unto them, Depart yet for three days, then come again to me. And the people departed. 6. And king Rehoboam took counsel with the old men, that had stood before Solomon his father while he yet lived, saying, What counsel give ye me to return answer to this people? 7. And they spake unto him, saying, If thou wilt be a servant unto this people this day, and wilt serve them, and answer them, and speak good words to them, then they will be thy servants for ever.

8. But he forsook the counsel of the old men which they had given him, and took counsel with the young men that were grown up with him, that stood before him. 9. And he said unto them, What counsel give ye, that we may return answer to this people, who have spoken to me, saying, Make the yoke that thy father did put upon us lighter? 10. And the young men that were grown up with him spake unto him, saying, Thus shalt thou say unto this people that spake unto thee, saying, Thy father made our yoke heavy, but make thou it lighter unto us; thus shalt thou speak unto them, My little finger is thicker than my father's loins. 11. And now whereas my father did lade you with a heavy yoke, I will add to your yoke: my father chastised you with whips, but I will chastise you with scorpions. 12. So Jere-

(II Chron. 9:) 29. Now the rest of the acts of Solomon, first and last, are they not written in the history of Nathan the prophet, and in the prophecy of Ahijah the Shilonite, and in the visions of Iddo the seer concerning Jereboam the son of Nebat?
30. And Solomon reigned in Jerusalem over all Israel forty years. 31. And Solomon slept with his fathers, and he was buried in the city of David his father: and Rehoboam his son reigned in his stead.
(II Chron. 10:) 1. And Rehoboam went to Shechem: for all Israel were come to Shechem to make him king. 2. And it came to pass, when Jereboam the son of Nebat heard of it, for he was yet in Egypt, whither he had fled from the presence of king Solomon, that Jereboam returned out of Egypt. 3. And they sent and called him; and Jereboam and all Israel came and they spake to Rehoboam, saying, 4. Thy father made our yoke grievous: now therefore make thou the grievous service of thy father, and his heavy yoke which he put upon us, lighter, and we will serve thee. 5. And he said unto them, Come again unto me after three days. And the people departed. 6. And king Rehoboam took counsel with the old men, that had stood before Solomon his father while he yet lived, saying, What counsel give ye me to return answer to this people? 7. And they spake unto him, saying, If thou be kind to this people and please them, and speak good words to them, then they will be thy servants for ever.

8. But he forsook the counsel of the old men which they had given him, and took counsel with the young men that were grown up with him, that stood before him. 9. And he said unto them, What counsel give ye, that we may return answer to this people, who have spoken to me, saying, Make the yoke that thy father did put upon us lighter? 10. And the young men that were grown up with him spake unto him, saying, Thus shalt thou say unto the people that spake unto thee, saying, Thy father made our yoke heavy, but make thou it lighter unto us; thus shalt thou say unto them, My little finger is thicker than my father's loins. 11. And now whereas my father did lade you with a heavy yoke, I will add to your yoke: my father chastised you with whips, but I will chastise you with scorpions. 12. So Jera-

Jereboam and all the people came to Rehoboam the third day, as the king bade, saying, Come to me again the third day.

And the king answered the people roughly, and king Rehoboam forsook the counsel of the old men which they had given him: and spake to them after the counsel of the young men, saying, My father made your yoke heavy, but I will add to your yoke: my father chastised you with whips, but I will chastise you with scorpions. So the king hearkened not unto the people; for it was a thing brought about of God, that the Lord might establish his word, which he spake by the hand of Ahijah the Shilonite to Jereboam the son of Nebat.

Rebellion of Israel And when all Israel saw that the king hearkened not unto them, the people answered the king, What portion have we in David? neither have we inheritance in the son of Jesse: every man to your tents, O Israel: now see to thine own house, David. So all Israel departed unto their tents. But as for the children of Israel which dwelt in the cities of Judah, Rehoboam reigned over them. Then king Rehoboam sent Adoram, who was over the levy; and the children of Israel stoned him with stones, that he died. And king Rehoboam made speed to get him up to his chariot, to flee to Jerusalem. So Israel rebelled against the house of David, unto this day.

boam and all the people came to Rehoboam the third day, as the king bade, saying, Come to me again the third day.

13. And the king answered the people roughly, and forsook the counsel of the old men which they had given him; 14. and spake to them after the counsel of the young men, saying, My father made your yoke heavy, but I will add to your yoke: my father chastised you with whips, but I will chastise you with scorpions. 15. So the king hearkened not unto the people; for it was a thing brought about of the Lord, that he might establish his word, which the Lord spake by the hand of Ahijah the Shilonite to Jereboam the son of Nebat.

16. And when all Israel saw that the king hearkened not unto them, the people answered the king, saying, What portion have we in David? neither have we inheritance in the son of Jesse: to your tents, O Israel: now see to thine own house, David. So Israel departed unto their tents. 17. But as for the children of Israel which dwelt in the cities of Judah, Rehoboam reigned over them. 18. Then king Rehoboam sent Adoram, who was over the levy; and all Israel stoned him with stones, that he died. And king Rehoboam made speed to get him up to his chariot, to flee to Jerusalem. 19. So Israel rebelled against the house of David, unto this day.

boam and all the people came to Rehoboam the third day, as the king bade, saying, Come to me again the third day.

13. And the king answered them roughly; and king Rehoboam forsook the counsel of the old men, 14. and spake to them after the counsel of the young men, saying, My father made your yoke heavy, but I will add thereto: my father chastised you with whips, but I will chastise you with scorpions. 15. So the king hearkened not unto the people; for it was brought about of God, that the Lord might establish his word, which he spake by the hand of Ahijah the Shilonite to Jereboam the son of Nabat.

16. And when all Israel saw that the king hearkened not unto them, the people answered the king, saying, What portion have we in David? neither have we inheritance in the son of Jesse: every man to your tents, O Israel: now see to thine own house, David. So all Israel departed unto their tents. 17. But as for the children of Israel that dwelt in the cities of Judah, Rehoboam reigned over them. 18. Then king Rehoboam sent Hadoram, who was over the levy; and the children of Israel stoned him with stones, that he died. And king Rehoboam made speed to get him up to his chariot, to flee to Jerusalem. 19. So Israel rebelled against the house of David, unto this day.

PART III
The Divided Kingdom

JUDAH		ISRAEL	
THE HOUSE OF DAVID		THE HOUSE OF JEREBOAM (First)	
B. C. 976-959 *		B. C. 976-953	
III Rehoboam (Shemaiah)	(Ahijah)	I Jereboam	(1)
B. C. 937-920		B. C. 937-915	
B. C. 959-956		B. C. 955-953	
IV Abijam		II Nadab	(2)
B. C. 920-917		B. C. 915-914	
B. C. 956-915			
V Asa			
B. C. 917-876			

SECTION XXII
Rival Houses of David and Jereboam

I Kings 12:20. And it came to pass, when all Israel heard that Jereboam was returned, that they sent and called him unto the congregation, and made him king over all Israel: there was none that followed the house of David, but the tribe of Judah only.

Civil War Forbidden
And when Rehoboam was come to Jerusalem, he assembled all the house of Judah, and the tribe of Benjamin, an hundred and fourscore thousand chosen men, which were warriors, to fight against the house of Israel, to bring the kingdom again to Rehoboam the son of Solomon. But the word of the Lord came to Shemaiah the man of God, saying, Speak unto Rehoboam the son of Solomon, king of Judah, and unto all the house of Judah and Benjamin, and to the rest of the people, saying, Thus saith the Lord, Ye shall not go up, nor fight against your brethren the children of Israel: return every man to his house; for this thing is of me. So they hearkened unto the words of the Lord, and returned from going against Jereboam, and went their way, according to the word of the Lord. Then Jereboam built Shechem in the hill

Initiatory Enterprises
country of Ephraim, and dwelt therein; and he went out from thence and built Penuel.

II Chron. 11:5. And Rehoboam dwelt in Jerusalem, and built cities for defence in Judah. 6. He built even Beth-lehem, and Etam and Tekoa, 7. and Beth-zur, and Soco, and Adullam, 8. and Gath, and Mareshah, and Ziph, 9. and Adoraim, and Lachish, and Azekah, 10. and Zorah, and Aijalon and Hebron, which are in Judah and in Benjamin, fenced cities. 11. And he fortified the strongholds, and put captains in them, and store of victual, and oil and wine. 12. And in every several city he put shields and spears, and made them exceeding strong. And Judah and Benjamin belonged to him. 13. And the priests and the Levites that were in all Israel resorted to him out of all their border. 14. For the Levites left their suburbs and their possession, and came to Judah and Jerusalem: for Jereboam and his sons cast them off, that they should not execute the priest's office unto the Lord: 15. and he appointed him priests for the high places, and for the he-goats, and for the calves which he had made. 16. And after them, out of all the tribes of Israel, such as set their hearts to seek the Lord, the God of Israel, came to Jerusalem to sacrifice unto the Lord, the God of their fathers. 17. So they strengthened the kingdom of Judah, and made Rehoboam the son of Solomon strong, three years: for they walked three years in the way of David and Solomon.

* See Chronology Appendix A. Both systems of chronology are used, e. g., Rehoboam $\frac{976}{937}$ (Usher) (Revised)

SECT. XXII   THE DIVIDED KINGDOM

(I Kings 12:) 21. And when Rehoboam was come to Jerusalem, he assembled all the house of Judah, and the tribe of Benjamin, an hundred and fourscore thousand chosen men, which were warriors, to fight against the house of Israel, to bring the kingdom again to Rehoboam the son of Solomon.	(II Chron. 11:) 1. And when Rehoboam was come to Jerusalem, he assembled the house of Judah and Benjamin, an hundred and fourscore thousand chosen men, which were warriors, to fight against Israel, to bring the kingdom again to Rehoboam.
22. But the word of God came unto Shemaiah the man of God, saying, 23. Speak unto Rehoboam the son of Solomon, king of Judah, and unto all the house of Judah and Benjamin, and to the rest of the people, saying, 24. Thus saith the Lord, Ye shall not go up, nor fight against your brethren the children of Israel: return every man to his house: for this thing is of me. So they hearkened unto the word of the Lord, and returned and went their way, according to the word of the Lord. 25. Then Jereboam built Shechem in the hill country of Ephraim, and dwelt therein; and he went out from thence and built Penuel.	2. But the word of the Lord came to Shemaiah the man of God, saying, 3. Speak unto Rehoboam the son of Solomon, king of Judah, and to all Israel in Judah and Benjamin, saying, 4. Thus saith the Lord, Ye shall not go up, nor fight against your brethren: return every man to his house: for this thing is of me. So they hearkened unto the words of the Lord, and returned from going against Jereboam.

Two Calves and Feast

I Kings 12:26. And Jereboam said in his heart, Now shall the kingdom return to the house of David: 27. if this people go up to offer sacrifices in the house of the Lord at Jerusalem, then shall the heart of this people turn again unto their lord, even unto Rehoboam king of Judah; and they shall kill me, and return to Rehoboam king of Judah. 28. Whereupon the king took counsel, and made two calves of gold; and he said unto them, It is too much for you to go up to Jerusalem; behold thy gods, O Israel, which brought thee up out of the land of Egypt. 29. And he set the one in Bethel, and the other put he in Dan. 30. And this thing became a sin: for the people went to worship before the one, even unto Dan. 31. And he made houses of high places, and made priests from among all the people, which were not of the sons of Levi.

32. And Jereboam ordained a feast in the eighth month, on the fifteenth day of the month, like unto the feast that is in Judah, and he went up unto the altar; so did he in Bethel, sacrificing unto the calves that he had made: and he placed in Bethel the priests of the high places which he had made. 33. And he went up unto the altar which he had made in Bethel on the fifteenth day in the eighth month, even in the month which he had devised of his own heart: and he ordained a feast for the children of Israel, and went up unto the altar to burn incense.

Prophecy of Man and God

I Kings 13:1. And, behold, there came a man of God out of Judah by the word of the Lord unto Bethel: and Jereboam was standing by the altar to burn incense. 2. And he cried against the altar by the word of the Lord, and said, O altar, altar, thus saith the Lord: * Behold, a child shall be born unto the house of David, Josiah by name; and upon thee shall he sacrifice the priests of the high places that burn incense upon thee, and men's bones shall they burn upon thee. 3. And he gave a sign the same day, saying, This is the sign which the Lord hath spoken: Behold, the altar shall be rent, and the ashes that are upon it shall be poured out. 4. And it came to pass, when the king heard the saying of the man of God, which he cried against the altar in Bethel, that Jereboam put forth his hand from the altar, saying, Lay hold on him. And his hand, which he put forth against him, dried up, so that he could not draw it back again to him. 5. The altar also was rent, and the ashes poured out from the altar, according to the sign which the man of God had given by the word of the Lord. 6. And the king answered and said unto the man of God, Intreat now the favour of the Lord thy God, and pray for me, that my hand may be restored me again. And the man of God intreated the Lord, and the king's hand was restored him again, and became as it was before. 7. And the king said unto the man of God, Come home with me, and refresh thyself, and I will give thee a reward. 8. And the man of God said unto the king, If thou wilt give me half thine house, I will not go in with thee, neither will I eat bread nor drink water in this place: 9. for so it was charged me by the word of the Lord, saying, Thou shalt eat no bread, nor drink water, neither return by the way that thou camest. 10. So he went another way, and returned not by the way that he came to Bethel.

---

* Prophecy fulfilled, II Kings 23:15-20. Moreover the altar that was at Bethel, and the high place which Jereboam the son of Nebat, who made Israel to sin, had made, even that altar and the high place he (Josiah) brake down; and he burned the high place and stamped it small to powder, and burned the Asherah. And as Josiah turned himself, he spied the sepulchres that were there in the mount; and he sent, and took the bones out of the sepulchres and burned them upon the altar, and defiled it, according to the word of the Lord which the man of God proclaimed, who proclaimed these things.

SECT. XXII   THE DIVIDED KINGDOM

Deception and Disobedience

11. Now there dwelt an old prophet in Bethel; and one of his sons came and told him all the works that the man of God had done that day in Bethel: the words which he had spoken unto the king, them also they told unto their father. 12. And their father said unto them, What way went he? Now his sons had seen what way the man of God went, which came from Judah. 13. And he said unto his sons, Saddle me the ass. So they saddled him the ass: and he rode thereon. 14. And he went after the man of God, and found him sitting under an oak: and he said unto him, Art thou the man of God that camest from Judah? And he said, I am. 15. Then he said unto him, Come home with me, and eat bread. 16. And he said, I may not return with thee, nor go in with thee: neither will I eat bread nor drink water with thee in this place: 17. for it was said to me by the word of the Lord, Thou shalt eat no bread nor drink water there, nor turn again to go by the way by which thou camest. 18. And he said unto him, I also am a prophet as thou art; and an angel spake unto me by the word of the Lord, saying, Bring him back with thee into thine house, that he may eat bread and drink water. 19. But he lied unto him. So he went back with him, and did eat bread in his house, and drank water. 20. And it came to pass, as they sat at the table, that the word of the Lord came unto the prophet that brought him back: 21. and he cried unto the man of God that came from Judah, saying, Thus saith the Lord, Forasmuch as thou hast been disobedient unto the mouth of the Lord, and hast not kept the commandment which the Lord thy God cammanded thee, 22. but camest back, and hast eaten bread and drunk water in the place of which he said to thee, Eat no bread and drink no water; thy carcase shall not come unto the sepulchre of thy fathers. 23. And it came to pass, after he had eaten bread, and after he had drunk, that he saddled for him the ass, to wit, for the prophet whom he had brought back. 24. And when he was gone, a lion met him by the way, and slew him: and his carcase was cast in the way, and the ass stood by it; the lion also stood by the carcase. 25. And, behold, men passed by, and saw the carcase cast in the way, and the lion standing by the carcase: and they came and told it in the city where the old prophet dwelt. 26. And when the prophet that brought him back from the way heard thereof, he said, It is the man of God, who was disobedient unto the mouth of the Lord: therefore the Lord hath delivered him unto the lion, which hath torn him, and slain him, according to the word of the Lord, which he spake unto him. 27. And he spake to his sons, saying, Saddle me the ass. And they saddled it. 28. And he went and found his carcase cast in the way, and the ass and the lion standing by the carcase: the lion had not eaten the carcase, nor torn the ass. 29. And the prophet took up the carcase of the man of God, and laid it upon the ass, and brought it back: and he came to the city of the old prophet, to mourn, and to bury him. 30. And he laid his carcase in his own grave; and they mourned over him, saying, Alas, my brother! 31. And it came to pass, after he had buried him, that he spake to his sons, saying, * When I am dead, then bury me in the sepulchre wherein the man of God is buried; lay my bones beside his bones. 32. For the saying which he cried by the word of the Lord against the altar in Bethel, and against all the houses of the high places which are in the cities of Samaria, shall surely come

---

* Then he said, What monument is that which I see? And the men of the city told him, It is the sepulchre of the man of God, which came from Judah, and proclaimed these things that thou hast done against the altar of Bethel. And he said, Let him be; let no man move his bones. So they let his bones alone, with the bones of the prophet that came out of Samaria. And all the houses also of the high places that were in the cities of Samaria, which the king of Israel had made to provoke the Lord to anger, Josiah took away, and did to them according to all the acts that he had done in Bethel. And he slew all the priests of the high places that were there, upon the altars, and burned men's bones upon them; and he returned to Jerusalem.

to pass. 33. After this thing Jereboam returned not from his evil way, but made again from among all the people priests of the high places: whosoever would, he consecrated him, that there might be priests of the high places. 34. And this thing became sin unto the house of Jereboam, even to cut it off, and to destroy it from off the face of the earth.

Rehoboam's Household

II Chron. 11:18. And Rehoboam took him a wife, Mahalath the daughter of Jerimoth the son of David, and of Abihail the daughter of Eliab the son of Jesse; 19. and she bare him sons Jeush, and Shemaraiah, and Zaham. 20. And after her he took * Maacah the daughter of Absalom; and she bare him Abijah, and Attai, and Ziza, and Shelomith. 21. And Rehoboam loved Maacah the daughter of Absalom above all his wives and his concubines: (for he took eighteen wives, and threescore concubines, and begat twenty and eight sons and threescore daughters.) 22. And Rehoboam appointed Abijah the son of Maacah to be chief, even the prince among his brethren: for he was minded to make him king. 23. And he dealt wisely, and dispersed of all his sons throughout all the land of Judah and Benjamin, unto every fenced city: and he gave them victual in abundance. And he sought for them many wives.

Forsaking God in Prosperity

II Chron. 12:1. And it came to pass, when the kingdom of Rehoboam was established, and he was strong, that he forsook the law of the Lord, and all Israel with him. And it came to pass in the fifth year of king Rehoboam, that Shishak king of Egypt came up against Jerusalem, because they had trespassed against the Lord, with twelve hundred chariots, and threescore thousand horsemen: and the people were without number that came with him out of Egypt; the Lubim, the Sukiim, and the Ethiopians. And he took the fenced cities which pertained to Judah, and came unto Jerusalem. Now Shemaiah the prophet came to Rehoboam, and to the princes of Judah, that were gathered together to Jerusalem because of Shishak, and said unto them, Thus saith the Lord, Ye have forsaken me, therefore also have I left you in the hand of Shishak. Then the princes of Israel and the king humbled themselves; and they said, The Lord is righteous. And when the Lord saw that they humbled themselves, the word of the Lord came to Shemaiah, saying, They have humbled themselves; I will not destroy them: but I will grant them some deliverance, and my wrath shall not be poured upon Jerusalem by the hand of Shishak. Nevertheless they shall be his servants; that they may know my service, and the service of the kingdoms of the countries. So Shishak king of Egypt came up against Jerusalem, and took away the treasures of the house of the Lord, and the treasures of the king's house; he even took away all: and he took away also the shields of gold which Solomon had made. And king Rehoboam made in their stead shields of brass, and committed them to the hands of the captains of the guard, that kept the door of the king's house. And it was so, that as often as the king entered into the house of the Lord, the guard came and bare them, and brought them back in to the guard chamber. And when he humbled himself, the wrath of the Lord turned from him, that he would not destroy him altogether: and moreover in Judah there were good things found. So king Rehoboam the son of Solomon strengthened

Summary of Rehoboam's Reign

himself in Jerusalem, and reigned in Judah. Rehoboam was forty and one years old when he began to reign, and he reigned seventeen years in Jerusalem, the city which the Lord had chosen out of all the tribes of Israel, to put his name there: and his mother's name was Naamah the Ammonitess. And he did that which was evil, because he set not his heart to seek the Lord. And Judah did that which was evil in the sight of the Lord; and

---

* Chronicles, Micaiah the daughter of Uriel.

SECT. XXII — THE DIVIDED KINGDOM

(I Kings 15:) 2b. and his (Abijah) mother's name was Maacah the daughter of Abishalom.	(II Chron. 13:) 2b. and his (Abijah) mother's name was Micaiah the daughter of Uriel of Gibeah.
(I Kings 14:) 25. And it came to pass in the fifth year of king Rehoboam, that Shishak king of Egypt came up against Jerusalem:	(II Chron. 12:) 2. And it came to pass in the fifth year of king Rehoboam, that Shishak king of Egypt came up against Jerusalem, because they had trespassed against the Lord, 3. with twelve hundred chariots, and threescore thousand horsemen: and the people were without number that came with him out of Egypt; the Lubim, the Sukiim, and the Ethiopians. 4. And he took the fenced cities which pertained to Judah, and came unto Jerusalem. 5. Now Shemaiah the prophet came to Rehoboam, and to the princes of Judah, that were gathered together to Jerusalem because of Shishak, and said unto them, Thus saith the Lord, Ye have forsaken me, therefore also have I left you in the hand of Shishak. 6. Then the princes of Israel and the king humbled themselves; and they said, The Lord is righteous. 7. And when the Lord saw that they humbled themselves, the word of the Lord came to Shemaiah, saying, They have humbled themselves; I will not destroy them: but I will grant them some deliverance, and my wrath shall not be poured upon Jerusalem by the hand of Shishak. 8. Nevertheless they shall be his servants; that they may know my service, and the service of the kingdoms of the countries. 9. So Shishak king of Egypt came up against Jerusalem, and took away the treasures of the house of the Lord, and the treasures of the king's house; he took all away:
26. and he took away the treasures of the house of the Lord, and the treasures of the king's house; he even took away all; and he took away all the shields of gold which Solomon had made. 27. And king Rehoboam made in their stead shields of brass, and committed them to the hands of the captains of the guard, which kept the door of the king's house. 28. And it was so, that as oft as the king went into the house of the Lord, the guard bare them, and brought them back into the guard chamber.	he took away also the shields of gold which Solomon had made. 10. And king Rehoboam made in their stead shields of brass, and committed them to the hands of the captains of the guard, that kept the door of the king's house. 11. And it was so that as oft as the king entered into the house of the Lord, the guard came and bare them, and brought them back into the guard chamber. 12. And when he humbled himself, the wrath of the Lord turned from him, that he would not destroy him altogether: and moreover in Judah there were good things found.
21. And Rehoboam the son of Solomon and reigned in Judah. Rehoboam was forty and one years old when he began to reign, and he reigned seventeen years in Jerusalem, the city which the Lord had chosen out of all the tribes of Israel, to put his name there: and his mother's name was Naamah the Ammonitess.	13. So king Rehoboam strengthened himself in Jerusalem, and reigned: for Rehoboam was forty and one years old when he began to reign, and he reigned seventeen years in Jerusalem, the city which the Lord had chosen out of all the tribes of Israel, to put his name there: and his mother's name was Naamah the Ammonitess. 14. And he did that which was evil, because he set not his heart to seek the Lord.
22. And Judah did that which was evil in the sight of the Lord; and	

they provoked him to jealousy with their sins which they had committed above all that their fathers had done. For they also built them high places, and pillars, and Asherim on every high hill, and under every green tree: and there were sodomites in the land: and they did according to all the abominations of the nations which the Lord drave out before the children of Israel.

Now the rest of the acts of Rehoboam, and all that he did first and last, are they not written in the book of the chronicles of the kings of Judah (the histories of Shemaiah the prophet and of Iddo the seer, after the manner of genealogies)? And there were wars between Rehoboam and Jereboam continually. And Rehoboam slept with his fathers, and was buried with his fathers in the city of David. And Abijah his son reigned in his stead.

Accession and Character of Abijah

Now in the eighteenth year of king Jereboam the son of Nebat began Abijah to reign over Judah. Three years reigned he in Jerusalem: and his mother's name was *Maacah the daughter of Abishalom. And he walked in all the sins of his father, which he had done before him: and his heart was not perfect with the Lord his God, as the heart of David his father. Nevertheless for David's sake did the Lord his God give him a lamp in Jerusalem, to set up his son after him, and to establish Jerusalem: because David did that which was right in the eyes of the Lord, and turned not aside from anything that he commanded him all the days of his life, save only in the matter of Uriah the Hittite. Now there was war between Rehoboam and Jereboam all the days of his life. And there was war between Abijah and Jereboam. II Chron. 13:3. And

Victory over Israel

Abijah joined battle with an army of valiant men of war, even four hundred thousand chosen men: and Jereboam set the battle in array against him with eight hundred thousand chosen men, who were mighty men of valour. And Abijah stood up upon mount Zemaraim, which is in the hill country of Ephraim, and said, Hear me, O Jereboam and all Israel; 5. ought ye not to know that the Lord, the God of Israel, gave the kingdom over Israel to David for ever, even to him and his sons by a covenant of salt? 6. Yet Jereboam the son of Nebat, the servant of Solomon the son of David, rose up, and rebelled against his lord. 7. And there were gathered unto him vain men, sons of Belial, which strengthened themselves against Rehoboam the son of Solomon, when Rehoboam was young and tenderhearted, and could not withstand them. 8. And now ye think to withstand the kingdom of the Lord in the hand of the sons of David; and ye be a great multitude, and there are with you the golden calves which Jereboam made you for gods. 9. Have ye not driven out the priests of the Lord, the sons of Aaron, and the Levites, and have made you priests after the manner of the peoples of other lands? so that whosoever cometh to consecrate himself with a young bullock and seven rams, the same may be a priest of them who are no gods. 10. But as for us, the Lord is our God, and we have not forsaken him; and we have priests ministering unto the Lord, the sons of Aaron, and the Levites in their work: 11. and they burn unto the Lord every morning and every evening burnt offerings and sweet incense: the shewbread also set they in order upon the pure table; and the candlestick of gold with the lamps thereof, to burn every evening: for we keep the charge of the Lord our God; but ye have forsaken him. 12. And, behold, God is with us at our head, and his priests with the trumpets of alarm to sound an alarm against you. O children of Israel, fight ye not against the Lord, the God of your fathers; for ye shall not prosper. 13. But Jereboam caused an ambushment to come about behind them: so they were before Judah, and the ambushment was behind them. 14. And when Judah looked back, behold, the battle was before and

---

* See Appendix C. Chronicles III, 2, (7).

SECT. XXII — THE DIVIDED KINGDOM

they provoked him to jealousy with their sins which they committed, above all that their fathers had done. 23. For they also built them high places, and pillars, and Asherim, on every high hill, and under every green tree; 24. and there were also sodomites in the land: and they did according to all the abominations of the nations which the Lord drave out before the children of Israel.

29. Now the rest of the acts of Rehoboam, and all that he did, are they not written in the ((book of the chronicles of the kings of Judah?))
30. And there was war between Rehoboam and Jereboam continually.
31 And Rehoboam slept with his fathers, and was buried with his fathers in the city of David: and his mother's name was Naamah the Ammonitess. And Abijam his son reigned in his stead.
(I Kings 15:) 1. Now in the eighteenth year of king Jereboam the son of Nebat began Abijam to reign over Judah. 2. Three years reigned he in Jerusalem: and his mother's name was (Maacah the daughter of Abishalom.))

3. And he walked in all the sins of his father, which he had done before him: and his heart was not perfect with the Lord his God, as the heart of David his father. 4. Nevertheless for David's sake did the Lord his God give him a lamp in Jerusalem, to set up his son after him, and to establish Jerusalem: 5. because David did that which was right in the eyes of the Lord, and turned not aside from any thing that he commanded him all the days of his life, save only in the matter of Uriah the Hittite. 6 Now there was war between Rehoboam and Jereboam all the days of his life. 7b. And there was war between Abijam and Jereboam.

15. Now the acts of Rehoboam, first and last, are they not written in the ((histories of Shemaiah the prophet and of Iddo the seer, after the manner of genealogies?)) And there were wars between Rehoboam and Jereboam continually.
16. And Rehoboam slept with his fathers, and was buried in the city of David:
And Abijah his son reigned in his stead.
(II Chron. 13:) 1. In the eighteenth year of king Jereboam began Abijah to reign over Judah. 2. Three years reigned he in Jerusalem: and his mother's name was (Micaiah the daughter of Uriel of Gibeah.))

And there was war between Abijah and Jereboam.

behind them: and they cried unto the Lord, and the priests sounded with the trumpets. 15. Then the men of Judah gave a shout: and as the men of Judah shouted, it came to pass, that God smote Jereboam and all Israel before Abijah and Judah. 16. And the children of Israel fled before Judah; and God delivered them into their hand. 17. And Abijah and his people slew them with a great slaughter: so there fell down slain of Israel five hundred thousand chosen men. 18. Thus the children of Israel were brought under at that time, and the children of Judah prevailed, because they relied upon the Lord, the God of their fathers. 19. And Abijah pursued after Jereboam, and took cities from him, Bethel with the towns thereof, and Jesanah with the towns thereof, and Ephron with the towns thereof. 20. Neither did Jereboam recover strength again in the days of Abijah: and the Lord smote him, and he died. 21. But Abijah waxed mighty, and took unto himself fourteen wives, and begat twenty and two sons, and sixteen daughters.

Summary of the Reign of Abijah

And the rest of the acts of Abijah, and his ways and his sayings and all that he did, are they not written in the book of the chronicles of the kings of Judah (the commentary of the prophet Iddo)? So Abijah slept with his fathers, and they buried him in the city of David: and Asa his son reigned in his stead.

Accession and Character of Asa

And in the twentieth year of Jereboam king of Israel began Asa to reign over Judah. And forty and one years reigned he in Jerusalem: and his mother's name was Maacah the daughter of Abishalom. And Asa did that which was good and right in the eyes of the Lord his God, as did David his father. And he put away the sodomites out of the land, and removed all the idols that his father had made, for he took away the strange altars, and the high places, and the pillars, and hewed down the Asherim. And also Maacah the mother of Asa the king, he removed from being queen, because she had made an abominable image for an Asherah; and Asa cut down her image, and made dust of it, and burnt it at the brook Kidron. But the high places were not taken away out of Israel: nevertheless the heart of Asa was perfect with the Lord all his days. And he brought into the house of the Lord the things which his father had dedicated, and the things that he himself had dedicated, silver and gold and vessels. And he commanded Judah to seek the Lord, the God of their fathers, and to do the law and the commandment. Also he took away out of all the cities of Judah the high places and the sun-images: and the kingdom was quiet before him. In his days the land was quiet ten years. And he built fenced cities in Judah: for the land was quiet, and he had no war in those years; because the Lord had given him rest. For he said unto Judah, Let us build these cities, and make about them walls, and towers, and gates, and bars; the land is yet before us, because we have sought the Lord our God; we have sought him, and he hath given us rest on every side. So they built and prospered.

Jereboam's Retributive Punishment

I Kings 14:1. At that time Abijam the son of Jereboam fell sick. 2. And Jereboam said to his wife, Arise, I pray thee, and disguise thyself, that thou be not known to be the wife of Jereboam; and get thee to Shiloh; behold, there is Ahijah the prophet which spake concerning me that I should be king over this people. 3. And take with thee ten loaves, and cracknels, and a cruse of honey, and go to him: he shall tell thee what shall become of the child. 4. And Jereboam's wife did so, and arose, and went to Shiloh, and came to the house of Ahijah. Now Ahijah could not see; for his eyes were set by reason of his age. 5. And the Lord said unto Ahijah, Behold, the wife of Jereboam cometh to inquire of thee concerning her son; for he is sick: thus and thus shalt thou say unto her: for it shall be,

SECT. XXII THE DIVIDED KINGDOM

(I Kings 15:) 7ᵃ. And the rest of the acts of Abijam, and all that he did, are they not written ((in the book of the chronicles of the kings of Judah?))

8. And Abijam slept with his fathers; and they buried him in the city of David: and Asa his son reigned in his stead. 9. And in the twentieth year of Jereboam king of Israel began Asa to reign over Judah. 10. And forty and one years reigned he in Jerusalem: and his mother's name was Maacah the daughter of Abishalom.
11. And Asa did that which was right in the eyes of the Lord, as did David his father. 12. (And he put away the sodomites out of the land, and removed all the idols that his father had made.)

13. And also Maacah his mother he removed from being queen, because she had made an abominable image for an Asherah; and Asa cut down her image, and burnt it at the brook Kidron. 14. But the high places were not taken away: nevertheless the heart of Asa was perfect with the Lord all his days. 15. And he brought into the house of the Lord the things that his father had dedicated, and the things that himself had dedicated, silver and gold and vessels

(II Chron. 13:) 22. And the rest of the acts of Abijah, and his ways and his sayings, are written ((in the commentary of the prophet Iddo.))

(II Chron. 14:) 1ᵃ. So Abijah slept with his fathers, and they buried him in the city of David, and Asa his son reigned in his stead.

2. And Asa did that which was good and right in the eyes of the Lord his God;

3. (for he took away the strange altars, and the high places, and brake down the pillars, and hewed down the Asherim;) 15:16. And also Maacah the mother of Asa the king, he removed her from being queen, because she had made an abominable image for an Asherah; and Asa cut down her image, and made dust of it, and burnt it at the brook Kidron. 17. But the high places were not taken away out of Israel: nevertheless the heart of Asa was perfect all his days. 18. And he brought into the house of God the things which his father had dedicated, and that he himself had dedicated, silver and gold and vessels.
14:4. And commanded Judah to seek the Lord, the God of their fathers, and to do the law and the commandment. 5. Also he took away out of all the cities of Judah the high places and the sun-images: and the kingdom was quiet before him. 1ᵇ. In his days the land was quiet ten years. 6. And he built fenced cities in Judah: for the land was quiet, and he had no war in those years; because the Lord had given him rest. 7. For he said unto Judah, Let us build these cities, and make about them walls, and towers, gates, and bars; the land is yet before us, because we have sought the Lord our God; we have sought him, and he hath given us rest on every side. So they built and prospered.

when she cometh in, that she shall feign herself to be another woman. 6. And it was so, when Ahijah heard the sound of her feet, as she came in at the door, that he said, Come in, thou wife of Jereboam; why feignest thou thyself to be another? for I am sent to thee with heavy tidings. 7. Go, tell Jereboam, Thus saith the Lord, the God of Israel: Forasmuch as I exalted thee from among the people, and made thee prince over my people Israel, 8. and rent the kingdom away from the house of David, and gave it to thee: and yet thou hast not been as my servant David, who kept my commandments, and who followed me with all his heart, to do that only which was right in mine eyes; 9. but hast done evil above all that were before thee, and hast gone and made thee other gods, and molten images, to provoke me to anger, and hast cast me behind thy back: 10. therefore, behold I will bring evil upon the house of Jereboam, and will cut off from Jereboam every man child, him that is shut up and him that is left at large in Israel, and will utterly sweep away the house of Jereboam, as a man sweepeth away dung, till it be all gone. 11. Him that dieth of Jereboam in the city shall the dogs eat; and him that dieth in the field shall the fowls of the air eat: for the Lord hath spoken it. 12. Arise thou therefore get thee to thine house: and when thy feet enter into the city, the child shall die. 13. And all Israel shall mourn for him, and bury him; for he only of Jereboam shall come to the grave: because in him there is found some good thing toward the Lord, the God of Israel, in the house of Jereboam. 14. Moreover the Lord shall raise him up a king over Israel, who shall cut off the house of Jereboam that day: but what? even now. 15. For the Lord shall smite Israel, as a reed is shaken in the water; and he shall root up Israel out of this good land, which he gave to their fathers, and shall scatter them beyond the River; because they have made their Asherim, provoking the Lord to anger. 16. And he shall give Israel up because of the sins of Jereboam, which he hath sinned, and wherewith he hath made Israel to sin. 17. And Jereboam's wife arose, and departed, and came to Tirzah: and as she came to the threshold of the house, the child died. 18. And all Israel buried him, and mourned for him; according to the word of the Lord, which he spake by the hand of his servant Ahijah the prophet.

Fulfillment of Prophecy in Nadab

19. And the rest of the acts of Jereboam, how he warred, and how he reigned, behold, they are written in the book of the chronicles of the kings of Israel. 20. And the days which Jereboam reigned were two and twenty years: and he slept with his fathers, and Nadab his son reigned in his stead. I Kings 15:25. And Nadab the son of Jereboam began to reign over Israel in the second year of Asa the king of Judah, and he reigned over Israel two years. 26. And he did that which was evil in the sight of the Lord, and walked in the way of his father, and in his sin wherewith he made Israel to sin. 27. And Baasha the son of Ahijah, of the house of Issachar conspired against him; and Baasha smote him at Gibbethon, which belonged to the Philistines; for Nadab and all Israel were laying siege to Gibbethon. 28. Even in the third year of Asa king of Judah did Baasha slay him, and reigned in his stead. And it came to pass that, as soon as he was king, he smote all the house of Jereboam; he left not to Jereboam any that breathed, until he had destroyed him; according unto the saying of the Lord, which he spake by the hand of his servant Ahijah the Shilonite: for the sins of Jereboam which he sinned, and wherewith he made Israel to sin; because of his provocation wherewith he provoked the Lord, the God of Israel, to anger. 31. Now the rest of the acts of Nadab, and all that he did, are they not written in the book of the chronicles of the king of Israel?

SECT. XXIII   THE DIVIDED KINGDOM   163

JUDAH	ISRAEL
THE HOUSE OF DAVID	THE HOUSE OF BAASHA (Second)
B. C. 956-915* (Azariah)	B. C. 953-931
V Asa	(Jehu) I Baasha (3)
B. C. 917-876 (Hanani)	B. C. 914-890
	B. C. 931-930
	II Elah (4)
	B. C. 890-889
	THE HOUSE OF ZIMRI (Third)
	B. C. 930
	I Zimri (5)
	B. C. 889

SECTION XXIII

Rival Houses of David, Baasha and Zimri

Accession and Character of Baasha

I Kings 15:33. In the third year of Asa king of Judah began Baasha the son of Ahijah to reign over all Israel in Tirzah, and reigned twenty and four years. 34. And he did that which was evil in the sight of the Lord, and walked in the way of Jereboam, and in his sin wherewith he made Israel to sin.

Asa's Victory over Zerah at Mareshah

II Chron. 14:8. And Asa had an army that bare bucklers and spears, out of Judah three hundred thousand; and out of Benjamin, that bare shields and drew bows, two hundred and fourscore thousand: all these were mighty men of valour. 9. And there came out against them Zerah the Ethiopian with an army of a thousand thousand, and three hundred chariots; and he came unto Mareshah. 10. Then Asa went out to meet him, and they set the battle in array in the valley of Zephathah at Mareshah. 11. And Asa cried unto the Lord his God, and said, Lord there is none beside thee to help, between the mighty and him that hath no strength: help us, O Lord our God; for we rely on thee, and in thy name are we come against this multitude. O Lord, thou art our God; let not man prevail against thee. 12. So the Lord smote the Ethiopians before Asa, and before Judah; and the Ethiopians fled. 13. And Asa and the people that were with him pursued them unto Gerar: and there fell of the Ethiopians so many that they could not recover themselves; for they were destroyed before the Lord, and before his host; and they carried away very much booty. 14. And they smote all the cities round about Gerar; for the fear of the Lord came upon them: and they spoiled all the cities; for there was much spoil in them. 15. They smote also the tents of cattle, and carried away sheep in abundance and camels, and returned to Jerusalem.

Azariah's Approval and Encouragement

II Chron. 15:1. And the spirit of God came upon Azariah the son of Oded: 2. and he went out to meet Asa, and said unto him, Hear ye me, Asa, and all Judah and Benjamin: the Lord is with you, while ye be with him; and if ye seek him, he will be found of you; but if ye forsake him, he will forsake you. 3. Now for long seasons Israel hath been without the true God, and without a teaching priest, and without law: but when in their distress they turned unto the Lord, the God of Israel, and sought him, he was found of them. 5. And in those times there was no peace to him that went out, nor to him that came

---

* See Chronology Appendix A. Both systems of chronology are used, e.g., Asa $\frac{956 \text{ (Usher)}}{917 \text{ (Revised)}}$

in, but great vexations were upon all the inhabitants of the lands. 6. And they were broken in pieces, nation against nation, and city against city: for God did vex them with all adversity. 7. But be ye strong, and let not your hand be slack: for your work shall be rewarded.

Reformation, Sacrifice, Covenant 8. And when Asa heard these words, and the prophecy of Oded the prophet, he took courage, and put away the abominations out of all the land of Judah and Benjamin, and out of the cities which he had taken from the hill country of Ephraim; and he renewed the altar of the Lord, that was before the porch of the Lord. 9. And he gathered all Judah and Benjamin, and them that sojourned with them out of Ephraim and Manasseh, and out of Simeon: for they fell to him out of Israel in abundance, when they saw that the Lord his God was with him. 10. So they gathered themselves together at Jerusalem in the third month, in the fifteenth year of the reign of Asa. 11. And they sacrificed unto the Lord in that day, of the spoil which they had brought, seven hundred oxen and seven thousand sheep. 12. And they entered into the covenant to seek the Lord, the God of their fathers, with all their heart, and with all their soul; 13. and that whosoever would not seek the Lord, the God of Israel, should be put to death, whether small or great, whether man or woman. 14. And they sware unto the Lord with a loud voice, and with shouting, and with trumpets, and with cornets. 15. And all Judah rejoiced at the oath: for they had sworn with all their heart, and sought him with their whole desire; and he was found of them: and the Lord gave them rest round about. 19. And there was no more war unto the five and * thirtieth year of the reign of Asa.

And there was war between Asa and Baasha king of Israel all their days. In the six and thirtieth year of the reign of Asa, Baasha king of Israel went up against Judah, and built Ramah that he might not suffer any to go out or come in to Asa king of Judah. Then Asa took all the silver and gold that were left in the treasures of the house of the Lord, and the treasures of the king's house, and delivered them into the hands of his servants: and sent them to Ben-hadad, the son of Tabrimmon, the son of Hezion, king of Syria, that dwelt at Damascus, saying, There is a league between me and thee, as there was between my father and thy father: behold, I have sent unto thee a present of silver and gold: go, break thy league with Baasha king of Israel, that he may depart from me. And Ben-hadad hearkened unto king Asa, and sent the captains of his armies against the cities of Israel, and they smote Ijon, and Dan, and Abel-beth-maacah, and all Chinneroth, and all the store cities of Naphtali. And it came to pass when Baasha heard thereof, that he left off building of Ramah, and let his work cease, and dwelt in Tirzah.

Alliance with Ben-hadad

Then king Asa made a proclamation unto all Judah; none was exempted: and they carried away the stones of Ramah, and the timber thereof, wherewith Baasha had builded; and king Asa built therewith Geba of Benjamin, and Mizpah.

---

* NOTE.—According to I Kings 16:8 Baasha's reign, ended in the *twenty* and sixth year of Asa, and this agrees with the other data given concerning Asa's reign. We must then either suppose that *thirtieth* in this verse, and in II Chron. 16:1 is an error for *twentieth*, or that the expression "reign of Asa," found in both verses, is to have the unusual interpretation "kingdom of Judah," and to date back to some event prior to the accession of Asa. This would make Baasha's building of Ramah, in his aggressive movement against Judah, to have occurred in the closing year of his reign.

SECT. XXIII THE DIVIDED KINGDOM

(I Kings 15:) 16, 32. And there was war between Asa and Baasha king of Israel all their days. 17. And Baasha king of Israel went up against Judah, and built Ramah that he might not suffer any to go out or come in to Asa king of Judah. 18. Then Asa took all the silver and gold that were left in the treasures of the house of the Lord, and the treasures of the king's house, and delivered them into the hands of his servants: and king Asa sent them to Ben-hadad, the son of Tabrimmon, the son of Hezion, king of Syria, that dwelt at Damascus, saying, 19. There is a league between me and thee, between my father and thy father: behold I have sent unto thee a present of silver and gold; go, break thy league with Baasha king of Israel, that he may depart from me. 20. And Ben-hadad hearkened unto king Asa, and sent the captains of his armies against the cities of Israel, and smote Ijon, and Dan, and Abelbeth-maacah, and all Chinneroth, with all the land of Naphtali. 21. And it came to pass, when Baasha heard thereof, that he left off building of Ramah, and dwelt in Tirzah. 22. Then king Asa made a proclamation unto all Judah; none was exempted; and they carried away the stones of Ramah, and the timber thereof, wherewith Baasha had builded; and king Asa built therewith Geba of Benjamin, and Mizpah.	(II Chron. 16:) 1. In the six and thirtieth year of the reign of Asa, Baasha king of Israel went up against Judah, and built Ramah that he might not suffer any to go out or come in to Asa king of Judah. 2. Then Asa brought out silver and gold out of the treasures of the house of the Lord, and of the king's house, and sent them to Ben-hadad, king of Syria, that dwelt at Damascus, saying, 3. There is a league between me and thee, as there was between my father and thy father: behold, I have sent thee silver and gold; go, break thy league with Baasha king of Israel, that he may depart from me. 4. And Ben-hadad hearkened unto king Asa, and sent the captains of his armies against the cities of Israel, and they smote Ijom, and Dan, and Abelmaim, and all the store cities of Naphtali. 5. And it came to pass, when Baasha heard thereof, that he left off building of Ramah, and let his work cease. 6. Then Asa the king took all Judah; and they carried away the stones of Ramah, and the timber thereof, wherewith Baasha had builded; and he built therewith Geba, and Mizpah.

Hanani's Reproof

II Chron. 16:7. And at that time Hanani the seer came to Asa king of Judah, and said unto him, Because thou hast relied on the king of Syria, and hast not relied on the Lord thy God, therefore is the host of the king of Assyria escaped out of thine hand. 8. Were not the Ethiopians and the Lubim a huge host, with chariots and horsemen exceeding many? yet, because thou didst rely on the Lord, he delivered them into thine hand. 9. For the eyes of the Lord run to and fro throughout the whole earth, to shew himself strong in the behalf of them whose heart is perfect toward him. Herein thou hast done foolishly; for from henceforth thou shalt have wars. 10. Then Asa was wroth with the seer, and put him in the prison house; for he was in a rage with him because of this thing. And Asa oppressed some of the people the same time.

Condemnation of Baasha by Jehu

I Kings 16:1. And the word of the Lord came to Jehu the son of Hanani against Baasha, saying, Forasmuch as I exalted thee out of the dust, and made thee prince over my people Israel; and thou hast walked in the way of Jereboam, and hast made my people Israel to sin, to provoke me to anger with their sins; 3. behold, I will utterly sweep away Baasha and his house; and I will make thy house like the house of Jereboam the son of Nebat. 4. Him that dieth of Baasha in the city shall the dogs eat; and him that dieth of his in the field shall the fowls of the air eat. 5. Now the rest of the acts of Baasha, and what he did, and his might, are they not written in the book of the chronicles of the kings of Israel? 6. And Baasha slept with his fathers, and was buried in Tirzah; and Elah his son reigned in his stead. 7. And moreover by the hand of the prophet Jehu the son of Hanani came the word of the Lord against Baasha, and against his house, both because of all the evil that he did in the sight of the Lord, to provoke him to anger with the work of his hands, in being like the house of Jereboam, and because he smote him.

Accession and Assassination of Elah

8. In the twenty and sixth year of Asa king of Judah began Elah the son of Baasha to reign over Israel in Tirzah, and reigned two years. 9. And his servant Zimri, captain of half his chariots, conspired against him: now he was in Tirzah, drinking himself drunk in the house of Arza, which was over the household in Tirzah: 10. and Zimri went in and smote him, and killed him, in the twenty and seventh year of Asa king of Judah, and reigned in his stead. 11. And it came to pass, when he began to reign, as soon as he sat on his throne, that he smote all the house of Baasha: he left him not a single man child, neither of his kinsfolks, nor of his friends. 12. Thus did Zimri destroy all the house of Baasha, according to the word of the Lord, which he spake against Baasha by Jehu the prophet, 13. for all the sins of Baasha, and the sins of Elah his son, which they sinned, and wherewith they made Israel to sin, to provoke the Lord, the God of Israel, to anger with their vanities. 14. Now the rest of the acts of Elah, and all that he did, are they not written in the book of the chronicles of the kings of Israel?

SECT. XXIV   THE DIVIDED KINGDOM   167

JUDAH	ISRAEL
THE HOUSE OF DAVID	THE HOUSE OF OMRI (Fourth)
B. C. 956-915*	B. C. 930-917
V Asa	I Omri (6)
B. C. 917-876	B. C. 889-887
B. C. 915-889 (Jehu)	B. C. 917-898
VI Jehoshaphat	(Elijah) II Ahab (7)
B. C. 876-851 (Eliezer)	(Micaiah) B. C. 887-855
B. C. 889-885	B. C. 898-897
VII Jehoram	(Elijah) III Ahaziah (8)
B. C. 851-843	B. C. 855-854
B. C. 885-883	B. C. 897-883
VIII Ahaziah	(Elisha) IV Jehoram (9)
B. C. 843-842	B. C. 854-842

SECTION XXIV

Rival Houses of David and Omri

Zimri's One Week's Reign

I Kings 16:15. In the twenty and seventh year of Asa king of Judah did Zimri reign seven days in Tirzah. Now the people were encamped against Gibbethon, which belonged to the Philistines. 16. And the people that were encamped heard say, Zimri had conspired, and had also smitten the king: wherefore all Israel made Omri, the captain of the host, king over Israel that day in the camp. 17. And Omri went up from Gibbethon, and all Israel with him, and they besieged Tirzah. 18. And it came to pass, when Zimri saw that the city was taken, that he went into the castle of the king's house, and burnt the king's house over him with fire, and died, 19. for his sins which he sinned in doing that which was evil in the sight of the Lord, in walking in the way of Jereboam, and in his sin which he did, to make Israel to sin. 20. Now the rest of the acts of Zimri, and his treason that he wrought, are they not written in the book of the chronicles of the kings of Israel?

21. Then were the people of Israel divided into two parts: half of the people followed Tibni the son of Ginath to make him king; and half followed Omri. 22. But the people that followed Omri prevailed against the people that followed Tibni the son of Ginath: so Tibni died and Omri reigned. 23. In the thirty and first year of Asa king of Judah began Omri to reign over Israel, and reigned twelve years: six years reigned he in Tirzah.

Accession and Character of Omri

24. And he bought the hill Samaria of Shemer for two talents of silver, and he built on the hill, and called the name of the city which he built, after the name of Shemer, the owner of the hill, Samaria.

25. And Omri did that which was evil in the sight of the Lord, and dealt wickedly above all that were before him. 26. For he walked in all the ways of Jereboam the son of Nebat, and in his sins wherewith he made Israel to sin, to provoke the Lord, the God of Israel, to anger with their vanities. 27. Now the rest of the acts of Omri which he did, and his might that he shewed, are they not written in the book of the chronicles of the kings of Israel? 28. So Omri slept with his fathers, and was buried in Samaria: and Ahab his son reigned in his stead.

Accession and Character of Ahab

29. And in the thirtieth and eighth year of Asa king of Judah began Ahab the son of Omri to reign over Israel: and Ahab the son of Omri reigned over Israel in Samaria twenty and two years. 30. And Ahab the son of Omri did that which was evil in the sight of

---

* See Chronology Appendix A. Both systems of chronology are used, e.g., Asa $\frac{956 \text{ (Usher)}}{917 \text{ (Revised)}}$

the Lord above all that were before him. 31. And it came to pass, as if it had been a light thing for him to walk in the sins of Jereboam the son of Nebat, that he took to wife Jezebel the daughter of Ethbaal king of the Zidonians, and went and served Baal, and worshipped him. 32. And he reared up an altar for Baal in the house of Baal, which he had built in Samaria. 33. And Ahab made the Asherah; and Ahab did yet more to provoke the Lord, the God of Israel, to anger than all the kings of Israel that were before him. 34. In his days did Hiel the Beth-elite build Jericho: he laid the foundation thereof with the loss of Abiram his firstborn, and set up the gates thereof with the loss of his youngest son Segub; according to the word of the Lord, which he spake by the hand of * Joshua the son of Nun.

Asa's Disease and Death Now the rest of all the acts of Asa, first and last, and all his might, and all that he did, and the cities which he built, lo, they are written in the book of the chronicles of the kings of Judah and Israel. And in the thirty and ninth year of his reign, in the time of his old age, Asa was diseased in his feet; his disease was exceeding great: yet in his disease he sought not to the Lord, but to the physicians.

And Asa slept with his fathers, and died in the one and fortieth year of his reign. And they buried him with his fathers, in his own sepulchres which he had hewn out for himself in the city of David his father, and laid him in the bed which was filled with sweet odours and divers kind of spices prepared by the apothecaries' art: and they made a great burning for him: and Jehoshaphat his son reigned in his stead.

Accession and Character of Jehoshaphat And Jehoshaphat the son of Asa began to reign over Judah in the fourth year of Ahab king of Israel. Jehoshaphat was thirty and five years old when he began to reign; and he reigned twenty and five years in Jerusalem: and his mother's name was Azubah the daughter of Shilhi. And he walked in all the ways of Asa his father; he turned not aside from it, doing that which was right in the eyes of the Lord. Howbeit the high places were not taken away; the people still sacrificed and burnt incense in the high places; neither as yet had the people set their hearts unto the God of their fathers. And the remnant of the sodomites, which remained in the days of his father Asa, he put away out of the land.

The Kingdom Stablished II Chron. 17:1ᵇ. And (Jehoshaphat) strengthened himself against Israel. 2. And he placed forces in all the fenced cities of Judah, and set garrisons in the land of Judah, and in the cities of Ephraim, which Asa his father had taken. 3. And the Lord was with Jehoshaphat, because he walked in the first ways of his father David, and sought not unto the Baalim; 4. but sought to the God of his father, and walked in his commandments, and not after the doings of Israel. 5. Therefore the Lord stablished the kingdom in his hand; and all Judah brought to Jehoshaphat presents; and he had riches and honour in abundance. 6. And his heart was lifted up in the ways of the Lord: and furthermore he took away the high places and the Asherim out of Judah.

Judah Taught 7. Also in the third year of his reign he sent his princes, even Benhail, and Obadiah, and Zechariah, and Nethanel, and Micaiah, to teach in the cities of Judah; 8. and with them the Levites, even Shemaiah, and Nethaniah, and Zebadiah, and Asahel, and Shemiramoth, and Jehonathan, and Adonijah, and Tobijah, and Tobadonijah, the Levites; and with them Elishama and Jehoram the priests. 9. And they taught in Judah, having the book of the law of the Lord with them: and they went about through all the cities of Judah, and taught among the people.

---
* Josh. 6:26.

SECT. XXIV THE DIVIDED KINGDOM 169

I Kings 15:) 23. Now the rest of all the acts of Asa, and all his might, and all that he did, and the cities which he built, are they not written in the book of the chronicles of the kings of Judah? But in the time of his old age he was diseased in his feet.

24. And Asa slept with his fathers and was buried with his fathers

in the city of David his father:

and Jehoshaphat his son reigned in his stead.
(I Kings 22:) 41. And Jehoshaphat the son of Asa began to reign over Judah in the fourth year of Ahab king of Israel. 42. Jehoshaphat was thirty and five years old when he began to reign; and he reigned twenty and five years in Jerusalem. And his mother's name was Azubah the daughter of Shilhi.

43. And he walked in all the ways of Asa his father; he turned not aside from it, doing that which was right in the eyes of the Lord: howbeit the high places were not taken away; (the people still sacrificed and burnt incense in the high places.) 46. And the remnant of the sodomites, which remained in the days of his father Asa, he put away out of the land.

(II Chron. 16:) 11. And, behold, the acts of Asa, first and last,

lo, they are written in the book of the kings of Judah and Israel. 12. And in the thirty and ninth year of his reign Asa was diseased in his feet; his disease was exceeding great: yet in his disease he sought not to the Lord, but to the physicians.

13. And Asa slept with his fathers, and died in the one and fortieth year of his reign. 14. And they buried him in his own sepulchres, which he had hewn out for himself in the city of David, and laid him in the bed which was filled with sweet odours and divers kind of spices prepared by the apothecaries' art: and they made a very great burning for him.
(II Chron. 17:) 1ª. And Jehoshaphat his son reigned in his stead.
(II Chron. 20:) 31. And Jehoshaphat reigned over Judah:
he was thirty and five years old when he began to reign; and he reigned twenty and five years in Jerusalem: and his mother's name was Azubah the daughter of Shilhi.

32. And he walked in the way of Asa his father, and turned not aside from it, doing that which was right in the eyes of the Lord. 33. Howbeit the high places were not taken away; (neither as yet had the people set their hearts unto the God of their fathers.)

Increasing Power and Greatness

10. And the fear of the Lord fell upon all the kingdoms of the lands that were round about Judah, so that they made no war against Jehoshaphat. 11. And some of the Philistines brought Jehoshaphat presents, and silver for tribute; the Arabians also brought him flocks, seven thousand and seven hundred rams, and seven thousand and seven hundred he-goats. 12. And Jehoshaphat waxed great exceedingly; and he built in Judah castles and cities of store. 13. And he had many works in the cities of Judah; and men of war, mighty men of valour, in Jerusalem. 14. And this was the numbering of them according to their father's houses: of Judah, the captains of thousands;

Adnah the captain, and with him mighty men of valour three hundred thousand; 15. and next to him Jehohanan the captain, and with him two hundred and fourscore thousand:

16. and next to him Amasiah the son of Zichri, who willingly offered himself unto the Lord; and with him two hundred thousand mighty men of valour: 17. and of Benjamin;

Eliada a mighty man of valour, and with him two hundred thousand armed with bow and shield:

18. and next to him Jehozabad, and with him an hundred and fourscore thousand ready prepared for war. 19. These were they that waited on the king, beside those whom the king put in the fenced cities throughout all Judah.

Prophecy and Hiding of Elijah

I Kings 17:1. And Elijah the Tishbite, who was of the sojourners of Gilead, said unto Ahab, As the Lord, the God of Israel, liveth, before whom I stand,[*1] there shall not be dew nor rain these years, but according to my word. 2. And the word of the Lord came unto him, saying, 3. Get thee hence, and turn thee eastward, and hide thyself by the brook Cherith, that is before Jordan. 4. And it shall be, that thou shalt drink of the brook; and I have commanded the ravens to feed thee there. 5. So he went and did according unto the word of the Lord: for he went and dwelt by the brook Cherith, that is before Jordan. 6. And the ravens brought him bread and flesh in the morning, and bread and flesh in the evening; and he drank of the brook. 7. And it came to pass after a while that the brook dried up, because there was no rain in the land. 8. And the word of the Lord came unto him, saying, 9. Arise, get thee to Zarephath, which belongeth to Zidon, and dwell there: behold, I have commanded a widow woman there to sustain thee.[*2] 10. So he arose and went to Zarephath; and when he came to the gate of the city, behold, a widow woman was there gathering sticks: and he called to her, and said, Fetch me, I pray thee, a little water in a vessel, that I may drink. 11. And as she was going to fetch it, he called to her, and said, Bring me, I pray thee, a morsel of bread in thine hand. 12. And she said, As the Lord thy God liveth, I have not a cake, but an handful of meal in a barrel, and a little oil in a cruse: and, behold, I am gathering two sticks, that I may go in and dress it for me and my son, that we may eat it, and die. 13. And Elijah said unto her, Fear not; go and do as thou hast said: but make me thereof a little cake first, and bring it forth unto me, and afterward make for thee and for thy son. 14. For thus saith the Lord, the God of Israel, The barrel of meal shall not waste, neither shall the cruse of oil fail, until the day that the Lord sendeth rain upon the earth. 15. And she went and did according to the saying of Elijah: and she, and he, and her house, did eat many days. 16. The barrel of meal wasted not, neither did the cruse of oil fail, according to the word of the Lord, which he spake by Elijah.

[*1] Used as an encouragement to prayer. James 5:16b-18.
[*2] Used as an illustration by Jesus. Luke 4:25, 26.

Reviving of the Widow's Dead Child

17. And it came to pass after these things, that the son of the woman, the mistress of the house, fell sick; and his sickness was so sore, that there was no breath left in him. 18. And she said unto Elijah, What have I to do with thee, O man of God? thou art come unto me to bring my sin to remembrance, and to slay my son! 19. And he said unto her, Give me thy son. And he took him out of her bosom, and carried him up into the chamber, where he abode, and laid him upon his own bed. 20. And he cried unto the Lord, and said, O Lord my God, hast thou also brought evil upon the widow with whom I sojourn, by slaying her son? 21. And he stretched himself upon the child three times, and cried unto the Lord, and said, O Lord my God, I pray thee, let this child's soul come into him again. 22. And the Lord hearkened unto the voice of Elijah; and the soul of the child came into him again, and he revived. 23. And Elijah took the child, and brought him down out of the chamber into the house, and delivered him unto his mother: and Elijah said, See, thy son liveth. 24. And the woman said to Elijah, Now I know that thou art a man of God, and that the word of the Lord in thy mouth is truth.

Meeting of Elijah and Ahab

I Kings 18:1. And it came to pass after many days, that the word of the Lord came to Elijah, in the third year, saying, Go, shew thyself unto Ahab; and I will send rain upon the earth. 2. And Elijah went to shew himself unto Ahab. And the famine was sore in Samaria. 3. And Ahab called Obadiah, which was over the household. (Now Obadiah feared the Lord greatly; 4. for it was so, when Jezebel cut off the prophets of the Lord, that Obadiah took an hundred prophets, and hid them by fifty in a cave, and fed them with bread and water.) 5. And Ahab said unto Obadiah, Go through the land, unto all the fountains of water, and unto all the brooks: peradventure we may find grass and save the horses and mules alive, that we lose not all the beasts. 6. So they divided the land between them to pass throughout it: Ahab went one way by himself, and Obadiah went another way by himself. 7. And as Obadiah was in the way, behold, Elijah met him: and he knew him, and fell on his face, and said, Is it thou, my lord Elijah? 8. And he answered him, It is I: go, tell thy lord, Behold, Elijah is here. 9. And he said, Wherein have I sinned, that thou wouldest deliver thy servant into the hand of Ahab, to slay me? 10. As the Lord thy God liveth, there is no nation or kingdom, whither my lord hath not sent to seek thee: and when they said, He is not here, he took an oath of the kingdom and nation, that they found thee not. 11. And now thou sayest, Go, tell thy lord, Behold, Elijah is here. 12. And it shall come to pass, as soon as I am gone from thee, that the spirit of the Lord shall carry thee whither I know not; and so when I come and tell Ahab, and he cannot find thee, he shall slay me: But I thy servant fear the Lord from my youth. 13. Was it not told my lord what I did when Jezebel slew the prophets of the Lord, how I hid an hundred men of the Lord's prophets by fifty in a cave, and fed them with bread and water? 14. And now thou sayest, Go, tell thy lord, Behold, Elijah is here: and he shall slay me. 15. And Elijah said, As the Lord of hosts liveth, before whom I stand, I will surely shew myself unto him to-day. 16. So Obadiah went to meet Ahab, and told him: and Ahab went to meet Elijah. 17. And it came to pass, when Ahab saw Elijah, that Ahab said unto him, Is it thou, thou troubler of Israel? 18. And he answered, I have not troubled Israel; but thou, and thy father's house, in that ye have forsaken the commandments of the Lord, and thou hast followed the Baalim. 19. Now therefore send, and gather to me all Israel unto Mount Carmel, and the prophets of Baal four hundred and fifty, and the prophets of the Asherah four hundred, which eat at Jezebel's table. 20. So Ahab sent unto all the children of Israel, and gathered the prophets together unto mount Carmel. 21. And Elijah came near unto all the people, and said, How long halt ye between two opinions? if the Lord be God, follow him: but if Baal, then follow him. And the people answered him not a word.

Challenge to Sacrifice with Test of Fire
22. Then said Elijah unto the people, I, even I only, am left a prophet of the Lord; but Baal's prophets are four hundred and fifty men. 23. Let them therefore give us two bullocks; and let them choose one bullock for themselves, and cut it in pieces, and lay it on the wood, and put no fire under: and I will dress the other bullock, and lay it on the wood, and put no fire under. 24. And call ye on the name of your god, and I will call upon the name of the Lord; and the God that answereth by fire, let him be God. And all the people answered and said, It is well spoken. 25. And Elijah said unto the prophets of Baal, Choose you one bullock for yourselves, and dress it first; for ye are many; and call on the name of your god, but put no fire under. 26. And they took the bullock which was given them, and they dressed it, and called on the name of Baal from morning even until noon, saying, O Baal, hear us. But there was no voice, nor any that answered. And they leaped about the altar which was made. 27. And it came to pass at noon, that Elijah mocked them, and said, Cry aloud: for he is a god; either he is musing, or he is gone aside, or he is in a journey, or peradventure he sleepeth, and must be awaked. 28. And they cried aloud, and cut themselves after their manner with knives and lances, till the blood gushed out upon them. 29. And it was so, when midday was past, that they prophesied until the time of the offering of the evening oblation; but there was neither voice, nor any to answer, nor any that regarded.

30. And Elijah said unto all the people, Come near unto me; and all the people came near unto him. And he repaired the altar of the Lord that was thrown down. 31. And Elijah took twelve stones, according to the number of the tribes of the sons of Jacob, unto whom the word of the Lord came, saying, Israel shall be thy name. 32. And with the stones he built an altar in the name of the Lord; and he made a trench about the altar, as great as would contain two measures of seed. 33. And he put the wood in order, and cut the bullock in pieces, and laid it on the wood. And he said, Fill four barrels with water, and pour it on the burnt offering, and on the wood. 34. And he said, Do it the second time; and they did it the second time. And he said, Do it the third time, and they did it the third time. 35. And the water ran about the altar; and he filled the trench also with water. 36. And it came to pass at the time of the offering of the evening oblation, that Elijah the prophet came near, and said, O Lord, the God of Abraham, of Isaac, and of Israel, let it be known this day that thou art God in Israel, and that I am thy servant, and that I have done all these things at thy word. 37. Hear me, O Lord, hear me, that this people may know that thou, Lord, art God, and that thou hast turned their heart back again. 38. Then the fire of the Lord fell, and consumed the burnt offering, and the wood, and the stones, and the dust, and licked up the water that was in the trench. 39. And when all the people saw it, they fell on their faces: and they said; the Lord, he is God; the Lord, he is God. 40. And Elijah said unto them, Take the prophets of Baal; let not one of them escape. And they took them: and Elijah brought them down to the brook Kishon, and slew them there. 41. And Elijah said unto Ahab, Get thee up, eat and drink; for there is the sound of abundance of rain. 42. So Ahab went up to eat and to drink. And Elijah went up to the top of Carmel; and he bowed himself down upon the earth, and put his face between his

knees. 43. And he said to his servant, Go up now, look toward the sea. And he went up, and looked, and said, There is nothing. And he said, Go again seven times. 44. And it came to pass, at the seventh time, that he said, Behold, there ariseth a cloud out of the sea, as small as a man's hand. And he said, Go up, say unto Ahab, Make ready thy chariot, and get thee down, that the rain stop thee not. 45. And it came to pass in a little while, that the heaven grew black with clouds and wind, and there was a great rain. And Ahab rode, and went to Jezreel. 46. And the hand of the Lord was on Elijah; and he girded up his loins, and ran before Ahab to the entrance of Jezreel.

Flight and Despondency of Elijah

I Kings 19:1. And Ahab told Jezebel all that Elijah had done, and withal how he had slain all the prophets with the sword. 2. Then Jezebel sent a messenger unto Elijah, saying, So let the gods do to me, and more also, if I make not thy life as the life of one of them by to-morrow about this time. 3. And when he saw that, he arose, and went for his life, and came to Beer-sheba, which belongeth to Judah, and left his servant there. 4. But he himself went a day's journey into the wilderness, and came and sat down under a juniper tree: and he requested for himself that he might die; and he said, It is enough; now, O Lord, take away my life; for I am not better than my fathers. 5. And he lay down and slept under a juniper tree; and, behold, an angel touched him, and said unto him, Arise and eat. 6. And he looked, and, behold, there was at his head a cake baken on the coals, and a cruse of water. And he did eat and drink, and laid him down again. 7. And the angel of the Lord came again the second time, and touched him, and said, Arise and eat; because the journey is too great for thee. 8. And he arose, and did eat and drink, and went in the strength of that meat forty days and forty nights unto Horeb the mount of God. 9. And he came thither unto a cave, and lodged there; and, behold, the word of the Lord came to him, and he said unto him, What doest thou here Elijah? 10. And he said I have been very jealous for the Lord, the God of hosts; for the children of Israel have forsaken thy covenant, thrown down thine altars, and slain thy prophets with the sword: and I, even I only, am left; and they seek my life to take it away.

Manifestation and Message of the Lord

11. And he said, Go forth and stand upon the mount before the Lord. And, behold, the Lord passed by, and a great and strong wind rent the mountains, and brake in pieces the rocks before the Lord; but the Lord was not in the wind: and after the wind an earthquake; but the Lord was not in the earthquake: 12. and after the earthquake a fire: but the Lord was not in the fire: and after the fire a still small voice. 13. And it was so, when Elijah heard it, that he wrapped his face in his mantle, and went out, and stood in the entering of the cave. And, behold, there came a voice unto him, and said, What doest thou here Elijah? 14. And he said, I have been very jealous for the Lord, the God of hosts; for the children of Israel have forsaken thy covenant, thrown down thine altars, and slain thy prophets with the sword; and I, even I only, am left; and they seek my life to take it away. 15. And the Lord said unto him, Go, return on thy way to the wilderness of Damascus: and when thou comest, thou shalt anoint Hazael to be king over Syria: 16. and Jehu the son of Nimshi shalt thou anoint to be king over Israel: and Elisha the son of Shaphat of Abel-meholah shalt thou anoint to be prophet in thy room. 17. And it shall come to pass, that him that escapeth from the sword of Hazael shall Jehu slay: and him that escapeth from the sword of Jehu, shall Elisha slay. 18. Yet will I leave me seven thousand in Israel, all the knees which have not bowed unto Baal, and every mouth which hath not kissed him.

Call of Elisha

19. So he departed thence, and found Elisha the son of Shaphat, who was plowing, with twelve yoke of oxen before him, and he with the twelfth: and Elijah passed over unto him, and cast his mantle upon him. 20. And he left the oxen, and ran after Elijah, and said, Let me, I pray thee, kiss my father and my mother, and then I will follow thee. And he said unto him, Go back again; for what have I done to thee? 21. And he returned from following him, and took the yoke of oxen, and slew them, and boiled their flesh with the instruments of the oxen, and gave unto the people, and they did eat. Then he arose, and went after Elijah, and ministered unto him.

Ben-hadad Besieges Samaria

I Kings 20:1. And Ben-hadad the king of Syria gathered all his host together: and there were thirty and two kings with him, and horses and chariots: and he went up and besieged Samaria, and fought against it. 2. And he sent messengers to Ahab king of Israel, into the city, and said unto him, Thus saith Ben-hadad, 3. Thy silver and thy gold is mine; thy wives also and thy children, even the goodliest are mine. 4. And the king of Israel answered and said, It is according to thy saying, my lord, O king; I am thine and all that I have. 5. And the messengers came again, and said, Thus speaketh Ben-hadad, saying, I sent indeed unto thee, saying, Thou shalt deliver me thy silver, and thy gold, and thy wives, and thy children; 6. but I will send my servants unto thee to-morrow about this time, and they shall search thine house, and the houses of thy servants; and it shall be, that whatsoever is pleasant in thine eyes, they shall put it in their hand, and take it away. 7. Then the king of Israel called all the elders of the land, and said, Mark, I pray you, and see how this man seeketh mischief: for he sent unto me for my wives, and for my children, and for my silver, and for my gold; and I denied him not. 8. And all the elders and all the people said unto him, Hearken thou not, neither consent. 9. Wherefore he said unto the messengers of Ben-hadad, Tell my lord the king, all that thou didst send for to thy servant at the first I will do: but this thing I may not do. And the messengers departed, and brought him word again. 10. And Ben-hadad sent unto him, and said, The gods do so unto me, and more also, if the dust of Samaria shall suffice for handfuls for all the people that follow me. 11. And the king of Israel answered and said, Tell him, Let not him that girdeth on his armour boast himself as he that putteth it off. 12. And it came to pass, when Ben-hadad heard this message, as he was drinking, he and the kings, in the pavilions, that he said unto his servants, Set yourselves in array. And they set themselves in array against the city.

Ahab's Victory

13. And, behold, a prophet came near unto Ahab king of Israel, and said, Thus saith the Lord, Hast thou seen all this great multitude? behold, I will deliver it into thine hand this day; and thou shalt know that I am the Lord. 14. And Ahab said, By whom? And he said, Thus saith the Lord, by the young men of the princes of the provinces. Then he said, Who shall begin the battle? And he answered, Thou. 15. Then he mustered the young men of the princes of the provinces, and they were two hundred and thirty two: and after that he mustered all the people, even all the children of Israel, being seven thousand. 16. And they went out at noon. But Ben-hadad was drinking himself drunk in the pavilions, he and the kings, the thirty and two kings that helped him. 17. And the young men of the princes of the provinces went out first; and Ben-hadad sent out, and they told him, saying, There are men come out from Samaria. 18. And he said, Whether they be come out for peace, take them alive; or whether they be come out for war, take them alive. 19. So these

went out of the city, the young men of the princes of the provinces, and the army which followed them. 20. And they slew every one his man; and the Syrians fled, and Israel pursued them: and Ben-hadad the king of Syria escaped on an horse with horsemen. 21. And the king of Israel went out, and smote the horses and chariots, and slew the Syrians with a great slaughter. 22. And the prophet came near to the king of Israel, and said unto him, Go, strengthen thyself, and mark, and see what thou doest: for at the return of the year the king of Syria will come up against thee.

Ben-hadad's Second Campaign

23. And the servants of the king of Syria said unto him, Their god is a god of the hills; therefore they were stronger than we: but let us fight against them in the plain, and surely we shall be stronger than they. 24. And do this thing; take the kings away, every man out of his place, and put captains in their room: 25. and number thee an army, like the army thou hast lost, horse for horse, and chariot for chariot: and we will fight against them in the plain, and surely we shall be stronger than they. And he hearkened unto their voice, and did so. 26. And it came to pass at the return of the year, that Ben-hadad mustered the Syrians, and went up to Aphek to fight against Israel. 27. And the children of Israel were mustered, and were victualled, and went against them: and the children of Israel encamped before them like two little flocks of kids; but the Syrians filled the country. 28. And a man of God came near and spake unto the king of Israel, and said, Thus saith the Lord, Because the Syrians have said, The Lord is a God of the hills, but he is not a God of the valleys; therefore will I deliver all this great multitude into thine hand, and ye shall know that I am the Lord.

Ahab's Second Victory

29. And they encamped one over against the other seven days. And so it was that in the seventh day the battle was joined; and the children of Israel slew of the Syrians an hundred thousand footmen in one day. 30. But the rest fled to Aphek, into the city; and the wall fell upon twenty and seven thousand men that were left. And Ben-hadad fled, and came into the city, into an inner chamber. 31. And his servants said unto him, Behold now, we have heard that the kings of the house of Israel are merciful kings: let us, we pray thee, put sackcloth on our loins, and ropes upon our heads, and go out to the king of Israel: peradventure he will save thy life. 32. So they girded sackcloth on their loins, and put ropes on their heads, and came to the king of Israel, and said, Thy servant Ben-hadad saith, I pray thee, let me live. And he said, Is he yet alive? he is my brother. 33. Now the men observed diligently, and hasted to catch whether it were his mind; and they said, Thy brother Ben-hadad. Then he said, Go ye, bring him. Then Ben-hadad came forth to him; and he caused him to come up into the chariot. 34. And Ben-hadad said unto him, The cities which my father took from thy father I will restore; and thou shalt make streets for thee in Damascus, as my father made in Samaria. And I, said Ahab, will let thee go with this covenant. So he made a covenant with him, and let him go.

Life Spared and Life Forfeited

35. And a certain man of the sons of the prophets said unto his fellow by the word of the Lord, Smite me, I pray thee. And the man refused to smite him. 36. Then said he unto him, Because thou hast not obeyed the voice of the Lord, behold, as soon as thou art departed from me, a lion shall slay thee. And as soon as he was departed from him, a lion found him, and slew him. 37. Then he found another man, and said, Smite me, I pray thee. And the man smote him, smiting and wounding him. 38. So the prophet departed,

and waited for the king by the way, and disguised himself with his headband over his eyes. 39. And as the king passed by, he cried unto the king: and he said, Thy servant went out into the midst of the battle; and, behold, a man turned aside, and brought a man unto me, and said, Keep this man: if by any means he be missing, then shall thy life be for his life, or else thou shalt pay a talent of silver. 40. And as thy servant was busy here and there, he was gone. And the king of Israel said unto him, So shall thy judgment be; thyself hast decided it. 41. And he hasted, and took the headband away from his eyes; and the king of Israel discerned him that he was of the prophets. 42. And he said unto him, Thus saith the Lord, Because thou hast let go out of thy hand the man whom I had devoted to destruction, therefore thy life shall go for his life, and thy people for his people.* 43. And the king of Israel went to his house heavy and displeased, and came to Samaria.

Ahab's Sin Against Naboth I Kings 21:1. And it came to pass after these things, that Naboth the Jezreelite had a vineyard, which was in Jezreel, hard by the palace of Ahab king of Samaria. 2. And Ahab spake unto Naboth, saying, Give me thy vineyard, that I may have it for a garden of herbs, because it is near unto my house; and I will give thee for it a better vineyard than it; or, if it seem good to thee, I will give thee the worth of it in money. 3. And Naboth said to Ahab, The Lord forbid it me, that I should give the inheritance of my fathers unto thee. 4. And Ahab came into his house heavy and displeased because of the word which Naboth the Jezreelite had spoken to him: for he had said, I will not give thee the inheritance of my fathers. And he laid him down upon his bed, and turned away his face, and would eat no bread. 5. But Jezebel his wife came to him, and said unto him, Why is thy spirit so sad, that thou eatest no bread? 6. And he said unto her, Because I spake unto Naboth the Jezreelite, and said unto him, Give me thy vineyard for money; or else, if it please thee, I will give thee another vineyard for it: and he answered, I will not give thee my vineyard. 7. And Jezebel his wife said unto him, Dost thou now govern the kingdom of Israel? arise, and eat bread, and let thine heart be merry: I will give thee the vineyard of Naboth the Jezreelite. 8. So she wrote letters in Ahab's name, and sealed them with his seal, and sent the letters unto the elders and to the nobles that were in his city, and that dwelt with Naboth. 9. And she wrote in the letters, saying, Proclaim a fast, and set Naboth on high among the people: and set two men, sons of Belial, before him, and let them bear witness against him, saying, Thou didst curse God and the king. And then carry him out, and stone him, that he die. 11. And the men of his city, even the elders and the nobles who dwelt in his city, did as Jezebel had sent unto them, according as it was written in the letters which she had sent unto them. 12. They proclaimed a fast, and set Naboth on high among the people. 13. And the two men sons of Belial, came in and sat before him; and the men of Belial bare witness against him, even against Naboth, in the presence of the people, saying, Naboth did curse God and the king. Then they carried him forth out of the city, and stoned him with stones, that he died. 14. Then they sent to Jezebel, saying, Naboth is stoned, and is dead. 15. And it came to pass, when Jezebel heard that Naboth was stoned, and was dead, that Jezebel said to Ahab, Arise, take possession of the vineyard of Naboth the Jezreelite, which he refused to give thee for money: for Naboth is not alive, but dead. 16. And it came to pass, when Ahab heard that Naboth was dead, that Ahab rose up to go down to the vineyard of Naboth the Jezreelite, to take possession of it,

---

* Fulfilled in the battle to recover Ramoth. I Kings 22:34-37.

Retributive Punishment Foretold

17. And the word of the Lord came to Elijah the Tishbite, saying, 18. Arise, go down to meet Ahab king of Israel, which dwelleth in Samaria: behold, he is in the vineyard of Naboth, whither he is gone down to take possession of it. 19. And thou shalt speak unto him, saying, Thus saith the Lord, Hast thou killed, and also taken possession? and thou shalt speak unto him, saying, Thus saith the Lord, In the place where dogs licked the blood of Naboth shall dogs lick thy blood, even thine. 20. And Ahab said to Elijah, Hast thou found me, O mine enemy? And he answered, I have found thee: because thou hast sold thyself to do that which is evil in the sight of the Lord. 21. Behold, I will bring evil upon thee, and will utterly sweep thee away, and will cut off from Ahab every man child, and him that is shut up and him that is left at large in Israel: 22. and I will make thine house like the house of Jereboam the son of Nebat, and like the house of Baasha the son of Ahijah, for the provocation wherewith thou hast provoked me to anger, and hast made Israel to sin. 23. And of Jezebel also spake the Lord, saying, The dogs shall eat Jezebel by the rampart of Jezreel. 24. Him that dieth of Ahab in the city the dogs shall eat; and him that dieth in the field shall the fowls of the air eat. 25. (But there was none like unto Ahab, which did sell himself to do that which was evil in the sight of the Lord, whom Jezebel his wife stirred up. 26. And he did very abominably in following idols, according to all that the Amorites did, whom the Lord cast out before the children of Israel.) 27. And it came to pass when Ahab heard those words, that he rent his clothes, and put sackcloth upon his flesh, and fasted, and lay in sackcloth, and went softly. 28. And the word of the Lord came to Elijah the Tishbite, saying, 29. Seest thou how Ahab humbleth himself before me? because he humbleth himself before me, I will not bring the evil in his days: but in his son's days will I bring the evil upon his house.

JUDAH	ISRAEL
THE HOUSE OF DAVID	**THE HOUSE OF OMRI** (Fourth)
B. C. 956-915*	B. C. 930-917
V Asa	I Omri (6)
B. C. 917-876	B. C. 889-887
B. C. 915-889 (Jehu)	B. C. 917-898
VI Jehoshaphat (Elijah)	II Ahab (7)
B. C. 876-851 (Eliezer) (Micaiah)	B. C. 887-855
B. C. 889-885	B. C. 898-897
VII Jehoram (Elijah)	III Ahaziah (8)
B. C. 851-843	B. C. 855-854
B. C. 885-883	B. C. 897-883
VIII Ahaziah (Elisha)	IV Jehoram (9)
B. C. 843-842	B. C. 854-842

SECTION XXV
Allied Houses of David and Omri (Elijah)

Alliance of Jehoshaphat and Ahab

And they continued three years without war between Syria and Israel. Now Jehoshaphat had riches and honour in abundance; and he joined affinity with Ahab. And it came to pass in the third year, that Jehoshaphat the king of Judah went down to Ahab the king of Israel to Samaria. And Ahab killed sheep and oxen for him in abundance, and for the people that were with him, and moved him to go up with him to Ramoth-gilead. And the king of Israel said unto his servants, Know ye that Ramoth-gilead is ours, and we be still, and take it not out of the hand of the king of Syria? And Ahab king of Israel said unto Jehoshaphat king of Judah, Wilt thou go with me to battle to Ramoth-gilead? And Jehoshaphat said to the king of Israel, I am as thou art, and my people as thy people, my horses as thy horses, and we will be with thee in the war. And Jehoshaphat said unto the king of Israel, Inquire, I pray thee, at the word of the Lord to-day. Then the king of Israel gathered the prophets together, about four hundred men, and said unto them, Shall we go to Ramoth-gilead to battle, or shall we forbear? And they said, Go up; for the Lord shall deliver it into the hand of the king.

Micaiah's Adverse Prediction

But Jehoshaphat said, Is there not here besides a prophet of the Lord, that we might inquire of him? And the king of Israel said unto Jehoshaphat, There is yet one man by whom we may inquire of the Lord, Micaiah the son of Imlah: but I hate him; for he doth not prophesy good concerning me, but always evil. And Jehoshaphat said, Let not the king say so. Then the king of Israel called an officer, and said, Fetch quickly Micaiah the son of Imlah. Now the king of Israel and Jehoshaphat the king of Judah sat each on his throne, arrayed in their robes, and they sat in an open place at the entrance of the gate of Samaria; and all the prophets prophesied before them. And Zedekiah the son of Chenaanah made him horns of iron, and said, Thus saith the Lord, With these shalt thou push the Syrians, until they be consumed. And all the prophets prophesied so, saying, Go up to Ramoth-gilead and prosper: for the Lord shall deliver it into the hand of the king. And the messenger that went to call Micaiah spake unto him, saying, Behold now, the words of the prophets declare good unto the king with one mouth: let thy word, I pray thee, be like the word of one of them, and speak thou good. And Micaiah said, As the Lord liveth, what the Lord saith unto me, that will I speak. And when he was come to the king, the king said unto him, Micaiah shall we go to Ramoth-gilead to battle, or shall we forbear? And he answered him, and said, Go up, and prosper: and the Lord shall deliver it into the hand of the king.

---

* See Chronology Appendix A. Both systems of chronology are used, *e.g.*, Asa $\frac{956}{917}$ (Usher) (Revised)

THE DIVIDED KINGDOM

(I Kings 22:) 1. And they continued three years without war between Syria and Israel.

2. And it came to pass in the third year, that Jehoshaphat the king of Judah came down to the king of Israel.

3. (And the king of Israel said unto his servants, Know ye that Ramoth-gilead is ours, and we be still, and take it not out of the hand of the king of Syria?) 4. And he said unto Jehoshaphat, Wilt thou go with me to battle to Ramoth-gilead? And Jehoshaphat said to the king of Israel, I am as thou art, my people as thy people, my horses as thy horses.

5. And Jehoshaphat said unto the king of Israel, Inquire, I pray thee, at the word of the Lord to-day. 6. Then the king of Israel gathered the prophets together, about four hundred men, and said unto them, Shall I go against Ramoth-gilead to battle, or shall I forbear? And they said, Go up; for the Lord shall deliver it into the hand of the king.

7. But Jehoshaphat said, Is there not here besides a prophet of the Lord, that we might inquire of him? 8. And the king of Israel said unto Jehoshaphat, There is yet one man by whom we may inquire of the Lord, Micaiah the son of Imlah: but I hate him; for he doth not prophesy good concerning me, but evil. And Jehoshaphat said, Let not the king say so. 9. Then the king of Israel called an officer, and said, Fetch quickly Micaiah the son of Imlah. 10. Now the king of Israel and Jehoshaphat the king of Judah sat each on his throne, arrayed in their robes, in an open place at the entrance of the gate of Samaria; and all the prophets prophesied before them. 11. And Zedekiah the son of Chenaanah made him horns of iron, and said, Thus saith the Lord, With these shalt thou push the Syrians, until they be consumed. 12. And all the prophets prophesied so, saying, Go up to Ramoth-gilead and prosper: for the Lord shall deliver it into the hand of the king. 13. And the messenger that went to call Micaiah spake unto him, saying, Behold now, the words of the prophets declare good unto the king with one mouth: let thy word, I pray thee, be like the word of one of them, and speak thou good. 14. And Micaiah said, As the Lord liveth, what the Lord saith unto me, that will I speak. 15. And when he was come to the king, the king said unto him, Micaiah shall we go to Ramoth-gilead to battle, or shall we forbear? And he answered him, Go up, and prosper; and the Lord shall deliver it into the hand of the king.

(II Chron. 18:) 1. Now Jehoshaphat had riches and honour in abundance; and he joined affinity with Ahab. 2. And after certain years he went down to Ahab to Samaria. And Ahab killed sheep and oxen for him in abundance, and for the people that were with him, (and moved him to go up with him to Ramoth-gilead.)

3 And Ahab king of Israel said unto Jehoshaphat king of Judah, Wilt thou go with me to Ramoth-gilead? And he answered him, I am as thou art, and my people as thy people, and we will be with thee in the war.

4. And Jehoshaphat said unto the king of Israel, Inquire, I pray thee, at the word of the Lord to-day. 5. Then the king of Israel gathered the prophets together, four hundred men, and said unto them, Shall we go to Ramoth-gilead to battle, or shall I forbear? And they said, Go up; for God shall deliver it into the hand of the king.

6. But Jehoshaphat said, Is there not here besides a prophet of the Lord, that we might inquire of him? 7. And the king of Israel said unto Jehoshaphat, There is yet one man by whom we may inquire of the Lord: but I hate him; for he never prophesieth good concerning me, but always evil: The same is Micaiah the son of Imla. And Jehoshaphat said, Let not the king say so. 8. Then the king of Israel called an officer, and said, Fetch quickly Micaiah the son of Imla. 9. Now the king of Israel and Jehoshaphat the king of Judah sat each on his throne, arrayed in their robes, and they sat in an open place at the entrance of the gate of Samaria; and all the prophets prophesied before them. 10. And Zedekiah the son of Chenaanah made him horns of iron, and said, Thus saith the Lord, With these shalt thou push the Syrians, until they be consumed. 11. And all the prophets prophesied so, saying, Go up to Ramoth-gilead, and prosper: for the Lord shall deliver it into the hand of the king. 12. And the messenger that went to call Micaiah spake to him, saying, Behold the words of the prophets declare good unto the king with one mouth: let thy word therefore, I pray thee, be like one of theirs, and speak thou good. 13. And Micaiah said, As the Lord liveth, what my God saith that will I speak. 14. And when he was come to the king, the king said unto him, Micaiah shall we go to Ramoth-gilead to battle, or shall I forbear? And he said, Go ye up and prosper; and they shall be delivered into your hand.

And the king said unto him, How many times shall I adjure thee that thou speak unto me nothing but the truth in the name of the Lord? And he said, I saw all Israel scattered upon the mountains, as sheep that have no shepherd: and the Lord said, These have no master; let them return every man to his house in peace. And the king of Israel said to Jehoshaphat, Did I not tell thee that he would not prophesy good concerning me, but evil? And he said, Therefore hear thou the word of the Lord: I saw the Lord sitting on his throne, and all the host of heaven standing by him on his right hand and on his left. And the Lord said, Who shall entice Ahab, that he may go up and fall at Ramoth-gilead? And one spake saying after this manner, and another saying after that manner.

And there came forth a spirit, and stood before the Lord, and said, I will entice him. And the Lord said, Wherewith? And he said, I will go forth, and will be a lying spirit in the mouth of all his prophets. And he said, Thou shalt entice him, and shalt prevail also: go forth, and do so. Now therefore, behold, the Lord hath put a lying spirit in the mouth of all these thy prophets; and the Lord hath spoken evil concerning thee.

Then Zedekiah the son of Chenaanah came near, and smote Micaiah on the cheek, and said, Which way went the spirit of the Lord from me to speak unto thee? And Micaiah said, Behold, thou shalt see on that day, when thou shalt go into an inner chamber to hide thyself.

Ahab Puts Micaiah in Prison

And the king of Israel said, Take ye Micaiah, and carry him back unto Amon the governor of the city, and to Joash the king's son: and say, Thus saith the king, Put this fellow in the prison, and feed him with bread of affliction and with water of affliction, until I return in peace. And Micaiah said, If thou return at all in peace, the Lord hath not spoken by me. And he said, Hear ye peoples, all of you.

Defiance, Disguise, and Death

So the king of Israel and Jehoshaphat the king of Judah went up to Ramoth-gilead. And the king of Israel said unto Jehoshaphat, I will disguise myself, and go into the battle; but put thou on thy robes. So the king of Israel disguised himself, and they went into the battle. Now the king of Syria had commanded the thirty and two captains of his chariots, saying, Fight neither with small nor great, save only with the king of Israel. And it came to pass, when the captains of the chariots saw Jehoshaphat, that they said, It is the king of Israel. Therefore they turned aside to fight against him: but Jehoshaphat cried out, and the Lord helped him; and God moved them to depart from him. And it came to pass when the captains of the chariots saw that it was not the king of Israel, that they turned back from pursuing him. And a certain man drew his bow at a venture, and smote the king of Israel between the joints of the harness: wherefore he said unto the driver of his chariot, Turn thine hand, and carry me out of the host: for I am sore wounded. And the battle increased that day: howbeit the king of Israel stayed himself up in his chariot against the Syrians until the even: and about the time of the going down of the sun he died, and the blood ran out of the wound into the bottom of the chariot.

And there went a cry throughout the host about the going down of the sun, saying, Every man to his city, and every man to his country. So the king died, and was brought to Samaria; and they buried the king in Samaria. And they washed the chariot by the pool of Samaria; and the dogs licked up his blood, (now the harlots washed themselves there;) according unto the word of the Lord which he spake.*

* Fulfillment of I Kings 20:42; 21:19.

16. And the king said unto him, How many times shall I adjure thee that thou speak unto me nothing but the truth in the name of the Lord? 17. And he said, I saw all Israel scattered upon the mountains, as sheep that have no shepherd: and the Lord said, These have no master; let them return every man to his house in peace. 18. And the king of Israel said to Jehoshaphat, Did I not tell thee that he would not prophesy good concerning me, but evil? 19. And he said, Therefore hear thou the word of the Lord: I saw the Lord sitting on his throne, and all the host of heaven standing by him on his right hand and on his left. 20. And the Lord said, Who shall entice Ahab, that he may go up and fall at Ramoth-gilead? And one said on this manner; and another said on that manner.

21. And there came forth a spirit, and stood before the Lord, and said, I will entice him. 22. And the Lord said unto him, Wherewith? And he said, I will go forth, and will be a lying spirit in the mouth of all his prophets. And he said, Thou shalt entice him, and shalt prevail also: go forth, and do so. 23. Now therefore, behold, the Lord hath put a lying spirit in the mouth of all these thy prophets; and the Lord hath spoken evil concerning thee. 24. Then Zedekiah the son of Chenaanah came near, and smote Micaiah on the cheek, and said, Which way went the spirit of the Lord from me to speak unto thee? 25. And Micaiah said, Behold, thou shalt see on that day, when thou shalt go into an inner chamber to hide thyself.

26. And the king of Israel said, Take Micaiah, and carry him back unto Amon the governor of the city, and to Joash the king's son; 27. and say, Thus saith the king, Put this fellow in the prison, and feed him with bread of affliction and with water of affliction, until I come in peace. 28. And Micaiah said, If thou return at all in peace, the Lord hath not spoken by me. And he said, Hear ye peoples, all of you.

29. So the king of Israel and Jehoshaphat the king of Judah went up to Ramoth-gilead. 30. And the king of Israel said unto Jehoshaphat, I will disguise myself, and go into the battle; but put thou on thy robes. And the king of Israel disguised himself, and went into the battle. 31. Now the king of Syria had commanded the thirty and two captains of his chariots, saying, Fight neither with small nor great, save only with the king of Israel. 32. And it came to pass, when the captains of the chariots saw Jehoshaphat, that they said, It is the king of Israel; and they turned aside to fight against him: and Jehoshaphat cried out. 33. And it came to pass, when the captains of the chariots saw that it was not the king of Israel, that they turned back from pursuing him. 34. And a certain man drew his bow at a venture, and smote the king of Israel between the joints of the harness: wherefore he said unto the driver of his chariot, Turn thine hand, and carry me out of the host; for I am sore wounded. 35. And the battle increased that day: and the king was stayed up in his chariot against the Syrians, and died at even, and the blood ran out of the wound into the bottom of the chariot. 36. And there went a cry throughout the host about the going down of the sun, saying, Every man to his city, and every man to his country. 37. So the king died, and was brought to Samaria; and they buried the king in Samaria. 38. And they washed the chariot by the pool of Samaria; and the dogs licked up his blood; (now the harlots washed themselves there;) according unto the word of the Lord which he spake.

15. And the king said to him, How many times shall I adjure thee that thou speak unto me nothing but the truth in the name of the Lord? 16. And he said, I saw all Israel scattered upon the mountains, as sheep that have no shepherd: and the Lord said, These have no master; let them return every man to his house in peace. 17. And the king of Israel said to Jehoshaphat, Did I not tell thee that he would not prophesy good concerning me, but evil? 18. And he said, Therefore hear thou the word of the Lord: I saw the Lord sitting upon his throne, and all the host of heaven standing on his right hand and on his left. 19. And the Lord said, Who shall entice Ahab, that he may go up and fall at Ramoth-gilead? And one spake saying after this manner, and another saying after that manner.

20. And there came forth a spirit, and stood before the Lord, and said, I will entice him. And the Lord said unto him, Wherewith? 21. And he said, I will go forth, and will be a lying spirit in the mouth of all his prophets. And he said, Thou shalt entice him, and shalt prevail also: go forth, and do so. 22. Now therefore the Lord hath put a lying spirit in the mouth of these thy prophets; and the Lord hath spoken evil concerning thee. 23. Then Zedekiah the son of Chenaanah came near, and smote Micaiah on the cheek, and said, Which way went the spirit of the Lord from me to speak unto thee? 24. And Micaiah said, Behold, thou shalt see on that day, when thou shalt go into an inner chamber to hide thyself.

25. And the king of Israel said, Take ye Micaiah, and carry him back unto Amon the governor of the city, and to Joash the king's son; 26. and say, Thus saith the king, Put this fellow in the prison, and feed him with bread of affliction and with water of affliction, until I return in peace. 27. And Micaiah said, If thou return at all in peace, the Lord hath not spoken by me. And he said, Hear ye peoples, all of you.

28. So the king of Israel and Jehoshaphat the king of Judah went up to Ramoth-gilead. 29. And the king of Israel said unto Jehoshaphat, I will disguise myself, and go into the battle; but put thou on thy robes. So the king of Israel disguised himself, and they went into the battle. 30. Now the king of Syria had commanded the captains of his chariots, saying, Fight neither with small nor great, save only with the king of Israel. 31. And it came to pass, when the captains of the chariots saw Jehoshaphat, that they said, It is the king of Israel. Therefore, they turned aside to fight against him: but Jehoshaphat cried out, and the Lord helped him; and God moved them to depart from him. 32. And it came to pass, when the captains of the chariots saw that it was not the king of Israel, that they turned back from pursuing him. 33. And a certain man drew his bow at a venture, and smote the king of Israel between the joints of the harness: wherefore he said to the driver of his chariot, Turn thine hand, and carry me out of the host; for I am sore wounded. 34. And the battle increased that day: howbeit the king of Israel stayed himself up in his chariot against the Syrians until the even: and about the time of the going down of the sun he died.

Rebuke of Jehoshaphat by Jehu

II Chron. 19:1. And Jehoshaphat the king of Judah returned to his house in peace to Jerusalem. 2. And Jehu the son of Hanani the seer went out to meet him, and said to king Jehoshaphat, Shouldest thou help the wicked, and love them that hate the Lord? for this thing wrath is upon thee from before the Lord. 3. Nevertheless there are good things found in thee, in that thou hast put away the Asheroth out of the land, and hast set thine heart to seek God.

Accession and Character of Ahaziah

I Kings 22:39. Now the rest of the acts of Ahab, and all that he did, and the ivory house which he built, and all the cities that he built, are they not written in the book of the chronicles of the kings of Israel? 40. So Ahab slept with his fathers; and Ahaziah his son reigned in his stead. 51. Ahaziah the son of Ahab began to reign over Israel in Samaria in the seventeenth year of Jehoshaphat king of Judah, and he reigned two years over Israel. 52. And he did that which was evil in the sight of the Lord, and walked in the way of his father, and in the way of his mother, and in the way of Jereboam the son of Nebat, wherein he made Israel to sin. 53. And he served Baal, and worshipped him, and provoked to anger the Lord, the God of Israel, according to all that his father had done.

Reforms of Jehoshaphat

II Chron. 19:4. And Jehoshaphat dwelt at Jerusalem: and he went out again among the people from Beer-sheba to the hill country of Ephraim, and brought them back unto the Lord, the God of their fathers. 5. And he set judges in the land throughout all the fenced cities of Judah, city by city, and said to the judges, 6. Consider what ye do: for ye judge not for man, but for the Lord; and he is with you in the judgement. 7. Now therefore let the fear of the Lord be upon you: take heed and do it; for there is no iniquity with the Lord our God, nor respect of persons, nor taking of gifts. 8. Moreover in Jerusalem did Jehoshaphat set of the Levites and the priests, and of the heads of the fathers' houses of Israel, for the judgement of the Lord, and for controversies, And they returned to Jerusalem. 9. And he charged them, saying, Thus shall ye do in the fear of the Lord, faithfully, and with a perfect heart. 10. And whensoever any controversy shall come to you from your brethren that dwell in their cities, between blood and blood, between law and commandment, statutes and judgements, ye shall warn them, that they be not guilty towards the Lord, and so wrath come upon you and upon your brethren: this do, and ye shall not be guilty. 11. And, behold, Amariah the chief priest is over you in all matters of the Lord; and Zebadiah the son of Ishmael, the ruler of the house of Judah, in all the king's matters: also the Levites shall be officers before you. Deal courageously, and the Lord be with the good.

Alliance of Jehoshaphat and Ahaziah

And there was no king in Edom; a deputy was king. And after this did Jehoshaphat make peace and join himself with Ahaziah king of Israel: the same did very wickedly: *[1] and he joined himself with him to make ships to go to Tarshish: *[2] and they made the ships in Ezion-geber. Then Eliezer the son of Dodavahu of Mareshah prophesied against Jehoshaphat, saying, Because thou hast joined thyself with Ahaziah, the Lord hath destroyed thy works. And the ships were broken at Ezion-geber, that they were not able to go to Tarshish. Then said Ahaziah the son of Ahab unto Jehoshaphat, Let my servants go with thy servants in the ships. But Jehoshaphat would not.

---

*[1] I Kings 22:48. "Jehoshaphat made ships of Tarshish to go to Ophir for gold." *[2] II Chron. 20:36. "Jehoshaphat and Ahaziah made ships to go to Tarshish: and they were made in Ezion-geber." See Appendix C. Chronicles III, 2, (8).

(I Kings 22:) 47. And there was no king in Edom; a deputy was king. 44. And　　　　　Jehoshaphat made peace with the king of Israel. 48. ((Jehoshaphat made ships of Tarshish to go to Ophir for gold　　　　　　　　　　　but they went not; for the ships were broken at Ezion-geber.　　　49. Then said Ahaziah the son of Ahab unto Jehoshaphat, Let my servants go with thy servants in the ships. But Jehoshaphat would not.))	(II Chron. 20:) 35. And after this did Jehoshaphat join himself with Ahaziah king of Israel: the same did very wickedly: 36. ((and he joined himself with him to make ships to go to Tarshish: and they made the ships in Ezion-geber. 37. Then Eliezer the son of Dodavahu of Mareshah prophesied against Jehoshaphat, saying, Because thou hast joined thyself with Ahaziah, the Lord hath destroyed thy works. And the ships were broken　　　　that they were not able to go to Tarshish.))

Sentence of Elijah upon Ahaziah

II Kings 1:2. And Ahaziah fell down through the lattice in his upper chamber that was in Samaria, and was sick: and he sent messengers, and said unto them, Go, inquire of Baal-zebub the god of Ekron whether I shall recover of this sickness. 3. But the angel of the Lord said to Elijah the Tishbite, Arise, go up to meet the messengers of the king of Samaria, and say unto them, Is it because there is no God in Israel, that ye go to inquire of Baal-zebub the god of Ekron? 4. Now therefore thus saith the Lord, Thou shalt not come down from the bed whither thou art gone up, but shalt surely die. And Elijah departed. 5. And the messengers returned unto him, and he said unto them, Why is it that ye are returned? 6. And they said unto him, There came up a man to meet us, and said unto us, Go, turn again unto the king that sent you, and say unto him, Thus saith the Lord, Is it because there is no God in Israel, that thou sendest to inquire of Baal-zebub the god of Ekron? therefore thou shalt not come down from the bed whither thou art gone up, but shalt surely die. 7. And he said unto them, What manner of man was he which came up to meet you, and told you these words? 8. And they answered him, He was an hairy man, and girt with a girdle of leather about his loins. And he said, It is Elijah the Tishbite. 9. Then the king sent unto him a captain of fifty with his fifty. And he went up to him: and, behold, he sat on the top of the hill. And he spake unto him, O man of God, the king hath said, Come down. 10. And Elijah answered and said to the captain of fifty, If I be a man of God, let fire come down from heaven, and consume thee and thy fifty. And there came down fire from heaven, and consumed him and his fifty. 11. And again he sent unto him another captain of fifty with his fifty, and he answered and said unto him, O man of God, thus hath the king said, Come down quickly. 12. And Elijah answered and said unto them, If I be a man of God, let fire come down from heaven, and consume thee and thy fifty. And the fire of God came down from heaven, and consumed him and his fifty. 13. And again he sent the captain of a third fifty with his fifty. And the third captain of fifty went up, and came and fell on his knees before Elijah, and besought him, and said unto him, O man of God, I pray thee, let my life, and the life of these fifty thy servants, be precious in thy sight. 14. Behold, there came fire down from heaven, and consumed the two former captains of fifty with their fifties: but now let my life be precious in thy sight. 15. And the angel of the Lord said unto Elijah, Go down with him: be not afraid of him. And he arose, and went down with him unto the king. 16. And he said unto him, Thus saith the Lord, Forasmuch as thou hast sent messengers to inquire of Baal-zebub the god of Ekron, is it because there is no God in Israel to inquire of his word? therefore thou shalt not come down from the bed whither thou art gone up, but shalt surely die. 17a. So he died according to the word of the Lord which Elijah had spoken. 18. Now the rest of the acts of Ahaziah which he did, are they not written in the book of the chronicles of the kings of Israel?

The Wondrous Deliverance by Prayer

II Chron. 20:1. And it came to pass after this, that the children of Moab, and the children of Ammon, and with them some of the Ammonites, came against Jehoshaphat to battle. 2. Then there came some that told Jehoshaphat, saying, There cometh a great multitude against thee from beyond the sea from Syria; and, behold, they be in Hazazon-tamar (the same is En-gedi). 3. And Jehoshaphat feared, and set himself to seek unto the Lord; and he proclaimed a fast throughout all Judah. 4. And Judah gathered themselves together, to seek help of the Lord: even out of all the cities of Judah they came to seek the Lord. 5. And Jehoshaphat stood in the congregation of Judah and Jerusalem, in the house of the Lord, before the new court; 6. and he said, O Lord, the God of our fathers, art not thou God in heaven? and art not thou ruler over all the kingdoms of the nations? and in thine hand is power and might, so that none is able to withstand thee. 7. Didst not thou, O our God, drive out the inhabitants of this land before thy people Israel, and gavest it to the seed of Abraham thy friend for ever? 8. And they dwelt therein, and have built thee a sanctuary therein for thy name, saying, 9. If evil come upon us, the sword, judgement, or pestilence, or famine, we will stand before this house, and before thee, (for thy name is in this house,) and cry unto thee in our affliction, and thou wilt hear and save. 10. And now, behold, the children of Ammon and Moab and mount Seir, whom thou wouldest not let Israel invade, when they came out of the land of Egypt, but they turned aside from them, and destroyed them not; 11. behold, how they reward us, to come to cast us out of our possession, which thou hast given us to inherit. 12. O our God, wilt thou not judge them? for we have no might against this great company that cometh against us; neither know we what to do: but our eyes are upon thee. 13. And all Judah stood before the Lord, with their little ones, their wives, and their children.*

14. Then upon Jehaziel, the son of Zechariah, the son of Benaiah, the son of Jeiel, the son of Mattaniah, the Levite, of the sons of Asaph, came the spirit of the Lord in the midst of the congregation, 15. and he said, Hearken ye, all Judah, and ye inhabitants of Jerusalem, and thou king Jehoshaphat: thus saith the Lord unto you, Fear not ye, neither be dismayed by reason of this great multitude; for the battle is not yours, but God's. 16. To-morrow go ye down against them: behold, they come up by the ascent of Ziz; and ye shall find them at the end of the valley, before the wilderness of Jeruel. 17. Ye shall not need to fight in this battle: set yourselves, stand ye still, and see the salvation of the Lord with you, O Judah and Jerusalem: fear not: nor be dismayed: to-morrow go out against them; for the Lord is with you. 18. And Jehoshaphat bowed his head with his face to the ground: and all Judah and the inhabitants of Jerusalem fell down before the Lord, worshipping the Lord.

Praise, Song, Thanksgiving and Blessing

19. And the Levites, of the children of the Kohathites and of the children of the Korahites, stood up to praise the Lord, the God of Israel, with an exceeding loud voice. 20. And they rose early in the morning, and went forth into the wilderness of Tekoa: and as they went forth, Jehoshaphat stood and said, Hear me, O Judah and ye inhabitants of Jerusalem; believe in the Lord your God, so shall ye be established, believe his prophets, so shall ye prosper. 21. And when he had taken counsel with the people, he appointed them that should sing unto the Lord, and praise the beauty of holiness, as they went out before the army, and say, Give thanks unto the Lord; for his mercy endureth for ever. †22. And when they began to sing and to praise, the Lord set liers in wait against the children of Ammon, Moab, and mount Seir, which were come against Judah; and they were smitten. 23. For the children of Ammon and Moab stood up against the inhabitants of mount Seir, utterly to slay and destroy them: and when they had made an end of the inhabitants of Seir, every one helped to destroy another. 24. And when Judah came to the watch-tower of the wilderness, they looked upon the multitude; and, behold, they were dead bodies fallen to the earth, and there were none that escaped. 25. And when Jehoshaphat and his people came to take the spoil of them, they found among them in abundance both riches and dead bodies, and precious jewels, which they stripped off for them-

---
* Read Psalm 83 : 1–18. Keep not thou silence, O God.
† Psalm 136 : 1–26. Refrain of each verse.

selves, more than they could carry away: and they were three days in taking of the spoil, it was so much. 26. And on the fourth day they assembled themselves in the valley of Beracah; for there they blessed the Lord: therefore the name of that place was called the valley of Beracah, unto this day. 27. Then they returned, every man of Judah and Jerusalem and Jehoshaphat in the forefront of them, to go again to Jerusalem with joy; for the Lord had made them to rejoice over their enemies. 28.* And they came to Jerusalem with psalteries and harps and trumpets unto the house of the Lord. 29. And the fear of God was on all the kingdoms of the countries, when they heard that the Lord fought against the enemies of Israel. 30. So the realm of Jehoshaphat was quiet: for his God gave him rest round about.

Mantle of Elijah Falls on Elisha
II Kings 2:1. And it came to pass, when the Lord would take up Elijah by a whirlwind into heaven, that Elijah went with Elisha from Gilgal. 2. And Elijah said unto Elisha, Tarry here, I pray thee; for the Lord hath sent me as far as Beth-el. And Elisha said, As the Lord liveth, and as thy soul liveth, I will not leave thee. So they went down to Beth-el. 3. And the sons of the prophets that were at Beth-el came forth to Elisha, and said unto him, Knowest thou that the Lord will take away thy master from thy head to-day? And he said, Yea, I know it; hold ye your peace. 4. And Elijah said unto him, Elisha, tarry here, I pray thee; for the Lord hath sent me to Jericho. And he said, As the Lord liveth, and as thy soul liveth, I will not leave thee. So they came to Jericho. 5. And the sons of the prophets that were at Jericho came near to Elisha, and said unto him, Knowest thou that the Lord will take away thy master from thy head to-day? And he answered, Yea, I know it; hold ye your peace. 6. And Elijah said unto him, Tarry here, I pray thee; for the Lord hath sent me to Jordan. And he said, As the Lord liveth, and as thy soul liveth, I will not leave thee. And they two went on. 7. And fifty men of the sons of the prophets went, and stood over against them afar off: and they two stood by Jordan. 8. And Elijah took his mantle, and wrapped it together, and smote the waters, and they were divided hither and thither, so that they two went over on dry ground. 9. And it came to pass, when they were gone over, that Elijah said unto Elisha, Ask what I shall do for thee, before I be taken from thee. And Elisha said, I pray thee, let a double portion of thy spirit be upon me. 10. And he said, Thou hast asked a hard thing: nevertheless, if thou see me when I am taken from thee, it shall be so unto thee; but if not, it shall not be so. 11. And it came to pass, as they still went on, and talked, that, behold, there appeared a chariot of fire, and horses of fire, which parted them both asunder; and Elijah went up by a whirlwind into heaven. 12. And Elisha saw it, and he cried, My father, my father, the chariots of Israel and the horsemen thereof! And he saw him no more: and he took hold of his own clothes, and rent them in two pieces. 13. He took up also the mantle of Elijah that fell from him, and went back, and stood by the bank of Jordan. 14. And he took the mantle of Elijah that fell from him, and smote the waters, and said, Where is the Lord, the God of Elijah? and when he also had smitten the waters, they were divided hither and thither; and Elisha went over. 15. And when the sons of the prophets which were at Jericho over against him saw him, they said, The spirit of Elijah doth rest on Elisha. And they came to meet him, and bowed themselves to the ground before him. 16. And they said unto him, Behold now, there be with thy servants fifty strong men; let them go, we pray thee, and seek thy master; lest peradventure the spirit of the Lord hath taken him up, and cast him upon some mountain, or into some valley. And he said, Ye shall not send. 17. And when they urged him till he was ashamed,

---
*Read Psalms 46, 47, and 48.

he said, Send. They sent therefore fifty men; and they sought three days, but found him not. 18. And they came back to him, while he tarried at Jericho; and he said unto them, Did I not say unto you, Go not?

Beginning of Elisha's Miracles

19. And the men of the city said unto Elisha, Behold, we pray thee, the situation of this city is pleasant, as my lord seeth: but the water is naught, and the land miscarrieth. 20. And he said, Bring me a new cruse, and put salt therein. And they brought it to him. 21. And he went forth unto the spring of the waters, and cast salt therein, and said, Thus saith the Lord, I have healed these waters: there shall not be from thence any more death or miscarrying. 22. So the waters were healed unto this day, according to the word of Elisha which he spake.

23. And he went up from thence unto Beth-el: and as he was going up by the way, there came forth little children out of the city, and mocked him, and said unto him, Go up, thou bald head; go up, thou bald head. 24. And he looked behind him and saw them, and cursed them in the name of the Lord. And there came forth two she-bears out of the wood, and tare forty and two children of them. 25. And he went from thence to mount Carmel, and from thence he returned to Samaria.

II Kings 4:1. Now there cried a certain woman of the wives of the sons of the prophets unto Elisha, saying, Thy servant my husband is dead: and thou knowest that thy servant did fear the Lord: and the creditor is come to take unto him my two children to be bondmen. 2. And Elisha said unto her, What shall I do for thee? tell me: What hast thou in the house? And she said, Thine handmaid hath not anything in the house, save a pot of oil. 3. Then he said, Go, borrow thee vessels abroad of all thy neighbours, even empty vessels; borrow not a few. 4. And thou shalt go in and shut the door upon thee and upon thy sons, and pour out into all those vessels; and thou shalt set aside that which is full. 5. So she went from him, and shut the door upon her and upon her sons; they brought the vessels to her, and she poured out. 6. And it came to pass, when the vessels were full, that she said unto her son, Bring me yet a vessel. And he said unto her, There is not a vessel more. And the oil stayed. 7. Then she came and told the man of God. And he said, Go, sell the oil, and pay thy debt, and live thou and thy sons of the rest.

38. And Elisha came again to Gilgal: and there was a dearth in the land, and the sons of the prophets were sitting before him; and he said unto his servant, Set on the great pot, and seethe pottage for the sons of the prophets. 39. And one went out into the field to gather herbs, and found a wild vine, and gathered thereof wild gourds his lap full, and came and shred them into the pot of pottage: for they knew them not. 40. So they poured out for the men to eat. And it came to pass, as they were eating of the pottage, that they cried out, and said, O man of God, there is death in the pot. And they could not eat thereof. 41. But he said, Then bring meal. And he cast it into the pot; and he said, Pour out for the people, that they may eat. And there was no harm in the pot.

42. And there came a man from Baal-shalishah, and brought the man of God bread of the first fruits, twenty loaves of barley, and fresh ears of corn in his sack. And he said, Give unto the people, that they may eat. 43. And his servants said, What, should I set this before an hundred men? But he said, Give the people, that they may eat; for thus saith the Lord, They shall eat, and shall leave thereof. 44. So he set it before them, and they did eat, and left thereof, according to the word of the Lord.

II Kings 6:1. And the sons of the prophet said unto Elisha, Behold now, the place where we dwell before thee is too strait for us. 2. Let us go, we pray thee, unto Jordan, and take thence every man a beam, and let us make us a place there, where we may dwell. And he answered, Go ye. 3. And one said, Be content, I pray thee, and go with thy servants. And he answered, I will go. 4. So he went with them. And when they came to Jordan, they cut down wood. 5. But as one was felling a beam, the axe-head fell into the water: and he cried, and said, Alas, my master! for it was borrowed. 6. And the man of God said, Where fell it? And he shewed him the place. And he cut down a stick, and cast it in thither, and made the iron to swim. 7. And he said, Take it up to thee. So he put out his hand, and took it.

JUDAH		ISRAEL	
THE HOUSE OF DAVID		THE HOUSE OF OMRI (Fourth)	
B. C. 956–915*		B. C. 930–917	
V Asa		I Omri	(6)
B. C. 917–876		B. C. 889–887	
B. C. 915–889 (Jehu)		B. C. 917–898	
VI Jehoshaphat	(Elijah) (Micaiah)	II Ahab	(7)
B. C. 876–851 (Eliezer)		B. C. 887–855	
B. C. 889–885		B. C. 898–897	
VII Jehoram	(Elijah)	III Ahaziah	(8)
B. C. 851–843		B. C. 855–854	
B. C. 885–883		B. C. 897–883	
VIII Ahaziah	(Elisha)	IV Jehoram	(9)
B. C. 843–842		B. C. 854–842	

SECTION XXVI

Allied Houses of David and Omri (Elisha)

Accession and Character of Jehoram

So (Ahaziah) died according to the word of the Lord which Elijah had spoken. And Jehoram the son of Ahab began to reign over Israel in Samaria in his stead, because he had no son, in the eighteenth year of Jehoshaphat king of Judah, in the *second* † year of Jehoram the son of Jehoshaphat, and he reigned twelve years. And he did that which was evil in the sight of the Lord; but not like his father, and like his mother: for he put away the pillar of Baal that his father had made. Nevertheless he cleaved unto the sins of Jereboam the son of Nebat, wherewith he made Israel to sin; he departed not therefrom. Now Mesha king of Moab was a sheepmaster; and he rendered unto the king of Israel the wool of an hundred thousand lambs, and an hundred thousand rams. But it came to pass that the king of Moab rebelled against the king of Israel when Ahab was dead.

---

* See Chronology Appendix A. Both systems of chronology are used, e.g., Asa $\frac{956 \text{ (Usher)}}{917 \text{ (Revised)}}$

† We are told (II Kings 8:16) "And in the *fifth* year of Joram the son of Ahab, Jehoshaphat being then king of Judah, Jehoram the son of Jehoshaphat began to reign." If now, as above stated, Jehoram the son of Jehoshaphat was in his *second* year when Joram the son of Ahab began to reign, then the *fifth* year of the latter would be the *seventh* year of the former, and not the *first*, when, as stated, he began to reign. This discrepancy can be reconciled on the supposition that Jehoram was co-regent with his father Jehoshaphat during this period. One passage refers to the beginning of his co-regency, and the other to the beginning of his reign, as sole king. This supposition finds some confirmation in II Chron. 21:1–4: "1. And Jehoshaphat slept with his fathers, and was buried with his fathers in the city of David; and Jehoram his son reigned in his stead. 2. And he had brethren the sons of Jehoshaphat, Azariah, and Jehiel, and Zechariah, and Azariah, and Michael, and Shephatiah: all these were the sons of Jehoshaphat king of Israel. 3. And their father gave them great gifts, of silver, and of gold, and of precious things, with fenced cities in Judah: but the kingdom gave he to Jehoram, because he was the firstborn. 4. Now when Jehoram was risen up over the kingdom of his father, and had strengthened himself, he slew all his brethren with the sword, and divers also of the princes of Israel."

Now it is natural to suppose that this division of great gifts and fenced cities to his six brothers was made when he became co-regent. This beneficent arrangement for all his children was put an end to when Jehoram became sole king, and slew all his brethren and divers princes.

SECT. XXVI. THE DIVIDED KINGDOM

(II Kings 1:) 17. So he died according to the word of the Lord which Elijah had spoken. And Jehoram began to reign in his stead in the second year of Jehoram the son of Jehoshaphat king of Judah; because he had no son.

(II Kings 1:) 1. And Moab rebelled against Israel after the death of Ahab.

(II Kings 3:) 1. Now Jehoram the son of Ahab began to reign over Israel in Samaria in the eighteenth year of Jehoshaphat king of Judah, and reigned twelve years. 2. And he did that which was evil in the sight of the Lord; but not like his father, and like his mother: for he put away the pillar of Baal that his father had made. 3. Nevertheless he cleaved unto the sins of Jereboam the son of Nebat, wherewith he made Israel to sin; he departed not therefrom.
4. Now Mesha king of Moab was a sheep-master; and he rendered unto the king of Israel the wool of an hundred thousand lambs, and an hundred thousand rams. 5. But it came to pass that the king of Moab rebelled against the king of Israel, when Ahab was dead.

Alliance of Jehoshaphat and Jehoram

II Kings 3:6. And king Jehoram went out of Samaria at that time, and mustered all Israel. 7. And he went and sent to Jehoshaphat the king of Judah, saying, The king of Moab hath rebelled against me: wilt thou go with me against Moab to battle? And he said, I will go up: I am as thou art, my people as thy people, my horses as thy horses. 8. And he said, Which way shall we go up? And he answered, The way of the wilderness of Edom. 9. So the king of Israel went, and the king of Judah, and the king of Edom: and they made a circuit of seven days' journey: and there was no water for the host, nor for the beasts that followed them. 10. And the king of Israel said, Alas! for the Lord hath called these three kings together to deliver them into the hand of Moab. 11. But Jehoshaphat said, Is there not here a prophet of the Lord, that we may inquire of the Lord by him? And one of the king of Israel's servants answered and said, Elisha the son of Shaphat is here, which poured water on the hands of Elijah. 12. And Jehoshaphat said, The word of the Lord is with him. So the king of Israel and Jehoshaphat and the king of Edom went down to him.

Prediction and Prophecy of Elisha

13. And Elisha said unto the king of Israel, What have I to do with thee? get thee to the prophets of thy father, and to the prophets of thy mother. And the king of Israel said unto him, Nay: for the Lord hath called these three kings together to deliver them into the hand of Moab. 14. And Elisha said, As the Lord of hosts liveth, before whom I stand, surely, were it not that I regard the presence of Jehoshaphat the king of Judah, I would not look toward thee, nor see thee. 15. But now bring me a minstrel. And it came to pass, when the minstrel played, that the hand of the Lord came upon him. 16. And he said, Thus saith the Lord, Make this valley full of trenches. 17. For thus saith the Lord, Ye shall not see wind, neither shall ye see rain, yet that valley shall be filled with water: and ye shall drink, both ye and your cattle and your beasts. 18. And this is but a light thing in the sight of the Lord: he will also deliver the Moabites into your hand. 19. And ye shall smite every fenced city, and every choice city, and shall fell every good tree, and stop all fountains of water, and mar every good piece of land with stones. 20. And it came to pass in the morning, about the time of offering the oblation, that, behold, there came water by the way of Edom, and the country was filled with water. 21. Now when all the Moabites heard that the kings were come up to fight against them, they gathered themselves together, all that were able to put on armour, and upward, and stood on the border. 22. And they rose up early in the morning, and the sun shone upon the water, and the Moabites saw the water over against them as red as blood: and they said, This is blood: the kings are surely destroyed, and they have smitten each man his fellow: now, therefore, Moab to the spoil. 24. And when they came to the camp of Israel, the Israelites rose up and smote the Moabites, so that they fled before them: and they went forward into the land smiting the Moabites. 25. And they beat down the cities; and on every good piece of land they cast every man his stone, and filled it; and they stopped all the fountains of water, and felled all the good trees: until in Kir-haraseth only they left the stones thereof; howbeit the slingers went about it, and smote it. 26. And when the king of Moab saw that the battle was too sore for him, he took with him seven hundred men that drew sword, to break through unto the king of Edom: but they could not. 27. Then he took his eldest son that should have reigned in his stead, and offered him for a burnt offering upon the wall. And there was great wrath against Israel: and they departed from him, and returned to their own land.

SECT. XXVI — THE DIVIDED KINGDOM

Prophet's Chamber at Shunem

II Kings 4:8. And it fell on a day, that Elisha passed to Shunem, where was a great woman; and she constrained him to eat bread. And so it was, that as oft as he passed by, he turned in thither to eat bread. 9. And she said unto her husband, Behold now, I perceive that this is an holy man of God, which passed by us continually. 10. Let us make, I pray thee, a little chamber on the wall; and let us set for him there a bed, and a table, and a stool, and a candlestick: and it shall be, when he cometh to us, that he shall turn in thither. 11. And it fell on a day, that he came thither, and he turned into the chamber and lay there. 12. And he said to Gehazi his servant, Call this Shunamite. And when he had called her, she stood before him.

Elisha's Appreciation and Reward

13. And he said unto him, Say now unto her, Behold, thou hast been careful for us with all this care; what is to be done for thee? wouldest thou be spoken for to the king, or to the captain of the host? And she answered, I dwell among mine own people. 14. And he said, What then is to be done for her? And Gehazi answered, Verily she hath no son, and her husband is old. 15. And he said, Call her. And when he had called her, she stood in the door. 16. And he said, At this season, when the time cometh round, thou shalt embrace a son. And she said, Nay, my lord, thou man of God, do not lie unto thine handmaid. 17. And the woman conceived, and bare a son at that season, when the time came round, as Elisha had said unto her. 18. And when the child was grown, it fell on a day, that he went out to his father to the reapers. 19. And he said unto his father, My head, my head. And he said to his servant, Carry him to his mother. 20. And when he had taken him, and brought him to his mother, he sat on her knees till noon, and then died. 21. And she went up, and laid him on the bed of the man of God, and shut the door upon him, and went out. 22. And she called unto her husband, and said, Send me, I pray thee, one of the servants, and one of the asses, that I may run to the man of God, and come again. 23. And he said, Wherefore wilt thou go to him to-day? it is neither new moon nor sabbath. And she said, It shall be well. 24. Then she saddled an ass, and said to her servant, Drive, and go forward; slacken me not the riding, except I bid thee. 25. So she went, and came unto the man of God to mount Carmel. And it came to pass, when the man of God saw her afar off, that he said to Gehazi his servant, Behold, yonder is the Shunamite: 26. run, I pray thee, now to meet her, and say unto her, Is it well with thee? is it well with thy husband? is it well with the child? And she answered, It is well. 27. And when she came to the man of God to the hill, she caught hold of his feet. And Gehazi came near to thrust her away; but the man of God said, Let her alone: for her soul is vexed within her; and the Lord hath hid it from me, and hath not told me. 28. Then she said, Did I desire a son of my lord? did I not say, Do not deceive me? 29. Then he said to Gehazi, Gird up thy loins, and take my staff in thine hand, and go thy way: if thou meet any man, salute him not; and if any salute thee, answer him not again: and lay my staff upon the face of the child. 30. And the mother of the child said, As the Lord liveth, and as thy soul liveth, I will not leave thee. And he arose, and followed her. 31. And Gehazi passed on before them, and laid the staff upon the face of the child; but there was neither voice, nor hearing. Wherefore he returned to meet him and told him, saying, The child is not awaked. 32. And when Elisha was come into the house, behold, the child was dead, and laid upon his bed. 33. He went in therefore, and shut the door upon them twain, and prayed unto the Lord. 34. And he went up and lay upon the child, and put his mouth upon his mouth, and his eyes upon his eyes, and his hands upon his hands: and he stretched himself upon him; and the

flesh of the child waxed warm. 35. Then he returned, and walked in the house once to and fro, and went up, and stretched himself upon him: and the child sneezed seven times, and the child opened his eyes. 36. And he called Gehazi, and said, Call this Shunamite. So he called her. And when she was come unto him, he said, Take up thy son. 37. Then she went in, and fell at his feet, and bowed herself to the ground; and she took up her son, and went out.

Saved from Famine and Loss of Land
II Kings 8:1. Now Elisha had spoken unto the woman, whose son he had restored to life, saying, Arise, and go thou and thine household, and so journey wheresoever thou canst sojourn: for the Lord hath called for a famine; and it shall also come upon the land seven years. 2. And the woman arose, and did according to the word of the man of God: and she went with her household, and sojourned in the land of the Philistines seven years. 3. And it came to pass at the seven years' end, that the woman returned out of the land of the Philistines: and she went forth to cry unto the king for her house and for her land. 4. Now the king was talking with Gehazi the servant of the man of God, saying, Tell me, I pray thee, all the great things that Elisha hath done. 5. And it came to pass, as he was telling the king how he had restored to life him that was dead, that, behold, the woman, whose son he had restored to life, cried to the king for her house and for her land. And Gehazi said, My lord, O king, this is the woman, and this is her son, whom Elisha restored to life. 6. And when the king asked the woman, she told him. So the king appointed unto her a certain officer, saying, Restore all that was hers, and all the fruits of the field since the day that she left the land, even until now.

The Healing of Naaman's Leprosy
II Kings 5:1. Now Naaman, captain of the host of the king of Syria, was a great man with his master, and honourable, because by him the Lord had given victory unto Syria: he was also a mighty man of valour, but he was a leper. 2. And the Syrians had gone out in bands, and had brought away captive out of the land of Israel a little maid; and she waited on Naaman's wife. 3. And she said unto her mistress, Would God my lord were with the prophet that is in Samaria! then would he recover him of his leprosy. 4. And one went in, and told his lord, saying, Thus and thus said the maid that is of the land of Israel. 5. And the king of Syria said, Go to, go, and I will send a letter unto the king of Israel. And he departed, and took with him ten talents of silver, and six thousand pieces of gold, and ten changes of raiment. 6. And he brought the letter to the king of Israel, saying, And now when this letter is come unto thee, behold, I have sent Naaman my servant to thee, that thou mayest recover him of his leprosy. 7. And it came to pass, when the king of Israel had read the letter, that he rent his clothes, and said, Am I God, to kill and to make alive, that this man doth send unto me to recover a man of his leprosy? but consider, I pray you, and see how he seeketh a quarrel against me. 8. And it was so, when Elisha the man of God heard that the king of Israel had rent his clothes, that he sent to the king, saying, Wherefore hast thou rent thy clothes? let him come now to me, and he shall know that there is a prophet in Israel. 9. So Naaman came with his horses and with his chariots, and stood at the door of the house of Elisha. 10. And Elisha sent a messenger unto him, saying, Go and wash in Jordan seven times, and thy flesh shall come again to thee, and thou shalt be clean. 11. But Naaman was wroth, and went away, and said, Behold, I thought, He will surely come out to me, and stand, and call on the name of the Lord his God, and wave his hand over the place, and recover the leper. 12. Are not Abanah and Pharper, the rivers of Damascus, better than all the waters of Israel? may I not wash

in them and be clean? So he turned and went away in a rage. 13. And his servants came near, and spake unto him, and said, My father, if the prophet had bid thee do some great thing, wouldest thou not have done it? how much rather then, when he saith to thee, Wash, and be clean? 14. Then went he down, and dipped himself seven times in Jordan, according to the saying of the man of God: and his flesh came again like unto the flesh of a little child, and he was clean. 15. And he returned to the man of God, he and all his company, and came, and stood before him: and he said, Behold now, I know that there is no God in all the earth, but in Israel: now therefore, I pray thee, Take a present of thy servant. 16. But he said, As the Lord liveth, before whom I stand, I will receive none. And he urged him to take it; but he refused. 17. And Naaman said, If not, yet I pray thee let there be given to thy servant two mules' burden of earth; for thy servant will henceforth offer neither burnt offering nor sacrifice unto other gods, but unto the Lord. 18. In this thing the Lord pardon thy servant; when my master goeth into the house of Rimmon to worship there, and he leaneth on my hand, and I bow myself in the house of Rimmon, when I bow myself in the house of Rimmon, the Lord pardon thy servant in this thing. 19. And he said unto him, Go in peace. So he departed from him a little way.

Leprosy of Naaman Put On Gehazi 20. But Gehazi, the servant of Elisha the man of God, said, Behold, my master hath spared this Naaman the Syrian, in not receiving at his hands that which he brought: as the Lord liveth, I will run after him, and take somewhat of him. 21. So Gehazi followed after Naaman. And when Naaman saw one running after him, he lighted down from the chariot to meet him, and said, Is all well? 22. And he said, All is well. My master hath sent me, saying, Behold, even now there be come to me from the hill country of Ephraim two young men of the sons of the prophets; give them, I pray thee, a talent of silver, and two changes of raiment. 23. And Naaman said, Be content, take two talents. And he urged him, and bound two talents of silver in two bags, with two changes of raiment, and laid them upon two of his servants; and they bare them before him. 24. And when he came to the hill, he took them from their hand, and bestowed them in the house: and he let the men go, and they departed. 25. But he went in, and stood before his master. And Elisha said unto him, Whence comest thou, Gehazi? And he said, Thy servant went no whither. 26. And he said unto him, Went not mine heart with thee, when the man turned again from his chariot to meet thee? Is it a time to receive money, and to receive garments, and oliveyards, and vineyards, and sheep and oxen, and menservants, and maidservants? 27. The leprosy therefore of Naaman shall cleave unto thee, and unto thy seed for ever. And he went out from his presence a leper as white as snow.

Syrian Bands Smitten with Blindness II Kings 6:8. Now the king of Syria warred against Israel; and he took counsel with his servants, saying, In such and such a place shall be my camp. 9. And the man of God sent unto the king of Israel, saying, Beware that thou pass not such a place; for thither the Syrians are coming down. 10. And the king of Israel sent to the place which the man of God told him and warned him of; and he saved himself there not once nor twice. 11. And the heart of the king of Syria was sore troubled for this thing; and he called his servants, and said unto them, Will ye not shew me which of us is for the king of Israel? 12. And one of his servants said, Nay, my lord, O king: but Elisha, the prophet that is in Israel, telleth the king of Israel the words that thou speakest in thy bedchamber. 13. And he said, Go and see where he is, that I may send and fetch him. And it was told him, saying, Behold, he is in Dothan. 14. Therefore sent he thither horses, and chariots, and a great host: and they came by night and compassed the city about. 15. And when the servant of the man of God was risen early and gone forth, behold, an host with horses and chariots was round about the city. And his servant said unto him, Alas, my master! how shall we do? 16. And he answered, Fear not; for they that be with us are more than they that be with them. 17. And Elisha prayed, and said, Lord, I pray thee, Open his eyes, that he may see. And the Lord opened the eyes of the young man; and he saw: and, behold, the mountain was full of horses and chariots of fire round about Elisha. 18. And when they came down to him, Elisha prayed unto the Lord, and said, Smite this people, I pray thee, with blindness. And he smote them with blindness according to the word of Elisha. 19. And Elisha said unto them, This is not the way, neither is this the city: follow me and I will bring you to the man whom ye seek. And he led them to Samaria. 20. And it came to pass, when they were come into Samaria, that Elisha said, Lord, open the eyes of these men, that they may see. And the Lord opened their eyes, and they saw; and, behold, they were in the midst of Samaria. 21. And the king of Israel said unto Elisha, when he saw them, My father, Shall I smite them? shall I smite them? 22. And he answered, Thou shalt not smite them: wouldst thou smite those whom thou hast taken captive with thy sword and with thy bow? set bread and water before them, that they may eat and drink, and go to their master. 23. And he prepared great provision for them: and when they had eaten and drunk, he sent them away, and they went to their master. And the bands of Syria came no more into the land of Israel.

Ben-hadad Besieges Samaria

24. And it came to pass after this, that Ben-hadad king of Syria gathered all his host, and went up and besieged Samaria. 25. And there was a great famine in Samaria: and, behold they besieged it, until an ass's head was sold for fourscore pieces of silver, and the fourth part of a kab of dove's dung for five pieces of silver. 26. And as the king of Israel was passing by upon the wall, there cried a woman unto him, saying, Help, my lord, O king. 27. And he said, If the Lord do not help thee, whence shall I help thee? out of the threshing floor, or out of the winepress? 28. And the king said unto her, What aileth thee? And she answered, This woman said unto me, Give thy son, that we may eat him to-day, and we will eat my son to-morrow. 29. So we boiled my son, and did eat him: and I said unto her on the next day, Give thy son that we may eat him: and she had hid her son. 30. And it came to pass, when the king heard the words of the woman, that he rent his clothes; (now he was passing by upon the wall;) and the people looked, and, behold, he had sackcloth within upon his flesh. 31. Then he said, God do so to me, and more also, if the head of Elisha the son of Shaphat shall stand on him this day. 32. But Elisha sat in his house, and the elders sat with him; and the king sent a man from before him: but ere the messenger came to him, he said to the elders, See ye how this son of a murderer hath sent to take away mine head? look, when the messenger cometh, shut the door, and hold the door fast against him: is not the sound of his master's feet behind him? 33. And while he yet talked with them, behold the messenger came down unto him: and he said, Behold, this evil is of the Lord; why should I wait for the Lord any longer?

Predicted Plenty and Deliverance

II Kings 7:1. And Elisha said, Hear ye the word of the Lord: thus saith the Lord, To-morrow about this time shall a measure of fine flour be sold for a shekel, and two measures of barley for a shekel, in the gate of Samaria. 2. Then the captain on whose hand the king leaned answered the man of God, and said, Behold, if the Lord should make windows in heaven, might this thing be? And he said, Behold, thou shalt see it with thine eyes, but shalt not eat thereof. 3. Now there were four leprous men at the entering in of the gate: and they said one to another, Why sit we here until we die? 4. If we say, We will enter into the city, then the famine is in the city, and we shall die there: and if we sit still here, we die also. Now therefore come, and let us fall unto the host of the Syrians: if they save us alive, we shall live; and if they kill us, we shall but die. 5. And they rose up in the twilight, to go unto the camp of the Syrians: and when they were come to the outermost part of the camp of the Syrians, behold, there was no man there. 6. For the Lord had made the host of the Syrians to hear a noise of chariots, and a noise of horses, even the noise of a great host: and they said one to another, Lo, the king of Israel hath hired against us the kings of the Hittites, and the kings of the Egyptians, to come upon us. 7. Wherefore they arose and fled in the twilight, and left their tents, and their horses, and their asses, even the camp as it was, and fled for their life. 8. And when these lepers came to the outermost part of the camp, they went into one tent, and did eat and drink, and carried thence silver and gold, and raiment, and went and hid it; and they came back, and entered into another tent, and carried thence also, and went and hid it. 9. Then they said one to another, We do not well: this day is a day of good tidings, and we hold our peace: if we tarry till the morning light, punishment will overtake us: now therefore come, let us go and tell the king's household. 10. So they came and called unto the porters of the city: and they told them, saying, We came to the camp of the Syrians, and, behold, there was no man there, neither voice of man, but the horses tied, and the asses tied, and the tents as they were. 11. And he called the porters; and they told it to the king's household within. 12. And the king arose in the night, and said unto his servants, I will now shew you what the Syrians have done to us. They know that we be hungry; therefore are they gone out of the camp to hide themselves in the field, saying, When they come out of the city, we shall take them alive, and get into the city. 13. And one of his servants answered and said, Let some take, I pray thee, five of the horses that remain, which are left in the city, (behold, they are as all the multitude of Israel that are left in it: behold, they are as all the multitude of Israel that are consumed:) and let us send and see. 14. They took therefore two chariots with horses; and the king sent after the host of the Syrians, saying, Go and see. 15. And they went after them unto Jordan: and, lo, all the way was full of garments and vessels, which the Syrians had cast away in their haste. And the messengers returned, and told the king. 16. And the people went out, and spoiled the camp of the Syrians. So a measure of fine flour was sold for a shekel, and two measures of barley for a shekel, according to the word of the Lord. 17. And the king appointed the captain on whose arm he leaned to have charge of the gate: and the people trode upon him in the gate, and he died as the man of God had said, who spake when the king come down to him. 18. And it came to pass, as the man of God had spoken to the king, saying, Two measures of barley for a shekel, and a measure of fine flour for a shekel, shall be to-morrow about this time in the gate of Samaria; 19. and that captain answered the man of God, and said, Now, behold, if the Lord should make windows in heaven, might such a thing be? and he said, Behold thou shalt see it with thine eyes, but shalt not eat thereof: 20. it came to pass even so unto him; for the people trode upon him in the gate, and he died.

II Kings 8:7. And Elisha came to Damascus; and Ben-hadad the king of Syria was sick; and it was told him, saying, The man of God is come hither.

Elisha's Word to Ben-hadad and Hazael

8. And the king said unto Hazael, Take a present in thine hand, and go meet the man of God, and inquire of the Lord by him, saying, Shall I recover of this sickness? 9. So Hazael went to meet him, and took a present with him, even of every good thing of Damascus, forty camels' burden, and came and stood before him, and said, Thy son Ben-hadad king of Syria hath sent me to thee, saying, Shall I recover of this sickness? 10. And Elisha said unto him, Go, say unto him, Thou shalt surely recover; howbeit the Lord hath shewed me that he shall surely die. 11. And he settled his countenance steadfastly upon him, until he was ashamed: and the man of God wept. 12. And Hazael said, Why weepeth my lord? And he answered, Because I know the evil that thou wilt do unto the children of Israel: their strongholds wilt thou set on fire, and their young men wilt thou slay with the sword, and wilt dash in pieces their little ones, and rip up their women with child. 13. And Hazael said, But what is thy servant, which is but a dog, that he should do this great thing? And Elisha answered, The Lord hath shewed me that thou shalt be king over Syria. 14. Then he departed from Elisha, and came to his master; who said to him, What said Elisha to thee? And he answered, He told me that thou shouldest surely recover. 15. And it came to pass on the morrow, that he took the coverlet, and dipped it in water, and spread it on his face, so that he died: and Hazael reigned in his stead.

Co-regency of Jehoram

And in the fifth year* of Joram the son of Ahab king of Israel, Jehoshaphat being then king of Judah, Jehoram the son of Jehoshaphat began to reign. And he had brethren the sons of Jehoshaphat, Azariah, and Jehiel, and Zechariah, and Azariah, and Michael, and Shephatiah: all these were the sons of Jehoshaphat king of Israel. And their father gave them great gifts, of silver, and of gold, and of precious things, with fenced cities in Judah: but the kingdom gave he to Jehoram, because he was the firstborn.

Now the rest of the acts of Jehoshaphat, first and last, and his might that he shewed, and how he warred, behold, they are written in the history of Jehu the son of Hanani, which is inserted in the book of the kings of Israel.† And Jehoshaphat slept with his fathers, and was buried with his fathers in the city of David his father: and Jehoram his son reigned in his stead.

Wicked and Disastrous Reign

Now when Jehoram was risen up over the kingdom of his father, and had strengthened himself, he slew all his brethren with the sword, and divers also of the princes of Israel. Jehoram was thirty and two years old when he began to reign; and he reigned eight years in Jerusalem. And he walked in the ways of the kings of Israel, as did the house of Ahab: for he had the daughter of Ahab to wife: and he did that which was evil in the sight of the Lord. Howbeit the Lord would not destroy the house of David, because of the covenant he had made with David, and as he promised him to give a lamp to him, and to his children alway. In his days Edom revolted from under the hand of Judah, and make a king over themselves. Then Jehoram passed over to Zair with his captains, and all his chariots with him: and he rose up by night, and smote the Edomites which compassed him about, and the captains of the chariots: and the people fled to their tents. So Edom revolted from under the hand of Judah, unto this day: then did Libnah revolt at the same time from under his hand: because he had forsaken the Lord, the God of his fathers. Moreover he made high places in the mountains of Judah, and made the inhabitants of Jerusalem to go a whoring, and led Judah astray.

* See note on Jehoram's Co-regency. Page 189.
† In Kings "the book of the chronicles of the kings of Judah."

SECT. XXVI — THE DIVIDED KINGDOM

(II Kings 8:) 16. And in the fifth year of Joram the son of Ahab king of Israel, Jehoshaphat being then king of Judah, Jehoram the son of Jehoshaphat king of Judah began to reign.

(II Chron. 21:) 2. And he had brethren the sons of Jehoshaphat, Azariah, and Jehiel, and Zechariah, and Azariah, and Michael, and Shephatiah: all these were the sons of Jehoshaphat king of Israel. 3. And their father gave them great gifts, of silver, and of gold, and of precious things, with fenced cities in Judah: but the kingdom gave he to Jehoram, because he was the firstborn.

(I Kings 22:) 45. Now the rest of the acts of Jehoshaphat, and his might that he shewed, and how he warred, are they not written in ((the book of the chronicles of the kings of Judah?))

50. And Jehoshaphat slept with his fathers, and was buried with his fathers in the city of David his father: and Jehoram his son reigned in his stead.

(II Chron. 20:) 34. Now the rest of the acts of Jehoshaphat, first and last, behold, they are written in ((the history of Jehu the son of Hanani, which is inserted in the book of the kings of Israel.))

1. And Jehoshaphat slept with his fathers, and was buried with his fathers in the city of David: and Jehoram his son reigned in his stead. 4. Now when Jehoram was risen up over the kingdom of his father, and had strengthened himself, he slew all his brethren with the sword, and divers also of the princes of Israel.

17. Thirty and two years old was he when he began to reign; and he reigned eight years in Jerusalem. 18. And he walked in the ways of the kings of Israel, as did the house of Ahab: for he had the daughter of Ahab to wife: and he did that which was evil in the sight of the Lord. 19. Howbeit the Lord would not destroy Judah, for David his servant's sake, as he promised him to give unto him a lamp for his children alway.

5. Jehoram was thirty and two years old when he began to reign; and he reigned eight years in Jerusalem. 6. And he walked in the way of the kings of Israel, as did the house of Ahab: for he had the daughter of Ahab to wife: and he did that which was evil in the sight of the Lord. 7. Howbeit the Lord would not destroy the house of David, because of the covenant that he had made with David, and as he promised to give a lamp to him, and to his children alway.

20. In his days Edom revolted from under the hand of Judah, and made a king over themselves. 21. Then Joram passed over to Zair and all his chariots with him: and he rose up by night, and smote the Edomites which compassed him about, and the captains of the chariots: and the people fled to their tents. 22. So Edom revolted from under the hand of Judah, unto this day. Then did Libnah revolt at the same time.

8. In his days Edom revolted from under the hand of Judah, and made a king over themselves. 9. Then Jehoram passed over with his captains, and all his chariots with him: and he rose up by night, and smote the Edomites which compassed him about, and the captains of the chariots. 10. So Edom revolted from under the hand of Judah, unto this day: then did Libnah revolt at the same time from under his hand: because he had forsaken the Lord, the God of his fathers. 11. Moreover he made high places in the mountains of Judah, and made the inhabitants of Jerusalem to go a whoring, and led Judah astray.

Posthumous Message from Elijah

II Chron. 21:12. And there came a writing to him from Elijah the prophet, saying, Thus saith the Lord, the God of David thy father, Because thou hast not walked in the ways of Jehoshaphat thy father, nor in the ways of Asa king of Judah; 13. but hast walked in the ways of the kings of Israel, and hast made Judah and the inhabitants of Jerusalem to go a whoring, like as the house of Ahab did; and also hast slain thy brethren of thy father's house, which were better than thyself: 14. behold, the Lord will smite with a great plague thy people, and thy children, and thy wives, and all thy substance: 15. and thou shalt have great sickness by disease of thy bowels, until thy bowels fall out by reason of the sickness, day by day.

16. And the Lord stirred up against Jehoram the spirit of the Philistines, and of the Arabians which are beside the Ethiopians: 17. and they came up against Judah, and brake into it, and carried away all the substance that was found in the king's house, and his sons also, and his wives; so that there was never a son left him, save Jehoahaz, the youngest of his sons. 18. And after all this the Lord smote him in his bowels with an incurable disease. 19. And it came to pass, in process of time, at the end of two years, that his bowels fell out by reason of his sickness, and he died of sore diseases. And his people made no burning for him, like the burning of his fathers. 20. Thirty and two years old was he when he began to reign, and he reigned in Jerusalem eight years: and he departed without being desired. And the rest of the acts of Joram, and all that he did are they not written in the book of the chronicles of the kings of Judah? And Joram slept with his fathers, and was buried with his fathers in the city of David, but not in the sepulchres of the kings.

Accession and Character of Ahaziah

And the inhabitants of Jerusalem made Ahaziah* his youngest son king in his stead: for the band of men that came with the Arabians to the camp had slain all the eldest. In the twelfth year †¹of Joram the son of Ahab king of Israel did Ahaziah the son of Jehoram king of Judah begin to reign. Two and twenty†² years old was Ahaziah when he began to reign; and he reigned one year in Jerusalem: and his mother's name was Athaliah the daughter of Omri king of Israel. And he walked in the ways of the house of Ahab; for his mother was his counsellor to do wickedly. And he did that which was evil in the sight of the Lord, as did the house of Ahab: for he was son in law to the house of Ahab, and they were his counsellors after the death of his father, to his destruction.

Alliance with Joram of Israel

He walked also after their counsel, and went with Jehoram the son of Ahab king of Israel to war against Hazael king of Syria at Ramoth-gilead: and the Syrians wounded Joram. And king Joram returned to be healed in Jezreel of the wounds which the Syrians had given him at Ramah, when he fought against Hazael king of Syria. And Ahaziah the son of Jehoram king of Judah went down to see Joram the son of Ahab in Jezreel, because he was sick.

Anointing of Jehu

II Kings 9:1. And Elisha the prophet called one of the sons of the prophets, and said unto him, Gird up thy loins, and take this vial of oil in thine hand, and go to Ramoth-gilead. 2. And when thou comest thither, look out there Jehu the son of Jehoshaphat the son of Nimshi, and go in, and make him arise up from among his brethren, and carry him into an inner chamber. 3. Then take the vial of oil, and pour it upon his head, and say, Thus

---
* II Kings 21:17. Jehoahaz. 22:6. Azariah.
† 1 In II Kings 9:29. In the *eleventh year*. See Appendix C, Chronicles III, 1, (14).
† 2 In II Chron. 22:2. *Forty-two years old.* See Appendix C, III, 1, (15).

SECT. XXVI — THE DIVIDED KINGDOM

(II Kings 8:) 23. And the rest of the acts of Joram, and all that he did, are they not written in the book of the chronicles of the kings of Judah? 24. and Joram slept with his fathers and was buried with his fathers in the city of David:

                          and
Ahaziah his son   reigned in his stead.

(II Chron. 21:) 20. and they buried him in the city of David, but not in the sepulchres of the kings.
(II Chron. 22:) 1. And the inhabitants of Jerusalem made Ahaziah his youngest son king in his stead: for the band of men that came with the Arabians to the camp had slain all the eldest.

25. ((In the twelfth year)) of Joram the son of Ahab king of Israel did Ahaziah the son of Joram begin to reign.

(II Kings 9:) 29. ((In the eleventh)) year of Joram the son of Ahab began Ahaziah to reign over Judah.

So Ahaziah the son of Jehoram king of Judah reigned.

26. ((Two and twenty years old)) was Ahaziah when he began to reign: and he reigned one year in Jerusalem. And his mother's name was Athaliah the daughter of Omri king of Israel.

2. ((Forty and two years old)) was Ahaziah when he began to reign: and he reigned one year in Jerusalem: and his mother's name was Athaliah the daughter of Omri.

27. And he walked in the way of the house of Ahab, and did that which was evil in the sight of the Lord, as did the house of Ahab: for he was the son in law of the house of Ahab.

3. He also walked in the ways of the house of Ahab: for his mother was his counsellor to do wickedly. 4. And he did that which was evil in the sight of the Lord, as did the house of Ahab: for they were his counsellors after the death of his father, to his destruction. 5. He walked after their counsel, and went

28. And he went with Joram the son of Ahab to war against Hazael king of Syria at Ramoth-gilead: and the Syrians wounded Joram. 29. And king Joram returned to be healed in Jezreel of the wounds which the Syrians had given him at Ramah, when he fought against Hazael king of Syria. And Ahaziah the son of Jehoram king of Judah went down to see Joram the son of Ahab in Jezreel, because he was sick.

with Jehoram the son of Ahab king of Israel to war against Hazael king of Syria at Ramoth-gilead: and the Syrians wounded Joram. 6. And he returned to be healed in Jezreel of the wounds which they had given him at Ramah, when he fought against Hazael king of Syria. And Azariah the son of Jehoram king of Judah went down to see Jehoram the son of Ahab in Jezreel, because he was sick.

saith the Lord, I have anointed thee king over Israel. Then open the door, and flee, and tarry not. 4. So the young man, even the young man the prophet, went to Ramoth-gilead. 5. And when he came, behold, the captains of the host were sitting; and he said, I have an errand to thee, O Captain. And Jehu said, Unto which of all us? And he said, To thee, O captain. 6. And he arose, and went into the house, and he poured the oil upon his head, and said unto him, Thus saith the Lord, the God of Israel, I have anointed thee king over the people of the Lord, even over Israel. 7. And thou shalt smite the house of Ahab thy master, that I may avenge the blood of my servants the prophets, and the blood of all the servants of the Lord, at the hand of Jezebel. 8. For the whole house of Ahab shall perish: and I will cut off from Ahab every man child, and him that is shut up, and him that is left at large in Israel. 9. And I will make the house of Ahab like the house of Jereboam the son of Nebat, and like the house of Baasha the son of Ahijah. 10. And the dogs shall eat Jezebel in the portion of Jezreel, and there shall be none to bury her. And he opened the door, and fled. 11. Then Jehu came forth to the servants of his lord; and one said unto him, Is all well? wherefore came this mad fellow to thee? And he said unto them, Ye know the man and what his talk was. 12. And they said, It is false; tell us now. And he said, Thus and thus spake he to me, saying, Thus saith the Lord, I have anointed thee king over Israel. 13. Then they hasted and took every man his garment, and put it under him on the top of the stairs, and blew the trumpet, saying, Jehu is king. 14. So Jehu the son of Jehoshaphat the son of Nimshi conspired against Joram. (Now Joram kept Ramoth-gilead, he and all Israel, because of Hazael king of Syria: 15. but king Joram was returned to be healed in Jezreel of the wounds which the Syrians had given him, when he fought with Hazael king of Syria.)

Conspiracy and Ride to Jezreel

And Jehu said, If this be your mind, then let none escape and go forth out of the city, to go and tell it in Jezreel. 16. So Jehu rode in a chariot, and went to Jezreel; for Joram lay there. And Ahaziah king of Judah was come down to see Joram. 17. Now the watchman stood on the tower in Jezreel, and he spied the company of Jehu as he came, and said, I see a company. And Joram said, Take an horseman, and send to meet them, and let him say, Is it peace? 18. So there went one on horseback to meet him, and said, Thus saith the king, Is it peace? And Jehu said, what hast thou to do with peace? turn thee behind me. And the watchman told, saying, The messenger came to them, but he cometh not again. 19. Then he sent out a second on horseback, which came to them, and said, Thus saith the king, Is it peace? And Jehu answered, What hast thou to do with peace? turn thee behind me. 20. And the watchman told, saying, He came even unto them, and cometh not again; and the driving is like the driving of Jehu the son of Nimshi; for he driveth furiously. 21. And Joram said, Make ready. And they made ready his chariot. And Joram king of Israel and Ahaziah king of Judah went out, each in his chariot, and they went out to meet Jehu, and found him in the portion of Naboth the Jezreelite. 22. And it came to pass, when Joram saw Jehu, that he said, Is it peace, Jehu? And he answered, What peace, so long as the whoredoms of thy mother Jezebel and her witchcrafts are so many? 23. And Joram turned his hands, and fled, and said to Ahaziah, There is treachery, O Ahaziah.

Jehoram Slain and Cast in Naboth's Plat

And Jehu drew his bow with his full strength, and smote Joram between his arms, and the arrow went out at his heart, and he sunk down in his chariot. 25. Then said Jehu to Bidkar his captain, Take up and cast him in the portion of the field of Naboth the Jezreelite: for remember how that, when I and thou rode together after Ahab his father, the Lord laid this burden upon him: 26. Surely I have seen yesterday the blood of Naboth, and the blood of his sons saith the Lord; and I will requite thee in this plat, saith the Lord. Now therefore take and cast him into the plat of ground, according to the word of the Lord.*

THE CONFLUENCE OF BLESSING AND CURSE IN JOASH.

*NOTE.—By the marriage of Jehoram of Judah and Athaliah of Israel, not only was the curse pronounced on Ahab's house extended so as to include the house of David, but it was also brought into direct antagonism with the blessing pronounced on David and his seed. By Jehu's execution of judgment on Ahab's house, together with a strange series of assassinations in David's house, the threatened curse of extermination of the former and the promised blessing of preservation of the latter, converged in one person, who was the only surviving male of either royal house, and hence the heir both of the curse and the blessing. If the word of curse be strictly kept, the word of blessing will be broken. One or the other must prevail. Succeeding history will show the triumph of mercy over judgment.

PROMISED BLESSING

(II Sam. 7:) 11. Moreover the Lord telleth thee that the Lord will make thee an house. 12. When thy days be fulfilled, and thou shalt sleep with thy fathers, I will set up thy seed after thee, which shall proceed out of thy bowels, and I will establish his kingdom. 13. He shall build an house for my name, and I will establish the throne of his kingdom for ever. 14. I will be his father, and he shall be my son: if he commit iniquity, I will chasten him with the rod of men, and with the stripes of the children of men; but my mercy shall not depart from him, as I took it from Saul whom I put away before thee. 16. And thine house and thy kingdom shall be made sure for ever before thee: thy throne shall be established for ever.

THREATENED CURSE

(I Kings 21:) 19. Thus saith the Lord, in the place where dogs licked the blood of Naboth shall dogs lick thy blood, even thine. 21. Behold, I will bring evil upon thee, and will utterly sweep thee away, and will cut off from Ahab every man child, and him that is shut up, and him that is left at large in Israel: 22. and I will make thine house like the house of Jereboam the son of Nebat, and like the house of Baasha the son of Ahijah, for the provocation wherewith thou hast provoked me to anger, and hast made Israel to sin.
29. Seest thou how Ahab humbleth himself before me? because he humbleth himself before me, I will not bring the evil in his days: but in his son's days will I bring the evil upon his house.

VIOLENT DEATHS IN DAVID'S HOUSE

Jehoram the son of Jehoshaphat slays his six brethren.
II Chron. 21:4.
Jehoram's sons, save the youngest, Ahaziah, slain by Arabians.
II Chron. 21:17.
II Chron. 22:1.
Jehoram smitten by the Lord with incurable disease.
II Chron. 21:12-15, 18, 19.
Ahaziah slain by Jehu when on a visit to Jezreel.
II Kings 9:26, 27.
II Chron. 22:7, 9.
Ahaziah's forty brethren slain near Jezreel.
II Kings 10:13, 14.
II Chron. 22:8.
Athaliah daughter of Ahab destroys all the seed royal of David, except the babe Joash hidden by his aunt.
II Kings 11:1-3.

VIOLENT DEATHS IN AHAB'S HOUSE

Ahab slain in battle at Ramoth-gilead.
I Kings 22:29-38.
II Chron. 18:30-34.
Ahaziah son of Ahab smitten by God for his sin.
II Kings 1:16, 17.
Jehoram son of Ahab slain by Jehu at Jezreel.
II Kings 9:21-26.
Ahab's seventy sons slain at Jehu's command.
II Kings 10:1-11.
Jehu smites all that remain of Ahab in Jezreel.
II Kings 10:11.
Jehu smites all that remain of Ahab in Samaria.
II Kings 10:15-17.

This babe Joash, rescued, and hidden in the house of the Lord seven years, by his aunt Jehoshabeath the wife of Jehoiada the priest was thus the only surviving male child both of the house of David and of the house of Ahab. If the curse pronounced on Ahab's house be executed on him as the last of Ahab's line, then the house of David will also become extinct. When Jehoram married Ahab's daughter and did evil in the sight of the Lord, we are told "Howbeit the Lord would not destroy the house of David, because of the covenant that he had made with David, and as he had promised to give a lamp to him and his children alway" II Chron. 21:7. This was in accordance with the condition "If he commit iniquity, I will chasten him with the rod of men and with the stripes of the children of men; but my mercy shall not depart from him, as I took it from

Jehu Slays Ahaziah and His Brethren

But when Ahaziah the king of Judah saw this, he fled by the way of the garden house. Now the destruction of Ahaziah was of God, in that he went unto Joram: for when he was come, he went out with Jehoram against Jehu the son of Nimshi, whom the Lord had appointed to cut off the house of Ahab. And Jehu followed after him, and said, Smite him also in the chariot: and they smote him at the ascent of Gur, which is by Ibleam.* And he fled to Megiddo and died there. And his servants carried him in a chariot to Jerusalem, and buried him in his sepulchre with his fathers in the city of David, for they said, He is the son of Jehoshaphat, who sought the Lord with all his heart. And the house of Ahaziah had no power to hold the kingdom. And it came to pass, when Jehu was executing judgement upon the house of Ahab, as he was at the shearing house of the shepherds in the way, that he met with the princes of Judah, and the sons of the brethren of Ahaziah king of Judah, ministering to Ahaziah, and said, Who are ye? And they answered, We are the brethren of Ahaziah: and we go down to salute the children of the king and the children of the queen. And he said, Take them alive. And they took them alive, and slew them at the pit of the shearing house, even two and forty men: neither left he any of them.

Death of Jezebel as Predicted

II Kings 9:30. And when Jehu was come to Jezreel, Jezebel heard of it; and she painted her eyes, and tired her head, and looked out of the window. 31. And as Jehu entered in at the gate, she said, Is it peace, thou Zimri, thy master's murderer? 32. And he lifted up his face to the window, and said, Who is on my side? who? And there looked out to him two or three eunuchs. 33. And he said, Throw her down. So they threw her down: and some of the blood was sprinkled on the wall, and on the horses: and he trode her under foot. 34. And when he was come in, he did eat and drink; and he said, See now to this cursed woman, and bury her: for she is a king's daughter. 35. And they went to bury her: but they found no more of her than the skull, and the feet, and the palms of her hands. 36. Wherefore they came again, and told him. And he said, This is the word of the Lord, which he spake by his servant Elijah the Tishbite, saying, In the portion of Jezreel shall the dogs eat the flesh of Jezebel: 37. and the carcase of Jezebel shall be as dung upon the face of the field in the portion of Jezreel; so that they shall not say, This is Jezebel.

---

* Chonicles says "they caught him hiding in Samaria, and brought him to Jehu and slew him."
See Appendix C. Chronicles III, 2, '9'.

Saul, whom I put away before thee." So now when Joash, the only surviving offspring of that fatal marriage, unites in himself not only all the ill deserts of the house of David, but also the curse of the more sinful house of Ahab, the Lord is still true to his covenant promise to give a lamp to David and his children alway. Although the foretold chastening with the rod and the stripes of men approaches to the very verge of extinction, and the final issue trembles in the balance, when the wicked Athaliah thinks she has destroyed all the seed royal of the house of David, and the fact that she has not done so is kept a secret in the house of the Lord, still mercy not only does not depart from David's house, but the blessing promised to that house prevails over the judgment threatened to the guilty house of Ahab. In the seventh year, Jehoiada with the captains of hundreds, brought out the king's son, and put the crown upon him, and gave him the testimony; and they made him king, and anointed him; and they clapped their hands, and said, God save the king.

SECT. XXVI THE DIVIDED KINGDOM 203

II King 9:) 27. But when Ahaziah the king of Judah saw this, he fled by the way of the garden house.

((And Jehu followed after him, and said, Smite him also in the chariot: and they smote him at the ascent of Gur, which is by Ibleam. And he fled to Megiddo and died there.))

28. And his servants carried him in a chariot to Jerusalem, and buried him in his sepulchre with his fathers in the city of David.

(II Kings 10:) 12^b. (And as he was at the shearing house of the shepherds in the way, Jehu met with the brethren of Ahaziah king of Judah, and said, Who are ye? And they answered, We are the brethren of Ahaziah: and we go down to salute the children of the king and the children of the queen. 14. And he said, Take them alive. And they took them alive, and slew them at the pit of the shearing house, even two and forty men; neither left he any of them.)

(II Chron 22:) 7. Now the destruction of Ahaziah was of God, in that he went unto Joram · for when he was come, he went out with Jehoram against Jehu the son of Nimshi, whom the Lord had anointed to cut off the house of Ahab.

9. ((And he sought Ahaziah, and they caught him, (now he was hiding in Samaria,) and they brought him to Jehu, and slew him:))

and they buried him,

for they said, He is the son of Jehoshaphat, who sought the Lord with all his heart. And the house of Ahaziah had no power to hold the kingdom. 8. (And it came to pass, when Jehu was executing judgement upon the house of Ahab, that he found the princes of Judah, and the sons of the brethren of Ahaziah, ministering to Ahaziah,

and slew them.)

Jehu Slays All Belonging to Ahab in Jezreel

II Kings 10:1. Now Ahab had seventy sons in Samaria. And Jehu wrote letters, and sent to Samaria, unto the rulers of Jezreel, even the elders, and unto them that brought up the sons of Ahab, saying. 2. And now as soon as this letter cometh to you, seeing your master's sons are with you, and there are with you chariots and horses, a fenced city also, and armour; 3. look ye out the best and meetest of your master's sons, and set him on his father's throne, and fight for your master's house. 4. But they were exceedingly afraid, and said, Behold, the two kings stood not before him: how then shall we stand? 5. And he that was over the household, and he that was over the city, the elders also, and they that brought up the children, sent to Jehu, saying, We are thy servants, and will do all that thou shalt bid us: we will not make any man king: do thou that which is good in thine eyes. 6. Then he wrote a letter the second time to them, saying, If ye be on my side, and if ye will hearken unto my voice, take ye the heads of the men your master's sons, and come to me to Jezreel by to-morrow this time. Now the king's sons, being seventy persons, were with the great men of the city, which brought them up. 7. And it came to pass, when the letter came to them, that they took the king's sons, and slew them, even seventy persons, and put their heads in baskets, and sent them unto him to Jezreel. 8. And there came a messenger, and told him, saying. They have brought the heads of the king's sons. And he said, Lay ye them in two heaps at the entering in of the gate until the morning. 9. And it came to pass in the morning, that he went out, and stood, and said to all the people, Ye be righteous: behold, I conspired against my master, and slew him: but who smote all these? 10. Know now that there shall fall unto the earth nothing of the word of the Lord, which the Lord spake concerning the house of Ahab: for the Lord hath done that which he spake by his servant Elijah. 11. So Jehu smote all that remained of the house of Ahab in Jezreel, and all his great men, and his familiar friends, and his priests, until he left him none remaining. 12ª. And he arose and departed and went to Samaria.

Jehu Smites All Belonging to Ahab in Samaria

15. And when he was departed thence, he lighted on Jehonadab the son of Rechab coming to meet him: and he saluted him, and said to him, Is thine heart right, as my heart is with thy heart? And Jehonadab answered, It is. If it be, give me thine hand. And he gave him his hand; and he took him up to him into the chariot. 16. And he said, Come with me, and see my zeal for the Lord. So they made him ride in his chariot. 17. And when he came to Samaria, he smote all that remained unto Ahab in Samaria, till he had destroyed him, according to the word of the Lord, which he spake to Elijah.

Jehu Commended and Condemned

30. And the Lord said unto Jehu, Because thou hast done well in executing that which was right in mine eyes, and hast done unto the house of Ahab according to all that was in mine heart, thy sons of the fourth generation shall sit on the throne of Israel. 31. But Jehu took no heed to walk in the law of the Lord, the God of Israel, with all his heart: he departed not from the sins of Jereboam, wherewith he made Israel to sin.

JUDAH		ISRAEL	
THE HOUSE OF DAVID		THE HOUSE OF JEHU (Fifth)	
	B. C. 883-877* (Usurping Queen)	B. C. 883-855	
Athaliah		I Jehu	(10)
	B. C. 842-856	B. C. 842-814	
	B. C. 877-838	B. C. 855-838	
IX Joash		II Jehoahaz	(11)
	B. C. 856-796	B. C. 814-797	
	B. C. 838-808	(Elisha) B. C. 838-823	
X Amaziah		(Jonah) III Jehoash	(12)
	B. C. 796-782 (Joel)	B. C. 797-781	
	B. C. 808-756 (Isaiah)	(Amos) B. C. 823-771	
XI Uzziah		(Hosea) IV Jeroboam II	(13)
	B. C. 782-737 (Micah)	B. C. 781-740	
	Jotham Co-regent	B. C. 771-770	
		V Zechariah	(14)
		B. C. 740	

SECTION XXVII

Rival Houses of David and Jehu

Jehu Subtilly Slays All Worshippers of Baal

II Kings 10:18. And Jehu gathered all the people together, and said unto them, Ahab served Baal a little; but Jehu shall serve him much. 19. Now therefore call unto me all the prophets of Baal, all his worshippers, and all his priests; let none be wanting: for I have a great sacrifice to do to Baal; whosoever shall be wanting, he shall not live. But Jehu did it in subtilty, to the intent that he might destroy the worshippers of Baal. 20. And Jehu said, Sanctify a solemn assembly for Baal. And they proclaimed it. 21. And Jehu sent through all Israel: and all the worshippers of Baal came, so that there was not a man left that came not. And they came into the house of Baal; and the house of Baal was filled from one end to another. 22. And he said unto him that was over the vestry, Bring forth vestments for all the worshippers of Baal. And he brought them forth vestments. 23. And Jehu went, and Jehonadab the son of Rechab, into the house of Baal; and he said unto the worshippers of Baal, Search, and look that there be here with you none of the servants of the Lord, but the worshippers of Baal only. 24. And they went in to offer sacrifices and burnt offerings. Now Jehu had appointed him fourscore men without, and said, If any of the men whom I bring into your hands escape, he that letteth him go, his life shall be for the life of him. 25. And it came to pass, as soon as he had made an end of offering the burnt offering, that Jehu said to the guard and to the captains, Go in, and slay them; let none come forth. And they smote them with the edge of the sword; and the guard and the captains cast them out, and went to the city of the house of Baal. 26. And they brought forth the pillars that were in the house of Baal, and burned them. 27. And they brake down the pillars of Baal, and brake down the house of Baal, and made it a draught house, unto this day. 28. Thus Jehu destroyed Baal out of Israel. 29. Howbeit from the sins of Jereboam the son of Nebat, wherewith he made Israel to sin, Jehu departed not from after them, to wit, the golden calves that were in Beth-el, and that were in Dan.

---

* See Chronology Appendix A. Both systems of chronology are used, *e.g.*, Athaliah $\frac{833 \text{ (Usher)}}{842 \text{ (Revised)}}$

Athaliah's Usurpation

Now when Athaliah the mother of Ahaziah saw that her son was dead, she arose and destroyed all the seed royal of the house of Judah. But Jehoshabeath * the daughter of king Joram, sister of Ahaziah, took Joash the son of Ahaziah, and stole him away from among the king's sons that were slain, even him and his nurse, and put them in the bedchamber. So Jehoshabeath, the daughter of king Jehoram, the wife of Jehoiada the priest, (for she was sister of Ahaziah,) hid him from Athaliah, so that she slew him not. And he was with her hid in the house of the Lord six years: and Athaliah reigned over the land.

Joash Made King

And in the seventh year Jehoiada strengthened himself, and took the captains of hundreds, of the Carites and of the guard, Azariah the son of Jeroham, and Ishmael the son of Jehohanan, and Azariah the son of Obed, and Maaseiah the son of Adaiah, and Elishaphat the son of Zichri, into covenant with him. And they went about in Judah, and gathered the Levites out of all the cities of Judah, and the heads of fathers' houses of Israel, and they came to Jerusalem, and brought them into the house of the Lord; and he made a covenant with them, and took an oath of them in the house of the Lord, and shewed them the king's son. And he said unto them, Behold, the king's son shall reign, as the Lord hath spoken concerning the sons of David. And he commanded them, saying, This is the thing that ye shall do: a third part of you, that come in on the sabbath, of the priests, and of the Levites, shall be keepers of the watch of the king's house: and a third part shall be at the gate Sur; and a third part at the gate behind the guard: so shall ye keep the watch of the house, and be a barrier, and all the people shall be in the courts of the house of the Lord. But let none come into the house of the Lord, save the priests, and they that minister of the Levites; they shall come in for they are holy: but all the people shall keep the watch of the Lord. And the two companies of you, even all that go forth on the sabbath, shall keep the watch of the Lord about the king. And the Levites shall compass the king round about, every man with his weapons in his hand; and he that cometh within the ranks, let him be slain: and be ye with the king when he goeth out and when he cometh in. And the captains over hundreds and all Judah did according to all that Jehoiada the priest commanded: and they took every man his men, those that were to come in on the sabbath, with those that were to go out on the sabbath, and came to Jehoiada the priest, for he dismissed not the courses. And Jehoiada the priest delivered to the captains over hundreds the spears and shields that had been king David's, which were in the house of the Lord. And the guard stood, every man with his weapons in his hand, from the right side of the house to the left side of the house, along by the altar and the house, by the king round about. Then he brought out the king's son, and put the crown upon him, and gave him the testimony; and made him king; and Jehoiada and his sons anointed him, and they clapped their hands, and said, God save the king.

Death of Athaliah

And when Athaliah heard the noise of the guard and of the people running and praising the king, she came to the people into the house of the Lord: and she looked, and, behold, the king stood by the pillar at the entrance, as the manner was, and the captains and the trumpets by the king: and all the people of the land rejoiced, and blew with trumpets; the singers also played on instruments of music, and led the singing of the praise. Then Athaliah rent her clothes, and said, Treason, Treason. And Jehoiada the priest commanded the captains of hundreds that were set over the host, and said unto them, Have her

* Kings Jehosheba.

SECT. XXVII — THE DIVIDED KINGDOM

(II Kings 11:) 1. Now when Athaliah the mother of Ahaziah saw that her son was dead, she arose and destroyed all the seed royal.
2. But Jehosheba, the daughter of king Joram, sister of Ahaziah, took Joash the son of Ahaziah, and stole him away from among the king's sons that were slain, even him and his nurse, and put them in the bedchamber and they hid him from Athaliah, so that he was not slain. 3. And he was with her hid in the house of the Lord six years: and Athaliah reigned over the land.

4. And in the seventh year Jehoiada sent and fetched the captains over hundreds, of the Carites and of the guard,

and brought them into the house of the Lord; and he made a covenant with them, and took an oath of them in the house of the Lord, and shewed them the king's son.

5. And he commanded them, saying, This is the thing that ye shall do: a third part of you, that come in on the sabbath, shall be keepers of the watch of the king's house: 6. and a third part shall be at the gate Sur; and a third part at the gate behind the guard: so shall ye keep the watch of the house, and be a barrier.

7. And the two companies of you, even all that go forth on the sabbath, shall keep the watch of the house of the Lord about the king. 8. And ye shall compass the king round about, every man with his weapons in his hand; and he that cometh within the ranks, let him be slain: and be ye with the king when he goeth out and when he cometh in. 9. And the captains over hundreds did according to all that Jehoiada the priest commanded: and they took every man his men, those that were to come in on the sabbath, with those that were to go out on the sabbath, and came to Jehoiada the priest.
10. And the priest delivered to the captains over hundreds the spears and shields that had been king David's, which were in the house of the Lord. 11. And the guard stood, every man with his weapons in his hand, from the right side of the house to the left side of the house, along by the altar and the house, by the king round about. 12. Then he brought out the king's son, and put the crown upon him, and gave him the testimony; and made him king, and anointed him, and they clapped their hands, and said, God save the king.
13. And when Athaliah heard the noise of the guard and of the people, she came to the people into the house of the Lord: 14. and she looked, and, behold, the king stood by the pillar, as the manner was, and the captains and the trumpets by the king; and all the people of the land rejoiced, and blew with trumpets.

Then Athaliah rent her clothes, and cried, Treason, Treason.
15. And Jehoiada the priest commanded the captains of hundreds that were set over the host, and said unto them, Have her

---

(II Chron. 22:) 10. Now when Athaliah the mother of Ahaziah saw that her son was dead, she arose and destroyed all the seed royal of the house of Judah.
11. But Jehoshabeath, the daughter of the king took Joash the son of Ahaziah, and stole him away from among the king's sons that were slain, and put him and his nurse in the bedchamber. So Jehoshabeath, the daughter of king Jehoram, the wife of Jehoiada the priest, (for she was the sister of Ahaziah,) hid him from Athaliah, so that she slew him not. 12. And he was with them hid in the house of God six years: and Athaliah reigned over the land.

23:1. And in the seventh year Jehoiada strengthened himself, and took the captains of hundreds, Azariah the son of Jeroham, and Ishmael the son of Jehohanan, and Azariah the son of Obed, and Maaseiah the son of Adaiah, and Elishaphat the son of Zichri, into covenant with him. 2. And they went about in Judah, and gathered the Levites out of all the cities of Judah, and the heads of fathers' houses of Israel, and they came to Jerusalem.
3. And all the congregation made a covenant with the king in the house of God. And he said unto them, Behold the king's son shall reign, as the Lord hath spoken concerning the sons of David.

4. This is the thing that ye shall do: a third part of you, that come in on the sabbath, of the priests and of the Levites, shall be porters of the doors; 5. and a third part shall be at the king's house: and a third part at the gate of the foundation: and all the people shall be in the courts of the house of the Lord. 6. But let none come into the house of the Lord, save the priests, and they that minister of the Levites; they shall come in, for they are holy: but all the people shall keep the watch of the Lord.

7. And the Levites shall compass the king round about, every man with his weapons in his hand; and whosoever cometh into the house, let him be slain: and be ye with the king when he cometh in, and when he goeth out. 8. So the Levites and all Judah did according to all that Jehoiada the priest commanded: and they took every man his men, those that were to come in on the sabbath, with those that were to go out on the sabbath,
For Jehoiada the priest dismissed not the courses.
9. And Jehoiada the priest delivered to the captains of hundreds the spears and shields that had been king David's, which were in the house of God. 10. And he set all the people, every man with his weapon in his hand, from the right side of the house to the left side of the house, along by the altar and the house, by the king round about. 11. Then they brought out the king's son, and put the crown upon him, and gave him the testimony; and made him king; and Jehoiada and his sons anointed him: and they said, God save the king.
12. And when Athaliah heard the noise of the people running and praising the king, she came to the people into the house of the Lord: 13. and she looked, and, behold, the king stood by his pillar at the entrance, and the captains and the trumpets by the king; and all the people of the land rejoiced, and blew with trumpets; the singers also played on instruments of music, and led the singing of praise. Then Athaliah rent her clothes, and said, Treason, Treason.
14. And Jehoiada the priest brought out the captains of hundreds that were set over the host, and said unto them, Have her

forth between the ranks; and him that followeth her slay with the sword: for the priest said, Let her not be slain in the house of the Lord. So they made way for her; and she went by the way of the horses' entry to the king's house: and there she was slain.

Jehoiada's Covenant And Jehoiada made a covenant between the Lord and the king and the people, that they should be the Lord's people; between the king also and the people. And all the people of the land went to the house of Baal, and brake it down; his altars and his images brake they in pieces thoroughly, and slew Mattan the priest of Baal before the altars. And Jehoiada appointed the officers of the house of the Lord under the hand of the priests the Levites, whom David had distributed in the house of the Lord, to offer the burnt offerings of the Lord, as it is written in the law of Moses, with rejoicing and singing, according to the order of David. And he set the porters at the gate of the house of the Lord, that none which was unclean in any thing should enter in. And he took the captains over hundreds, and the Carites, and the guard and all the people of the land; and they brought down the king from the house of the Lord, and came by the way of the gate of the guard unto the king's house, and set the king upon the throne of the kingdom. So all the people of the land rejoiced, and the city was quiet: and they slew Athaliah with the sword at the king's house.

Accession and Character of Joash Joash was seven years old when he began to reign. In the seventh year of Jehu began Joash to reign; and he reigned forty years in Jerusalem: and his mother's name was Zibiah of Beer-sheba. And Joash did that which was right in the eyes of the Lord all his days wherein Jehoiada the priest instructed him. Howbeit the high places were not taken away; the people still sacrificed and burnt incense in the high places. And Jehoiada took for him two wives; and he begat sons and daughters. And it came to pass after this, that Joash was minded to restore the house of the Lord. For the sons of Athaliah, that wicked woman, had broken up the house of God: and also all the dedicated things of the house of the Lord did they bestow upon the Baalim. And he gathered together the priests and the Levites, and said unto them, * All the money of the hallowed things that is brought into the house of the Lord, in current money, the money of the persons for whom each man is rated, and all the money that it cometh into any man's heart to bring into the house of the Lord, let the priests take it to them, every man from his acquaintance: and they shall repair the breaches of the house, wheresoever any breach shall be found, and see that ye hasten the matter.

Transjordanic Raid of Hazael
Death of Jehu II Kings 10:32. In those days the Lord began to cut Israel short: and Hazael smote them in all the coasts of Israel: 33. from Jordan eastward, all the Land of Gilead, the Gadites, and the Reubenites, and the Manassites, from Aroer, which is by the valley of Arnon, even Gilead and Bashan. 34. Now the rest of the acts of Jehu, and all that he did, and all his might, are they not written in the book of the chronicles of the kings of Israel? 35. And Jehu slept with his fathers: and they buried him in Samaria. And Jehoahaz his son reigned in his stead. 36. And the time that Jehu reigned over Israel in Samaria was twenty and eight years.

Accession and Character of Jehoahaz II Kings 13:1. In the three and twentieth year of Joash the son of Ahaziah, king of Judah, Jehoahaz the son of Jehu, began to reign over Israel in Samaria, and reigned seventeen years. 2. And he did that which was evil in the sight of the Lord, and followed the sins of Jereboam the son of Nebat, wherewith he made Israel to sin; he departed not therefrom.

---
* In Chronicles, Go out and gather money.

SECT. XXVII — THE DIVIDED KINGDOM

forth between the ranks; and him that followeth her slay with the sword: for the priest said, Let her not be slain in the house of the Lord. 16. So they made way for her; and she went by the way of the horses' entry to the king's house: and there was she slain.
17. And Jehoiada made a covenant between the Lord and the king and the people, that they should be the Lord's people; between the king also and the people. 18. And all the people of the land went to the house of Baal, and brake it down; his altars and his images brake they in pieces thoroughly, and slew Mattan the priest of Baal before the altars. And the priest appointed officers over the house of the Lord.

19. And he took the captains over hundreds, and the *Carites*, and the *guard* and all the people of the land; and they brought down the king from the house of the Lord, and came by the way of the gate of the guard unto the the king's house. And he sat on the throne of the kings.
20. So all the people of the land rejoiced, and the city was quiet: and they slew Athaliah with the sword at the king's house.

21. Jehoash was seven years old when he began to reign.
(II Kings 12:) 1. In the seventh year of Jehu began Jehoash to reign; and he reigned forty years in Jerusalem: and his mother's name was Zibiah of Beer-sheba. 2. And Jehoash did that which was right in the eyes of the Lord all his days wherein Jehoiada the priest instructed him. 3. Howbeit the high places were not taken away; the people still sacrificed and burnt incense in the high places.

4. And Jehoash

said to the priests, (All the money of the hallowed things that is brought into the house of the Lord, in current money, the money of the persons for whom each man is rated,
and all the money that it cometh into any man's heart to bring into the house of the Lord, 5. let the priests take it to them, every man from his acquaintance: and they shall repair the breaches of the house, wheresoever any breach shall be found.)

---

forth between the ranks; and whoso followeth her, let him be slain with the sword: for the priest said, Slay her not in the house of the Lord. 15 So they made way for her; and she went to the entry of the horse gate to the king's house: and they slew her there.
16. And Jehoiada made a covenant between himself, and all the people, and the king, that they should be the Lord's people. 17. And all the people went to the house of Baal, and brake it down; and brake his altars and his images in pieces, and slew Mattan the priest of Baal, before the altars. 18. And Jehoiada appointed the offices of the house of the Lord under the hand of the priests the Levites, whom David had distributed in the house of the Lord, to offer the burnt offerings of the Lord, as it is written in the law of Moses, with rejoicing and with singing, according to the order of David.

19. And he set the porters at the gate of the house of the Lord, that none which was unclean in anything should enter in.
20. And he took the captains of hundreds, and the *nobles*, and the *governors* of the people, and all the people of the land; and brought down the king from the house of the Lord: and they came through the upper gate unto the king's house, and set the king upon the throne of the kingdom.
21. So all the people of the land rejoiced, and the city was quiet: and they slew Athaliah with the sword.

(II Chron. 24.) 1. Joash was seven years old when he began to reign.

and he reigned forty years in Jerusalem: and his mother's name was Zibiah of Beer-sheba. 2. And Joash did that which was right in the eyes of the Lord all the days of Jehoiada the priest.

3. And Jehoiada took for him two wives; and he begat sons and daughters.
4. And it came to pass after this that Joash was minded to restore the house of the Lord. 7. For the sons of Athaliah, that wicked woman, had broken up the house of God; and also all the dedicated things of the house of the Lord did they bestow upon the Baalim. 5. And he gathered together the priests and the Levites, and said to them,

(Go out unto the cities of Judah, and gather of all Israel money to repair the house of your God from year to year,

and see that ye hasten the matter.)

Renewal and Repairs by King Joash

Howbeit the Levites hastened it not, but it was so, that in the three and thirtieth year of king Joash the priests had not repaired the breaches of the house. Then king Joash called for Jehoiada the priest, and for the other priests, and said unto him, Why hast thou not required of the Levites to bring in out of Judah and out of Jerusalem the tax of Moses the servant of the Lord, and of the congregation of Israel, for the tent of the testimony? Why repair ye not the breaches of the house? Now therefore take no more money from your acquaintance, but deliver it for the breaches of the house. And the priests consented that they should take no more money from the people, neither repair the breaches of the house.

New Device of a Chest for Gifts

So the king commanded, and Jehoiada the priest took a chest, and bored a hole in the lid of it, and set it beside the altar, on the right side as one cometh into the house of the Lord: and the priests that kept the door put therein all the money that was brought into the house of the Lord. And they made a proclamation through Judah and Jerusalem, to bring in for the Lord the tax that Moses the servant of God laid upon Israel in the wilderness. And all the princes and the people rejoiced, and brought in, and cast into the chest, until they had made an end. And it was so, that at what time the chest was brought into the king's office by the hand of the Levites, and when they saw that there was much money in the chest, that the king's scribe and the chief priest's officer came and emptied the chest, and having put up in bags and told the money that was found in the house of the Lord, they took it, and carried it to its place again, Thus they did day by day and gathered money in abundance.

And the king and Jehoiada gave the money that was weighed out into the hands of them that did the work that had the oversight of the house of the Lord: and they paid it out to the carpenters and the builders that wrought upon the house of the Lord, and to the masons and the hewers of stone, and for buying timber and hewn stone to repair the breaches of the house of the Lord, and for all that was laid out for the house to repair it.

But there was not made for the house of the Lord cups of silver, snuffers, basons, trumpets, any vessels of gold, or vessels of silver, of the money that was brought into the house of the Lord: for they gave that to them that did the work, and repaired therewith the house of the Lord. Moreover they reckoned not with the men, into whose hand they delivered the money to give to them that did the work: for they dealt faithfully. The money for the guilt offerings, and the money for the sin offerings, was not brought into the house of the Lord: it was the priests'.

So the workmen wrought, and the work was perfected by them, and they set up the house of God in its state, and strengthened it. And when they had made an end, they brought the rest of the money before the king and Jehoiada, whereof were made vessels for the house of the Lord, even vessels to minister, and to offer withal, and spoons, and vessels of gold and silver. And they offered burnt offerings in the house of the Lord continually, all the days of Jehoiada.

Oppression by Hazael and Ben-hadad

II Kings 13:3. And the anger of the Lord was kindled against Israel, and he delivered them into the hand of Hazael king of Syria, and into the hand of Ben-hadad the son of Hazael, continually. 4. And Jehoahaz besought the Lord, and the Lord hearkened unto him: for he saw the oppression of Israel, how that the king of Syria oppressed them. (5. And the Lord gave Israel a saviour so that they went out from under the hand of the

SECT. XXVII   THE DIVIDED KINGDOM

6. (But it was so, that in the three and twentieth year of king Jehoash the priests had not repaired the breaches of the house.) 7. Then king Jehoash called for Jehoiada the priest, and for the other priests, and said unto them, (Why repair ye not the breaches of the house?)	(Howbeit the Levites hastened it not.) 6. And the king called for Jehoiada the chief, and said unto him, (Why hast thou not required of the Levites to bring in out of Judah and out of Jerusalem the tax of Moses the servant of the Lord, and of the congregation of Israel, for the tent of the testimony?)
Now therefore take no more money from your acquaintance, but deliver it for the breaches of the house. 8. And the priests consented that they should take no more money from the people, neither repair the breaches of the house.	
9. But Jehoiada the priest took a chest, and bored a hole in the lid of it, and set it beside the altar, on the right side as one cometh into the house of the Lord: and the priests that kept the door put therein all the money that was brought into the house of the Lord.	8. So the king commanded, and they made a chest, and set it without the gate of the house of the Lord.
10. And it was so, when they saw that there was much money in the chest, that the king's scribe and the *high priest* came up, and they put up in bags and told the money that was found in the house of the Lord.	9. And they made a proclamation through Judah and Jerusalem, to bring in for the Lord the tax that Moses the servant of God laid upon Israel in the wilderness. 10. And all the princes and all the people rejoiced, and brought in, and cast into the chest, until they had made an end. 11. And it was so, that at what time the chest was brought unto the king's office by the hand of the Levites, and when they saw that there was much money the king's scribe and the *chief priest's officer* came and emptied the chest, and took it, and carried it to its place again. Thus they did day by day, and gathered money in abundance.
11. And they gave the money that was weighed out into the hands of them that did the work that had the oversight of the house of the Lord: (and they paid it out to the carpenters and builders that wrought upon the house of the Lord, 12. and to the masons and the hewers of stone, and for buying timber and hewn stone to repair the breaches of the house of the Lord, and for all that was laid out for the house to repair it.)	12. And the king and Jehoiada gave it to such as did the work of the service of the house of the Lord; (and they hired masons and carpenters to restore the house of the Lord, and also such as wrought iron and brass to repair the house of the Lord.)
13. But there were not made for the house of the Lord cups of silver, snuffers, basons, trumpets, any vessels of gold, or vessels of silver, of the money that was brought into the house of the Lord: 14. for they gave that to them that did the work, and repaired therewith the house of the Lord. 15. Moreover they reckoned not with the men, into whose hand they delivered the money to give to them that did the work: for they dealt faithfully. 16. The money for the guilt offerings, and the money for the sin offerings, was not brought into the house of the Lord: it was the priests'.	
	13. So the workmen wrought, and the work was perfected by them, and they set up the house of God in its state, and strengthened it. 14. And when they had made an end, they brought the rest of the money before the king and Jehoiada, whereof were made vessels for the house of the Lord, even vessels to minister, and to offer withal, and spoons, and vessels of gold and silver. And they offered burnt offerings in the house of the Lord continually all the days of Jehoiada.

Syrians: and the children of Israel dwelt in their tents, as beforetime. 6. Nevertheless they departed not from the sins of the house of Jereboam, wherewith he made Israel to sin, but walked therein; and there remained the Asherah also in Samaria.) 7. For he left not to Jehoahaz of the people save fifty horsemen, and ten chariots, and ten thousand footmen; for the king of Syria destroyed them, and made them like the dust in threshing.

Jehoiada's Death
Judah's Apostacy

II Chron. 24:15. But Jehoiada waxed old and was full of days, and he died; an hundred and thirty years old was he when he died. 16. And they buried him in the city of David among the kings, because he had done good in Israel, and toward God and his house. 17. Now after the death of Jehoiada came the princes of Judah, and made abeisance to the king. Then the king hearkened unto them.

18. And they forsook the house of the Lord, the God of their fathers, and served the Asherim and the idols: and wrath came upon Judah and Jerusalem for this their guiltiness. 19. Yet he sent prophets to them, to bring them again unto the Lord; and they testified against them: but they would not give ear. 20. And the spirit of God came upon Zechariah the son of Jehoiada the priest; and he stood above the people, and said unto them, Thus saith God, Why transgress ye the commandments of the Lord, that ye cannot prosper? because ye have forsaken the Lord, he hath also forsaken you. 21. And they conspired against him, and stoned him with stones at the command of the king in the court of the house of the Lord. 22. Thus Joash the king remembered not the kindness which Jehoiada his father had done to him, but slew his son. And when he died, he said, The Lord look upon it, and require it.

Joash's Triple Retributive Punishment

Then Hazael king of Syria went up, and fought against Gath, and took it: and Hazael set his face to go up to Jerusalem. And it came to pass at the end of the year, that the army of the Syrians came up against Joash: and they came to Judah and Jerusalem, and destroyed all the princes of the people from among the people. And Joash king of Judah took all the hallowed things that Jehoshaphat, and Jehoram, and Ahaziah, his fathers, kings of Judah, had dedicated, and his own hallowed things, and all the gold that was found in the treasures of the house of the Lord, and of the king's house, and sent all the spoil of them, unto Hazael king of Syria [1]: and he went away from Jerusalem.

For the army of the Syrians came with a small company of men; and the Lord delivered a very great host into their hand, because they had forsaken the Lord, the God of their fathers. So they executed judgement upon Joash. And when they were departed from him, (for they left him in great diseases,) his own servants arose and conspired against him for the blood of the sons of Jehoiada the priest, and slew him on his bed, at the house of Millo, on the way that goeth down to Silla. And these are they that conspired against him; Jozacar[2] the son of Shimeath the Ammonitess, and Jehozabad the son of Shomer[3] the Moabitess, his servants. And he died, and they buried him with his fathers in the city of David, but they buried him not in the sepulchres of the kings.

Now concerning his sons, and the rest of the acts of Joash, and all that he did, and the greatness of the burdens laid upon him, and the rebuilding of the house of God, behold, are they not written in the book of the chronicles of the kings of Judah?[4] and Amaziah his son reigned in his stead.

---

[1] In Chronicles, king of Damascus. [2] Zabad. [3] Shimrith. [4] Commentary of the book of kings. See Appendix C. III.

Sect. XXVII — THE DIVIDED KINGDOM

(II Kings 12:) 17. Then Hazael king of Syria went up, and fought against Gath: and took it: (and Hazael set his face to go up to Jerusalem.

18. And Jehoash king of Judah took all the hallowed things, that Jehoshaphat, and Jehoram, and Ahaziah, his fathers, kings of Judah, had dedicated, and his own hallowed things, and all the gold that was found in the treasures of the house of the Lord, and of the king's house, and sent it to Hazael king of *Syria*: and he went away from Jerusalem.)

20. And his servants arose, and made a conspiracy and smote Joash at the house of Millo, on the way that goeth down to Silla.

21[a]. For *Jozacar* the son of Shimeath and Jehozabad the son of *Shomer* his servants, smote him, and he died; and they buried him with his fathers in the city of David;

19. Now the rest of the acts of Joash, and all that he did, are they not written *in the book of the chronicles of the* kings of Judah? 21[b]. and Amaziah his son reigned in his stead.

(II Chron. 24:) 23. And it came to pass at the end of the year, that the army of the Syrians came up against him: (and they came to Judah and Jerusalem, and destroyed all the princes of the people from among the people,

and sent all the spoil of them unto the king of *Damascus*.)

24. For the army of the Syrians came with a small company of men; and the Lord delivered a very great host into their hand, because they had forsaken the Lord, the God of their fathers. So they executed judgement upon Joash.

25[a]. And when they were departed from him, for they left him in great diseases, his own servants conspired against him for the blood of the sons of Jehoiada the priest, and slew him on his bed,

26. And these are they that conspired against him; *Zabad* the son of Shimeath the Ammonitess, and Jehozabad the son of Shimrith the Moabitess, 25[b]. and he died; and they buried him in the city of David, but they buried him not in the sepulchres of the kings.

27. Now concerning his sons, and the greatness of the burdens laid upon him, and the rebuilding of the house of God, behold, they are written *in the commentary of the book of the* kings, and Amaziah his son reigned in his stead.

Oppression by Hazael, Death of Jehoahaz

II Kings 13:22. And Hazael king of Syria oppressed Israel all the days of Jehoahaz. 23. But the Lord was gracious unto them, and had compassion on them, and had respect unto them, because of his covenant with Abraham, Isaac, and Jacob, and would not destroy them, neither cast he them from his presence as yet. 8. Now the rest of the acts of Jehoahaz, and all that he did, and his might, are they not written in the book of the chronicles of the kings of Israel? 9. And Jehoahaz slept with his fathers; and they buried him in Samaria; and Joash reigned in his stead.

Accession and Character of Jehoash

10. In the thirty and seventh year of Joash king of Judah began Jehoash the son of Jehoahaz to reign over Israel in Samaria, and reigned sixteen years. 11. And he did that which was evil in the sight of the Lord; he departed not from all the sins of Jereboam the son of Nebat, wherewith he made Israel to sin: but he walked therein.

Accession and Character of Amaziah

In the second year of Joash son of Joahaz king of Israel began Amaziah the son of Joash king of Judah to reign. He was twenty and five years old when he began to reign; and he reigned twenty and nine years in Jerusalem: and his mother's name was Jehoaddin of Jerusalem. And he did that which was right in the eyes of the Lord, but not with a perfect heart like David his father: he did according to all that Joash his father had done. Howbeit the high places were not taken away: the people still sacrificed and burnt incense in high places. And it came to pass, as soon as the kingdom was established in his hand, that he slew his servants which had slain the king his father. But the children of the murderers he put not to death, but did according to that which is written in the book of the law of Moses, as the Lord commanded, saying, The fathers shall not be put to death for the children, neither the children for the fathers: but every man shall die for his own sin.

Military Preparations

II Chron. 25:5. Moreover Amaziah gathered Judah together, and ordered them according to their father's houses, under captains of thousands and captains of hundreds, even all Judah and Benjamin: and he numbered them from twenty years old and upward, and found them three hundred thousand chosen men, able to go forth to war, that could handle spear and shield.

An Israelite Army Hired but Returned

6. He hired also an hundred thousand mighty men of valour out of Israel for an hundred talents of silver. 7. But there came a man of God to him, saying, O king, let not the army of Israel go with thee; for the Lord is not with Israel, to wit, with all the children of Ephraim. 8. But if thou wilt go, do valiantly, be strong for the battle: God shall cast thee down before the enemy; for God hath power to help, and to cast down. 9. And Amaziah said to the man of God, But what shall we do for the hundred talents which I have given to the army of Israel? And the man of God answered, The Lord is able to give thee much more than this. 10. Then Amaziah separated them, to wit, the army that was come to him out of Ephraim, to go home again: wherefore their anger was greatly kindled against Judah, and they returned home in fierce anger. And Amaziah took courage, and led forth his people, and went to the Valley of Salt, and smote of the children of Seir ten thousand, and took Sela by war, and called the name of it Joktheel, unto this day. 12. And other ten thousand did the children of Judah carry away alive, and brought them unto the top of the rock, and cast them down from the top of the rock, that they all were broken in pieces. 13. But the men of the army which Amaziah sent back,

SECT. XXVII   THE UNITED KINGDOM

(II Kings 14:) 1. In the second year of Joash son of Joahaz king of Israel began Amaziah the son of Joash king of Judah to reign. 2. He was twenty and five years old when he began to reign; and he reigned twenty and nine years in Jerusalem: and his mother's name was Jehoaddin of Jerusalem. 3. And he did that which was right in the eyes of the Lord, yet not like David his father: he did according to all that Joash his father had done. 4. Howbeit the high places were not taken away: the people still sacrificed and burnt incense in the high places.	
5. And it came to pass, as soon as the kingdom was established in his hand, that he slew his servants which had slain the king his father: 6. but the children of the murderers he put not to death: according to that which is written in the book of the law of Moses, as the Lord commanded, saying, The fathers shall not be put to death for the children, nor the children be put to death for the fathers: but every man shall die for his own sin.	(II Chron. 25:) 1. Amaziah was twenty and five years old when he began to reign: and he reigned twenty and nine years in Jerusalem: and his mother's name was Jehoaddin of Jerusalem. 2. And he did that which was right in the eyes of the Lord, but not with a perfect heart. 3. Now it came to pass, when the kingdom was established unto him, that he slew his servants which had killed the king his father. 4. But he put not their children to death, but did according to that which is written in the law in the book of Moses, as the Lord commanded, saying, The fathers shall not die for the children, neither the children die for the fathers: but every man shall die for his own sin.
7. He slew of Edom in the Valley of Salt ten thousand and took Sela by war, and called the name of it Joktheel, unto this day.	11. Then Amaziah took courage, and led forth his people, and went to the Valley of Salt, and smote of the children of Seir ten thousand.

that they should not go with him to battle, fell upon the cities of Judah, from Samaria even unto Beth-horon, and smote of them three thousand, and took much spoil.

Amaziah's Idolatry Rebuked

14. Now it came to pass, after that Amaziah was come from the slaughter of the Edomites, that he brought the gods of the children of Seir, and set them up to be his gods, and bowed down himself before them, and burned incense unto them. 15. Wherefore the anger of the Lord was kindled against Amaziah, and he sent unto him a prophet, which said unto him, Why hast thou sought after the gods of the people, which have not delivered their own people out of thine hand? 16. And it came to pass, as he talked with him, that the king said unto him, Have we made thee of the king's counsel? forbear; why shouldest thou be smitten? Then the prophet forbare, and said I know that God hath determined to destroy thee, because thou hast done this, and hast not hearkened unto my counsel.

Elisha and Joash King of Israel

II Kings 13:14. Now Elisha was fallen sick of his sickness whereof he died: and Joash the king of Israel came down unto him, and wept over him, and said, My father, My father, the chariots of Israel and the horsemen thereof! 15. And Elisha said unto him, Take bow and arrows: and he took unto him bow and arrows. 16. And he said to the king of Israel, Put thine hand upon the bow: and he put his hand upon it. And Elisha laid his hand upon the king's hands. 17. And he said, Open the window eastward: and he opened it. Then Elisha said, Shoot: and he shot. And he said, The Lord's arrow of victory, even the arrow of victory over Syria: for thou shalt smite the Syrians in Aphek, till thou have consumed them. 18. And he said, Take the arrows: and he took them. And he said unto the king of Israel, Smite upon the ground: and he smote thrice, and stayed. 19. And the man of God was wroth with him, and said, Thou shouldest have smitten five or six times; then hadst thou smitten Syria till thou hadst consumed it: whereas now thou shalt smite Syria but thrice.

Death and Burial of Elisha

20. And Elisha died, and they buried him. Now the bands of the Moabites invaded the land at the coming of the year. 21. And it came to pass, as they were burying a man, that, behold, they spied a band; and they cast the man into the sepulchre of Elisha: and as soon as the man touched the bones of Elisha, he revived and stood up on his feet.

24. And Hazael king of Syria died; and Ben-hadad his son reigned in his stead. 25. And Jehoash the son of Jehoahaz took again out of the hand of Ben-hadad the son of Hazael the cities which he had taken out of the hand of Jehoahaz his father by war. Three times did Joash smite him, and recovered the cities of Israel.

Amaziah's Boastful Challenge

Then Amaziah king of Judah took advice, and sent messengers to Joash the son of Jehoahaz son of Jehu the king of Israel, saying, Come, let us look one another in the face. And Joash the king of Israel sent to Amaziah king of Judah, saying, The thistle that was in Lebanon sent to the cedar that was in Lebanon, saying, Give thy daughter to my son to wife: and there passed by a wild beast that was in Lebanon, and trode down the thistle. Thou sayest, Lo thou hast indeed smitten Edom, and thine heart lifteth thee up to boast: glory thereof, and abide now at home; for why shouldest thou meddle to thy hurt, that thou shouldest fall, even thou, and Judah with thee? But Amaziah would not hear; for it was of God, that he might deliver them into the hand of their enemies, because they had sought after the gods of Edom. So Joash king of Israel went up; and he and Amaziah king of Judah looked one an-

SECT. XXVII   THE DIVIDED KINGDOM

(II Kings 14 :) 8. Then Amaziah sent messengers to Jehoash, the son of Jehoahaz son of Jehu, the king of Israel, saying, Come, let us look one another in the face. 9. And Jehoash the king of Israel sent to Amaziah king of Judah, saying, The thistle that was in Lebanon sent to the cedar that was in Lebanon, saying, Give thy daughter to my son to wife: and there passed by a wild beast that was in Lebanon, and trode down the thistle. 10. Thou hast indeed smitten Edom, and thine heart hath lifted thee up : glory thereof, and abide at home ; for why shouldest thou meddle to thy hurt, that thou shouldest fall, even thou, and Judah with thee? 11. But Amaziah would not hear. So Jehoash king of Israel went up; and he and Amaziah king of Judah looked	(II Chron. 25 :) 17. Then Amaziah king of Judah took advice, and sent to Joash, the son of Jehoahaz the son of Jehu, king of Israel, saying, Come, let us look one another in the face. 18. And Joash king of Israel sent to Amaziah king of Judah, saying, The thistle that was in Lebanon sent to the cedar that was in Lebanon, saying, Give thy daughter to my son to wife : and there passed by a wild beast that was in Lebanon, and trode down the thistle. 19. Thou sayest, Lo thou hast smitten Edom, and thine heart lifteth thee up to boast: abide now at home ; why shouldest thou meddle to thy hurt, that thou shouldest fall, even thou, and Judah with thee? 20. But Amaziah would not hear ; for it was of God, that he might deliver them into the hand of their enemies, because they had sought after the gods of Edom. So Joash king of Israel went up, and he and Amaziah king of Judah looked

other in the face at Beth-shemesh, which belongeth to Judah.

Amaziah's Disastrous Defeat

And Judah was put to the worse before Israel, and they fled every man to his tent. And Joash king of Israel took Amaziah king of Judah, the son of Joash the son of Ahaziah at Beth-shemesh, and brought him to Jerusalem, and brake down the wall of Jerusalem from the gate of Ephraim unto the corner gate, four hundred cubits. And he took all the gold and silver, and all the vessels that were found in the house of the Lord with Obed-edom, and the treasures of the king's house, the hostages also, and returned to Samaria.

Death of Jehoash and Amaziah

Now the rest of the acts of Joash, and all that he did, and his might wherewith he fought against Amaziah king of Judah, are they not written in the book of the chronicles of the kings of Israel? And Joash slept with his fathers; and was buried in Samaria with the kings of Israel; and Jereboam his son reigned in his stead. And Amaziah the son of Jehoash king of Judah lived after the death of Joash the son of Jehoahaz king of Israel fifteen years.

Now the rest of the acts of Amaziah, first and last, behold, are they not written in the book of the chronicles of the kings of Israel?[*1] Now from the time that Amaziah did turn away from following the Lord, they made a conspiracy against him in Jerusalem; and he fled to Lachish: but they sent after him to Lachish, and slew him there. And they brought him upon horses: and he was buried with his fathers in the city of David.[*2]

Accession and Character of Jereboam II.

II Kings 14:23. In the fifteenth year of Amaziah the son of Joash king of Judah Jereboam the son of Joash king of Israel began to reign in Samaria, and reigned forty and one years.

24. And he did that which was evil in the sight of the Lord; he departed not from all the sins of Jereboam the son of Nebat, wherewith he made Israel to sin. 25. He restored the border of Israel from the entering in of Hamath unto the sea of Arabah, according to the word of the Lord, the God of Israel, which he spake by the hand of his servant Jonah † the son of Amittai, the prophet, which was of Gath-hepher. 26. For the Lord saw the affliction of Israel, that it was very bitter: for there was none shut up nor left at large, neither was there any helper for Israel. 27. And the Lord said not that he would blot out the name of Israel from under heaven: but he saved them by the hand of Jereboam the son of Joash.

[*1]. In Chronicles, the book of the kings of Judah and Israel. [*2]. the City of Judah.

† THE PROPHETS OF THE ASSYRIAN PERIOD.

Chronologically, they probably stand thus, Jonah, Joel, Amos, Hosea, Isaiah, Micah. Jonah prophesied in the days of Jereboam. (II Kings 14:25.) Amos in the days of Uzziah king of Judah, and of Jereboam king of Israel. (Amos 1:1.) Hosea in the days of Uzziah, Jotham, Ahaz, and Hezekiah, kings of Judah, and Jereboam king of Israel. (Hosea 1:1.) Isaiah in the days of Uzziah, Jotham, Ahaz, and Hezekiah, kings of Judah. (Isaiah 1:1.) Micah in the days of Jotham, Ahaz, and Hezekiah, kings of Judah. (Micah 1:1.) As to the time of Joel's prophesying, there is the greatest divergence of opinion, some putting him before Jonah, while others put him in the post-exilic period. A comparison of Joel 3:16, 18. and Amos 1:2. 9:13. furnishes presumptive evidence, based on the similarity of the prophecies, that Joel prophesied before Amos,

(Joel 3:) 16, 18. And the Lord shall roar from Zion, and utter his voice from Jerusalem; 18. And it shall come to pass in that day, that the mountains shall drop down sweet wine, and the hills shall flow with milk, and all the brooks of Judah shall flow with waters; and a fountain shall come forth of the house of the Lord, and shall water the valley of Shittim.	(Amos 1:) 2. And he said, The Lord shall roar from Zion, and utter his voice from Jerusalem; 9:13. Behold, the days come, saith the Lord, that the plowman shall overtake the reaper, and the treader of grapes him that soweth seed; and the mountains shall drop sweet wine, and all the hills shall melt.

one another in the face at Beth-shemesh, which belongeth to Judah. 12. And Judah was put to the worse before Israel; and they fled every man to his tent. 13. And Jehoash king of Israel took Amaziah king of Judah, the son of Jehoash the son of Ahaziah, at Beth-shemesh, and came to Jerusalem, and brake down the wall of Jerusalem from the gate of Ephraim unto the corner gate, four hundred cubits. 14. And he took all the gold and silver, and all the vessels that were found in the house of the Lord, and in the treasures of the king's house, the hostages also, and returned to Samaria. 15. Now the rest of the acts of Jehoash which he did, and his might, and how he fought with Amaziah king of Judah, are they not written in the book of the chronicles of the kings of Israel? 16. And Jehoash slept with his fathers; and was buried in Samaria with the kings of Israel; and Jeroboam his son reigned in his stead. 17. And Amaziah the son of Joash king of Judah lived after the death of Jehoash son of Jehoahaz king of Israel fifteen years.

18. Now the rest of the acts of Amaziah, are they not written in the book of the *chronicles of the kings of Judah?* 19. And they made a conspiracy against him in Jerusalem; and he fled to Lachish: but they sent after him to Lachish, and slew him there. 20. And they brought him upon horses: and he was buried with his fathers in the city of *David*.

one another in the face at Beth-shemesh, which belongeth to Judah. 22. And Judah was put to the worse before Israel; and they fled every man to his tent. 23. And Joash king of Israel took Amaziah king of Judah, the son of Joash the son of Jehoahaz, at Beth-shemesh, and brought him to Jerusalem, and brake down the wall of Jerusalem from the gate of Ephraim unto the corner gate, four hundred cubits. 24. And he took all the gold and silver, and all the vessels that were found in the house of God with Obed-edom, and the treasures of the king's house, the hostages also, and returned to Samaria. (II Kings 13:) 12. Now the rest of the acts of Joash, and all that he did, and his might wherewith he fought against Amaziah king of Judah, are they not written in the book of the chronicles of the kings of Israel? 13. And Joash slept with his fathers; and Joash was buried in Samaria with the kings of Israel, and Jeroboam his son reigned in his stead. (II Chron. 25:) 25. And Amaziah the son of Joash king of Judah lived after the death of Joash son of Jehoahaz king of Israel fifteen years.

26. Now the rest of the acts of Amaziah, first and last, behold, are they not written in the book of the *kings of Judah and Israel?* 27. Now from the time that Amaziah did turn away from following the Lord they made a conspiracy against him in Jerusalem; and he fled to Lachish: but they sent after him to Lachish, and slew him there. 28. And they brought him upon horses: and buried him with his fathers in the city of *Judah*.

Jonah and Hosea were certainly prophets of the Northern kingdom. Amos was of Judah, but he prophesied in Israel, until prohibited. (Amos 7:10) "Then Amaziah the priest of Beth-el sent to Jeroboam king of Israel, saying, Amos hath conspired against thee in the midst of the house of Israel: the land is not able to bear all his words. 11. For thus Amos saith, Jeroboam shall die by the sword, and Israel shall surely be led away captive out of his land. 12. And Amaziah said unto Amos, O thou seer, go, flee thee away into the land of Judah, there eat bread, and prophesy there: 13. but prophesy not again any more at Beth-el: for it is the king's sanctuary, and it is a royal house." All the other prophets prophesied in the Southern kingdom.

The conquests of Jeroboam II over Syria greatly extending Israel eastward, brought his kingdom into direct contact with the great military empire of Assyria. Uzziah's conquests westward, so that his name spread abroad even to the entering in of Egypt, attracted the attention of that great empire. Amos' prophecy (6:14) "For, behold, I will raise up against you a

Accession and Character of Uzziah

And all the people of Judah took Uzziah,[*1] who was sixteen years old, and made him king in the room of his father Amaziah. He built Eloth,[*2] and restored it to Judah, after that the king slept with his fathers. In the twenty and seventh year of Jereboam king of Israel began Uzziah the son of Amaziah king of Judah to reign. Sixteen years old was he when he began to reign; and he reigned fifty and two years in Jerusalem: and his mother's name was Jechiliah[*3] of Jerusalem. And he did that which was right in the eyes of the Lord, according to all that Amaziah his father had done. Howbeit the high places were not taken away: the people still sacrificed and burnt incense in the high places. And he set himself to seek God in the days of Zechariah, who had understanding in the vision of God: and as long as he sought the Lord, God made him to prosper.

Subjection of Philistines, Arabians and Ammonites

II Chron. 26:6. And he went forth and warred against the Philistines, and brake down the wall of Gath, and the wall of Jabneh, and the wall of Ashdod; and he built cities in the country of Ashdod, and among the Philistines. 7. And God helped him against the Philistines, and against the Arabians that dwelt in Gur-baal, and the Meunim. 8. And the Ammonites gave gifts to Uzziah: and his name spread abroad even to the entering in of Egypt; for he waxed exceeding strong. 9. Moreover Uzziah built towers in Jerusalem at the corner gate, and at the valley gate, and at the turning of the wall, and fortified them. 10. And he built towers in the wilderness, and hewed out many cisterns, for he had much cattle; in the lowland also, and in the plain: and he had husbandmen and vinedressers in the mountains and in the fruitful fields; for he loved husbandry. 11. Moreover Uzziah had an army of fighting men, that went out to war by bands, according to the number of their reckoning made by Jeiel the scribe and Masseiah the officer, under the hand of Hananiah, one of the king's captains. 12. The whole number of the heads of the fathers' houses, even the mighty men of valour, was two thousand and six hundred. 13. And under their hand was a trained army, three hundred thousand and seven thousand and five hundred, that made war with mighty power, to help the king against the enemy. 14. And Uzziah prepared for them, even for all the host, shields, and spears, and helmets, and coats of mail, and bows, and stones for slinging. 15. And he made in Jerusalem engines, invented by cunning men, to be on the towers and upon the battlements, to shoot arrows and great stones withal. And his name spread far abroad; for he was marvellously helped, till he was strong.

---

* In Kings [1] Azariah. [2] Elath. [3] Jecoliah.

---

nation, saith the Lord, the God of hosts; and they shall afflict you from the entering of Hamath unto the brook of Arabah, uses the same language to describe Assyria's advance westward, as was used (II Kings 14:25) to describe Jereboam's earlier advance eastward. The absorption of both the Northern and the Southern kingdoms could be prevented only by special help from their Covenant-God; or by playing the rival kingdoms of Assyria and Egypt against each other; or by tributary alliances with Assyria, the most aggressive of the two empires. The prophets of this period condemn and denounce in severest terms the last two remedies, and foretell their failure if tried, and constantly preach reliance on Jehovah to avert the impending destruction. This leads them to portray in vivid colors the sinful internal conditions of both Israel and Judah, which demand their repentance and reformation before they can hope for Jehovah's help. With this condemnation of the present, they predict a bright and glorious future for God's people after they have been purified by deserved punishment.

Sect. XXVII THE DIVIDED KINGDOM

(II Kings 14:) 21. And all the people of Judah took *Azariah*, who was sixteen years old, and made him king in the room of his father Amaziah.
22. He built *Elath*, and restored it to Judah, after that the king slept with his fathers. (II Kings 15:) 1. In the twenty and seventh year of Jereboam king of Israel began Azariah the son of Amaziah king of Judah to reign.
2. Sixteen years old was he when he began to reign; and he reigned two and fifty years in Jerusalem: and his mother's name was *Jecoliah* of Jerusalem. 3. And he did that which was right in the eyes of the Lord, according to all that his father Amaziah had done. 4. Howbeit the high places were not taken away: the people still sacrificed and burnt incense in the high places.

(II Chron. 26:) 1. And all the people of Judah took *Uzziah*, who was sixteen years old, and made him king in the room of his father Amaziah.
2. He built *Eloth*, and restored it to Judah, after that the king slept with his fathers.

3. Sixteen years old was Uzziah when he began to reign; and he reigned fifty and two years in Jerusalem: and his mother's name was *Jechiliah* of Jerusalem. 4. And he did that which was right in the eyes of the Lord, according to all that his father Amaziah had done.

5. And he set himself to seek God in the days of Zechariah, who had understanding in the vision of God: and as long as he sought the Lord, God made him to prosper.

Uzziah's Presumption and Leprosy

16. But when he was strong, his heart was lifted up so that he did corruptly, and he trespassed against the Lord his God; for he went into the temple of the Lord to burn incense upon the altar of incense. 17. And Azariah the priest went in after him, and with him fourscore priests of the Lord, that were valiant men: 18. and they withstood Uzziah the king, and said unto him, It pertaineth not unto thee, Uzziah, to burn incense unto the Lord, but to the priests the sons of Aaron, that are consecrated to burn incense: go out of the sanctuary; for thou hast trespassed; neither shall it be for thine honour from the Lord God. 19. Then Uzziah was wroth; and he had a censer in his hand to burn incense; and while he was wroth with the priests, the leprosy brake forth in his forehead before the priests in the house of the Lord, beside the altar of incense. 20ª. And Azariah the chief priest, and all the priests, looked upon him, and, behold, he was leprous in his forehead, and they thrust him out quickly from thence; yea, himself hasted also to go out, because the Lord had smitten him. And Uzziah the king was a leper unto the day of his death, and dwelt in a several house, being a leper; for he was cut off from the house of the Lord: and Jotham his son was over the king's house, judging the people of the land.

Jereboam's Death and Burial

II Kings 14:28. Now the rest of the acts of Jereboam, and all that he did, and his might, how he warred, and how he recovered Damascus, and Hamath, which had belonged to Judah, for Israel, are they not written in the book of the chronicles of the kings of Israel? 29. And Jereboam slept with his fathers, even with the kings of Israel; and Zechariah his son reigned in his stead.

Accession and Character of Zechariah

II Kings 15:8. In the thirty and eighth year of Azariah king of Judah did Zechariah the son of Jereboam reign over Israel in Samaria six months. 9. And he did that which was evil in the sight of the Lord, as his fathers had done: he departed not from the sins of Jereboam the son of Nebat, wherewith he made Israel to sin. 10. And Shallum the son of Jabesh conspired against him, and smote him before the people, and slew him, and reigned in his stead.

11. Now the rest of the acts of Zechariah, behold, they are written in the book of the chronicles of the kings of Israel. 12. This was the word of the Lord which he spake unto Jehu, saying, Thy sons to the fourth generation shall sit upon the throne of Israel.* And so it came to pass.

---

* II Kings 10:30. And the Lord said unto Jehu, Because thou hast done well in executing that which is right in mine eyes and hast done unto the house of Ahab according to all that was in mine heart, thy sons of the fourth generation shal sit on the throne of Israel.

(II Kings 15:) 5. And the Lord smote the king, so that he was a leper unto the day of his death, and dwelt in a several house. And Jotham the king's son was over the household, judging the people of the land.

(II Chron. 26:) 20ᵇ. because the Lord had smitten him. 21. And Uzziah the king was a leper unto the day of his death, and dwelt in a several house, being a leper; for he was cut off from the house of the Lord: and Jotham his son was over the king's house, judging the people of the land.

JUDAH	ISRAEL
THE HOUSE OF DAVID.	B. C. 770
B. C. 808–756*	(Amos) THE HOUSE OF SHALLUM (Sixth) (15)
XI Uzziah (Isaiah)	B. C. 740
B. C. 782–737	(Hosea) THE HOUSE OF MENAHEM (Seventh) (16)
Jotham Co-Regent (Micah)	I Menahem { B. C. 770–761 / B. C. 740–737
B. C. 756–742	
XII Jotham	II Pekahiah { B. C. 761–759 / B. C. 737–735 (17)
B. C. 737–735	
B. C. 742–726	B. C. 759–730
XIII Ahaz	THE HOUSE OF PEKAH (Eighth) (18)
B. C. 735–725 or 715	B. C. 735–733
B. C. 726	B. C. 730–721
XIV Hezekiah	THE HOUSE OF HOSHEA (Ninth) (19)
B. C. 725 or 715	B. C. 733–722

SECTION XXVIII
House of David and Last Four Houses of Israel

Shallum's One Month's Reign

II Kings 15:13. Shallum the son of Jabesh began to reign in nine and thirtieth year of Uzziah king of Judah; and he reigned the space of a month in Samaria. 14. And Menahem the son of Gadi went up from Tirzah, and came to Samaria, and smote Shallum the son of Jabesh in Samaria, and slew him, and reigned in his stead. 15. Now the rest of the acts of Shallum, and his conspiracy which he made, behold, they are written in the book of the chronicles of the kings of Israel. 16. Then Menahem smote Tiphsah, and all that were therein, and the borders thereof, from Tirzah: because they opened not to him, therefore he smote it; and all the women therein that were with child he ripped up.

Accession and Character of Menahem

17. In the nine and thirtieth year of Azariah king of Judah began Menahem the son of Gadi to reign over Israel, and reigned ten years in Samaria. 18. And he did that which was evil in the sight of the Lord: he departed not all his days from the sins of Jereboam the son of Nebat, wherewith he made Israel to sin. 19. There came against the land Pul the king of Assyria; and Menahem gave Pul a thousand talents of silver, that his hand might be with him to confirm the kingdom in his hand. 20. And Menahem exacted the money of Israel, even of all the mighty men of wealth, of each man fifty shekels of silver, to give to the king of Assyria. So the king of Assyria turned back, and stayed not there in the land. 21. Now the rest of the acts of Menahem, and all that he did, are they not written in the book of the chronicles of the kings of Israel? 22. And Menahem slept with his fathers; and Pekahiah his son reigned in his stead.

Accession and Character of Pekahiah and of Pekah

23. In the fiftieth year of Azariah king of Judah Pekahiah the son of Menahem began to reign over Israel in Samaria, and reigned two years. 24. And he did that which was evil in the sight of the Lord: he departed not from the sins of Jereboam the son of Nebat, wherewith he made Israel to sin. 25. And Pekah the son of Remaliah, his captain, conspired against him, and smote him in Samaria, in the castle of the king's house, with Argob and Arieh; and with him were fifty men of the Gileadites: and he slew him, and reigned in his stead. 26. Now the rest of the acts of Pekahiah and all that he did, behold, they are written in the book of the chronicles of the kings of Israel.

27. In the two and fiftieth year of Azariah king of Judah Pekah the son of Remaliah began to reign over Israel in Samaria, and reigned twenty years. 28. And he did that which was evil in the sight of the Lord: he departed not from the sins of Jereboam the son of Nebat, wherewith he made Israel to sin.

Now the rest of the acts of Uzziah,† and all that he did, first and last, did Isaiah the prophet, the son of Amoz, write. Are they not written in the book of the chronicles of the kings of Judah?

---
* See Chronology Appendix A. Both systems of chronology are used, *e. g.*, Uzziah 808 (Usher) / 782 (Revised)
† In Kings, Azariah.

(II Kings 15:) 6. Now the rest of the acts of Azariah, and all that he did, ((are they not written in the book of the chronicles of the kings of Judah?))	(II Chron. 26:) 22. Now the rest of the acts of Uzziah, first and last, ((did Isaiah the prophet, the son of Amos, write.))

	And Uzziah slept with his fathers* and they buried him with his

Death and Burial of Uzziah / **Jotham Reigns Alone**

And Uzziah slept with his fathers* and they buried him with his fathers in the city of David, in the field of burial which belonged to the kings; for they said, He is a leper: and Jotham his son reigned in his stead. In the second year of Pekah the son of Remaliah king of Israel began Jotham the son of Uzziah king of Judah to reign. Five and twenty years old was he when he began to reign; and he reigned sixteen years in Jerusalem: and his mother's name was Jerusha the daughter of Zadok.

Character, Works, and Wars

And he did that which was right in the eyes of the Lord, according to all that his father Uzziah had done. Howbeit he entered not into the temple of the Lord, the high places were not taken away; the people still sacrificed and burnt incense in the high places, and did yet corruptly. He built the upper gate of the house of the Lord, and on the wall of Ophel he built much. Moreover he built cities in the hill country of Judah, and in the forests he built castles and towers. He fought also with the king of the children of Ammon, and prevailed against them. And the children of Ammon gave him the same year an hundred talents of silver, and ten thousand measures of wheat, and ten thousand of barley. So much did the children of Ammon render unto him, in the second year also, and in the third. So Jotham became mighty, because he ordered his ways before the Lord his God. Now the rest of the acts of Jotham, and all that he did, and all his wars, and his ways, behold, they are written in the book of the kings of Israel and Judah. He was five and twenty years old when he began to reign, and reigned sixteen years in Jerusalem. And Jotham slept with his fathers, and they buried him with his fathers in the city of David his father: and Ahaz his son reigned in his stead.

THE CALL, CONSECRATION, AND COMMISSION OF ISAIAH.

* Isaiah 6: 1-13. In the year that king Uzziah died I saw the Lord sitting upon a throne, high and lifted up, and his train filled the temple. Above him stood the Seraphim: each one had six wings; with twain he covered his face, and with twain he covered his feet, and with twain he did fly. And one cried unto another, and said,

"Holy, holy, holy, is the Lord of Hosts!"
"The whole earth is full of his glory!"

And the foundations of the thresholds were moved at the voice of him that cried, and the house was filled with smoke.

Then said I, "Woe is me! for I am undone; because I am a man of unclean lips, and I dwell in the midst of a people of unclean lips: Mine eyes have seen the king, the Lord of Hosts!"

Then flew one of the Seraphim unto me, having a live coal in his hand, which he had taken with the tongs from off the altar: and he touched my mouth with it, and said, "Lo, this hath touched thy lips; and thine iniquity is taken away, and thy sin is purged."

And I heard the voice of the Lord, saying, "Whom shall I send, and who will go for us?" Then I said, "Here am I, send me."

And he said, "Go, and tell this people, Hear ye indeed, but understand not; and see ye indeed, but perceive not. Make the heart of this people fat, and make their ears heavy, and shut their eyes; lest they see with their eyes, and hear with their ears, and understand with their heart, and turn again, and be healed." "Then said I, Lord, how long?"

"And he answered, Until cities be waste without inhabitant, and houses without man, and the land become utterly waste, and the Lord have removed men far away, and the forsaken places be many in the midst of the land. And if there be yet a tenth in it, it shall again be eaten up: as a terebinth, and as an oak, whose stock remaineth, when they are felled; so the holy seed is the stock thereof."

SECT. XXVIII   THE DIVIDED KINGDOM   227

(II Kings 15:) 7. And Azariah slept with his fathers; and they buried him with his fathers in the city of David; and Jotham his son reigned in his stead.
(II Kings 15:) 32. In the second year of Pekah the son of Remaliah king of Israel began Jotham the son of Uzziah king of Judah to reign. 33. Five and twenty years old was he when he began to reign; and he reigned sixteen years in Jerusalem: and his mother's name was Jerusha the daughter of Zadok.
34. And he did that which was right in the eyes of the Lord: he did according to all that his father Uzziah had done.
35. Howbeit the high places were not taken away: the people *still sacrificed and burnt incense* in the high places. He built the upper gate of the house of the Lord.

36. Now the rest of the acts of Jotham, and all that he did, are they not written ((in the book of the *chronicles of the kings of Judah?*))

38. And Jotham slept with his fathers, and was buried with his fathers in the city of David his father: and Ahaz his son reigned in his stead.

(II Chron. 26:) 23. So Uzziah slept with his fathers; and they buried him with his fathers in the field of burial which belonged to the kings; for they said, He is a leper: and Jotham his son reigned in his stead.

(II Chron. 27:) 1. Jotham was twenty and five years old when he began to reign; and he reigned sixteen years in Jerusalem; and his mother's name was Jerusha the daughter of Zadok.
2. And he did that which was right in the eyes of the Lord according to all that his father Uzziah had done, howbeit he entered not into the temple of the Lord. And the people *did yet corruptly*.

3. He built the upper gate of the house of the Lord, and on the wall of Ophel he built much. 4. Moreover he built cities in the hill country of Judah, and in the forests he built castles and towers. 5. He fought also with the king of the children of Ammon, and prevailed against them. And the children of Ammon gave him the same year an hundred talents of silver, and ten thousand measures of wheat, and ten thousand of barley. So much did the children of Ammon render unto him, in the second year also, and in the third. 6. So Jotham became mighty, because he ordered his ways before the Lord his God. 7. Now the rest of the acts of Jotham, and all his wars, and his ways, behold, they are written ((in the book of the *kings of Israel and Judah*.)) 8. He was five and twenty years old when he began to reign, and he reigned sixteen years in Jerusalem. 9. And Jotham slept with his fathers, and they buried him in the city of David: and Ahaz his son reigned in his stead.

Accession and Character of Ahaz

In the seventeenth year of Pekah the son of Remaliah Ahaz the son of Jotham began to reign. Twenty years old was Ahaz when he began to reign; and he reigned sixteen years in Jerusalem: and he did not that which was right in the eyes of the Lord his God, like David his father: but he walked in the ways of the kings of Israel, and made also molten images for the Baalim.

Moreover he burnt incense in the valley of the son of Hinnom, and made his son to pass through the fire, according to the abominations of the heathen, whom the Lord cast out before the children of Israel. And he sacrificed and burnt incense in the high places, and on the hills and under every green tree.

Rezin and Pekah Besiege Jerusalem

In those days the Lord began to send against Judah Rezin the king of Syria, and Pekah the son of Remaliah. And it came to pass in the days of Ahaz the son of Jotham, the son of Uzziah, king of Judah, that *Rezin king of Syria, and Pekah the son of Remaliah king of Israel went up to Jerusalem to war against it: but could not prevail against it: and they besieged Ahaz, but could not overcome him. And it was told the house of David, saying, Syria is confederate with Ephraim. *And his heart was moved, and the heart of his people, as the trees of the forest are moved with the wind.

Isaiah's First Message to Ahaz

Then said the Lord unto Isaiah, Go forth now to meet Ahaz, thou, and Shear-jashub thy son, at the end of the conduit of the upper pool, in the high way of the fuller's field; and say unto him, Take heed, and be quiet; fear not, neither let thine heart be faint, because of these two tails of smoking firebrands, for the fierce anger of Rezin and Syria, and of the son of Remaliah. Because Syria hath counselled evil against thee, Ephraim also, and the son of Remaliah, saying, Let us go up against Judah, and vex it, and let us make a breach therein for us, and set up a king in the midst of it, even the son of Tabeel: * thus saith the Lord God, It shall not stand, neither shall it come to pass. For the head of Syria is Damascus, and the head of Damascus is Rezin: and within threescore and five years shall Ephraim be broken in pieces, that it be not a people: and the head of Ephraim is Samaria, and the head of Samaria is Remaliah's son. If ye will not believe, surely ye shall not be established.

Isaiah's Second Message

Is. 7: 10. And the Lord spake again unto Ahaz, saying, 11. Ask thee a sign of the Lord thy God; ask it either in the depth, or in the height above. 12. But Ahaz said, I will not ask, neither will I tempt the Lord. 13. And he said, Hear ye now, O house of David: is it a small thing for you to weary men, that ye will weary my God also? 14. Therefore the Lord himself shall give you a sign: behold, a virgin shall conceive, and bear a son, and shall call his name Immanuel. 15. Butter and honey shall he eat, when he knoweth to refuse the evil, and choose the good. 16. For before the child shall know to refuse the evil, and choose the good, the land whose two kings thou abhorrest shall be forsaken. 17. The Lord shall bring upon thee, and upon thy people, and upon thy father's house, days that have not come, from the day that Ephraim departed from Judah; even the king of Assyria.

Ahaz Punished for Idolatry and Unbelief

II Chron. 28:5. Wherefore the Lord his God delivered him into the hand of the king of Syria; and they smote him, and carried away of him a great multitude of captives, and brought them to Damascus. And he was also delivered into the hand of the king of Israel, who smote him with a great slaughter. 6. For Pekah the son of Remaliah slew in

---
* NOTE.—It is probable that Rezin and Pekah joined together to make war on Ahaz, because he had refused to ally

SECT. XXVIII   THE DIVIDED KINGDOM   229

(II Kings 16:) 1. In the seventeenth year of Pekah the son of Remaliah Ahaz the son of Jotham began to reign.

2. Twenty years old was Ahaz when he began to reign; and he reigned sixteen years in Jerusalem: and he did not that which was right in the eyes of the Lord his God, like David his father. 3. But he walked in the way of the kings of Israel,

yea, and made his son to pass through the fire, according to the abominations of the heathen, whom the Lord cast out from before the children of Israel. 4. And he sacrificed and burnt incense in the high places, and on the hills and under every green tree.

(II Kings 15:) 37.   In those days the Lord began to send against Judah Rezin the king of Syria, and Pekah the son of Remaliah. (II Kings 16:) 5. Then Rezin king of Syria and Pekah the son of Remaliah king of Israel came up to Jerusalem to war: and they besieged Ahaz, but could not overcome him.

(II Chron. 28:) 1. Ahaz was twenty years old when he began to reign; and he reigned sixteen years in Jerusalem: and he did not that which was right in the eyes of the Lord,   like David his father: 2. but he walked in the ways of the kings of Israel, and made also molten images for the Baalim. 3. Moreover he burnt incense in the valley of the son of Hinnom, and burnt his children in the fire, according to the abominations of the heathen, whom the Lord cast out before the children of Israel. 4. And he sacrificed and burnt incense in the high places, and on the hills and under every green tree.

(Isaiah 7:) 1. And it came to pass in the days of Ahaz the son of Jotham, the son of Uzziah, king of Judah,

that Rezin the king of Syria and Pekah the son of Remaliah king of Israel went up to Jerusalem to war against it;   but could not prevail against it. 2. And it was told the house of David, saying, Syria is confederate with Ephraim. And his heart was moved, and the heart of his people, as the trees of the forest are moved with the wind.

(Isaiah 7:) 3. Then said the Lord unto Isaiah, Go forth now to meet Ahaz, thou, and Shear-jashub thy son, at the end of the conduit of the upper pool, in the high way of the fuller's field; 4. and say unto him, Take heed, and be quiet; fear not, neither let thine heart be faint, because of these two tails of smoking firebrands, for the fierce anger of Rezin and Syria, and of the son of Remaliah. 5. Because Syria hath counselled evil against thee, Ephraim also, and the son of Remaliaht saying, 6. Let us go up against Judah, and vex it, and let us make a breach therein for us, and set up a king in the midst of it, even the son of Tabeel: 7. thus saith the Lord God, It shall not stand, neither shall it come to pass. 8. For the head of Syria is Damascus, and the head of Damascus is Rezin: and within threescore and five years shall Ephraim be broken in pieces, that it be not a people: 9. and the head of Ephraim is Samaria, and the head of Samaria is Remaliah's son. If ye will not believe, surely ye shall not be established.

---

himself with them against the king of Assyria. Unable to secure his co-operation, they banded together to dethrone him, and set up a king in his place, even the son of Tabeel, (Isaiah 7:6) who would form a triple alliance with them against Assyria. We are told (II Kings 16:5) (Isaiah 7:1) that they failed. The Lord sends messages to Ahaz in his great trepidation, to "be quiet, fear not, neither be faint," and warns him, (Isaiah 7:9) "If ye believe not, surely ye shall not be established." He further tells him, (7:11-16) to ask for a sign, and when he refuses to ask for one, he gives him one unasked, and announces the retribution the Lord will send upon his people, and his father's house. (Isaiah 7:17.)

For this unbelief, added to his previous outrageous idolatry, we have given in Chronicles, (II Chron. 28:5-15) what is omitted in Kings and Isaiah, how the Lord his God delivered him into the hand of king of Syria and the king of Israel, both of whom smote him with great slaughter and carried a great multitude away captives, "because they had forsaken the Lord, the God of their fathers." Through the protest of Oded the prophet, Israel returned all their captives to Jericho. After this terrible defeat and loss, still refusing to trust in God, he halted between two alternatives, viz., either form alliance with Syria and Israel, which he had refused to do at the first, or, call on the king of Assyria for help. In respect to this, Isaiah (8:5-8) says, "And the Lord spake unto me yet again, saying, Forasmuch as this people hath refused the waters of Shiloah that go softly, and rejoice in Rezin and Remaliah's son; now therefore, behold, the Lord bringeth up upon them the waters of the River, strong and many, even the king of Assyria and all his glory: and he shall come up over all his channels and go over all his banks: and he shall sweep onward into Judah; he shall overthrow and pass through; he shall reach even to the neck; and the stretching out of his wings shall fill the breadth of thy land, O Immanuel."

This message seems to have prevented the forming of this alliance with Syria and Israel. After still more repulses and defeats from the Syrians, Edomites and Philistines, he took the other horn of the dilemma, and called the king of Assyria to his help, which led to still greater distresses of him and his people, "and in the time of his distress did he trespass ye more against the Lord."

Judah an hundred and twenty thousand in one day, all of them valiant men; because they had forsaken the Lord, the God of their fathers. 7. And Zichri, a mighty man of Ephraim, slew Maaseiah the king's son, and Azrikam the ruler of the house, and Elkanah that was next to the king. 8. And the children of Israel carried away captive of their brethren two hundred thousand, women, sons, and daughters, and took also away much spoil from them, and brought the spoil to Samaria. 9. But a prophet of the Lord was there, whose name was Oded: and he went out to meet the host that came to Samaria, and said unto them, Behold, because the Lord, the God of your fathers, was wroth with Judah, he hath delivered them into your hand, and ye have slain them in a rage which hath reached up to heaven. 10. And now ye purpose to keep under the children of Judah and Jerusalem for bondmen and bondwomen unto you: but are there not even with you trespasses of your own against the Lord your God? 11. Now hear me therefore, and send back the captives, which ye have taken captive of your brethren: for the fierce wrath of the Lord is upon you. 12. Then certain of the heads of the children of Ephraim, Azariah the son of Johanan, Berechiah the son of Meshillemoth, and Jehizkiah the son of Shallum, and Amasa the son of Hadlai, stood up against them that came from the war, 13. and said unto them, Ye shall not bring in the captives hither: for ye purpose that which will bring upon us a trespass against the Lord, to add unto our sins and to our trespass: for our trespass is great, and there is fierce wrath against Israel. 14. So the armed men left the captive and the spoil before the princes and all the congregation. 15. And the men which have been expressed by name rose up, and took the captives, and with the spoil clothed all that were naked among them, and arrayed them, and shod them, and gave them to eat and to drink, and anointed them, and carried all the feeble of them upon asses, and brought them to Jericho, the city of palm trees, unto their brethren: then they returned to Samaria.

At that time Rezin king of Syria recovered Elath to Syria, and drave the Jews from Elath: and the Syrians came to Elath, and dwelt there unto this day. At that time did king Ahaz send unto Tiglath-pileser king of Assyria to help him, saying, I am thy servant and thy son: come up, save me out of the hand of the king of Syria, and out of the hand of the king of Israel which rise up against me. For again the Edomites had come and smitten Judah, and carried away captives. The Philistines also had invaded the cities of the lowland, and of the South of Judah, and had taken Beth-shemesh, and Aijalon, and Gederoth, and Soco with the towns thereof, and Timnah with the towns thereof, Gimzo also and the towns thereof; and they dwelt there. For the Lord brought Judah low because of Ahaz king of Israel; for he had dealt wantonly in Judah, and trespassed against the Lord. And Ahaz took the silver and gold that was found in the house of the Lord, and in the treasures of the king's house, and of the princes, and sent it for a present to the king of Assyria; but it helped him not.

Ahaz Sends to Tiglath-pileser for Help

And Tiglath-pileser king of Assyria hearkened (and) came unto him, and distressed him, but strengthened him not. And in the time of his distress did he trespass yet more against the lord, this same king Ahaz. For he sacrificed unto the gods of Damascus, which smote him: and he said, Because the gods of the king of Syria helped them, therefore will I sacrifice to them, that they may help me. But they were the ruin of him, and of all Israel. And the king of Assyria went up against Damascus,* and took it, and carried the people of it to Kir, and slew Rezin.

Material Gain but Spiritual Loss

---

* Cf. Isaiah's Prophecy concerning Syria and Israel (Is. 7:1-9, 8:1-8).

SECT. XXVIII   THE DIVIDED KINGDOM   231

(II Kings 16:) 6. At that time Rezin king of Syria recovered Elath to Syria, and drave the Jews from Elath: and the Syrians came to Elath, and dwelt there unto this day.
7. So Ahaz sent messengers to Tiglath-pileser king of Assyria, saying, I am thy servant and thy son: come up, and save me out of the hand of the king of Syria, and out of the hand of the king of Israel, which rise up against me.

(II Chron. 28:) 16. At that time did king Ahaz send unto the kings of Assyria to help him.

17. For again the Edomites had come and smitten Judah and carried away captives. 18. The Philistines also had invaded the cities of the lowland, and of the South of Judah, and had taken Beth-shemesh, and Aijalon, and Gederoth, and Soco with the towns thereof, and Timnah with the towns thereof, Gimzo also and the towns thereof; and they dwelt there. 19. For the Lord brought Judah low because of Ahaz king of Israel; for he had dealt wantonly in Judah, and trespassed against the Lord.

8. And Ahaz *took the silver and gold that was found in the house of the Lord*, and in the treasures of the king's house, and sent it for a present to the king of Assyria.
9. And the king of Assyria hearkened unto him:

21. For Ahaz *took away a portion out of the house of the Lord*, and out of the house of the king, and of the princes, and gave it unto the king of Assyria, but it helped him not.

20. And Tiglath-pileser king of Assyria came unto him, and distressed him, but strengthened him not. 22. And in the time of his distress did he trespass yet more against the Lord, this same king Ahaz. 23. For he sacrificed unto the gods of Damascus, which smote him: and he said, Because the gods of the kings of Syria helped them, therefore will I sacrifice to them, that they may help me. But they were the ruin of him, and of all Israel.

and the king of Assyria went up against Damascus, and took it, and carried the people of it captive to Kir, and slew Rezin.

II Kings 16:10. And king Ahaz went to Damascus to meet Tiglath-pileser king of Assyria, and saw the altar that was at Damascus: and king Ahaz sent to Urijah the priest the fashion of the altar, and the pattern of it, according to all the workmanship thereof. 11. And Urijah the priest built an altar: according to all that king Ahaz had sent from Damascus, so did Urijah the priest make it against king Ahaz came from Damascus. 12. And when the king was come from Damascus, the king saw the altar: and the king drew near unto the altar, and offered thereon. 13. And he burnt his burnt offering and his meal offering, and poured his drink offering, and sprinkled the blood of his peace offerings, upon the altar. 14. And the brasen altar, which was before the Lord, he brought from the forefront of the house, from between his altar and the house of the Lord, and put it on the north side of his altar. 15. And king Ahaz commanded Urijah the priest, saying, Upon the great altar burn the morning burnt offering, and the evening meal offering, and the king's burnt offering, and his meal offering, with the burnt offering of all the people of the land, and their meal offering, and their drink offerings; and sprinkle upon it all the blood of the burnt offering, and all the blood of the sacrifice: but the brasen altar shall be for me to inquire by. 16. Thus did Urijah the priest, according to all that king Ahaz commanded. 17. And king Ahaz cut off the borders of the bases, and removed the laver from off them; and took down the sea from off the brasen oxen that were under it, and put it upon a pavement of stone. 18. And the covered way for the sabbath that they had built in the house, and the king's entry without, turned he unto the house of the Lord, because of the king of Assyria. II Chron. 28:24. And Ahaz gathered together the vessels of the house of God, and cut in pieces the vessels of the house of God, and shut up the doors of the house of the Lord; and he made him altars in every corner of Jerusalem. 25. And in every several city of Judah he made high places to burn incense unto other gods, and provoked to anger the Lord, the God of his fathers.

Israel's First Captivity and Conspiracy of Hoshea against Pekah

II Kings 15:29. In the days of Pekah king of Israel came Tiglath-pileser king of Assyria and took Ijon, and Abel-bethmaachah, and Janoah, and Kedesh, and Hazor, and Gilead, and Galilee, all the land of Naphtali;* and he carried them captive to Assyria. 30. And Hoshea the son of Elah made a conspiracy against Pekah the son of Remaliah, and smote him, and slew him, and reigned in his stead, in the † twentieth year of Jotham the son of Uzziah. 31. Now the rest of the acts of Pekah, and all that he did, behold, they are written in the book of the chronicles of the kings of Israel.

Accession and Character of Hoshea

II Kings 17:1. In the twelfth year of Ahaz king of Judah began Hoshea the son of Elah to reign in Samaria over Israel, and reigned nine years. 2. And he did that which was evil in the sight of the Lord, yet not as the kings of Israel that were before him. 3. Against him came up Shalmaneser king of Assyria; and Hoshea became his servant, and brought him presents.

Death and Burial of Ahaz

Now the rest of the acts of Ahaz which he did, and all his ways, first and last, behold, they are written in the book of the kings of Judah and Israel. And Ahaz slept with his fathers, and was buried with his fathers in the city of David, even in Jerusalem; for they brought him not into the sepulchres of the kings of Israel: and Hezekiah his son reigned in his stead.

---

* Cf. Isaiah's prophecy of a brighter day dawning (9:1-7).
† "Twentieth year of Jotham," i.e., since he became Co-Regent with his father Uzziah, at the time he was smitten of God with leprosy.

SECT. XXVIII THE DIVIDED KINGDOM

| (II Kings 16:) 19. Now the rest of the acts of Ahaz which he did, are they not written in the book of the chronicles of the kings *of Judah?*
20. And Ahaz slept with his fathers, and was buried with his fathers in the city of David:

and Hezekiah his son reigned in his stead. | (II Chron. 28:) 26. Now the rest of his acts, and all his ways, first and last, behold, they are written in the book of the kings *of Judah and Israel?*
27. And Ahaz slept with his fathers, and they buried him in the city, even in Jerusalem; for they brought him not into the sepulchres of the kings of Israel: and Hezekiah his son reigned in his stead. |

Accession and Character of Hezekiah Now it came to pass in the third year of Hoshea son of Elah king of Israel, that Hezekiah the son of Ahaz began to reign. Twenty and five years old was he when he began to reign; and he reigned twenty and nine years in Jerusalem: and his mother's name was Abi the daughter of Zechariah. And he did that which was right in the eyes of the Lord, according to all that David his father had done. II Chron. 29:3. He in the first year of his reign, in the first month, opened the doors of the house of the Lord, and repaired them. 4. And he brought in the priests and the Levites, and gathered them together into the broad place on the east, and said unto them, 5. Hear me, ye Levites: now sanctify yourselves, and sanctify the house of the Lord, the God of your fathers, and carry forth the filthiness out of the holy place. 6. For our fathers have trespassed, and done that which was evil in the sight of the Lord our God, and have forsaken him, and have turned away their faces from the habitation of the Lord, and turned their backs. 7. Also they have shut up the doors of the porch, and put out the lamps, and have not burned incense nor offered burnt offerings in the holy place unto the God of Israel. 8. Wherefore the wrath of the Lord was upon Judah and Jerusalem, and he hath delivered them to be tossed to and fro, to be an astonishment, and an hissing, as ye see with your eyes. For, lo, our fathers have fallen by the sword, and our sons and our daughters and our wives are in captivity for this. 10. Now it is in mine heart to make a covenant with the Lord, the God of Israel, that his fierce anger may turn away from us. 11. My sons, be not now negligent: for the Lord hath chosen you to stand before him, to minister unto him, and that ye should be his ministers, and burn incense.

Sixteen Days' Cleansing of the Temple 12. Then the Levites arose, Mahath the son of Amasi, and Joel the son of Azariah, of the sons of the Kohathites: and of the sons of Merari, Kish the son of Abdi, and Azariah the son of Jehallelel: and of the Gershonites, Joah the son of Zimmah, and Eden the son of Joah: 13. and of the sons of Elizaphan, Shimri and Jeuel; and of the sons of Asaph, Zechariah and Mattaniah: 14. and of the sons of Heman, Jehuel and Shimei: and of the sons of Jeduthun, Shemaiah and Uzziel. 15. And they gathered their brethren, and sanctified themselves and went in, according to the commandment of the king by the words of the Lord, to cleanse the house of the Lord. 16. And the priests went in unto the inner part of the house of the Lord, to cleanse it, and brought out all the uncleanness that they found in the temple of the Lord into the court of the house of the Lord. And the Levites took it, to carry it out abroad to the brook Kidron. 17. Now they began on the first day of the first month to sanctify, and on the eighth day of the month came they to the porch of the Lord; and they sanctified the house of the Lord in eight days: and on the sixteenth day of the first month they made an end. 18. Then they went in to Hezekiah the king within the palace, and said, We have cleansed all the house of the Lord, and the altar of burnt offering, with all the vessels thereof, and the table of shewbread, with all the vessels thereof. 19. Moreover all the vessels, which king Ahaz in his reign did cast away when he trespassed, have we prepared and sanctified; and behold, they are before the altar of the Lord.

Hezekiah and the People Offer Sacrifices 20. Then Hezekiah the king arose early, and gathered the princes of the city, and went up to the house of the Lord. 21. And they brought seven bullocks, and seven rams, and seven lambs, and seven he-goats, for a sin offering for the kingdom and for the sanctuary and for Judah. And he commanded the priests the sons of Aaron to

(II Kings 18:) 1. Now it came to pass in the third year of Hoshea son of Elah king of Israel, that Hezekiah the son of Ahaz began to reign. 2. Twenty and five years old was he when he began to reign; and he reigned twenty and nine years in Jerusalem: and his mother's name was Abi the daughter of Zechariah. 3. And he did that which was right in the eyes of the Lord, according to all that David his father had done.

(II Chron. 29:) 1. Hezekiah began to reign when he was five and twenty years old; and he reigned nine and twenty years in Jerusalem: and his mother's name was Abijah the daughter of Zechariah. 2. And he did that which was right in the eyes of the Lord, according to all that David his father had done.

offer them on the altar of the Lord. 22. So they killed the bullocks, and the priests received the blood, and sprinkled it on the altar: and they killed the rams, and sprinkled the blood upon the altar: they killed also the lambs, and sprinkled the blood upon the altar. 23. And they brought near the he-goats for the sin offering before the king and the congregation; and they laid their hands upon them: 24. and the priests killed them, and they made a sin offering with their blood upon the altar, to make atonement for all Israel: for the king commanded that the burnt offering and the sin offering should be made for all Israel. 25. And he set the Levites in the house of the Lord with cymbals, with psalteries, and with harps, according to the commandment of David, and of Gad the king's seer, and Nathan the prophet: for the commandment was of the Lord by his prophets. 26. And the Levites stood with the instruments of David, and the priests with the trumpets. 27. And Hezekiah commanded to offer the burnt offering upon the altar. And when the burnt offering began, the song of the Lord began also, and the trumpets, together with the instruments of David king of Israel. 28. And all the congregation worshipped, and the singers sang, and the trumpeters sounded; all this continued until the burnt offering was finished. 29. And when they had made an end of offering, the king and all that were present with him bowed themselves and worshipped. 30. Moreover Hezekiah the king and the princes commanded the Levites to sing praises unto the Lord with the words of David, and of Asaph the seer. And they sang praises with gladness, and they bowed their heads and worshipped.

Congregation Bring Thank Offerings

31. Then Hezekiah answered and said, Now ye have consecrated yourselves unto the Lord, come near and bring sacrifices and thank offerings into the house of the Lord. And the congregation brought in sacrifices and thank offerings: and as many as were of a willing heart brought burnt offerings. 32. And the number of the burnt offerings, which the congregation brought, was threescore and ten bullocks, an hundred rams, and two hundred lambs: all these were for a burnt offering to the Lord. 33. And the consecrated things were six hundred oxen and three thousand sheep. 34. But the priests were too few, so that they could not flay all the burnt offerings: wherefore their brethren the Levites did help them, till the work was ended, and until the priests had sanctified themselves: for the Levites were more upright in heart to sanctify themselves than the priests. 35. And also the burnt offerings were in abundance, with the fat of the peace offerings, and with the drink offerings for every burnt offering. So the service of the house of the Lord was set in order. 36. And Hezekiah rejoiced, and all the people, because of that which God had prepared for the people: for the thing was done suddenly.

Proclamation for Passover Second Month

II Chron. 30:1. And Hezekiah sent to all Israel and Judah, and wrote letters also to Ephraim and Manasseh, that they should come to the house of the Lord at Jerusalem, to keep the passover unto the Lord, the God of Israel. 2. For the king had taken counsel, and his princes, and all the congregation in Jerusalem, to keep the passover in the second month. 3. For they could not keep it at that time, because the priests had not sanctified themselves in sufficient number, neither had the people gathered themselves together to Jerusalem. 4. And the thing was right in the eyes of the king and of all the congregation. 5. So they established a decree to make proclamation throughout all Israel, from Beer-sheba even to Dan, that they should come to keep the passover unto the Lord, the God of Israel, at Jerusalem: for they had not kept it in great numbers in such sort as it is written.

6. So the posts went with the letters from the king and his princes throughout all Israel

and Judah, and according to the commandment of the king, saying, Ye children of Israel, turn again unto the Lord, the God of Abraham, Isaac and Israel, that he may return to the remnant that are escaped of you out of the hands of the kings of Assyria. 7. And be not like your fathers, and like your brethren, which trespassed against the Lord, the God of their fathers, so that he gave them up to desolation, as ye see. 8. Now be ye not stiff-necked, as your fathers were: but yield yourselves unto the Lord, and enter into his sanctuary, which he hath sanctified forever, and serve the Lord your God, that his fierce anger may turn away from you. 9. For if ye turn again unto the Lord, your brethren and your children shall find compassion before them that led them captive, and shall come again into this land: for the Lord your God is gracious and merciful, and will not turn away his face from you, if ye return unto him.

Israel Divided, Judah United, Passover Kept 10. So the posts passed from city to city through the country of Ephraim and Manasseh, even unto Zebulun: but they laughed them to scorn, and mocked them. 11. Nevertheless divers of Asher and Manasseh and of Zebulun humbled themselves, and came to Jerusalem. 12. Also in Judah was the hand of God to give them one heart, to do the commandment of the king and of the princes by the word of the Lord. 13. And there assembled at Jerusalem much people to keep the feast of unleavened bread in the second month, a very great congregation. 14. And they arose and took away the altars that were in Jerusalem, and all the altars for incense took they away, and cast them into the brook Kidron. 15. Then they killed the passover on the fourteenth day of the second month: and the priests and the Levites were ashamed, and sanctified themselves, and brought burnt offerings into the house of the Lord. 16. And they stood in their place after their order, according to the law of Moses the man of God: the priests sprinkled the blood, which they received of the hand of the Levites. 17. For there were many in the congregation that had not sanctified themselves: therefore the Levites had the charge of killing the passovers for every one that was not clean, to sanctify them unto the Lord. 18. For a multitude of the people, even many of Ephraim and Manasseh, Issachar and Zebulun, had not cleansed themselves, yet did they eat the passover otherwise than it is written. For Hezekiah had prayed for them, saying, The good Lord pardon every one that setteth his heart to seek God, the Lord the God of his fathers, though he be not cleansed according to the purification of the sanctuary. 20. And the Lord hearkened to Hezekiah, and healed the people. 21. And the children of Israel that were present at Jerusalem kept the feast of unleavened bread seven days with great gladness: and the Levites and the priests praised the Lord day by day, singing with loud instruments unto the Lord. 22. And Hezekiah spake comfortably unto all the Levites that were well skilled in the service of the Lord. So they did eat throughout the feast for the seven days, offering sacrifices of peace offerings, and making confession to the Lord, the God of their fathers. 23. And the whole congregation took counsel to keep other seven days: and they kept other seven days with gladness. 24. For Hezekiah king of Judah did give to the congregation for offerings a thousand bullocks and seven thousand sheep; and the princes gave to the congregation a thousand bullocks and ten thousand sheep: and a great number of priests sanctified themselves. 25. And all the congregation of Judah, with the priests and the Levites, and all the congregation that came out of Israel, and the strangers that came out of the land of Israel, and that dwelt in Judah rejoiced. 26. So there was great joy in Jerusalem: for since the time of Solomon the son of David king of Israel there was not the like in Jerusalem. 27. Then the priests the Levites arose and blessed the people: and their voice was heard, and their prayer came up to his holy habitation, even unto heaven.

II Chron. 31: 1. Now when all this was finished, all Israel that were present went out to the cities of Judah, and brake in pieces the pillars, and hewed down the Asherim, and brake down the high places and the altars out of all Judah and Benjamin, in Ephraim also and Manasseh, until they had destroyed them all. Then all the children of Israel returned, every man to his possession, into their own cities.

Hezekiah's and People's Portions
2. And Hezekiah appointed the courses of the priests and the Levites after their courses, every man according to his service, both the priests and the Levites, for burnt offerings and for peace offerings, to minister, and to give thanks, and to praise in the gates of the camp of the Lord. 3. He appointed also the king's portion of his substance for the burnt offerings, to wit, for the morning and the evening burnt offerings, and the burnt offerings for the sabbaths, and for the new moons, and for the set feasts, as it is written in the law of the Lord. 4. Moreover he commanded the people that dwelt in Jerusalem to give the portion of the priests and the Levites, that they might give themselves to the law of the Lord. 5. And as soon as the commandment came abroad, the children of Israel gave in abundance the first-fruits of corn, wine, and oil, and honey, and of all the increase of the field; and the tithe of all things brought they in abundantly. 6. And the children of Israel and Judah, that dwelt in the cities of Judah, they also brought in the tithe of oxen and sheep, and the tithe of dedicated things which were consecrated unto the Lord their God, and laid them by heaps. 7. In the third month they began to lay the foundation of the heaps, and finished them in the seventh month. 8. And when Hezekiah and the princes came and saw the heaps, they blessed the Lord, and his people Israel.

Oblations and Tithes Stored, Distributed
9. Then Hezekiah questioned with the priests and the Levites concerning the heaps. 10. And Azariah the chief priest, of the house of Zadok, answered him and said, Since the people began to bring the oblations into the house of the Lord, we have eaten and had enough, and have left plenty: for the Lord hath blessed his people; and that which is left is this great store. 11. Then Hezekiah commanded to prepare chambers in the house of the Lord: and they prepared them. 12. And they brought in the oblations and the tithes and the dedicated things faithfully: and over them Conaniah the Levite was ruler, and Shimei his brother was second. 13. And Jehiel, and Azaziah, and Nahath, and Asahel, and Jerimoth, and Jozabad, and Eliel, and Ismachiah, and Mahath, and Benaiah, were overseers under the hand of Conaniah and Shimei his brother, by the appointment of Hezekiah the king, and Azariah the ruler of the house of God. 14. And Kore the son of Imnah the Levite, the porter at the east gate, was over the free-will offerings of God, to distribute the oblations of the Lord, and the most holy things. 15. And under him were Eden, and Miniamin, and Jeshua, and Shemaiah, Amariah, and Shecaniah, in the cities of the priests, in their set office, to give to their brethren by courses, as well to the great as to the small; 16. beside them that were reckoned by genealogy of males, from three years old and upward, even every one that entered into the house of the Lord, as the duty of every day required, for their service in their charges according to their courses; 17. and them that were reckoned by genealogy of the priests by their fathers' houses, and the Levites from twenty years old and upward, in their charges by their courses; 18. and them that were reckoned by genealogy of all their little ones, their wives, and their sons, and their daughters, through all the congregation: for in their set office they sanctified themselves in holiness: 19. also for the sons of Aaron the priests, which were in the fields of the suburbs of their cities, in every

(II Kings 18:) 4ᵃ. *He removed the high places, and brake the pillars, and cut down the Asherah:

(II Chron. 31:) 1. Now when all this was finished, all Israel that were present went out to the cities of Judah, and brake in pieces the pillars, and hewed down the Asherim, and brake down the high places and the altars out of all Judah and Benjamin, in Ephraim and Manasseh, until they had destroyed them all. Then all the children of Israel returned, every man to his own possession, into their own cities.

---

* Kings, he—*i.e.*, Hezekiah.

several city, there were men that were expressed by name, to give portions to all the males among the priests, and to all that were reckoned by genealogy among the Levites.

Commendation of Hezekiah's Early Reign
And thus did Hezekiah throughout all Judah; and he wrought that which was good and right and faithful before the Lord his God. And he brake in pieces the brasen serpent that Moses had made; for unto those days the children of Israel did burn incense to it; and he called it Nehustan. He trusted in the Lord, the God of Israel; so that after him was none like him among all the kings of Judah, nor among them that were before him. For he clave to the Lord, he departed not from following him, but kept his commandments, which the Lord commanded Moses. And in every work that he began in the service of the house of God, and in the law, and in the commandments, to seek his God, he did it with all his heart. And the Lord was with him; whithersoever he went forth he prospered: and he rebelled against the king of Assyria, and served him not. He smote the Philistines unto Gaza and the borders thereof, from the tower of the watchmen to the fenced city.

Hoshea's Conspiracy and Imprisonment
And the king of Assyria found conspiracy in Hoshea; for he had sent messengers to So king of Egypt, and offered no presents to the king of Assyria, as he had done year by year: therefore the king of Assyria shut him up, and bound him in prison. And it came to pass in the fourth year of Hezekiah, which was the seventh year of Hoshea son of Elah king of Israel, that Shalmaneser the king of Assyria came up throughout all the land, and went up to Samaria, and besieged it three years.

Shalmaneser Besieges and Takes Samaria
And at the end of three years they took it, even in the sixth year of Hezekiah, which was the ninth year of Hoshea king of Israel. And the king of Assyria carried Israel away unto Assyria, and placed them in Halah, and in Habor, and on the river of Gozan, and in the cities of the Medes. And it was so, because the children of Israel had sinned against the Lord

Lord's Bitter Indictment against Israel
their God, which brought them up out of the land of Egypt from under the hand of Pharaoh king of Egypt, and obeyed not the voice of the Lord their God, but transgressed his covenant, even all that Moses the servant of the Lord had commanded, and would not hear it, and do it, and had feared other gods, and walked in the statutes of the nations, whom the Lord cast out from before the children of Israel, and of the kings of Israel, which they made.

II Kings 17:9. And the children of Israel did secretly things that were not right against the Lord their God, and they built them high places in all their cities, from the tower of the watchman to the fenced city. 10. And they set them up pillars and Asherim upon every high hill, and under every green tree: 11. and there they burnt incense in all the high places, as did the nations whom the Lord carried away before them; and wrought wicked things to provoke the Lord to anger: 12. and they served idols, whereof the Lord had said unto them, Ye shall not do this thing.

13. Yet the Lord testified unto Israel, and unto Judah, by the hand of every prophet, and of every seer, saying, Turn ye from your evil ways, and keep my commandments and my statutes, according to all the law which I commanded your fathers, and which I sent to you by the hand of my servants the prophets. 14. Notwithstanding they would not hear, but hardened their neck, like to the neck of their fathers, who believed not in the Lord their God. 15. And they rejected his statutes, and his covenant that he made with their fathers, and his testimonies which he testified unto them; and they followed vanity, and became vain, and went after the nations that were round about them, concerning whom

(II Kings 18:) 4ᵇ. and he brake in pieces the brasen serpent that Moses had made; for unto those days the children of Israel did burn incense to it; and he called it Nehustan. 5. He trusted in the Lord, the God of Israel; so that after him was none like him among all the kings of Judah, nor among them that were before him. 6. For he clave to the Lord, he departed not from following him, but kept his commandments, which the Lord commanded Moses.

7. And the Lord was with him; whithersoever he went forth he prospered: and he rebelled against the king of Assyria, and served him not. 8. He smote the Philistines unto Gaza and the borders thereof, from the tower of the watchmen to the fenced city.

(II Kings 17:) 4. And the king of Assyria found conspiracy in Hoshea; for he had sent messengers to So king of Egypt, and offered no present to the king of Assyria, as he had done year by year: therefore the king of Assyria shut him up, and bound him in prison.

5. Then the king of Assyria came up throughout all the land, and went up to Samaria, and besieged it three years. 6. In the ninth year of Hoshea, the king of Assyria took Samaria, and carried Israel away unto Assyria, and placed them in Halah, and in Habor, on the river of Gozan, and in the cities of the Medes. 7. And it was so, because the children of Israel had sinned against the Lord their God, which brought them up out of the land of Egypt from under the hand of Pharaoh king of Egypt,

and had feared other gods, 8. and walked in the statutes of the nations, whom the Lord cast out from before the children of Israel, and of the kings of Israel, which they made.

(II Chron. 31:) 20. And thus did Hezekiah throughout all Judah; and he wrought that which was good and right and faithful before the Lord his God.

21. And in every work that he began in the service of the house of God, and in the law, and in the commandments, to seek his God, he did it with all his heart,

and prospered.

(II Kings 18:) 9. And it came to pass in the fourth year of Hezekiah, which was the seventh year of Hoshea son of Elah king of Israel, that Shalmaneser king came up against Samaria, and besieged it. 10. And at the end of three years they took it, even in the sixth year of Hezekiah, which was the ninth year of Hoshea king of Israel, Samaria was taken. 11. And the king of Assyria carried Israel away unto Assyria, and put them in Halah, and in Habor, on the river of Gozan, and in the cities of the Medes: 12. because they

obeyed not the voice of the Lord their God, but transgressed his covenant, even all that Moses the servant of the Lord had commanded, and would not hear it, nor do it.

the Lord had charged them that they should not do like them. 16. And they forsook all the commandments of the Lord their God, and made them molten images, even two calves, and made an Asherah, and worshipped all the host of heaven, and served Baal. 17. And they caused their sons and their daughters to pass through the fire, and used divinations and enchantments, and sold themselves to do that which was evil in the sight of the Lord, to provoke him to anger.

Israel Removed by Jehovah

18. Therefore the Lord was very angry with Israel, and removed them out of his sight: there was none left but the tribe of Judah only. 19. Also Judah kept not the commandments of the Lord their God, but walked in the statutes of Israel which they made. 20. And the Lord rejected all the seed of Israel, and afflicted them, and delivered them into the hand of spoilers, until he had cast them out of his sight. 21. For he rent Israel from the house of David; and they made Jereboam the son of Nebat king: And Jereboam drove Israel from following the Lord, and made them sin a great sin. 22. And the children of Israel walked in all the sins of Jereboam which he did: they departed not from them; 23. until the Lord removed Israel out of his sight, as he spake by the hand of all his servants the prophets. So Israel was carried away out of their own land to Assyria, unto this day.

Other Nations Brought into Samaria

24. And the king of Assyria brought men from Babylon, and from Cuthah, and from Avva, and from Hamath and Sevarvaim, and placed them in the cities instead of the children of Israel: and they possessed Samaria, and dwelt in the cities thereof. 25. And so it was, at the beginning of their dwelling there, that they feared not the Lord: therefore the Lord sent lions among them, which killed some of them.

A Priest Sent Back from the Captives

26. Wherefore they spake to the king of Assyria, saying, The nations which thou hast carried away, and placed in the cities of Samaria, know not the manner of the God of the land: therefore he hath sent lions among them, and, behold, they slay them, because they know not the manner of the God of the land. 27. Then the king of Assyria commanded, saying, Carry thither one of the priests whom ye brought from thence; and let them go and dwell there, and let him teach them the manner of the God of the land. 28. So one of the priests whom they had carried away from Samaria came and dwelt in Beth-el, and taught them how they should fear the Lord. 29. Howbeit every nation made gods of their own, and put them in the houses of the high places which the Samaritans had made, every nation in their cities wherein they dwelt. 30. And the men of Babylon made Succoth-benoth, and the men of Cuth made Nergal, and the men of Hamath made Ashima, and the Avvites made Nibhaz and Tartak, and the Sepharvites burnt their children in the fire to Adrammelech and Anammelech, the gods of Sepharvaim.

Priests Made and Their Own Gods Served

32. So they feared the Lord, and made unto them from among themselves priests of the high places, which sacrificed for them in the houses of the high places. 33. They feared the Lord, and served their own gods, after the manner of the nations from among whom they had been carried away. 34. Unto this day they do after their former manners: they fear not the Lord, neither do they after their statutes, or after their ordinances, or after the law or after the commandments which the Lord commanded the children of Jacob, whom he named Israel; 35. with whom the Lord had made a covenant, and charged them, saying, Ye shall not fear other gods, nor bow yourselves to them, nor serve them, nor sacrifice to them: 36. but the Lord, which brought you up out of the land of

Egypt with great power and with a stretched out arm, him shall ye fear, and unto him shall ye bow yourselves, and to him shall ye sacrifice: 37. and the statutes and the ordinances, and the law and the commandment, which he wrote for you, ye shall observe to do for evermore: and ye shall not fear other gods: 38. and the covenant that I have made with you ye shall not forget; neither shall ye fear other gods: 39. but the Lord your God shall ye fear; and he shall deliver you out of the hand of all your enemies. 40. Howbeit they did not hearken, but they did after their former manner. 41. So these nations feared the Lord, and served their graven images; their children likewise, and their children's children, as did their fathers, so do they unto this day.

THE HOUSE OF DAVID
    B. C. 726 -697 Isaiah.*
  XIV Hezekiah
    B. C. 725 or 715-686 Micah.

PART IV

The Surviving Southern Kingdom

SECTION XXIX

The Reign of Hezekiah After Captivity of Israel

Sickness and Recovery

In those days † Hezekiah was sick even unto death. And Isaiah the prophet the son of Amoz came to him and said, Set thine house in order: for thou shalt die, and not live. Then Hezekiah turned his face to the wall, and prayed unto the Lord, and said, Remember now, O Lord, I beseech thee, How I have walked before thee in truth and with a perfect heart, and have done that which was good in thy sight. And Hezekiah wept sore. And it came to pass, afore Isaiah was gone out into the middle part of the city, that the word of the Lord came to him, saying, Turn again, and say to Hezekiah the prince of my people, Thus saith the Lord, the God of David thy father, I have heard thy prayer, I have seen thy tears: behold, I will heal thee: on the third day thou shalt go up unto the house of the Lord. And I will add unto thy days fifteen years: and I will deliver thee, and this city out of the hand of the king of Assyria: and I will defend this city, for mine own sake, and for my servant David's sake. Now Isaiah had said, Let them take a cake of figs, and lay it for a plaster upon the boil, and he shall recover. And they took and laid it on the boil, and he recovered. Hezekiah also had said unto Isaiah, What shall be the sign that the Lord will heal me, and that I shall go up unto

Return of the Shadow Ten Steps

the house of the Lord the third day? And Isaiah said, This shall be the sign unto thee from the Lord, that the Lord will do the thing that he hath spoken: shall the shadow go forward ten steps, or go back ten steps? And Hezekiah answered, It is a light thing for the shadow to decline ten steps: nay, but let the shadow return ten steps. And he spake unto him and gave him a sign, behold, I will cause the shadow on the steps, which is gone down on the dial of Ahaz with the sun, to return backward ten steps. And Isaiah the prophet cried unto the Lord: and he brought the shadow ten steps backward, by which it had gone down on the dial of Ahaz.

---

* See Chronology Appendix A. Both systems of chronology are used, e.g., Hezekiah $\frac{726 \text{ (Usher)}}{725 \text{ (Revised)}}$

† "In those days" refers to the period when "he rebelled against the king of Assyria and served him not," and so was pleased with the embassy from Babylon, which suggested a possible alliance against a common enemy. See The Higher Criticism and the Monuments. Sayce, pp. 423-447.

SECT. XXIX THE SURVIVING SOUTHERN KINGDOM

(II Kings 20:) 1. In those days was Hezekiah sick unto death. And Isaiah the prophet the son of Amoz came to him, and said unto him, Thus saith the Lord, Set thine house in order; for thou shalt die, and not live. 2. Then he turned his face to the wall, and prayed unto the Lord, saying, Remember now, O Lord, I beseech thee, how I have walked before thee in truth and with a perfect heart, and have done that which was good in thy sight. And Hezekiah wept sore.
4. And it came to pass, afore Isaiah was gone out into the middle part of the city, that the word of the Lord came to him, saying, 5. Turn again, and say to Hezekiah the prince of my people, Thus saith the Lord, the God of David thy father, I have heard thy prayer, I have seen thy tears: behold, I will heal thee: on the third day thou shalt go up unto the house of the Lord. 6. And I will add unto thy days fifteen years; and I will deliver thee and this city out of the hand of the king of Assyria: and I will defend this city, for mine own sake, and for my servant David's sake.
7. And Isaiah said, take a cake of figs. And they took and laid it on the boil, and he recovered. 8. And Hezekiah said unto Isaiah, What shall be the sign that the Lord will heal me, and that I shall go up unto the house of the Lord the third day? 9. And Isaiah said, This shall be the sign unto thee from the Lord, that the Lord will do the thing that he hath spoken: shall the shadow go forward ten steps, or go back ten steps? 10. And Hezekiah answered, It is a light thing for the shadow to decline ten steps: nay, but let the shadow return ten steps.

11. And Isaiah the prophet cried unto the Lord: and he brought the shadow ten steps backward, by which it had gone down on the dial of Ahaz.

(Isaiah 38:) 1. In those days was Hezekiah sick unto death. And Isaiah the prophet the son of Amoz came to him and said unto him, Thus saith the Lord, Set thine house in order; for thou shalt die, and not live. 2. Then Hezekiah turned his face to the wall, and prayed unto the Lord, and said, 3. Remember now, O Lord, I beseech thee, how I have walked before thee in truth and with a perfect heart, and have done that which is good in thy sight. And Hezekiah wept sore.

Isaiah, saying, 5. Go, Thus saith the Lord, the God of David thy father, I have heard thy prayer, I have seen thy tears: behold, I will add unto thy days fifteen years. 6. And I will deliver thee and this city out of the hand of the king of Assyria: and I will defend this city.
21. Now Isaiah had said, Let them take a cake of figs, and lay it for a plaster upon the boil, and he shall recover. 22. Hezekiah also had said, What is the sign that I shall go up to the house of the Lord? 7. and this shall be the sign unto thee from the Lord, that the Lord will do the thing that he hath spoken:

8. behold, I will cause the shadow on the steps, which is gone down on the dial of Ahaz with the sun, to return backward ten steps.
So the sun returned ten steps on the dial whereon it was gone down.

(II Chron. 32:) 24^a. In those days was Hezekiah sick even unto death:

and he prayed unto the Lord:

4. Then came the word of the Lord to and say to Hezekiah,

I will add unto thy days fifteen years. 6. And I will deliver thee and this city out of the hand of the king of Assyria: and I will defend this city.

(II Chron. 32:) 24^b. and he spake unto him and gave him a sign.

Isaiah 38: 9. The writing of Hezekiah king of Judah, when he had been sick, and was recovered of his sickness.

10. I said, In the noontide of my days, I shall go into the gates of the grave:
I am deprived of the residue of my years.
11. I said, I shall not see the Lord, even the Lord in the land of the living:
I shall behold man no more with the inhabitants of the world.
12. Mine age is removed, and is carried away from me as a shepherd's tent;
I have rolled up like a weaver my life; he will cut me off from the loom;
From day even to night wilt thou make an end of me.
13. I quieted myself until morning; as a lion, so he breaketh all my bones:
From day even to night wilt thou make an end of me.
14. Like a swallow or a crane, so did I chatter;
I did mourn as a dove: mine eyes fail with looking upward;
O Lord, I am oppressed, be thou my surety.
15. What shall I say? he hath both spoken unto me, and himself hath done it:
I shall go softly all my years because of the bitterness of my soul.
16. O Lord, by these things men live.
And wholly therein is the life of my spirit;
Wherefore recover thou me, and make me to live.
17. Behold, it was for my peace that I had great bitterness:
But thou hast in love to my soul delivered it from the pit of corruption;
For thou hast cast all my sins behind thy back.
18. For the grave cannot praise thee, death cannot celebrate thee:
They that go down into the pit cannot hope for thy truth.
19. The living, the living, he shall praise thee, as I do this day:
The father to the children shall make known thy truth.
20. The Lord is ready to save me:
Therefore we will sing my songs to the stringed instruments
All the days of our life in the house of the Lord.

II Chron. 32: 25. But Hezekiah rendered not again according to the benefit done unto him; for his heart was lifted up: therefore there was wrath upon him, and upon Judah and Jerusalem.

Ambassadors from Babylon At that time * Berodach-baladan, the son of Baladan, king of Babylon, sent letters and a present unto Hezekiah: for he had heard that he had been sick, and was recovered. And Hezekiah was glad of them, and shewed them all the house of his precious things, the silver, and the gold, and the spices, and the precious oil, and all the house of his armour, and all that was found in his treasures: there was nothing in his house, nor in all his dominion, that Hezekiah shewed them not.

Babylonian Captivity Foretold Then came Isaiah the prophet unto king Hezekiah, and said unto him, What said these men? and from whence came they unto thee? And Hezekiah said, They are come from a far country unto me, even from Babylon. Then said he, What have they seen in thine house? And Hezekiah answered, All that is in mine house have they seen: there is nothing among my treasures that I have not shewed them. Then Isaiah said unto Hezekiah, Hear the word of the Lord of hosts. Behold, the days come, that all that is in thine house, and all that which thy

---
* In Chronicles, Merodach-baladan.

SECT. XXIX THE SURVIVING SOUTHERN KINGDOM

(II Kings 20:) 12. At that time Berodach-baladan, the son of Baladan king of Babylon, sent letters and a present unto Hezekiah: for he had heard that Hezekiah had been sick.	(Isaiah 39:) 1. At that time Merodach-baladan, the son of Baladan king of Babylon, sent letters and a present to Hezekiah: for he heard that he had been sick, and was recovered.
13. And Hezekiah hearkened unto them, and shewed them all the house of his precious things, the silver, and the gold, and the spices, and the precious oil, and the house of his armour, and all that was found in his treasures: there was nothing in his house, nor in all his dominion, that Hezekiah shewed them not.	2. And Hezekiah was glad of them, and shewed them the house of his precious things, the silver, and the gold, and the spices, and the precious oil, and all the house of his armour, and all that was found in his treasures: there was nothing in his house, nor in all his dominion, that Hezekiah shewed them not.
14. Then came Isaiah the prophet unto king Hezekiah, and said unto him, What said these men? and from whence came they unto thee? And Hezekiah said, They are come from a far country, even from Babylon. 15. And he said, What have they seen in thine house? And Hezekiah answered, All that is in mine house have they seen: there is nothing among my treasures that I have not shewed them.	3. Then came Isaiah the prophet unto king Hezekiah, and said unto him, What said these men? and from whence came they unto thee? And Hezekiah said, They are come from a far country, unto me, even from Babylon. 4. Then said he, What have they seen in thine house? And Hezekiah answered, All that is in mine house have they seen: there is nothing among my treasures that I have not shewed them.
16. And Isaiah said unto Hezekiah, Hear the word of the Lord, 17. Behold, the days come, that all that is in thine house, and that which thy	5. Then said Isaiah to Hezekiah, Hear the word of the Lord of hosts, 6. Behold, the days come, that all that is in thine house, and that which thy

fathers have laid up in store unto this day, shall be carried to Babylon: nothing shall be left, saith the Lord. And of thy sons that shall issue from thee, which thou shalt beget, shall they take away; and they shall be eunuchs in the palace of the king of Babylon. Notwithstanding Hezekiah humbled himself for the pride of his heart, both he and the inhabitants of Jerusalem, so that the wrath of the Lord came not upon them in the days of Hezekiah. Then said Hezekiah unto Isaiah, Good is the word of the Lord which thou hast spoken. He said moreover, Is it not so, if peace and truth shall be in my days? Howbeit in the business of the ambassadors of the princes of Babylon, who sent unto him to inquire of the wonder that was done in the land, God left him to try him, that he might know all that was in his heart.

Prosperous End of Life and Reign

And Hezekiah had exceeding much riches and honour; and he provided him treasuries for silver, and for gold, and for precious stones, and for spices, and for shields, and for all manner of goodly vessels; storehouses also for the increase of corn and wine and oil; and stalls for all manner of beasts, and flocks in folds. Moreover he provided him cities, and possessions of flocks, and herds in abundance: for God had given him very much substance. This same Hezekiah also stopped the upper spring of the waters of Gihon, and brought them straight down on the west side of the city of David. And Hezekiah prospered in all his works.

Sennacherib Invades Judah

Now it came to pass after these things, and this faithfulness, in the fourteenth year of king Hezekiah that Sennacherib king of Assyria came, and entered into Judah, and encamped against all the fenced cities of Judah, *and thought to win them for himself.** And when Hezekiah saw that Sennacherib was come, and that he was purposed to fight against Jerusalem, he took counsel with his princes and his mighty men to stop the waters of the fountains which were without the city; and they helped him. So there was gathered much people together, and they stopped all the fountains, and the brook that flowed through the midst of the land, saying, Why should the kings of Assyria come, and find much water? And he took courage and built up all the wall that was broken down, and raised it up to the towers, and the other wall without, and strengthened Millo in the city of David, and made weapons and shields in abundance. And he set captains of war over the people, and gathered them together to him in the broad place at the gate of the city, and spake comfortably to them, saying, Be strong and of a good courage, be not afraid or dismayed for the king of Assyria, nor for all the multitude that is with him: with him is an arm of flesh; but with us is the Lord our God to help us, and to fight our battles. And the people rested themselves upon the words of Hezekiah king of Judah.

Brave Words to the People

Humble Words to the King of Assyria

And Hezekiah king of Judah sent to the king of Assyria to Lachish, saying, I have offended; return from me; that which thou puttest on me will I bear. And the king of Assyria appointed unto Hezekiah king of Judah three hundred talents of silver and thirty talents of gold. And Hezekiah gave him all the silver that was found in the house of the Lord, and in the treasures of the king's house. At that time did Hezekiah cut off the gold from the doors of the temple of the Lord, and from the pillars which Hezekiah king of Judah overlaid, and gave it to the king of Assyria.

---

* Kings and Isaiah read "*and took them,*" which statement is harder to reconcile with the context.

Sect. XXIX THE SURVIVING SOUTHERN KINGDOM

fathers have laid up in store unto this day, shall be carried to Babylon: nothing shall be left, saith the Lord. 18. And of thy sons that shall issue from thee, which thou shalt beget, shall they take away: and they shall be eunuchs in the palace of the king of Babylon.

19 Then said Hezekiah unto Isaiah, Good is the word of the Lord which thou hast spoken. He said moreover, Is it not so, if peace and truth shall be in my days?

fathers have laid up in store unto this day, shall be carried to Babylon: nothing shall be left, saith the Lord. 7. And of thy sons that shall issue from thee, which thou shalt beget, shall they take away; and they shall be eunuchs in the palace of the king of Babylon.

8. Then said Hezekiah unto Isaiah, Good is the word of the Lord which thou hast spoken. He said moreover, For there shall be peace and truth in my days.

(II Chron. 32:) 26. Notwithstanding Hezekiah humbled himself for the pride of his heart, both he and the inhabitants of Jerusalem, so that the wrath of the Lord came not upon them in the days of Hezekiah. 31. Howbeit in the business of the ambassadors of the princes of Babylon, who sent unto him to inquire of the wonder that was done in the land, God left him to try him, that he might know all that was in his heart.

27. And Hezekiah had exceeding much riches and honour: and he provided him treasuries for silver, and for gold, and for precious stones, and for spices, and for shields, and for all manner of goodly vessels; 28. storehouses also for the increase of corn and wine and oil; and stalls for all manner of beasts, and flocks in folds. 29. Moreover he provided him cities, and possessions of flocks and herds in abundance: for God had given him very much substance. 30. This same Hezekiah also stopped the upper spring of the waters of Gihon, and brought them straight down on the west side of the city of David. And Hezekiah prospered in all his works. (II Chron. 32:) 1. (After these things, and this faithfulness,)

(II Kings 18:) 13. (Now in the fourteenth year of king Hezekiah) did Sennacherib king of Assyria come up against all the fenced cities of Judah, ((and took them.))

(Isaiah 36:) 1. (Now it came to pass in the fourteenth year of king Hezekiah) that Sennacherib king of Assyria came up against all the fenced cities of Judah, ((and took them.))

Sennacherib king of Assyria came and entered into Judah, and encamped against the fenced cities, ((and thought to win them for himself.))

2. And when Hezekiah saw that Sennacherib was come, and that he was purposed to fight against Jerusalem, 3. he took counsel with his princes and his mighty men to stop the waters of the fountains which were without the city; and they helped him. 4. So there was gathered much people together, and they stopped all the fountains, and the brook that flowed through the midst of the land, saying, Why should the kings of Assyria come, and find much water? 5. And he took courage, and built up all the wall that was broken down, and raised it up to the towers, and the other wall without, and strengthened Millo in the city of David, and made weapons and shields in abundance. 6. And he set captains of war over the people, and gathered them together to him in the broad place at the gate of the city, and spake comfortably to them, saying, 7. Be strong and of good courage, be not afraid nor dismayed for the king of Assyria, nor for all the multitude that is with him: for there is a greater with us than with him: 8. with him is an arm of flesh; but with us is the Lord our God to help us, and to fight our battles. And the people rested themselves upon the words of Hezekiah king of Judah.

14. And Hezekiah king of Judah sent to the king of Assyria to Lachish, saying, I have offended; return from me; that which thou puttest on me will I bear. And the king of Assyria appointed unto Hezekiah king of Judah three hundred talents of silver and thirty talents of gold. 15. And Hezekiah gave him all the silver that was found in the house of the Lord, and in the treasures of the king's house. 16. At that time did Hezekiah cut off the gold from the doors of the temple of the Lord, and from the pillars which Hezekiah king of Judah had overlaid, and gave it to the king of Assyria.

Sennacherib's Messengers

After this did Sennacherib send his servants, Tartan and Rabsaris and Rabshakeh, from Lachish to Jerusalem (now he was before Lachish, and all his power with him) unto Hezekiah king of Judah, and unto all Judah that were at Jerusalem, with a great army. And they went up and came to Jerusalem. And when they were come up, they came and stood by the conduit of the upper pool, which is in the high way of the fuller's field. And when they had called to the king, there came out to them Eliakim the son of Hilkiah, which was over the household, and Shebna the scribe, and Joah the son of Asaph the recorder.

Rabshakeh's Insulting Message

And Rabshakeh said unto them, Say ye now to Hezekiah, Thus saith Sennacherib the great king, the king of Assyria. What confidence is this wherein thou trustest, that ye abide the siege in Jerusalem? I say, thy counsel and strength for the war are but vain words: now on whom dost thou trust, that thou hast rebelled against me? Now behold thou trustest upon the staff of this bruised reed, even upon Egypt; whereon if a man lean, it will go into his hand and pierce it: so is Pharaoh king of Egypt unto all that trust on him.

Doth not Hezekiah persuade you, to give you over to die by famine and by thirst, saying, The Lord our God shall deliver us out of the hand of the king of Assyria? Hath not the same Hezekiah taken away his high places and his altars, and hath said to Judah and to Jerusalem, saying, Ye shall worship before one altar, and upon it shall ye burn incense?

Know ye not what I and my fathers have done unto all the peoples of the lands? Now therefore, I pray thee, give pledges to my master the king of Assyria, and I will give thee two thousand horses, if thou be able on thy part to set riders upon them. How then canst thou turn away the face of one captain of the least of my master's servants, and put thy trust on Egypt for chariots and for horsemen? Am I now come up without the Lord against this place to destroy it? The Lord said unto me, Go up against this land, and destroy it. Then said Eliakim the son of Hilkiah, and Shebnah, and Joah, unto Rabshakeh, Speak, I pray thee, unto thy servants in the Syrian language; for we understand it: and speak not to us in the Jew's language, in the ears of the people that are on the wall.

But Rabshakeh said unto them, Hath my master sent me to thy master, and to thee, to speak these words? hath he not sent me to the men which sit on the wall to eat their own dung, and to drink their own water with you?

SECT. XXIX THE SURVIVING SOUTHERN KINGDOM

17. And the king of Assyria sent Tartan and Rabsaris and Rabshakeh from Lachish to king Hezekiah with a great army unto Jerusalem. And they went up and came to Jerusalem. And when they were come up, they came and stood by the conduit of the upper pool, which is in the high way of the fuller's field.

18. And when they had called to the king, there came out to them Eliakim the son of Hilkiah, which was over the household, and Shebna the scribe, and Joah the son of Asaph the recorder.

19. And Rabshakeh said unto them, Say ye now to Hezekiah, Thus saith the great king, the king of Assyria, What confidence is this wherein thou trustest?
20. Thou sayest, but they are but vain words, there is counsel and strength for the war. Now on whom dost thou trust, that thou hast rebelled against me?
21. Now, behold, thou trustest upon the staff of this bruised reed, even upon Egypt; whereon if a man lean, it will go into his hand, and pierce it: so is Pharaoh king of Egypt unto all that trust on him.

22. But if ye say unto me, We trust in the Lord our God:
is not that he, whose high places and whose altars Hezekiah hath taken away, and hath said to Judah and to Jerusalem Ye shall worship before this altar in Jerusalem?

23. Now therefore, I pray thee, give pledges to my master the king of Assyria, and I will give thee two thousand horses, if thou be able on thy part to set riders upon them. 24. How then canst thou turn away the face of one captain of the least of my master's servants, and put thy trust on Egypt for chariots and for horsemen? 25. Am I now come up without the Lord against this place to destroy it? The Lord said unto me, Go up against this land, and destroy it.
26. Then said Eliakim the son of Hilkiah, and Shebnah, and Joah, unto Rabshakeh, Speak, I pray thee, to thy servants in the Syrian language; for we understand it: and speak not with us in the Jew's language, in the ears of the people that are on the wall.

27. But Rabshakeh said unto them, Hath my master sent me to thy master, and to thee, to speak these words? hath he not sent me to the men which sit on the wall to eat their own dung, and to drink their own water with you?

---

2. And the king of Assyria sent Rabshakeh from Lachish to Jerusalem unto king Hezekiah with a great army.
and he stood by the conduit of the upper pool in the high way of the fuller's field.

3. Then came forth unto him Eliakim the son of Hilkiah, which was over the household, and Shebna the scribe, and Joah the son of Asaph the recorder.

4. And Rabshakeh said unto them, Say ye now to Hezekiah, Thus saith the great king, the king of Assyria, What confidence is this wherein thou trustest?
5. I say, thy counsel and strength for the war are but vain words:
now on whom dost thou trust, that thou hast rebelled against me?
6. Behold, thou trustest upon the staff of this bruised reed, even upon Egypt; whereon if a man lean, it will go into his hand, and pierce it: so is Pharaoh king of Egypt to all that trust on him.

7. But if thou say unto me, We trust in the Lord our God:
is not that he, whose high places and whose altars Hezekiah hath taken away, and hath said to Judah and to Jerusalem, Ye shall worship before this altar?

8. Now therefore, I pray thee, give pledges to my master the king of Assyria, and I will give thee two thousand horses, if thou be able on thy part to set riders upon them. 9. How then canst thou turn away the face of one captain of the least of my master's servants, and put thy trust on Egypt for chariots and for horsemen? 10. And am I now come up without the Lord against this land to destroy it? The Lord said unto me, Go up against this land, and destroy it.
11. Then said Eliakim and Shebna and Joah unto Rabshakeh, Speak, I pray thee, unto thy servants in the Syrian language; for we understand it: and speak not to us in the Jew's language, in the ears of the people that are on the wall.

12. But Rabshakeh said, Hath my master sent me to thy master, and to thee, to speak these words? hath he not sent me to the men which sit upon the wall to eat their own dung, and to drink their own water with you?

---

9. After this did Sennacherib king of Assyria send his servants to Jerusalem (now he was before Lachish, and all his power with him) unto Hezekiah king of Judah, and unto all Judah that were at Jerusalem,

saying, 10. Thus saith Sennacherib king of Assyria, Whereon do ye trust, that ye abide the siege in Jerusalem?

11. Doth not Hezekiah persuade you, to give you over to die by famine and by thirst, saying, The Lord our God shall deliver us out of the hand of the king of Assyria?
12. Hath not the same Hezekiah taken away his high places and his altars, and commanded Judah and Jerusalem, saying, Ye shall worship before one altar, and upon it shall ye burn incense? 13. Know he not what I and my fathers have done unto all the peoples of the lands?

Insolent Repetition of Insult

Then Rabshakeh stood, and cried with a loud voice in the Jew's language unto the people of Jerusalem that were on the wall to affright them, and to trouble them; that they might take the city; and said, Hear ye the word of the great king, the king of Assyria. Thus saith the king, Now therefore let not Hezekiah deceive you; for he shall not be able to deliver you out of his hand: neither let Hezekiah make you trust in the Lord, saying, The Lord will surely deliver us, and this city shall not be given into the hand of the king of Assyria.

Hearken not to Hezekiah: for thus saith the king of Assyria, Make your peace with me, and come out to me; and eat ye every one of his vine, and every one of his fig tree, and drink ye every one the waters of his own cistern; until I come and take you away to a land like your own land, a land of corn and wine, a land of bread and vineyards, a land of oil olive and of honey, that ye may live and not die. Beware lest Hezekiah persuade you on this manner, saying, The Lord will deliver us; neither believe ye him: for no god of any nation or kingdom was able to deliver his people out of mine hand, and out of the hand of my fathers: how much less shall your God deliver you out of mine hand?

Were any of the gods of the nations of the lands any ways able to deliver their land out of the hand of the king of Assyria? Where are the gods of Hamath and Arpad? where are the gods of Sepharvaim, of Hena, and Ivvah? and have they delivered Samaria out of my hand?

Who are they among all the gods of those nations which my fathers utterly destroyed, that could deliver his people out of mine hand that the Lord your God should be able to deliver Jerusalem out of mine hand?

And his servants spake yet more against the Lord God, and against his servant Hezekiah. He wrote also letters, to rail on the Lord, the God of Israel, and to speak against him, saying, As the gods of the nations of the lands, which have not delivered their people out of mine hand, so shall not the God of Hezekiah deliver his people out of mine hand. And they spake of the God of Jerusalem as of the gods of the peoples of the earth, which are the work of men's hands. But the people held their peace, and answered him not a word: for the king's commandment was, saying, Answer him not. Then came Eliakim the son of Hilkiah, which was over the household, and Shebna the scribe, and Joah the son of Asaph the recorder, to Hezekiah with their clothes rent, and told him the words of Rabshakeh.

SECT. XXIX THE SURVIVING SOUTHERN KINGDOM

(II Kings 18:) 28. Then Rabshakeh stood, and cried with a loud voice in the Jew's language, saying, Hear ye the word of the great king, the king of Assyria. 29. Thus saith the king, Let not Hezekiah deceive you; for he shall not be able to deliver you out of his hand: 30. neither let Hezekiah make you trust in the Lord, saying, The Lord will surely deliver us, and this city shall not be given into the hand of the king of Assyria. 31. Hearken not to Hezekiah: for thus saith the king of Assyria, Make your peace with me, and come out to me; and eat ye every one of his vine, and every one of his fig tree, and drink ye every one of the waters of his own cistern; 32. until I come and take you away to a land like your own land, a land of corn and wine, a land of bread and vineyards, a land of oil olive and of honey, that ye may live, and not die: and hearken not unto Hezekiah, when he persuadeth you, saying, The Lord will deliver us.	(Isaiah 36:) 13. Then Rabshakeh stood, and cried with a loud voice in the Jew's language, and said, Hear ye the word of the great king, the king of Assyria. 14. Thus saith the king, Let not Hezekiah deceive you; for he shall not be able to deliver you: 15. neither let Hezekiah make you trust in the Lord, saying, The Lord will surely deliver us; this city shall not be given into the hand of the king of Assyria. 16. Hearken not to Hezekiah: for thus saith the king of Assyria, Make your peace with me, and come out to me; and eat ye every one of his vine, and every one of his fig tree, and drink ye every one of the waters of his own cistern; 17. until I come and take you away to a land like your own land, a land of corn and wine, a land of bread and vineyards. 18. Beware lest Hezekiah persuade you, saying, The Lord will deliver us.	(II Chron. 32:) 18. And they cried with a loud voice in the Jew's language unto the people of Jerusalem that were on the wall, to affright them, and to trouble them; that they might take the city. 15. Now therefore let not Hezekiah deceive you, nor persuade you on this manner, neither believe ye him: for no god of any nation or kingdom was able to deliver his people out of mine hand, and out of the hand of my fathers: how much less shall your God deliver you out of mine hand?
33. Hath any of the gods of the nations ever delivered his land out of the hand of the king of Assyria? 34. Where are the gods of Hamath and Arpad? where are the gods of Sepharvaim, of Hena, and Ivvah? have they delivered Samaria out of my hand?	Hath any of the gods of the nations delivered his land out of the hand of the king of Assyria? 19. Where are the gods of Hamath and Arpad? where are the gods of Sepharvaim? and have they delivered Samaria out of my hand?	13b. Were the gods of the nations of the lands any ways able to deliver their land out of mine hand?
35. Who are they among all the gods of the countries, that have delivered their country out of my hand? that the Lord should deliver Jerusalem out of my hand?	20. Who are they among all the gods of these countries, that have delivered their country out of my hand? that the Lord should deliver Jerusalem out of my hand?	14. Who was there among all the gods of those nations which my fathers utterly destroyed, that could deliver his people out of mine hand that your God should be able to deliver you out of mine hand?
		16. And his servants spake yet more against the Lord God, and against his servant Hezekiah. 17. He wrote also letters, to rail on the Lord, the God of Israel, and to speak against him, saying, as the gods of the nations of the lands, which have not delivered their people out of mine hand, so shall not the God of Hezekiah deliver his people out of mine hand. 19. And they spake of the God of Jerusalem, as of the gods of the peoples of the earth, which are the work of men's hands.
36. But the people held their peace, and answered him not a word: for the king's commandment was, saying, Answer him not. 37. Then came Eliakim the son of Hilkiah, which was over the household, and Shebna the scribe, and Joah the son of Asaph the recorder, to Hezekiah with their clothes rent, and told him the words of Rabshakeh.	21. But they held their peace, and answered him not a word: for the king's commandment was, saying, Answer him not. 22. Then came Eliakim the son of Hilkiah, which was over the household, and Shebna the scribe, and Joah the son of Asaph the recorder, to Hezekiah with their clothes rent, and told him the words of Rabshakeh.	

Hezekiah's Message to Isaiah

And it came to pass, when king Hezekiah heard it, that he rent his clothes and covered himself with sackcloth, and went into the house of the Lord. And Hezekiah, the king, and Isaiah the prophet the son of Amoz prayed because of this, and cried to heaven. And he sent Eliakim, who was over the household, and Shebna, the scribe, and the elders of the priests, covered with sackcloth, unto Isaiah the prophet the son of Amoz. And they said unto him, Thus saith Hezekiah, This day is a day of trouble, and of rebuke, and of contumely: for the children are come to the birth, and there is not strength to bring forth.

It may be the Lord thy God will hear all the words of Rabshakeh, whom the king of Assyria his master hath sent to reproach the living God, and will rebuke the words which the Lord thy God hath heard: wherefore lift up thy prayer for the remnant that is left. So the servants of king Hezekiah came to Isaiah.

Isaiah's Prediction

And Isaiah said unto them, Thus shall ye say to your master, Thus saith the Lord, Be not afraid of the words that thou hast heard wherewith the servants of the king of Assyria have blasphemed me. Behold, I will put a spirit in him, and he shall hear a rumour, and shall return to his own land; and I will cause him to fall by the sword in his own land. So Rabshakeh returned and found the king of Assyria warring against Libnah: for he had heard that he was departed from Lachish. And he heard say of Tirhakah king of Ethiopia, He is come out to fight against thee. And when he heard it, he sent messengers again unto Hezekiah, saying, Thus shall ye speak to Hezekiah king of Judah, saying, Let not thy God in whom thou trusteth deceive thee, saying Jerusalem shall not be given into the hand of the king of Assyria. Behold, thou hast heard what the kings of Assyria have done to all lands, by destroying them utterly: and shall thou be delivered? Have the gods of the nations delivered them, which my fathers have destroyed, Gozan, and Haran, and Rezeph, and the children of Eden which were in Talassar? Where is the king of Hamath, and the king of Arpad, and the king of the city of Sepharvaim, of Hena, and Ivvah? And Hezekiah received the letter from the hand of the messengers, and read it: and Hezekiah went unto the house of the Lord, and spread it before the Lord.

Prayer of Hezekiah

And Hezekiah prayed before the Lord, and said, O Lord of hosts, the God of Israel, that sittest upon the cherubim, thou art the God, even thou alone, of all the kingdoms of the earth. Incline thine ear, O Lord, and hear; open thine eyes, O Lord, and see: and hear all the words of Sennacherib, wherewith he hath sent him to reproach the living God. Of a truth, O Lord, the kings of Assyria have laid waste the nations and their lands, and have cast their gods into the fire; for they were no gods, but the work of men's hands, wood and stone; therefore they have destroyed them. Now therefore, O Lord our God, save thou us, I beseech thee, out of his hand, that all the kingdoms of the earth may know that thou art the Lord, even thou only.

God's Answer By Isaiah

Then Isaiah the son of Amoz sent to Hezekiah, saying, Thus saith the Lord, the God of Israel, Whereas thou hast prayed to me against Sennacherib king of Assyria, I have heard thee. This is the word that the Lord hath spoken concerning him: The virgin daughter of Zion hath despised thee and laughed thee to scorn; the daughter of Jerusalem hath shaken her head at thee. Whom hast thou reproached and blasphemed? and against whom hast thou exalted thy voice and lifted up thine eyes on high? even against the Holy One of Israel. By thy

SECT. XXIX — THE SURVIVING SOUTHERN KINGDOM

(II Kings 19:) 1. And it came to pass, when king Hezekiah heard it, that he rent his clothes, and covered himself with sackcloth, and went into the house of the Lord.

(Isaiah 37:) 1. And it came to pass, when king Hezekiah heard it, that he rent his clothes, and covered himself with sackcloth, and went into the house of the Lord.

(II Chron. 32:) 20. And Hezekiah, the king and Isaiah the prophet the son of Amoz, prayed because of this, and cried to heaven.

(II Kings 19:) 2. And he sent Eliakim, which was over the household, and Shebna the scribe, and the elders of the priests, covered with sackcloth, unto Isaiah the prophet the son of Amoz. 3. And they said unto him, Thus saith Hezekiah, This day is a day of trouble, and of rebuke, and of contumely: for the children are come to the birth, and there is not strength to bring forth. 4. It may be the Lord thy God will hear all the words of Rabshakeh, whom the king of Assyria his master hath sent to reproach the living God, and will rebuke the words which the Lord thy God hath heard: wherefore lift up thy prayer for the remnant that is left. 5. So the servants of king Hezekiah came to Isaiah.

6. And Isaiah said unto them, Thus shall ye say to your master, Thus saith the Lord, Be not afraid of the words that thou hast heard wherewith the servants of the king of Assyria have blasphemed me.

7. Behold, I will put a spirit in him, and he shall hear a rumour, and shall return to his own land; and I will cause him to fall by the sword in his own land. 8. So Rabshakeh returned, and found the king of Assyria warring against Libnah: for he had heard that he was departed from Lachish. 9. And when he heard say of Tirhakah king of Ethiopia, Behold, he is come out to fight against thee: he sent messengers again unto Hezekiah, saying, 10. Thus shall ye speak to Hezekiah king of Judah, saying, Let not thy God in whom thou trustest deceive thee, saying, Jerusalem shall not be given into the hand of the king of Assyria. 11. Behold, thou hast heard what the kings of Assyria have done to all lands, by destroying them utterly: and shalt thou be delivered? 12. Have the gods of the nations delivered them, which my fathers have destroyed, Gozan, and Haran, and Rezeph, and the children of Eden which were in Telassar? 13. Where is the king of Hamath, and the king of Arpad, and the king of the city of Sepharvaim, of Hena, and Ivvah? 14. And Hezekiah received the letter from the hand of the messengers, and read it: and Hezekiah went up unto the house of the Lord, and spread it before the Lord.

(Isaiah 37:) 2. And he sent Eliakim, who was over the household, and Shebna the scribe, and the elders of the priests, covered with sackcloth, unto Isaiah the prophet the son of Amoz. 3. And they said unto him, Thus saith Hezekiah, This day is a day of trouble, and of rebuke, and of contumely: for the children are come to the birth, and there is not strength to bring forth. 4. It may be the Lord thy God will hear the words of Rabshakeh, whom the king of Assyria his master hath sent to reproach the living God, and will rebuke the words which the Lord thy God hath heard: wherefore lift up thy prayer for the remnant that is left. 5. So the servants of king Hezekiah came to Isaiah.

6. And Isaiah said unto them, Thus shall ye say to your master, Thus saith the Lord, Be not afraid of the words that thou hast heard wherewith the servants of the king of Assyria have blasphemed me.

7. Behold, I will put a spirit in him, and he shall hear a rumour, and shall return unto his own land; and I will cause him to fall by the sword in his own land. 8. So Rabshakeh returned, and found the king of Assyria warring against Libnah: for he had heard that he was departed from Lachish. 9. And he heard say concerning Tirhakah king of Ethiopia, He is come out to fight against thee. And when he heard it, he sent messengers to Hezekiah, saying, 10. Thus shall ye speak to Hezekiah king of Judah, saying, Let not thy God in whom thou trustest deceive thee, saying, Jerusalem shall not be given into the hand of the king of Assyria. 11. Behold, thou hast heard what the kings of Assyria have done to all lands, by destroying them utterly: and shalt thou be delivered? 12. Have the gods of the nations delivered them, which my fathers have destroyed, Gozan, and Haran, and Rezeph, and the children of Eden which were in Telassar? 13. Where is the king of Hamath, and the king of Arpad, and the king of the city of Sepharvaim, of Hena, and Ivvah? 14. And Hezekiah received the letter from the hand of the messengers, and read it: and Hezekiah went up to the house of the Lord, and spread it before the Lord.

15. And Hezekiah prayed before the Lord, and said, O Lord, the God of Israel, that sittest upon the cherubim, thou art the God, even thou alone, of all the kingdoms of the earth: thou hast made heaven and earth. 16. Incline thine ear, O Lord, and hear; open thine eyes O Lord and see: and hear the words of Sennacherib, wherewith he hath sent him to reproach the living God. 17. Of a truth Lord, the kings of Assyria have laid waste the nations and their lands, 18. and have cast their gods into the fire; for they were no gods, but the work of men's hands, wood and stone; therefore they have destroyed them. 19. Now therefore, O Lord our God, save thou us, I beseech thee, out of his hand, that all the kingdoms of the earth may know that thou art the Lord, even thou only.

15. And Hezekiah prayed unto the Lord, saying, 16. O Lord of hosts, the God of Israel, that sittest upon the cherubim, thou art the God, even thou alone, of all the kingdoms of the earth; thou hast made heaven and earth. 17. Incline thine ear, O Lord, and hear; open thine eyes O Lord and see: and hear all the words of Sennacherib, which he hath sent to reproach the living God. 18. Of a truth, Lord, the kings of Assyria have laid waste all the countries and their land, 19. and have cast their gods into the fire; for they were no gods, but the work of men's hands, wood and stone; therefore they have destroyed them. 20. Now therefore, O Lord our God, save us, from his hand, that all the kingdoms of the earth may know that thou art the Lord, even thou only.

20. Then Isaiah the son of Amoz sent to Hezekiah, saying, Thus saith the Lord, the God of Israel, Whereas thou hast prayed to me against Sennacherib king of Assyria, I have heard thee. 21. This is the word that the Lord hath spoken concerning him: The virgin daughter of Zion hath despised thee and laughed thee to scorn; the daughter of Jerusalem hath shaken her head at thee.

21. Then Isaiah the son of Amoz sent unto Hezekiah, saying, Thus saith the Lord, the God of Israel, Whereas thou hast prayed to me against Sennacherib king of Assyria, 22. this is the word which the Lord hath spoken concerning him: The virgin daughter of Zion hath despised thee and laughed thee to scorn; the daughter of Jerusalem hath shaken her head at thee.

22. Whom hast thou reproached and blasphemed? and against whom hast thou exalted thy voice and lifted up thine eyes on high? even against the Holy One of Israel. 23. By thy

23. Whom hast thou reproached and blasphemed? and against whom hast thou exalted the voice and lifted up thine eyes on high? even against the Holy One of Israel. 24. By thy

messengers thou hast reproached the Lord, and hast said, With the multitude of my chariots am I come up to the height of the mountains, to the innermost parts of Lebanon; and I will cut down the tall cedars thereof, and the choice fir trees thereof; and I will enter into his farthest lodging place, the forest of his fruitful field. I have digged and drunk strange waters, and with the sole of my feet will I dry up all the rivers of Egypt.

Hast thou not heard how I have done it long ago, and formed it of ancient times? now have I brought it to pass, that thou shouldest be to lay waste fenced cities into ruined heaps. Therefore their inhabitants were of small power, they were dismayed and confounded; they were as the grass of the field, and as the green herb, as the grass on the housetops, and as corn blasted before it is grown up. But I know thy sitting down, and thy going out, and thy coming in, and thy raging against me. Because of the raging against me, and for that thy arrogancy is come up into mine ears, therefore will I put my hook in thy nose, and my bridle in thy lips, and I will turn thee back by the way by which thou camest. And this shall be the sign unto thee: ye shall eat this year that which groweth of itself, and in the second year that which springeth of the same; and in the third year sow ye, and reap, and plant vineyards, and eat the fruit thereof. And the remnant that is escaped of the house of Judah shall again take root downward, and bear fruit upward. For out of Jerusalem shall go forth a remnant, and out of mount Zion they that shall escape: the zeal of the Lord of hosts shall perform this.

Prophecy and Fulfillment

Therefore thus saith the Lord concerning the king of Assyria, He shall not come into this city, nor shoot an arrow there, neither shall he come before it with a shield, nor cast a mount against it. By the way that he came, by the same shall he return, and he shall not come unto this city, saith the Lord. For I will defend this city to save it, for mine own sake, and for my servant David's sake. And it came to pass that night, that the Lord sent an angel which cut off all the mighty men of valour, and the leaders and the captains, and smote in the camp of the Assyrians an hundred and fourscore and five thousand: and when men arose early in the morning, behold, they were all dead corpses. So Sennacherib king of Assyria departed, and went, and returned with shame of face to his own land, and dwelt at Nineveh. And it came to pass, as he was worshipping in the house of Nisroch his god, that Adrammelech and Sharezer, they that came forth of his own bowels, slew him there with the sword: and they escaped into the land of Ararat. And Esar-haddon his son reigned in his stead. Thus the Lord saved Hezekiah and the inhabitants of Jerusalem from the hand of Sennacherib the king of Assyria, and from the hand of all other, and guided them on every side. And many brought gifts unto the Lord to Jerusalem, and precious things to Hezekiah king of Judah: so that he was exalted in the sight of all nations from henceforth. Now the rest of the acts of Hezekiah, and his good deeds, and all his might, and how he made the pool, and the conduit, and brought the water into the city, behold, they are written in the vision of Isaiah the prophet the son of Amoz, in the book of the chronicles of the kings of Judah and Israel. And Hezekiah slept with his fathers, and they buried him in the ascent of the sepulchres of the sons of David: and all Judah and the inhabitants of Jerusalem did him honour at his death. And Manasseh his son reigned in his stead.

SECT. XXIX THE SURVIVING SOUTHERN KINGDOM

messengers thou hast reproached the Lord, and hast said, With the multitude of my chariots am I come up to the height of the mountains, to the innermost parts of Lebanon; and I will cut down the tall cedars thereof, and the choice fir trees thereof: and I will enter into his farthest lodging place, the forest of his fruitful field. 24. I have digged and drunk strange waters, and with the sole of my feet will I dry up all the rivers of Egypt.	servants hast thou reproached the Lord, and hast said With the multitude of my chariots am I come up to the height of the mountains, to the innermost parts of Lebanon; and I will cut down the tall cedars thereof, and the choice fir trees thereof: and I will enter into his farthest height, the forest of his fruitful field. 25. I have digged and drunk water, and with the sole of my feet will I dry up all the rivers of Egypt.	
25. Hast thou not heard how I have done it long ago, and formed it of ancient times? now have I brought it to pass, that thou shouldest be to lay waste fenced cities into ruinous heaps. 26. Therefore their inhabitants were of small power, they were dismayed and confounded; they were as the grass of the field, and as the green herb, as the grass on the housetops, and as corn blasted before it be grown up. 27. But I know thy sitting down, and thy going out, and thy coming in, and thy raging against me. 28. Because of the raging against me, and for that thy arrogancy is come up into mine ears, therefore will I put my hook in thy nose, and my bridle in thy lips, and I will turn thee back by the way by which thou camest. 29. And this shall be the sign unto thee: ye shall eat this year that which groweth of itself, and in the second year that which springeth of the same; and in the third year sow ye, and reap, and plant vineyards, and eat the fruit thereof. 30. And the remnant that is escaped of the house of Judah shall again take root downward, and bear fruit upward. 31. For out of Jerusalem shall go forth a remnant, and out of mount Zion they that shall escape: the zeal of the Lord shall perform this.	26. Hast thou not heard how I have done it long ago, and formed it of ancient times? now have I brought it to pass, that thou shouldest be to lay waste fenced cities into ruinous heaps. 27. Therefore their inhabitants were of small power, they were dismayed and confounded; they were as the grass of the field, and as the green herb, as the grass on the housetops, and as a field of corn before it is grown up. 28. But I know thy sitting down, and thy going out, and thy coming in, and thy raging against me. 29. Because of thy raging against me, and for that thy arrogancy is come up into mine ears, therefore will I put my hook in thy nose, and my bridle in thy lips, and I will turn thee back by the way by which thou camest. 30. And this shall be the sign unto thee: ye shall eat this year that which groweth of itself, and in the second year that which springeth of the same, and in the third year sow ye, and reap, and plant vineyards, and eat the fruit thereof. 31. And the remnant that is escaped of the house of Judah shall again take root downward, and bear fruit upward. 32. For out of Jerusalem shall go forth a remnant, and out of mount Zion they that shall escape: the zeal of the Lord shall perform this.	
32. Therefore thus saith the Lord concerning the king of Assyria, He shall not come into this city, nor shoot an arrow there, neither shall he come before it with shield, nor cast a mount against it. 33. By the way that he came, by the same shall he return, and he shall not come unto this city, saith the Lord. 34. For I will defend this city to save it, for mine own sake, and for my servant David's sake.	33. Therefore thus saith the Lord concerning the king of Assyria, He shall not come into this city, nor shoot an arrow there, neither shall he come before it with a shield, nor cast a mount against it. 34. By the way that he came, by the same shall he return, and he shall not come unto this city, saith the Lord. 35. For I will defend this city to save it, for mine own sake, and for my servant David's sake.	
35. And it came to pass that night, that the angel of the Lord went forth, (and smote in the camp of the Assyrians an hundred fourscore and five thousand: and when men arose early in the morning, behold, they were all dead corpses.)	36. And the angel of the Lord went forth, (and smote in the camp of the Assyrians an hundred and fourscore and five thousand: and when men arose early in the morning, behold, they were all dead corpses.)	(II Chron. 32:) 21. And the Lord sent an angel, (which cut off all the mighty men of valour, and the leaders and the captains, in the camp of the king of Assyria.)
36. So Sennacherib king of Assyria departed, and went and returned, and dwelt at Nineveh.	37. So Sennacherib king of Assyria departed, and went and returned, and dwelt at Nineveh.	So he returned with shame of face to his own land.
37. And it came to pass, as he was worshipping in the house of Nisroch his god, that Adrammelech and Sharezer smote him with the sword: and they escaped into the land of Ararat. And Esar-haddon his son reigned in his stead.	38. And it came to pass, as he was worshipping in the house of Nisroch his god, that Adrammelech and Sharezer his sons smote him with the sword: and they escaped into the land of Ararat. And Esar-haddon his son reigned in his stead.	And when he was come into the house of his god, they that came forth of his own bowels slew him there with the sword.
		22. Thus the Lord saved Hezekiah and the inhabitants of Jerusalem from the hand of Sennacherib the king of Assyria, and from the hand of all other, and guided them on every side. 23. And many brought gifts unto the Lord to Jerusalem, and precious things to Hezekiah king of Judah: so that he was exalted in the sight of all nations from henceforth.
	(II Kings 20:) 20. Now the rest of the acts of Hezekiah, and all his might, and how he made the pool, and the conduit, and brought water into the city, are they not written in the book of the chronicles of the kings of Judah? 21. And Hezekiah slept with his fathers: and Manasseh his son reigned in his stead.	32. Now the rest of the acts of Hezekiah, and his good deeds, behold, they are written in the vision of Isaiah the prophet the son of Amoz, in the book of the kings of Judah and Israel. 33. And Hezekiah slept with his fathers, and they buried him in the ascent of the sepulchres of the sons of David: and all Judah and the inhabitants of Jerusalem did him honour at his death. And Manasseh his son reigned in his stead.

THE HOUSE OF DAVID
B. C. 697-642 *
XV Manasseh   Nahum.
B. C. 686-641
B. C. 642-640
XVI Amon
B. C. 641-639

SECTION XXX

The Wicked Reigns of Manasseh and Amon

Accession and Character of Manasseh

Manasseh was twelve years old when he began to reign; and he reigned fifty and five years in Jerusalem: and his mother's name was Hephzi-bah. And he did that which was evil in the sight of the Lord, after the abominations of the heathen, whom the Lord cast out before the children of Israel. For he built again the high places which Hezekiah his father had destroyed; and he reared up altars for the Baalim, and made an Asherah, as did Ahab king of Israel, and worshipped all the host of heaven, and served them. And he built altars in the house of the Lord, whereof the Lord said, in Jerusalem will I put my name for ever. And he built altars for all the host of heaven in the two courts of the house of the Lord. He also made his children to pass through the fire, in the valley of the son of Hinnom; and he practised augury, and used enchantments, and practised sorcery, and dealt with them that had familiar spirits, and with wizards; he wrought much evil in the sight of the Lord, to provoke him to anger. And he set the graven image of Asherah, that he had made in the house of God, of which the Lord said to David and to Solomon his son, In this house, and in Jerusalem, which I have chosen out of all the tribes of Israel, will I put my name for ever: neither will I any more remove the foot of Israel from off the land which I have appointed for your fathers: if only they will observe to do according to all that I have commanded them, even all the law, and the statutes, and the ordinances by the hand of Moses. But they hearkened not: and Manasseh made Judah and the inhabitants of Jerusalem to err, so that they did evil more than did the nations, whom the Lord destroyed before the children of Israel.

The Lord's Indictment and Sentence

And the Lord spake, by his servants the prophets, to Manasseh and his people, saying, Because Manasseh king of Judah hath done these abominations and hath done wickedly above all that the Amorites did, which were before him, and hath made Judah also to sin with his idols: therefore thus saith the Lord, the God of Israel, Behold, I bring such evil upon Jerusalem and Judah, that whosoever heareth of it, both his ears shall tingle. And I will stretch over Jerusalem the line of Samaria, and the plummet of the house of Ahab: and I will wipe Jerusalem as a man wipeth a dish, wiping it and turning it upside down. And I will cast off the remnant of mine inheritance, and deliver them into the hand of their enemies; and they shall become a prey and a spoil to all their enemies; because they have done that which is evil in my sight, and have provoked me to anger, since the day their fathers came

---

* See Chronology Appendix A. Both systems of chronology are used, e.g., Manasseh $\frac{697 \text{ (Usher)}}{686 \text{ (Revised)}}$

SECT. XXX THE SURVIVING SOUTHERN KINGDOM

(II Kings 21:) 1. Manasseh was twelve years old when he began to reign; and he reigned five and fifty years in Jerusalem: and his mother's name was Hephzi-bah. 2. And he did that which was evil in the sight of the Lord, after the abominations of the heathen whom the Lord cast out before the children of Israel. 3. For he built again the high places which Hezekiah his father had destroyed; and he reared up altars for Baal, and made an Asherah, as did Ahab king of Israel, and worshipped all the host of heaven, and served them. 4. And he built altars in the house of the Lord, whereof the Lord said, in Jerusalem will I put my name. 5. And he built altars for all the host of heaven in the two courts of the house of the Lord. 6. And he made his son to pass through the fire, and practised augury, and used enchantments, and dealt with them that had familiar spirits, and with wizards; he wrought much evil in the sight of the Lord, to provoke him to anger. 7. And he set the graven image of Asherah, that he had made in the house of which the Lord said to David and to Solomon his son, In this house and in Jerusalem, which I have chosen out of all the tribes of Israel, will I put my name for ever: 8. (neither will I cause the feet of Israel to wander any more out of the land which I gave their fathers;) if only they will observe to do according to all that I have commanded them, and (according to all the law that my servant Moses commanded them.) 9. But they hearkened not: and Manasseh seduced them to do that which is evil more than did the nations, whom the Lord destroyed before the children of Israel.

10. And the Lord spake, by his servants the prophets, saying, 11. Because Manasseh king of Judah hath done these abominations and hath done wickedly above all that the Amorites did, which were before him, and hath made Judah also to sin with his idols: 12. therefore thus saith the Lord, the God of Israel, Behold, I bring such evil upon Jerusalem and Judah, that whosoever heareth of it, both his ears shall tingle. 13. And I will stretch over Jerusalem the line of Samaria, and the plummet of the house of Ahab: and I will wipe Jerusalem as a man wipeth a dish, wiping it and turning it upside down. 14. And I will cast off the remnant of mine inheritance, and deliver them into the hand of their enemies; and they shall become a prey and a spoil to all their enemies; 15. because they have done that which is evil in my sight, and have provoked me to anger, since the day their fathers came

(II Chron. 33:) 1. Manasseh was twelve years old when he began to reign; and he reigned fifty and five years in Jerusalem; 2. And he did that which was evil in the sight of the Lord, after the abominations of the heathen, whom the Lord cast out before the children of Israel. 3. For he built again the high places which Hezekiah his father had broken down; and he reared up altars for the Baalim, and made Ashteroth, and worshipped all the host of heaven, and served them. 4. And he built altars in the house of the Lord, whereof the Lord said, in Jerusalem shall my name be for ever. 5. And he built altars for all the host of heaven in the two courts of the house of the Lord. 6. He also made his children to pass through the fire, in the valley of the son of Hinnom; and he practised augury, and used enchantments, and practised sorcery, and dealt with them that had familiar spirits, and with wizards: he wrought much evil in the sight of the Lord, to provoke him to anger. 7. And he set the graven image of the idol, which he had made in the house of God, of which God said to David and to Solomon his son, In this house and in Jerusalem, which I have chosen out of all the tribes of Israel, will I put my name for ever; 8. (neither will I any more remove the foot of Israel from off the land which I have appointed for your fathers: if only they will observe to do according to all that I have commanded them, (even all the law and the statutes, and the ordinances by the hand of Moses.) 9. and Manasseh made Judah and the inhabitants of Jerusalem to err, so that they did evil more than did the nations, whom the Lord destroyed before the children of Israel.

10. And the Lord spake to Manasseh and his people:

forth out of Egypt, even unto this day:*¹ but they gave no heed. Moreover Manasseh shed innocent blood very much, till he had filled Jerusalem from one end to another; beside his sin wherewith he made Judah to sin, in doing that which was evil in the sight of the Lord. Wherefore the Lord brought upon them the captains of the host of the king of Assyria, which took Manasseh in chains, and bound him with fetters, and carried him to Babylon.*²

Repentance Remission Reformation   *³ And when he was in distress, he besought the Lord his God, and humbled himself greatly before the God of his fathers. And he prayed unto him; and he was intreated of him, and heard his supplication, and brought him again to Jerusalem into his kingdom. Then Manasseh knew that the Lord he was God. Now after this he built an outer wall to the city of David, on the west side of Gihon, in the valley, even to the entering in at the fish gate; and he compassed about Ophel, and raised it up a very great height; and he put valiant captains in all the fenced cities of Judah.

And he took away the strange gods, and the idol out of the house of the Lord, and all the altars that he had built in the mount of the house of the Lord, and in Jerusalem, and cast them out of the city. And he built up the altar of the Lord, and he offered thereon sacrifices of peace offerings and of thanksgiving, and commanded Judah to serve the Lord, the God of Israel. Nevertheless, the people did sacrifice still in the high places, but only unto the Lord their God. Now the rest of the acts of Manasseh, and all that he did, and his sin that he sinned, and his prayer unto his God, and the word of the seers that spake to him in the name of the Lord, the God of Israel, behold, are they not written in the book of the chronicles of the kings of Judah? His prayer also, and how God was intreated of him, and all his sin and his trespass, and the places wherein he built high places, and set up the Asherim, and the graven images, before he humbled himself: behold they are written in the history of the book of Hozai. And Manasseh slept with his fathers, and they buried him in his own house, in the garden of Uzza: and Amon his son reigned in his stead.

---

*¹ Read what Jeremiah the prophet says, Jer. 15:1-6. 1. Then said the Lord unto me, Though Moses and Samuel stood before me, yet my mind could not be toward this people: cast them out of my sight, and let them go forth. 2. And it shall come to pass, when they say unto thee, Whither shall we go forth? then thou shalt tell them, Thus saith the Lord: Such as for death, to death; and such as for the sword, to the sword: and such as are for the famine, to the famine: and such as for captivity, to captivity. 3. And I will appoint over them four kinds, saith the Lord: the sword to slay, and the dogs to tear, and the fowls of the heaven, and the beasts of the earth, to devour and to destroy. 4. And I will cause them to be tossed to and fro among all the kingdoms of the earth, *because of Manasseh the son of Hezekiah king of Judah*, for that which he did in Jerusalem. 5. For who shall have pity upon thee, O Jerusalem? or who shall bemoan thee? or who shall turn aside to ask of thy welfare? 6. Thou hast rejected me, saith the Lord, thou art gone backward: therefore have I stretched out my hand against thee, and destroyed thee; I am weary with repenting.

*² After being taken, rebuilt and refitted as Capital by king of Assyria.

*³ This is the most remarkable of all the additions made by the chronicler to the narrative found in Kings. He cites as his authority for this radical reversal of the final estimate Scripture puts upon Manasseh, as man and king, "the history of the book

Sect. XXX — THE SURVIVING SOUTHERN KINGDOM

forth out of Egypt, even unto this day.

16. Moreover Manasseh shed innocent blood very much, till he had filled Jerusalem from one end to another: beside his sin wherewith he made Judah to sin, in doing that which was evil in the sight of the Lord.

but they gave no heed.

11. Wherefore the Lord brought upon them the captains of the host of the king of Assyria, which took Manasseh in chains, and bound him with fetters, and carried him to Babylon.

12. And when he was in distress, he besought the Lord his God, and humbled himself greatly before the God of his fathers. 13. And he prayed unto him; and he was intreated of him, and heard his supplication, and brought him again to Jerusalem into his kingdom.

Then Manasseh knew that the Lord he was God. 14. Now after this he built an outer wall to the city of David, on the west side of Gihon, in the valley, even to the entering in at the fish gate; and he compassed about Ophel, and raised it up a very great height: and he put valiant captains in all the fenced cities of Judah.

15. And he took away the strange gods, and the idol out of the house of the Lord, and all the altars that he had built in the mount of the house of the Lord, and in Jerusalem, and cast them out of the city. 16. And he built up the altar of the Lord, and he offered thereon sacrifices of peace offerings and of thanksgiving, and commanded Judah to serve the Lord, the God of Israel.

17. Nevertheless the people did sacrifice still in the high places, but only unto the Lord their God.

17. Now the rest of the acts of Manasseh, and all that he did, and his sin that he sinned,

are they not written ((in the book of the chronicles of the kings of Judah?))

18. Now the rest of the acts of Manasseh, and his prayer unto his God, and the words of the seers that spake to him in the name of the Lord, the God of Israel, behold, they are written ((among the acts of the kings of Israel.))

19. His prayer also, and how God was intreated of him, and all his sin and his trespass, and the places wherein he built high places, and set up the Asherim, and the graven images, before he humbled himself: behold, they are written in the history of Hozai.

18. And Manasseh slept with his fathers, and was buried in the garden of his own house, in the garden of Uzza: and Amon his son reigned in his stead.

20. So Manasseh slept with his fathers, and they buried him in his own house: and Amon his son reigned in his stead.

---

of Hozai." The Chronicler gives full details of the remarkable repentance and reformation of Manasseh, as preceding and following the merciful remission and restoration to country and throne after captivity by Jehovah. Of all the incidents recorded in the Old Testament, it most nearly corresponds with the story of the thief on the cross, both as to time and place when and where the repentance for and remission of his sin was secured; and to the transformation of Saul the persecutor to Paul the preacher, as to the completeness of the change wrought in him. Kings record the Lord's terrible indictment and sentence of the wicked king; Chronicles record the king's greatly humbling himself before, and his supplication and prayer to, the Lord his God and its gracious answer by the God of his fathers. They are thus the complements of each other, as are the Law and the Gospel as seen in the first thirty-nine and the last twenty-seven Chapters of Isaiah, or in the first thirty-nine and the last twenty-seven Books of the Old and New Testament. See Appendix C. Chronicles II for other Additions.

The Prayer of Manasses (Apocryphal).

O Lord Almighty, God of our fathers, Abraham, Isaac, and Jacob, and of their righteous seed; who hast made heaven and earth, with all the ornament thereof; who hast bound the sea by the word of thy commandment; who hast shut up the

Accession and Character of Amon

Amon was twenty and two years old when he began to reign; and he reigned two years in Jerusalem: and his mother's name was Meshullemeth the daughter of Haruz of Jotbah. And he did that which was evil in the sight of the Lord, as did Manasseh his father. And Amon walked in all the way that his father walked in, and sacrificed unto all the graven images which Manasseh his father had made, and served the idols that his father served, and worshipped them: and he forsook the Lord, the God of his fathers, and walked not in the way of the Lord.

And he humbled not himself before the Lord, as Manasseh his father had humbled himself; but the same Amon trespassed more and more.

Violent Death and Burial

And the servants of Amon conspired against him, and put the king to death in his own house. But the people of the land slew all them that conspired against king Amon: and the people of the land made Josiah his son king in his stead. Now the rest of the acts of Amon which he did, are they not written in the book of the chronicles of the kings of Judah? And he was buried in his sepulchre in the garden of Uzza: and Josiah his son reigned in his stead.

---

deep, and sealed it by thy terrible and glorious name; whom all men fear, and tremble before thy power; for the majesty of thy glory cannot be borne, and thy angry threatening toward sinners is importable; but thy merciful promise is unmeasurable and unsearchable; for thou art the most high Lord, of great compassion, long-suffering, very merciful, and repentest of the evils of men. Thou, O Lord, according to thy great goodness has promised repentance and forgiveness to them that have sinned against thee, and of thine infinite mercies hast appointed repentance unto sinners that they may be saved. Thou therefore, O Lord, thou art the God of the just, hast not appointed repentance to the just, as to Abraham, and Isaac, and Jacob, which have not sinned against thee; but thou hast appointed repentance unto me that am a sinner. For I have sinned above the number of the sands of the sea. My transgressions, O Lord, are multiplied; my transgressions are multiplied, and I am not worthy to behold and see the height of heaven for the multitude of mine iniquities. I am bowed down with many iron bands, that I cannot lift up mine head, neither have any release: for I have provoked thy wrath and done evil before thee: I did not thy will, neither kept I thy commandments: I have set up abominations, and have multiplied offences

Sect. XXX THE SURVIVING SOUTHERN KINGDOM

(II Kings 21:) 19. Amon was twenty and two years old when he began to reign; and he reigned two years in Jerusalem: and his mother's name was Meshulemeth the daughter of Haruz of Jotbah. 20. And he did that which was evil in the sight of the Lord, as did Manasseh his father.
21. And he walked in all the way that his father walked in, and served the idols that his father served, and worshipped them: 22. and he forsook the Lord, the God of his fathers, and walked not in the way of the Lord.

23. And the servants of Amon conspired against him, and put the king to death in his own house. 24. But the people of the land slew all them that conspired against king Amon: and the people of the land made Josiah his son king in his stead. 25. Now the rest of the acts of Amon which he did, are they not written in the book of the chronicles of the kings of Judah? 26. And he was buried in his sepulchre in the garden of Uzza: and Josiah his son reigned in his stead.

(II Chron. 33:) 21. Amon was twenty and two years old when he began to reign; and he reigned two years in Jerusalem:

22. And he did that which was evil in the sight of the Lord, as did Manasseh his father.
And Amon sacrificed unto all the graven images which Manasseh his father had made, and served them.

23. And he humbled not himself before the Lord, as Manasseh his father had humbled himself; but this same Amon trespassed more and more.
24. And his servants conspired against him, and put him to death in his own house. 25. But the people of the land slew all them that conspired against king Amon; and the people of the land made Josiah his son king in his stead.

THE HOUSE OF DAVID
B. C. 640-609 * Zephaniah, Jeremiah
XVII Josiah
B. C. 639-609 Habakkuk, Huldah

SECTION XXXI

Josiah's Piety and Reformations

Accession and Character of Josiah

Josiah was eight years old when he began to reign; and he reigned thirty and one years in Jerusalem: and his mother's name was Jedidah the daughter of Adaiah of Bozkath. And he did that which was right in the eyes of the Lord and walked in all the way of David his father, and turned not aside to the right hand or to the left. For in the eighth year of his reign, while he was yet young, he began to seek after the God of David his father: and in the twelfth year he began to purge Judah and Jerusalem from the high places, and the Asherim, and the graven images, and the molten images. And they brake down the altars of the Baalim in his presence; and the sun images, that were on high above them, he hewed down; and the Asherim, and the graven images, and the molten images, he brake in pieces, and made dust of them, and strowed it upon the graves of them that had sacrificed unto them. And he burnt the bones of the priests upon their altars, and purged Judah and Jerusalem. And so did he in the cities of Manasseh and Ephraim and Simeon, even unto Naphtali, in their ruins round about. And he brake down the altars, and beat the Asherim and the graven images into powder, and hewed down all the sun images throughout all the land of Israel, and returned to Jerusalem.

Repairs of the House of the Lord

And it came to pass in the eighteenth year of king Josiah, that, when he purged the land, and the house, the king sent Shaphan the son of Azaliah, the son of Meshullam, the scribe, and Maaseiah the governor of the city, and Joah the son of Joahaz the recorder, to repair the house of the Lord his God. And they came to Hilkiah the high priest, and delivered the money that was brought into the house of God, which the Levites, the keepers of the door had gathered of the hand of Manasseh and Ephraim, and of all the remnant of Israel, and of all Judah and Benjamin, and of the inhabitants of Jerusalem. And they delivered it into the hand of the workmen that had the oversight of the house of the Lord; and the workmen that wrought in the house of the Lord gave it to amend and repair the breaches of the house; even to the carpenters and to the builders, and to the masons, gave they it, to buy hewn stone, and timber for couplings, and to make beams for the houses which the kings of Judah had destroyed. Howbeit there was no reckoning made with them of the money that was delivered into their hand; for they dealt faithfully. And the overseers of them were Jahath and Obadiah, the Levites, of the sons of Merari: and Zechariah and Meshullam, of the sons of Kohathites to set

* See Chronology Appendix A. Both systems of chronology are used, e.g., Josiah $\frac{640 \text{ (Usher)}}{639 \text{ (Revised)}}$

SECT. XXXI THE SURVIVING SOUTHERN KINGDOM

(II Kings 22:) 1. Josiah was eight years old when he began to reign; and he reigned thirty and one years in Jerusalem: and his mother's name was Jedidah the daughter of Adaiah of Bozkath. 2. And he did that which was right in the eyes of the Lord, and walked in all the way of David his father, and turned not aside to the right hand or to the left.

3. And it came to pass in the eighteenth year of king Josiah, that the king sent Shaphan the son of Azaliah, the son of Meshullam, the scribe, to the house of the Lord, saying, 4. Go up to Hilkiah the high priest, that he may sum the money which is brought into the house of the Lord, which the keepers of the door have gathered of the people:

5. and let them deliver it into the hand of the workmen that have the oversight of the house of the Lord; and let them give it to the workmen which are in the house of the Lord, to repair the breaches of the house; 6. unto the carpenters, and to the builders, and to the masons; and for buying timber and hewn stone to repair the house.

7. Howbeit there was no reckoning made with them of the money that was delivered into their hand; for they dealt faithfully.

(II Chron. 34:) 1. Josiah was eight years old when he began to reign; and he reigned thirty and one years in Jerusalem.

2. And he did that which was right in the eyes of the Lord, and walked in the ways of David his father, and turned not aside to the right hand or to the left. 3. For in the eighth year of his reign, while he was yet young, he began to seek after the God of David his father: and in the twelfth year he began to purge Judah and Jerusalem from the high places, and the Asherim, and the graven images, and the molten images. 4. And they brake down the altars of the Baalim in his presence; and the sun images that were on high above them, he hewed down; and the Asherim, and the graven images and the molten images, he brake in pieces, and made dust of them, and strowed it upon the graves of them that had sacrificed unto them. 5. And he burnt the bones of the priests upon their altars, and purged Judah and Jerusalem. 6. And so did he in the cities of Manasseh and Ephraim and Simeon, even unto Naphtali, in their ruins round about. 7. And he brake down the altars, and beat the Asherim and the graven images into powder, and hewed down all the sun images throughout all the land of Israel, and returned to Jerusalem.

8. Now in the eighteenth year of his reign, when he had purged the land, and the house, he sent Shaphan the son of Azaliah, and Maaseiah the governor of the city, and Joah the son of Joahaz the recorder, to repair the house of the Lord his God. 9 And they came to Hilkiah the high priest, and delivered the money that was brought into the house of God, which the Levites, the keepers of the door had gathered of the hand of Manasseh and Ephraim, and of all the remnant of Israel, and of all Judah and Benjamin, and of the inhabitants of Jerusalem. 10. And they delivered it into the hand of the workmen that had the oversight of the house of the Lord; and the workmen that wrought in the house of the Lord gave it to amend and repair the house; 11. even to the carpenters and to the builders, gave they it, to buy hewn stone, and timber for couplings, and to make beams for the houses which the kings of Judah had destroyed.

12. And the men did the work faithfully: and the overseers of them were Jahath and Obadiah, the Levites, of the sons of Merari; and Zechariah and Meshullam, of the sons of Kohathites, to set

it forward: and other of the Levites, all that could skill of instruments of music. Also they were over the bearers of burdens, and set forward all that did the work in every manner of service: and of the Levites there were scribes, and officers, and porters.

Finding Book of the Law of the Lord

And when they brought out the money that was brought into the house of the Lord, Hilkiah the priest found the book of the law of the Lord given by Moses. And Hilkiah the high priest answered and said unto Shaphan the scribe, I have found the book of the law in the house of the Lord. And Hilkiah delivered the book to Shaphan, and he read it. And Shaphan the scribe carried the book to the king, and moreover brought the king word again, saying, All that was committed to thy servants, they do it. And they have emptied out the money that was found in the house of the Lord, and have delivered it into the hand of the overseers, and into the hand of the workmen that have the oversight of the house of the Lord. And Shaphan the scribe told the king, saying, Hilkiah the priest hath delivered me a book. And Shaphan read therein before the king.

King Inquires of Huldah the Prophetess

And the king commanded Hilkiah the priest, and Ahikam the son of Shaphan, and Achbor the son of Micaiah, and Shaphan the scribe, and Asaiah the king's servant, saying, Go ye, inquire of the Lord for me, and for them that are left in Israel, and in Judah, concerning the words of the book that is found: for great is the wrath of the Lord that is kindled against us, because our fathers have not hearkened unto the words of this book, to do according to all that is written corcerning us.

So Hilkiah the priest, and they whom the king had commanded, Ahikam, and Achbor, and Shaphan, and Asaiah, went unto Huldah the prophetess, the wife of Shallum the son of Tikvah, the son of Harhas, keeper of the wardrobe; (now she dwelt in Jerusalem in the second quarter;) and they communed with her, and spake to her to that effect.

Huldah's Answer

And she said unto them, Thus saith the Lord, the God of Israel: Tell ye the man that sent you unto me, Thus saith the Lord, Behold, I will bring evil upon this place, and upon the inhabitants thereof, even all the curses that are written in the book which they have read before the king of Judah: because they have forsaken me, and have burned incense unto other gods, that they might provoke me to anger with all the works of their hands: therefore is my wrath poured upon this place, and it shall not be quenched. But unto the king of Judah, who sent you to inquire of the Lord, thus shall ye say to him, Thus saith the Lord, the God of Israel: As touching the word which thou hast heard, because thine heart was tender, and thou didst humble thyself before the Lord, when thou heardest his words against this place, and against the inhabitants thereof, that they should become a desolation and a curse, and hast humbled thyself before me, and hast rent thy clothes, and wept before me; I also have heard thee, saith the Lord. Therefore, behold, I will gather thee to thy fathers, and thou shalt be gathered to thy grave in peace, neither shall thine eyes see all the evil which I will bring upon this place. And they brought the king word again.

National Renewal of the Covenant

Then the king sent and gathered together unto him all the elders of Judah and Jerusalem. And the king went up to the house of the Lord, and all the men of Judah and the inhabitants of Jerusalem with him, and the priests, and the prophets, and the Levites, and all the people, both great and small: and he read in their ears all the words of the book of the covenant which was found in the house of the Lord.

SECT. XXXI THE SURVIVING SOUTHERN KINGDOM

	it forward: and other of the Levites, all that could skill of instruments of music. 13. Also they were over the bearers of burdens, and set forward all that did the work in every manner of service: and of the Levites there were scribes, and officers, and porters.
	14. And when they brought out the money that was brought into the house of the Lord, Hilkiah the priest found the book of the law of the Lord given by Moses.
8. And Hilkiah the high priest said unto Shaphan the scribe, I have found the book of the law in the house of the Lord. And Hilkiah delivered the book to Shaphan, and he read it. 9. And Shaphan the scribe came to the king, and brought the king word again, and said, Thy servants have emptied out the money that was found in the house, and have delivered it into the hands of the workmen that have the oversight of the house of the Lord.	15. And Hilkiah answered and said to Shaphan the scribe, I have found the book of the law in the house of the Lord. And Hilkiah delivered the book to Shaphan. 16. And Shaphan carried the book to the king, and moreover brought the king word again, saying, All that was committed to thy servants, they do it. 17. And they have emptied out the money that was found in the house of the Lord, and have delivered it into the hand of the overseers, and into the hand of the workmen.
10. And Shaphan the scribe told the king, saying, Hilkiah the priest hath delivered me a book. And Shaphan read it before the king	18. And Shaphan the scribe told the king, saying, Hilkiah the priest hath delivered me a book. And Shaphan read therein before the king.
11. And it came to pass, when the king had heard the words of the book of the law, that he rent his clothes. 12. And the king commanded Hilkiah the priest, and Ahikam the son of Shaphan, and *Achbor* the son of *Micaiah*, and Shaphan the scribe, and Asaiah the king's servant, saying, 13. Go ye, inquire of the Lord for me, and for the people, and for all Judah concerning the words of this book that is found: for great is the wrath of the Lord that is kindled against us, because our fathers have not hearkened unto the words of this book, to do according unto all that which is written concerning us.	19. And it came to pass, when the king had heard the words of the law, that he rent his clothes. 20. And the king commanded Hilkiah and Ahikam the son of Shaphan, and *Abdon* the son of *Micah*, and Shaphan the scribe, and Asaiah the king's servant, saying, 21. Go ye, inquire of the Lord for me, and for them that are left in Israel, and in Judah, concerning the words of the book that is found: for great is the wrath that is poured out upon us, because our fathers have not kept the word of the Lord, to do according to all that is written in this book.
14. So Hilkiah the priest, and Ahikam, and Achbor, and Shaphan, and Asaiah, went unto Huldah the prophetess, the wife of Shallum the son of *Tikvah* the son of *Harhas*, keeper of the wardrobe; (now she dwelt in Jerusalem in the second quarter;) and they communed with her.	22. So Hilkiah, and they whom the king had commanded, went to Huldah the prophetess, the wife of Shallum the son of *Tokhath* the son of *Hasrah*, keeper of the wardrobe; (now she dwelt in Jerusalem in the second quarter;) and they spake to her to that effect.
15. And she said unto them, Thus saith the Lord, the God of Israel: Tell ye the man that sent you unto me, 16. Thus saith the Lord, Behold, I will bring evil upon this place, and upon the inhabitants thereof, even all the words of the book which the king of Judah hath read: 17. because they have forsaken me, and have burned incense unto other gods, that they might provoke me to anger with all the work of their hands; therefore my wrath shall be kindled against this place, and it shall not be quenched.	23. And she said unto them, Thus saith the Lord, the God of Israel: Tell ye the man that sent you unto me, 24. Thus saith the Lord, Behold, I will bring evil upon this place, and upon the inhabitants thereof, even all the curses that are written in the book which they have read before the king of Judah: 25. because they have forsaken me, and have burned incense unto other gods, that they might provoke me to anger with all the works of their hands; therefore is my wrath poured out upon this place, and it shall not be quenched.
18. But unto the king of Judah, who sent you to inquire of the Lord, thus shall ye say to him, Thus saith the Lord, the God of Israel: As touching the words which thou hast heard, 19. because thine heart was tender, and thou didst humble thyself before the Lord, when thou heardest what I spake against this place, and against the inhabitants thereof, that they should become a desolation and a curse, and hast rent thy clothes, and wept before me; I also have heard thee, saith the Lord. 20. Therefore, behold, I will gather thee to thy fathers, and thou shalt be gathered to thy grave in peace, neither shall thine eyes see all the evil which I will bring upon this place. And they brought the king word again.	26. But unto the king of Judah, who sent you to inquire of the Lord, thus shall ye say to him, Thus saith the Lord, the God of Israel: As touching the words which thou hast heard, 27. because thine heart was tender, and thou didst humble thyself before God, when thou heardest his words against this place, and against the inhabitants thereof, and hast humbled thyself before me, and hast rent thy clothes, and wept before me; I also have heard thee, saith the Lord. 28. Behold, I will gather thee to thy fathers, and thou shalt be gathered to thy grave in peace, neither shall thine eyes see all the evil that I will bring upon this place, and upon the inhabitants thereof. And they brought the king word again.
(II Kings 23:) 1. And the king sent, and they gathered unto him all the elders of Judah and Jerusalem. 2. And the king went up to the house of the Lord, and all the men of Judah and the inhabitants of Jerusalem with him, and the priests, and the prophets, and all the people, both small and great: and he read in their ears all the words of the book of the covenant which was found in the house of the Lord.	29. Then the king sent and gathered together all the elders of Judah and Jerusalem. 30. And the king went up to the house of the Lord, and all the men of Judah and the inhabitants of Jerusalem and the priests, and the Levites, and all the people, both great and small: and he read in their ears all the words of the book of the covenant that was found in the house of the Lord.

And the king stood in his place by the pillar, and made a covenant before the Lord, to walk after the Lord, and to keep his commandments, and his testimonies, and his statutes, with all his heart, and with all his soul, to perform the words of this covenant that were written in this book: And he caused all the people that were found in Jerusalem and Benjamin to stand to the covenant. And the inhabitants of Jerusalem did according to the covenant of God, the God of their fathers.

Suppression of Idolatry in Jerusalem And Josiah took away all the abominations out of all the countries that pertained to the children of Israel, and made all that were found in Israel to serve, even to serve the Lord their God. All his days they departed not from following the Lord, the God of their fathers. II Kings 23:4. And the king commanded Hilkiah the high priest, and the priests of the second order, and the keepers of the door, to bring forth out of the temple of the Lord all the vessels that were made for Baal, and for the Asherah, and for all the host of heaven: and he burned them without Jerusalem in the fields of Kidron, and carried the ashes of them unto Bethel. 5. And he put down the idolatrous priests, whom the kings of Judah had ordained to burn incense in the high places in the cities of Judah, and in the places round about Jerusalem; them also that burned incense unto Baal, to the sun, and to the moon, and to the planets, and to all the host of heaven. 6. And he brought out the Asherah from the house of the Lord, without Jerusalem, unto the brook Kidron, and burned it at the brook Kidron, and stamped it small to powder, and cast the powder thereof upon the graves of the common people. 7. And he brake down the house of the sodomites, that were in the house of the Lord, where the women wove hangings for the Asherah. 8. And he brought all the priests out of the cities of Judah, and defiled the high places where the priests had burned incense, from Geba to Beer-sheba; and he brake down the high places of the gates that were at the entering in of the gate of Joshua the governor of the city, which were on a man's left hand at the gate of the city. 9. Nevertheless the priests of the high places came not up to the altar of the Lord in Jerusalem, but they did eat unleavened bread among their brethren. 10. *And he defiled Topheth, which is in the valley of the children of Hinnom,** that no man might make his son or his daughter to pass through the fire to Moloch.

---

* Compare Jeremiah's prophecy (Jer. 19:1-15) proclaimed in the valley of the son of Hinnom. 1. Thus saith the Lord, Go, and buy a potter's earthen bottle, and take of the elders of the people, and of the elders of the priests; 2. and go forth unto the valley of the son of Hinnom, which is by the entry of the gate Harsith, and proclaim there the words that I shall tell thee: 3. and say, Hear ye the word of the Lord, O kings of Judah, and inhabitants of Jerusalem; thus saith the Lord of hosts, the God of Israel, Behold, I will bring evil upon this place, the which whosoever heareth, his ears shall tingle. 4. Because they have forsaken me, and have estranged this place, and have burned incense in it unto other gods, whom they knew not, they and their fathers and the kings of Judah; and have filled this place with the blood of innocents; 5. and have built the high places of Baal, to burn their sons in the fire for burnt offerings unto Baal; which I commanded not, nor spake it, neither came it into my mind: 6. therefore behold, the days come, saith the Lord, that this place shall no more be called Topheth, nor The valley of the son of Hinnom, but The valley of Slaughter. 7. And I will make void the counsel of Judah and Jerusalem in this place; and I will cause them to fall by the sword before their enemies, and by the hand of them that seek their life: and their carcasses will I give to be meat for the fowls of the heaven, and for the beasts of the earth. 8. And I will make this city an astonishment,

SECT. XXXI THE SURVIVING SOUTHERN KINGDOM 269

3. And the king stood by the pillar, and made a covenant before the Lord, to walk after the Lord, and to keep his commandments, and his testimonies, and his statutes, with all his heart, and all his soul, to confirm the words of this covenant that were written in this book: and all the people stood to the covenant.

31. And the king stood in his place, and made a covenant before the Lord, to walk after the Lord, and to keep his commandments, and his testimonies, and his statutes, with all his heart, and with all his soul, to perform the words of this covenant that were written in this book. 32. And he caused all that were found in Jerusalem and Benjamin to stand to it. And the inhabitants of Jerusalem did according to the covenant of God, the God of their fathers.

33. And Josiah took away all the abominations out of all the countries that pertained to the children of Israel, and made all that were found in Israel to serve, even to serve the Lord their God. All his days they departed not from following the Lord, the God of their fathers.

---

and an hissing; every one that passeth thereby shall be astonished and hiss because of all the plagues thereof. 9. And I will cause them to eat the flesh of their sons and the flesh of their daughters, and they shall eat every one the flesh of his friend, in the siege and in the straitness, wherewith their enemies, and they that seek their life, shall straiten them. 10. Then shalt thou break the bottle in the sight of the men that go with thee, and shall say unto them, 11. Thus saith the Lord of hosts: Even so will I break this people and this city, as one breaketh a potter's vessel, that cannot be made whole again: and they shall bury in Topheth, till there be no place to bury. 12. Thus will I do unto this place, saith the Lord, and to the inhabitants thereof, even making this city as Topheth: 13. and the houses of Jerusalem, and the houses of the kings of Judah, which are defiled, shall be as the place of Topheth, even all the houses upon whose roofs they have burned incense unto all the host of heaven, and have poured out drink offerings unto other gods. 14. Then came Jeremiah from Topheth, whither the Lord had sent him to prophesy; and he stood in the court of the Lord's house, and said to all the people: 15. Thus saith the Lord of hosts, the God of Israel, Behold, I will bring upon this city and upon all her towns all the evil that I have pronounced against it; because they have made their neck stiff, that they might not hear my words.

11. And he took away the horses that the kings of Judah had given to the sun, at the entering in of the house of the Lord, by the chamber of Nathanmelech the chamberlain, which was in the precincts; and he burned the chariots of the sun with fire. 12. And the altars that were on the roof of the upper chamber of Ahaz, which the kings of Judah had made, and the altars which Manasseh had made in the two courts of the house of the Lord, did the king break down, and beat them down from thence, and cast the dust of them into the brook Kidron. 13. And the high places that were before Jerusalem which were on the right hand of the mount of corruption, which Solomon the king of Israel had builded for Ashteroth the abomination of the Zidonians, and for Chemosh the abomination of Moab, and for Milcom the abomination of the children of Ammon, did the king defile. 14. And he brake in pieces the pillars, and cut down the Asherim, and filled their places with the bones of men. 15. Moreover the altar that was at Beth-el, and the high place which Jereboam the son of Nebat, who made Israel to sin, had made, even that altar and the high place he brake down: and he burned the high place and stamped it small to powder, and burned the Asherah.

Fulfillment of Prophecy on the Altar

16. And as Josiah turned himself, he spied the sepulchres that were there in the mount; and he sent and took the bones out of the sepulchres, and burned them upon the altar, and defiled it, according to the word of the Lord which the man of God proclaimed, who proclaimed these things. * 17. Then he said, What monument is that which I see? And the men of the city told him, It is the sepulchre of the man of God, which came from Judah, and proclaimed these things that thou hast done against the altar of Beth-el. 18. And he said, Let him be; let no man move his bones. So they let his bones alone, with the bones of the prophet that came out of Samaria. 19. And all the houses also of the high places that were in the cities of Samaria, which the kings of Israel had made to provoke the Lord to anger, Josiah took away, and did to them according to all the acts that he had done in Beth-el. 20. And he slew all the priests of the high places that were there, upon the altars, and burned men's bones upon them; and he returned to Jerusalem.

Josiah's Great Passover

And the king commanded all the people, saying, Keep the passover unto the Lord your God, as it is written in this book of the covenant. And Josiah kept a passover unto the Lord in Jerusalem: and they killed the passover on the fourteenth day of the first month. II Chron. 35:2. And he set the priests in their charges, and encouraged them to the service of the house of the Lord. 3. And he said unto the Levites that taught all Israel, which were holy unto the Lord, Put the holy ark in the house which Solomon the son of David king of Israel did build; there shall no more be a burden upon your shoulders: now serve the Lord your God, and his people Israel.

4. And prepare yourselves after your father's houses by your courses, according to the writing of David king of Israel, and according to the writing of Solomon his son. 5. And stand in the holy place according to the divisions of the father's houses of your brethren the childern of the people, and let there be for each a portion of a father's house of the Levites. 6. And kill the passover and sanctify yourselves, and prepare for your brethren, to do according to the word of the Lord by the hand of Moses.

7. And Josiah gave to the children of the people, of the flock, lambs and kids, all of them for the passover offerings, unto all that were present, to the number of thirty thousand, and three thousand bullocks: these were of the king's substance. 8. And his princes gave for a

---
* See I Kings 13: 1-32. Pp. 155-157.

(II Kings 23:) 21. And the king commanded all the people, saying, Keep the passover unto the Lord your God, as it is written in this book of the covenant.

(II Chron. 35:) 1. And Josiah kept a passover unto the Lord in Jerusalem: and they killed the passover on the fourteenth day of the first month.

freewill offering unto the people, to the priests, and to the Levites. Hilkiah and Zechariah and Jehiel, the rulers of the house of God, gave unto the priests for the passover offerings two thousand and six hundred small cattle, and three hundred oxen. 9. Conaniah also, and Shemaiah and Nethanel, his brethren, and Hashabiah and Jeiel and Jozabad, the chiefs of the Levites, gave unto the Levites for the passover offerings five thousand small cattle, and five hundred oxen. 10. So the service was prepared, and the priests stood in their place, and the Levites by their courses, according to the king's commandment. 11. And they killed the passover, and the priests sprinkled the blood, which they received of their hand, and the Levites flayed them. 12. And they removed the burnt offerings, that they might give them according to the divisions of the fathers' houses of the children of the people, to offer unto the Lord, as it is written in the book of Moses. And so did they with the oxen.

13. And they roasted the passover with fire according to the ordinance: and the holy offerings sod they in pots, and in caldrons, and in pans, and carried them quickly to all the children of the people. 14. And afterward they prepared for themselves, and for the priests; because the priests the sons of Aaron were busied in offering the burnt offerings and the fat until night: therefore the Levites prepared for themselves, and for the priests the sons of Aaron. 15. And the singers the sons of Asaph were in their place according to the commandment of David, and Asaph, and Heman, and Jeduthun the king's seer; and the porters were at every gate: they needed not to depart from their service, for their brethren the Levites prepared for them. 16. So all the service of the Lord was prepared the same day, to keep the passover, and to offer burnt offerings upon the altar of the Lord, according to the commandment of king Josiah. 17. And the children of Israel that were present kept the passover at that time, and the feast of unleavened bread seven days.

Surely there was not kept such a passover in Israel from the days of the judges that judged Israel, neither did any of the kings of Israel, nor of the kings of Judah, keep such a passover as Josiah kept, and the priests, and the Levites, and all Judah and Israel that were present, and the inhabitants of Jerusalem. In the eighteenth year of the reign of king Josiah was this passover kept to the Lord in Jerusalem. II Kings 23:24. Moreover them that had familiar spirits, and the wizards, and the teraphim, and the idols, and all the abominations that were spied in the land of Judah and in Jerusalem, did Josiah put away, that he might confirm the words of the law which were written in the book that Hilkiah the priest found in the house of the Lord. 25. And like unto him there was no king before him, that turned to the Lord with all his heart, and with all his soul, and with all his might, according to all the law of Moses; neither after him arose there any like him. 26. Notwithstanding the Lord turned not from the fierceness of his great wrath wherewith his anger was kindled against Judah, because of all the provocations that Manasseh had provoked him withal. 27. And the Lord said, I will remove Judah also out of my sight, as I have removed Israel, and I will cast off this city, which I have chosen, even Jerusalem, and the house of which I said, My name shall be there.*

Summary of Josiah's Reforms

---

* Compare Jeremiah 3:6-11. 6. Moreover the Lord said unto me in the days of Josiah the king, Hast thou seen that which backsliding Israel hath done? she is gone up upon every high mountain and under every green tree, and there hath played the harlot. 7. And I said after she had done all these things, She will return unto me; but she returned not: and her treacherous sister Judah saw it. 8. And I saw, when, for this very cause that backsliding Israel had committed adultery, I had put her away and given her a bill of divorcement, yet treacherous Judah her sister feared not; but she also went and played the harlot. 9. And it came to pass through the lightness of her whoredom, that the land was polluted, and she committed adultery with stones and with stocks. 10. And yet for all this her treacherous sister Judah hath not returned unto me with her whole heart, but feignedly, saith the Lord. 11. And the Lord said unto me, Backsliding Israel hath shewn herself more righteous than treacherous Judah.

II Kings 23 :) 22. Surely there was not kept such a passover from the days of the judges that judged Israel, nor in all the days of the kings of Israel, nor of the kings of Judah;	(II Chron. 35:) 18. And there was no passover like to that kept in Israel from the days of Samuel the prophet; neither did any of the kings of Israel keep such a passover as Josiah kept, and the priests, and the Levites, and all Judah and Israel that were present, and the inhabitants of Jerusalem.
23. but in the eighteenth year of king Josiah was this passover kept to the Lord in Jerusalem.	19. In the eighteenth year of the reign of Josiah was this passover kept.

Disastrous Attack on Pharaoh-Necoh

After all this, when Josiah had prepared the temple, Pharaoh-necoh king of Egypt went up against the king of Assyria to fight against Carchemish by the river Euphrates: and king Josiah went out against him. But he sent ambassadors to him, saying, What have I to do with thee thou king of Judah? I come not against thee this day, but against the house wherewith I have war; and God hath commanded me to make haste: forbear thee from meddling with God who is with me, that he destroy thee not. Nevertheless Josiah would not turn his face from him, but disguised himself, that he might fight with him, and hearkened not unto the words of Neco, from the mouth of God, and came to fight in the valley of Megiddo. And when he had seen him, the archers shot at king Josiah; and the king said unto his servants, Have me away; for I am sore wounded. So his servants took him out of the chariot, and put him in the second chariot that he had, and brought him from Megiddo to Jerusalem: and he died, and was buried in his own sepulchre, in the sepulchres of his fathers. And all Judah and Jerusalem mourned for Josiah.* And Jeremiah lamented for Josiah: and all the singing men and singing women spake of Josiah in their lamentations, unto this day, and they made them an ordinance in Israel: and, behold, they are written in the lamentations.

Now the rest of the acts of Josiah, and his good deeds, according to that which is written in the law of the Lord, and all that he did, first and last, behold, they are written in the book of the chronicles of the kings of Israel and Judah.

---

* "The kingdom of Judah virtually perished with Josiah. Of Josiah's successors, the two who came to the throne in independence, Jehoahaz and Jehoiachim, reigned for only three months apiece. The two who reigned eleven years each, Jehoiakim and Zedekiah, were but creatures of a foreign power. There was no longer 'a question of independence, but of choice between two foreign sovereigns. When Judah recovered from the shock of Josiah's death, it found itself in the grasp of the Egyptian Necho.' (Stanley) From Necho's interference to the end, 'the kingdom of Judah fell into a state of alternate vassalage to the two conflicting powers of the valleys of the Nile and Euphrates. The shadows of kings were dismissed at the breath of their liege lord. It is a deplorable period of misrule and imbecility. Without ability to defend them, these kings had only the power of entailing the miseries of siege and conquest on their people by rebellions which had none of the dignity but all the melancholy consequences of a desperate struggle for independence' (Milman)."—Wood.

SECT. XXXI THE SURVIVING SOUTHERN KINGDOM

(II Kings 23:) 29. In his days Pharaoh-necoh king of Egypt went up against the king of Assyria to the river Euphrates: and king Josiah went against him:	(II Chron. 35:) 20. After all this, when Josiah had prepared the temple, Neco king of Egypt went up to fight against Carchemish by Euphrates: and Josiah went out against him. 21. But he sent ambassadors to him, saying, What have I to do with thee, thou king of Judah? I come not against thee this day, but against the house wherewith I have war; and God hath commanded me to make haste; forbear thee from meddling with God, who is with me, that he destroy thee not.
	22. Nevertheless Josiah would not turn his face from him, but disguised himself, that he might fight with him, and hearkened not unto the words of Neco, from the mouth of God, and came to fight in the valley of Megiddo.
and he slew him at Megiddo, when he had seen him. 30a. And his servants carried him in a chariot dead from Megiddo, and brought him to Jerusalem, and buried him in his own sepulchre.	23. And the archers shot at king Josiah; and the king said to his servants, Have me away; for I am sore wounded. 24. So his servants took him out of the chariot, and put him in the second chariot that he had, and brought him to Jerusalem; and he died, and was buried in the sepulchres of his fathers. And all Judah and Jerusalem mourned for Josiah. 25. And Jeremiah lamented for Josiah: and all the singing men and singing women spake of Josiah in their lamentations, unto this day; and they made them an ordinance in Israel: and, behold, they are written in the lamentations.
28. Now the rest of the acts of Josiah, and all that he did, are they not written in the book of the chronicles of the kings of Judah?	26 Now the rest of the acts of Josiah, and his good deeds, according to that which is written in the law of the Lord, 27. and his acts, first and last, behold, they are written in the book of the kings of Israel and Judah.

THE HOUSE OF DAVID
XVIII Jehoahaz { B. C. 609*
              { B. C. 609
XIX Jehoiakim { B. C. 609-599
              { B. C. 609-597   Jeremiah
XX   Jehoiachin { B. C. 599
               { B. C. 597
XXI Zedekiah { B. C. 599-588
             { B. C. 597-586

SECTION XXXII

Josiah's Successors the Vassals of Babylon

Jehoahaz Made King by People   And the people of the land took Jehoahaz the son of Josiah, and anointed him, and made him king in his father's stead in Jerusalem. Jehoahaz was twenty and three years old when he began to reign; and he reigned three months in Jerusalem: and his mother's name was Hamutal the daughter of Jeremiah of Libnah. And he did that which was evil in the sight of the Lord, according to all that his fathers had done. And Pharaoh-necoh the king of Egypt put him in bands at Riblah in the land of Hamath, that he might not reign in Jerusalem: and put the land to a tribute of an hundred talents of silver, and a talent of gold.

Jehoiakim Made King by Neco   And Pharaoh-necoh the king of Egypt made Eliakim the son of Josiah his brother king over Judah and Jerusalem, in the room of Josiah his father, and changed his name to Jehoiakim. And Neco took Jehoahaz his brother and carried him to Egypt. For thus saith the Lord concerning the house of the King of Judah: Weep ye not for the dead, neither bemoan him: but weep sore for him that goeth away; for he shall return no more, nor see his native country. For thus saith the Lord touching Shallum † the son of Josiah, king of Judah, which reigned instead of Josiah his father, which went forth out of this place: he shall not return thither any more; but in the place whither they have led him captive, there shall he die, and he shall see the land no more. And he came to Egypt, and died there. And Jehoiakim gave the silver and the gold to Pharaoh; but he taxed the land to give the money according to the commandment of Pharaoh: he exacted the silver and the gold of the people of the land, of every one according to his taxation, to give it unto Pharaoh-necoh. Jehoiakim was twenty and five years old when he began to reign; and he reigned eleven years in Jerusalem: and his mother's name was Zebidah the daughter of Padaiah of Rumah. And he did that which was evil in the sight of the Lord his God, according to all that his fathers had done.

Jeremiah Foretells Captivity   Jer. 25:1. The word of the Lord that came to Jerusalem concerning all the people of Judah in the fourth year of Jehoiakim the son of Josiah, king of Judah; the same was the first year of Nebuchad-rezzar king of Babylon; 2. the which Jeremiah the prophet spake unto all the people of Judah, and to all the inhabitants of Jerusalem, saying, 3. From the thir-

---
* See Chronology Appendix A. Both systems of chronology are used, e.g., Jehoahaz $\frac{609 \text{ (Usher)}}{609 \text{ (Revised)}}$

† In Kings and Chronicles, Jehoahaz.

SECT. XXXII   THE SURVIVING SOUTHERN KINGDOM

(II Kings 23:) 30b. And the people of the land took Jehoahaz the son of Josiah, and anointed him, and made him king in his father's stead. 31. Jehoahaz was twenty and three years old when he began to reign; and he reigned three months in Jerusalem: and his mother's name was Hamutal the daughter of Jeremiah of Libnah. 32. And he did that which was evil in the sight of the Lord, according to all that his fathers had done.

33. And Pharaoh-necoh put him in bands at Riblah in the land of Hamath, that he might not reign in Jerusalem; and put the land to a tribute of an hundred talents of silver, and a talent of gold.

34. And Pharaoh-necoh made Eliakim the son of Josiah king in the room of Josiah his father, and changed his name to Jehoiakim: but he took Jehoahaz away;

and he came to Egypt and died there.

35. And Jehoiakim gave the silver and the gold to Pharaoh; but he taxed the land to give the money according to the commandment of Pharaoh: he exacted the silver and the gold of the people of the land, of every one according to his taxation, to give it unto Pharaoh-necoh.

36. Jehoiakim was twenty and five years old when he began to reign and he reigned eleven years in Jerusalem: and his mother's name was Zebidah the daughter of Pedaiah of Rumah. 37. And he did that which was evil in the sight of the Lord, according to all that his fathers had done.

(II Chron. 36:) 1. Then the people of the land took Jehoahaz the son of Josiah, and made him king in his father's stead in Jerusalem. 2. Joahaz was twenty and three years old when he began to reign; and he reigned three months in Jerusalem.

3. And the king of Egypt deposed him at Jerusalem, and amerced the land in an hundred talents of silver, and a talent of gold.

4. And the king of Egypt made Eliakim his brother king over Judah and Jerusalem, and changed his name to Jehoiakim. And Neco took Joahaz his brother, and carried him to Egypt.

(Jer. 23:) 6a. For thus saith the Lord concerning the house of the king of Judah: 10. Weep ye not for the dead, neither bemoan him: but weep sore for him that goeth away; for he shall return no more, nor see his native country. 11. For thus saith the Lord touching Shallum the son of Josiah, king of Judah, which reigned instead of Josiah his father, which went forth out of this place: he shall not return thither any more; 12. but in the place whither they have led him captive, there shall he die, and he shall see the land no more.

5. Jehoiakim was twenty and five years old when he began to reign; and he reigned eleven years in Jerusalem:

and he did that which was evil in the sight of the Lord his God.

teenth year of Josiah, the son of Amon king of Judah, even unto this day, these three and twenty years, the word of the Lord hath come unto me, and I have spoken unto you, rising up early and speaking; but ye have not hearkened. 4. And the Lord hath sent unto you all his servants the prophets, rising up early and sending them; but ye have not hearkened nor inclined your ear to hear; saying, 5. Return ye now every one from his evil way, and from the evil of your doings, and dwell in the land that the Lord hath given unto you and to your fathers, from of old, and even for evermore: 6. and go not after other gods to serve them, and to worship them, and provoke me not to anger with the work of your hands; and I will do thee no hurt. 7. Yet ye have not hearkened unto me, saith the Lord; that ye might provoke me to anger with the work of your hands to your own hurt.

8. Therefore thus saith the Lord of hosts: Because ye have not heard my words, 9. behold, I will send and take all the families of the north, saith the Lord, and I will send unto Nebuchadrezzar the king of Babylon, my servant, and will bring them against this land, and against the inhabitants thereof, and against all these nations round about; and I will utterly destroy them, and make them an astonishment, and an hissing, and perpetual desolations. 10. Moreover I will take from them the voice of mirth and the voice of gladness, the voice of the bridegroom and the voice of the bride, the sound of the millstones, and the light of the candle. 11. And this whole land shall be a desolation, and an astonishment; and these nations shall serve the king of Babylon seventy years. 12. And it shall come to pass, when seventy years are accomplished, that I will punish the king of Babylon, and that nation, saith the Lord, for their iniquity, and the land of the Chaldeans: and I will make it desolate for ever. 13. And I will bring upon that land all my words which I have pronounced against it, even all that is written in this book, which Jeremiah hath prophesied against all the nations. 14. For many nations and great kings shall serve themselves of them, even of them: and I will recompense them according to their deeds, and according to the work of their hands.

Words Put in the Roll of a Book

Jer. 36: 1. And it came to pass in the fourth year of Jehoiakim the son of Josiah, king of Judah, that this word came unto Jeremiah from the Lord, saying, Take thee a roll of a book, and write therein all the words that I have spoken unto thee against Israel, and against Judah, and against all the nations, from the day I spake unto thee, from the days of Josiah, even unto this day. 3. It may be that the house of Judah will hear all the evil which I purpose to do unto them; that they may return every man from his evil way; that I may forgive their iniquity and their sin. 4. Then Jeremiah called Baruch the son of Neriah; and Baruch wrote from the mouth of Jeremiah all the words of the Lord, which he had spoken unto him, upon a roll of a book.

Roll Read in the House of the Lord

5. And Jeremiah commanded Baruch, saying, I am shut up; I cannot go into the house of the Lord: 6. therefore go thou, and read in the roll, which thou hast written from my mouth, the words of the Lord in the ears of the people in the Lord's house upon the fast day: and also thou shalt read them in the ears of all Judah that come out of their cities. 7. It may be they will present their supplication before the Lord, and will return every one from his evil way: for great is the anger and the fury that the Lord hath pronounced against this people. 8. And Baruch the son of Neriah did according to all that Jeremiah the prophet commanded him, reading in the book the words of the Lord in the Lord's house. 9. Now it came to pass

in the fifth year of Jehoiakim the son of Josiah, king of Judah, in the ninth month, that all the people in Jerusalem, and all the people that came from the cities of Judah unto Jerusalem, proclaimed a fast before the Lord. 10. Then read Baruch in the book the words of Jeremiah in the house of the Lord, in the chamber of Gemariah the son of Shaphan the scribe, in the upper court, at the entry of the new gate of the Lord's house, in the ears of all the people. 11. And when Micaiah the son of Gemariah, the son of Shaphan, had heard out of the book all the words of the Lord, 12. he went down into the king's house, into the scribe's chamber: and lo, all the princes sat there, even Elishama the scribe, and Delaiah the son of Shemaiah, and Elnathan the son of Achbor, and Gemariah the son of Shaphan, and Zedekiah the son of Hananiah, and all the princes. 13. Then Micaiah declared unto them all the words that he had heard, when Baruch read the book in the ears of the people.

Roll Read to Princes by Baruch 14. Therefore all the princes sent Jehudi the son of Nethaniah, the son of Shelemiah, the son of Cushi, unto Baruch, saying, Take in thine hand the roll wherein thou hast read in the ears of the people, and come. So Baruch the son of Neriah took the roll in his hand, and came unto them. 15. And they said unto him, Sit down now, and read it in our ears. So Baruch read it in their ears. 16. Now it came to pass, when they had heard all the words, they turned in fear one toward another, and said unto Baruch, We will surely tell the king of all these words. 17. And they asked Baruch, saying, Tell us now, How didst thou write all these words at his mouth? 18. Then Baruch answered them, He pronounced all these words unto me with his mouth, and I wrote them with ink in the book. 19. Then said the princes unto Baruch, Go, hide thee, thou and Jeremiah; and let no man know where ye be. 20. And they went in to the king into the court; but they had laid up the roll in the chamber of Elishama the scribe; and they told all the words in the ears of the king.

Roll Read to and Burned by the King 21. So the king sent Jehudi to fetch the roll: and he took it out of the chamber of Elishama the scribe. And Jehudi read it in the ears of the king, and in the ears of all the princes which stood beside the king. 22. Now the king sat in the winter house in the ninth month: and there was a fire in the brasier burning before him. 23. And it came to pass, when Jehudi had read three or four leaves, that the king cut it with the penknife, and cast it into the fire that was in the brasier, until all the roll was consumed in the fire that was in the brasier. 24. And they were not afraid, nor rent their garments, neither the king, nor any of his servants that heard all these words. 25. Moreover Elnathan and Delaiah and Gemariah had made intercession to the king that he would not burn the roll: but he would not hear them. 26. And the king commanded Jerahmeel the king's son, and Seraiah the son of Azriel, and Shelemiah the son of Abdeel, to take Baruch the scribe and Jeremiah the prophet: but the Lord hid them.

Second Roll. Denunciation of the King 27. Then the word of the Lord came to Jeremiah, after that the king had burned the roll, and the words which Baruch wrote at the mouth of Jeremiah, saying, 28. Take thee again another roll, and write in it all the former words that were in the first roll, which Jehoiakim the king of Judah hath burned. 29. And concerning Jehoiakim king of Judah thou shalt say, Thus saith the Lord: Thou hast burned this roll, saying, Why hast thou written therein, saying,

The king of Babylon shall certainly come and destroy this land, and shall cause to cease from thence man and beast? 30. Therefore thus saith the Lord concerning Jehoiakim king of Judah: He shall have none to sit upon the throne of David: and his dead body shall be cast out in the day to the heat, and in the night to the frost. 31. And I will punish him and his seed and his servants for their iniquity: and I will bring upon them, and upon the inhabitants of Jerusalem, and upon the men of Judah, all the evil that I have pronounced against them, but they hearkened not. 32. Then took Jeremiah another roll, and gave it to Baruch the scribe, the son of Neriah; who wrote therein from the mouth of Jeremiah all the words of the book which Jehoiakim king of Judah had burned in the fire: and there were added besides unto them many like words.

II Kings 24:2. And the Lord sent against him bands of the Chaldeans, and bands of the Syrians, and bands of the Moabites, and bands of the children of Ammon, and sent them against Judah to destroy it, according to the word of the Lord, which he spake by the hand of his servants the prophets. 3. Surely at the commandment of the Lord came this upon Judah, to remove them out of his sight, for the sins of Manasseh, according to all that he did; 4. and also for the innocent blood that he shed; for he filled Jerusalem with innocent blood: and the

The First Captivity

In the third year of the reign of Jehoiakim king of Judah, Nebuchadnezzar king of Babylon came up against him unto Jerusalem, and besieged it, and Jehoiakim became his servant three years: then he turned and rebelled against him. And the Lord gave Jehoiakim king of Judah into his hand, with part of the vessels of the house of God, and Nebuchadnezzar bound him in fetters to carry him to Babylon. Nebuchadnezzar also carried of the vessels of the house of the Lord into the land of Shinar to the house of his god: and he brought them into the treasure house of his god, and put them in his temple at Babylon.

Daniel, Hananiah, Mishael, and Azariah

Daniel 1:3. And the king spake unto Ashpenaz the master of his eunuchs, that he should bring in certain of the children of Israel, even of the seed royal and the nobles, 4. youths in whom was no blemish, but well favoured, and skilful in all wisdom, and cunning in knowledge, and understanding science, and such as had ability to stand in the king's palace; and that he should teach them the learning and the tongue of the Chaldeans. 5. And the king appointed for them a daily portion of the king's meat, and of the wine which he drank, and that they should be nourished three years; that at the end thereof they might stand before the king. 6. Now among these were, of the children of Judah, Daniel, Hananiah, Mishael, and Azariah. 7. And the prince of the eunuchs gave names unto them: unto Daniel he gave the name of Belteshazzar; and to Hananiah, of Shadrach; and to Mishael, of Meshach; and to Azariah, of Abednego. 17. Now as for these four youths, God gave them knowledge and skill in all learning and wisdom: and Daniel had understanding in all visions and dreams. 18. And at the end of the days which the king had appointed for bringing them in, the prince of the eunuchs brought them in before Nebuchadnezzar. 19. And the King communed with them; and among them all was found none like Daniel, Hananiah, Mishael, and Azariah: therefore stood they before the king. 20. And in every matter of wisdom and understanding,

SECT. XXXII — THE SURVIVING SOUTHERN KINGDOM

| (II Kings 24:) 1. In his days Nebuchadnezzar king of Babylon came up, and Jehoiakim became his servant three years: then he turned and rebelled against him. | (II Chron. 36:) 6. Against him came up Nebuchadnezzar king of Babylon, and bound him in fetters to carry him to Babylon. 7. Nebuchadnezzar also carried of the vessels of the house of the Lord to Babylon, and put them in his temple at Babylon. | (Daniel 1:) 1. In the third year of the reign of Jehoiakim king of Judah came Nebuchadnezzar king of Babylon unto Jerusalem, and besieged it. 2. And the Lord gave Jehoiakim king of Judah into his hand, with part of the vessels of the house of God; and he carried them into the land of Shinar to the house of his god: and he brought the vessels into the treasure house of his god. |

concerning which the king inquired of them, he found them ten times better than all the magicians and enchanters that were in all his realm. 21. And Daniel continued even unto the first year of king Cyrus.

Now the rest of the acts of Jehoiakim, and all that he did, and his abominations which he did, and that which was found in him, behold, they are written in the book of the chronicles of the kings of Israel and Judah.

Accession and Character of Jehoiachin

Jehoiachin was *eighteen* [*1] years old when he began to reign; and he reigned three months and ten days in Jerusalem; and his mother's name was Nehusta the daughter of Elnathan of Jerusalem. And he did that which was evil in the sight of the Lord, according to all that his father had done.

As I live, saith the Lord, though Coniah † the son of Jehoiakim king of Judah were the signet upon my right hand, yet would I pluck thee from thence; and I will give thee into the hand of them that seek thy life, and into the hand of them of whom thou art afraid, even into the hand of Nebuchadrezzar king of Babylon, and into the hand of the Chaldeans.

And I will cast thee out, and thy mother that bare thee, into another country, where ye were not born; and there shall ye die. But to the land whereunto their soul longeth to return, thither shall they not return.

Is this man Coniah a despised broken vessel? is he a vessel wherein is no pleasure? wherefore are they cast out, he and his seed, and are cast into the land which they know not? O earth, earth, earth, hear the words of the Lord. Thus saith the Lord, Write this man childless, a man that shall not prosper in his days: for no man of his seed shall prosper, sitting upon the throne of David, and ruling any more in Judah.

At that time the servants of Nebuchadnezzar king of Babylon came up to Jerusalem, and the city was besieged. And Nebuchadnezzar came unto the city while his servants were besieging it; and Jehoiachin the king of Judah went out to the king of Babylon, he, and his mother, and his servants, and his princes, and his officers: and the king of Babylon took him in the eighth year of his reign. And he carried out thence all the treasures with the goodly vessels of the house of the Lord, and the treasures of the king's house, and cut in pieces of the vessels of gold which Solomon king of Israel made in the temple of the Lord, as the Lord had said. And he carried away all Jerusalem, and all the princes, and all the mighty men of valour, even ten thousand captives, and all the craftsmen and the smiths; none remained save the poorest sort of the people of the land.

The Second Captivity

And at the return of the year king Nebuchadnezzar sent, and carried away Jehoiachin to Babylon; and the king's mother, and the king's wives, and his officers, and the chief men of the land, carried he into captivity from Jerusalem to Babylon. And all the men of might, even seven thousand, and the craftsmen, and the smiths a thousand, all of them strong and apt for war, even them the king of Babylon brought captive to Babylon.

And the king of Babylon made *Mattaniah his father's brother* [*2] king in his stead, over Judah and Jerusalem, and changed his name to Zedekiah.

And it came to pass in the seven and thirtieth year of the captivity of Jehoiachin king of Judah, in the twelfth month, in the *five* [*3] and twentieth day of the month, that Evil-merodach king of Babylon, in the first year of his reign, lifted up the head of Jehoiachin king of Judah.

[*1] In Chronicles, "Eight."   [*2] In Chronicles, "his brother."   [*3] In Kings, Seven.

† In I Chron. 3:16 and in Jer. 24:1, Jeconiah. In Kings and Chronicles, Jehoiachin.

SECT. XXXII — THE SURVIVING SOUTHERN KINGDOM

(II Kings 24:) 5. Now the rest of the acts of Jehoiakim, and all that he did, are they not written in the book of the chronicles of the kings of Judah? 6. So Jehoiakim slept with his fathers: and Jehoiachin his son reigned in his stead.
8. Jehoiachin was ((eighteen)) years old when he began to reign; and he reigned in Jerusalem three months: and his mother's name was Nehusta the daughter of Elnathan of Jerusalem. 9. And he did that which was evil in the sight of the Lord, according to all that his father had done.

10. At that time the servants of Nebuchadnezzar king of Babylon came up to Jerusalem, and the city was besieged.
11. And Nebuchadnezzar king of Babylon came unto the city, while his servants were besieging it; 12. and Jehoiachin the king of Judah went out to the king of Babylon, he, and his mother, and his servants, and his princes, and his officers: and the king of Babylon took him in the eighth year of his reign. 13. And he carried out thence all the treasures of the house of the Lord, and the treasures of the king's house, and cut in pieces all the vessels of gold which Solomon king of Israel had made in the temple of the Lord, as the Lord had said. 14. And he carried away all Jerusalem, and all the princes, and all the mighty men of valour, even ten thousand captives, and all the craftsmen and the smiths; none remained save the poorest sort of the people of the land.

15. And he carried away Jehoiachin to Babylon; and the king's mother, and the king's wives, and his officers, and the chief men of the land, carried he into captivity from Jerusalem to Babylon.

16. And all the men of might, even seven thousand, and the craftsmen and the smiths a thousand, all of them strong and apt for war, even them the king of Babylon brought captive to Babylon.

17. And the king of Babylon ((made Mattaniah his father's brother king in his stead, and changed his name to Zedekiah.))
(II Kings 25:) 27. And it came to pass in the seven and thirtieth year of the captivity of Jehoiachin king of Judah, in the twelfth month, on the ((seven)) and twentieth day of the month, that Evil-Merodach king of Babylon, in the year that he began to reign, did lift up the head of Jehoiachin king of Judah.

(II Chron. 36:) 8. Now the rest of the acts of Jehoiakim, and his abominations which he did, and that which was found in him, behold, they are written in the book of the kings of Israel and Judah: and Jehoiachin his son reigned in his stead.
9. Jehoiachin was ((eight)) years old when he began to reign; and he reigned three months and ten days in Jerusalem. and he did that which was evil in the sight of the Lord.

(Jer. 22:) 24. As I live, saith the Lord, though Coniah the son of Jehoiakim king of Judah were the signet upon my right hand, yet would I pluck thee from thence; 25. and I will give thee into the hand of them that seek thy life, and into the hand of them of whom thou art afraid, even into the hand of Nebuchadrezzar king of Babylon, and into the hand of the Chaldeans.

26. And I will cast thee out, and thy mother that bare thee, into another country, where ye were not born; and there shall ye die. 27. But to the land whereunto their soul longeth to return, thither shall they not return.

28. Is this man Coniah a despised broken vessel? is he a vessel wherein is no pleasure? wherefore are they cast out, he and his seed, and are cast into the land which they know not? 29. O earth, earth, earth, hear the word of the Lord. 30. Thus saith the Lord, Write ye this man childless, a man that shall not prosper in his days: for no man of his seed shall prosper, sitting upon the throne of David, and ruling any more in Judah.

(II Chron. 10^b.) with the goodly vessels of the house of the Lord.

10^a. And at the return of the year king Nebuchadnezzar sent, and brought him to Babylon.

and ((made Zedekiah his brother king over Judah and Jerusalem.))
(Jeremiah 52:) 31. And it came to pass in the seven and thirtieth year of the captivity of Jehoiachin king of Judah, in the twelfth month, in the ((five)) and twentieth day of the month, that Evil-merodach king of Babylon, in the first year of his reign, lifted up the head of Jehoiachin king of Judah,

and brought him forth out of prison; and he spake kindly to him, and set his throne above the throne of the kings that were with him in Babylon. And he changed his prison garments, and did eat bread before him continually all the days of his life. And for his allowance, there was a continual allowance given him of the king of Babylon, every day a portion until the day of his death, all the days of his life.

Vision of Good and Bad Figs

Jer. 24: 1. The Lord shewed me, and, behold, two baskets of figs set before the temple of the Lord; after that Nebuchadrezzar king of Babylon had carried away captive Jeconiah the son of Jehoiakim, king of Judah, and the princes of Judah, with the craftsmen and smiths, from Jerusalem, and had brought them to Babylon. 2. One basket had very good figs, like the figs that are first ripe: and the other basket had very bad figs, which could not be eaten, they were so bad. 3. Then said the Lord unto me, What seest thou Jeremiah? And I said, Figs; the good figs, very good; and the bad, very bad, that cannot be eaten, they are so bad. 4. And the word of the Lord came unto me, saying, 5. Thus saith the Lord, the God of Israel; Like these good figs, so will I regard the captives of Judah, whom I have sent out of this place into the land of the Chaldeans, for good. 6. For I will set mine eyes upon them for good, and I will bring them again to this land: and I will build them, and not pull them down; and I will plant them and not pluck them up. 7. And I will give them an heart to know me, that I am the Lord: and they shall be my people, and I will be their God: for they shall return unto me with their whole heart. 8. And as the bad figs, which cannot be eaten, they are so bad; surely this saith the Lord, So will I give up Zedekiah the king of Judah, and his princes, and the residue of Jerusalem, that remain in this land, and them that dwell in the land of Egypt: 9. I will even give them up to be tossed to and fro among all the kingdoms of the earth for evil; to be a reproach and a proverb, a taunt and a curse, in all places whither I shall drive them. 10. And I will send the sword, the famine, and the pestilence, among them, till they be consumed from off the land that I gave unto them and to their fathers.

Reign of Zedekiah

Zedekiah was twenty and one years old when he began to reign; and he reigned eleven years in Jerusalem: and his mother's name was Hamutal the daughter of Jeremiah of Libnah. And he did that which was evil in the sight of the Lord his God, according to all that Jehoiakim had done. He humbled not himself before, neither did he, nor his servants, nor the people of the land hearken unto Jeremiah the prophet speaking from the mouth of the Lord.

Hananiah's False Predictions

Jer. 28: 1. And it came to pass the same year, in the beginning of the reign of Zedekiah king of Judah, in the fourth year, in the fifth month, that Hananiah the son of Azzur the prophet, which was of Gibeon, spake unto me in the house of the Lord, in the presence of the priests and of all the people, saying, 2. Thus speaketh the Lord of hosts, the God of Israel, saying, I have broken the yoke of the king of Babylon. 3. Within two full years will I bring again into this place all the vessels of the Lord's house, that Nebuchadnezzar king of Babylon took away from this place, and carried them to Babylon: 4. and I will bring again to this place Jeconiah the son of Jehoiakim, king of Judah, with all the captives of Judah, that went to Babylon, saith the Lord: for I will break the yoke of the king of Babylon.

out of prison; 28. and he spake kindly to him, and set his throne above the throne of the kings that were with him in Babylon. 29. And he changed his prison garments, and did eat bread before him continually all the days of his life. 30. And for his allowance, there was a continual allowance given him of the king, every day a portion, all the days of his life.	and brought him forth out of prison; 32. and he spake kindly to him, and set his throne above the throne of the kings that were with him in Babylon. 33. And he changed his prison garments, and did eat bread before him continually all the days of his life. 34. And for his allowance, there was a continual allowance given him of the king of Babylon, every day a portion until the day of his death, all the days of his life.	

| (II Kings 24:) 18. Zedekiah was twenty and one years old when he began to reign; and he reigned eleven years in Jerusalem: and his mother's name was Hamutal the daughter of Jeremiah of Libnah. 19. And he did that which was evil in the sight of the Lord, according to all that Jehoiakim had done. | (II Chron. 36:) 11. Zedekiah was twenty and one years old when he began to reign; and he reigned eleven years in Jerusalem: 12. and he did that which was evil in the sight of the Lord his God; he humbled not himself before Jeremiah the prophet speaking from the mouth of the Lord. | (Jeremiah 52:) 1. Zedekiah was one and twenty years old when he began to reign; and he reigned eleven years in Jerusalem: and his mother's name was Hamutal the daughter of Jeremiah of Libnah. 2. And he did that which was evil in the sight of the Lord, according to all that Jehoiakim had done. (Jer. 37:) 2. But neither he nor his servants, nor the people of the land, did hearken unto the words of the Lord, which he spake by the prophet Jeremiah. |

Jeremiah's True Prophecies

5. Then the prophet Jeremiah said unto the prophet Hananiah in the presence of the priests, and in the presence of all the people that stood in the house of the Lord, 6. even the prophet Jeremiah said, Amen: the Lord do so: the Lord perform thy words which thou hast prophesied, to bring again the vessels of the Lord's house, and all them of the captivity, from Babylon unto this place. 7. Nevertheless hear thou now this word that I speak in thine ears, and in the ears of all the people: 8. The prophets that have been before me and before thee of old prophesied against many countries, and against great kingdoms, of war, and of evil, and of pestilence. 9. The prophet which prophesieth of peace, when the word of the prophet shall come to pass, then shall the prophet be known, that the Lord hath truly sent him. 10. Then Hananiah the prophet took the bar from off the prophet Jeremiah's neck, and break it. 11. And Hananiah spake in the presence of all the people, saying, Thus saith the Lord: Even so will I break the yoke of Nebuchadnezzar king of Babylon within two full years from off the neck of all the nations. And the prophet Jeremiah went his way. 12. Then the word of the Lord came unto Jeremiah, after that Hananiah the prophet had broken the bar from off the neck of the prophet Jeremiah, saying, 13. Go and tell Hananiah, saying, Thus saith the Lord: Thou hast broken the bars of wood; but thou shalt make in their stead bars of iron. 14. For thus saith the Lord of hosts, the God of Israel: I have put a yoke of iron upon the neck of all these nations, that they may serve Nebudchadnezzar king of Babylon; and they shall serve him: and I have given him the beasts of the field also. 15. Then said the prophet Jeremiah unto Hananiah the prophet, Hear now, Hananiah; the Lord hath not sent thee; but thou makest this people to trust in a lie. 16. Therefore thus saith the Lord, Behold, I will send thee away from the face of the earth: this year thou shalt die, because thou hast spoken rebellion against the Lord. 17. So Hananiah the prophet died the same year in the seventh month.

The Prophet Consulted the First Time

Jer. 21: 1. The word which came unto Jeremiah from the Lord, when king Zedekiah sent unto him Pashur the son of Malchiah, and Zephaniah the son of Maaseiah the priest, saying, 2. Inquire, I pray thee, of the Lord for us; for Nebuchadrezzar king of Babylon maketh war against us: peradventure the Lord will deal with us according to all his wondrous works, that he may go up from us.

3. Then said Jeremiah unto them, Thus shall ye say to Zedekiah: 4. Thus saith the Lord, the God of Israel, Behold, I will turn back the weapons of war that are in your hands, wherewith ye fight against the king of Babylon, and against the Chaldeans which besiege you, without the walls, and I will gather them into the midst of this city. 5. And I myself will fight against you with an outstretched hand and with a strong arm, even in anger, and in fury, and in great wrath. 6. And I will smite the inhabitants of this city, both man and beast: they shall die of a great pestilence. 7. And afterward, saith the Lord, I will deliver Zedekiah king of Judah, and his servants, and the people, even such as are left in this city from the pestilence, from the sword, and from the famine, into the hand of Nebuchadrezzar king of Babylon, and into the hand of their enemies, and into the hand of those that seek their life: and he shall smite them with the edge of the sword; he shall not spare them, neither have pity, nor have mercy. 8. And unto this people thou shalt say, Thus saith the Lord: Behold, I set before you the way of life and the way of death. 9. He that abideth in this city shall die by the sword, and by the famine, and by the pestilence; but he that goeth out, and falleth away to the Chaldeans that besiege you, he shall live, and his life shall be unto him for a prey. 10. For I

have set my face upon this city for evil, and not for good, saith the Lord: it shall be given into the hand of the king of Babylon, and he shall burn it with fire.

The Prophet Consulted the Second Time

Jer. 37: 3. And Zedekiah the king sent Jehucal the son of Shelemiah, and Zephaniah the son of Maaseiah the priest, to the prophet Jeremiah, saying, Pray now unto the Lord our God for us. 4. Now Jeremiah came in and went out among the people: for they had not put him into prison. 5. And Pharaoh's army was come forth out of Egypt: and when the Chaldeans that besieged Jerusalem heard tidings of them, they brake up from Jerusalem. 6. Then came the word of the Lord unto the prophet Jeremiah, saying, 7. Thus saith the Lord, the God of Israel: Thus shall ye say to the king of Judah, that sent you unto me to inquire of me; Behold, Pharaoh's army, which is come forth to help you, shall return to Egypt into their own land. 8. And the Chaldeans shall come again, and fight against this city; and they shall take it, and burn it with fire.

9. Thus saith the Lord: Deceive not yourselves, saying, The Chaldeans shall surely depart from us: for they shall not depart. 10. For though ye had smitten the whole army of the Chaldeans that fight against you, and there remained but wounded men among them, yet should they rise up every man in his tent, and burn this city with fire.

Jeremiah Put in Prison

Jer. 38: 1. And Shephatiah the son of Mattan, and Gedaliah the son of Pashur, and Jucal the son of Shelemiah, and Pashur the son of Malchiah, heard the words that Jeremiah spake unto all the people, saying, 2. Thus saith the Lord, He that abideth in this city shall die by the sword, by the famine, and by the pestilence: but he that goeth forth to the Chaldeans shall live, and his life shall be unto him for a prey, and he shall live. 3. Thus saith the Lord, This city shall surely be given into the hand of the army of the king of Babylon, and he shall take it. 4. Then the princes said unto the king, Let this man, we pray thee, be put to death; forasmuch as he weakeneth the hands of the men of war that remain in this city, and the hands of all the people, in speaking such words unto them: for this man seeketh not the welfare of this people, but the hurt. 5. And Zedekiah the king said, Behold, he is in your hand: for the king is not he that can do anything against you. 6. Then took they Jeremiah, and cast him into the dungeon of Malchiah the king's son, that was in the court of the guard: and they let down Jeremiah with cords. And in the dungeon there was no water, but mire: and Jeremiah sank in the mire.

Jeremiah Released

7. Now when Ebed-melach the Ethiopian, an eunuch, which was in the king's house, heard that they had put Jeremiah in the dungeon; the king then sitting in the gate of Benjamin; 8. Ebed-melech went forth out of the king's house, and spake to the king, saying, 9. My lord the king, these men have done evil in all that they have done to Jeremiah the prophet, whom they have cast into the dungeon; and he is like to die in the place where he is because of the famine: for there is no more bread in the city. 10. Then the king commanded Ebed-melach the Ethiopian, saying, Take from hence thirty men with thee, and take up Jeremiah the prophet out of the dungeon, before he die. 11. So Ebed-melech took the men with him, and went into the house of the king under the treasury, and took thence old cast clouts and old rotten rags, and let them down by cords into the dungeon to Jeremiah. 12. And Ebed-melech the Ethiopian said unto Jeremiah, Put now these old cast clouts and rotten rags under thine

armholes under the cords. And Jeremiah did so. 13. So they drew up Jeremiah with the cords, and took him up out of the dungeon: and Jeremiah remained in the court of the guards.

The Prophet Consulted the Third Time 14. Then Zedekiah the king sent, and took Jeremiah the prophet unto him into the third entry that is in the house of the Lord: and the king said unto Jeremiah, I will ask thee a thing; hide nothing from me. 15. Then Jeremiah said unto Zedekiah, If I declare it unto thee, wilt thou not surely put me to death? and if I give thee counsel, thou wilt not hearken unto me. 16. So Zedekiah the king sware secretly unto Jeremiah, saying, As the Lord liveth, that made us this soul, I will not put thee to death, neither will I give thee into the hand of these men that seek thy life. 17. Then said Jeremiah unto Zedekiah, Thus saith the Lord, the God of hosts, the God of Israel: If thou wilt go forth unto the king of Babylon's princes, then thy soul shall live, and thine house: 18. but if thou wilt not go forth to the king of Babylon's princes, then shall this city be given into the hand of the Chaldeans, and they shall burn it with fire, and thou shalt not escape out of their hand.

Zedekiah's Rebellion For through the anger of the Lord did it come to pass in Jerusalem and Judah, until he had cast them out from his presence. And Zedekiah rebelled against Nebuchadnezzar the king of Babylon, who had made him swear by God:* but he stiffened his neck, and hardened his heart, from turning unto the Lord, the God of Israel.

Jerusalem Besieged And it came to pass, when Jerusalem was taken, in the ninth year of Zedekiah king of Judah, in the tenth month, in the tenth day of the tenth month, that Nebuchadnezzar king of Babylon came, he and all his army against Jerusalem, and encamped against it; and they built forts against it round about.

Jer. 34:1. The word which came unto Jeremiah from the Lord, when Nebuchadrezzar king of Babylon, and all his army, and all the kingdoms of the earth that were under his dominion, and all the peoples, fought against Jerusalem, and against all the cities thereof, saying: 2. Thus saith the Lord, the God of Israel, Go, and speak to Zedekiah king of Judah, and tell him, Thus saith the Lord, Behold, I will give this city into the hand of the king of Babylon, and he shall burn it with fire: 3. and thou shalt not escape out of his hand, but shall surely be taken, and delivered into his hand: and thine eyes shall behold the eyes of the king of Babylon, and he shall speak with thee mouth to mouth and thou shalt go to Babylon. Jer. 32:1. The word that came to Jeremiah in the tenth year of Zedekiah king of Judah, which was the eighteenth year of Nebuchadrezzar. 2. Now at that time the king of Babylon's army besieged Jerusalem: and Jeremiah the prophet was shut up in the court of the guard, which was in the king of Judah's house. 3. For Zedekiah king of Judah had shut him up, saying, Wherefore dost thou prophesy, and say, Thus saith the Lord, Behold, I will give this city into the hand of the king of Babylon, and he shall take it; 4. and Zedekiah king of Judah shall not escape out of the hand of the Chaldeans, but shall surely be delivered into the hand of the king of Babylon, and shall speak with him mouth to mouth, and his eyes shall behold his eyes; 5. and he shall lead Zedekiah to Babylon, and there shall he be until I visit him, saith the Lord: though ye fight with the Chaldeans, ye shall not prosper.

---
* Ezekiel 17:11-21. See God's condemnation of and punishment for his rebellion and breaking the Covenant.

Sect. XXXII — THE SURVIVING SOUTHERN KINGDOM

(II Kings 24:) 20. For through the anger of the Lord did it come to pass in Jerusalem and Judah, until he had cast them out from his presence: and Zedekiah rebelled against the king of Babylon.		(Jer. 52:) 3. For through the anger of the Lord did it come to pass in Jerusalem and Judah, until he had cast them out from his presence: and Zedekiah rebelled against the king of Babylon.
	(II Chron. 36:) 13. And he also rebelled against king Nebuchadnezzar, who had made him swear by God: but he stiffened his neck, and hardened his heart, from turning unto the Lord, the God of Israel.	
(II Kings 25:) 1. And it came to pass in the ninth year of his reign in the tenth month, in the tenth day of the month, that Nebuchadnezzar king of Babylon came, he and all his army, against Jerusalem, and encamped against it; and they built forts against it round about.	(Jer. 39:) 1. And it came to pass when Jerusalem was taken, in the ninth year of Zedekiah king of Judah, in the tenth month, in the tenth day of the month, came Nebuchadnezzar king of Babylon and all his army against Jerusalem, and besieged it;	4. And it came to pass in the ninth year of his reign in the tenth month, in the tenth day of the month that Nebuchadnezzar king of Babylon came, he and all his army, against Jerusalem, and encamped against it; and they built forts against it round about.

Death and Burial Foretold

Jer. 34: 4. Yet hear the word of the Lord, O Zedekiah king of Judah; thus saith the Lord concerning thee, Thou shalt not die by the sword; 5. thou shalt die in peace: and with the burnings of thy fathers, the former kings which were before thee, so shall they make a burning for thee; and they shall lament thee, saying, Ah lord! for I have spoken the word, saith the Lord. 6. Then Jeremiah the prophet spake all these words unto Zedekiah king of Judah in Jerusalem, 7. when the king of Babylon's army fought against Jerusalem, and against all the cities of Judah that were left, against Lachish and against Azekah; for these alone remained of the cities of Judah as fenced cities.

Jerusalem Captured

So the city was besieged unto the eleventh year of king Zedekiah. In the fourth month, in the ninth day of the month, the famine was sore in the city, so that there was no bread for the people of the land. Then a breach was made in the city; that all the princes of the king of Babylon came in, and sat in the middle gate, even Nergal-sharezer, Samgar-nebo, Sarsechim, Rab-saris, Nergal-sharezer, Rabmag, with all the rest of the princes of the king of Babylon.

Zedekiah's Punishment

And it came to pass that when Zedekiah the king of Judah, and all the men of war saw them, then they fled, and went forth out of the city by night, by the way of the gate between the two walls, which was by the king's garden; (now the Chaldeans were against the city round about;) and the king went by the way of the Arabah. But the army of the Chaldeans pursued after them, and overtook Zedekiah in the plains of Jericho; and all his army was scattered from him. Then they took the king, and carried him up to Nebuchadnezzar king of Babylon to Riblah in the land of Hamath, and he gave judgement upon him. Then the king of Babylon slew the sons of Zedekiah in Riblah before his eyes: he slew also all the princes of Judah. Moreover he put out the eyes of Zedekiah, and the king of Babylon bound him in fetters, and carried him to Babylon, and put him in prison till the day of his death.

Jerusalem's Houses Burnt

Now in the fifth month, on the *seventh*[*] day of the month, which was the nineteenth year of king Nebuchadnezzar king of Babylon, came Nebuzaradan the captain of the guard, a servant of the king of Babylon, unto Jerusalem: and *he* burned the house of the Lord, and the king's house, and all the houses of the people of Jerusalem, even every great house, burned he with fire. And all the army of the Chaldeans, that were with the captain of the guard, brake down all the walls of Jerusalem round about. Then Nebuzaradan the captain of

The Final Captivity

the guard carried away captive into Babylon of the poorest sort of the people, and the residue of the people that were left in the city, the deserters also, and those that fell away, that fell to the king of Babylon, and the residue of the multitude that remained.

---

[*] In Jeremiah 52: 12, the *tenth* day. See Appendix C. III, 1.

SECT. XXXII — THE SURVIVING SOUTHERN KINGDOM

(II Kings 25:)	(Jer. 39:)	(Jer. 52:)
2. So the city was besieged unto the eleventh year of king Zedekiah. 3. On the ninth day of the fourth month, the famine was sore in the city, so that there was no bread for the people of the land. 4. Then a breach was made in the city,	2. In the eleventh year of Zedekiah, in the fourth month, the ninth day of the month,	5. So the city was besieged unto the eleventh year of king Zedekiah. 6. In the fourth month, in the ninth day of the month, the famine was sore in the city, so that there was no bread for the people of the land. 7. Then a breach was made in the city,
	3. a breach was made in the city; that all the princes of the king of Babylon came in, and sat in the middle gate, even Nergal-sharezer, Samgar-nebo, Sarsechim, Rab-saris, Nergal-sharezer, Rab-mag, with all the rest of the princes of the king of Babylon.	
	4. And it came to pass that when Zedekiah the king of Judah, and all the men of war saw them, then they fled, and went forth out of the city by night, by the way of the king's garden, by the gate betwixt the two walls:	
and all the men of war fled by night, by the way of the gate between the two walls, which was by the king's garden: now the Chaldeans were against the city round about: and the king went by the way of the Arabah.	and he went out the way of the Arabah.	and all the men of war fled and went forth out of the city by night, by the way of the gate between the two walls which was by the king's garden; now the Chaldeans were against the city round about: and they went by the way of the Arabah.
5. But the army of the Chaldeans pursued after the king, and overtook him in the plains of Jericho; and all his army was scattered from him. 6. Then they took the king, and carried him up unto the king of Babylon to Riblah; and they gave judgement upon him. 7. And they slew the sons of Zedekiah before his eyes,	5. But the army of the Chaldeans pursued after them, and overtook Zedekiah in the plains of Jericho: and when they had taken him, they brought him up to Nebuchadnezzar king of Babylon to Riblah in the land of Hamath, and he gave judgement upon him. 6. Then the king of Babylon slew the sons of Zedekiah in Riblah before his eyes: also the king of Babylon slew all the nobles of Judah.	8. But the army of the Chaldeans pursued after the king, and overtook Zedekiah in the plains of Jericho; and all his army was scattered from him. 9. Then they took the king, and carried him up unto the king of Babylon to Riblah in the land of Hamath, and he gave judgement upon him. 10. And the king of Babylon slew the sons of Zedekiah before his eyes: he slew also all the princes of Judah in Riblah.
and put out the eyes of Zedekiah, and bound him in fetters, and carried him to Babylon.	7. Moreover he put out Zedekiah's eyes, and bound him in fetters to carry him to Babylon.	11. And he put out the eyes of Zedekiah, and the king of Babylon bound him in fetters, and carried him to Babylon, and put him in prison till the day of his death.
8. Now in the fifth month, on the *seventh* day of the month, which was the nineteenth year of king Nebuchadnezzar king of Babylon, came Nebuzaradan the captain of the guard, a servant of the king of Babylon, unto Jerusalem: 9. and he burnt the house of the Lord, and the king's house; and all the houses of Jerusalem, even every great house, burnt he with fire. 10. And all the army of the Chaldeans, that were with the captain of the guard, brake down the walls of Jerusalem round about.	8. And the Chaldeans burned the king's house, and the houses of the people with fire, and brake down the walls of Jerusalem.	12. Now in the fifth month, in the *tenth* day of the month, which was the nineteenth year of king Nebuchadrezzar king of Babylon, came Nebuzaradan the captain of the guard, a servant of the king of Babylon, into Jerusalem 13. and he burned the house of the Lord, and the king's house, and all the houses of Jerusalem, even every great house, burned he with fire. 14. And all the army of the Chaldeans that were with the captain of the guard, brake down the walls of Jerusalem round about.
11. (And the residue of the people that were left in the city, and those that fell away, that fell to the king of Babylon, and the residue of the multitude, did Nebuzaradan the captain of the guard carry away captive.)	9. (Then Nebuzaradan the captain of the guard carried away captive into Babylon the residue of the people that remained in the city, the deserters also, that fell away to him, and the residue of the people that remained.)	15. (Then Nebuzaradan the captain of the guard carried away captive of the poorest sort of the people, and the residue of the people that were left in the city, and those that fell away, that fell to the king of Babylon, and the residue of the multitude.)

But Nebuzaradan the captain of the guard left of the poorest of the people of the land, which had nothing, in the land of Judah, and gave them vineyards and fields at the same time to be vinedressers and husbandmen.

The Temple Despoiled
And the pillars of brass that were in the house of the Lord, and the bases, and the brasen sea that were in the house of the Lord, did the Chaldeans break in pieces, and carried all the brass of them to Babylon. The pots also, and the shovels, and the snuffers, and the basons, and the spoons, and all the vessels of brass wherewith they ministered, took they away. And the cups, and the firepans, and the basons, and the pots, and the candlesticks, and the spoons, and the bowls; that which was of gold, in gold, and that which was of silver, in silver, the captain of the guard took away.

The two pillars, the one sea, and the twelve brasen bulls that were under the bases, which king Solomon had made for the house of the Lord; the brass of all these vessels was without weight. And as for the pillars, the height of the one pillar was eighteen cubits; and a line of twelve cubits did compass it; and the thickness thereof was four fingers: it was hollow. And a chapiter of brass was upon it; and the height of the one chapiter was *three* [*1] cubits; with network and pomegranates upon the chapiter round about, all of brass: and like unto these had the second pillar with network and pomegranates. And there were ninety and six pomegranates on the sides; all the pomegranates were an hundred upon the network round about.

Treatment and Number Captives
And the captain of the guard took Seraiah the chief priest, and Zephaniah the second priest, and the three keepers of the door; and out of the city he took an officer that was set over the men of war; and *five* [*2] men of them that saw the king's face, which were found in the city; and the scribe of the captain of the host, who mustered the people of the land, and threescore men of the people of the land, that were found in the city. And Nebuzaradan the captain of the guard took them, and brought them to the king of Babylon to Riblah. And the king of Babylon smote them, and put them to death at Riblah in the land of Hamath. So Judah was carried away captive out of his land. This is the people whom Nebuchadrezzar carried away captive: in the seventh year three thousand Jews and three and twenty: in the eighteenth year of Nebuchadrezzar he carried away captive from Jerusalem eight hundred thirty and two persons: in the three and twentieth year of Nebuchadrezzar, Nebuzaradan the captain of the guard carried away captive of the Jews seven hundred and forty-five persons: all the persons were four thousand and six hundred.

The Final Indictment and Sentence
II Chron. 36: 14. Moreover all the chiefs of the priests, and the people, trespassed very greatly after all the abominations of the heathen; and they polluted the house of the Lord which he had hallowed in Jerusalem. 15. And the Lord, the God of their fathers, sent to them by his messengers, rising up early and sending; because he had compassion on his people, and on his dwelling place: 16. but they mocked the messengers of God, and despised his words, and scoffed at his prophets, until the wrath of the Lord arose against his people, till there was no remedy. 17. Therefore he brought upon them the king of the Chaldeans, who slew their young men with the sword in the house of their sanctuary, and had no compassion upon young man or maiden, old man or ancient: he gave them all into his hand. 18. And all the vessels of the house of God, great and small, and the treasures of the house of the Lord, and

---

[*1] In Jeremiah, five.   [*2] In Jeremiah, seven.

SECT. XXXII — THE SURVIVING SOUTHERN KINGDOM

12. But the captain of the guard left of the poorest of the land to be vinedressers and husbandmen.	10. But Nebuzaradan the captain of the guard left of the poor of the people, which had nothing, in the land of Judah, and gave them vineyards and fields at the same time.	16. But Nebuzaradan the captain of the guard left of the poorest of the land to be vinedressers and husbandmen.
13. And the pillars of brass that were in the house of the Lord, and the bases and the brasen sea that were in the house of the Lord, did the Chaldeans break in pieces, and carried the brass of them to Babylon. 14. And the pots, and the shovels, and the snuffers, and the spoons, and all the vessels of brass wherewith they ministered, took they away. 15. And the firepans, and the basons; that which was of gold, in gold, and that which was of silver, in silver, the captain of the guard took away.		17. And the pillars of brass that were in the house of the Lord, and the bases and the brasen sea that were in the house of the Lord, did the Chaldeans break in pieces, and carried all the brass of them to Babylon. 18. The pots also, and the shovels, and the snuffers, and the basons, and the spoons, and all the vessels of brass wherewith they ministered, took they away. 19. And the cups, and the firepans, and the basons, and the pots, and the candlesticks, and the spoons, and the bowls; that which was of gold, in gold, and that which was of silver, in silver, the captain of the guard took away.
16. The two pillars, the one sea, and the bases, which Solomon had made for the house of the Lord; the brass of all these vessels was without weight. 17. The height of the one pillar was eighteen cubits, and a chapiter of brass was upon it: and the height of the chapiter was ((three)) cubits; with network and pomegranates upon the chapiter round about, all of brass: and like unto these had the second pillar with network.		20. The two pillars, the one sea, and the twelve brasen bulls that were under the bases, which king Solomon had made for the house of the Lord; the brass of all these vessels was without weight. 21. And as for the pillars, the height of the one pillar was eighteen cubits; and a line of twelve cubits did compass it; and the thickness thereof was four fingers: it was hollow. 22. And a chapiter of brass was upon it; and the height of the one chapiter was ((five)) cubits, with network and pomegranates upon the chapiter round about, all of brass: and the second pillar also had like unto these and pomegranates. 23. And there were ninety and six pomegranates on the sides; all the pomegranates were an hundred upon the network round about.
18. And the captain of the guard took Seraiah the chief priest, and Zephaniah the second priest, and the three keepers of the door: 19. and out of the city he took an officer that was set over the men of war; and ((five)) men of them that saw the king's face, which were found in the city; and the scribe, the captain of the host, which mustered the people of the land; and threescore men of the people of the land, that were found in the city.		24. And the captain of the guard took Seraiah the chief priest, and Zephaniah the second priest, and the three keepers of the door: 25. and out of the city he took an officer that was set over the men of war; and ((seven)) men of them that saw the king's face, which were found in the city; and the scribe of the captain of the host, who mustered the people of the land, and threescore men of the people of the land that were found in the midst of the city.
20. And Nebuzaradan the captain of the guard took them, and brought them to the king of Babylon to Riblah. 21. And the king of Babylon smote them, and put them to death at Riblah in the land of Hamath. So Judah was carried away captive out of his land.		26. And Nebuzaradan the captain of the guard took them, and brought them to the king of Babylon to Riblah. 27. And the king of Babylon smote them, and put them to death at Riblah in the land of Hamath. So Judah was carried away captive out of his land. 28. This is the people whom Nebuchadrezzar carried away captive: in the seventh year three thousand Jews and three and twenty: in the eighteenth year of Nebuchadrezzar he carried away captive from Jerusalem eight hundred thirty and two persons: 30. in the three and twentieth year of Nebuchadrezzar Nebuzaradan the captain of the guard carried away captive of the Jews seven hundred forty and five persons: all the persons were four thousand and six hundred.

the treasures of the king and of his princes; all these he brought to Babylon. 19. And they burnt the house of God, and brake down the wall of Jerusalem, and burnt all the palaces thereof with fire, and destroyed all the goodly vessels thereof. 20. And them that had escaped from the sword carried he away to Babylon; and they were the servants to him and his sons until the reign of the kingdom of Persia: 21. to fulfill the word of the Lord by the mouth of Jeremiah, until the land had enjoyed her sabbaths: for as long as she lay desolate she kept sabbath, to fulfil threescore and ten years.

Gedaliah the Governor and Jeremiah And as for the people that were left in the land of Judah, whom Nebuchadnezzar king of Babylon had left, even over them he made Gedaliah the son of Ahikam, the son of Shaphan, governor. And the captain of the guard took Jeremiah and said unto him, The Lord thy God pronounced this evil upon this place; and the Lord hath brought it, and done according as he spake; because ye have sinned against the Lord, and have not obeyed his voice, therefore this thing has come upon you. And now, behold, I loose thee this day from the chains which are upon thine hand. If it seem good unto thee to come with me into Babylon, come, and I will look well unto thee, but if it seem ill unto thee to come with me into Babylon, forbear; behold, all the land is before thee; whither it seemeth good and convenient unto thee to go, thither go. Now while he was not yet gone back, Go back then, said he, to Gedaliah the son of Ahikam, the son of Shaphan, whom the king of Babylon hath made governor over the cities of Judah, and dwell with him among the people: or go wheresoever it seemeth convenient unto thee to go. So the captain of the guard gave him victuals and a present, and let him go. Then went Jeremiah unto Gedaliah the son of Ahikam to Mizpah, and dwelt with him among the people that were left in the land. Now when all the captains of the forces which were in the fields, even they and their men, heard that the king of Babylon had made Gedaliah the son of Ahikam governor in the land, and committed unto him men, and women, and children, and of the poorest of the land, of them that were not carried away captive to Babylon; then they came to Gedaliah to Mizpah, even Ishmael the son of Nethaniah, and Johanan and Jonathan the sons of Kareah, and Seraiah the son of Tanhumeth, and the sons of Ephai the Neophathite, and Jazaniah the son of the Maacathite, they and their men. And Gedaliah the son of Ahikam, the son of Shaphan sware unto them and unto their men, saying, Fear not because of the servants of the Chaldeans: dwell in the land, and serve the king of Babylon, and it shall be well with you. Jer. 40: 10. As for me, behold, I will dwell at Mizpah, to stand before the Chaldeans, which shall come unto us: but ye, gather ye wine and summer fruits and oil, and put them in your vessels, and dwell in your cities that ye have taken. 11. Likewise when all the Jews that were in Moab, and among the children of Ammon, and in Edom, and that were in all the countries, heard that the king of Babylon had left a remnant of Judah, and that he had set over them Gedaliah the son of Ahikam, the son of Shaphan; 12. then all the Jews returned out of all places whither they were driven, and came to the land of Judah, to Gedaliah, unto Mizpah, and gathered wine and summer fruits very much.

13. Moreover Johanan the son of Kareah, and all the captains of the forces that were in the fields, came to Gedaliah to Mizpah, and said unto him, 14. Dost thou know that Baalis the king of the children of Ammon hath sent Ishmael the son of Nethaniah to take thy life?

SECT. XXXII THE SURVIVING SOUTHERN KINGDOM

(I Kings 25:) 22. And as for the people that were left in the land of Judah, whom Nebuchadnezzar king of Babylon had left, even over them he made Gedaliah the son of Ahikam, the son of Shaphan, governor.

(Jer. 40:) 2. And the captain of the guard took Jeremiah and said unto him, The Lord thy God pronounced this evil upon this place: 3. and the Lord hath brought it, and done according as he spake; because ye have sinned against the Lord, and have not obeyed his voice, therefore this thing has come upon you.

4. And now, behold, I loose thee this day from the chains which are upon thine hand. If it seems good unto thee to come with me into Babylon, come, and I will look well unto thee; but if it seem ill unto thee to come with me into Babylon, forbear: behold, all the land is before thee; whither it seemeth good and convenient unto thee to go, thither go. 5. Now while he was not yet gone back, Go back then, said he, to Gedaliah the son of Ahikam, the son of Shaphan, whom the king of Babylon hath made governor over the cities of Judah, and dwell with him among the people: or go wheresoever it seemeth convenient unto thee to go. So the captain of the guard gave him victuals and a present, and let him go. 6. Then went Jeremiah unto Gedaliah the son of Ahikam to Mizpah, and dwelt with him among the people that were left in the land.

23. Now when all the captains of the forces, they and their men, heard that the king of Babylon had made Gedaliah governor, they came to Gedaliah to Mizpah, even Ishmael the son of Nethaniah, and Johanan the son of Kareah, and Seraiah the son of Tanhumeth the Netophathite, and Jaazaniah the son of the Maacathite, they and their men.

7. Now when all the captains of the forces which were in the fields, even they and their men, heard that the king of Babylon had made Gedaliah the son of Ahikam governor in the land, and had committed unto him men, and women, and children, and of the poorest of the land, of them that were not carried away captive to Babylon; 8. then they came to Gedaliah to Mizpah, even Ishmael the son of Nathaniah, and Johanan and Jonathan the sons of Kareah, and Seraiah the son of Tanhumeth, and the sons of Ephai, the Netophathite, son of Tanhumeth, and the sons of Ephai, the Netophathite, and Jazaniah the son of the Maacathite, they and their men.

24. And Gedaliah sware to them and to their men, and said unto them, Fear not because of the servants of the Chaldeans: dwell in the land, and serve the king of Babylon, and it shall be well with you

9. And Gedaliah the son of Ahikam the son of Shaphan sware unto them and to their men, saying, Fear not to serve the Chaldeans: dwell in the land, and serve the king of Babylon,

But Gedaliah the son of Ahikam believed them not. 15. Then Johanan the son of Kareah spake to Gedaliah in Mizpah secretly, saying, Let me go, I pray thee, and I will slay Ishmael the son of Nethaniah, and no man shall know it: wherefore should he take thy life, that all the Jews which are gathered unto thee should be scattered, and the remnant of Judah perish? 16. But Gedaliah the son of Ahikam said unto Johanan the son of Kareah, Thou shalt not do this thing: for thou speakest falsely of Ishmael.

Gedaliah Murdered

Now it came to pass in the seventh month, that Ishmael the son of Nethaniah, the son of Elishama, of the seed royal, and one of the chief officers of the king, and ten men with him, came unto Gedaliah the son of Ahikam to Mizpah; and there they did eat together in Mizpah. Then arose Ishmael the son of Nethaniah, and the ten men that were with him, and smote Gedaliah the son of Ahikam the son of Shaphan with the sword, and slew him, whom the king of Babylon had made governor over the land. Ishmael also slew all the Jews that were with him, even with Gedaliah, at Mizpah, and the Chaldeans that were found there, even the men of war. Jer. 41:4. And it came to pass the second day after he had slain Gedaliah, and no man knew it, 5. that there came certain from Shechem, from Shiloh, and from Samaria, even fourscore men, having their beards shaven and their clothes rent, and having cut themselves, with *oblations and frankincense in their hand, to bring them to the house of the Lord. 6. And Ishmael the son of Nethaniah went forth from Mizpah to meet them, weeping all along as he went: and it came to pass, as he met them, he said unto them, Come to Gedaliah the son of Ahikam. 7. And it was so, when they came into the midst of the city, that Ishmael the son of Nethaniah slew them, *and cast them* into the midst of the pit, he, and the men that were with him. 8. But ten men were found among them that said unto Ishmael, Slay us not: for we have stores hidden in the field, of wheat, and of barley, and of oil, and of honey. So he forbare, and slew them not among their brethren. 9. Now the pit wherein Ishmael cast all the dead bodies of the men whom he had slain, by the side of Gedaliah, (the same was that which Asa the king had made for fear of Baasha king of Israel,) Ishmael the son of Nethaniah filled it with them that were slain.

10. Then Ishmael carried away captive all the residue of the people that were in Mizpah, even the king's daughters, and all the people that remained in Mizpah, whom Nebuzaradan the captain of the guard had committed to Gedaliah the son of Ahikam: Ishmael the son of Nethaniah carried them away captive, and departed to go over to the children of Ammon.

Johanan Rescues Captives

11. But when Johanan the son of Kareah, and all the captains of the forces that were with him, heard of all the evil that Ishmael the son of Nethaniah had done, 12. then they took all the men, and went to fight with Ishmael the son of Nethaniah, and found him by the great waters that are in Gibeon. 13. Now it came to pass that when all the people which were with Ishmael saw Johanan the son of Kareah, and all the captains of the forces that were with him, then they were glad. 14. So all the people that Ishmael had carried away captive from Mizpah cast about and returned, and went unto Johanan the son of Kareah. 15. But Ishmael the son of Nethaniah escaped from Johanan with eight men, and went to the children of Ammon. 16. Then took Johanan the son of Kareah, and all the captains of the forces that were with him, all the remnant of the people whom he had recovered from Ishmael the son of Nethaniah, from Mizpah, after that he had slain Gedaliah the son of Ahikam, even the men of war, and the

SECT. XXXII THE SURVIVING SOUTHERN KINGDOM

(II Kings 25:) 25. But it came to pass in the seventh month, that Ishmael the son of Nethaniah, the son of Elishama, of the seed royal, came, and ten men with him,

and smote Gedaliah, that he died,

and the Jews that were with him at Mizpah, and the Chaldeans,

(Jer. 41:) 1. Now it came to pass in the seventh month that Ishmael the son of Nethaniah, the son of Elishama, of the seed royal, and one of the chief officers of the king, and ten men with him, came unto Gedaliah the son of Ahikam to Mizpah; and there they did eat bread together in Mizpah. 2. Then arose Ishmael the son of Nethaniah, and the ten men that were with him, and smote Gedaliah the son of Ahikam the son of Shaphan with the sword, and slew him, whom the king of Babylon had made governor over the land. 3. Ishmael also slew all the Jews that were with him, even with Gedaliah, at Mizpah, and the Chaldeans that were found there, even the men of war, women, and the children, and the eunuchs, whom he had brought again from Gibeon: And all the people, both small and great, arose, departed, and dwelt in Geruth Chimham, which is by Beth-lehem, to go into Egypt, for they were afraid of the Chaldeans; because Ishmael the son of Nethaniah had slain Gedaliah the son of Ahikam, whom the king of Babylon made governor over the land.

Inquiry and Answer

Jer. 42: 1. Then all the captains of the forces, and Johanan the son of Kareah, and Jezaniah the son of Hoshaiah, and all the people from the least even unto the greatest, came near, 2. and said unto Jeremiah the prophet, Let, we pray thee, our supplication be accepted before thee, and pray for us unto the Lord thy God, even for all this remnant; for we are left but a few of many, as thine eyes do behold us: 3. that the Lord thy God may shew us the way wherein we should walk, and the thing that we should do. 4. Then Jeremiah the prophet said unto them, I have heard you; behold, I will pray unto the Lord your God according to your words; and it shall come to pass that whatsoever thing the Lord shall answer you, I will declare it unto you; I will keep nothing back from you. 5. Then they said to Jeremiah, The Lord be a true and faithful witness amongst us, if we do not even according to all the word wherewith the Lord thy God shall send thee to us. 6. Whether it be good, or whether it be evil, we will obey the voice of the Lord our God, to whom we send thee; that it may be well with us, when we obey the voice of the Lord our God.

7. And it came to pass after ten days, that the word of the Lord came unto Jeremiah. 8. Then called he Johanan the son of Kareah, and all the captains of the forces which were with him, and all the people from the least even to the greatest, 9. and said unto them, Thus saith the Lord, the God of Israel, unto whom ye sent me to present your supplication before him: 10. If ye will still abide in this land, then will I build you, and not pull you down, and I will plant you, and not pluck you up: for I repent me of the evil that I have done unto you. 11. Be not afraid of the king of Babylon, of whom ye are afraid; be not afraid of him, saith the Lord: for I am with you to save you, and to deliver you from his hand. 12. And I will grant you mercy, that he may have mercy upon you, and cause you to return to your own land. 13. But if ye say, We will not dwell in this land; so that ye obey not the voice of the Lord your God; 14. saying, No; but we will go into the land of Egypt, where we shall see no war, nor hear the sound of the trumpet, nor have hunger of bread; and there will we dwell: 15. now therefore hear ye the word of the Lord, O remnant of Judah: thus saith the Lord of hosts, the God of Israel, If ye wholly set your faces to enter into Egypt, and go to sojourn there; 16. then it shall come to pass, that the sword, which ye fear, shall overtake you there in the land of Egypt, and the famine, whereof ye are afraid, shall follow hard after you there in Egypt; and there ye shall die. 17. So shall it be with all the men that set their faces to go into Egypt to sojourn there; they shall die by the sword, by the famine, and by the pestilence: and none of them shall remain or escape from the evil that I will bring upon them. 18. For thus saith the Lord of hosts, the God of Israel; As mine anger and my fury hath been poured forth upon the inhabitants of Jerusalem, so shall my fury be poured forth upon you, when ye shall enter into Egypt: and ye shall be an execration, and an astonishment, and a curse, and a reproach; and ye shall see this place no more. 19. The Lord hath spoken concerning you, O remnant of Judah, Go ye not into Egypt: know certainly that I have testified unto you this day. 20. For ye have dealt deceitfully against your own souls; for ye sent me unto the Lord your God, saying, Pray for us unto the Lord our God; and according unto all that the Lord our God shall say, so declare unto us, and we will do it: 21. and I have this day declared it

Sect. XXXII — THE SURVIVING SOUTHERN KINGDOM

| (II Kings 25:) 26. And all the people, both small and great, and the captains of the forces, arose, and came to Egypt, for they were afraid of the Chaldeans. | (Jer. 41:) 17. And they departed, and dwelt in Geruth Chimham, which is by Beth-lehem, to go into Egypt, 18. because of the Chaldeans; for they were afraid of them, because Ishmael the son of Nethaniah had slain Gedaliah the son of Ahikam, whom the king of Babylon made governor over the land. |

to you; but ye have not obeyed the voice of the Lord your God in anything for the which he hath sent me unto you. 22. Now therefore know certainly that ye shall die by the sword, by the famine, and by the pestilence, in the place whither ye desire to go to sojourn there.

Disobedience and Destruction

Jer. 43: 1. And it came to pass that when Jeremiah had made an end of speaking unto all the people all the words of the Lord their God, wherewith the Lord their God hath sent him to them, even all these words, 2. then spake Azariah the son of Hoshaiah, and Johanan the son of Kareah, and all the proud men, saying unto Jeremiah, Thou speakest falsely: the Lord our God hath not sent thee to say, Ye shall not go into Egypt to sojourn there: 3. but Baruch the son of Neriah setteth thee on against us, for to deliver us into the hand of the Chaldeans, that they may put us to death, and carry us away captives to Babylon. 4. So Johanan the son of Kareah, and all the captains of the forces, and all the people, obeyed not the voice of the Lord, to dwell in the land of Judah. 5. But Johanan the son of Kareah, and all the captains of the forces, took all the remnant of Judah, that were returned from all the nations whither they had been driven to sojourn in the land of Judah; 6. the men, and the women, and the children, and the king's daughters, and every person that Nebuzaradan the captain of the guard had left with Gedaliah the son of Ahikam, the son of Shaphan, and Jeremiah the prophet, and Baruch the son of Neriah; 7. and they came into the land of Egypt; for they obeyed not the voice of the Lord: and they came even to Tahpanhes. 8. Then came the word of the Lord unto Jeremiah in Tahpanhes, saying, 9. Take great stones in thine hand, and hide them in mortar in the brickwork, which is at the entry of Pharaoh's house in Tahpanhes, in the sight of the men of Judah; 10. and say unto them, Thus saith the Lord of hosts, the God of Israel: Behold, I will send and take Nebuchadrezzar the king of Babylon, my servant, and will set his throne upon these stones that I have hid; and he shall spread his royal pavilion over them. 11. And he shall come, and shall smite the land of Egypt; such as are for death *shall be given* to death, and such as are for captivity to captivity, and such as are for the sword to the sword. 12. And I will kindle a fire in the houses of the gods of Egypt; and he shall burn them, and carry them away captives: and he shall array himself with the land of Egypt, as a shepherd putteth on his garment; and he shall go forth from thence in peace. 13. He shall also break the pillars of Bethshemesh, that is in the land of Egypt; and the houses of the gods of Egypt shall he burn with fire.

Idolatry Denounced

Jer. 44: 1. The word that came to Jeremiah concerning all the Jews which dwelt in the land of Egypt, which dwelt at Migdol, and at Tahpanhes, and at Noph, and in the country of Pathros, saying, 2. Thus saith the Lord of hosts, the God of Israel: Ye have seen all the evil that I have brought upon Jerusalem, and upon all the cities of Judah; and, behold, this day they are a desolation, and no man dwelleth therein; 3. because of their wickedness which they have committed to provoke me to anger, in that they went to burn incense, *and* to serve other gods, whom they knew not, neither they, nor ye, nor your fathers. 4. Howbeit I sent unto you all my servants the prophets, rising up early and sending them, saying, Oh, do not this abominable thing that I hate. 5. But they hearkened not, nor inclined their ear to turn from their wickedness, to burn no incense unto other gods. 6. Wherefore my fury and mine anger was poured forth, and was kindled in the cities of Judah and in the streets of Jerusalem; and they are wasted and desolate, as it is this day. 7. Therefore now thus saith the Lord, the God of hosts, the God of Israel: Wherefore commit ye *this* great evil against your own souls, to cut off from you man and woman, infant and suckling, out of the midst of Judah, to leave you none remaining; 8. in that ye provoke me unto anger with the works of your hands, burning incense unto other gods in the land of Egypt, whither ye be gone to sojourn; that ye may be cut off, and that ye may be a curse and a reproach among all the nations of the earth? 9. Have ye forgotten the wickedness of your fathers, and the wickedness of the kings of Judah, and the wickedness of their wives, and your own wickedness, and the wickedness of your wives, which they committed in the land of Judah, and in the streets of Jerusalem? 10. They are not humbled even unto this day, neither have they feared, nor walked in my law, nor in my statutes, that I set before you and before your fathers. 11. Therefore thus saith the Lord of hosts, the God of Israel: Behold, I will set my face against you for evil, even to cut off all Judah. 12. And I will take the remnant of Judah, that have set their faces to go into the land of Egypt to sojourn there, and they shall all be consumed; in the land of Egypt shall they fall; they shall be consumed by the sword and by the famine; they shall die, from the least even unto the greatest, by the sword and by the famine; and they shall be an execration, *and* an astonishment, and a curse, and a reproach. 13. For I will punish them that dwell in the land of Egypt, as I have punished Jerusalem, by the sword, by the famine, and by the pestilence: 14. so that none of the remnant of Judah, which are gone into the land of Egypt to sojourn there, shall escape or remain, that they should return into the land of Judah, to the which they have a desire to return to dwell there: for none shall return save such as shall escape.

15. Then all the men which knew that their wives burned incense unto other gods, and all the women that stood by, a great assembly, even all the people that dwelt in the land of Egypt, in Pathros, answered Jeremiah, saying, 16. As for the word that thou hast spoken unto us in the name of the Lord, we will not hearken unto thee. 17. But we will certainly perform every word that is gone forth out of our mouth, to burn incense unto the queen of heaven, and to pour out drink offerings unto her, as we have done, we and our fathers, our kings and our princes, in the cities of Judah, and in the streets of Jerusalem: for then had we plenty of victuals, and were well, and saw no evil. 18. But since we left off to burn incense to the queen of heaven, and to pour out drink offerings unto her, we have wanted all things, and have been consumed by the sword and by the famine. 19. And when we burned incense to the queen of heaven, and poured out drink offerings unto her, did we make her cakes to worship her, and pour out drink offerings unto her, without our husbands?

Retributive Punishment

20. Then Jeremiah said unto all the people, to the men, and to the women; even to all the people which had given him that answer, saying, 21. The incense that ye burned in the cities of Judah, and in the streets of Jerusalem, ye and your fathers, your kings and your princes, and the people of the land, did not the Lord remember them, and came it not into his mind? 22. so that the Lord could no longer bear, because of the evil of your doings, and because of the abominations which ye have committed; therefore is your land become a desolation, and an astonishment, and a curse, without inhabitant, as it is this day. 23. Because ye have burned incense, and because ye have sinned against the Lord, and have not obeyed the voice of the Lord, nor walked in his law, nor in his statutes, nor in his testimonies; therefore this evil is happened unto you, as it is this day.

24. Moreover Jeremiah said unto all the people, and to all the women, Hear the word of the Lord, all Judah that are in the land of Egypt: 25. thus saith the Lord of hosts, the God of Israel, saying: Ye and your wives have both spoken with your mouths, and with your hands have fulfilled it, saying, We will surely perform our vows that we have vowed, to burn incense to the queen of heaven, and to pour out drink offerings unto her: establish then your

vows, and perform your vows. 26. Therefore hear ye the word of the Lord, all Judah that dwell in the land of Egypt: Behold, I have sworn by my great name, saith the Lord, that my name shall no more be named in the mouth of any man of Judah in all the land of Egypt, saying, As the Lord God liveth. 27. Behold, I watch over them for evil, and not for good: and all the men of Judah that are in the land of Egypt shall be consumed by the sword and by the famine, until there be an end of them. 28. And they that escape the sword shall return out of the land of Egypt into the land of Judah, few in number; and all the remnant of Judah, that are gone into the land of Egypt to sojourn there, shall know whose word shall stand, mine, or theirs. 29. And this shall be the sign unto you, saith the Lord, that I will punish you in this place, that ye may know that my words shall surely stand against you for evil: 30. thus saith the Lord: Behold, I will give Pharaoh Hophra king of Egypt into the hand of his enemies, and into the hand of them that seek his life; as I gave Zedekiah king of Judah into the hand of Nebuchadrezzar king of Babylon, his enemy, and that sought his life.

Captivity and Promised Return

Jer. 29: 1. Now these are the words of the letter that Jeremiah the prophet sent from Jerusalem unto the residue of the elders of the captivity, and to the priests, and to the prophets, and to all the people, whom Nebuchadnezzar had carried away captive from Jerusalem to Babylon: 4. saying, Thus saith the Lord of hosts, the God of Israel, unto all the captivity, whom I have caused to be carried away captive from Jerusalem unto Babylon: 5. Build ye houses, and dwell in them; and plant gardens, and eat the fruit of them; 6. take ye wives, and beget sons and daughters; and take wives for your sons, and give your daughters to husbands, that they may bear sons and daughters; and multiply ye there, and be not diminished. 7. And seek the peace of the city whither I have caused you to be carried away captive, and pray unto the Lord for it: for in the peace thereof shall ye have peace. 8. For thus saith the Lord of hosts, the God of Israel: Let not your prophets that be in the midst of you, and your diviners, deceive you, neither hearken ye to your dreams which ye cause to be dreamed. 9. For they prophesy falsely unto you in my name: I have not sent them, saith the Lord. 10. For thus saith the Lord, After seventy years be accomplished for Babylon, I will visit you, and perform my good word toward you, in causing you to return to this place. 11. For I know the thoughts that I think toward you, saith the Lord, thoughts of peace, and not of evil, to give you hope in your latter end. 12. And ye shall call upon me, and ye shall go and pray unto me, and I will hearken unto you. 13. And ye shall seek me, and find me, when ye shall search for me with all your heart. 14. And I will be found of you, saith the Lord, and I will turn again your captivity, and I will gather you from all the nations, and from all the places whither I have driven you, saith the Lord; and I will bring you again unto the place whence I caused you to be carried away captive.

Proclamation for Return

Now in the first year of Cyrus king of Persia, that the word of the Lord by the mouth of Jeremiah the prophet might be accomplished, the Lord stirred up the spirit of Cyrus king of Persia, that he made a proclamation throughout all his kingdom, and put it also in writing, saying, Thus saith Cyrus king of Persia. All the kingdoms of the earth hath the Lord, the God of heaven, given me; and hath charged me to build him an house in Jerusalem, which is in Judah. Whosoever there is among you of all his people, the Lord his God be with him, and let him go up to Jerusalem, which is in Judah, and build the house of the Lord, the God of Israel, (he is God) which is in Jerusalem. And whosoever is left, in any place where he sojourneth, let the men of his place help him with silver, and with gold, and with goods, and with beasts, beside the free will offering for the house of God which is in Jerusalem.

(II Chron. 36:) 22. Now in the first year of Cyrus king of Persia, that the word of the Lord by the mouth of Jeremiah the prophet might be accomplished, the Lord stirred up the spirit of Cyrus king of Persia, that he made a proclamation throughout all his kingdom, and put it also in writing, saying, 23. Thus saith Cyrus king of Persia, All the kingdoms of the earth hath the Lord, the God of heaven, given me; and he hath charged me to build him an house in Jerusalem, which is in Judah.

Whosoever there is among you of all his people, the Lord his God be with him, and let him go up.

(Ezra 1:) 1. Now in the first year of Cyrus king of Persia, that the word of the Lord by the mouth of Jeremiah might be accomplished, the Lord stirred up the spirit of Cyrus king of Persia, that he made a proclamation throughout all his kingdom, and put it also in writing, saying, 2. Thus saith Cyrus king of Persia, All the kingdoms of the earth hath the Lord, the God of heaven, given me; and he hath charged me to build him an house in Jerusalem, which is in Judah.

3. Whosoever there is among you of all his people, his God be with him, and let him go up to Jerusalem, which is in Judah, and build the house of the Lord, the God of Israel, (he is God) which is in Jerusalem.
4. And whosoever is left in any place where he sojourneth, let the men of his place help him with silver, and with gold, and with goods, and with beasts, beside the free will offering for the house of God which is in Jerusalem.

The Return

Ezra 1:5. Then rose up the heads of the fathers' houses of Judah and Benjamin, and the priests and the Levites, even all whose spirit God had stirred to go up to build the house of the Lord which is in Jerusalem. 6. And all they that were round about them strengthened their hands with vessels of silver, with gold, with goods, and with beasts, and with precious things, beside all that was willingly offered. 7. Also Cyrus the king brought forth the vessels of the house of the Lord, which Nebuchadnezzar had brought forth out of Jerusalem, and had put them in the house of his gods; 8. even those did Cyrus king of Persia bring forth by the hand of Mithredath the treasurer, and numbered them unto Shesbazzar,* the prince of Judah. 9. And this is the number of them: thirty charges of gold, a thousand charges of silver, nine and twenty knives; 10. thirty bowls of gold, silver bowls of a second sort four hundred and ten, and other vessels a thousand. 11. All the vessels of gold and of silver were five thousand and four hundred. All these did Shesbazzar* bring up, when they of the captivity were brought up from Babylon unto Jerusalem.

---
* In other places called Zerubbabel.

APPENDIX A
Chronology

The necessity for and the difficulty of revising the chronology of the Old Testament have both been so plainly apparent, that they have served to counteract each other. The scheme of Biblical chronology propounded by Archbishop Usher, in a work published in 1650-64, the Annales Veteris et Novi Testamenti, whose dates were inserted by some unknown authority in the margin of reference editions of the authorized version, has until very recently been allowed to remain unimproved although its correctness has long been disproved. Sayce,* writing of the period of the Monarchy, says, "The inconsistent character of Biblical chronology of the royal houses of Judah and Israel, has been known ever since chronologists have set to work upon it. System after system has been proposed to reduce it to harmony. The systems have been unsatisfactory because the materials on which they rested were insufficient to solve the chronological problem. To-day all is changed. The Assyrian records have given us fixed points of departure for dating the reigns of the Jewish and Israelitish kings; from Ahab to Hezekiah we can check the chronological statements of the Books of Kings and determine the value to be attached to them." He gives the following tables to show how great are the discrepancies between them.

USHER	ASSYRIAN RECORDS
Ahab B. C. 918-897.	Ahab fights at Qarqara B. C. 853.
Jehu 884-856.	Jehu pays tribute to Assyria 842.
Benhadad murdered by Hazael Cir. 880.	Hadadezer murdered by Hazael 843.
Azariah of Judah 810-758.	Azariah defeated by Tiglath Pileser 737.
Pekah 759-739.	War with Pekah 734.
Accession of Hoshea 739.	Death of Pekah and Accession of Hoshea 729.
War with Rezin of Damascus 741.	War with Rezin 734.
Capture of Damascus 740.	Capture of Damascus 732.
Ahaz of Judah 742-726.	Submission of Jeho-ahaz of Judah 734.
Capture of Samaria 721.	Capture of Samaria 722.
Invasion of Judah by Sennacherib 712.	Sennacherib invades Judah 701.

The historic facts, as stated in the Scriptures, are thus fully corroborated by the Assyrian records, but the dates of their occurrence are widely at variance. In determining the true meaning of the chronological statements of the Scriptures, in distinction from their apparent meaning, we must take into consideration:

First. The variety of methods in reckoning periods of time. According to Hebrew usage, a portion of time is reckoned as the whole, a fraction as the unit, *e.g.*, the three days Christ remained in the tomb. David's reign in Hebron is the only one of all the kings of Israel or Judah whose duration is given in years and in fractions of the year. All the rest, whose reign lasted a year or more, are given in full calendar years. It is impossible for this to have been literally true. There must have been broken years in which one reign ended and another one began. In such cases, we find a variable method of reckoning. Generally it was counted

---
* The Higher Criticism and the Monuments Page 407.

for the reign that ended. The following year was called "the first year" for the reign that began, and the fraction of the year was designated as "the beginning of his reign." The effect of this reckoning was to make the reign that ended longer, and the one that began shorter, than they really were. This is called post-dating. Sometimes the broken year, in which a king died, was reckoned as his own last year and the first year of his successor. This was called pre-dating. The result of this variable reckoning is made apparent in the period between the beginning of the reigns of Rehoboam and Athaliah, and those of Jereboam and Jehu, which began at the same time in the Southern and Northern kingdoms respectively. The following table of the kings of this intervening period shows a difference of three years in the two kingdoms when they should be the same:

Rehoboam	17	Jereboam	22
Abijam	3	Nadab	2
Asa	41	Baasha	24
Jehoshaphat	25	Elah	2
Joram	8	Omri	12
Ahaziah	1	Ahab	22
	—	Ahaziah	2
	95	Joram	12
			98

This difference is the result of post-dating the reigns of three of the kings of the Southern kingdom, and so shortening each of them one year, and pre-dating the reigns of the Northern kingdom.

Second. We must consider the cross-reckoning of time between the two kingdoms, giving the synchronisms of reigns that were contemporaneous. The commencement of each reign is dated by the year of the reign of the contemporaneous king, in the other kingdom. The inconsistencies of these synchronisms are plainly seen, and to explain them we are obliged to infer the overlapping of reigns in some form of a co-regency, which is not definitely stated, *e.g.*, We read

In I Kings 22:51. Ahaziah the son of Ahab began to reign over Israel in Samaria in the *seventeenth* year of Jehoshaphat of Judah, *and he reigned two years.*	In II Kings 3:1. Now Jehoram the son of Ahab began to reign over Israel in Samaria in the *eighteenth* year of Jehoshaphat king of Judah.

Now the only way to reconcile these two conflicting statements is to suppose that the elder brother Ahaziah was co-regent with his father Ahab one of the two years of his reign. Contrast again

II Kings 1:17b. And Jehoram (the son of Ahab) began to reign in his stead (Azariah) in the *second year of Jehoram* the son of Jehoshaphat king of Judah.	II Kings 3:1. Now Jehoram the son of Ahab began to reign over Israel in Samaria in the *eighteenth year of Jehoshaphat* king of Judah.

Here is a discrepancy of nine years, as Jehoshaphat is said to have reigned twenty-five years.

With the two above inconsistent synchronisms, consider a third. II Kings 8:16. And in the fifth year of Joram the son of Ahab king of Israel, Jehoshaphat being then king of Judah, Jehoram the son of Jehoshaphat king of Judah began to reign. These passages can be harmonized only by inferring that Jehoshaphat associated his son Jehoram with him on the throne.

It is thought by some that this is intimated in II Chron. 21: 1-3. Now Jehoshaphat slept with his fathers, and was buried with his fathers in the city of David: and Jehoram his son reigned in his stead. (Margin A. V. Alone) 2. And he had brethren the sons of Jehoshaphat, ... 3. And their father gave them great gifts of silver, and of gold, and of precious things, with fenced cities in Judah, but the kingdom gave he to Jehoram, (Marg. Jehoram made partner of the kingdom with his father) because he was the first-born. The interpretation, thus put in the margin, is that the first verse describes what occurred at the death of his father. The third verse refers to an arrangement made by Jehoshaphat several years prior to his death. The fourth verse tells how he slew his six brethren and divers also of the princes of Israel in order to secure undivided power for himself. These co-regencies reduce the time between Solomon and Athaliah to 90 years, instead of either 98 or 95, as given in the table. These samples of the confusion arising from the modes of reckoning and cross-reckoning the time of the reigns of the kings of the two kingdoms are sufficient to show that the apparent meaning of the chronological statements of the Bible is not always the true meaning, and that the materials furnished us in the Scriptures are not sufficient alone to solve the chronological problem. We must look to another source for determining the chronology of this period. Such a source, in a limited degree, has been found in the Assyrian Inscriptions.

The Assyrian Eponym Canon is a list of officers, one officer for every year, containing about 265 names in a series backward from about 650 B. C. If they are continuous they go back to about 900 B. C., but if not continuous to less than 800 B. C. The Canon exists in several copies, all of which substantially agree, and is in a high degree trustworthy. Light is thrown on this Canon by the Assyrian records, consisting of the Annals of Shalmanezer II, Sargon, Sennacherib, Esar-haddon, Assur-bani-pal, and other kings, giving dated accounts of their exploits year by year. Calculated eclipses, especially the great eclipse of the sun B. C. 763, in the tenth year of Assur-daan king of Assyria, help to verify the assigned dates of this period. Back to this point there is substantial agreement, and we have independent lines of evidence, one confirming the other. Professor Beecher * claims that all back of this is conjectural and in dispute. Assyriologists insist that the list of Eponyms is continuous, and if it is, it makes the interval between Jehu and Hezekiah about fifty years less than the numbers in the Bible apparently make it. The revised chronology † gives the date for the accession of Rehoboam and Jereboam at the division of the kingdom as 937 B. C. We must choose between this and Usher's 975 B. C. With our present knowledge, there is no way of harmonizing these two systems of the chronology of this period. The overlapping of reigns is used as a variable factor in lessening the difference between them. In II Chron. 26: 21 (cf. II Kings 15: 5) we are told, And Uzziah the king was a leper unto the day of his death, and dwelt in a several house, being a leper; for he was cut off from the house of the Lord: and Jotham his son was over the king's house, judging the people of the land. At the death of Uzziah, we are further told (26: 23), and Jotham reigned in his stead, and (27: 1) he reigned sixteen years in Jerusalem. It is impossible to decide how much of the sixteen years overlapped the fifty-two years of Uzziah, and how much was left for his own independent reign. The uncertainties and inconsistencies of Usher's system and the disagreement of those who attempt to correct it, make it less satisfactory than the revised chronology, which has the substantial agreement of scholars whose prepared tables vary only in details. For the sake of convenient comparison, both systems are used in this work.

---

* Butler's Bible Work, Vol. VII, pp. 41-45. Chronology by Prof. Willis Judson Beecher, D.D. Hastings Dictionary of the Bible. Art. Chronology.
† Student's Chart of Biblical History by Charles F. Kent, Ph.D. Table in Hastings Dictionary of the Bible.

APPENDIX B

The Duplications of Incidents in I Samuel

I and II Samuel counted as one book, and I and II Kings counted as one book, are found in the first section of the second division of the Hebrew canon, called the Prophets. In the LXX the two books in the Hebrew canon are divided into the four books of Kings.

They form a continuous history of the Hebrew people, from Samuel the last judge to Zedekiah the last king. Beginning with the last Chapter of I Samuel (XXXI) this history is duplicated in I and II Chronicles, and in parts of Psalms, Ezra, Isaiah, Jeremiah, and Daniel.

The first thirty Chapters of I Samuel are not duplicated in any other Scripture, and is thus our only source of information concerning the pivotal transition period from the Judges to the Kings, and the trio of remarkable characters, Samuel, Saul, and David, that figure so largely in that period. All that we know of the first two from their birth to their death, and all that we know of the third from his birth to his being chosen as king at Hebron, we learn from I Samuel. But while I Samuel, with the exception of the thirteen verses of the last Chapter, is not duplicated in any other Scripture, it is largely made up of duplications of incidents and events, "a redaction of a manifold historical material." (Lange.) In this it is like Kings and Chronicles; but it is very unlike them in that it does not cite any of its sources as they do.

These duplications are:
1. Two denunciations of Eli (2: 27-36) (3: 11-18).
2. Three appointments of Saul as king (10: 1-8) (10: 17-24) (11: 14, 15).
3. Two instances of Saul's prophesying (10: 10-12) (19: 22-24).
4. Two rejections of Saul (13: 13, 14) (15: 16-29).
5. Two introductions of David at court (16: 14-23) (17: 17-39).
6. Two attempts of Saul to smite David (18: 10, 11) (19: 9, 10).
7. Two negotiations to make David the king's son-in-law (18: 12-19) (18: 20-27).
8. Two flights of David to Achish (21: 10-16) (27: 1-12. 28: 1-3. 29: 1-11).
9. Two betrayals of David by the Ziphites (23: 19-23) (26: 1-5).
10. Two instances of sparing Saul's life (24: 1-22) (26: 6-25).

An examination of this list of duplications shows: (1) There is only one in which there is any sequence of consecutive events that necessitates a succession of narratives to complete the biography, viz.: the three appointments of Saul as king, which stand related to each other as anointing, election and coronation. (2) In only three of these cases is there any allusion in one narrative that implies there is any other, viz.: 3: 12, 18: 11, 18: 21. (3) In only one case is there any unmistakable evidence of the interweaving of different accounts of the same incident or event, viz. (16: 14-23) (17: 17-39). (4) In no one of these duplications is there any after retrospective allusion or reference to it found in any other Scripture, comparing or contrasting their likenesses or unlikenesses, *e.g.*, Mark 8: 19-21, where Jesus points out four contrasts between the two miracles of feeding the multitude. The above statements prepare us for the inquiry whether they are duplications of like incidents or events, or duplicate accounts of the same event. Rev. H. P. Smith [*1] says, "The simplest way to account for them is to suppose that they are real duplicates, variant accounts of the same series of events, put together by a compiler who wished to preserve for us whatever he found of interest in both (or all) his sources." Over against this, it may be said, the simplest way is not necessarily the most convincing, nor the most satisfactory, nor the most impressive and instructive way.

Rev. A. F. Kirkpatrick, B.D., [*2] says of one of these duplications, "If the narratives are closely examined, it will be found that the differences outweigh the resemblances, and the difficulty of reconciling the narratives, if they refer to the same occurrence, is far greater than that of supposing that somewhat similar events happened twice." His treatment of the cases separately shows that this would be his judgment of most all of the cases, as well as of this one.

A brief consideration of each of the cases in their order of occurrence will help each one to decide for himself between these two extremes of interpretation about this and other kindred questions that may arise.†

1. Two denunciations of Eli (2: 27-36) (3: 11-18).

In the first (2: 27-36), there came a man of God unto Eli, who declared God's indictment and sentence, with a God-given sign.

In the second (3: 1-18), God speaks for the first time through the boy Samuel, who ministered unto the Lord before Eli, knowing how the Lord had called Samuel in the night, Eli in the morning adjures him to tell what the Lord had spoken unto him. When he had told him every whit, and hid nothing from him, then Eli said, "It is the Lord: let him do what seemeth him good." Had there been a doubt before, as likely there was, whether the Lord would do all that he had spoken, and would not let Eli's iniquity be expiated with sacrifice nor offering forever, that doubt was now entirely removed. Eli is wholly resigned, since God's word by the man of God has been verified by his word to Samuel. Smith says, "Two denunciations of Eli's course are related, either one of which abundantly answers the author's purpose. One of the denunciations is superfluous." This statement could only be true if they were repetitions of each other by the same person, but even then the second would serve as a forcible reminder. But the two denunciations of Eli were by two different persons of very different rank and standing. The first was by a nameless unknown man of God, the second was by Samuel, the greatest of the Judges.

God said to Samuel, "I will perform against Eli all that I have spoken concerning his house." This is not a repetition of an announcement, but a confirmation and a verification. The two were cumulative in their effect, making assurance doubly sure, on the principle of the divine injunction, "at the mouth of two witnesses, or at the mouth of three witnesses shall a matter be established." (Deut. 19: 15.)

2. Three appointments of Saul as king (10: 1-8) (10: 17-24) (11: 14, 15). These are narratives of separate, and closely connected, consecutive events that were climactic steps in the complete confirmation of Saul as king. The first was the private anointment by Samuel. The second was the public election, where the choice of tribe, family, and person was severally

---

[*1] The International Critical Commentary. Samuel. Introduction XV-XVI.
[*2] The Cambridge Bible for Schools and Colleges. Appendix Note VII.
† See Bibliotheca Sacra, April, 1899. "Old Testament Books Versus Their Sources," by Prof. Willis J. Beecher, D.D.

made by lot. The third was the confirmation by the people. There were three similar appointments of David as king. The private anointing (I Sam. 16:13). The anointing as king over Judah (II Sam. 2:4). The anointing as king over Israel (II Sam. 5:3).

3. Two instances of Saul's prophesying (10:10-12) (19:22-24).

There is no resemblance between the two, aside from the bare fact of prophesying, and the repetition of the proverb, Is Saul also among the prophets? The first prophesying was the closing part of the third sign confirmatory of his call. Although a plain citizen, he was made to prophesy among the trained recipients of divine inspiration, as a forcible way of manifesting God's encouragement for him to go on in the way of his appointment, as announced by Samuel.

The second prophesying was for the very opposite purpose, viz.: to discourage and restrain him from going on in the way of his own choosing. Saul sent messengers to Ramah, to take David from under the protection of Samuel, to whom he had fled for safety; and when they saw the company of the prophets prophesying, and Samuel standing as appointed over them, the spirit of God was upon the messengers of Saul, and they also prophesied. The same thing occurred when he sent the messengers the second and the third time, God thus thrice making Saul's messengers forget their errand of violence to David.

Saul then came down himself, and he too was made to prophesy. He was struck down more completely than his servants, and lay a day and a night unconscious. The proverb, Is Saul also among the prophets? received a fresh exemplification. The first prophesying was a special manifestation of divine approval and help in carrying out the work to which he had been called. The second prophesying, following that of the messengers thrice sent, was a signal manifestation of divine disapproval restraining him from doing that which was antagonistic to and destructive of God's will.

4. Two rejections of Saul (13:13, 14) (15:16-29).

This is plainly a duplication that is cumulative in its evidence of Saul's unworthiness. When Samuel anointed Saul, he predicted three things that should happen unto him as confirmatory signs. He then gave him two commands, with a reason assigned to each, viz.: "And thou shalt go down before me to Gilgal; and behold, I will come down unto thee, to offer and to sacrifice." (2) "Seven days shalt thou tarry, till I come unto thee, and shew thee what thou shalt do."

Saul tarried seven days, but when Samuel came not, and the people were scattered from him, he himself offered. In justifying himself to Samuel, he ignores altogether the second purpose of his coming, viz.: to shew him what he should do. He not only offered, but he followed his own judgment in repelling the Philistines. As the commands were connected with the signs that had all come true, he had every reason to trust God, but he distrusted him. He utterly failed to meet the test of confidence. His conduct was in striking contrast with that of David, who had to wait not days, but weeks, months, and years when it seemed certain that his life would be taken.

The cause of his second rejection was deliberate, wilful, flagrant disobedience, coupled with an excuse which arrayed sacrifice and disobedience as things equally pleasing to God, so that he could at pleasure choose between them. But Samuel affirms that to obey is better than sacrifice and announces that as he has rejected the word of the Lord, so the Lord had rejected him. The chronicler (I Ch. 10:13, 14) adds a third ground for Saul's rejection, "So Saul died because of the word of the Lord, which he kept not, and also for that he asked counsel of one that had a familiar spirit, to inquire thereby, and inquired not of the Lord." This third sin shews the same spirit as the other two, and the mention of it by the chronicler shews that the trend of Scripture is towards a duplication of incidents and events as well as duplicates of the same incident or event.

5. Two introductions of David at court (16: 14-23) (17: 17-39).

This is plainly a duplicate, and one of the hardest to harmonize in the Scriptures. One of the mysterious features of this case is that the oldest and most authoritative copy of the LXX (the Vatican) omits the second introduction and all that follows it which disagrees with the first introduction.* (Some difficult questions arise in connection with these omissions, *e.g.*, Did this first translation omit for any reason what it found in the Hebrew Bible? or were these passages not then in the Hebrew Bible? Has the Alexandrine copy, written a century later, added these passages to make it correspond with the Hebrew Bible?) † The omitted parts are (17: 12-31) David's visit to his brethren; (17: 41) Goliath's shield bearer going before him; (17: 55-58) Saul and Abner's dialogue about the son of Jesse; (18: 1-5) Jonathan's and David's mutual covenant; (18: 10, 11) Saul's first attempt to smite David; (18: 17-19) Saul's negotiation to give David his eldest daughter Merab.

The two introductions are not themselves contradictory, and a clue to the harmonizing is given (17: 15). "Now David went to and from Saul to feed his father's sheep." The real insurmountable difficulty is found (17: 55-58) in the dialogue between Saul and Abner after the defeat and death of Goliath, which manifests an utter ignorance of David by both the king and the captain of the host. Some find a solution in the fact that they do not ask, Who David is? but whose son is he? But 16: 18, 19 distinctly states that David was introduced to and sent for by Saul as Jesse's son. Others suggest that Saul in his frenzied state would not notice David sufficiently to recognize him, but 16: 21 states that in addition to playing for Saul, "he stood before him and became his armour bearer." Others suggest that 16: 14-23, the sending for David to play for Saul belongs chronologically after the triumph of David over Goliath, but the ignorance concerning David shown at the time of sending for him would be impossible after the notoriety of his victory. Moreover, 18: 2 definitely states that David's residence at court after the defeat of Goliath was continuous. With our present light it seems impossible to harmonize the conflicting accounts. We must choose between the alternatives, either the two accounts have been put together so that we cannot understand them correctly, or 17: 55-58 is an interpolation in the text.

6. Two attempts of Saul to smite David (18: 10, 11) (19: 9, 10).

The two narratives are very much alike, both in the facts described, and in the language used. But the first account distinctly states that "David avoided out of his presence twice," and the second one may well be that recorded in the next chapter.

There is an evident increase in Saul's jealous anger that shows itself in an increased intensity of feeling and action that corresponds with the progress of events. Each fits exactly in its place. The triumphant song of the women aroused Saul's jealousy so that he "eyed David from that day forward." As he nursed his grievance, it happened one day that having a spear in his hand, he said, "I will smite David even to the wall." He cast his spear, but we are not told with what force or result. Then follows the twofold effort to make David the king's son-in-law, which only resulted in making Saul "yet the more afraid of David." Jonathan effects a reconciliation between Saul and David, but David's victory over the Philistines opens the wound afresh, and Saul makes the second attempt on David's life.

It is very unlike the first in the intensity of the effort, for he smote the spear with such force that it went into the wall where David stood, but David slipped away out of Saul's presence, and fled and escaped. The first time Saul sent David away from him. The second

---

* The Septuagint H. B. Swete University Press, Cambridge, 1895, with the Vatican recension (B) in the text, and the Alexandrine (A) in footnote.

† Cambridge Bible. Introduction, page 15, and Appendix Note VI, 4, 5, page 243.

time David escaped and fled that night to Michal his wife, and she let him down from the wall before Saul's messengers reached him.

7. Two negotiations to make David Saul's son-in-law (18: 12-19) (18: 20-27).

The first negotiation for the eldest daughter Merab is omitted in the Septuagint. Again Adriel, to whom it is said Merab was given, after she was promised to David, is spoken of in II Samuel 21:8, as the husband of Michal, but Merab was evidently intended, because (1) Michal was made the wife of Palti, and (2) while it was natural that David should take the five sons of Merab to appease the wrath of Gibeonites against Saul, it would be very unnatural to take the sons of his wife Michal whom he took back from Palti to whom Saul had given her.

In favour of two negotiations are the words of Saul to David in reference to Michal, " Thou shalt this day be my son-in-law the *second time*" (A. V. in the twain). Again, in the first there is no mention made of a dowry being demanded, which accords with the promise made to the one who should defeat the giant Philistine.

Saul starts the second negotiation as an entirely new thing, and when David objects " that he is a poor man, and lightly esteemed," Saul sends word that he will accept an hundred foreskins of the Philistines in the place of a dowry, in the hope that he will be slain in his effort to obtain them. The two proposals to David far better accords with Saul's character than one, and also furnishes a better explanation of the anger and fear that made him cast his spear at David a second time with increased venom and hate, and henceforth hunt him as an enemy.

8. Two flights of David to Achish (21: 10-16) (27: 1-12. 28: 1, 2. 29: 1-11).

The circumstances of the two are very unlike, and correspond exactly to the difference between the two occasions.

In the first flight, he went alone and had no welcome from Achish, but being recognized as Israel's hero who had slain their champion, and therefore distrusted by the king's servants, he feigned madness which disgusted the king, and escaped as soon as possible.

In his second flight, he went with six hundred men, and is welcomed by the king as a leader of stalwart soldiers who will make a potent ally. In this rôle, he asks for and obtains Ziglag as a perpetual residence and possession, and dwelt there a full year and four months. After this long residence among them, when returning with the spoils of a successful raid against Israel's enemies, in answer to the king's question, " whither have ye made a raid to-day? David deliberately falsifies in his reply, " Against the south of Judah, of the Jerahmelites, and of the Kenites." This deception led to the king's announced purpose to take David and his men with him to battle, and on David's assuring response, Achish said, " Therefore will I make thee the keeper of my head for ever." The next battle proves to be the one in which Saul is defeated and slain. David is extricated from his false position, where he would have been forced to be a traitor either to the Philistines or to Israel, by the persistent distrust and jealousy of the princes of the Philistines, which compelled Achish to dismiss him from the army. David protests, appealing to his past loyalty, " but must have inwardly rejoiced that God had delivered him out of so perplexing a dilemma."

9. Two betrayals of David by the Ziphites (23: 19-23) (26: 1-5).

In the first instance, the Ziphites came up to Saul to Gibeah, saying, Doth not David hide himself with us in strong holds in the wood, in the hill of Hachilah, which is on the south of Jeshimon? They bid him come down and their part shall be to deliver him into the king's hand.

Saul blesses them, and tells them to know and see where his haunt is, and come again to him with a certainty, and he will go with them. This co-operation proved to be so successful that David was completely encompassed, but at the critical moment Saul was providentially called away to repel a Philistine invasion.

In the second instance, the Ziphites inform Saul where David is hiding, in almost the same language as in the first case, but they do not promise to deliver David into his hand as before, and Saul does not succeed in encompassing David, as in the first case.

10. Two instances of sparing Saul's life (24: 1-22) (26: 6-25).

When Saul was returned from the Philistines, *he came* with three thousand men in pursuit of David in the wilderness of Engedi, and unknowingly went into the cave where David and his men were hiding.

David's men think it is the Lord's providential deliverance of his enemy into his hand, but David having cut off the skirt of Saul's robe privily, said, The Lord forbid that I should do this thing unto my master, seeing he is anointed of the Lord, and stayed his servants, and suffered them not to rise against Saul. When Saul and his men went out, David followed and cried after him, pleading his innocence, holding up the skirt of his robe which he had cut off as proof, and called upon the Lord to judge between them and to avenge him. Saul filled with a momentary remorse, acknowledges that David is more righteous than he, and avows his belief that David will be king, and exacts a pledge from him that he will not cut off his seed.

In the second instance, *David came* to the place where Saul had pitched his camp, and looking down upon him and his people as they lay asleep, he calls for some one to go with him to the camp.

Abishai volunteers, and together they go and find Saul sleeping with his spear stuck in the ground at his bolster; and Abner and the people lay about him. David refuses to let Abishai smite him, avowing his conviction that the Lord will smite him; or his day shall come to die, or he shall perish in battle, but he bids Abishai take his spear and the cruse of water, and they gat them away without any one seeing or knowing it; because a deep sleep from the Lord was fallen upon them. Then David went and stood upon the top of a hill afar off with a great space between them, and holding up the spear and cruse, taunted Abner for his neglect.

Saul recognizes his voice and calls upon him, confessing his sin, folly, and error, and promises that he will no more do him harm, because his soul was precious in his eyes that day. David prays the Lord to save his life, as he has saved Saul's life, and to deliver him out of all tribulation. Saul blesses David, avowing his belief that he will do mightily and prevail. So they separate never to meet again, but David believing that this very sparing of Saul's life will increase Saul's fear of and anger against him, promptly decides to quit the land as long as Saul lives, and so escape out of his hands.

Rev. A. F. Kirkpatrick, B.D.,* commenting upon the last two duplications, viz.: The two flights of David to Achish and the sparing of the life of Saul that followed each flight, says, " The main points of agreement between the narratives are, (1) the conduct of the Ziphites; (2) Saul's pursuit of David; (3) David's generous refusal to take Saul's life. Besides these there are several minor coincidences, both of circumstance and language. But on the other hand, It is natural that in the accounts of two similar events there should be several close coincidences. Further, if the narratives are closely examined, it will be found that the differences outweigh the resemblances, and the difficulty of reconciling the narratives, if they refer to the same occurrence, is far greater than that of supposing that somewhat similar events

---
* Cambridge Bible, Samuel. Appendix Note VII.

happened twice during a pursuit which lasted several years, and was confined to a small district." He adds: " The following points should be noticed:

(a) The section XXIII. 19-XXIV. 22 contains a narrative of what took place upon two distinct occasions, *separated by Saul's being called away to repel a Philistine raid* (XXIII. 27); here there is no indication of such an *interval* between Saul's arrival at Hachilah and David's visit to his camp.

(b) The *scene* of the interview is different in each case. Here it is the camp at Hachilah: there a cave at En-gedi.

(c) The *circumstances* differ. Here David deliberately enters Saul's camp and takes his spear, &c.: there he accidentally gets Saul into his power in the cave in which he was concealed, and deprives him of the lappet of his robe.

(d) The *persons* concerned here are mentioned by name: there only 'the men' in general are spoken of.

(e) The *point of conversation* is different: here Saul only uses general language; there he acknowledges that David will be king and exacts an oath from him: here David indignantly demands to know why he is persecuted; there he lays stress on his having spared the king's life as a proof of his innocence.

(f) The general circumstances of this narrative correspond to *a later period of David's life, when David was bolder, and Saul more hardened;* and it would appear from XXVII. 1 that this pursuit was the final act of persecution which drove David to quit the country and take refuge at Gath."

APPENDIX C.

The Peculiarities of Chronicles

I and II Chronicles, taken as one, but separated from Ezra and Nehemiah to which it was originally joined as one work, is placed last in the Hebrew canon, and also last in the third division of the canon, the Kethubhim (the Writings), Hagiographa (Sacred Writings), and so stands as a sort of historical appendix to the O. T. This triple division of the Hebrew canon, Law, Prophets, Writings, is claimed by some to be based upon the time the different books were received into the canon, and so was formed progressively. This would account for the not putting Chronicles in second division with Samuel and Kings; and for placing it after and not before Ezra and Nehemiah, where it naturally belongs, in the third division. It is claimed by others that it is based upon the official status of their authors. The books written by Prophets stand in second division; those written by inspired men, not belonging to the prophetic order, in the third division. In Hebrew, the name is taken from the oft repeated phrase, "Dibhěrě Hayyâmim" (lit. acts of days) which Jerome renders in Latin "verba dierum," and gives as equivalent in Greek "chronikon." The LXX, followed by Vulgate, adopted the name "ta paralei pomera," the usual interpretation of which is, "the things passed over" by Samuel and Kings. Much of the contents of Chronicles is identical with these earlier histories, but the writer does not refer to them by name, but he gives at the end of each reign a list of authorities for the recorded acts of each king of the house of David.

For David, histories of Samuel the seer, Nathan the prophet, Gad the seer, I Ch. 29: 29.

For Solomon, history of Nathan the prophet, prophecy of Ahijah the Shilonite, visions of Iddo the seer concerning Jereboam the son of Nebat, II Ch. 9: 29.

For Rehoboam, histories of Shemaiah the prophet, Iddo the seer, II Ch. 12: 15.

For Abijah, commentary of prophet Iddo, II Ch. 13: 22.

For Asa, Amaziah, Ahaz, book of the kings of Judah and Israel, II Ch. 16: 11, 25: 26, 26: 26.

For Jotham, Josiah, Jehoiakim, book of the kings of Israel and Judah, 27: 7, 35: 27, 36: 8.

For Jehoshaphat, history of Jehu the son of Hanani, which is inserted in the books of the kings of Israel, II Ch. 20: 34.

For Joash, commentary of the book of kings, II Ch. 24: 27.

For Uzziah, Isaiah the prophet the son of Amoz, II Ch. 26: 22.

For Hezekiah, vision of Isaiah the son of Amoz, in book of kings of Judah and Israel, II Ch. 32: 32.

For Manasseh, words of the seers among the acts of the king of Israel, history of Hozai, (marg. the seers) II Ch. 33: 18, 19.

If we examine the parallel passages in Kings, we shall find opposite these lists of many authorities that the writer of Kings cites, for his one authority, the chronicles of the kings of Judah. We shall also find that where the chronicler gives no authorities, as in the reigns of Ahaziah,

Athaliah, Jehoahaz, Jehoiachin and Zedekiah, there is none cited in Kings. A fair inference from this is that, for the most part, the many authorities of Chronicles, are sections of the one authority of Kings. Again, the book of kings of Judah and Israel, and of Israel and Judah, are the union of the two books of the chronicles of the kings of Judah, and of the kings of Israel, cited separately by Kings, for the Southern and Northern kingdoms. The history of Hozai seems to be singled out as something additional (cf. II Ch. 33: 19, with ver. 18). Of this, and other similar books, containing facts not recorded in Kings, scholars like Ewald and Sayce claim that the chronicler was not confined to the writings of the canonical prophets for the sources of his history, but had also more or less contemporary documents, recent works composed in the manner of the old prophets, based on older unused writings or traditions, from which he made new and trustworthy extracts and quotations, and found new explanations and interpretations of old facts, which were suited to the special purpose and plan of his work. Although we do not know who was the author of the Chronicles, yet as like produces like, we know from the product what he was and what was his purpose in giving his supplement to the already existing histories of the Samuels and the Kings. He was an enthusiastic admirer and panegyrist of the House of David, idealising its founder and his successor Solomon in the united kingdom. After the division, he follows David's line in the Southern kingdom, recording only so much of history of Israel as threw light on that of Judah, until the Hebrew Monarchy ends in captivity and exile. Again, he was a man of sterling religious character, earnest piety, and serene faith; in all probability a Levite and musician, imbued with all the spirit, and possessed of all the lore of the priestly class. Moreover he lived in an age when the temporal power of King and State was only a memory of the past; and the Church, separate from king and state, was rehabilitating itself on the lofty ideals of past glory when it was united with them. Hence it is, that in tracing the history of the House of David, from the first gaining to the final losing of the throne, it is not the temporal and material that is most magnified, but the spiritual. In the foreground of the graphic portrayal of the greatness of David's House, is the bringing up the ark to Jerusalem, the royal preparation for the building of the Temple, its construction and dedication, its liturgical and musical services conducted by the appointed monthly classes, its sacrifices and burnt offerings performed by the priests, and the periodical and annual feasts. It is an ecclesiastical rather than a political history.

Again, he was a representative embodiment of the ritualistic habit of religious thought prevailing at the date of writing. With the downfall of Jerusalem and the destruction of the Temple, the prophetical element, with its exaltation of righteousness above sacrifice, developed rapidly during the period of exile. But with the return to Jerusalem and the rebuilding of the Temple, the pendulum of religious thought swung back to the ritualistic. As the latter increased, the former decreased, until religion became the mere shell that Jesus found it. At the date of writing, the two elements were more evenly balanced, but the ritualistic was waxing and the prophetical was waning. This contemporaneous habit of thought is reproduced in the Chronicles in the very large additions to earlier histories, of the mention and description of the sacrificial and liturgical services of the Temple.

A comparative analysis of the synoptic histories of the royal houses of Israel and Judah, shew that in many respects they are remarkably alike, and in many other respects they are remarkably unlike. The correspondence amounts in some cases to identity, and the disagreement in other cases amounts to contradiction. The characteristic peculiarities of the Chronicles are as follows:

I The first of these peculiarities is seen in the plainly intentional omissions of the blameworthy in the history of the reigns of David and Solomon. The Chronicles, as a panegyric, can be compared to the eleventh chapter of Hebrews, where the one praiseworthy quality of faith, in the different persons mentioned, is appropriately lauded; while their many blameworthy qualities are passed over, although known to exist. To have narrated them would not only have marred the picture, but have defeated the purpose of the writer, by drawing away the attention of the readers from the one thing he was impressing upon them.

So Bennet says of the Chronicles,* "Large omissions were absolutely necessary." "During the six or seven centuries that elapsed between the death of David and the chronicler, the name of David had come to have a symbolic meaning, which was largely independent of the personal character and career of the actual king. His reign had become idealised by the magic of antiquity; it was a glory of the good old times." "The chronicler brings out all that was best in the history of the ancient kings of Judah, that this ideal picture of the state and its rulers might encourage and inspire to future hope and effort. The character and achievements of David and his successors were of permanent significance. The grace and favour accorded to them symbolised the Divine promise for the future, and this promise was to be realised through a son of David."

1. The omission of all things said or done by others, or even themselves, that does not present them in the most favourable light, and so casts a reflection upon them.

(1) The whole life of Saul prior to his downfall and death, and of David prior to his accession to the throne. He thus gets rid of all disparaging or discreditable antecedents of David, either in the relation of pursuer and pursued, or in his own conduct as outlaw, freebooter, or ally of the Philistines. (2) The seven years' reign over Judah in Hebron, with Ishbosheth as rival king over Israel, and the "long war between the house of Saul and the house of David," I Sam. 2: 1, 3: 1. The bare fact of this divided reign is told by the chronicler in the genealogy of David, I Chron. 3: 4, and in the summary of his reign, I Chron. 29: 27, but it is not in the body of his narrative, nor is the fact anywhere explained. There he is represented as coming abruptly to the throne of the whole kingdom, I Chron. 11: 1. (3) The confession of David at the assassination of Abner, II Sam. 3: 39. "And I am this day weak, though anointed king; and these men the sons of Zeruiah are too hard for me: the Lord reward the wicked doer according to his wickedness." (4) The turning over the punishment of Joab and Shimei to Solomon, I Kings 2: 5-9. This acknowledged weakness and shifting of responsibility does not present David in an enviable light.

(5) The taunting challenge of the Jebusites, that "only the lame and the blind" defend the walls. "which was hated of David's soul," II Sam. 5: 6-8. In its place, the chronicler inserts David's making Joab chief for first going up and smiting the Jebusites, I Chron. 11: 6, cf. I Chron. 11: 4-6.

(6) At the siege of Ramah, Joab's boasting message, sent to David at Jerusalem, "I have fought against Rabbah, yea, I have taken the city of waters. Now therefore gather the rest of the people together, and encamp against the city, and take it: lest I take the city, and it be called after my name," II Sam. 11: 27, 28, cf. I Chron. 20: 1-3.

(7) The recovery of his wife, Michal, Saul's daughter, who had been taken away and given to Phatiel, II Sam. 3: 13-16. And the avenging of the Gibeonites for Saul's massacre, in putting to death the five sons of Merab, and two of Rizpah, II Sam. 21: 1-14.

(8) Michael's sarcastic criticism and rebuke of David's dancing before the ark, his apt reply, and Michal's punishment, II Sam. 6: 20-23, cf. I Chron. 15: 25.

* W. H. Bennett, The Books of Chronicles. The Expositor's Bible.

(9) Unfavourable comments, as *e.g.* I Kings 1:6. In explanation of Adonijah's rebellion " And his father had not displeased him at any time in saying, Why hast thou done so ? "

2. The omission of all immoral and sinful acts and their sad consequences. The only wrong doing of David the chronicler records is (1) carrying the ark of God upon a new cart, I Chron. 13:7, and (2) Numbering Israel, I Chron. 21:1, 2. We can account for these two exceptions, not only because they were irreligious rather than immoral acts, but also because they were redeemed by such humble repentance and righting the wrong done, as to secure God's full forgiveness and approval; but, more than all, because there is traced back to these, the building of the Temple in mount Moriah, and the appointment of the offerings and services by the Levites and singers, which in the estimation of the chronicler, was the crowning act of the House of David. But he omits

(1) The adultery with Bath-sheba, the wife of Uriah, II Sam. 11:1-5.

(2) The effort to conceal his guilt, and escape its consequences by calling her husband home from the army, II Sam. 11:6-13.

(3) The deliberate murder of Uriah, through instructions to Joab, by which he puts himself in the power of his powerful but unscrupulous chief, II Sam. 11:14-26.

(4) The displeasure of the Lord, and through Nathan, the foretelling of the death of the child, and the retributive punishment of the sword and evil in his own house, II Sam. 12:7-14.

(5) Amnon's adultery with his sister Tamar, and king David's wroth, but failure to punish. II Sam. 13:1-21.

(6) Absalom's revenge after two years, in the killing of Amnon, and his flight to Geshur, II Sam. 13:22-37.

(7) David's mourning for, but not recalling of Absalom, for three years, and then only through Joab's shrewd planning, II Sam. 13:37-39, 14:1-27.

(8) David's recalling Absalom to Jerusalem, but not seeing his face in two years, and then only under pressure, II Sam. 14:28-33.

(9) Absalom's rebellion, and dishonouring David's wives, and death by Joab through disobedience of king's command, II Sam. Chapters 15-19.

(10) Revolt of Israel under Sheba, and the assassination of Amasa by Joab, II Sam. 20:1-22.

(11) Adonijah's rebellion and defection of Joab and Abiathar, I Kings, 1:53. If we had only the Chronicles, we would have no intimation, much less record, of these sins of David himself or of his sons for which he was largely responsible, and which were sent of God as a merited retribution for his own guilty acts.

(12) Solomon's making affinity with Pharaoh king of Egypt, and his marriage with his daughter, I Kings 3:1.

(13) Solomon's loving many strange women of the Moabites, Ammonites, Edomites, Zidonians, and Hittites, in disobedience of God's command (Deut. 7:1-6). The turning away his heart, when he was old, by his 700 wives and 300 concubines, so that he went after Ashtoreth, and Milcom, and built an high place for Chemosh in the mount that is before Jerusalem, and for Molech, and permitting the burning of incense and sacrifices to them, I Kings 11:1-8.

(14) God's anger with Solomon, and rending the kingdom from him, in the days of his son, giving him but one tribe, and this only for David's and Jerusalem's sake, I Kings 11:9-13.

(15) The Lord's raising up the adversaries, Hadad the Edomite, Rezon of Zobah, and Jereboam the son of Nebat to whom Ahijah the Shilonite announced that God would rend the kingdom out of the hand of Solomon, and give ten tribes to him, I Kings 1:14-40. As with

David, so with Solomon, there is not a single defect, error or sin recorded in Chronicles.

II The second peculiarity of the Chronicles is seen in the additions of the praiseworthy in the history of the reigns of David and Solomon.

1 Of moral reflections and pious comments.

The first of the parallel passages is that which tells of the death of Saul. They are almost identical in the narrative, but the chronicler adds " So Saul died for his trespass which he committed against the Lord, because of the word of the Lord, which he kept not; and also for that he asked counsel of one that had a familiar spirit, to inquire thereby, and inquired not of the Lord: therefore he slew him, and turned the kingdom unto David the son of Jesse," I Chron. 10: 13, 14. This first addition reveals the animus of the writer, and the purpose of his writing, cf. I Chron. 14: 17. " And the fame of David went out into all lands: and the Lord brought the fear of him upon all nations." II Chron. 8: 11.

2 The addition of words and deeds of David and Solomon, not recorded in the Samuels and Kings that magnify, honour, and exalt them. In this respect also, the Chronicles may be compared to the eleventh chapter of Hebrews. Of Abraham's offering up of Isaac, it adds " accounting that God is able to raise up, even from the dead; from whence he did also in a parable receive him back," 11: 19. So of Moses, " refusing to be called the son of Pharaoh's daughter; choosing rather to be evil entreated with the people of God, than to enjoy the pleasures of sin for a season; accounting the reproach of Christ greater riches than the treasures of Egypt; for he looked unto the recompense of reward," 11: 25-27. So the Chronicles.

(1) David's bringing up the ark, I Chron. 13: 3, " for we sought not unto it in the days of Saul," 15: 13, 15. " For because ye bare it not at the first, the Lord our God made a breach upon us, for that we sought him not according to the ordinance. And the children of the Levites bare the ark of God upon their shoulders with the staves thereon, as Moses commanded according to the word of the Lord." This refers back to the frank acknowledgment of previous wrong, 15: 2. " None ought to carry the ark of God but the Levites: for them hath God chosen to carry the ark of God, and to minister unto him for ever." While the writer of Samuel condenses the account into eight verses, II Sam. 6: 12-19, the chronicler gives two long chapters, 15: 1-29, 16: 1-43, telling of David's preparing a place for the ark, his sanctification of the Levites, his appointment of the singers and players on instruments, his arrangement for Levites to minister before the ark, and to celebrate and to thank and praise the Lord, and his composing of the Psalms, CV, CVI, XCVI, to be used for giving thanks unto the Lord. These additions not only greatly increase our interest in the present act, but they indissolubly link it with the future, making it the first step towards the building of the Temple.

(2) David's offering at the threshing floor of Araunah. To the narrative common to both histories, the chronicler adds, I Chron. 21: 26, " and he answered him from heaven by fire upon the altar of burnt offering," 28. " At that time, when David saw that the Lord had answered him in the threshing floor of Ornan the Jebusite, then he sacrificed there." A second reason is given in verse 29, " For the tabernacle of the Lord, which Moses made in the wilderness, and the altar of burnt offering, were at that time in the high place of Gibeon, 30." But David could not go before it to inquire of God; for he was afraid of the sword of the angel of the Lord, cf. 16, 20. Thus the encouragement of fire upon the altar, and the discouragement of the feared sword of the angel of the Lord, make him decide to sacrifice there instead of Gibeon, not only for this one time in an emergency, but always; for we are told, 22: 1. " Then David said, This is the house of the Lord God, and this is the altar of burnt offering for Israel." This is confirmed, II Chron. 3: 1. " Then Solomon began to build the house of the

Lord at Jerusalem in mount Moriah, where the Lord appeared unto David his father, which he made ready in the place that David had appointed, in the threshing floor of Ornan the Jebusite." There is not an intimation of all this in Samuel. So the chronicler furnishes us the second step towards the building of the Temple in mount Moriah.

(3) Preparation for the Temple, its sacrifices and services. This is found in the closing 8 Chapters of I Chron. 22-29.

Chap. 22 tells of David preparing abundantly before his death for the Temple, and his first charge and directions to Solomon. In Chap. 28 we have an account of his assembling a general convention, with an address and charge to them; and giving to Solomon a pattern of the Temple, in all its parts and appurtenances, and his second charge. In Chap. 29 we have an account of David's address to the congregation, telling of his official and liberal personal contribution, with his appeal to them and the generous response of princes and people, and the universal rejoicing, concluding with David's thanksgiving and prayer to God, and the abundant sacrifices and offerings. All this which has been so helpful in building of churches ever since would have been entirely lost but for the chronicler.

In Chaps. 23-27 we have an account of the numbering and distribution of the 38,000 Levites into 24 courses according to the sons of Levi, the 24 courses of priests, the 24 classes of singers, the courses of doorkeepers, the officers of the treasuries and outer business, the 12 captains of the army, the chiefs of the 12 tribes and other rulers and officers.

(4) Description of services in the temple.

II Chron. 5: 11-13. When Solomon brought up the ark, the chronicler tells how the priests had sanctified themselves, how also the Levite singers Asaph, Heman, Jeduthun, and their sons and their brethren, arrayed in fine linen, with cymbals and psalteries and harps, stood at the east end of the altar, and with them an hundred and twenty priests sounding with trumpets: it came even to pass, when the trumpeters and singers were as one, to make one sound in praising and thanking the Lord, (using Psalm 136, with the same refrain in each of its 26 verses, For his mercy endureth for ever;) that then the cloud filled the house, so that the priests could not stand to minister by reason of the cloud. In Kings 8: 10, 11, all these interesting details are omitted.

So again when Solomon had finished his dedicatory prayer, we are told in II Chron. 7: 1 the fire came down from heaven, and consumed the burnt offering and the sacrifices. And all the children of Israel looked on, when the fire came down, and the glory of the Lord was upon the house; and they bowed themselves with their faces to the ground upon the pavement, and worshipped, and gave thanks to the Lord, saying, For he is good; for his mercy endureth for ever. So again when Solomon dedicated the house with the sacrifice of many thousands of oxen and of sheep, the chronicler, in the sixth verse, repeats the story of the priests standing in their offices, the Levites with their instruments of music, giving thanks unto the Lord, with the same words of the psalm, which was doubtlessly sung antiphonally; and the priests sounded trumpets before them; and all Israel stood.

All these were special services, and we read in I Kings 9: 25 that three times in a year Solomon offered burnt and peace offerings on the altar, but the chronicler enlarges and expands this statement and includes in II Chron. 8: 12-15 all the periodical and annual feasts. "Then Solomon offered, even as every day required, offering according to the commandment of Moses, on the sabbaths, and on the new moons, and on the set feasts, three times in the year, even in the feasts of unleavened bread, of weeks, and of tabernacles. And he appointed, according to the ordinance of David his father, the courses of the priests to their service, and the

THE PECULIARITIES OF CHRONICLES

Levites to their charges, to praise, and to minister before the priests, as the duty of every day required: the doorkeepers also by their courses at every gate. And they departed not from the commandment of the king unto the priests and Levites concerning any matter, or concerning the treasures." He thus gives us a brief epitome of temple services as described and provided for in (Chapters 23-27) (in I Chronicles).

III The third peculiarity of the Chronicles is seen in the disagreements between them and the previously written histories of Samuel and Kings. We have seen how the chronicler intentionally omits many things which for his purpose he thinks unnecessary to be rewritten; and how he adds other things, omitted by Samuel and Kings, which he thinks should be written; but he not only thus differs from them as to what he will put in his history, but he frequently disagrees with them when they write about the same things, that the same persons said or did.

1 There are discrepancies in numbers. The chronicler generally gives the larger number, but sometimes the smaller.

(1) II Sam. 10:18 David slew the men of "700" chariots, I Chron. 19:18 "7000."
(2) II Sam. 23:8 Jashobeam slew "800" at one time, I Chron. 11:11 "300."
(3) II Sam. 8:4 David took from Hadadezer "1700" horsemen, I Chron. 18:4 "7000."
(4) II Sam. 24:9 Number of Israel, "800,000" that drew sword. Of Judah "500,000."
    I Chron. 21:5   of Israel "1,000,000"   of Judah   "470,000."
(5) II Sam. 24:13 Shall "7" years famine came? II Chron. 21:11 "3" years famine.
(6) II Sam. 24:24 David paid Araunah "50 shekels of silver."
    I Chron. 21:25   "600 shekels of gold."
(7) I Kings 4:26 Solomon had "40,000" stalls of horses, II Chron. 9:25 "4000."
(8) II Kings 5:11 Solomon gave Hiram "20,000 measures of wheat, 20 pure oil."
    II Chron. 2:10   "20,000 measures of wheat, 20,000 measures of barley, 20,000 baths of wine, and 20,000 baths of oil."
(9) I Kings 9:28 Hiram brought from Ophir "420 talents gold."
    II Chron. 8:18   "450 talents gold."
(10) I Kings 5:16 Solomon had "3300 overseers," II Chron. 2:18 "3600."
(11) I Kings 7:15 Hiram made two pillars "of 18 cubits high apiece."
    II Chron. 3:15   "of 35 cubits high."
(12) I Kings 7:26 Molten sea held "2000 baths," II Chron. 4:5 "3000 baths."
(13) I Kings 9:23 Solomon's "chief officers 550," II Chron. 8:10 "250."
(14) II Kings 8:25 In "twelfth year" of Joram, II Chron. 22:1 "eleventh year."
(15) II Kings 8:26 "22 years old was Ahaziah when he began to reign." II Chron. 22:2 "42 years."

2 Conflicting statements.

(1) II Sam. 21:19. Elhanan slew Goliath, the staff of whose spear was like a weaver's beam. I Chron. 20:5 slew Lahmi the brother of Goliath.
(2) II Sam. 24:1. The Lord moved David to number Israel and Judah. I Chron. 21:1. Satan moved David.
(3) I Kings 7:13. Hiram the son of a widow woman of the tribe of Naphtali. II Chron. 2:14. Huram the son of a woman of the daughters of Dan.
(4) I Kings 10:13. Solomon gave queen of Sheba all her desire, beside that which Solomon gave her of his royal bounty. II Chron. 9:12, beside that which she had brought unto the king.

(5) I Kings 9:11. Solomon gave Hiram 20 cities. 12. Hiram came to see them and they pleased him not. 13. And he called them Cabul, *i.e.*, displeasing. II Chron. 8:2 the cities which Huram had given to Solomon, Solomon built them, and caused the children of Israel to dwell there.

(6) I Kings 15:2^b. Abijah's mother's name was Maacah daughter of Abishalom.

II Chron. 13:2^b. Abijah's mother's name was Micaiah daughter of Uriel of Gibeah.

(7) I Kings 22:48. Jehoshaphat made ships of Tarshish to go to Ophir for gold: but they went not; for the ships were broken at Ezion-geber. II Chron. 20:36. And he (Jehoshaphat) joined himself with him (Ahaziah) to make ships to go to Tarshish: and they made the ships in Ezion-geber. 37^b. And the ships were broken that they were not able to go to Tarshish.

(8) II Kings 9:27. But when Ahaziah the king of Judah saw this, he fled by the way of the garden house. And Jehu followed after him, and said, Smite him also in the chariot: and they smote him at the ascent of Gur, which is by Ibleam. And he fled to Megiddo and died there. II Chron. 22:9. And he (Jehu) sought Ahaziah, and they caught him, (now he was hiding in Samaria,) and they brought him to Jehu, and slew him.

(9) II Kings 12:21. Jozacar son of Shimeath, Jehozabad son of Shomer. II Chron. 24:26. Zabad son of Shimeath, Jehozabad son of Shimrith.

IV The fourth peculiarity of the Chronicles is seen in the striking contrast between its mode of treatment of David and Solomon, and that of their successors after the disruption. We have seen the omission of the blameworthy, and the addition of the praiseworthy, in the idealized royal house of David. All this ends abruptly with Solomon. There is no longer any omission of sinfulness, in the kings of Judah. The seeming exceptions to this are Jotham, Abijah, and Jehoahaz. In the brief record of Jotham (II Chron. 27:1-9) there is only approval. v. 6. "So Jotham became mighty, because he ordered his ways before the Lord his God." In the record of Abijah, (II Chron. 13:1-22) the chronicler omits the statement of his " walking in all the sins of his father, and not having a perfect heart as David," (I Kings 15:3-6) and adds his rebuke of Jereboam and Israel, and his victory over them, "because they relied upon the Lord, the God of their fathers." In the short account of Jehoahaz, (II Chron. 36:1-3) the record of his evil doing is omitted, but his punishment is given. These exceptions only strengthen the rule, and seem to be rather an oversight than an intentional omission.

The purpose and plan of the Chronicles appears to be first, to give a running commentary on the qualifying statement, inserted in the promise God made to David, II Sam. 7:14. "I will be his father, and he shall be my son: *if he commit iniquity, I will chasten him* with the rod of men, and with the stripes of the children of men; *but my mercy shall not depart from him*, as I took it from Saul, whom I put away before thee." This is the text, on which the chronicler's history from Rehoboam to Zedekiah is written as a sermon. The spirit of the sermon is that of Heb. 12:6-11, on chastening, and I Cor. 11:32. "But when we are judged, we are chastened of the Lord, that we may not be condemned with the world." The Chronicles passes over the history of Israel, as if in the latter class, *i.e.*, apostate; but dwells minutely on the history of Judah, as being in the former. Instead of omitting the sins of the kings of Judah, he now rather adds to them, that he may shew the mercy of God in rebuking, reproving, punishing and forgiving of their sins, in their chastisement as sons. Out of the nineteen kings (leaving out the usurping queen Athaliah), seven of them were wholly bad, viz.: Jehoram, Ahaziah, Ahaz, Amon, Jehoiakim, Jehoiachin, and Zedekiah. The chronicler's story of them is just the reverse of his story of David and Solomon, inasmuch as he portrays them as

THE PECULIARITIES OF CHRONICLES

more wicked than they are described in Kings, and sinning against greater light, and in spite of God's loving mercy shown them. 1. Of Jehoram, he tells us, that on coming to the throne, "he slew all his brethren and divers princes; that Edom revolted because he had forsaken the Lord God of his fathers; that the writing of Elijah came to him, foretelling of his long and loathsome sickness; and that the Lord stirred up the Philistines, Arabians, and Ethiopians, who brought terrible defeat, damage and death to his people and family; and finally that when he died there was no burning for him, and he departed without being desired." (II Chron. 21: 2-20.)

2. Of Ahaziah, and his sinful ways and death by Jehu, we are told, "Now the destruction of Ahaziah was of God." (II Chron. 22: 7.)

Of Ahaz, the chronicler adds to the common account of his idolatry, and burning his children in the fire as the heathen did, given in both histories; how that "the Lord delivered him into the hand of the king of Syria, and the king of Israel, both of whom smote him and carried away many captives; how that through the prophet Oded, Israel was compelled to return the 200,000 captives taken from Judah; how that when the Edomites and the Philistines came and smote Judah, and Ahaz sent unto the kings of Assyria for help, Tiglath-pileser came, but distressed him, and in the time of his distress, he trespassed yet more against the Lord. For he sacrificed unto the gods of Damascus which smote him: and he said, Because the gods of the kings of Syria helped them, therefore will I sacrifice unto them, that they may help me. But they were the ruin of him, and of all Israel. But yet in spite of all this, he cut in pieces the vessels of the house of God, and shut up the doors of the house of the Lord, and he made him altars in every corner of Jerusalem, and provoked the Lord to anger." (II Chron. 28: 1-27.)

3. Of Amon, Chronicles adds to the statement in both histories, "that he did evil in the sight of the Lord, and sacrificed unto all the graven images which Manasseh his father had made and served them; that he humbled not himself before the Lord, as Manasseh his father had humbled himself, but trespassed more and more." (II Chron. 33: 21-25.)

4. Of Jehoiakim, Jehoiachin and Zedekiah, Chronicles with Kings make record that they did evil in the sight of the Lord, and as a punishment, Nebudchadnezzar came up against them and carried them captives to Babylon. (II Chron. 36: 5-21.)

5. Of Zedekiah the chronicler says, he "humbled not himself before Jeremiah the prophet speaking from the mouth of the Lord." (II Chron. 36: 12.)

In its treatment of these and the remaining kings of Judah, the Chronicles shew a second underlying principle of judgment, closely associated with that of chastening, which is fully elaborated by Ezekiel (18: 1-32). "The word of the Lord came unto me again, saying, What mean ye, that ye use this proverb in the land of Israel, saying, The fathers have eaten sour grapes, and the children's teeth are set on edge? As I live, saith the Lord God, ye shall not have occasion any more to use this proverb in Israel. Behold, all souls are mine; as the soul of the father, so also the soul of the son is mine; the soul that sinneth, it shall die." The prophet then gives in detail six specifications. (1) A righteous man who continues righteous. (2) A righteous man who begets a bad son. (3) A wicked man who continues wicked. (4) A wicked man who begets a righteous son. (5) A wicked man who becomes righteous. (6) A righteous man who becomes wicked. The conclusion of all this is "Therefore I will judge you, O house of Israel, every one according to his ways, saith the Lord God." This teaching of the prophet reveals the later trend of thought, during and after the exile, as contrasted with the views held in earlier times, II Ch. 25: 3, 4. It is hence the contemporaneous mode of thought, with which the Chronicles is more affected than the earlier histories. The chronicler rings all the changes on these six specifications of this underlying principle of God's judgment, and selects and arranges all his material so as to sustain and substantiate the abstract principle applied in the concrete, to the nineteen kings of Judah, each one of which may be labelled as belonging to one of the six classes.

Four good kings (Jehoshaphat, Jotham, Hezekiah, Josiah) had bad sons.
Four bad kings (Abijam, Amaziah, Ahaz, Amon) had good sons.
One king (Rehoboam) had bad beginning and end, with some good in the middle.
One king (Manasseh) began badly, but ended well.
Seven kings (Asa, Jehoshaphat, Joash, Amaziah, Uzziah, Hezekiah, Josiah) began well, but did badly later in their reigns, and generally ended badly.

Every man's life, and every part of every man's life, stands out independently, and is judged by God for what it is. Whatever a man's father has been, or whatever his own life has been, it can be, and it may be different. This is the constantly reiterated lesson that the Chronicles teach; and from authorities in his possession, he adduces not only the old but also many new facts to illustrate and enforce this lesson.

A brief glance at the additions in the narrative of Chronicles, about these reigns, will make this and two previous principles, apparent to all.

1. Rehoboam. He lost ten tribes by following foolish advice. But the priests and levites of Israel, that were cast out by Jereboam, and such as set their hearts to seek the Lord God, resorted to him, and strengthened the kingdom, and made Rehoboam strong for three years, for they walked in the ways of David and Solomon. But when the kingdom was established, and he was strong, he forsook the law of the Lord, and because he trespassed against the Lord Shishak of Egypt came up against him. Then Shemaiah the prophet pointed out to him his sin and his punishment, the king and princes humbled themselves, and said, The Lord is righteous. When they humbled themselves, the Lord sent word by Shemaiah, that he would not destroy them, but they became servants to Shishak, and were spoiled of the treasures of the Lord's and the king's house. But he went back again and did evil the rest of his reign, because he set not his heart to seek the Lord. (II Chron. 11: 5-17, 12: 1-12.)

2. Manasseh. Next to Ahaz, he was the most wicked of Judah's kings, in the practice of heathen idolatry and superstition. He even put a graven image in the house of the Lord, and made Judah to do more evil than the nations that God destroyed. This is the only picture of him given in Kings. But the Chronicles record that when the Lord brought the Assyrians upon them, and he was carried captive to Babylon, and was in distress, he besought the Lord, and humbled himself greatly before God. And he prayed unto him, and he was intreated of him, and God heard his supplication, and brought him again to Jerusalem into his kingdom. Then Manasseh knew that the Lord was God. He did works meet for repentance, taking the graven image and idol out of the house of the Lord, and all the altars out of Jerusalem, and offered sacrifices and thanksgiving, and commanded Judah to serve the Lord. In this story of the turning of this prodigal king to the Lord, the chronicler has given us an Old Testament companion picture to Jesus's parable of the prodigal son. The narrative has what the parable has not, the complete reinstatement to former dignity and power. (II Chron. 33: 1-13.)

3. Of the seven good kings, I will not even refer to the chronicler's account of their good deeds and works, which are the glory of Judah. The aggregate of their reigns was 246 years, (an average of over 35 years for each reign) which was nearly two-thirds of the existence of

the Southern Kingdom. They all began well, and continued well, but late in their reigns, and generally at the end, they did badly.

4. Asa, about the middle of his reign, in order to protect himself against Baasha of Israel sent to Ben-hadad to ask his help. Hanani the seer rebukes him for not relying upon God, and contrasts it with his former conduct, when God delivered him from the huge host of the Ethiopians and Lubim, because of his reliance on him; and then announces that from henceforth he shall have wars. Then Asa was wroth with the seer, and put him in the prison house; for he was in a rage with him because of this thing. He also oppressed some of the people at this same time. Again in the thirty-ninth year of his reign, Asa had an exceeding great disease in his feet; yet he sought not to the Lord, but to his physicians. (II Chron. 14: 9-15, 16: 1-14.)

5. Of Jehoshaphat, the Chronicles tell us that he walked in the first ways of his father David, the Lord was with him, and stablished his kingdom. But after certain years he joined affinity with wicked Ahab of Israel. And Jehu the son of Hanani the seer said to him, Shouldest thou help the wicked, and love them that hate the Lord? for this thing wrath is upon thee from before the Lord. Later on in his reign, we have the account of his miraculous victory over children of Ammon, Moab and mount Seir, when in belief in God and in his prophets they sang thanks and praises to the Lord, in the place of fighting, and God gave him rest round about; yet after this did Jehoshaphat join himself with Ahaziah in making ships, and was rebuked by Eliezer, saying, Because thou hast joined thyself with Ahaziah, the Lord hath destroyed thy works. (II Chron. 18: 1, 19: 1, 20: 35-37.)

6. Of Joash the boy king, we have only good till after the death of Jehoiada the priest, when under the influence of the princes they forsook the Lord and served Asherim and the idols, and wrath came upon them for their guiltiness. God sent prophets unto them to bring them again to the Lord, but they gave no ear to them. Then Zechariah, the son of Jehoiada reproved them, saying, Because ye have forsaken the Lord, the Lord hath forsaken you. At the commandment of the king, they stoned him with stones. Thus Joash remembered not the kindness of his benefactor Jehoiada, and his dying son said The Lord look upon it, and require it. At the end of the year, the Syrians came up and destroyed the princes of Judah and sent the spoil to Damascus. The Lord delivered the very great host of Judah into the hand of the small company of the Syrians, because they had forsaken the Lord. So they executed judgment upon him, and when they left him in great diseases, his own servants slew him on his bed, for the blood of Zechariah. (II Chron. 24: 17-27.)

7. Amaziah having hired 100,000 men of Israel, followed the counsel and advice of the man of God, and returned them, losing the 100,000 talents of silver he had paid them, trusting the assurance that the Lord is able to give much more than this, and gained a great victory in the Valley of Salt. But on his return, he brought back their gods, and set them up to be his gods, and bowed and burned incense before them. He then provoked a quarrel with Joash king of Israel and in his headstrong folly joined in battle with him, and was defeated and despoiled. For it was of God, that he might deliver them, because they had sought after the gods of Edom. Now from the time that Amaziah did turn away from following the Lord they made a conspiracy against him in Jerusalem; and fifteen years later he fled to Lachish; but they sent after him and slew him there. (II Chron. 25: 14-28.)

8. Of Uzziah, the chronicler tells us of his fifty-two years' reign, as long as he sought the Lord, God made him to prosper. But when he was strong, his heart was lifted up, so that he did corruptly, and he trespassed against the Lord his God; for he went into the temple

of the Lord to burn incense. Azariah the priest and fourscore priests of the Lord withstood him, saying, It pertaineth not unto thee to burn incense, but to the priests the sons of Aaron, that are consecrated to burn incense: go out of the sanctuary; for thou hast trespassed; neither shall it be for thine honour from the Lord God. Then Uzziah was wroth; and he had a censer in his hand to burn incense; and while he was wroth with the priests, the leprosy broke forth, and they thrust him out quickly from thence; yea, himself hasted to go out, because the Lord had smitten him. And Uzziah remained a leper unto the day of his death, and dwelt in a several house; for he was cut off from the house of the Lord. (II Chron. 26: 16-23.)

9. Hezekiah, at the very acme of his prosperity was recovered from his sickness through prayer. But, according to Chronicles, he rendered not again according to the benefit done unto him; for his heart was lifted up: therefore there was wrath upon him, and upon Judah and Jerusalem. Notwithstanding Hezekiah humbled himself for the pride of his heart, both he and the inhabitants of Jerusalem, so that the wrath of the Lord came not in his days. And Hezekiah prospered in all his works. Howbeit in the business of the ambassadors of the princes of Babylon, who sent unto him to inquire of the wonder that was done in the land, God left him, to try him, that he might know all that was in his heart. (II Chron. 32: 24-31.) Contrary to the rule, it is the Kings and not Chronicles that contains Isaiah's announcement of God's retributive punishment. (II Kings 23: 14-21.)

10. Of Josiah the Kings tell us, And like unto him was there no king before him, that turned to the Lord with all his heart, and with all his soul, and with all his might, according to all the law of Moses; neither after him arose there any like him. Nevertheless he intercepted Neco of Egypt, on his way to the Euphrates, in spite of his warning to forbear from meddling with God, that he destroy thee not, and was slain. The chronicler's sentence is, Nevertheless Josiah would not turn his face from him, but disguised himself, that he might fight with him, and hearkened not unto the words of Neco, from the mouth of God. (II Chron. 35: 20-27.)

This brief rehearsal of the kings of Judah shows us that we get from Chronicles *alone* the inside view of their reigns from God's standpoint as revealed by his prophets; we get the authoritative cause for each of the bare facts recorded by Kings, which thus become logical results; we get the clue that solves the mysterious riddle of the otherwise puzzling and perplexing histories.

In the closing summary of the book, we have brought out a third principle of judgment, in accordance with which the purpose and plan of the book is plainly framed, viz.: divine retribution, which is clearly stated in Isaiah. (33: 1.) Woe to thee that spoilest, and thou wast not spoiled: and dealest treacherously, and they dealt not treacherously with thee! When thou hast ceased to spoil, thou shalt be spoiled; and when thou hast made an end to deal treacherously, they shall deal treacherously with thee.

The chronicler's conclusion is, Therefore he brought upon them the king of the Chaldeans, who slew all their young men, took away to Babylon all their treasures, burnt the house of God and all the palaces and destroyed all the goodly vessels thereof, brake down the wall of Jerusalem, and carried away captive those not slain, to fulfill the word of the Lord by the mouth of Jeremiah, until the land had enjoyed her sabbaths: for as long as she lay desolate she kept sabbath, to fulfill threescore and ten years.

As Moses and Aaron said to Israel by the word of the Lord, And your children shall be wanderers in the wilderness forty years. After the number of the days in which ye spied out the land, even forty days, for every day a year, shall ye bear your iniquities, even forty years, and ye shall know my alienation. (Numbers 14: 33, 34.) So Chronicles teach us that to fulfill the word of the Lord by Jeremiah, seventy years of captivity was the punishment for seventy periods of six years each, during which no sabbatical years had been observed, *i.e.*, a year of captivity for every sabbatical year neglected. According to revised chronology, the time between David's reign in Jerusalem and the going into captivity is four hundred and twenty-four years, almost exactly seventy times six, 420. The Chronicles, as distinct from Kings, will be found profitable in proportion as we bear constantly in mind, that every fact recorded, illustrates one or more of the three principles of judgment that underlie it, viz.: chastisement of the Lord in mercy, vs. condemnation; independent commendation or condemnation of every life, and of every part of every life in and for itself; and divine retribution, where each calamity is viewed as the punishment for some lapse into sin.

The prophet Zechariah says, (14:7, l.c.) but it shall come to pass, that at evening time there shall be light. The chronicler in his complete work, including Ezra and Nehemiah, gives as the complement of the sad story of captivity and exile, the bright one of return and restoration. And as Bennett well says, " The editor who separated Chronicles from the books of Ezra and Nehemiah was loath to allow the first part of the history to end in a gloomy record of sin and ruin. So he has appended two verses from the opening of the book of Ezra, which contain the decree of Cyrus authorizing the return from captivity and restoration of Jerusalem." Thus Chronicles concludes in the middle of the sentence, " Who is there among you of all his people? Jehovah his God be with him, and let him go up . . . ." which is completed in the book of Ezra . . . . " to Jerusalem, which is in Judah, and build the house of the Lord, the God of Israel, (he is God) which is in Jerusalem." This is the more noticeable in the Hebrew where Chronicles is put after and not before Ezra and Nehemiah, and at the end of the canon. " Thus the final editor of Chronicles has shown himself unwilling that the book should conclude with a gloomy record of sin and ruin, and has appended a few lines to remind his readers of the new life of faith and hope that lay beyond the Captivity. In so doing, he has echoed the keynote of prophecy: ever beyond man's transgression and punishment the prophets saw the vision of his forgiveness and restoration to God." To this agrees, the closing verses of Isaiah (66:22, 23). For as the new heavens and the new earth, which I shall make, shall remain before me, saith the Lord, so shall your seed remain. And it shall come to pass, that from one new moon to another, and from one sabbath to another, shall all flesh come to worship before me, saith the Lord. So also the closing words of Malachi (3:5, 6), the ending of Old Testament prophecy, Behold, I will send you Elijah the prophet before the great and terrible day of the Lord come. And he shall turn the hearts of the fathers to the children, and the hearts of the children to their fathers; lest I come and smite the earth with a curse.